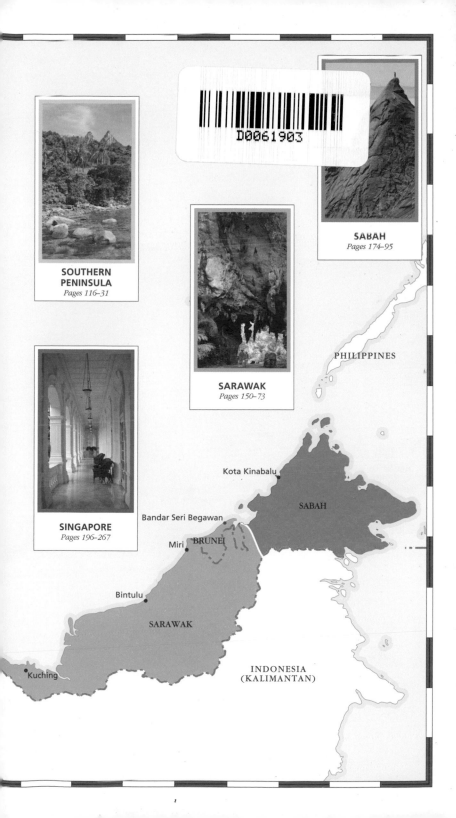

**SOUTHERN
PENINSULA**
Pages 116–31

SARAWAK
Pages 150–73

SABAH
Pages 174–95

SINGAPORE
Pages 196–267

PHILIPPINES

Kota Kinabalu

Bandar Seri Begawan

SABAH

Miri   BRUNEI

Bintulu

SARAWAK

Kuching

INDONESIA
(KALIMANTAN)

D0061903

EYEWITNESS TRAVEL

MALAYSIA &
SINGAPORE

EYEWITNESS TRAVEL
MALAYSIA & SINGAPORE

DK

LONDON, NEW YORK,
MELBOURNE, MUNICH AND DELHI
www.dk.com

MANAGING EDITOR Aruna Ghose
EDITORIAL MANAGER Ankita Awasthi
DESIGN MANAGER Priyanka Thakur
PROJECT EDITORS Sandhya Iyer, Shonali Yadav
PROJECT DESIGNERS Neha Beniwal, Shipra Gupta
EDITORS Jayashree Menon, Ipshita Nandi
DESIGNERS Pramod Bharti, Anchal Kaushal
SENIOR CARTOGRAPHIC MANAGER Uma Bhattacharya
CARTOGRAPHER Alok Pathak
SENIOR DTP DESIGNER Vinod Harish
SENIOR PICTURE RESEARCHER Taiyaba Khatoon
PICTURE RESEARCHER Sumita Khatwani

CONTRIBUTORS
David Bowden, Ron Emmons, Andrew Forbes,
Naiya Sivaraj, Richard Watkins

CONSULTANTS
David Bowden, Nick White

PHOTOGRAPHERS
Demetrio Carrasco, Nigel Hicks, Linda Whitwam

ILLUSTRATORS
Chapel Design and Marketing Ltd, Arun Pottirayil,
T. Gautam Trivedi

Reproduced in Singapore by Colourscan
Printed and bound by L. Rex Printing Company Limited, China

First American Edition, 2008
08 09 10 9 8 7 6 5 4 3 2 1

Published in the United States by Dorling Kindersley Publishing,
Inc., 375 Hudson Street, New York 10014

Copyright © 2008 Dorling Kindersley Limited, London
A Penguin Company

ALL RIGHTS RESERVED UNDER INTERNATIONAL AND PAN-AMERICAN COPYRIGHT
CONVENTIONS. NO PART OF THIS PUBLICATION MAY BE REPRODUCED, STORED IN
A RETRIEVAL SYSTEM, OR TRANSMITTED IN ANY FORM OR BY ANY MEANS,
ELECTRONIC, MECHANICAL, PHOTOCOPYING, RECORDING OR OTHERWISE WITHOUT
THE PRIOR WRITTEN PERMISSION OF THE COPYRIGHT OWNER.

Published in Great Britain by Dorling Kindersley Limited.

A CATALOGING IN PUBLICATION RECORD IS
AVAILABLE FROM THE LIBRARY OF CONGRESS.

ISSN 1542-1554
ISBN: 978-0-7566-2835-2

Front cover main image: Pantai Kok Beach, Pulau Langkawi

**The information in this
DK Eyewitness Travel Guide is checked regularly.**
Every effort has been made to ensure that this book is as up-to-date
as possible at the time of going to press. Some details, however,
such as telephone numbers, opening hours, prices, gallery hanging
arrangements and travel information are liable to change. The
publishers cannot accept responsibility for any consequences arising
from the use of this book, nor for any material on third party
websites, and cannot guarantee that any website address in this
book will be a suitable source of travel information. We value the
views and suggestions of our readers very highly. Please write to:
Publisher, DK Eyewitness Travel Guides, Dorling Kindersley,
80 Strand, London WC2R 0RL.

◁ Entrance to Batu Caves, the largest cave temple in Malaysia

CONTENTS

Pendant, Islamic Arts Museum,
Kuala Lumpur

INTRODUCING MALAYSIA AND SINGAPORE

An Orang Asli boy climbing a tree
in Taman Negara

Visitors strolling along the sandy Pantai Cenang beach, Pulau Langkawi

Statue of the Seated Buddha in Georgetown, Penang

The grand Raffles Hotel in Singapore

INTRODUCING MALAYSIA & SINGAPORE

DISCOVERING MALAYSIA AND SINGAPORE

Malaysia and Singapore have an astounding range of attractions for visitors, offering experiences and activities that appeal to all tastes. Malaysia's national parks, with their superb landscapes and unusual animals, are a magnet for nature-lovers, while its islands attract divers eager to explore the mysteries of the deep. The major cities of this region, particularly Singapore and Kuala Lumpur, offer the chance to see historical monuments, witness cultural shows, shop for local crafts, and sample the delights of Malay, Chinese, and Indian cuisine. These pages present the highlights of some of Southeast Asia's most intriguing destinations.

KUALA LUMPUR

- Colonial architecture
- Towering skyscrapers
- Superb shopping
- Vibrant nightlife

Although Kuala Lumpur is Southeast Asia's youngest capital and has developed beyond recognition during the past few decades, vestiges of its colonial past still exist. This is in evidence particularly around **Merdeka Square** *(see pp60–61)* where the **Royal Selangor Club** *(see p62)* and **Sultan Abdul Samad Building** *(see p62)* display British and Islamic influences on the city's early architecture. Several museums, such as the **National Museum** *(see p66)* and the **Islamic Arts Museum** *(see pp68–9)*, offer insights into Malaysia's history and its complex ethnic composition. While an effort has been made to preserve the

city's colonial past, Kuala Lumpur is essentially a modern city, and few visitors can resist the urge to admire the panoramic view from the dizzying heights of the **Petronas Towers** *(see p72)* or **Menara KL** *(see p74)*.

Kuala Lumpur is a shopper's paradise and for serious shopping it is necessary to become steeped in the city's shopping mall culture. Most of the biggest malls are in the **Golden Triangle** *(see p74)*, which is also the hub of the trendiest restaurants, bars, and clubs. Night owls can choose between watching live bands and listening to DJs play the latest trance and techno in state-of-the-art nightclubs.

It is well worth taking a stroll around **Chinatown** *(see p64)*, **Little India** *(see p70)*, and the Malay-dominated **Kampung Baru** *(see p72)* to explore their busy markets and to get a sense of the city's vibrant ethnic diversity.

Rolling hills of the Cameron Highlands, Northwest Peninsula

NORTHWEST PENINSULA

- Gorgeous beaches
- Cool hill stations
- Historic Georgetown

After Kuala Lumpur, the most visited region of Malaysia is the Northwest Peninsula, and it is not difficult to see why. With fabulous offshore islands, refreshing breezes at the hill stations, historic forts and churches, and ancient shophouses in the older towns, the region has abundant attractions. The region is also home to the archaeologically significant **Lembah Bujang** *(see p110)*, the site of an old Hindu-Buddhist empire.

Situated just south of Malaysia's border with Thailand, **Pulau Langkawi** *(see pp112–15)* is Malaysia's foremost island retreat. The

The Sultan Abdul Samad Building at Merdeka Square, Kuala Lumpur

◁ Detail from Nikhrodharam Thai Temple at Alor Star, Northwest Peninsula, Malaysia

island's luxury resorts and hotels provide all kinds of activities for visitors, such as snorkeling excursions, watersports, and boat trips to other islands in the archipelago. It is also worth exploring the main island's beautiful mountains and waterfalls.

Popular beaches off Malaysia's west coast are **Batu Ferringhi** *(see p108)* on Penang and Coral Bay on **Pulau Pangkor** *(see pp94–5)*.

After sizzling in the sun, the cool climate of the hill stations is irresistible, and places such as **Cameron Highlands** *(see pp92–3)* and **Fraser's Hill** *(see p91)* remain as popular with visitors today as they were with the British in the past, who established weekend retreats here to escape the heat of Kuala Lumpur. The most popular activities here are trekking, visiting tea plantations, playing golf, evenings by a roaring fire in a mock-Tudor hotel.

Although there are many cities of interest in the northwest, many people consider **Georgetown** *(see pp100–5)*, the capital of Penang, to be not only the most fascinating town in Malaysia, but in all of Asia. Its reputation is largely due to its heritage, which includes colonial buildings such as **Fort Cornwallis** *(see p100)*, ancient Chinese shophouses, temples, and museums. Excellent shopping and eateries combine to make it one of the most visited places in the country.

Striking red façade of the Dutch Christ Church in Malacca

SOUTHERN PENINSULA

- **Rich heritage of Malacca**
- **Traditional Minangkabau architecture**
- **Diving at Pulau Tioman**

The Southern Peninsula has some of Malaysia's most historically and culturally significant towns as well as some of its most popular offshore beaches. Culture buffs should head directly for **Malacca** *(see pp122–7)* on the southwest coast to see evidence of Portuguese, Dutch, and British colonization. Of particular interest are the **Stadthuys** *(see p122)*, the former Dutch town hall which now houses the **Museum of History and Ethnography**, the nearby **Christ Church** *(see p123)*, and the **Baba-Nonya Heritage Museum** *(see pp126–7)*, which offers a glimpse of a traditional Peranakan house. Peranakan culture resulted

from the intermarriage of Chinese traders with local Malay women. Among the other immigrants to the Southern Peninsula were the Minangkabau people from Sumatra, who settled around the towns of **Seremban** *(see p120)* and **Sri Menanti** *(see p120)*. These towns are well worth visiting for the unique signature motif of **Minangkabau architecture** *(see p121)* – the sweeping, saddle-shaped roofs that adorn their houses and palaces, the most spectacular example in the area is the **Istana Lama** *(see p120)*.

Off the southeast coast, **Pulau Tioman** *(see pp130–31)* in the **Seribuat Archipelago** *(see p129)* is often regarded as one of the world's most beautiful islands. A trip to the island is rewarded with visions of mountain peaks swathed in clouds, inviting sandy beaches, and some of the best diving and snorkeling in Malaysia.

White-sand beach framed by forested hills on Pulau Langkawi

EASTERN AND CENTRAL PENINSULA

- **Trekking in Taman Negara**
- **Picturesque Perhentian Islands**
- **Riding the Jungle Railway**

This region's appeal lies in its spectacular natural beauty. It is also the area that is most Malay in character, with Kelantan and Terengganu being the repositories of Malay culture and artistry.

Nature-lovers flock to **Taman Negara** *(see pp138–9)*, Malaysia's oldest and biggest national park, to view its wildlife, climb mountains, and take trips on Sungai Tembeling. Less visited than other national parks, **Endau-Rompin National Park** *(see p137)*, a huge tract of protected rainforest, offers the chance to escape the crowds. Visitors come here to see the hornbills, mouse deer, wild pigs, and tree frogs that inhabit the area.

Small offshore islands, such as the **Perhentian Islands** *(see p142)* and **Pulau Redang** *(see p142)*, which are surrounded by colorful coral reefs and shoals of tropical

A boatman steers his way across the waters, Taman Negara

fish, are increasing in popularity with divers and snorkelers. For the moment, however, they still evoke a sensation of getting away from it all. Also an experience is a boat trip on the 12 interlocking lakes that constitute **Tasik Chini** *(see p136)*.

Kota Bharu *(see pp146–7)* and **Kuala Terengganu** *(see p141)* are centers of local handicrafts. They also boast some of Malaysia's best street markets and offer delicious Malay cuisine.

A wonderful way to explore this remote region is on the **Jungle Railway** *(see p149)*, which runs between Gemas and Kota Bharu.

The train stops at tiny towns along the way and its passengers are mostly local villagers. A ride along the railroad's length provides a perfect introduction to the hospitality of the Malays.

SARAWAK

- **Historic Kuching**
- **Encounters with orangutans**
- **Visiting a longhouse**
- **Superb national parks**

Located in Malaysian Borneo, Sarawak is Malaysia's largest state and a prime destination for nature-lovers, as well as those with an interest in the history of the region or the traditions of its indigenous communities. **Kuching** *(see pp154–7)*, the capital, is undoubtedly one of Asia's most intriguing cities, and its town center still has many well-preserved colonial buildings and monuments, including the Sarawak Museum *(see p154)*, the Courthouse *(see p155)*, and the Astana *(see p157)*.

Kuching is also ideally situated to explore the rest of the state. Just a short day trip away are **Semenggoh Nature Reserve** *(see p161)* and **Bako National Park** *(see pp162–3)*, with easy walking trails and an abundance of wildlife. A visit to the longhouses of the indigenous people of Sarawak is another highlight and day trips and overnight stays are easily organized in Kuching. A trip

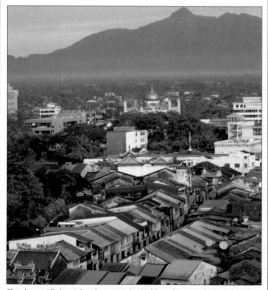

Shophouses lining Jalan Carpenter in Kuching, the capital of Sarawak

to a longhouse includes a journey by longboat along the mighty **Batang Rajang** *(see p164)*, which is the only way to reach the settlements.

Some of Sarawak's most spectacular attractions are scattered in the northeast of the state and are best accessed from the town of **Miri** *(see p168)*. Among these are the **Niah Caves National Park** *(see p168)* and **Mulu National Park** *(see pp170–71)*, These are sites of some of the world's biggest caves, which are also of archaeological significance. Mulu National Park offers treks to the limestone Pinnacles and the summit of Gunung Mulu. The remote **Kelabit Highlands** *(see p169)* have some of the most unspoilt natural beauty in Sarawak.

While in the region, curious travelers might like to visit the tiny Sultanate of **Brunei** *(pp172–3)*, with its glittering mosques, deserted beaches, and unspoilt interior.

A view of Singapore harbor and city

SABAH

- **Climbing Gunung Kinabalu**
- **Fantastic dive sites**
- **Rewarding wildlife watching**

Nicknamed the Land below the Wind, Sabah lacks the historic monuments of Sarawak, but makes up for this with a rich mosaic of ethnic groups, an exciting choice of adventure activities, and a sophisticated capital in **Kota Kinabalu** *(see p178)*. Sabah's principal attraction is **Kinabalu National Park** *(see p184–7)*, which encompasses Malaysia's highest peak. While some visitors attempt to conquer Kinabalu, others are content to simply enjoy the refreshing breezes and abundance of rare plants on its slopes.

Kota Kinabalu is also the access point for the **Tunku Abdul Rahman National Park** *(see p179)*, made up of five beautiful islands whose coral reefs are rich with marine life. Other popular activities include exciting white-water

rafting, especially on the **Padas River** *(see p181)*.

On the east coast are excellent opportunities for wildlife-watching. Visitors can observe green and hawksbill turtles laying their eggs at the **Turtle Island National Park** *(see pp190–91)*, orangutans at **Sepilok Orangutan Rehabilitation Center** *(see p190)*, and an amazing variety of fauna at the **Kinabatangan Wildlife Sanctuary** *(see p191)*. Wildlife-watching and thrilling treks are also possible at **Danum Valley** *(see p192)*. Off the state's east coast, **Pulau Sipadan** *(see pp194–5)* and **Pulau Lankayan** *(see p191)* are some of the best dive sites in the world.

Orangutan at the Semenggoh Nature Reserve

SINGAPORE

- **Visiting historic buildings**
- **Shopping on Orchard Road**
- **Sentosa Island**
- **Dining at Boat Quay**

While Malaysia's main draw is its natural wonders, the attractions of Singapore are mostly man-made. The city's skyline gleams with tall skyscrapers giving one the impression of modernity and sophistication. Its history is reflected in the many buildings which fill the Colonial Core, among them the world-famous **Raffles Hotel** *(see pp214–15)*. A more contemporary attraction is the nearby **Esplanade – Theaters on the Bay** *(see p210)*. The **Thian Hock Keng Temple** *(see pp222–3)* in Chinatown, **Sri Srinivasa Perumal Temple** *(see pp230–31)* in Little India, and the Islamic **Kampung Glam** *(see pp226–7)* are also frequently visited. The shops, temples, and mosques in these areas are a major draw for visitors. For day trips, there are plenty of offshore islands, the most popular being the island theme park of **Sentosa** *(see pp244–5)*.

A visit to Singapore would hardly be complete without a shopping spree, especially at **Orchard Road** *(see pp232–5)*, or without indulging in its fabulous food scene, from hawker stalls to chic eateries.

Putting Peninsular Malaysia on the Map

Bordered by Thailand to the north and connected to Singapore in the south by a causeway and a bridge, Peninsular Malaysia occupies the extreme south of mainland Southeast Asia, lying between 2 and 7 degrees north of the Equator. Off the west coast is the Strait of Malacca, while the east coast looks out onto the South China Sea. The majority of Malaysia's 25 million inhabitants live on the peninsula, heavily concentrated on the west coast, which includes the capital Kuala Lumpur. A mountainous ridge runs down the center of the peninsula, separating the densely forested and sparsely populated east coast from the west.

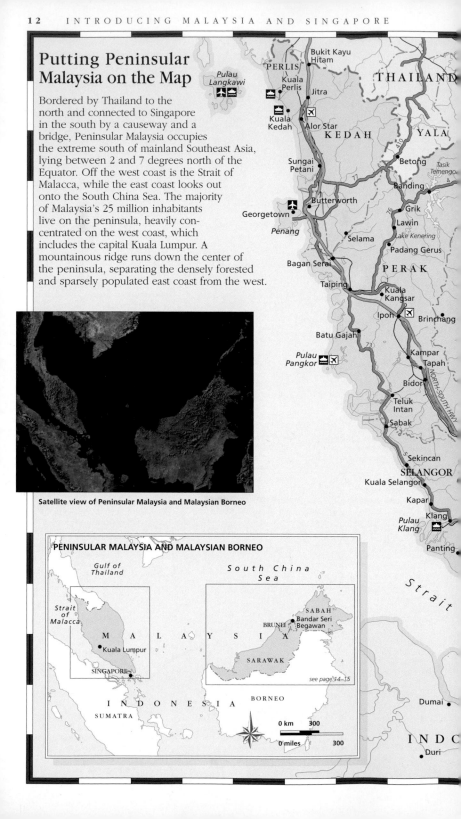

Satellite view of Peninsular Malaysia and Malaysian Borneo

PERLIS
Pulau Langkawi
Bukit Kayu Hitam
Kuala Perlis
Jitra
THAILAND
Kuala Kedah
Alor Star
KEDAH
YALA
410
Sungai Petani
Betong
Tasik Temengo
Banding
Butterworth
Georgetown
Penang
77
Grik
Lawin
Lake Kenering
Selama
Padang Gerus
Bagan Serai
PERAK
Taiping
Kuala Kangsar
Ipoh
Brinchang
Batu Gajah
Kampar
Pulau Pangkor
Tapah
73
Bidor
NORTH–SOUTH HWY
Teluk Intan
Sabak
Sekincan
SELANGOR
Kuala Selangor
Kapar
Pulau Klang
Klang
Panting

PENINSULAR MALAYSIA AND MALAYSIAN BORNEO

Gulf of Thailand
South China Sea
Strait of Malacca
MALAYSIA
Kuala Lumpur
SINGAPORE
SABAH
Bandar Seri Begawan
BRUNEI
SARAWAK
see page 14–15
INDONESIA
SUMATRA
BORNEO
Dumai

0 km 300
0 miles 300

Strait
INDO
Duri

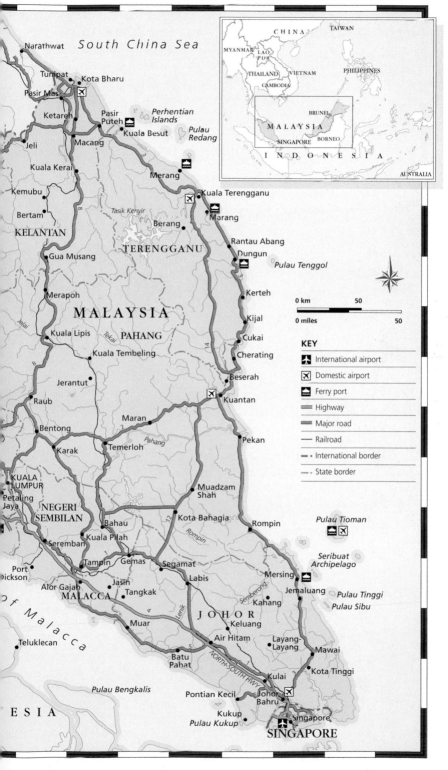

Putting Malaysian Borneo on the Map

Generally referred to as East Malaysia, Malaysian Borneo comprises the states of Sarawak, the largest in Malaysia, and Sabah, which together occupy more than half of the country's 127,445 sq miles (330,000 sq km). The states are located in the northern part of Borneo, the world's third-largest island, which they share with tiny Brunei and Kalimantan, Indonesia. Borneo lies about 373 miles (600 km) east of Peninsular Malaysia, from which it is separated by the South China Sea. The region is rich in natural resources, particularly oil and gas, and much of it is covered by rain forest and is sparsely populated. Of a population of 5 million people, most live in the provincial capitals, Kuching in Sarawak and Kota Kinabalu in Sabah, while many indigenous communities occupy remote outposts in the interior of the states.

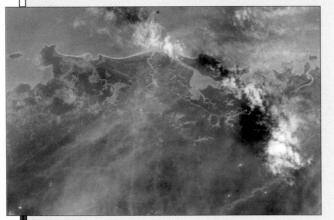

Astronaut's photograph of Gaya Bay, Kota Kinabalu

South China Sea

Kuala Belait

Miri

Beluru

Suai   Long Teru

Bintulu   Labang

Mukah   Rumah Melap

Belaga

Nanga Tamin   Rumah China   Long Geng

Daro   Matu

Sibu   SARAWAK

Binatang   Rumah Kam   Rumah Kulit

Sarikei   Kanowit   MALAYSIA

Kabong   Julau   Son   Kapit   Rumah Ary

Sematan   Saratok   Rumah Besi

Santubong   Rumah Layang   Rumah Mau

Lundu   Sebangan

Kuching

Bau   Gedong   Bandar Sri Aman   Batang Ai

Engkilili   INDONESIA

Danau Luar   Nahabuan

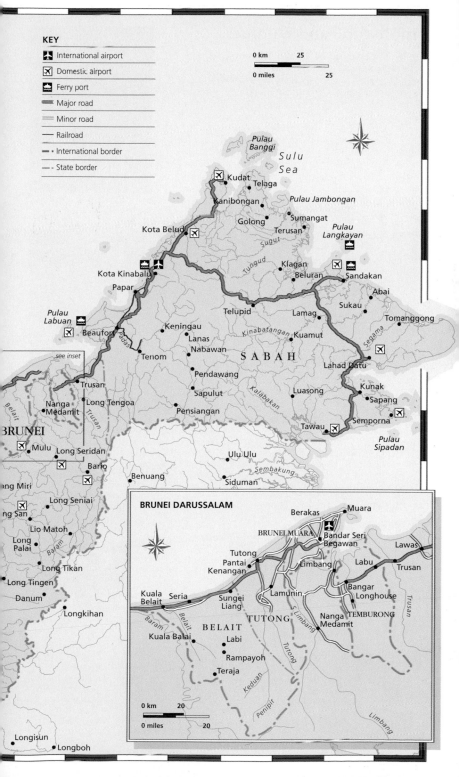

KEY

International airport
Domestic airport
Ferry port
Major road
Minor road
Railroad
International border
State border

0 km 25
0 miles 25

Pulau Banggi

Sulu Sea

Kudat
Telaga
Kanibongan
Pulau Jambongan
Golong
Sumangat
Kota Belud
Terusan
Pulau Langkayan
Sugut
Kota Kinabalu
Klagan
Beluran
Sandakan
Papar
Tungud
Abai
Pulau Labuan
Telupid
Lamag
Sukau
Beaufort
Keningau
Kinabatangan
Kuamut
Tomanggong
Lanas
Nabawan
Segama
SABAH
Tenom
Lahad Datu
Pendawang
Kalabakan
Luasong
Kunak
Trusan
Sapulut
Sapang
Nanga
Medamit
Long Tengoa
Pensiangan
Semporna
BRUNEI
Mulu
Long Seridan
Belait
Tawau
Pulau Sipadan
Trusan
Ulu Ulu
Sembakung
ng Miri
Bario
Benuang
Siduman
ng San
Long Seniai
Lio Matoh
Baram
Long
Palai
Long Tikan
Long Tingen
Danum
Longkihan
Longisun
Longboh

BRUNEI DARUSSALAM

Berakas
Muara
BRUNEI MUARA
Bandar Seri Begawan
Lawas
Tutong
Pantai Kenangan
Limbang
Labu
Trusan
Kuala Belait
Seria
Sungei Liang
Lamunin
Bangar Longhouse
Baram
Belait
BELAIT
TUTONG
Nanga Medamit
TEMBURONG
Kuala Balai
Labi
Limbang
Trusan
Rampayoh
Teraja
Keduan
Penpir
Limbang

0 km 20
0 miles 20

Landscape and Wildlife

Although separated by the South China Sea, Peninsular Malaysia and Malaysian Borneo form a part of the Sunda Shelf, a tectonic plate that once joined them in a single land mass. As a result, they share many geological features such as mountains, river networks, pristine offshore islands, and some of the world's oldest rain forests. These rain forests provide a habitat for a wealth of flora and fauna, including more than 15,000 types of flowering plants and nearly 200,000 species of animals. Among these are well-known endemic species, such as the orangutan, proboscis monkey, and rafflesia. Singapore retains pockets of primary rain forest in its northern region, while three-quarters of Brunei is still covered by native forest.

The *tualang* tree, one of the tallest plants in Malaysia

RAIN FORESTS

The rain forests of Malaysia are about 130 million years old and nurture a phenomenal range of plant life, from the 262-ft (80-m) tall *tualang* tree to an array of ferns, mosses, fungi, and orchids. They also provide a home for orangutans, proboscis monkeys, tapirs, binturongs or Malay civet cats, and honey bears, as well as hundreds of species of birds and butterflies.

LIMESTONE OUTCROPS

Many of Malaysia's mountains are formed of limestone, often rising dramatically out of the surrounding plain and containing massive cave networks caused by erosion. The most spectacular limestone outcrops are found in Sarawak's Niah Caves *(see p168)* and in Gunung Mulu National Park *(see pp170–71)*.

Malaysian tapirs *are distinguished by their black and white coloring and pig-like snout. These vegetarian mammals are most active at night.*

Bats, *such as the wrinkle-lipped bat, are common residents of limestone caves. Each evening, millions of bats take flight, filling the sky with a fantastic display.*

The orangutan *is the only great ape found outside Africa. These red-haired primates now face extinction and are rarely seen in the wild.*

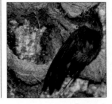

Cave swiftlets *are unusual birds that use echolocation to navigate the pitch-dark interiors of the caves. White nest swiftlets are prized in Malaysia for their edible nests.*

MALAYSIA'S ENDANGERED SPECIES

Malaysia's population has doubled since the 1970s, and the growing demand for living space is gradually destroying the habitat of several wildlife species. In greatest danger is the Sumatran rhinoceros, whose numbers are now thought to be fewer than 100. Several other species, including the clouded leopard, Asian elephant, and the country's national animal, the tiger, have also seen a dramatic decline. Among marine life, leatherback turtles and dugongs face a similar threat.

The Sumatran rhinoceros *is critically endangered. Its last remaining habitats include Sabah and Endau-Rompin National Park (see p137).*

Clouded leopards*, tawny or silver-colored cats, are hunted for their pelt, teeth, and bones, the latter being used in traditional Asian medicines.*

COASTAL PLAINS

The west coast of Peninsular Malaysia constitutes a long plain that provides an ideal environment for human inhabitation. These plains were the site of the earliest British settlements. Most of the country's important towns and cities, such as Kuala Lumpur, were established here.

Mangroves *are trees and shrubs that form swampy forests in saline coastal waters and provide a vital habitat for a number of wildlife species such as the proboscis monkey.*

Fiddler crabs *are critical to the wetland environment as they help aerate the soil by their feeding action. Males have asymmetrical and often brightly-colored claws.*

OFFSHORE ISLANDS

The seas around both Peninsular Malaysia and Malaysian Borneo are studded with stunning islands, many of them surrounded by coral reefs that sustain an incredible wealth of marine life. Divers are drawn to islands such as Tioman and Sipadan to observe the thriving underwater world.

Dugongs *take their name from the Malay word* duyung, *which means mermaid. Persistent hunting has resulted in the near extinction of these large sea mammals.*

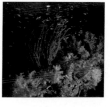

Coral reefs*, formed by tiny marine animals called polyps and other organisms, are beautiful living structures. They are essential to the preservation of marine life.*

Marine Life

Sea slug

The waters around both Peninsular Malaysia and Malaysian Borneo contain a huge diversity of marine life that attracts divers and snorkelers from around the world to gaze at brilliantly colored parrotfish, lionfish, and clownfish flitting around the vibrant coral reefs. For much of the year, the superb clarity of the water makes it easy to spot even the tiniest fish. The Malaysian government has designated 38 of its coral islands as protected areas to preserve their unique and biologically sensitive ecosystems.

Snorkeler examining underwater life on a coastal reef

Sea anemones, *named for a species of garden flower, are brightly colored, predatory animals that eat fish, mussels, and zooplankton.*

CORAL LIFE

Over 350 species of coral have been identified in Malaysian waters, making the country's reefs some of the most diverse in the world. Sadly, they are under threat from sediment build-up caused by ongoing logging, blast and cyanide fishing, and anchoring.

Gorgonian fan corals *reach up to 16.5 ft (5 m) in height in the warm waters of the tropics, filtering out the plankton and zooxanthellae on which they live.*

Brain corals are usually found in colonies and bear an uncanny resemblance to the human brain.

The star coral has a stone-like calcium skeleton and star-shaped polyp.

Yellow soft corals, *so called because of their lack of a hard external skeleton, have polyps with eight tentacles, and come in a stunning kaleidoscope of colors.*

Sunflower corals *have long polyps tipped with stinging tentacles to catch plankton.*

Mandarin fish *live camouflaged in broken coral bottoms eating small crustaceans called copepods. The male is larger than the female and has a spiked dorsal fin which it uses to threaten other males.*

Coleman shrimp, *always found in pairs, live on the toxic fire urchin. They clear a resting area of poisonous spines and sit protected from predators.*

Clownfish *live in a symbiotic relationship with sea anemones, which defend them from predatory fish.*

Sea ferns are a type of gorgonian coral with varied shapes and colors.

The lionfish, *a reef dweller of spectacular appearance, is a deadly killer, armed with venomous spines that it uses to stun small fish.*

Sea horses *are unusual in that it is the males that give birth. Many species are almost transparent and hard to spot. Their use in Chinese medicine has put them under threat of extinction.*

Lettuce coral is named for its green color and spiraling plates that resemble a growing lettuce.

Shoals of big-eye trevallies in the South China Sea

TURTLE CONSERVATION

Until recently, turtles were among the most conspicuous forms of marine life in Malaysia. Of the four species of turtle known to breed in these waters – the green, the hawksbill, the olive ridley, and the leatherback – only the green is now commonly seen and the leatherback is an endangered species. There is ample evidence that human intervention is destroying the habitat and damaging the life cycle of these turtles. Throughout their lives, adult turtles are prone to getting caught in fishing lines and nets, while the increasing development of beaches has adverse effects on the numbers of nesting females, eggs, and hatchlings.

Green turtle swimming in the warm waters near Malaysia

Peoples of Malaysia and Singapore

The indigenous people of Malaysia settled in the region some 40,000 years ago. Owing to its key position on maritime trade routes from around 2,500 years ago, the region acquired a large immigrant population. Today, Malays form 51 percent of the country's 27 million inhabitants, with the Chinese making up about a quarter, and the Indians, about 7 percent. Indigenous groups comprise the remainder of the population. By contrast, the Chinese form a strong majority in Singapore, where there are fewer Malays and Indians.

A group of Orang Asli, the indigenous people of Malaysia

THE MALAY

The largest ethnic group of Malaysia is, by definition, a Muslim group. Believed to have arrived on the peninsula from Sumatra, the Malays began converting to Islam in the 15th century, owing to the rise of the Malay sultanates. Today, they predominate on the east coast of Peninsular Malaysia, while in Singapore, they constitute about 14 percent of the population.

Malays *celebrate Hari Raya Puasa, also known as Hari Raya Aidilfitri (see p52), the Muslim New Year. Here, men are dressed in traditional Malaysian finery at a formal reception.*

Traditional Malay culture *revolves around village compounds called* kampung, *where inhabitants farm, fish, and practice crafts. Today, many Malays have migrated to urban centers.*

THE CHINESE

Originally from southern China, most Chinese immigrants arrived in Malaysia during the 19th century to work as laborers in the burgeoning tin-mining industry. Since then, they have dominated all aspects of commerce and today, Malaysia has several Chinatowns, where Chinese businesses thrive. In Singapore, more than three-quarters of the population is Chinese.

The Peranakans, *also known as Straits Chinese or Baba-Nonya, are a community born out of marriages between Chinese and Malays from the 16th century onwards.*

Chinese traders *can be seen selling artifacts in Kuala Lumpur. The Chinese have historically played a major role in the Malaysian economy.*

SOUTH ASIANS

Indians have been trading with Malaysia for over 2,000 years. However, most Malaysians of Indian origin settled here, like the Chinese, during the 19th century. Although the immigrants came largely from southern India, there are also people of northern Indian descent, notably the Sikhs.

Asian women *of Indian descent sell vibrantly colored handmade silk at market stalls in Kuala Lumpur. The ethnic enclave of Little India (see p70) is packed with such stalls.*

A rubber tapper *of south Indian origin collects latex from a rubber tree. Indians have also traditionally been employed on tea estates.*

INDIGENOUS PEOPLES OF MALAYSIA

The indigenous peoples of Peninsular Malaysia, the Orang Asli, are among the minority of the peninsula's population, and generally live in its more inaccessible areas. In contrast, indigenous tribes make up half the population of Sarawak and 66 percent of Sabah. Many of these groups, including the Iban and Bidayuh of Sarawak, live in longhouses and hold animist beliefs. Some, like the Kelabit and Bajau, have converted to Christianity or Islam. The tribes of Sabah, such as the Kadazan Dusun, are traditionally agriculturalists, but most other groups were semi-nomadic hunter-gatherer communities. They are now being encouraged by the government to live in towns and villages.

The Bajau *are predominantly Muslim and are the second largest ethnic group in Sabah. Noted horsemen, the Bajau dress in elaborate costumes at the annual Tamu Besar in Kota Belud (see p53).*

The Penan, *the only true nomadic indigenous group in Malaysia, are skilled hunter-gatherers. The Penan consist of about 10,000 individuals who live in the upper Rajang and Limbang areas of Sarawak.*

The Rungus *are an indigenous people of northern Sabah. They are skilled in beadwork, weaving, and gong-making. Rungus people live communally in longhouses around Kudat (see p183).*

The Kadazan Dusun *are the largest ethnic group in Sabah, made up of a number of subgroups, constituting about 25 percent of Sabah's population. They traditionally wear black silk outfits on festive occasions such as the Dusun Harvest Dance.*

The Bidayuh, *or Land Dayaks, build their longhouses on hillsides, rather than near water as the other groups in Sarawak do. The third largest of Sarawak's indigenous peoples, they predominantly inhabit the region around Kuching (see p159).*

The Orang Ulu, *or upriver people, is an unofficial generic name for about 27 small and ethnically diverse groups, such as the Kayan and Kenyah, living in the interior of Sarawak.*

BUMIPUTRAS

The Malaysian authorities make an important distinction between migrant peoples and the *bumiputra*, or sons of the soil. The latter group includes all Malays and indigenous peoples of the country. This recognition was brought in as part of the New Economic Policy, following race riots in 1969, to boost the *bumiputra's* economic standing in society. Though it was much criticized by the Chinese and Indian migrants who then dominated commerce, the policy has ultimately led to more stability as it gave rise to a rich Malay group, whose financial interests lie in maintaining political and economic harmony.

The Iban, *also known as Sea Dayaks, are the largest ethnic group of Sarawak. They have an enduring reputation as fierce warriors and good hunters. The men are often heavily tattooed.*

Islam

While Malaysia is home to people of many different faiths, Islam is the official religion. So closely bound is Malay cultural identity with Islam that the Bahasa Malaysia phrase for adopting Islam, *masok melayu*, means "to become a Malay." Arab and Indian-Muslim merchants, who doubled as missionaries, began converting the local population from the 11th century onwards. Most Malay Muslims are orthodox Sunnis of the Shafi'i school but there are also smaller numbers of Shia Muslims and Sufi mystics. Just over 60 percent of Malaysia's population is Muslim; in Singapore, they form around 14 percent of the population.

Domes *are a characteristic feature of all mosques. They are generally onion-shaped structures and are often crowned by a crescent moon, the universal symbol of Islam.*

The courtyard *of a mosque is designed to accommodate a large number of worshipers. This courtyard at Johor Bahru's Sultan Abu Bakar Mosque holds 2,000 people.*

A minaret *is a lofty tower usually located in one of the corners of a mosque. From here the* muezzin, *or caller to prayer, summons the faithful five times a day.*

ISLAMIC ARCHITECTURE

Despite the flamboyant exteriors of some Islamic architecture, its real beauty lies in the inner spaces of the courtyard and rooms. This has often led to it being called the architecture of the veil. With its gleaming golden dome and striking minarets, Ubudiah Mosque *(right)* in Kuala Kangsar is among Malaysia's finest mosques.

This crenellated arch *at Masjid Kapitan Kling (see pp101) in Georgetown, Penang, is Moorish in style, borrowing from the architectural tradition of Islamic Spain and the North African Maghreb.*

Colorful Islamic tilework *is characterized by intricate geometric patterns and graceful floral motifs. Traditional Malay Muslim houses and mosques are adorned with these tiles.*

ISLAMIC FAITH

Islam, which means "submission to the will of God" in Arabic, was first revealed to the Prophet Muhammad at Mecca in Arabia, in AD 622. The principle of Islam rests on an unshakeable faith in a single deity, Allah, and on his word delivered by Muhammad in the Koran. The five pillars of Islamic faith are *shahadah,* witnessing that there is only one God; *salat,* performing the five daily prayers; *sawm,* fasting during the month of Ramadan; *zakat,* the giving of alms; and *hajj,* or performing the pilgrimage to Mecca at least once in a lifetime.

The Koran *is the central religious text of Islam, believed to be the inspired and immutable Word of God. Divided into 114 units and written in the Arabic script, it is often memorized verbatim by the faithful.*

Salat *is the name given to the obligatory prayers that are performed five times a day. The faithful always pray in the direction of Mecca. Salat is believed to establish a direct link between the worshiper and the worshiped.*

Wuzu *is the first step of the ablutions performed before commencing the* salat. *This is an essential act of spiritual and physical cleansing, as no prayer is acceptable without the complete* wuzu.

ISLAMIC ART

Architecture and calligraphy are the two most distinctive and elegant art forms in Islam. Both have developed to levels of great sophistication because of the general prohibition of representational art forms. The *hadith,* or Traditions of the Prophet Muhammad, decree that "the house which contains pictures will not be entered by the angels." Geometry also plays a major role in both architecture and calligraphy.

The Jawi script *is a Malay variant of Arabic writing. It is one of the two official scripts in Brunei and is also used in Malaysia and Singapore, particularly in religious calligraphy.*

Zapin *is a traditional Malay folk dance, with dancers usually performing in pairs accompanied by Islamic devotional chanting. Believed to have been introduced by 14th-century Muslim missionaries from the Middle East, it is commonly performed in Johor Bahru* (see p128).

Batik, *the art of wax-resist dyeing on textiles, is commonly used to pattern garments such as sarongs with bright designs. The most popular of such designs are floral prints* (see p30).

Hinduism and Buddhism

Hinduism and Buddhism are the major religions of Malaysia and Singapore's South Asian and Chinese communities respectively. Although Hinduism dates back to at least 1,500 years in both countries, the religion only took root when contract laborers from India were recruited to work in rubber and coffee plantations in Malaysia in the late 19th and 20th centuries. Buddhism became a permanent feature in Malaysia and Singapore after Chinese immigrants spread the religion to every part of the country in the 19th century.

Figure at Sri Krishna Temple

Monk praying at a shrine of Kuan Yin, goddess of mercy

HINDUISM

Hinduism in Malaysia and Singapore, complete with its many rituals and deities, is directly taken from Indian Hindu traditions, especially those of southern India from where most Indian migrants originated.

Statues of deities are enshrined at the central altar.

Fresh flower garlands are used to venerate the gods.

Devotees come to temples for individual or communal *puja*, or worship, ritual occasions, and to make offerings to honor the gods.

Offerings may include flowers, incense, and fruit such as coconuts, which are sprinkled with holy water during prayers.

Components of a prayer ritual include frankincense, myrrh, and other aromatic combustibles.

Hindu priests are Brahmins who belong to the highest of the four main castes. They tend to the temple and officiate at ceremonies.

The gopuram, *or entrance gateway to Hindu temples, is often multitiered and elegantly decorated with colorful sculptures from the vast pantheon of Hindu gods.*

SHAIVISM

Shaivism is a form of Hinduism which worships Lord Shiva as the main manifestation of the supreme being. His consort, Parvati, and their two sons, Murugan and Ganapati, are also worshiped by Shaivites. Shaivism grew prominent in Malaysia and Singapore as the Indian immigrants who settled there in the 19th century were mainly from southern India where the worship of Shiva is popular. The Sri Shivan temples in Singapore and Malaysia are especially revered by Shaivites.

Vibrant portrait of Lord Shiva

BUDDHISM

In both Malaysia and Singapore the Chinese communities follow the Mahayana school of Buddhism practiced in China, Japan, Korea, and Vietnam. The Thais of Singapore and the Orang Syam, or indigenous Thais of Malaysia, follow Theravada Buddhism, practiced in Thailand, Lao PDR (formerly Laos), Cambodia, Myanmar, and Sri Lanka. Buddhism in both countries is a fusion of different beliefs. In Singapore it is combined with Confucianism, Taoism, and ancestor worship. Buddhism is also personalized and centers around Kuan Yin, the goddess of mercy. Belief in luck and filial piety are also central features of Buddhism.

Buddhist monks *shave their heads, wear saffron robes, and generally go barefoot to indicate a life of austerity.*

The Buddha's halo, or nimbus, commonly depicted in Buddhist art, signifies enlightenment and spiritual development.

An urna, or a small protuberance between the Buddha's eyes, represents the "third eye" of spiritual vision, a mark of a holy man.

The Buddha is often depicted with a serene expression and a faint smile.

The wheel turning pose represents the Wheel of Law, or *dhammachakra*, set in motion by the Buddha's first sermon at Sarnath, India.

Bare feet with both soles turned upward and resting on opposite thighs signifies meditation.

The Buddha's hair is generally arranged in the form of snail shell curls, and surmounted by a *ushnisa*, or topknot.

Elongated earlobes are thought to be the result of heavy earrings worn by the Buddha as a prince.

A simple monk's robe represents the Buddha's life of renunciation.

The cross-legged posture is the position in which Buddha is most commonly portrayed.

Devout Buddhists *burn incense and make offerings at temples across Malaysia and Singapore to show respect to the Buddha, the sangha, or order of monks, and the dhamma, or teachings of the Buddhist cannon. Offerings often include fruit and flowers. Worshipers usually ask for good health and prosperity.*

PRINCIPLES OF BUDDHISM

Despite the existence of two main schools and different sects that have evolved over the centuries, the central principles of Buddhism are common to most forms of the religion. These include the Four Noble Truths, the Eight Fold Path, *karma*, or the moral law of cause and effect, which is symbolized by the Wheel of Law, and *nirvana*, or enlightenment. The Mahayana, or Greater Vehicle, school stresses the role of the *bodhisattva* or religious adept who, having gained *nirvana*, voluntarily renounces it to enlighten others. The Theravada, or Lesser Vehicle, school emphasizes the role of the *arhat*, or worthy one, who has attained *nirvana*.

Buddhist Wheel of Law

Secular Architecture

The traditional vernacular architecture of Malaysia and Singapore is mainly Malay and Straits Chinese, but a strong colonial influence is also apparent in buildings constructed during periods of British, Portuguese, and Dutch rule. In contrast, both countries boast stunning modern architecture, most prominently seen in their soaring skyscrapers. This is particularly true of Kuala Lumpur and Singapore.

The Singapore skyline is dominated by spectacular high-rise buildings

STRAITS CHINESE

Straits Chinese architecture centers on the ubiquitous shophouse, found throughout Malaysia and Singapore. Buildings of this style were introduced by immigrants from the Guangdong province of southern China.

Five Foot Way forming a sheltered passage (see p105)

Characteristic gabled roof

Flower motif *on a Peranakan shophouse tile.*

Classic shophouses *comprise a ground floor, whose street-facing portion is used to conduct business, and upper floors that serve as living quarters.*

TRADITIONAL MALAY HOUSE

The traditional Malay house tends to be raised on stilts, with extensions added when necessary. The house is centered around the *rumah ibu*, or main living room.

Pitched roof with gables

Serambi gantung, or hanging veranda

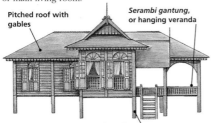

Stilts that protect the house from floods

The interiors *are ventilated by many open spaces such as verandas and windows. Traditionally, the houses have wooden walls and thatched roofs.*

LONGHOUSES

Indigenous peoples of Sabah and Sarawak traditionally live in longhouse communities (see p167), with each family occupying a separate apartment under a single contiguous roof. The entire structure is raised on stilts.

Living quarters occupied by individual families

Bamboo and rattan, the traditional building materials

Open veranda or *tanju*

Longhouses *commonly have a covered veranda, or* ruai, *which runs the length of the building, backed by a series of living quarters, or* bileks. *There is also a* tanju, *or open veranda.*

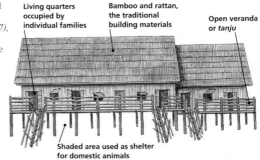

Shaded area used as shelter for domestic animals

MINANGKABAU

The spectacular architecture of the Minangkabau people, concentrated in the state of Negeri Sembilan, is chiefly distinguished by upswept roofs rising to pointed peaks that represent the horns of a victorious buffalo, or *minangkabau (see p121)*. Traditionally, the roofs were thatched with the fronds of the *nipa* palm, but today they are more usually shingled, or even made from galvanized iron.

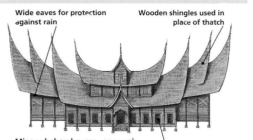

Wide eaves for protection against rain

Wooden shingles used in place of thatch

Minangkabau houses, *or* rumah minangkabau, *are recognizable by the distinctive style of their roofs.*

Windows permitting air circulation

COLONIAL BUILDINGS

Colonial buildings in both Malaysia and Singapore combine British Indian, Dutch East Indian, and Portuguese styles, often combined with indigenous Malay elements, Islamic motifs, and classical European flourishes. Elaborate decorations and wooden traceries lend individuality and style.

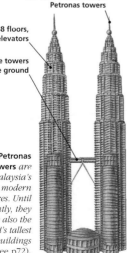

Mock-Tudor bungalows *are not uncommon in the hill stations of Peninsular Malaysia. These were built by British plantation owners.*

Classical façade

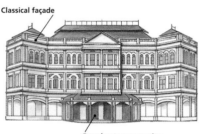

Grand entrance portico

The Raffles Hotel in Singapore *dates from 1887 and is named after Sir Stamford Raffles, the founder of Singapore (see pp214–15). It is the epitome of colonial elegance.*

MODERN ARCHITECTURE

Both Malaysia and Singapore are distinguished by their steel and concrete skyscrapers, often with façades of light- and heat-reflecting mirrored glass. While contemporary buildings in Malaysia incorporate elements of traditional Islamic architecture, Singaporean designs remain entirely modernistic.

The 1,483-ft (452-m) tall Petronas towers

Tower consisting of 88 floors, 10 escalators, and 76 elevators

Skybridge connecting the towers at 558 ft (170 m) off the ground

The Petronas Towers *are Malaysia's famous modern structures. Until recently, they were also the world's tallest buildings (see p72).*

The futuristic Esplanade – Theaters on the Bay, *with twin domes (see p210), adds to Singapore's ultramodern cityscape, in contrast with the city's traditional Indian, Chinese, and colonial architecture.*

Festivals of Malaysia and Singapore

Life in Malaysia and Singapore is punctuated with festivals, which are both frequent and spectacular. Although some festivals have a fixed date according to the international calendar, the Malay Muslim, Hindu, and Chinese traditions all set their festive days according to the lunar calendar *(see p333)*, making these celebrations movable events. Fortunately, the Malaysia and Singapore tourist boards regularly publish calendars of national and local festivals.

Giant banners in abundance, marking the beginning of the Chinese New Year

The traditional dinner *with the entire family is perhaps the most important aspect of the celebrations at the New Year, which is also considered the time for new beginnings.*

The dragon is a mythical beast symbolizing justice, wealth, and good fortune.

The colors used are predominantly red and gold, representing prosperity and long life.

Seven poles support the body, although more may be needed if the dragon is long.

CHINESE NEW YEAR

The most significant festival for the Chinese is the Lunar New Year. In Singapore and in some parts of Malaysia, such as Kuala Lumpur, Ipoh, Taiping, and Johor Bahru, this 15-day festival is marked by *chingay*, a joyous street parade with lion dancers, stilt-walkers, giant banners, music, and colorful floats. Almost all the festival rituals are focused on bringing good luck and prosperity.

The leader of the team must be the most skilled and experienced of the dancers as the others follow him.

The display of fireworks *in the night skies above the Petronas Towers is a spectacular highlight of the extravagant New Year's Eve celebrations in Kuala Lumpur.*

The lion dance *is a traditional dance form that dates back more than a thousand years. A pair of dancers trained in martial arts form the fore and hind legs of the lion, mimicking its motions.*

HARI RAYA PUASA

For Malay Muslims, the most important festival of the year is Hari Raya Puasa, also known as Aidilfitri in Malay, marking the end of the fasting month of Ramadan. Throughout the ninth month of the Muslim calendar, believers abstain from eating and drinking between sunrise and sunset. With the sighting of the new moon on the 30th day of the ninth month, Ramadan ends and the tenth month is ushered in with feasting on traditional fare such as *ketupat*, or rice cakes, and *lemang*, or glutinous rice.

The long, narrow body of the dragon is designed for sinuous movement.

Dragon dancers must be fit and need to practice regularly to put on a good show.

Muslim men start the day *by congregating at mosques for morning prayers, dressed in their finest clothes. Graves are cleaned and quarrels forgiven before the festivities begin.*

Muslim children *light firecrackers on Hari Raya Puasa and are given* duit raya, *or gifts of money, in small green envelopes. For three days, family, friends, and neighbors visit each other.*

THAIPUSAM

Celebrated by the southern Indian communities of Malaysia and Singapore, Thaipusam honors the Hindu god Murugan, youngest son of the gods Shiva and Parvati. It is held in the Tamil month of Thai (between January and February). The largest Thaipusam festival takes place at the Batu Caves, with over one million devotees and 10,000 tourists attending it. Worshipers shave their heads and undertake a pilgrimage along a set route, performing various acts of devotion along the way.

Kavadi carriers *hold elaborately decorated metal frames called* kavadi. *Adorned with peacock feathers, these portable altars are attached to devotees with skewers pierced into the skin.*

The Batu Caves (see p90), *dedicated to Lord Murugan, are one of the prime pilgrimage sites for Malaysia's Hindus. A spectacular scene unfolds here during Thaipusam, when an estimated one million pilgrims climb the 272 steps to the temple at the summit.*

Arts and Crafts of Malaysia

Malaysia has a wealth of indigenous artistic traditions, many dating back centuries, but its arts and crafts have also been enriched by the cultural influences of Chinese, Indians, and other peoples. While Peninsular Malaysia excels at metalwork, Malaysian Borneo produces the most spectacular woodcarvings. Besides pottery, ceramic, brass, and silverware, a wide range of regional artistry, such as kite-making in Kota Bharu, is available. The country has a flourishing art scene, influenced by Hindu, Buddhist, Islamic, and Chinese cultures, and more recently by Western art.

Labu sayong water pots from Sayong, near Kuala Kangsar

MALAYASIAN TEXTILES

Batik, which means writing in wax, is extremely popular in Malaysia, forming part of the Malay national dress. Among the best places to buy traditional *batik* is Kuching in Sarawak. The country's textile traditions also encompass fine silk and cotton cloth originally created for the royal courts. These include *kain lemar*, or silk brocade interwoven with *ikat; kain sutera*, or woven silk; *kain songket*, or rich brocade; and *kain mastuli*, or heavy silk.

Ikat *cloth is made using a tie-and-dye technique on the threads before they are woven into elaborate patterns. Today, the best* ikat, *such as this decorative Iban blanket, comes from Sarawak.*

Batik motifs are usually floral or geometric.

Melted wax is applied to the cloth to prevent dyes from penetrating.

Pua kumbu *cloths are woven by the Iban for use in ceremonies and for decoration. Weaving is done primarily by women and the motif they use once showed their status. Today, motifs vary from plant and animal themes to more abstract patterns.*

SONGKET SILK

The term *songket* is derived from the Malay *menyongket*, which means to embroider with silver or gold thread. The metallic thread inserted between the silk strands stands out on the background cloth, creating a shimmering effect.

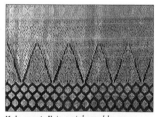

Kain sutera *is a type of* songket *used for sarongs traditionally worn on formal or ceremonial occasions.*

Kain mastuli *is a rich and heavy variety of* songket *silk thread that is used when making traditional garments and decorative fabrics.*

WOODCARVING

Malaysian Borneo boasts the best and most varied forms of woodcarving in the country. Indigenous people of the region are known for their carving of spirit and totem figures, masks, and good luck charms.

Malay woodcarvers *work deftly and with confident speed. Some of the best are found in Kuching and Kota Bharu.*

Elaborate wooden masks *are carved by the indigenous peoples of Malaysian Borneo to fend off evil and bad luck.*

This gilt carving *of a bat on the window frame of a Malaccan house is a Peranakan symbol of good fortune.*

A tribal grave post *with a totemic figure is displayed at Kuching's Sarawak Museum.*

Intricately carved shields *were traditionally carried by Iban warriors into battle. The heavy wooden shields were often decorated with hideous faces to demoralize foes.*

METALWORK

Traditional Malaysian silverware and jewelry has been influenced by the Peranakan. Metalware produced and sold in the markets of Penang, Malacca, and Kuching often shows considerable southern Indian influence. The products include gongs produced in Sumangkap (*see p182*), a range of brass items, and *keris*.

Brass *is used for making household, decorative, and ceremonial objects. This brass screen in Kuala Lumpur's Sri Kanthaswamy Hindu Temple shows the intricate detailing that is typical of Malaysian craftsmanship.*

Keris, *or daggers, are weapons unique to Malay culture. They are said to possess magical powers that protect their owners and bring death to enemies.*

Silverware *of the finest quality is produced in Kelantan and Terengganu. Malaysian silverware is known for its intricate filigree work and designs.*

THE HISTORY OF MALAYSIA AND SINGAPORE

The early history of the Malay peninsula is shrouded in mystery. But records of the subsequent centuries depict a great trading nation beleaguered by foreign invaders attracted by its abundant natural wealth and strategic position between the key maritime trade centers of India and China. Following their independence, Malaysia and Singapore have rapidly emerged as models of economic progress and modernization.

The discovery, in 1958, of a human skull at Niah Caves in Sarawak and stone tools from Perak point towards human occupation of the region as far back as 40,000 BC. Findings of pottery and stone objects from both the peninsula and Malaysian Borneo, dating between 2800 and 500 BC, prove the existence of a Neolithic culture in this region.

Perak Man, reconstruction at Lenggong museum

Although few iron and bronze objects have been found in Malaysia, evidence in the form of huge Bronze Age Dongson drums links Peninsular Malaysia to northern Vietnam at around 500–300 BC. The drums, together with beads and pottery from India and China also found on the peninsula and dating back to the same time, indicate that international trade networks were already well-established and foreign goods were being exchanged for the region's rich resources, including tin, gold, aromatic woods, and spices. So rich was this trade that the Indians seem to have referred to the peninsula

as *suvarnabhumi*, or the land of gold, from as early on as 200 BC. The growth of trade relations with India brought the coastal peoples of the Strait of Malacca into contact with Buddhism and Hinduism, as well as with Indian notions of kingship. For example, the Malay word for ruler, *rajah*, was borrowed from Sanskrit. Significant archaeological finds, such as Sanskrit inscriptions and Hindu and Buddhist statues (especially in Kedah in northwest Malaysia), suggest that Indian influence was well-established in a number of settlements along the west coast of the peninsula by the 5th century AD.

Chinese trade was significant too, beginning from the 2nd century, via the Cambodian kingdom of Funan which extended its influence into the northern peninsula. The growing use of the sea to transport goods from western Asia to China gave further impetus to the emergence of port kingdoms in the Malaysian world.

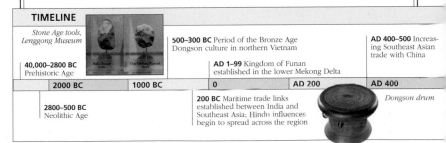

TIMELINE

Stone Age tools, Lenggong Museum

40,000–2800 BC Prehistoric Age

500–300 BC Period of the Bronze Age Dongson culture in northern Vietnam

AD 1–99 Kingdom of Funan established in the lower Mekong Delta

AD 400–500 Increasing Southeast Asian trade with China

2000 BC	1000 BC	0	AD 200	AD 400

2800–500 BC Neolithic Age

200 BC Maritime trade links established between India and Southeast Asia; Hindu influences begin to spread across the region

Dongson drum

◁ **Panoramic Sketch of Prince of Wales Island by William Daniell, 1821**

SRIVIJAYA

The first of the port kingdoms to become a great pan-Malay confederation was the Hindu-Buddhist, maritime trade-based empire of Srivijaya. It emerged in the course of the 7th century and established its capital near Palembang in southeastern Sumatra.

Arrival of Arab merchants and missionaries in SE Asia

Srivijaya evolved into a wealthy and powerful Malay kingdom, dominating maritime passages around the Strait of Malacca and the Sunda Strait (between Java and Sumatra), as well as the overland portage routes across Peninsular Malaysia as far north as Nakhon Si Thammarat in present-day Thailand. From its strategic position, Srivijaya was able to attract and monopolize overseas commerce between India and China, acting as a great entrepôt for Southeast Asian shipping as well as a source for rare and valuable goods, from scented woods to gold.

The rulers of Srivijaya developed methods of government which became popular with succeeding kingdoms such as Malacca. Paramount among these concepts was complete loyalty to the ruler, who was associated with divine powers – disloyalty was severely punished. While a mixture of Hinduism, Buddhism, and indigenous spirit belief was practiced in Srivijaya, it gained prominence as a center of Buddhist learning.

Terengganu Stone

Srivijaya prospered until the 11th century, after which it began to decline, weakened by wars both with Java and the south Indian Chola kingdom. The power of the Hindu-Buddhist *rajahs* was also being undermined by Islam. At the same time, the increasing presence of Chinese ships encouraged Srivijaya's vassals to break away from Palembang's grip. By the late-13th century, the Thai kingdoms of Sukhothai and Ayutthaya had acquired considerable influence over the peninsula, as had the Hindu Majapahit empire of Java over southeast Sumatra.

THE SPREAD OF ISLAM

Islam came to Southeast Asia as a religion of trade, not one of conquest. Introduced by Arab merchants and missionaries around the 11th century, the religion spread rapidly across Peninsular Malaysia with Indian-Muslim traders. The Terengganu Stone, discovered in the peninsula's northeastern province in 1899, bears an inscription in the Malay Arabic script, suggesting that Islamic law was established here as early as 1303. However, Islam received its greatest boost when it was made state religion of the Sultanate of Malacca in the 15th century. Spreading to the farthest corners of the Malaccan empire, Islam gradually came to be associated with the national identity of Malays.

TIMELINE

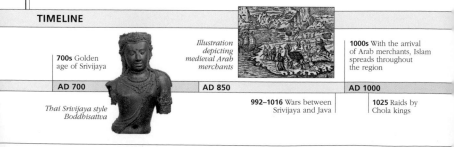

700s Golden age of Srivijaya

Thai Srivijaya style Boddhisattva

Illustration depicting medieval Arab merchants

1000s With the arrival of Arab merchants, Islam spreads throughout the region

AD 700	AD 850	AD 1000

992–1016 Wars between Srivijaya and Java

1025 Raids by Chola kings

THE RISE OF MALACCA

Around 1400, Parameswara, the prince of Palembang, attempted to throw off Javanese domination over his realm by fleeing to Tumasik in present-day Singapore, before finally establishing a new kingdom at Malacca. Ideally located on the Strait of Malacca and within easy reach of the spice islands of Indonesia, the new state attracted trade from across Asia.

Plan of the city of Malacca by Pedro Baretti de Resende, c.1511.

In 1405, Zheng He, the great Chinese Ming admiral, launched his explorations of Southeast Asia and the Indian Ocean, and made Malacca the foremost outpost for his fleet. This helped secure a trade agreement with China as well as protection from its emperor against the constant threat of Siamese attacks. The city of Malacca became truly cosmopolitan: given the seasonal winds, ships from China, Japan, India, and Persia might spend at least a year in the port.

The spread of Islam in Malacca is believed to have taken place between 1425 and 1445, when Parameswara's successors made Islam the state religion and took the title of Sultan, thus giving rise to the Sultanate of Malacca. The adoption of Islam helped link Malacca to the vast Muslim trading world, and by the end

of the 15th century it was the region's major entrepôt, dominating much of the Malay world. Though ties with the Imperial Court in China were fostered for added protection, the sultanate developed into an independent and centralized administration with the sultan as absolute ruler. He oversaw a fairly complex legal and administrative structure which ensured the stability of the kingdom. High-ranking officials of the state included the *bendahara*, or prime minister, the *laksamanas*, or admirals, who commanded the army and navy, the *temenggung*, or minister responsible for defense and justice, and the *syahbandar*, or harbor master. Government was formalized in the *Undang-Undang Malacca*, or codified laws of Malacca, which constantly evolved under successive sultans. The basis for Malaccan law was threefold – Hindu-Buddhist tradition, Islamic tradition, and *adapt*, or indigenous tradition. Concurrently, Malacca became a center for Islamic dissemination throughout present-day Malaysia, Indonesia, and Brunei. The state's influence was reflected in the emergence of the Malay language as the language of trade in the region.

Relief of Zheng He, Chinese temple in Semarang, Java

Sukhothai-style vessel with lid

1400 Parameswara founds the kingdom of Malacca

1425–45 Malacca ruler adopts Islam and takes the title of Sultan

| 1150 | 1300 | 1450 |

1238 Foundation of the Thai Kingdom of Sukhothai

1303 Terengganu Stone records the establishment of Islamic law

Malacca tin coin, the earliest known indigenous coins of the Malay States

PORTUGUESE CONQUEST

By the 15th century, the Portuguese were eager to challenge Venice's position as the sole suppliers of spices in Europe, as well as to break the monopoly of the Arab and Indian Muslim traders over the immensely valuable spice trade. In 1509, an initial Portuguese expedition under Admiral Lopez de Sequeira arrived in Malacca, but was driven off by the sultan's army. A much larger and better-equipped fleet, led by Admiral Alfonso de Albuquerque in 1511, succeeded in capturing Malacca after a 40-day siege, ushering in the era of European colonial powers in the region. Sultan Mahmud Shah escaped to the interior of the peninsula, where his elder son, Muzaffar Shah, eventually established the Sultanate of Perak in the north, and his younger son, Alauddin Riyat Shah, founded the Johor Sultanate in the south. This period also saw the rise of the Sumatran state of Aceh as a regional power.

Alfonso de Albuquerque

Although Malacca remained a Portuguese colony for over a century, the period saw a three-way struggle between Aceh, the sultanates of Johor and Perak, and the Portuguese, for the control of Malacca, which lasted most of the 16th century.

THE DUTCH ERA

The new kingdom of Johor faced its own share of assaults, from both the Portuguese and Aceh, and it was not until the arrival of the Dutch, toward the end of the 16th century, that it succeeded in consolidating its position.

Looking to protect itself against its enemies, the sultan forged an alliance with the Dutch. In 1602, all the Dutch trading enterprises in Asia combined to form The United Netherlands Chartered East India Company (VOC), which recognized the need to seize control of Malacca to gain monopoly of the spice trade. In 1640, the Dutch, with the help of the Sultan of Johor, attacked Malacca and after a year-long siege succeeded in displacing the Portuguese. In return for its support, Johor was granted trading privileges and by the end of the 17th century it had grown into a powerful kingdom. At the height of its power it controlled southern Peninsular Malaysia and part of eastern Sumatra.

When the Dutch took over, much of Malacca lay in ruin owing to the 1640–41 siege. During their rule, the Dutch rebuilt the city and many of these structures survive to this day. Among the prominent buildings is the Stadthuys (see p122), the oldest Dutch building in Southeast Asia. Yet, over the next 180 years under the Dutch, Malacca's prosperity declined as the new colonial rulers concentrated on

Dutch ships attacking a Portuguese vessel on the Indian Ocean

TIMELINE

1511 Portuguese Admiral Alfonso d'Albuquerque seizes Malacca

1550s Rise of Aceh in north Sumatra

1602 United Netherlands Chartered East India Company (VOC) formed

1641 Dutch capture Malacca from Portugal

1500

1560

1620

1528–35 Sultanates of Johor and Perak founded

Coat of arms of the VOC above one of the gates on Galle Fort, Ceylon (Sri Lanka)

Dutch merchant and VOC ships at Jakarta, 17th century

developing their main base at Batavia, which is now Jakarta in Indonesia.

BORNEO

Until the arrival of the British, the areas that now comprise Sarawak, Sabah, and the tiny, oil-rich state of Brunei had little to do with the Malay peninsula. Most of Borneo, as well as part of the neighboring Sulu Archipelago (present-day Philippines), was ruled by the powerful Brunei Sultanate. In 1704, during a period of internal unrest, Brunei appears to have ceded part of Sabah to the Sultan of Sulu in return for the latter's military assistance. The territory eventually passed to Malaysia via the British, but the Philippines tried to reclaim Sabah as their land after the formation of Malaysia in 1963.

ARRIVAL OF THE BRITISH

Things changed dramatically in Malaysia with the arrival of the British in the 18th century. The British East India Company (EIC) needed a halfway base for their maritime trade with India and China. In 1786, Sir Francis Light *(see p103)* signed a treaty and acquired Penang from the Sultan of Kedah on behalf of the company and established it as a

commercial and naval base. He also declared it as a free trading port and Penang soon thrived. After Europe's Napoleonic Wars (1800–15), Britain emerged as the leading power in Asia. In 1819, Sir Stamford Raffles *(see p38)* repeated Light's work at Penang with considerable success in Singapore, which also became a booming trade port. In 1824, Britain and the Netherlands signed the Anglo-Dutch Treaty dividing the Malay world, with the Malay peninsula passing to Britain and the bulk of the Indonesian Archipelago to the Dutch. Thus, Malacca passed to the British in exchange for Bengkulu on Sumatra, which went to Holland.

Initial British policy towards Malaysia was determinedly one of "trade, not territory," and also like the Dutch, but unlike the Portuguese, the British were not interested in spreading Christianity, but rather in free trade and profit. They limited their direct control to the Straits Settlements *(see pp38–9)*, formed in 1826. The Malay Peninsula became part of Britain's sphere of influence, but remained largely self-governing and independent.

British ships arriving to take control of Malacca in 1824

Sir Stamford Raffles

1704 Brunei cedes part of Borneo to Sulu

1819 Sir Stamford Raffles founds Singapore

1826 Formation of the Straits Settlements

1680   1740   1800

Detail of Borneo from Peter Plancius's chart of Borneo, 1595

1786 Sir Francis Light acquires Penang for the British East India Company

1824 Malacca passes to Britain under the Anglo-Dutch Treaty

The Straits Settlements

Between 1826 and 1946, the British Crown held a group of geographically separate territories consisting of Penang, Malacca, Singapore, Province Wellesley, and surrounding islands, under the collective name of the Straits Settlements. Colonial influence in the area, however, began as early as 1786, when the Sultan of Kedah ceded Penang to the British East India Company in exchange for protection from Siam and Burma. As other areas came under colonial power, they were built up to promote trade. The consequent close association of the region is still visible today in the racial and cultural ties of its mixed ethnic communities and the legacies of its architectural style and landmarks.

British East India vessel off Malacca, early 19th century

The British in Penang *employed Chinese and Indian migrants, and sometimes indigenous Malays, as laborers on road construction projects throughout the island.*

COLONIZATION

The British did not arrive at the Straits Settlements in large numbers, instead establishing themselves as the ruling elite and employing migrants from India, China, and other parts of the British Empire to administer the new colonies and serve as soldiers, laborers, and tradesmen.

Chinese junks were used extensively for trade between the Settlements.

STAMFORD RAFFLES

Sir Stamford Raffles

One of the British Empire's most celebrated statesmen, Sir Thomas Stamford Raffles (1781–1826) began his career at the age of 14 as a clerk with the British East India Company in London. He worked his way up to Lieutenant-Governor of Java in 1811 and was knighted in 1817. In 1819, Raffles signed a treaty with a local sultan, laying the foundation for modern Singapore. Also a founder and first president of the Zoological Society of London, he is remembered in the name of the largest flower in the world, the rafflesia.

Sultan Abdul Hamid Halim Shah of Kedah *and his entourage in 1900. Like all sultans who reigned after the British took control of Penang in 1786, he had no real power in the island's government.*

TRADE

The Straits Settlements were acquired by the British to function as free trade ports, not to promote territorial ambitions. By establishing such ports, Britain sought to dominate trade routes between Europe and Asia.

Spice plantations *were set up in Penang to grow mace, nutmeg, cinnamon, and pepper, which were rare and valuable commodities in 18th-century Europe.*

Penang's first coin, *bearing the British East India Company crest, was minted in 1787 in Calcutta. Sir Francis Light is said to have fired cannons loaded with coins into the jungle to coax laborers to clear it.*

1/4 cent coins, *bearing the head of Queen Victoria, were struck in 1826, the year the Straits Settlements passed into the hands of the British Government.*

A new port at Singapore *was envisaged by Raffles as a free port astride the sea lanes between Europe and the Far East. Today, it is one of the busiest ports in the world.*

Gas lighting was one of many innovations brought by the British to the Settlements.

CULTURE

The Straits Settlements developed as a fascinating melting pot of cultures. Immigrants from Asia lived side by side with Portuguese, Dutch, and British settlers, as well as indigenous Malays.

Peranakan culture *grew alongside the development of the Settlements. New customs were born out of the marriages between the Chinese and Malay, which blended the traditions of each culture. At Peranakan weddings, for example, couples traditionally wore Chinese dress.*

Early Chinese settlers, *as well as Peranakan men, wore their hair in distinctive long ponytails, or queues, well into the late-19th century. This was a sign of their allegiance to the Qing Empire.*

Kling *is an outdated name for early Tamil settlers originating from southern India. They formed the majority of South Asian migrants to the Straits Settlements.*

A lithograph depicting the scene of a battle with pirates during James Brooke's rule

THE RISE OF THE WHITE RAJAHS

Britain did not include Borneo in the Anglo-Dutch Treaty, preferring to concentrate their interests on the peninsula. By the late 18th century, Brunei was in decline and faced increasing unrest from the indigenous peoples as well as territorial claims from the Sulu Sultanate. In 1838, James Brooke, an explorer and former officer with the East India Company, set out to seek his fortune in the East Indies. En route he passed through Singapore and was asked by the British governor to deliver a message to Rajah Muda Hashim, Governor of Kuching in Sarawak. Brooke arrived in Sarawak in 1839 to find the territory in a state of revolt, with the indigenous Dayaks rising up against the Sultan of Brunei. He was enlisted to help the sultan and together they crushed the rebellion within a year.

James Brooke, the first White Rajah of Sarawak

As a reward, in 1841, the sultan made Brooke the Rajah of Sarawak, the first of three White Rajahs (*see p157*). Brooke, backed by British naval power, used his position to

consolidate his rule over the indigenous people, as well as ward off unruly Malay pirates who wreaked havoc on the coast. Brooke's rule was remarkably progressive, and he sought to establish law and order as well as welfare for the local people. He gradually won the trust of the indigenous communities, although he faced and put down a rebellion by Chinese migrants in 1857. When he died in 1868, James Brooke was succeeded as rajah by his nephew, Charles Brooke (1829–1917) who was responsible for expanding the territory of Sarawak at the expense of the shrinking Brunei Sultanate. During his reign, Sarawak also became a British protectorate in 1888, with the Brooke family retaining control of the internal administration.

EXPANSION OF BRITISH CONTROL

In the mid-19th century, Sabah remained under the loose control of Brunei (with Sulu chiefs exercising authority at a local level). Enfeebled by internal disputes, Brunei sought to

TIMELINE

Signing the treaty for the cession of Labuan, Borneo, in 1846

1847 Signing of the treaty of Labuan

1865 Brunei leases Sabah to Claude Lee Moses, the American consul

1874 Treaty of Pangkor signed; first British Resident installed in Perak

1840	1850	1860	1870

1841 James Brooke becomes the first White Rajah

1857 Brooke puts down Chinese rebellion

Charles Brooke, second White Rajah of Sarawak

1868 Death of James Brooke, Charles Brooke succeeds

lease the territory, first to Claude Lee Moscs, the American consul in Brunei, in 1865, then to Baron von Overbeck, the Austrian consul in Hong Kong in 1875, and finally to Englishman Alfred Dent, who established the British North Borneo Company in 1881. In 1888, Sabah, along with Sarawak, came under British government protection. Like the White Rajahs, however, the company retained control of internal

British officials with the sultans of the Federated Malay States

administration. A resistance movement started by Mat Salleh in 1895 against the company's rule was not defeated until 1905 (five years after Mat Salleh's death). Following that, Sabah remained a quiet colonial backwater.

At about the same time, the British began to refine their policies of non-intervention in the Malay peninsular states. The booming tin industry had attracted large numbers of Chinese immigrants to the states of Perak and Selangor. This led to ethnic clashes with the Malays, as well as to civil disorders caused by Chinese criminal gangs. Infighting also raged in various Malay sultanates. The British feared that another major European power, notably Germany, might exploit these weaknesses to gain a foothold on the Malaysian mainland. Hence, in 1874, through the Treaty of Pangkor, the first British Resident was appointed in Perak, whom the sultan agreed to consult on all issues except those involving Muslim religion and Malay custom. However, increased British control of judicial and financial affairs sparked unrest amongst the Perak Malays and led to the murder of the first Resident, J.W.W. Birch, in 1875.

This revolt was quickly quashed, and the process of appointing British

Residents continued. In 1896, the states of Pahang, Selangor, and Negeri Sembilan joined Perak as part of the British-controlled Federated Malay States, which were administered from the Sultan Abdul Samad Building in Kuala Lumpur. In 1909, under the terms of the Anglo-Siamese Treaty, the former Thai tributaries of Kelantan, Terengganu, Kedah, and Perlis, joined by Johor in 1914, came under the system of British Residents, becoming known as the Unfederated Malay States. Thus, together with the Straits Settlements and Sabah, Sarawak, and Brunei, British consolidation of power over Malaya was complete by World War I.

Sultan Abdul Samad Building, Kuala Lumpur

1877 Brunei renews lease on Sabah to Overbeck

STATE OF NORTH BORNEO
ONE CENT

Stamp issued by the North Borneo Company

1888 British Resident appointed in Pahang

1895 Mat Salleh resistance movement begins in Sabah

1896 Creation of the Federated Malay States

1909 Unfederated Malay States formed

| 1880 | 1890 | 1900 | 1910 |

1881 Alfred Dent sets up the BNBC

1888 Sarawak and Sabah become British protectorates

1914 Johor joins the Unfederated Malay States

1877 Rubber tree introduced via Brazil, Kew Gardens, and Ceylon (Sri Lanka), to the Botanic Gardens in Singapore

Sir Frank Swettenham, first Resident-General of the Federated Malay States

A British rubber planter overseeing Indian workers, Malaysia

COLONIAL LIFE

Having taken charge of the entire peninsula, the British turned their energies towards developing a productive economy. Peninsular Malaysia emerged in the 20th century as the world's leading producer of both rubber and tin. In Borneo, Sarawak was a securely established and relatively prosperous territory by the time Charles Vyner Brooke took over as the third White Rajah in 1917, while Sabah was profiting from the timber, rubber, and tobacco industries. Large-scale immigration from India and China was encouraged to supply the workforce for the colonial economy. The Malays were recognized as indigenous people, but were largely encouraged to stay in their villages. By the late 1930s, ordinary Malays were less well off than the urban Chinese, and in danger of becoming a minority in their own homeland. The stage had been set for decades of racial tensions. Politicization and elite sentiment for independence along ethnic lines also began to grow.

The advent of World War II ensured that colonial life would never be the same.

WORLD WAR II

Troops of the Japanese Imperial Army landed on the east coast of the peninsula in December 1941. Within two months, they had conquered it, and Singapore, and Borneo as well. For the next three years they would unleash a particularly ruthless regime. The *sook ching* (purification by elimination) massacres in the first months of Japanese rule involved the deaths of between 40,000 and 70,000 ethnic Chinese in Singapore alone. About 75,000 Malaysians, mostly Indian Tamils, were recruited to work on the Burma-Thailand "Death" Railway. With malnourishment, appalling working conditions, and the brutality of the

Japanese troops marching through downtown Singapore in December 1941

Japanese overseers, death rates escalated to 40 percent.

Some Malaysians resisted, notably the guerrilla units of the Malayan Communist Party (MCP), armed by British saboteurs in the underground Force 136. At the same time, to bolster their rule, the Japanese encouraged radical Malayan nationalists to organize paramilitary and political organizations. Hopelessly overstretched throughout Asia and the Pacific, Japanese rule had induced economic chaos in the Malay peninsula and Borneo by 1944. But it was the dropping of atomic bombs on Hiroshima and Nagasaki in August 1945 that finally forced Japan to surrender.

TIMELINE

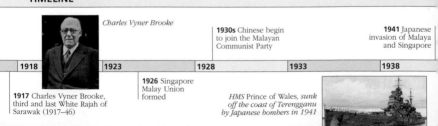

Charles Vyner Brooke

1930s Chinese begin to join the Malayan Communist Party

1941 Japanese invasion of Malaya and Singapore

| 1918 | 1923 | 1928 | 1933 | 1938 |

1917 Charles Vyner Brooke, third and last White Rajah of Sarawak (1917–46)

1926 Singapore Malay Union formed

HMS Prince of Wales, *sunk off the coast of Terengganu by Japanese bombers in 1941*

Declaration of independence from British rule by Tunku Abdul Rahman in August 1957

THE EMERGENCY

In the reoccupation, the first British step was to establish the Malayan Union in 1946. This united all the peninsular states into a central administration under British rule and granted equal citizenship rights to all ethnic groups. Singapore, Sabah, and Sarawak were to be governed separately as crown colonies.

The union was strongly opposed by the Malay population and led to the formation of the first Malay political party, the United Malays National Organisation (UMNO). The Malayan Union was subsequently replaced by the Federation of Malaya, which excluded Singapore, and granted special rights to the Malays. However, the Chinese were dissatisfied with this development, and in June 1948, the Malayan Races Liberation Army (MRLA), the armed wing of the MCP, returned to the jungle to begin an insurgency against the British, under the leadership of Chin Peng. So began the hard-fought Emergency.

Chin Peng's war was ultimately doomed. Few Malays or Indians supported the MCP, while the resettlement of 400,000 rural Chinese cut off the guerrillas from food and intelligence supplies. The MCP leaders finally fled to Thailand in the late 1950s, and by 1960 the government of independent Malaya declared the Emergency over.

MERDEKA (INDEPENDENCE)

Parallel to their campaign against the MRLA, the British pursued talks with anti-communist Malay nationalists, promising independence. In 1955, elections were held to determine the government for the new country. This was won by the Alliance Party, formed by the UMNO, the Malayan Chinese Association, and the Malayan Indian Congress. On August 31, 1957, Malaya gained independence, with Tunku Abdul Rahman as its first prime minister. Sarawak, Sabah, and Singapore remained crown colonies, although Singapore became self-governing in 1959. In 1961, a new federation uniting the peninsular states, Singapore, Sarawak, Sabah, and Brunei, was proposed. Despite the opposition from Indonesia and the Philippines, the planned union went ahead, and Malaysia was proclaimed on September 16, 1963, but without Brunei, which opted out.

1946 Malayan Union established; UMNO set up

1948 State of Emergency declared, which lasts until 1960; Federation of Malaya replaces the Malayan Union

Tunku Abdul Rahman signing Federation of Malaya (Independence) Agreement, 1957

1961 Tunku Abdul Rahman proposes a new Malaysian Federation

1943	1948	1953	1958	1963

1945 Japanese surrender; British reoccupy Borneo, Malaya, and Singapore

1953 Alliance Party formed

1957 Malaya attains independence; Tunku Abdul Rahman becomes first prime minister

1959 Singapore granted internal self-government; Lee Kuan Yew is first prime minister

1963 Malaysia established; Brunei opts out

Malay Royal Regiment troops patrolling the streets of Kuala Lumpur following the May 13, 1969 riots

KONFRONTASI

Both Indonesia and the Philippines immediately severed diplomatic relations with the new state of Malaysia. Indonesian president Sukarno began a policy of Konfrontasi, or confrontation, involving infiltration and sabotage. Indonesian armed troops crossed into Sabah and Sarawak, and even landed in Peninsular Malaysia and Singapore. Over the next four years the Malaysian army, backed by British, New Zealand, and Australian forces, defeated Indonesian attempts to subvert the new federation. Malaysia was thus established as a secure, internationally recognized state. However, in 1965, Singapore

Inaugural meeting of ASEAN members in August 1967

reluctantly left the Malaysian Federation due to continuing political disagreements and became an independent country. Still, the two neighbors remained closely associated. In 1967, Malaysia and Singapore joined the Association of Southeast Asian Nations (ASEAN) and were two of its five original members.

ETHNIC AND ECONOMIC TENSIONS

In the late 1960s, Malaysia and Singapore were still relatively impoverished by the effects of war and also riven with ethnic tensions. The departure of Singapore from the Federation of Malaysia ensured a Malay Muslim majority within Malaysia, but Malay politicians and the ethnic Malay population were still concerned by the economic power wielded by the Chinese. In 1967, the National Language Act was passed to ensure the primacy of the Malay language. The move was resented by the Chinese. Ethnic tensions first came to a head in Singapore, where there was rioting between the Malays and Chinese in 1964. In the 1969 general elections, the Alliance Party

TIMELINE

1963 Sukarno starts policy of Konfrontasi

1967 Malaysia and Singapore join ASEAN

1969 Race riots in Kuala Lumpur

1981 Mahathir Mohamad becomes Malaysia's fourth prime minister

1964		1974		1984

1965 Singapore leaves Malaysia and becomes an independent state

1970 Tun Abdul Razak takes over as Malaysia's prime minister; NEP introduced favoring the *bumiputra*

Offshore oil rig in Sarawak

polled less than 50 percent of the popular vote, but retained its majority in the parliament. A celebration march by the opposition parties led to an outbreak of race riots in Kuala Lumpur on May 13, 1969, when hundreds of ethnic Chinese were massacred.

The Malaysian government, under Tun Abdul Razak, who had taken over from Tunku Abdul Rahman in 1970, was badly shaken. It responded by introducing the New Economic Policy (NEP) in 1970, which was designed to favor the *bumiputra (see pp20–21)* and improve their economic standing in society. At the same time, the authorities made it clear that no further racial attacks on ethnic Chinese would be tolerated. The Alliance Party also broadened its coalition to include members of the opposition and formed the Barisan Nasional (National Front), which continues to be in power today.

Kuala Lumpur's soaring skyline, dominated by the Petronas Towers, a symbol of economic prosperity

MALAYSIA AND SINGAPORE TODAY

Over the next 20 years, using a cautious mixture of financial inducements and firm paternalism, both Malaysia and Singapore remained peaceful as their economies soared. Malaysia prospered due to world demand for its traditional products – rubber, palm oil, tea, and tin – and by the end of the 1970s, the development of light industries and the discovery of oil and natural gas reserves in the South China Sea provided an extra boost. A period of remarkable economic and social development in the 1980s and 1990s was overseen by Prime Minister Mahathir Mohamad, who came to power in 1981.

At its independence in 1965, Singapore seemed to face a bleak economic future. However, under Lee Kuan Yew, Prime Minister from 1959 to 1990, it grew and prospered as a powerhouse of light industry and high technology. It also became one of the world's greatest sea ports.

In 2003, Abdullah Ahmad Badawi took over from Mahathir Mohamad as prime minister of Malaysia. In Singapore, Lee Kuan Yew's successor, Goh Chok Tong, was replaced by Yew's son, Lee Hsien Loong, in 2004. Both governments have now entered a less authoritarian era, although one where media and freedom of speech are still tightly monitored. The two countries remain close despite an ongoing dispute over the construction of a new causeway between Johor Bahru and Singapore, and their economies continue to surge ahead, as do living standards, higher education, health, and social services.

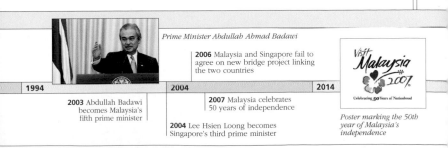

Prime Minister Abdullah Ahmad Badawi

2006 Malaysia and Singapore fail to agree on new bridge project linking the two countries

| 1994 | 2004 | 2014 |

2003 Abdullah Badawi becomes Malaysia's fifth prime minister

2007 Malaysia celebrates 50 years of independence

2004 Lee Hsien Loong becomes Singapore's third prime minister

Visit *Malaysia* 2007
Celebrating 50 Years of Nationhood

Poster marking the 50th year of Malaysia's independence

MALAYSIA REGION BY REGION

A PORTRAIT OF MALAYSIA

W*ith its magnificent natural beauty and unique cultural heritage, Malaysia is a fascinating Southeast Asian destination. A relatively young country that celebrated 50 years of independence in 2007, it has progressed remarkably and has emerged as one of the most successful economies in Asia.*

Situated at the crossroads of ancient maritime trade routes, Malaysia has long been a cultural melting pot. The bulk of the population lives on Peninsular Malaysia. While about half the country's 27 million people are of Malay origin, there are significant Chinese and Indian minorities, as well as many indigenous communities. The country's diversity is apparent in its social customs and festivals, and its many cuisines and languages.

Performers at a cultural show in Penang

SOCIETY AND POLITICS

Malaysia is a constitutional monarchy, based on the political system of its former colonial ruler, Britain. In practice, however, there is more power vested in the executive branch of government than the judiciary. The country is headed nominally by a supreme ruler, a rotating position that is held for a five-year term by sultans of nine hereditary Malay sultanates, while the government is led by an elected prime minister, currently Datuk Seri Abdullah Ahmad Badawi, who is assisted by a cabinet of ministers. The government's two-tier parliament consists of a lower house with 219 elected representatives and an upper house with 70 senators. Elections are held every five years. Since independence, the country has been ruled by a multiracial coalition named Barisan Nasional (National Front), of which the United Malays National Organization (UMNO) is the largest political party.

ECONOMY

From the early 1970s through the late 1990s, Malaysia transformed itself from an economy based on mining and agriculture to one dominated by manufacturing and exports, particularly of electronic components. Palm oil also continues to be one of the most important exports. Other prominent contributors to the economy are oil and gas production, timber, and tourism. The country has maintained steady economic growth over the past couple

The port and the stunning Masjid Negeri in Kuantan, Pahang

A pair of rhinoceros hornbills, the state bird of Sarawak, in the lush Malaysian rain forest

of decades, fueling rapid development in the major cities. Its main trading partners are the USA, China, and Japan, all of which are significant sources of foreign investment.

ENVIRONMENT

Malaysia, like many developing nations, faces its own set of environmental issues, including air and water pollution, deforestation, and the depletion of wildlife species. Although stretches of the country's ancient rain forests, and the wildlife they shelter, are protected in national parks, intense logging is changing the face of the country, transforming jungles into barren hillsides. Fortunately, several international bodies, such as WWF, the global conservation organization, are very active in Malaysia and their persistent campaigning has at least slowed down the rate of environmental degradation. Despite their efforts, the Sumatran rhinoceros and the leatherback turtle face extinction.

CULTURE AND ARTS

Malaysia's ethnic mosaic endows it with an infinitely varied and cosmopolitan culture, assimilating Malay, Chinese, and Indian customs, traditions, and beliefs, as well as those of its indigenous peoples. The ethnic diversity is also reflected in the variety of religions followed here. Although Islam is the state religion, Buddhism, Hinduism, and Christianity, among others, are practiced freely. Traditional Malay performing arts, including the fascinating *wayang kulit*, or shadow-puppet plays, continue to thrive and can be seen during festivals or at cultural shows. Local pastimes such as kite-flying and top-spinning are still practiced, particularly on the east coast of the peninsula. The country has a vibrant handicrafts tradition, ranging from exquisitely woven textiles to basketware and woodcarving. Malaysia is also gaining a healthy contemporary art scene, with work by the country's leading artists on display in galleries.

Puppeteer maneuvering figures during a show

MALAYSIA THROUGH THE YEAR

Ｗith its unique blend of diverse ethnic groups and cultures, Malaysia hosts a range of festivals and events throughout the year. The country's religious festivals include the Islamic Hari Raya Puasa and Hindu Deepavali. Sporting events, such as Formula 1 racing, and traditional pastimes such as kite flying are also enjoyed. In addition to nationwide events, an array of state-specific festivals are celebrated. As many people visit family during major festivals, all forms of transport become congested. Many religious festivals are based on the lunar calendar, so dates can vary. Islamic festivals, for example, move forward by about ten days each year in relation to the Gregorian calendar. For exact dates, check with Malaysia Tourism.

Iban warrior performing a traditional dance

JANUARY TO MARCH

Seasons vary little in Malaysia, with only the early months of the year distinguished by heavy rain on the east coast of Peninsular Malaysia. Still, spirits are far from dampened by the rain and festivals such as the Chinese New Year are celebrated with enthusiasm.

Ponggal *(Jan/Feb)*, nationwide. A Tamil (southern Indian) harvest festival celebrated by boiling rice, sugar, and milk until the pot overflows, symbolizing prosperity. This is offered to gods at Hindu temples.
Thaipusam *(Jan/Feb)*, nationwide. A Hindu festival honoring Lord Murugan, in which thousands of devotees carry *kavadis*, or steel arches, attached to their skin by hooks, and walk in a massive procession from the Sri Maha Mariamman Temple *(see p64)* to the Batu Caves *(see p90)*, one of the largest temple caves in the country.

Flora Fest *(Jan/Feb)*, Klang Valley and Putrajaya. Floats decked in flowers are paraded through the streets, accompanied by cultural performances.
Federal Territory Day *(Feb 1)*, Kuala Lumpur, Labuan, and Putrajaya. Malaysia's three federal territories put on parades, firework displays, and cultural shows.
Le Tour de Langkawi *(Feb)*, Langkawi to Merdeka Square in Kuala Lumpur. Top cyclists from around the world compete in Asia's version of the Tour de France.
Malaysian Open Golf Championship *(Feb)*, nationwide. An international golfing event that takes place at the top golf courses in the country, including the Royal Selangor Golf and Country Club and the Kuala Lumpur Golf and Country Club.
Hari Raya Haji *(variable)*, nationwide. This Islamic festival celebrates the return of pilgrims from the Haj to Mecca with prayers and animal sacrifices. This is a

Worshipers lighting candles at a church during Easter

public holiday in the states of Kedah, Kelantan, Perlis, and Terengganu.
Chinese New Year *(Jan/Feb)*, nationwide. The streets come alive to see out the old year and welcome the new, with dragon dances and Chinese opera performances. Debts are paid off, children are given presents of money, and mandarin oranges – a symbol of good luck – are eaten. Many shops and businesses close for a week.
Chap Goh Mei *(usually Feb)*, nationwide. The fifteenth day after the start of the Chinese New Year is marked by feasts and prayers.
Malaysian Grand Prix *(usually Mar)*, Selangor. The world's fastest Formula 1 drivers compete at the Sepang International Circuit.
Easter *(Mar/Apr)*, nationwide. The biggest ceremonies are held in Malacca with candle-lit processions at churches on Good Friday, which is a public holiday in Sabah and Sarawak.

Rubens Barrichello, for Ferrari, in the lead at the Malaysian Grand Prix

APRIL TO JUNE

This is the peak of the festival calendar especially for the Dayaks of Sarawak who celebrate the Gawai festival. Other highlights include the Buddhist Vesak.

KL International Arts Festival *(Apr)*, Kuala Lumpur. A showcase for Malaysian art with some eye-catching street art.
Pesta Kaul *(Apr)*, Mukah. A festival of the Melanau fishing communities to mark the beginning of the fishing season. Dare-devil acts are performed on *tibau,* or huge rattan swings.
Prophet Muhammad's Birthday *(variable)*, nationwide. Processions and Koran recitations are held to commemorate the birth of the Prophet Muhammad.
World Harvest Festival *(2nd weekend of May)*, Sarawak Cultural Village, located near Kuching. A cultural extravaganza in anticipation of the Gawai festival, with dance, music, and a beauty pageant.
Labuan International Sea Challenge *(May)*, Pulau Labuan. An international competition that includes fishing, swimming, and kayaking events.
Johor International Orchid Show *(May)*, Johor. An exhibition of rare orchids from around the globe.

Orang Ulu dancers in vibrant ethnic costumes at the Harvest Festival

Orchid at the Johor International Orchid Show

Colors of Malaysia *(May)*, nationwide. A month-long celebration of Malaysian culture, this event takes place in the big cities and features street parades, music, dance, and food festivals.
Miri International Jazz Festival *(May)*, Miri. Musicians from Europe, Australia, Africa, and Asia perform funk, fusion, Latin, and blues.
Tadau Kaamatan *(end of May)*, Penampang (Sabah). A festival for the Kadazan Dusun and Murut communities, who give thanks for a successful rice crop by singing, dancing, and electing a harvest queen.
Vesak *(May/Jun)*, nationwide. The most important festival of the year for Buddhists, honoring the birth, enlightenment, and death of the Buddha.
King's Birthday *(1st Sat in Jun)*, nationwide. There are processions in the streets

of Kuala Lumpur to celebrate the birthday of the king.
Gawai *(early Jun)*, across Sarawak. Marking the end of the rice harvest, this festival is the highlight of the year for the Dayaks of Sarawak and an occasion for feasting and dancing. There are many versions of Gawai, such as Gawai Padi, celebrated by the Bidayuh, one of the Dayak groups. It is an ideal time to visit a longhouse.
Fiesta San Pedro *(Jun)*, Malacca. The Eurasian community, who came here during the Portuguese occupation in the 16th century, decorate their boats to pay homage to St. Peter.
Penang International Dragon Boat Festival *(Jun/Jul)*, Penang. Long rowing boats, each decorated with a dragon's head and tail, participate in races to honor the memory of Chinese poet Qu Yuan, who drowned himself in 278 BC in a protest against corrupt politics.

Spectacular celebrations at the Colors of Malaysia festival

AVERAGE MONTHLY RAINFALL (KUALA LUMPUR)

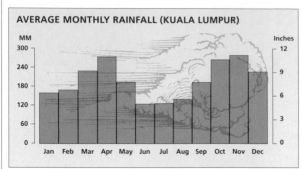

Rainfall Chart
Rainfall across the country is variable and it is difficult to show a national average. The wettest period for the east coast of the Malaysian Peninsula and Malaysian Borneo is November to March. The west coast of the peninsula sees rain from April to October.

JULY TO SEPTEMBER

The focus of festivities during these months are Merdeka Eve and National Day at the end of August, commemorating Malaysia's independence. Other colorful and unique events include the Rainforest Music Festival in Sarawak, the Sarawak Regatta, and the Mount Kinabalu Climbathon.

Malaysia Mega Sale Carnival *(Jul to Sep)*, nationwide. Substantial discounts are offered on everything from designer clothing to electronic gadgets at shopping malls and stores.
Rainforest World Music Festival *(Jul)*, Sarawak Cultural Village, near Kuching. An annual global event featuring music workshops and performances by renowned musicians from as far away as Madagascar, Albania, and Mongolia as well as rarely heard indigenous musicians from across the country *(see p159)*.

Fireworks display during National Day celebrations

Kuching Festival *(Aug)*, Kuching. This celebration of Sarawak's culture comprises concerts, exhibitions, theater performances, and food fairs, and lasts for a month.
Merdeka Eve *(Aug 30)*, nationwide. Fireworks displays and cultural performances in major towns and cities herald National Day.
National Day *(Aug 31)*, nationwide. Parades, pop music shows, and a plethora of competitions are among the celebrations that mark the anniversary of the country's independence.
Festival of the Hungry Ghosts *(Aug/Sep)*, nationwide. This Chinese festival is held to appease the spirits of the dead released from purgatory during the seventh lunar month. Joss sticks, candles, and paper money are burnt outside homes and Chinese street opera is performed.
Ramadan *(variable)*, nationwide. This is the Muslim holy month during which Muslims fast in daylight hours and eat only after sunset. Street stalls set up outside mosques in the evening offer many Muslim delicacies.
Hari Raya Puasa *(variable)*, nationwide. Also known as Aidilfitri, this Muslim festival marks the end of Ramadan, with feasts that feature special food preparations. Families get together and pay respect to their elders, and packets of money are given to children as presents.
Sarawak Regatta *(Sep)*, Kuching. An annual regatta of paddleboat, powerboat, and canoe competitions on the Sungai Sarawak between the various indigenous people of Sarawak.
Mount Kinabalu Climbathon *(Sep/Oct)*, Sabah. Most people take two full days to climb this massive mountain but the skilled climbers in this climbathon, the world's toughest mountain race, take less than three hours to complete the climb and descend.

Malaysia Mega Sale Carnival at Soga department store in Kuala Lumpur

AVERAGE MONTHLY TEMPERATURE (KUALA LUMPUR)

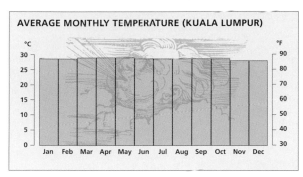

°C: 30, 25, 20, 15, 10, 5, 0
°F: 90, 80, 70, 60, 50, 40, 30

Jan Feb Mar Apr May Jun Jul Aug Sep Oct Nov Dec

Temperature Chart
The temperature in Malaysia does not vary much. Hot and humid all year round, the temperature hovers around 30° C (86° F) during the day, with a slight drop in the evenings. The hill stations may get as cool as 15° C (59° F).

OCTOBER TO DECEMBER

Due to heavy rain and rough seas on the east coast, boat travel to small islands is tough. Some national parks are also closed. The two important religious festivals during this season are the Mooncake Festival and Deepavali. Although there are only a few Christians in Malaysia, Christmas is still a much celebrated event.

Borneo Cultural Festival
(Oct), Sibu. A week-long celebration of music and dance with participants that include local ethnic groups, and visiting performers from countries including China and Indonesia. The festival also attracts visitors from Thailand, Brunei, and nearby countries.
Mooncake Festival *(variable)*, nationwide. Also known as the Mid-Autumn Festival, this day is celebrated by the Chinese who exchange and consume mooncakes, made of lotus and sesame seeds,

Energetic dances at the KL International Buskers Festival

to mark the fall of the Mongol dynasty in China in the 12th century. In the evening, lanterns are lit and areas with large Chinese communities hold a lantern parade.
Deepavali *(Oct/Nov)*, nationwide. The festival of lights commemorates Lord Krishna's victory over Narakasura, the triumph of good over evil and light over dark. Hindu homes and temples around the country are decorated with oil lamps to welcome the goddess of prosperity. Hindus pray for happiness and stability.
Tamu Besar *(Nov)*, Kota Belud. Held annually at one of Sabah's biggest markets and tourist attractions, Tamu Besar features cultural performances and handicraft demonstrations. The highlight, however, is to see Bajau horsemen, dressed in colorful traditional costumes. They ride their bedecked horses around town *(see p182)*.
KL International Buskers Festival *(Dec)*, Kuala Lumpur. For over a week, street performers from around the world, including musicians, dancers, comedians, jugglers, and acrobats, put on shows to demonstrate their talents.
Christmas *(Dec 25)*, nationwide. Largely unmarked in predominantly Muslim regions, such as the peninsula's eastern coast and parts of Sabah, Christmas is a major commercial event in

Towering Christmas tree at a shopping center in Kuala Lumpur

the big cities with lavish decorations in hotels and shopping malls. Midnight Mass is celebrated in churches nationwide.

PUBLIC HOLIDAYS

New Year's Day (Jan 1)

Chinese New Year (Jan/Feb)

Thaipusam (Jan/Feb)

Good Friday (Mar/Apr)

Birthday of the Prophet Muhammad (variable)

Labor Day (May 1)

Vesak (May/Jun)

King's Birthday (Jun)

Hari Raya Puasa (variable)

National Day (Aug 31)

Deepavali (Oct/Nov)

Christmas (Dec 25)

Malaysia at a Glance

Malaysia consists of two geographical regions, Peninsular Malaysia and Malaysian Borneo, which are divided by the South China Sea. A range of mountains runs down the center of the peninsula, dividing the developed plains of the west from the more rural east coast. Malaysian Borneo, comprising the states of Sarawak and Sabah, is a land of rain forests and great rivers. Sandwiched between these two states is the oil-rich independent Sultanate of Brunei.

The Perhentian Islands (see p142) *off the coast of Terengganu have pristine beaches and offer excellent swimming and diving in the clear waters of the South China Sea.*

Taman Negara *(see pp138–9)*, Malaysia's largest national park, contains the peninsula's highest peak and an incredible variety of birds and wildlife.

Cameron Highlands (see pp92–3) *is the country's largest and most popular hill station, with a consistently pleasant climate, rolling hills, lush tea plantations, and a distinctively colonial character.*

NORTHWEST PENINSULA *(see pp86–115)*

EASTERN AND CENTRAL PENINSULA *(see pp132–49)*

KUALA LUMPUR *(see pp56–85)*

SOUTHERN PENINSULA *(see pp116–31)*

SINGAPORE *(see pp196–267)*

The Sultan Abdul Samad Building (see p62) *is one of busy Kuala Lumpur's most magnificent colonial structures. The city's other attractions include interesting museums, pleasant gardens, and lively local markets.*

Seremban (see p120), *the state capital of Negeri Sembilan, is the center of Minangkabau culture in Malaysia. Striking buildings with roofs shaped like buffalo horns, such as the State Museum, can be seen throughout town.*

Pulau Sipadan (see pp194–5), *off the east coast of Sabah, is surrounded by a stunning coral reef and is rated among the world's top diving destinations.*

Brunei's Sultan Omar Ali Saifuddien Mosque, *an icon for the tiny Sultanate of Brunei (see pp172–3), stands on an island in an artificial lagoon in the heart of the capital city of Bandar Seri Begawan.*

Turtle Island National Park *(see p190)* is a prime spot for viewing the green and hawksbill turtles that come ashore to nest.

Mulu National Park *(see pp170–71)* has picturesque walking trails in a forested landscape rich in wildlife.

SABAH
(see pp174–95)

SARAWAK
(see pp150–73)

0 km   150

0 miles   150

Kuching *(see pp154–7),* the historic capital of Sarawak, is set on the banks of the Sungai Sarawak.

Lambir Hills National Park (see p169) *protects the forested areas around Lambir Hills. Visited most often for its scenic waterfalls, the park reflects the natural heritage of Sarawak, a state that owes its considerable global significance to its many spectacular and species rich forests.*

KUALA LUMPUR

The capital of Malaysia, Kuala Lumpur, is the nation's biggest city with a population of 1.5 million people. A relatively young city, it has evolved from a humble town in the 1850s to the financial and commercial capital and principal gateway of the country. A vision of modernity with its skyscrapers and the best restaurants and nightlife in the country, Kuala Lumpur also possesses a rich cultural heritage that is revealed in its colonial architecture, temples, and mosques.

Kuala Lumpur sits in the Klang Valley, and its name, which means muddy confluence in Malay, is derived from its location at the point where the Klang and Gombak rivers meet. Established here in 1857, the city began as a ramshackle trading post for the burgeoning tin industry, and was constantly plagued by floods, fires, and civil wars. Chinese miners and traders formed a large part of its early population, governed by a Kapitan China, or headman. The most famous of them was Yap Ah Loy *(see p65)* who was responsible for the city's early growth.

A building boom began when the British took control in the 1880s, and in 1896, Kuala Lumpur was made the capital of the newly formed Federated Malay States. A multiracial population began to settle here, congregating in ethnic enclaves that remain even today. In 1999, Putrajaya became the new administrative capital, but Kuala Lumpur remains the country's financial and commercial center.

Some of the country's rich history can be seen in the 19th-century architecture of the old colonial district and in neighboring Chinatown, with its incense-filled temples and chatter-filled *kedai kopi*, or coffee shops. Little India, Kampung Baru, and Chow Kit are the best places to find Indian, Malay, and Chinese cuisines. A closer look reveals that the city blends the old with the new. Flanked by glitzy shops and trendy bars, the Golden Triangle is the hub of the city's nightlife, while the Petronas Towers dominate the business district of KLCC. The Lake Gardens are a perfect escape from the urban clutter.

Entrance to Chan See Shu Yuen Temple in Kuala Lumpur

◁ Asy-Syakirin mosque with the gleaming Petronas Towers in the background, Kuala Lumpur

Exploring Kuala Lumpur

Kuala Lumpur's old colonial core is centered on Merdeka Square, which is ringed with elegant colonial buildings. To the southwest are the tranquil Lake Gardens. Across the river, to the east, Chinatown, Little India, Chow Kit, and Kampung Baru boast some of the best street markets. To the west is the Putra World Trade Center (PWTC), one of the city's convention and exhibition centers. Farther northeast is the modern Kuala Lumpur City Center (KLCC) dominated by the Petronas Towers. The Golden Triangle is the business and entertainment hub of the capital. Close by is the soaring Menara KL at the foot of which is the Bukit Nanas Forest Reserve, a patch of rain forest in the center of the city.

SIGHTS AT A GLANCE

Historic Streets, Buildings, and Neighborhoods
Badan Warisan **31**
Carcosa Seri Negara **16**
Chinatown **7**
The Golden Triangle **29**
Jalan Tuanku Abdul Rahman **20**
Kuala Lumpur Railway Station **11**
Little India **19**
Malaysian Tourism
  Information Complex **28**
Menara KL and Bukit Nanas
  Forest Reserve **30**
Petronas Towers **25**
Royal Selangor Club **3**
Sultan Abdul Samad Building **1**

Museums and Galleries
*Islamic Arts Museum
  see pp68–9* **13**
National Art Gallery **22**
National History Museum **4**
National Museum **14**

Shopping and Markets
Central Market **5**
Chow Kit Market **21**
Jalan Petaling Market **8**
Kampung Baru and
  Pasar Minggu Market **24**
Suria KLCC and KLCC Gardens **26**

Places of Worship
Chan See Shu Yuen Temple **10**
Masjid India **18**
Masjid Jamek **2**
Masjid Negara **12**
Sze Ya Temple **6**
Sri Maha Mariamman
  Temple **9**
Thean Hou Temple **17**

Islands
Pulau Ketam **36**

Gardens and Themed Attractions
Aquaria KLCC **27**
FRIM **33**
Kompleks Budaya Kraf **32**
Lake Gardens **15**
Titiwangsa Lake
  Gardens **23**

Towns and Cities
Klang **35**
Putrajaya **37**
Shah Alam **34**

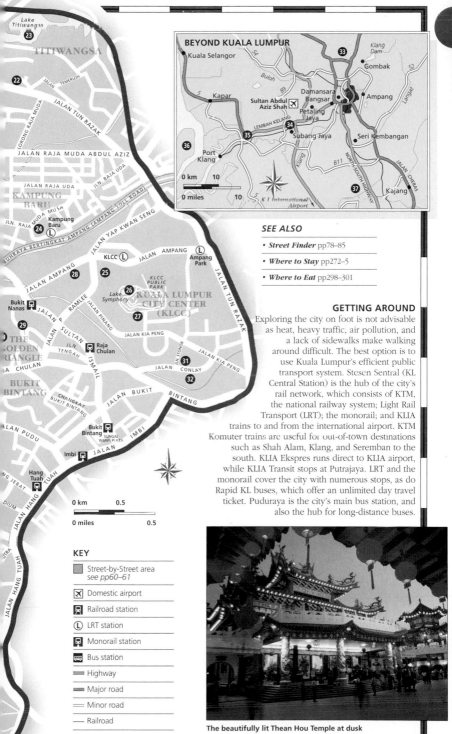

Lake Titiwangsa
23
TITIWANGSA
22
JALAN TEMERLOH
LORONG RAJA MUDA
JALAN TUN RAZAK
JALAN RAJA MUDA ABDUL AZIZ
JALAN RAJA UDA
JLN. RAJA UDA
KAMPUNG BARU
JLN. RAJA MUDA MUSA
Kampung Baru 24
BUHRAYA BERTINGKAT AMPANG AMPANG (AMPANG) (OIL ROAD)
JALAN YAP KWAN SENG
KLCC 25
JALAN AMPANG
Ampang Park
JALAN AMPANG 28
JALAN P. RAMLEE
JALAN PINANG
JALAN AMPANG
JALAN TUN RAZAK
Bukit Nanas 29
JALAN P.
KLCC PUBLIC PARK
Lake Symphony 26
KUALA LUMPUR CITY CENTER (KLCC)
27
THE GOLDEN TRIANGLE
JALAN SULTAN
JLN. TENGAH
JALAN ISMAIL
Raja Chulan
JALAN KIA PENG
JALAN KIA PENG
JLN STONOR
31
JALAN CONLAY
32
CHULAN
BUKIT BINTANG
CHANGKAT BUKIT BINTANG
JALAN BUKIT BINTANG
JALAN BUKIT BINTANG
LAN PUDU
Bukit Bintang
SUNGAI WANG PLAZA
IMBI
Imbi
JALAN IMBI
Hang Tuah
JALAN HANG TUAH
NG JEBAT
DIUM
JALAN HANG TUAH
UTRA

SEE ALSO

• **Street Finder** pp78–85

• **Where to Stay** pp272–5

• **Where to Eat** pp298–301

GETTING AROUND

Exploring the city on foot is not advisable as heat, heavy traffic, air pollution, and a lack of sidewalks make walking around difficult. The best option is to use Kuala Lumpur's efficient public transport system. Stesen Sentral (KL Central Station) is the hub of the city's rail network, which consists of KTM, the national railway system; Light Rail Transport (LRT); the monorail; and KLIA trains to and from the international airport. KTM Komuter trains are useful for out-of-town destinations such as Shah Alam, Klang, and Seremban to the south. KLIA Ekspres runs direct to KLIA airport, while KLIA Transit stops at Putrajaya. LRT and the monorail cover the city with numerous stops, as do Rapid KL buses, which offer an unlimited day travel ticket. Puduraya is the city's main bus station, and also the hub for long-distance buses.

BEYOND KUALA LUMPUR

Kuala Selangor
Klang Dam
33
Gombak
Buloh
Kapar
Damansara
Bangsar
Ampang
Sultan Abdul Aziz Shah
Petaling Jaya
LEMBAH KELANG
35
34
Subang Jaya
Seri Kembangan
36
Port Klang
Kajang
0 km 10
0 miles 10
KL International Airport
37
Kajang

KEY

	Street-by-Street area see pp60–61
✕	Domestic airport
🚉	Railroad station
Ⓛ	LRT station
🚈	Monorail station
🚌	Bus station
▬▬	Highway
▬▬	Major road
═══	Minor road
───	Railroad

0 km 0.5
0 miles 0.5

The beautifully lit Thean Hou Temple at dusk

Street-by-Street: Merdeka Square

Located in the heart of Kuala Lumpur's colonial district, Dataran Merdeka, or Independence Square, is a vast rectangular grassy field that once hosted cricket matches and parades. Surrounded by the mock-Tudor Royal Selangor Club, the National History Museum, St. Mary's Cathedral, and the Sultan Abdul Samad Building, the square offers a rare glimpse into the city's past. The venue for many national events, it was here that the Union Flag was finally lowered on August 31, 1957, when independent Malaysia was born. Today, the Malaysian flag flies at the southern end of the square.

Pitcher Plant Fountain
Standing in a small garden north of the square, this unique water feature is styled as a series of pitcher plants.

St. Mary's Cathedral
Built in the English Gothic style by A.C. Norman, this whitewashed cathedral is home to an exceptional English pipe organ, installed in 1895.

— JLN. RAJA LAUT —

PITCHER PLANT FOUNTAIN ←

JLN. RAJA

0 meters 50
0 yards 50

KEY
- - - Suggested route

★ **Royal Selangor Club**
Affectionately known as The Spotted Dog and once the focus of colonial life in Kuala Lumpur, this grand mock-Tudor edifice is the city's most prestigious private club ❸

STAR SIGHTS

- ★ Royal Selangor Club
- ★ Sultan Abdul Samad Building
- ★ National History Museum

★ **Sultan Abdul Samad Building**
This flamboyant Moorish-style building dates from 1897. Dominating the eastern side of Merdeka Square, it now houses a division of the Malaysian High Court ❶

Masjid Jamek

Built in 1909 in stately Mughal style, the Masjid Jamek, or Friday Mosque, is the oldest surviving mosque in the capital. It stands at the confluence of the Klang and Gombak rivers, where the city's first arrivals settled in the 1850s **2**

Central Market

Once the city's main fresh produce market, the 1930s Art Deco building of the Central Market is now a shopping mall with Indian, Straits Chinese, and Malay ethnic arts and craft shops **5**

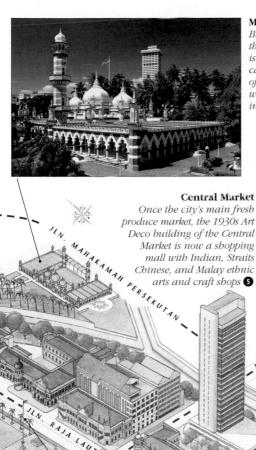

JLN. MAHAKAMAH PERSEKUTAN

LEBUH PASAR BESAR

CHINATOWN →

JLN. RAJA LAUT

Kuala Lumpur Memorial Library

The Flagpole

The 328-ft (100-m) high free-standing flagpole is believed to be the tallest in the world. The Malaysian flag is raised here on National Day.

★ National History Museum

Originally home to the Chartered Bank of India, Australia, and China, this 19th-century building is now a museum. Artifacts include a seven-armed Buddha, coral-encrusted porcelain, and coins in animal shapes **4**

The Royal Selangor Club, once the focus of colonial life

Sultan Abdul Samad Building ❶

Jalan Raja Laut. **Map** 4 E2.
Ⓛ *Masjid Jamek.* 🚌 *R101, R109.*

A magnificent Moorish edifice presiding over the eastern flank of Merdeka Square, the Sultan Abdul Samad Building was built in 1897 to serve as the headquarters of colonial administration and named in honor of the ruler of Selangor at the time. Designed by A.C. Norman, a British architect who also designed the nearby St. Mary's Cathedral, the building is made of red brick and white stone and draws upon Mughal, Egyptian, and traditional Islamic styles. Its architectural features include

Sultan Abdul Samad Building with its grand clock tower

elegantly arched windows, cupolas, an imposing porch, and a soaring 133-ft (41-m) clock tower, flanked by two smaller towers crowned with gleaming copper domes. The building is the focus for midnight celebrations on the eve of National Day *(see p52)* and New Year's Eve. Today, it houses the commercial division of Malaysia's High Court and although it is not open to the public, its striking façade makes it one of the capital's most photographed landmarks.

Masjid Jamek ❷

Off Jalan Tun Perak. **Map** 4 E2.
Ⓛ *Masjid Jamek.* 🚌 *R101.*
🕗 *8:30am–12:20pm, 2:30–4pm daily.* 🌙 *11am–2:30pm Fri.* ♿

Standing at the confluence of the Klang and Gombak rivers, the site where Kuala Lumpur was founded, the beautiful Masjid Jamek is the city's oldest mosque. Masjid Jamek, which means Friday Mosque, was built in 1909 by architect A.B. Hubbock, who was responsible for many of the country's colonial cityscapes. The red brick and marble building, with three large onion-shaped domes, two minarets, and arched colonnades, was inspired by Mughal architecture. Surrounded by palm groves, and with unrivaled views downstream, the mosque

forms a tranquil haven in the middle of the city. The main prayer hall is open only to Muslims. Visitors to the mosque must be dressed appropriately with arms and legs covered, and women must cover their heads. Gowns are supplied free of charge and shoes must be removed before entering.

Royal Selangor Club ❸

Merdeka Square. **Map** 4 E2. *Tel (03) 2692-7166.* Ⓛ *Masjid Jamek.* 🚌 *R101, R109.* www.rscweb.org.my

Established in 1884, the Royal Selangor Club was at the center of colonial social life in Kuala Lumpur. Expatriates and officials gathered here to relax, play billiards, and watch cricket on the padang, now a part of **Merdeka Square** *(see pp60–61)*. The club also hosted traveling plays and musicals. In 1970, the original building was destroyed by a fire, which was soon followed by a flood. The present black and white mock-Tudor building, an authentic reproduction of the old club, was built in 1980. Still referred to as The Spotted Dog, the club remains the preserve of the city's elite. The origin of its nickname attracted several theories, including one that traces it to a pet Dalmatian that belonged to a former member.

National History Museum [4]

29 Jalan Raja. **Map** 4 E2. ***Tel*** *(03) 2694-4590.* Ⓛ *Masjid Jamek.* 🚌 *R101, R109.* 🕒 *daily.* 🛍 **www**.nationalhistorymuseum.gov.my

Completed in 1891, this grand Moorish-style building at the southern end of Merdeka Square was built to house Kuala Lumpur's first bank. During World War II, the structure was requisitioned as a telecommunications base by the then occupying Japanese army. In 1991, it was converted into the Muzium Sejarah Nasional, or National History Museum, which gives an overview of the country's history by compiling and chronicling key events and artifacts from the Stone Age until independence.

Museum displays include a collection of Paleolithic tools, Neolithic pottery, replicas of megaliths that have been found around the country, and exquisite bronze Buddhas. Upstairs, the timeline continues into the medieval and colonial eras, focusing on the Portuguese and Dutch forays into Malacca, with displays of ceramics, coins, and weapons. Artifacts from the Japanese occupation during World War II, including army uniforms and a Samurai sword, are displayed on the top floor, along with photographs, documents, and video footage from the independence movement. Also on display is the flag of the first Federation of Malay States *(see p43)*, first unfurled on August 31, 1957, at Merdeka Square, as well as the table on which the 1874 Pangkor Treaty was signed.

The imposing façade of the National History Museum

Central Market [5]

Jalan Hang Kasturi. **Map** 4 E2. ***Tel*** *(03) 2031-0399.* Ⓛ *Pasar Seni.* 🚌 *R101, R110, R111.* 🕒 *10am–10pm daily.* ♿ *first floor only.* 🚻

Housed in a powder-blue Art Deco building dating from the 1930s, the Central Market was formerly the city's main fresh-produce market. It was rescued from dereliction and reopened as a modern shopping complex in the 1980s.

Also known as the Cultural Bazaar, the building has arts and crafts shops that sell an array of products including wood carvings, *batik*, pottery, paintings, and traditional kites. Prices tend to be high and haggling is necessary to get reasonable deals. There are a number of other outlets that sell an eclectic assortment of goods ranging from guitars to ladies' wigs.

Upstairs, there is a good food court with separate counters offering dishes from various Malaysian states. A few restaurants are scattered on both floors. The Central Market is also a venue for free cultural performances.

Sze Ya Temple [6]

Lebuh Pudu. **Map** 4 F3. Ⓛ *Pasar Seni* 🚌 *R110, R111.* 🕒 *7am–5pm daily.*

Located halfway down a narrow alley off Lebuh Pudu, the small Sze Ya Temple is built at an awkward angle to the road, a position said to have been decided by the principles of feng shui. The oldest Taoist temple in Kuala Lumpur, it was founded in 1864 by Yap Ah Loy, the third Kapitan China *(see p65)*, who also funded its construction. Inside the temple, a statue of Loy is installed left of the main altar, while images of the patron deities Si Sze Ya and Sin Sze Ya occupy the right. The interior is filled with elaborate carvings and the smell of burning incense. The temple entrance is guarded by statues of fierce lions, a common feature in Chinese and Taoist temples, accompanied by statues of storks. For an extra charge visitors can have their fortunes told inside the temple.

Colorful interior of the Sze Ya Temple, one of the oldest in the capital

Gateway to Jalan Petaling in Chinatown

Chinatown ❼

Map 4 F3. Ⓛ *Pasar Seni.*
🚌 *Maharajalela.* 🚍 *R102, R110.*
🎭 *Chinese New Year (Jan/Feb).*

Kuala Lumpur's relatively small but vibrant Chinatown is roughly bordered by Jalan Hang Kasturi to the west and Jalan Sultan to the east, with Masjid Jamek and the Chan See Shu Yuen Temple marking its northern and southern limits respectively. The area is a maze of narrow streets and alleyways, dotted with small Chinese temples and lined with old shophouses, medicine stores, and traditional family-run *kedai kopi*, or coffee shops, where locals gather to socialize. At the heart of Chinatown is **Jalan Petaling**, with its bustling market and crowded cafés. Numerous modern shops and chain stores add a contemporary touch to this ethnic enclave. Chinatown is also home to much of the city's budget accommodation. The area, however, is not exclusively Chinese. Located on

Jalan Tun HS Lee, a major thoroughfare, is the city's principal Hindu temple, **Sri Maha Mariamman Temple**.

Jalan Petaling Market ❽

Jalan Petaling. **Map** 4 F3. Ⓛ *Pasar Seni.* 🚍 *R110.* ⏱ *10am–11pm.*

The scene of the capital's most famous and lively street market, Jalan Petaling is a partly roofed string of stalls specializing in fake designer goods. Watches, clothes, wallets, handbags, and a profusion of pirated CDs and DVDs are all sold openly. There are few fixed prices, and with initial offers often set unreasonably high, buyers are expected to haggle. Interspersed with the stalls are a few shops that sell an assortment of other goods such as a variety of dried meats and traditional medicines. At the northern end is a vegetable and fruit market and plenty of cheap cafés.

Jalan Petaling is just a normal shop-lined street in Chinatown until around 4 or 5pm everyday, when the area is closed off to traffic and transformed into a *pasar malam*, or night market. Many of the daytime stalls pack up and are replaced by food stalls that sell a tempting array of Indian, Malay, and Chinese delicacies. Local souvenirs are also available. Both the day and night markets attract large crowds and visitors must be careful of their belongings.

Colorful *gopuram* of Sri Maha Mariamman Temple

Sri Maha Mariamman Temple ❾

163 Jalan Tun HS Lee. **Map** 4 F3.
***Tel** (03) 2078-3467.* Ⓛ *Pasar Seni.*
🚍 *R102.* ⏱ *6am–9pm daily.*
🎭 *Thaipusam (Jan/Feb).*

Established in 1873 as the private shrine of a Tamil family from southern India, Sri Maha Mariamman Temple was rebuilt on its present site in 1885. Today, it is Kuala Lumpur's main Hindu temple. The building is said to be laid out in the form of a reclining human body, with the head pointing to the west, and the feet to the east. The feet are represented by a five-tiered *gopuram*, or entrance gate, which is decorated with intricately carved statues of various Hindu deities. During an extensive renovation of the temple in the 1960s, gold and precious stones as well as Spanish and Italian tiles were added to the *gopuram*.

Inside the temple are several altars displaying images of Hindu gods. The temple also houses the ornate silver chariot used in a procession during the fascinating annual Thaipusam festival *(see p29)*. The chariot is brought out from the temple's vault during the celebration, when up to a million devotees converge here and make their way up to the Hindu shrine at Batu Caves *(see p90)*. Visitors must remove their shoes before entering the temple.

Traditional tea shop at the Jalan Petaling street market

For hotels and restaurants in this region see pp272–5 and pp298–301

Chan See Shu Yuen Temple ⑩

172 Jalan Petaling. **Map** 4 F4.
Tel (03) 2078-1461. Ⓛ *Pasar Seni.*
🚇 *Maharajalela.* 🚌 *R110.*
www.cssykl.com

Built between 1897 and 1906, Chan See Shu Yuen Temple is said to be one of the finest examples of southern Chinese architecture in Malaysia. It features an elaborate pottery-tiled roof and undulating gables as well as superbly sculpted green- and blue-glazed ceramic friezes depicting mythological scenes on the façade. Decorating the edges of the temple are blue ceramic vases. On either side of the main entrance are shrines to the female and male guardians of the doorway, with incense burning continually before them.

The temple is essentially a clan association, representing families bearing the related names of Chan, Chen, or Tan, and is dedicated to the family ancestors. Enshrined at the central altar of the temple are images of the clan founders, Chan Siow Ling, Chan Xin Xi, and Chan Zai Tian, while above the altar, to the right and left, are a series of black and white photographs of deceased clan members. Framing the central shrine are gilded wooden panels painted with scenes of warriors battling lions and mythical creatures.

Detail of friezes carved on the façade of the Chan See Shu Yuen Temple

Kuala Lumpur Railway Station ⑪

Jalan Sultan Hishamuddin.
Map 4 E4. 🚌 *R109.* ♿ 🖵 📷

Among the best examples of colonial architecture in Malaysia, the ornate Kuala Lumpur Railway Station is a majestic, gleaming white building with Moorish arches, balustrades, minarets, and cupolas. Completed in 1911, it was designed by the British architect A.B. Hubbock, who is also known for the striking Masjid Jamek *(see p62).* Beneath the Islamic exterior, the building was constructed according to specifications for railroad stations in England and included an iron roof capable of withstanding up to 3 ft (1 m) of snow. The concrete structure was built to replace an *attap,* or thatch-roofed shed, which had served as the railroad terminal since 1886 when the first railroad line was constructed.

For 90 years it was the city's main intercity rail terminal, until it was replaced in 2001 by the state-of-the-art KL Sentral Station, a few streets to the south. Now only KTM Komuter trains pass through this historic station. Still, it remains one of the city's most notable landmarks. Some of the best views of the building are from Jalan Kinabalu.

The colonial-era Heritage Station Hotel *(see p275),* one of the grandest in its time, continues to occupy a section of the station.

KAPITAN CHINA

The office of Kapitan China, or headman of the Chinese community of Kuala Lumpur, was instituted in 1858 by Rajah Abdullah, Chief of Selangor state, as a way of imposing order on the fractious Chinese immigrants and their secret societies. In 1869, Yap Ah Loy, a fierce and ambitious immigrant from southern China, became the third Kapitan China. He soon found himself at the center of a bloody civil war between different Chinese groups and local Malays, but a major victory led by him in Kuala Lumpur in 1873, along with the arrival of the first British Resident in 1874 *(see p41),* put an end to the fighting. He remained headman until his death in 1885. Also credited with establishing the city as a major economic powerhouse, Yap Ah Loy is considered the founding father of modern Kuala Lumpur.

**Kapitan China
Yap Ah Loy**

The magnificent edifice of the Kuala Lumpur Railway Station

The striking 18-pointed roof of Masjid Negara, the national mosque

Masjid Negara ⑫

Jalan Perdana. **Map** 4 D3. **Tel** (03)
2693-7784. 🚇 KL Railway Station.
🚌 R109. ⏰ 9am–noon, 3–4pm
and 5:30–6:30pm daily. 🌙 2:45–
6:30pm Fri.

Built in 1965, Masjid Negara
is Malaysia's national mosque.
Set in sprawling gardens that
contain pools and fountains,
it is a vast modern building
with room for up to 15,000
worshipers. The main prayer
hall is open only to Muslims.
    The hall is covered with a
distinctive dome in the shape
of a stylized 18-point star,
representing the 13 states of
Malaysia and the five pillars
of Islam. Towering over the
mosque is a slender 240-ft
(73-m) high minaret. Visitors
are welcome to explore the
entire complex but must be
appropriately dressed at all
times and headscarves are
mandatory for women. Shoes
must be removed before
entering the building.

Islamic Arts Museum ⑬

See pp68–9.

National Museum ⑭

Jalan Damansara. **Map** 3 C4.
Tel (03) 2282-6255. 🚇 KL Stesen
Sentral, then a short walk. Ⓛ Stesen
Sentral, then a short walk. 🚌 R109.
⏰ daily. 📷 ♿ 🛍 🍴
www.museum.gov.my **KLTA
Tourist Information Center
Tel** (03) 2287-1830.

Opened in 1963, the
National Museum, or
Muzium Negara, is
built on the site of the
old Selangor Museum
which was destroyed
by Allied bombing
during World War II.
It is housed in a repro-
duction of a traditional
Malay palace and its façade
is adorned with murals

Chinese ceramic
vase at the
National Museum

depicting scenes from the
nation's history. Inside, four
themed galleries provide an
introduction to Malaysia's
ethnography and natural
history. The Cultural Gallery
and Faces of Malaysia Gallery
both exhibit colorful traditional costumes as well as
handicrafts such as kites and
shadow-puppets. Dioramas
illustrating some unique
rituals of the Malay, Chinese,
and Indian communities are
also on display. The Natural
History Gallery is filled with
examples of native animals,
insects, and flora. The fourth
gallery has an impressive collection of antique weapons,
musical instruments, and
Southeast Asian ceramics.
The small **KLTA Tourist
Information Center** is within
the museum grounds.

Lake Gardens ⑮

Jalan Perdana. **Map** 3 B3.
🚇 KL Railway Station. Ⓛ Stesen
Sentral. 🚌 R109. ♿ 🛍 🍴
Bird Park Tel (03) 2272-1010.
⏰ 9am–7pm daily. 📷 **Bird
feeding and shows** check
website for times.
www.birdpark.com.my
Butterfly Park Tel (03) 2693-
4799. ⏰ daily. 📷 **National
Planetarium Tel** (03) 2273-
4303. ⏰ 9:30am–4:15pm
Tue–Sun. 🌙 Mon. 📷
www.angkasa.gov.my

Lying on the western
edge of the city center
is the Lake Gardens,
known in Malay as Taman
Tasik Perdana. It is a beautiful
expanse of greenery laid out
in the late 19th century as a
tranquil residential area for
the governing British elite.
Today, the Lake Gardens is
the capital's biggest and most
popular park, with a large
lake at its center where boats
can be hired. Plenty of walking trails crisscross the park.
    Within the gardens are a
number of other attractions,
the highlight of which is
the **Bird Park**. Said to be the
world's largest walk-in free-
flight aviary, the park houses
around 3,000 tropical birds
including flamingos, hornbills,
and parrots. There is also a
Butterfly Park which is home

A gallery at the Muzium Negara, or National Museum

For hotels and restaurants in this region see pp272–5 and pp298–301

to over 6,000 butterflies of at least 120 different species. Close by is the **Orchid Garden**, which showcases over 800 species of Malay orchids, which are for sale during the weekend. On the southern edge of the Lake Gardens is the **National Planetarium**, which stages various shows and screens IMAX movies. The 50-ft (15-m) high bronze **National Monument** which commemorates the defeat of the Communist insurgency dominates the northern end of the park. It was created in 1966 by Felix de Weldon, who was best known for the Iwo Jima monument in Washington, D.C. Among the fine colonial mansions built here is **Carcosa Seri Negara**, which presides over the western boundary of the gardens. The smaller museums around the park are dedicated to the police, civil service, banking, and former political leaders.

Carcosa Seri Negara **⑯**

Lake Gardens. **Map** 3 B3. **Tel** (03) 2295-0888. 🚆 KL Railway Station. Ⓛ Stesen Sentral. 🔌 🍴 🖂 **www.**carcosa.com.my

This exquisite pair of colonial mansions set in their own grounds on the edge of the Lake Gardens were built between 1896 and 1904. The first building, Carcosa,

Plush dining room at Carcosa Seri Negara, a luxury hotel

formerly known as The House on the Hill, was constructed as a home for Sir Frank Swettenham, the first British Resident-General of the Federation of Malay States (see p41), a function it continued to serve for subsequent British governors. The second building, Seri Negara, earlier known as the King's House, was the official home of the Governor of the Straits Settlements. After independence and until 1987, Carcosa was the official residence of the British High Commissioner while Seri Negara functioned as a state guesthouse for visiting foreign dignitaries. Today, the two buildings together form one of Kuala Lumpur's finest boutique hotels (see p275), and contain two award-winning restaurants including the elegant, colonial Mahsuri Dining Room (see p301).

Thean Hou Temple **⑰**

62 Persiaran Indah, off Jalan Syed Putra. **Tel** (03) 2274-7088. 🚌 from Stesen Sentral. ◯ 8am–10pm; 6am–midnight during Chinese New Year. 🖻 🚹 📷 Chinese New Year (Jan/Feb).

Perched on a hill southwest of the city center, the Thean Hou Temple is a striking 3-tier Chinese temple. Built in the 1980s, this is one of the biggest Chinese temples in Malaysia. It is dedicated to Thean Hou, or heavenly mother, the patron deity of sailors and fishermen. An image of the goddess, also known as Ma Zu, is enshrined in the main hall, flanked by statues of Sui Wei, goddess of the waterfront, and Kuan Yin, goddess of mercy. Statues of the Laughing Buddha and other Buddhist and Taoist images are also kept here.

The temple has a series of traditional Chinese-style roofs decorated with golden dragons, phoenix, and a canopy of red paper lanterns. Built on four levels, it has food outlets and shops on the ground level, while the main shrine is on the third floor. The temple also serves as a community center, and a hall on the second level forms the venue for social gatherings such as weddings. Outside the building stand twelve statues, which represent the twelve animals of the Chinese zodiac.

The extravagant Thean Hou Temple, with a series of tiled, Chinese-style roofs

Islamic Arts Museum ⑬

Coin tree, Malay World Gallery

Situated on the eastern edge of the Lake Gardens *(see p66)*, the Islamic Arts Museum houses fascinating exhibits from the Muslim world. Opened in 1998, the museum has the largest collection of its kind in Southeast Asia with over 7,000 artifacts. The building itself is an impressive modern construction topped by turquoise domes, with Iranian tilework on columns at the entrance. Inside, five elegant domes created by Uzbek craftsmen decorate the ceilings.

The emphasis of the exhibits here is on Asian arts in addition to those from Persia and the Middle East.

The magnificent dome at the Inverted Dome Pavilion

The state-of-the-art auditorium seats up to 250 people and is used for seminars and lectures.

The Inverted Dome Pavilion is an airy exhibition hall with its unique dome executed in white and gold, bearing extracts from the Koran.

The Architecture Gallery
The main focus of this gallery is the collection of scale models of mosques, including the Dome on the Rock, Taj Mahal, and the Al-Haram Mosque.

Ground floor

Fountain garden

Lower Ground

Preview room

Main entrance

Briefing hall

Children's library

The Education Department conducts workshops on art and activities for children.

Woodwork Gallery
Located on Level 2, the gallery exhibits elaborately crafted wooden artifacts often embellished with ivory and mother-of-pearl.

STAR EXHIBITS

- ★ Turkish Iznik Tiles
- ★ Jewelry Gallery
- ★ Standard Chartered Ottoman Room

GALLERY GUIDE

The permanent displays begin on Level 1 with the Architecture Gallery, which has detailed scale models of mosques. Nearby is the Manuscript Gallery, a reconstructed Ottoman Room, and galleries dedicated to China, India, and Malaysia. Level 2 has the Jewelry, Arms and Armor, Coin, Metalwork, Woodwork, Ceramics, and Textile galleries. On the Ground and Lower Ground floors are two galleries for temporary exhibitions. The non-exhibition area has facilities for research and education.

Qur'an and Manuscript Gallery

This gallery features handwritten Korans, Sultans' decrees, miniature paintings, and scholarly works on botany and astronomy.

VISITORS' CHECKLIST

Jalan Lembah Perdana.
Map 4 D3. **Tel** *(03) 2274-2020.*
Kuala Lumpur Railway Station. 10am–6pm Tue–Sun.
www.iamm.org.my

The Coin Gallery displays gold and silver Islamic coins, noted for intricate Ottoman and Mughal calligraphy.

Library

★ **Turkish Iznik Tiles**
These glazed tiles with stylized trees, fruits, and foliage in vibrant hues were first produced in the Turkish city of Iznik in the 16th and 17th centuries.

Level 2

Level 1

Main dome and viewing terrace

★ **Jewelry Gallery**
Ornaments from across Asia are housed here, including Iranian gold anklets and a 19th-century gold and ruby necklace from Mughal India.

The Architecture Gallery

The China Gallery displays Chinese manuscripts, a Koran, and blue and white porcelain with Arabic script.

★ **Standard Chartered Ottoman Room**
This room once belonged to a lavish house built in Syria in 1820 and has now been restored to its original appearance. It is spectacularly decorated with painted wood paneling.

KEY

- Jewelry Gallery
- Arms and Armor Gallery
- Textile Gallery
- Woodwork Gallery
- Coin Gallery
- Metalwork Gallery
- Ceramics and Glassware Gallery
- Architecture Gallery
- Qur'an and Manuscript Gallery
- India Gallery
- China Gallery
- Malay World Gallery
- Temporary exhibitions
- Non-exhibition space

Key to Symbols *see back flap*

Masjid India ⑱

Jalan Masjid India. **Map** 4 F1.
Ⓛ *Masjid Jamek.* 🚌 *R109.* ♿

Originally built as a modest
wooden structure in 1863,
Masjid India has been rebuilt
and upgraded a number of
times over the years. The
present building was com-
pleted in 1966, and designed
in southern Indian style, with
onion-domed cupolas and
elegant arched windows.
The three-story mosque, is
the main place of worship
for Kuala Lumpur's Indian
Muslims. It has the capacity
to accommodate up to 3,500
devotees, with separate floors
for men and women.

Vibrant silk cloth and garments on
sale at a Little India stall

Little India ⑲

Jalan Masjid India and environs.
Map 1 B5. Ⓛ *Masjid Jamek,*
Bandaraya. 🚌 *R101 to Jalan Tuanku*
Abdul Rahman. 🎎 *Deepavali (Oct).*

Although tiny in comparison
with the Indian enclaves of
Singapore or even Georgetown
in Penang, Kuala Lumpur's
Little India is equally lively
and colorful, steeped in the
history and culture of the
capital's Indian community.
Jalan Masjid India is the
main street of this ethnic
quarter, which takes its name
from Masjid India. Rows of
shops and stalls line the
street, and are crammed with
Indian merchandise such as
saris, silk cloth and other

fabric, jewelry, flowers, and
spices. There are also a number of hawker stalls that sell
a variety of delicious and traditional Indian snacks such
as *pakoras* and *samosas*.
At the end of Jalan Masjid
India is Lorong Bunus, which
marks the northern limit of
Little India. It leads to Lorong
Tuanku Abdul Rahman, a
narrow lane that is the venue
of another of the capital's popular *pasar malams,* or night
markets. An assortment of
Indian goods are sold here,
including household items
and brassware, and it is also
one of the best places in the
city to sample authentic
Indian street food. During
the day, artisans, including
garland makers, can be seen
at work all along the street.

Jalan Tuanku Abdul Rahman ⑳

Map 1 B3. Ⓛ *Bandaraya.* 🚌 *R101,*
R109. **Coliseum Cinema** 96 Jalan
Tuanku Abdul Rahman. **Tel** (03)
2692-5995.

Named for the first king of
independent Malaysia, and
commonly known as Jalan
TAR, Jalan Tuanku Abdul
Rahman is one of the busiest
roads in Kuala Lumpur and is
constantly choked with traffic.
Stretching north from Merdeka
Square to Little India, it is
one of the city's most popular
shopping destinations, particularly known for silk shops

Poster of a feature film screened
at the Coliseum Cinema

such as the Global Silk Store
(*see p318*) as well as the
small, bazaar-style carpet
shops clustered around its
southern end. The Japanese
department store Sogo is
also located on this road.
Despite a lot of modern
development in recent years,
Jalan TAR has retained much
of its historic architecture,
revealed in many of the
striking 19th- and early 20th-
century façades that still exist
above the gaudy shop signs.
Among the most interesting
and significant of these structures is the **Coliseum Cinema**.
Barring a few years during
World War II, the cinema has
been in business since 1921,
making it Kuala Lumpur's
oldest running movie hall.
These days, it screens Hindi
and southern Indian Tamil
films. Visitors are free to

Façade of the Coliseum Cinema, which dates back to the colonial era

For hotels and restaurants in this region see pp272–5 and pp298–301

explore the building. Next door to the cinema, and built around the same time, the **Coliseum Café and Hotel** was once the favorite haunt of colonial planters and tin miners. It also counts English author Somerset Maugham among its early patrons.

The Coliseum Café and Hotel still offers cheap meals, budget accommodation, and an authentic early 20th-century atmosphere that has changed little over the years.

Chow Kit Market ㉑

Jalan Haji Hussein. **Map** 1 B4.
🚇 *Chow Kit.* 🚌 *R109.* 🕐 *10am–2am daily.*

Strung out along the narrow lanes and alleys just to the east of Jalan Tuanku Abdul Rahman, Chow Kit Market is one of the city's biggest and most popular street markets. It is divided into various sections and is especially known for its fresh produce, which includes everything from exotic fruits and vege-tables to live seafood, dried anchovies, and meat. Stall owners shout out their wares to vie for attention while porters busily ferry trays and carts laden with goods between the stalls. Although the smells can be overpower-ing and the narrow wooden walkways wet and slippery, the market offers an interest-ing glimpse of everyday life in Kuala Lumpur. Chow Kit Market is also one of the best places to buy secondhand clothes. Numerous other stalls selling household goods, shoes, watches, and a wide variety of everyday items fill the market.

Most of Chow Kit Market, especially the fresh produce sections, closes before 6pm, which is when the night mar-ket takes over. A profusion of hawker stalls set up shop, offering a variety of Malay snacks, as well as inexpensive but substantial meals, cooked in the traditional way. Indian and Chinese food, authenti-cally prepared, is also on offer. The market is always

Roadside vendor at Chow Kit Market, one of the city's largest day markets

bustling, and often lasts into the early hours. As with other crowded areas, visitors should be vigilant of pickpockets, especially after dark.

National Art Gallery ㉒

Jalan Temerloh. **Map** 2 D1. *Tel (03) 4025-4990.* 🚇 *Titiwangsa.* 🚌 *R104.* 🕐 *10am–6pm Tue–Sun.* 🕐 *11am & 2:30pm Tue–Sun, 10:30am & 3pm Fri.* 🚫 📷 🎦 www.artgallery. gov.my **National Theater Tel** *(03) 4026-5555.* 🕐 *box office: 10am–6pm Mon–Fri.* ♿

Home to the city's finest permanent collection of con-temporary Malaysian art, the National Art Gallery also hosts temporary exhibitions of Asian and international art. The permanent collection is on the second floor with the paintings arranged into themes such as Spirituality and Work. Highlights include Patrick Ng Kah Onn's *Spirit of the Earth, Sky and Water*; Samjis Mat Jan's portrait of a boy in *Rendezvous*; Ismail Mat Hussein's *batik* canvases depicting traditional village life; and Ooi Kooi Hin's *It's So Quiet*, in which a woman screams in a room filled with corpses. The temporary shows of modern Asian art include photography, sculp-ture, and installation art.

Next door, the striking **National Theater**, designed in the shape of a *wau bulan*, or Malay kite, hosts several interesting cultural shows as well as national and inter-national theater, and also features a traditional Malay theater costume gallery.

Contemporary art exhibits at the National Art Gallery

Titiwangsa Lake Gardens ㉓

Jalan Temerloh. Ⓛ *Titiwangsa*.
🚉 *Titiwangsa*. 🚌 *R106*.
♿ 🍴 🖥️

Located on the northern
fringes of the city, these
peaceful, manicured gardens
are a great escape from the
urban bustle and a popular
recreational space. Laid out
around a vast man-made
lake, the lush gardens are a
visual treat and also a perfect
place to relax, go jogging, or
even go boating. There is a
herb garden, a lovely lotus
pond, and a playground for
children. The garden's
Nelayan Restaurant hosts
cultural performances on
most evenings.

Kampung Baru and Pasar Minggu Market ㉔

Jalan Raja Muda Musa. **Map** 2 D4.
Ⓛ *Kampung Baru*. 🚌 *R102 & R103
to Jalan Raja Muda Abdul Aziz*.

Established in 1899, the
village of Kampung Baru
is the oldest Malay residential
area in Kuala Lumpur. Its
traditional wooden houses,
some on stilts, are still found
throughout this small settlement which lies to the north
of the Sungai Klang, roughly
between Jalan Raja Muda
Musa and Jalan Raja Muda
Abdul Aziz, with Jalan Raja
Abdullah and the incredibly

**Street food being prepared at
Pasar Minggu**

Petronas Towers, the tallest twin structures in the world, until recently

busy Chow Kit area marking
its western boundary. While
the old-fashioned kampung-
style houses and the 1920s
Masjid Jamek on Jalan Raja
Abdullah are worth a visit, the
real highlight of Kampung
Baru is the glimpse it offers of
an older, more leisurely way
of life that seems to be
rapidly disappearing under
the increasingly fast pace of
modern Kuala Lumpur.

The area comes alive
on Saturday nights for
the locally popular
Pasar Minggu, or
Sunday Market. Stalls
are set up along Jalan
Raja Muda Musa and
Jalan Raja Alang at
about 6pm on Saturday
evening, and stay open until
1am, or the early hours of
Sunday morning. On sale
are a wide variety of clothes,
jewelry, handicrafts, and
textiles, including reasonably
priced *batik* and locally
woven *songket* fabric. Plenty
of food and fresh produce is
available, as well as numerous hawker stalls tempting
shoppers with delicious, traditional Malay street food. A
few basic cafés offer visitors
more substantial meal options.

**Starfruit at
Pasar Minggu**

Petronas Towers ㉕

Jalan Ampang. **Map** 2F4. **Tel** (03)
2331-8080. Ⓛ *KLCC*. 🚌 *R109*.
⬜ *Skybridge: 8:30am–5pm Tue–Sun*.
● *Mon, 1–2:30pm Fri*. ♿ 🎫
www.petronastwintowers.com.my

Soaring to a height of 1,483 ft
(452 m), the 88-story Petronas
Towers are an internationally
recognized symbol of modern
Malaysia. Designed by the
famous Argentinian
architect Cesar Pelli, who
also designed the
Canary Wharf Tower
in London, the Petronas
Towers were com-
pleted in 1998. Built
with heat-reflecting
stainless steel and laminated
glass, and crowned by steel
pinnacles, the towers resemble
a pair of minarets. The eight-
sided star of the floorplan and
the overall architecture reflect
Islamic principles of unity and
harmony. The towers house
the national petroleum and
oil company, Petronas. The
skybridge, linking the towers
at the 41st floor, offers visitors
a bird's-eye view of the city.
Only 800 free tickets for the
skybridge are issued daily,
and visitors must line up early.

Suria KLCC and KLCC Gardens ㉖

Jalan Ampang. **Map** 2 F5.
Tel (03) 2382-3326. Ⓛ KLCC.
🚌 R106. ◯ daily. 🔽 free hire
inside Suria KLCC. 🍴 🖥 🏛
www.suriaklcc.com.my **KLCC**
Gardens ◯ 7am–10pm. **Galeri**
Petronas Tel (03) 2051-7770. ◯
Tue–Sun. 🔽 🏛 **Petrosains Tel** (03)
2331-8181. ◯ 9:30am–4pm
Tue–Thu, 1:30–4pm Fri, 9:30am–5pm
Sat–Sun. 📷 🏛

Spread out over six floors inside the Petronas Towers, Suria KLCC is one of the city's busiest and glitziest shopping malls, with numerous chain stores, restaurants, coffee bars, and a cinema, as well as banks, ATMs, and a post office. A range of giant international department stores have branches here, including Isetan and Parkson, along with specialist retailers and fast-food outlets.

On the third floor is the **Galeri Petronas**, which hosts rotating exhibitions of traditional and contemporary art, both from Asia and farther afield. **Petrosains**, on the fourth floor, is an excellent interactive science discovery center. Young visitors can learn about petroleum science and technology through a range of engaging hands-on exhibits, and can also visit a mock oil rig, try a helicopter flight simulator, and learn about prehistory in the geotime diorama. Of interest to

The glitzy interior of the Suria KLCC shopping mall

both young and adult visitors are the demonstrations and interactive sessions at the science stations.

The lush KLCC Gardens sprawling in front of the complex offer a welcome respite from city traffic. The gardens are laid out with benches and shelters, a jogging track for the more energetic, and a children's playground. Planted with over 1,900 native trees, many bearing explanation plaques, and centered on an artificial lake with dancing fountains, the gardens are a cool and pleasant place to wander around in the evenings. However, whistle-blowing security guards discourage visitors from lingering in the gardens beyond closing time.

Aquaria KLCC ㉗

Jalan Pinang. **Map** 2 F5. **Tel** (03)
2333-1888. Ⓛ KLCC. 🚌 R105,
R106. ◯ 11am–8pm daily. 📷
🔽 🏛 www.klaquaria.com

Occupying two levels within the Kuala Lumpur Convention Center, a short walk from the Petronas Towers, Aquaria KLCC is a visual treat. This enormous state-of-the-art aquarium is home to over 5,000 creatures, both aquatic and terrestrial, including around 150 different species of fish from across the world.

Conceptualized around the route that water takes from the mountains to the sea, the aquarium recreates various ecosystems. The journey begins in the highlands and is followed by a flooded forest display where giant catfish can be seen lurking among tree roots. Other ecosystems include mangroves, coral reefs, and the spectacular open ocean. A highlight is the 295-ft (90-m) long moving walkway underwater tunnel, which offers views of a simulated natural habitat and a shipwreck colonized by reef inhabitants, as well as close-up sightings of stingrays, eels, and rare sand tiger sharks.

A theater screens films on Malaysia's marine life, and a touch pool lets children handle aquatic creatures. More adventurous visitors can even swim with sharks, but advance booking is essential.

Visitors observing a school of fish through the glass of a giant tank at the Aquaria KLCC

Malaysian Tourism Information Complex, housed in a colonial mansion

Malaysian Tourism Information Complex ㉘

109 Jalan Ampang. **Map** 2 E5.
Tel *(03) 2163-3664.* Ⓛ *KLCC.*
🚇 *Bukit Nanas.* 🚌 *R106.* ⏱ *7am–10pm daily; cultural shows: 2–2:30pm Tue, Thu, Sat & Sun, traditional games: 4pm Sat & Sun* ♿ 🍴 📷
www.mtc.gov.my

The largest tourist center in Kuala Lumpur, the Malaysian Tourism Information Complex is housed in an impressive colonial mansion. Built on the site of an old rambutan orchard in 1935, it was formerly the home of Eu Tong Seng, a wealthy Chinese tin and rubber businessman. Not long after its construction, World War II broke out and the house was taken over by the British military and used as their war office. It was subsequently captured by the Japanese army, who converted it into their headquarters in Malaysia for the remainder the war. After independence, the building housed several government agencies and also witnessed the coronation ceremonies of four successive Malaysian kings.

Today, the main building in the complex houses the Malaysia tourist information office, while several annexes contain a tourist police office, restaurant, and a concert hall where regular cultural shows are performed *(see p321)*. Traditional games, such as top-spinning, are also hosted here over the weekends.

The Golden Triangle ㉙

Map 1 C5. 🚇 *Bukit Bintang, Imbi.*
🚌 *R107, R108.*

Spread over a large, roughly triangular area with its apex at Jalan Ampang in the north and its base formed by Jalan Imbi in the south, the Golden Triangle is Kuala Lumpur's main business, shopping, and nightlife district. Among the sea of glitzy high-rise buildings are most of the city's prominent shopping malls, along with countless bars, restaurants, cafés, and premier hotels, including the **Mandarin Oriental** *(see p275)*, which is located opposite the Petronas Towers. At the heart of the Golden Triangle is Jalan Bukit Bintang with its trendy bars, eateries, and the biggest concentration of shopping

Mandarin Oriental, a luxury hotel in the Golden Triangle

malls, including Lot 10 and Sungai Wang Plaza. Adding local flavor are pavement reflexologists and Middle-Eastern cafés where locals puff hookahs, or tobacco pipes. Changkat Bukit Bintang is another street offering chic bars and restaurants. The country's biggest shopping mall, Berjaya Times Square, dominates Jalan Imbi while most of the top-end hotels lie on Jalan Sultan Ismail.

Menara KL and Bukit Nanas Forest Reserve ㉚

2 Jalan Punchak, off Jalan P Ramlee.
Map 5 A1. ***Tel*** *(03) 2020-5444.*
🚇 *Bukit Nanas.* ⏱ *9am–10pm daily; cultural shows: 11am & 4pm Thu–Sun.* 🅿 🍴 🖥 📷 **www**.
menarakl.com.my **Bukit Nanas Forest Reserve** ⏱ *7am–6pm daily.*
🎫 *arranged by Menara KL.* ♿

Built as a communications tower between 1991 and 1996, Menara KL, or KL tower, is among the five tallest towers in the world. It stands at a height of 1,380 ft (421 m). Its lobby has several shops, restaurants, and a theater where a video of the tower's construction is screened. A lift whisks visitors up to the observation deck for a panoramic view of the city. At a dizzying height of 905 ft (276 m), it is more than 328 ft (100 m) higher than the skybridge at the Petronas Towers. Even farther up is a revolving restaurant, Seri Angkasa, which features afternoon teas and also traditional music and dance performances.

At the base of the tower is Malaysia's oldest nature reserve, the **Bukit Nanas Forest Reserve**, gazetted in 1906. This legal status saved the 27-acre (11-ha) slice of rain forest from destruction when the tower was built, and even resulted in a reworking of the architectural plans to avoid the cutting down of a 100-year old *jelutong* tree. Although small, the preserve supports a rich variety of wildlife, including monkeys and squirrels, as well as numerous

View of Kuala Lumpur from the soaring heights of the Menara KL observation deck

tropical trees. Visitors can explore this patch of rain forest by its three short walking trails.

Badan Warisan ③

2 Jalan Stonor. **Map** 6 E1. **Tel** (03) 2144-9273. 🚇 Raja Chulan. 🚌 R108. ⏰ 10am–5:30pm Mon–Sat. 🌑 Sun. 📷 🎟 11am & 3pm Mon–Sat. ♿ limited. 🖥 www. badanwarisan.org.my

Founded in 1983 for the conservation of Malaysia's architectural heritage, Badan Warisan is a non-government organization that runs regular campaigns and projects to save historical buildings from neglect and destruction. In 1995, it renovated a colonial bungalow on Jalan Stonor and turned it into a heritage center, with exhibition facilities for art and craft shows as well as a resource center with books, drawings, slides, and photographs for those keen to learn more about the organization's conservation work. The highlight is **Rumuh Penghulu Abu Seman**, a traditional Malay wooden house dating from the 1920s. It was brought to this site in a state of serious disrepair from a village in Kedah. Since then, it has been expertly restored and now serves as a showpiece for modern conservation methods.

Kompleks Budaya Kraf ③

63 Jalan Conlay. **Map** 6 E1. **Tel** (03) 2162-7459. 🄻 KLCC. 🚇 Raja Chulan. 🚌 R108. ⏰ daily. 📷 ♿ 🖥 🏛 www.kraftangan.gov.my

Located on the eastern edge of the Golden Triangle, Kompleks Budaya Kraf is a handicrafts complex that showcases a wide range of traditional arts and crafts from the various states of Peninsular Malaysia and Malaysian Borneo. It is made up of four separate buildings that house shops and stalls, a museum, exhibition areas, and several workshops. The museum traces the history and development of age-old crafts and

Earthenware at Budaya Kraf

features dioramas of artisans creating their wares with displays of the various tools they would have used.

In the exhibition areas and workshops, craftspeople demonstrate ethnic art and craft skills, such as weaving, *batik*-printing, and silver and copperwork. Visitors are welcome to try their hand and can also receive lessons in a particular craft. The complex is one of the best places in Kuala Lumpur to buy these local handicrafts, with a number of shops and stalls selling pewter, silverwork, pottery, woodcarvings, hand-woven textiles, *batik*, and beadwork, alongside more unusual items such as rattan fishtraps, birdcages, and tribal blowpipes.

An array of traditional handicrafts on sale at the Kompleks Budaya Kraf

Sultan Salahuddin Abdul Aziz Shah Mosque in Shah Alam

FRIM ⑬

Kepong, 10 miles (16 km) NW of Kuala Lumpur. *Tel (03) 6279-7000.* 🚌 to Kepong, then taxi. ⬜ *park: 5am–7:30pm; museum: 8am–4:30pm.* for vehicles; canopy tours. limited. **www**.frim.gov.my

Occupying 2 sq miles (5 sq km) of parkland within the Bukit Lagong Forest Reserve, the Forest Research Institute of Malaysia (FRIM) was founded in 1929 as a research and development center for tropical forests, with a special emphasis on sustainable forest management. An on-site museum explains the center's work. There are several arboreta of native trees, including the most comprehensive collection of dipterocarp (hardwood) species in the world. Also in the grounds is a traditional Malay house brought here from Terengganu *(see p141).* Among the highlights of a visit to FRIM is the 656-ft (200-m) long canopy walkway suspended 98 ft (30 m) above ground, which offers a fascinating close-up view of the treetops. There are also a number of easy walking trails, a more strenuous mountain bike trail, camping, bird-watching, and picnic areas.

FRIM logo

Shah Alam ⑭

11 miles (18 km) W of Kuala Lumpur. 🚶 *319,600.* 🚌 🚏 ℹ *Jalan Indah 14, (03) 5513-2000.* 🎉 *Bon Odori Festival (Jul).* **Museum Sultan Azlan Shah** Persian Bandaraya. *Tel (03) 5519-0050.* ⬜ *9:30am–5:30pm Tue–Sun.* ⬤ *Mon, noon–2:45pm Fri.* 🚻 **Galeri Shah Alam** Persiaran Tasik. *Tel (03) 5510-5344.* ⬜ *8:30am–5:30pm daily.* ⬤*12:15–2:45pm Fri.* **Wet World Water Park** *Tel (03) 5513-2020.* ⬜ *1–7pm Mon, Tue, Thu, Fri; 10am–8pm Sat & Sun.*

Designated the state capital of Selangor in 1978, Shah Alam is a well-planned modern city sprawled over a large area. It is essentially an industrial and administrative center, and is rarely visited by tourists. Still, the area's few sights of interest, most of which are within walking distance of each other, make it a pleasant day trip. Located in a park at the center of town is the city's main attraction, the **Sultan Salahuddin Abdul Aziz Shah Mosque**, more popularly known as the Blue Mosque owing to its large blue and silver aluminum dome. Its four 466-ft (142-m) high minarets are said to be the tallest in the world. The mosque can accommodate up to 24,000 worshipers and is reputed to

be one of the largest mosques in Southeast Asia and the largest in Malaysia.

Nearby is the **Museum Sultan Azlan Shah** with extensive displays covering the history of Selangor from prehistoric times to the present day. It also contains galleries dedicated to the state's wildlife as well as its sporting achievements. To the west of the museum is the attractively landscaped Lake Gardens, home to the **Galeri Shah Alam**, a modern art gallery located in a traditional Malay wooden building which hosts temporary exhibitions of modern art over three separate galleries. On the opposite side of the lake is the **Wet World Water Park**, a water theme park with pools, slides, and rides *(see p321).*

Klang ⑮

18 miles (30 km) SW of Kuala Lumpur. 🚶 *563,200.* 🚌 🚏 **www**.mpklang.gov.my **Gedung Raja Abdullah** Jalan Raja Abdullah. *Tel (03) 5519-0050.* ⬜ *10am–6pm Tue–Sun.*

The former royal capital of Selangor, the city of Klang, flourished during the 19th-century boom in the tin industry. However, in 1867, civil war erupted owing to the rivalry between the two local chieftains, Rajah Mahadi and Rajah Abdullah. The fighting was ended in 1874 when the British authorities intervened and installed the first Resident in the town. The discovery of new tin deposits in Kuala

Inscribed mausoleum at Masjid Di Raja Sultan Suleiman in Klang

Lumpur in 1880 further diminished the importance of Klang. Today, the city is a commercial center, with most sights of interest located in the old town, south of the Sungai Klang.

Built in 1857, **Gedung Raja Abdullah** was the former residence of Rajah Abdullah. The building now houses the Tin Museum, which traces the history of the local mining industry through archived photographs and other artifacts. Nearby are the remains of Rajah Mahadi's fort. Also located in the old quarter is the attractive **Masjid Di Raja Sultan Suleiman**, the former state mosque, behind which is **Istana Alam Shah**, the royal palace of the Sultan of Selangor. Although closed to the public, visitors can view the pleasing façade of the palace which is a blend of Islamic and modern architecture. **Port Klang**, or North Port, lies 5 miles (8 km) to the west, close to South Port, Malaysia's main seaport, and is the access point for Pulau Ketam.

Pulau Ketam 36

34 miles (55 km) SW of Kuala Lumpur. 8,000. from Port Klang. www.pulauketam.com

First inhabited by Hainanese fishermen in the 1870s, Pulau Ketam, or Crab Island, remains largely populated by Chinese. The majority of the inhabitants still make their living by fishing. Although Pulau Ketam village is a simple settlement of stilt houses built over the water with narrow wooden walkways in place of roads, it contains a number of basic amenities including a bank and hospital. It is well known for its superb seafood restaurants, specializing in crab dishes, which make it a popular weekend dining venue for city residents. There are also ornate Chinese temples, such as the **Nang Thiam Keng Temple**, where locals host wedding feasts. The many floating fish farms offshore are worth visiting and can be reached by a short boat ride from the island jetty.

Putrajaya 37

15 miles (25 km) SW of Kuala Lumpur. 45,000. KLIA Transit from Stesen Sentral. Precinct 1, (03) 8888-7272. www.ppj.gov.my **Botanic Garden** Precinct 1. 7am–7pm daily. **Putrajaya Wetlands** Precinct 13. **Tel** (03) 8925-3817. 10am–6pm Tue–Fri, 7am–7pm Sat & Sun.

Founded in 1995, Putrajaya is the new federal administrative capital of Malaysia. Lying at the heart of the Multimedia Super Corridor (MSC), an area designated to attract information technology companies, and with huge swathes of green spaces, it is a planned "intelligent" garden city. Putrajaya is built on cleared forest land and centered around a huge artificial lake. The city is designed to create a sense of vastness and with so much water around, great attention has been paid to building massive bridges. These include the Putra Bridge, inspired by the Khaju Bridge in Iran, and the 787-ft (240-m) long Seri Gemilang Bridge.

Government departments and ministries began the move here from Kuala Lumpur in 1999. These include the Prime Minister's office, known as **Perdana Putra**, built in a flamboyant Malay-Palladian style,

Constructed of rose-tinted granite, the Putra Mosque is a landmark

and the equally grand **Palace of Justice**, topped with a gigantic dome. The **Putra Mosque** with its 380-ft (116-m) high minaret looms over one edge of the lake and is one of the city's most impressive buildings, blending architectural styles from Iraq, Iran, and Morocco. Other sights worth exploring include the **Botanic Garden** with its collection of tropical flora, and the **Putrajaya Wetlands**, which were constructed to help cleanse river water. Paddleboats can be hired for trips on the wetlands and lake.

Lying on the outskirts of Putrajaya is its twin town, **Cyberjaya**. Conceived as a center for high-tech companies, it has been under construction for over ten years now.

Palace of Justice, Putrajaya, with its distinctive Islamic-style architecture

KUALA LUMPUR STREET FINDER

The key map below shows the area of Kuala Lumpur covered in this Street Finder. Map references given for sights, shops, and entertainment venues in the Kuala Lumpur section refer to the maps on the following pages. Map references are also provided for some of Kuala Lumpur's hotels and restaurants. An index of the street names and places of interest shown on the maps can be found on the facing page. The first figure in the map reference indicates which Street Finder map to turn to, and the letters and numbers that follow refer to the map's grid. The symbols used to represent sights and useful information on the Street Finder maps are listed in the key below. Common street names have been abbreviated – Jalan to Jln. and Lorong to Lrg.

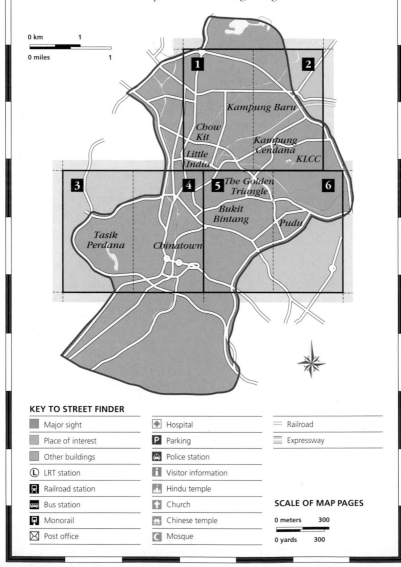

KEY TO STREET FINDER

Major sight	Hospital	Railroad
Place of interest	Parking	Expressway
Other buildings	Police station	
LRT station	Visitor information	
Railroad station	Hindu temple	**SCALE OF MAP PAGES**
Bus station	Church	0 meters 300
Monorail	Chinese temple	0 yards 300
Post office	Mosque	

Street Finder Index

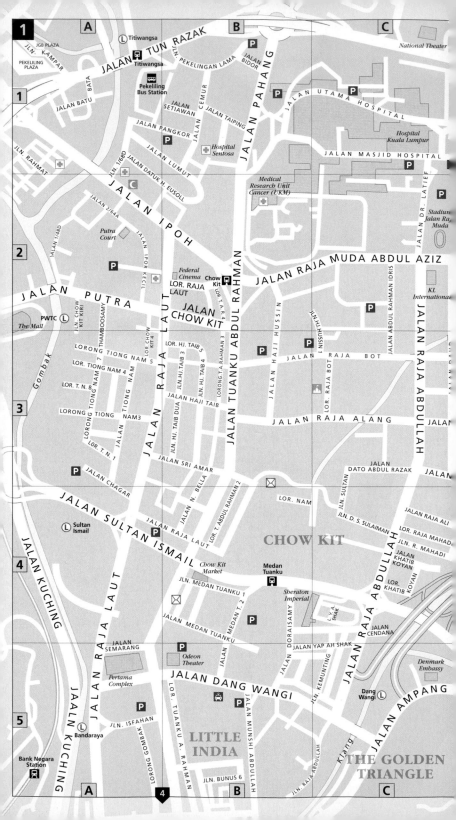

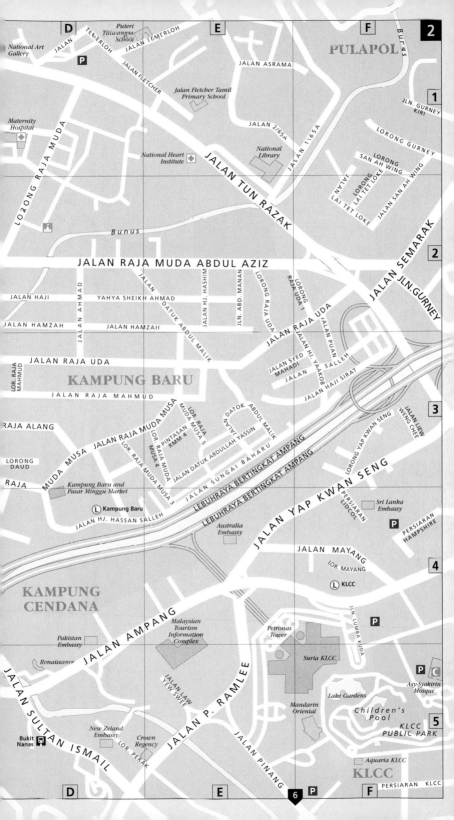

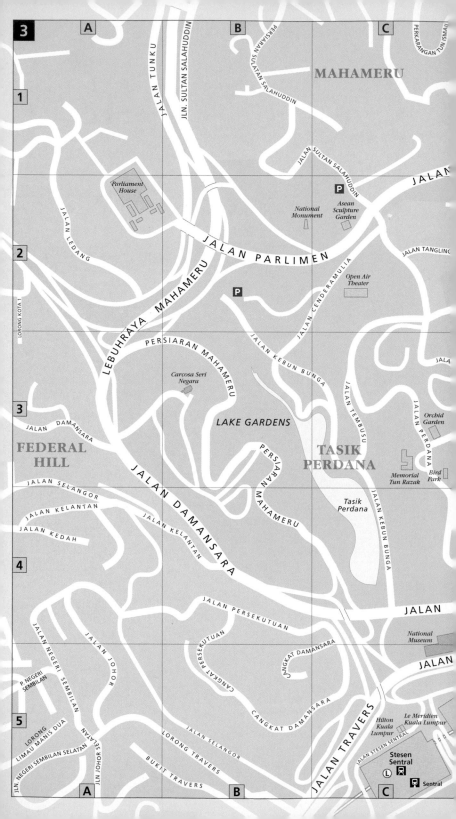

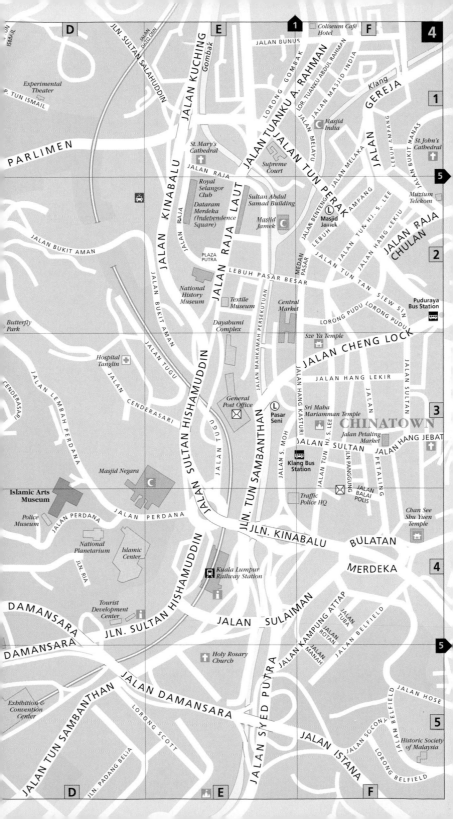

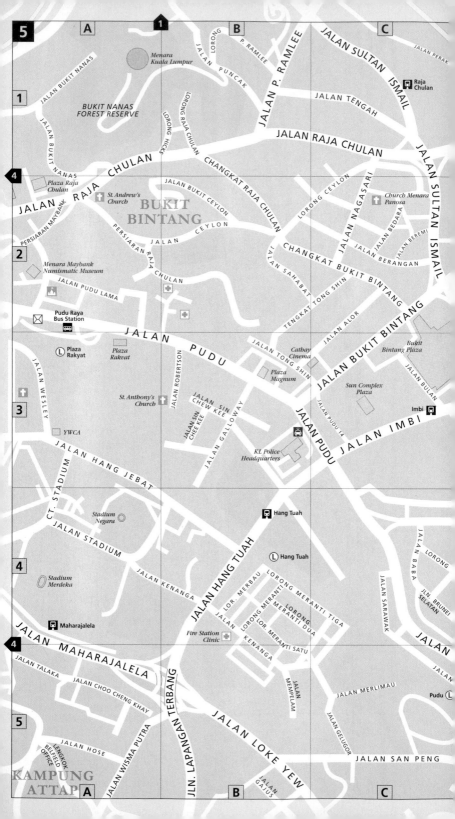

NORTHWEST PENINSULA

The northwestern states of Malaysia are among the most geographically diverse and historically significant in the country. The landscape encompasses everything from coastal plains and lushly forested mountains to jutting limestone cliffs and pristine islands. A long legacy of immigrants and rulers, attracted by the region's strategic geographical position and its natural wealth, has bequeathed a fascinating mix of cultures.

Archaeological remains found at the coastal site of Lembah Bujang provide evidence of a Hindu-Buddhist kingdom that dates back to the 4th century AD. In the 7th and 8th centuries, the region was ruled by the Srivijaya empire and later by Siam (now Thailand), while the 15th century saw the rise of the Sultanate of Malacca. With the beginning of the 17th century, a power struggle ensued between colonial powers in the area until the British finally gained control.

By the mid-19th century, the growing importance of tin mining in the states of Perak and Selangor brought with it far-reaching economic, political, and social repercussions. It fueled Malaysia's tremendous economic rise in the 20th century and also attracted a huge influx of Chinese immigrants. As a result of these varied early influences and economic developments, the Northwest Peninsula is more cosmopolitan and less culturally conservative than other parts of Malaysia. It is also one of the most developed and populous regions in the country, comprising not only ethnic Malays, Chinese, and Indians, but also indigenous groups such as the Orang Asli and the Orang Syam in the interior jungles and far north. The old royal capital of Kuala Kangsar and the vibrant, historic, and culturally diverse city of Georgetown in Penang are on the itinerary of most visitors to the Northwest Peninsula. More laid-back tourists head for the region's pristine beaches or the soothing environs of its tea plantations and cool hill stations.

The palm-fringed white sands of Pantai Cenang Beach, Langkawi

◁ Old rickshaws on display at the beautifully restored Cheong Fatt Tze Mansion in Georgetown, Penang

Exploring the Northwest Peninsula

Few regions in the country offer the range of attractions found in the Northwest Peninsula. The interiors feature cool hill stations, such as the celebrated Cameron Highlands, limestone cliffs riddled with cave temples, including the Batu Caves, and Chinese dominated tin-rush towns such as Ipoh. The most popular destinations are along the coast, including Penang, which is an ideal base for exploring the region and a fascinating destination in itself, and the islands of Langkawi and Pangkor. The archaeologically important Lembah Bujang lies in Kedah which, together with Perlis, is carpeted with paddy fields.

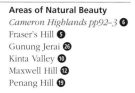

SIGHTS AT A GLANCE

Towns and Cities
Alor Star **27**
Batu Maung **24**
Georgetown *pp100–105* **14**
Ipoh **7**
Kuala Kangsar **13**
Kuala Kedah **28**
Kuala Selangor **4**
Taiping **11**

Places of Worship
Batu Caves **1**
Dhammikarama Temple **15**
Kek Lok Si Temple **18**
Snake Temple **23**
Wat Chayamangkalaram **16**

Gardens and Themed Attractions
Genting Highlands **3**
Penang Botanic Gardens **17**

Museums and Galleries
Orang Asli Museum **2**
Universiti Sains Malaysia Museum and Art Gallery **22**

Areas of Natural Beauty
Cameron Highlands *pp92–3* **6**
Fraser's Hill **5**
Gunung Jerai **26**
Kinta Valley **10**
Maxwell Hill **12**
Penang Hill **19**

Historical Sites and Buildings
Kellie's Castle **8**
Lembah Bujang **25**

Islands and Beaches
Batu Ferringhi **20**
Pulau Langkawi *pp112–5* **29**
Pulau Pangkor **9**
Teluk Bahang **21**

0 km   50

0 miles   50

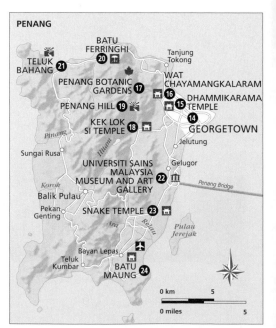

PENANG

BATU FERRINGHI **20**

Tanjung Tokong

TELUK BAHANG **21**

PENANG BOTANIC GARDENS **17**

WAT CHAYAMANGKALARAM **16**

DHAMMIKARAMA TEMPLE **15**

PENANG HILL **19**

KEK LOK SI TEMPLE **18**

GEORGETOWN **14**

Pinang

Hitam

Jelutung

Sungai Rusa

Korok

Gelugor

UNIVERSITI SAINS MALAYSIA MUSEUM AND ART GALLERY **22**

Penang Bridge

Balik Pulau

Pekan Genting

SNAKE TEMPLE **23**

Ara

Relau

Pulau Jerejak

Bayan Lepas

Teluk Kumbar

BATU MAUNG **24**

0 km   5

0 miles   5

Palm-fringed Pelangi Beach, Pulau Langkawi

GETTING AROUND

A good domestic flight network covers Ipoh, Pulau Pangkor, Langkawi, Georgetown, and Alor Star. The North-South Highway and Route 1, the region's two major roads, and the national railway (KTM) run almost parallel with each other, tracing the length of the west coast and linking the major towns. Driving is a good option; roads are safe and traffic is law-abiding. The Penang Bridge connects Butterworth with Penang, as do regular car and passenger ferries. Lumut is the ferry point for Pukau Pangkor, while ferries to Pulau Langkawi are available at Kuala Kedah and Kuala Perlis.

Kek Lok Si Temple in Penang, the largest Buddhist temple in Malaysia

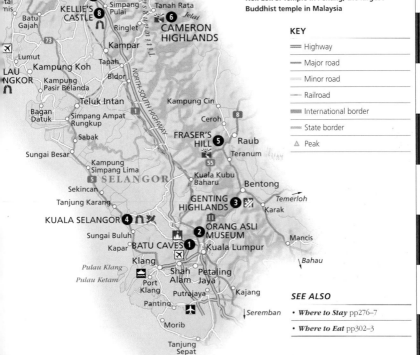

KEY

- ▬ Highway
- ▬ Major road
- ▭ Minor road
- ╌ Railroad
- ▬ International border
- ▬ State border
- △ Peak

SEE ALSO

Vibrant paintings of Hindu deities on the walls at one of the Batu Caves

Batu Caves ❶

8 miles (13 km) N of Kuala Lumpur
on Middle Ring Road 2. 🚌 🅿 8am–
8pm daily. 🍴 📷 🎎 Thaipusam
Festival (Jan/Feb).

Set high in a range of rugged
limestone cliffs, the Batu
Caves are a vast cavern complex that has become one of
the most popular attractions
near the capital. Long known
to the indigenous Orang Asli
people, the caves only gained
worlwide popularity when
American naturalist William
Hornaday came upon them in
1878. Deeply impressed by
the extent and beauty of the
largest cave, he compared it
to a grand cathedral. In the
1890s, it was converted into a
shrine dedicated to the Hindu
deity Lord Murugan, and soon
became the most important
pilgrimage site for Malaysia's
Hindus. During the annual
Thaipusam festival, held in
late January or early February,
a spectacular scene unfolds
here, when an estimated
one million pilgrims visit
the caves (see p29).
    Dominating the entrance to
the caves is a 141-ft (43-m)
tall golden statue of Lord
Murugan. From here a steep
flight of 272 steps leads up to
the main cave. Also known as
Temple or **Cathedral Cave**, it
is 328 ft (100 m) high and is
partially lit by shafts of light
that stream through gaps in
the roof. The cave walls are
lined with numerous statues
of Lord Murugan, along with
those of other Hindu gods,
including Shiva, Ganesh, and
Durga. The dome of the cave

is richly painted with scenes
from the Hindu scriptures. In
a chamber behind the central
shrine is the statue of another
deity, Lord Rama.
    There are a number of
other caves, including a small
one at the cliff's base containing elaborately painted
sculptures of Hindu gods.

Orang Asli
Museum ❷

Jalan Pahang, Gombak, 18 miles
(30 km) N of Kuala Lumpur. **Tel** (03)
6189-2113. 🚌 🅿 9am–5pm
Sat–Thu. 📷 🅿

Though visited by few
people, the Orang Asli
Museum provides a superb
introduction to the customs,
traditions, and material culture of Malaysia's almost
100,000 Orang Asli people,
the earliest known indigenous
inhabitants of the peninsula.
Run by the Orang Asli Affairs

Department, the museum
presents the history of the
18 distinct groups within the
Orang Asli community along
with their geographical distribution, musical instruments,
ornaments, medicines, models
of their dwellings, and a collection of traditional hunting
weapons, such as blowpipes
and poison spoons. Among
the most impressive of these
is the display of traditional
handicrafts, which includes
wooden head carvings with
fierce facial expressions.
Details of daily life, including
wedding rites and religious
practices, are also described.

Genting
Highlands ❸

31 miles (50 km) NE of Kuala
Lumpur. 🚌 from Kuala Lumpur,
then cable car (optional). 🍴
🅿 www.genting.com.my.
Cable Cars run every 20 min;
after midnight every hour.

Unlike most conventional
hill-station retreats, the 6,562-ft
(2,000-m) high Genting
Highlands, located in the
Titiwangsa Mountain Range,
is an extensive entertainment
and gambling complex which
features Malaysia's biggest
theme park as well as its only
casino. The glitzy 24-hour
Casino de Genting, one of the
largest in the world, contains
endless rows of Chinese and
Western games tables, a computerized racetrack, and slot
machines, while the **Genting
Theme Park** offers more than

The graceful entrance to the Orang Asli Museum

The sprawling entertainment complex at Genting Highlands

40 rides including Grand Prix Go Kart, the Cork-screw roller coaster, and a 185-ft (56-m) Turbo Drop which reaches the ground in less than five seconds. The resort, considered to be the largest in the world, has over 6,000 rooms, a shopping arcade, a golf course, and several concert halls that host international performing artists. An indoor leisure zone provides an excellent alternative on rainy days.

An attraction in itself is the cable car ride, which is a popular alternative to the bus journey for the final 2.5-mile (4-km) trip to the top. Genting Skyway and Awana Skyway are the two cable car operators that regularly organize these scenic trips.

🍁 **Genting Theme Park**
🕒 *daily.* 👋

Kuala Selangor ❹

42 miles (67 km) NW of Kuala Lumpur on Hwy 4, then 5.
👥 *39,200.* 🚌

The small and quiet district capital of Selangor, located at the mouth of the Sungai Selangor, was once the royal capital of the Sultanate of Selangor. It was conquered by the Dutch in 1784, and soon became the scene of a number of intense battles. During their invasion, the Dutch destroyed the sultan's fort and rebuilt it, naming it **Fort Atlingsburg** after their governor general. Perched atop Bukit Melawati, a hill overlooking the town, the fort was fought over repeatedly, and all that remains today are sections of the wall and cannons. Directly below the fort lies the boundary of **Taman Alam Kuala Selangor Nature Park**, a mangrove forest, home to over 150 species of birds. This is the only area in Malaysia to record sightings of the spoonbill sandpiper. It is also home to a variety of fish and crabs, found in the mangroves along the park's coastline. Several artificial ponds are surrounded by nature trails and observation hides.

Foliage-covered clock tower at Fraser's Hill

A particular highlight of Kuala Selangor is the chance to see the dazzling *kelip kelip,* or fireflies, along the banks of the Sungai Selangor at **Kampung Kuantan**, 6 miles (10 km) east of the capital.

⛫ **Fort Altingsburg**
Bukit Melawati. 🕒 *daily.*

🐦 **Taman Alam Kuala Selangor Nature Park**
Jalan Klinik. ***Tel*** *(03) 3289-2294.*
🕒 *daily.*

Fraser's Hill ❺

62 miles (100 km) N of Kuala Lumpur. 🚌 to Kuala Kubu Bharu, then Fraser's Hill. ℹ *WWF Nature Education Center, Jalan Genting, (09) 362-2517.* 👋 *nature walks.* 🍴

A hill station sprawling across seven forested hills, the 4,921-ft (1,500-m) Fraser's Hill is named after British pioneer Louis James Fraser. A mule-train driver and tin-ore trader, he arrived here in the late 1890s, but then mysteriously disappeared around 1910. Shortly after, Fraser's Hill was developed as a refreshing retreat for the British expatriate community.

A picturesque journey leads to Fraser's Hill, passing through giant bamboo groves and tree ferns, and climbing steeply through the Gap, a mountain pass between Kubu Bharu and Raub.

Of all the hill stations set in the Titiwangsa mountains, Fraser's Hill retains the most distinct colonial ambience with Tudor-style buildings and neat rose gardens. It is a quiet, relaxed place, perfect for jungle strolls and afternoon teas. At the center of town is a market square and a clock tower. This small area is surrounded by dense woods, which contain several nature trails. One of the hill station's main attractions is its abundant flora and fauna. Over 265 species of birds have been recorded in the area. Every June, Fraser's Hill hosts the annual International Bird Race, in which teams of ornithologists compete to spot as many bird varieties as possible over a 24-hour period.

Golfing at the Fraser's Hill Golf Course is a popular sport, as is horseback riding. It is possible to fish on **Allan's Waters**, a tiny lake located in town. About 3 miles (5 km) northwest of the center, passing by a lookout tower, is **Jeriau Waterfall**, which flows into a small stream.

Lush, meandering route to the summit of Fraser's Hill

Cameron Highlands ⑥

The largest and most popular hill station in Malaysia, Cameron Highlands is located on the northwest corner of Pahang. It is named for the British surveyor William Cameron who charted the area in 1885. Dotted with lush tea plantations and farms, the region is renowned for its flowers and fresh produce. The temperature here rarely exceeds 22° C (72° F) and is accompanied by mists and light rainfall, which makes it a great getaway from the hot plains. It is also a popular destination for trekkers. Cameron Highlands retains a distinct colonial ambience, with its principal settlement located in Tanah Rata.

KEY

☐   Cameron Highlands

★ **Ye Olde Smokehouse**
A mock-Tudor building on the outskirts of Tanah Rata, Ye Olde Smokehouse typifies the colonial architecture that adds to the appeal of Cameron Highlands. It is popular with visitors for its real Devonshire cream teas.

Gunung Jasar, at 5,564 ft (1,696 m), offers fine views across Cameron Highlands from its bald summit and is easily accessible by a carefully marked trail from Tanah Rata.

Gunung Perdah at 5,171 ft (1,576 m), rises above an Orang Asli village to the north of Tanah Rata and dominates the northwestern horizon.

All Souls' Church, erected in 1958, serves as a civilian church as well as the Anglican retreat center at Cameron Highlands.

Strawberry Park Resort

Kampung Orang Asli

Cameron Highlands Resort

Gunung Perdah 5,171 ft

Weather Station

Golf Club

Gunung Jasar 5,564 ft

Kampu Taman S

Tanah Rata

Bharat Tea Estate   RINGLET

JIM THOMPSON

Jim Thompson shortly before his disappearance

In March 1967, James H.W. Thompson, a successful US-born Thai businessman, disappeared while on holiday in the Cameron Highlands. He simply walked out of the cottage where he was staying, and never came back. At the time, and for months afterwards, the media was filled with speculation about his fate. With his disappearance, he became a legendary figure, leaving behind him a resurrected and resilient Thai silk industry and a traditional teak home in Bangkok. Jim Thompson's home is now an exquisite museum of Southeast Asian art.

STAR SIGHTS

★ Ye Olde Smokehouse

★ Sungai Palas Tea Plantation

★ Sam Poh Temple

★ **Sungai Palas Tea Plantation**
This stunning estate offers free daily tours. Visitors can purchase teas and enjoy fine views across the surrounding hills while sampling tea and cakes in the estate tearoom.

VISITORS' CHECKLIST

56 miles (90 km) E of Ipoh.
🏘 12,000. 🚌 *from Penang and Kuala Lumpur.* ℹ *Jalan Besar, Tanah Rata; (012) 657-1084.* **www.**cameronhighlands.com.my

Butterfly Garden
Almost 300 species of butterfly are on show here, alongside scorpions, giant rhinoceros beetles, and camouflaged stick insects.

Rose Garden
This garden has an immense appeal for locals as well as tourists who visit to see the exotic roses in bloom. The flowers flourish only in temperate upland areas such as the Cameron Highlands.

Map labels:
ung bang 5 ft
/IPOH
Blue Valley Tea Estate
Kuala Terla
Rose Valley
ncle Sam's Farm
Brinchang
Gunung Beremban 6,037 ft
ardi Agricultural ation
obinson alls
inson Falls er Station

0 km 1
0 miles 1

KEY

━━	Major road
━━	Minor road
‑ ‑	Trail
ℹ	Visitor information
🏛	Buddhist temple
✝	Church
▲	Peak

★ **Sam Poh Temple**
This ornate Chinese-Buddhist temple is situated on a hill overlooking the town of Brinchang. Protected by gilded lions and temple guardians, it serves as the main place of worship for the local Chinese.

Birch Memorial Clock Tower standing in Ipoh's Old Town

Ipoh ❼

128 miles (205 km) N of Kuala Lumpur on North-South Hwy.
🏘 625,000. ✈ 🚉 🚌 🛈 7–9 Jalan Medan Istana 3, (05) 255-2772.
🎭 International Orchid Festival (Jun/Aug). www.ipoh-online.com.my

Nestled in the limestone cliffs of Kinta Valley, Ipoh is the state capital of Perak and Malaysia's third largest city. It was built on profits from the valley's rich tin mines, which were developed by immigrant Chinese workers in the late-19th century. This influx of people bequeathed to the city some of the finest Peranakan architecture seen in the country.

The Kinta River divides Ipoh into two neat halves. Occupying the left bank is the **Old Town**, the most atmospheric part of the city. It boasts elegant Chinese mansions and shophouses, as well as grand colonial buildings. Built in 1917, Ipoh Station is a blend of late Victorian and Moorish-Islamic styles. Directly opposite stands the Dewan Bandaran, or Town Hall, a dazzling white Neoclassical structure. Other prominent landmarks near the station include the mock-Tudor Royal Ipoh Club with its half-timbered walls and mullioned windows, and the historical landmark Birch Memorial Clock Tower erected in memory of James

Birch, the first British Resident in Perak. A short distance from the Old Town center is **Darul Ridzuan Museum**. Set in a stately 1920s mansion, it recounts the history of Ipoh and the rise of the tin mining industry in Perak.

The **New Town**, on the right bank of the river, contains some splendid Chinese shophouses and most of the city's accommodations.

🏛 **Darul Ridzuan Museum**
Jalan Panglima. *Tel* (05) 253-8906.
⏰ 9am–5pm Sat–Thu.

Kellie's Castle ❽

19 miles (30 km) S of Ipoh. 🚌
⏰ 8:30am–6pm daily. 🎫 📷 📹

A unique fusion of Scottish castle and Moorish architecture, Kellie's Castle is an unfinished colonial structure. It was built by Scotsman William Kellie-Smith, who made a fortune in the rubber business in the 19th century. The mansion was envisioned as a spectacular edifice, complete with an elevator, and work began in 1915. However, Smith died of pneumonia in 1926 while in Portugal, leaving his grand home incomplete. During World War II, the castle grounds were used as an execution site by the Japanese. Today, it is a well-preserved attraction set in a park with fig and banyan trees. Also on the grounds is a Hindu temple built by Smith for his largely Tamil labor force. The temple was built after many Tamil workers were killed in an epidemic of

influenza during the mansion's construction. Grateful for this act, the workers added a small statue of Smith amid the Hindu deities on the temple roof.

Pulau Pangkor ❾

51 miles (83 km) SW of Ipoh.
🏘 25,000. ✈ ⛴ from Lumut.
🛈 Jalan Sultan Idris Shah, Lumut, (05) 683-4057. www.pulau-pangkor.com

Endowed with a laid-back feel and some of the best beaches on the west coast of the peninsula, Pulau Pangkor is a popular destination. The island is inhabited by a thriving fishing community. Most of the local villages, including Pangkor Town, the main settlement, lie on its east coast, while the resorts and stunning powder-white beaches are strung out on the west, around Teluk Nipah. The main beaches include Pasir Bogak, Coral Bay, and Pantai Puteri Dewi, which is privately owned and requires an entrance fee. The beach at Teluk Ketapang, or Turtle Bay, at the northern end of the island, is named for the increasingly rare sea turtles that come ashore here in the summer months to lay their eggs.

Offering a change of scene from the beaches is the historical site of **Kota Belanda**, a 17th-century Dutch fort 2 miles (3 km) south of Pangkor Town. The fort was built mainly to protect Dutch interests in the tin trade from Malay pirates. There are a few Hindu and Chinese temples

Remains of the striking Kellie's Castle

The picturesque Lake Gardens in Taiping, near the foot of Bukit Larut

Kinta Valley ⑩

9 miles (15 km) N of Ipoh, off North-South Hwy. 🚌 from Ipoh. 🚹

Once rich with tin ore, the magnificent jungle-topped limestone cliffs of Kinta Valley shelter a number of caves, which, over the years, have been converted into Buddhist temples and are now popular pilgrimage centers. The oldest and largest cave temple is **Sam Poh Tong**. Established by a Buddhist monk in the late-19th century, it features Chinese-style Mahayana Buddhist images. More impressive is **Perak Tong**, one of the largest Chinese temples in Malaysia, founded in 1926. Its interior walls are adorned with murals done by artists from across Southeast Asia. The main chamber contains over 40 Buddha statues and a huge bell believed to be more than a century old. A series of 400 steps leads up and through the cave to a balcony which offers splendid views across the valley. The temple also doubles as a Chinese art center. A more recent temple, **Kek Lok Tong**, is set in a two-tiered cavern and has a bronze Laughing Buddha.

Bronze Buddha at Kek Lok Tong

Taiping ⑪

40 miles (70 km) N of Ipoh.
🏘 220,000. 🚉 from Ipoh. 🚌
🛈 355 Jalan Kota; (05) 806-9487.
🎏 Taiping Festival Month (Sep).
www.perak.gov.my/en

Although the name Taiping means everlasting peace in Chinese, the old state capital of Perak traces its origins to a turbulent past, marked by bitter feuds between rival Chinese secret societies. The country's first tin mining center and the most important town in Perak in the mid-19th century, it began to be overshadowed by Ipoh and Kinta Valley in the 1890s. Now a low-key town, with a distinctly Chinese feel, Taiping is best known for its vast, tranquil **Lake Gardens**, or Taman Tasik Taiping. A stroll around the town will reveal some attractive colonial architecture, best exemplified by the District Office. It is also home to **Perak Museum**, the oldest museum in the country, built in 1883. Housed in a grand colonial building, it is noted for its natural history and ethnological exhibits, as well as a fine collection of *keris*, or traditional Malay daggers. Next door to the museum is the colorful **Ling Nam Temple**, the oldest Chinese temple in Perak, as well as **All Saints' Church**, the oldest church in Malaysia. Taiping also has a number of well-preserved Chinese shophouses.

🏛 **Perak Museum**
Tel (05) 807-2057. ⭘ daily.
⏺ 12:15–2:45pm Fri.

Maxwell Hill ⑫

6 miles (10 km) NW of Taiping.
🚙 government-run Land Rovers from Taiping. 🚹 (05) 807-7243.
🖥 **www**.perak.gov.my/en

Now officially called Bukit Larut, Maxwell Hill is the oldest and smallest hill station in Malaysia. It is also the wettest, receiving the highest rainfall in the country. Once a tea plantation, Maxwell Hill was founded in the 1870s. It was named after William Edward Maxwell, the Assistant Resident of Perak. The 3,340-ft (1,020-m) mist-shrouded hill station is still developing. Its greatest appeal lies in the bucolic charm of its surroundings and the stunning vistas that stretch across the plains to the Strait of Malacca.

Activities here revolve around trekking and bird- and butterfly-watching. The steep climb to the summit of Bukit Larut, with its spectacular views on the way up, is a popular day trip from Taiping. It twists through more than 70 hairpin bends, dense jungles, and a crumbling, old tea garden.

One of the many bungalows on peaceful Maxwell Hill

---

as well. Pangkor's compact size makes it ideal for walking and cycling, although its densely forested interior remains largely inaccessible.

The resorts arrange fishing and snorkeling day trips to the small islands nearby. Among these is Pangkor Laut, home to Emerald Bay, one of Malaysia's most beautiful beaches, though access is restricted to residents of the island's resort.

Kuala Kangsar ⑬

31 miles (50 km) NW of Ipoh, off
North-South Hwy. 🚗 40,000.
🚌 from Kuala Lumpur and
Georgetown. 🚆 from Ipoh and
Taiping. 📅 Sultan's Birthday (Apr
19). www.perak.gov.my/en

Kuala Kangsar in Perak has
been the royal capital of the
Sultans of Perak for the last
200 years. In the 1870s, it
became the first foothold
for the British in Malaysia,
who initiated their control
of the peninsula by installing
Residents, or colonial officers,
at the royal courts. During
the same period, the town
became the birthplace of
Malaysia's rubber industry
when Sir Hugh Low, then
British Resident in Perak,
planted the first seeds
of rubber. By the
1890s, however, the
town's prestige as an
administrative and
financial center was
eclipsed by the tin-
trading towns of Ipoh
and Taiping.

Today a tranquil
town, Kuala Kangsar
remains steeped in
Malay tradition and is home
to one of the most attractive
royal districts in the country,
as well as some fine colonial
architecture and lovely gardens. All the main sights are
within walking distance
of each other and can be
explored in half a day.

The small town center can
be divided into old and new
sections. The older part, close
to the banks of the Sungai
Perak, is a good place to buy

The distinctive clock tower at the Kuala Kangsar town center

traditional Malay handicrafts,
such as *mengkuang* woven
cloth, bamboo products, and
the celebrated *labu*, or gourd-
shaped earthenware pots.
These are manufactured in
the village of Sayong, which

Crafting *labu*,
Sayong village

is located across the
river and can be
reached by boat. The
new town is domi-
nated by Chinese
shophouses and mod-
ern buildings, includ-
ing most of Kuala
Kangsar's restaurants.
Marking the center of
town are two colonial-
era structures, the
distinctive clock tower and
the **District Office**, whose
grounds still contain one of
the town's first rubber trees.

To the north of the town
center is one of the most
impressive colonial buildings
in Kuala Kangsar, the **Malay
College**. Opened in 1905
during the reign of Sultan
Idris, it was the first Malay
school to provide English
education to the local elite
who were hoping to join the

colonial administrative
service. Across the road from
the Malay College stands
Pavilion Square Tower. Built
in 1930, this small wooden
three-story structure, designed
in colonial and Malay styles,
enabled the royal family and
British dignitaries to view
polo matches and other
sports events in privacy.

🅲 Masjid Ubudiah
Jalan Istana.
To the east of Kuala Kangsar,
along the wide Sungai Perak,
an ornamental gateway leads
to Masjid Ubudiah, Perak's
royal mosque and one of the
finest examples of Islamic
architecture in Malaysia.
Gracing the slopes of the
grassy Bukit Chandan, the
striking mosque is built in
Moorish style. Its magnificent
golden onion-shaped dome is
closely surrounded by four
soaring white minarets, each
crowned with its own small
dome. Construction of the
mosque began during the
reign of Sultan Idris but was
not completed until 1917, the
first year of the reign of his
successor, Sultan Abdul Jalil.
The delays were partly due to
World War I, and partly due
to two royal elephants running amok and destroying the
imported Italian marble floor.
Next to the mosque is the
Royal Mausoleum, where
rulers of Perak have been
interred since the 18th century.

The interior of the mosque
is officially closed to non-
Muslims. However, visitors
are free to explore the
grounds of the mosque and
are permitted to photograph
the building.

The magnificient Masjid Ubudiah, Perak's royal mosque

For hotels and restaurants in this region see pp276–7 and pp302–3

⛫ Istana Iskandariah

Jalan Istana.

Perched at the summit of Bukit Chandan, overlooking the Sungai Perak and Masjid Ubudiah, the modern Istana Iskandariah was built in 1933 and is the official residence of the present royal family. Set amid rolling lawns, the imposing white marble palace, with its series of towers topped by golden domes, reflects a fusion of Moorish and 1930s colonial Art Deco styles. A less impressive annex was added on the southern side in 1984. Although the palace is not open to visitors, a stroll along the two small roads that form its boundary provides excellent views of the building and its lawns, especially from the riverside.

⛫ Istana Kenangan

Jalan Istana. ☐ *9:30am–5pm Sat–Thu.* ◉ *12:15–2:45pm Fri.* 🖼

Just to the southwest of Istana Iskandariah stands the smaller but more captivating Istana Kenangan, or Palace of Memories. This palace was built in 1931 for Sultan Iskandar Shah (1876–1938) as a temporary royal residence while the Istana Iskandariah was being constructed. It is a superb example of traditional Malay architecture. The structure is built entirely of wood without the use of an architectural plan, nails, or steel, and is decorated with geometric-patterned bamboo

Façade of the grand Galeri Sultan Azlan Shah, a state museum

panels and intricate friezes. The roof features five ridges and is surmounted by a symbolic row of bananas. The ground floor of the palace features extensive verandas that allow cool breezes to flow through the entire space. The erstwhile palace now houses the **Perak Royal Museum**, popularly known as Muzium Di Raja, which traces the history of Perak and its royal family through images and artifacts.

⛫ Istana Hulu

Jalan Istana. ☐ *9:30am–5pm daily.* 🖼

The beautiful Victorian-style Istana Hulu is another former palace that was built in 1903 for Sultan Idris, the 28th Sultan of Perak. When the palace ceased to function as a royal residence, it became the location of the prestigious girls' college Sekolah Raja Perempuan Mazwin, or Mazwin School for Ladies, for several decades. The palace has now been converted into the **Galeri Sultan Azlan Shah**, or Sultan Azlan Shah Museum, a Perak state museum. Exhibits showcase traditional handicrafts of the state including a fine collection of traditional *keris*, or Malay daggers, and examples of *tekat* embroidery. Most significant, however, is the museum's extensive collection of royal gifts, photographs, and other personal effects belonging to Azlan Shah, the present Sultan of Perak, who has also served as the ninth Yang di-Pertaun Agong, or King of Malaysia, from 1984 to 1994, a rotating position held by sultans of the various states.

The beautiful Istana Kenangan, built in traditional Malay style, now housing the Perak Royal Museum

Sprawling tea plantation in the Cameron Highlands ▷

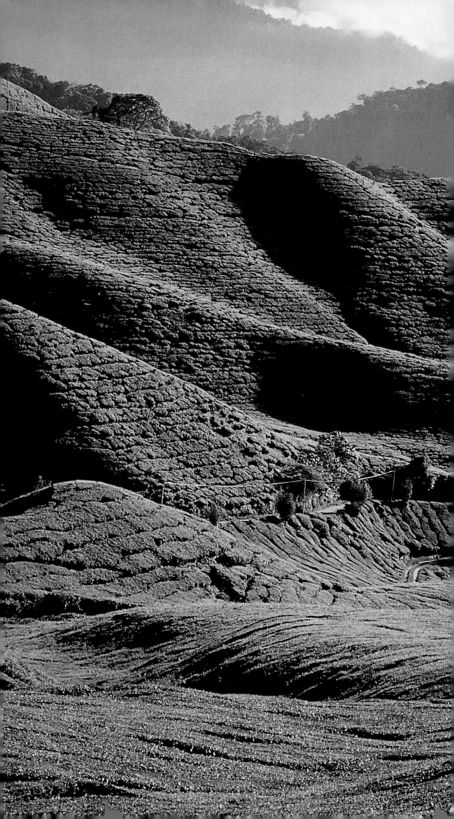

Georgetown ⑭

Located on the northeastern coast of Penang, Georgetown is one of Malaysia's most visited cities. Founded in 1786 by Captain Francis Light as a base for the British East India Company in the Malay states, the town, which was named after the Prince of Wales, soon developed into the state's economic and cultural hub. An essentially Chinese city today, Georgetown has an authentic Straits Settlement atmosphere, enhanced by its well-preserved colonial architecture, traditional wooden shophouses, and the diverse cuisine developed by its Indian, Malay, Peranakan, Thai, and European communities.

🏛 Fort Cornwallis

Lebuh Light. 🚌 *from KOMTAR via Weld Quay.* ◯ *9am–7pm daily.*

The spot where Sir Francis Light (*see p103*) stepped ashore in 1786, Fort Cornwallis, in the colonial core of Georgetown, is a great place to start an exploration of the city on foot, by bicycle, or by trishaw. The original fort was a simple palm-tree stockade, but in 1805 this was replaced by a star-shaped brick and mortar structure complete with moat and crenellated walls to shelter cannon guarding the harbor. As the first headquarters of the British East India Company in Penang, Fort Cornwallis contained barracks for troops, a signal station, administrative offices, and a Christian chapel. Today, little remains of the fort apart from its outer fortifications. The inner area is a park liberally scattered with cannon. The oldest of these,

Victoria Memorial Clock Tower

Seri Rambai, is of Dutch origin and dates back to 1603.

In a small traffic circle to the southeast of the fort stands the **Victoria Memorial Clock Tower**, an elegant colonial edifice crowned by a Moorish-style dome. Built in 1897 with funds donated by a Georgetown *towkay*, or Chinese businessman, it commemorates the diamond jubilee of Queen Victoria's reign. The memorial stands 60-ft (18-m) high in honor of the 60 years of the monarch's reign. To the west of the fort are the parklands of the **Padang Kota Lama**, or the Old City Green. Among the fine colonial buildings to the south and west are the Supreme Court, the Dewan Undangan Negeri, or State Legislative Building, and the grand **Dewan Bandaran**, or City Hall. To the north, facing the northern channel of the Strait of Malacca, runs the **Esplanade**, named Jalan Tun Syed Sheh Barakbah.

🏛 Weld Quay Clan Piers

Pengkalan Weld. 🚌 *from KOMTAR.* 🚗

South of Little India, along Weld Quay and projecting into the southern channel of the Strait of Malacca, stand long rows of jetties on which are built low houses, religious shrines, and shops. These are the clan jetties of Georgetown, dating back to the late-19th century. There are seven such jetties, all but one home to a different

[Map showing Georgetown streets including JALAN SULTAN AHMAD SHAH, LEBUH FARQ, JALAN ARGYLL, JALAN SRI BAHARI, Cheong Fatt Tze Mansion, JLN. ARIFFIN, JALAN TRANSFER, JALAN ARGYLL, JALAN HUTTON, JLN. D'KOYAH, Bengali Mosque, Hai Tem, 100 Cintra Street ⑬, LEBUH DICKENS, JALAN CHOWRASTA, LEBUH CAMBELL, LEBUH CINTRA, JALAN PHEE CHOON, Market, LEBUH KUALA KANGSAR, JALAN PINTAL, LEBUH PHEE CHOON, JALAN DRUM CHWEE LEONG, KIMBERLEY, KOMTAR ℹ, LEBUH TEK SOON, JALAN RIA, JALAN MAXWELL, JALAN CHWEE LEONG, LEBUH CARNAV, JALAN PRANGIN, JALAN MAGAZINE, LEBUH NOORDIN, LE, LEBUH PRESSGRAVE, LEBUH TYE SIN, Airport 7.5 miles (12 km)]

Chinese clan, originally from the Tong An district of China's Fujian province.

The oldest and largest is the Chew Jetty, founded in the 1870s, followed by the Lee, Tan, Yeoh, and Koay jetties. The most recent, the Mixed Clan and Peng Aun jetties, date from the 1960s. Six are home to Sino-Malaysian Buddhist clans, while the last, Koay Jetty, is Muslim, being home to around 30 Chinese Hui Muslim families. All the jetties, except Koay, terminate in small temples. The most important one, on Chew Jetty, is dedicated to the Jade Emperor.

Replica of 18th-century British camp and cannon, Fort Cornwallis

For hotels and restaurants in this region see pp276–7 and pp302–3

One of the jetties at Weld Quay Clan Piers

Khoo Kongsi Temple

Medan Cannon. *from KOMTAR.* 9am–5pm daily. www.khookongsi.com.my

Penang's greatest historical attraction, the gloriously ornate Khoo Kongsi Temple, was founded in 1835 by wealthy Hokkien merchants of the influential Khoo clan. The temple's full name, Leong San Tong Khoo Kongsi, or Dragon Mountain Hall, was chosen in honor of the merchants' ancestral village of Leong San in southern China.

VISITORS' CHECKLIST

Penang Island. 220,000. to Butterworth, then ferry. KOMTAR, (04) 264-3494. Penang International Dragon Boat Festival (Jun), Pesta Pulau Penang (Nov–Dec), Chingay (Dec). www.tourismpenang.gov.my

The clan took this as an indication of divine wrath at the building of a temple too grand for ancestor worship, so the temple was built again, but on a less lavish scale.

Rebuilt in Qing dynasty style, with elaborate wall carvings, detailed frescoes, and fine roof decorations, the building is adorned with painted dragons and other auspicious figures.

Altar at the Khoo Kongsi Temple, decorated with intricate carvings

Map labels

Dewan Bandaran
JALAN TUN SYED SHEH
Green Hill
Penang Library
Supreme Court
Fort Cornwallis (1)
Cathedral of the Assumption (12)
Penang Museum & Art Gallery (11)
St.George's Church (10)
LIGHT
Clocktower
Kuan Yin Temple (9)
Masjid Kapitan Kling (6)
Sri Mariamman Temple (7)
Little India (8)
Acheen Street Mosque (4)
Syed Alatas Mansion (5)
MPP Bus Station
Yeoh Kongsi
Yellow and Blue Bus Station
Khoo Kongsi Temple (3)
Weld Quay Clan Piers (2)
Ferry Terminal
BUTTERWORTH
E & O Hotel

0 meters 300
0 yards 300

GEORGETOWN

Key to Symbols *see back flap*

Kongsis are designed to function as places of worship and community centers for members of the clan that built them. This *kongsi*, however, became a center not just for the Khoos, but for four other powerful Hokkien-speaking families, the Cheah, Lim, Tan, and Yeoh clans, who ran an influential secret society.

The original temple, thought too modest for the thriving Khoo clan, was demolished in 1894. A magnificent new temple was constructed over the next eight years, but it burned to the ground within a month of its completion.

Acheen Street Mosque

Lebuh Aceh. *from Lebuh Chulia.*

One of the oldest buildings in Georgetown, the Acheen Street Mosque was founded in 1808 by a prosperous Sumatran pepper merchant. It was originally built to serve the burgeoning Muslim community of Lebuh Aceh, Penang's first urban Malay village. It is more commonly known as Masjid Melayu, or the Malay Mosque, to distinguish it from the nearby **Masjid Kapitan Kling**, which was built by Indian-Muslim migrants.

The mosque, a 5-minute walk from Lebuh Chulia, has an Egyptian-style minaret and an Achenese-style roof. The hole halfway up its minaret was the result of a cannonball fired in a clan riot in Penang.

The 19th-century Syed Alatas Mansion, a museum and information center

Syed Alatas Mansion

128 Lebuh Armenian. ***Tel** (04) 261-6606.* *9:30am–6:30pm Wed–Mon.* **www**.penang-islamicmuseum.net

Syed Mohammed Alatas was a wealthy and influential 19th-century Achenese businessman and leader of Penang's Malay community. In the 1860s he built a magnificent *rumah besar*, or great house, on Armenian Street where he lived with his family until his death in the early 20th century. Set in a walled compound, the two-story Syed Alatas Mansion is an eclectic mix of Malay, Indian, and European architectural and cultural influences. It features a terra-cotta hipped roof that slopes down to the eaves and a carriage porch with a gable roof. The building is elaborately decorated with molded cornices and elegant stuccowork. Although considered one of the finest examples of upper-class Malay Muslim residences in Penang, it fell into a state of disrepair when it was abandoned in the 1930s and remained virtually forgotten for most of the 20th century.

In 1993, the mansion was taken over and restored by the Penang State Government and eventually reopened as the Penang Islamic Museum. It houses various collections of Islamic and Malay artifacts, and also functions as an information center. The exhibits are displayed thematically, and include Arabic calligraphy, ceramics, carpets and upholstery, and items used in religious rituals. One of the most unusual artifacts on display is a ceremonial Malay circumcision chair. Facets of Malay wedding rituals are also chronicled. The Personalities Room has exhibits on iconic Malay figures of the past. The entrance displays a *beduk*, or a long wooden drum, used to sound the call to prayer five times a day.

Masjid Kapitan Kling

Jalan Masjid Kapitan Kling. ***Tel** (04) 261-6663.* *Islamic Information Center. daily. prayer times.*

Masjid Kapitan Kling, the oldest and best-known historic mosque in Penang, was founded around 1800 by Caudeer Mohudeen. He was a prominent member of the island's Indian Muslim community and bore the title Kapitan Kling, or Captain of the Klings. Kling was a term employed at that time to describe Tamil Muslims, also called Chulia, who formed the bulk of Penang's Indian Muslims. Mohudeen, officially named headman of the Chulias in 1801, died in 1834. His tomb is located at the nearby Kampung Kolam.

The Masjid has been restored and altered on several occasions, most notably in 1910 when it was given its present appearance with the addition of Indian-style copper domes, turrets, and a minaret. A *madrassa*, or religious school, was added in 1916. In 1935, the height of the central prayer hall was doubled, allowing more natural light and air into the interior. The most recent renovation took place in 2003, when Arabic calligraphy was added to the interior of the main dome and to the walls, which were originally decorated with intricate floral motifs.

Sri Mariamman Temple

Jalan Masjid Kapitan Kling. *6am–9pm daily. Thaipusam (Jan/Feb), Navaratri (Oct/Nov).*

On the opposite side of the street from Masjid Kapitan Kling is the Sri Mariamman Temple, a typical southern Indian temple with an elaborately carved and painted *gopuram*, or tiered entrance gateway of a Hindu temple. Dedicated to the deity Mariamman, or Great Powerful Mother, this is Penang's oldest Hindu temple.

Established by pious local Tamils as a simple shrine, it became a fully-fledged temple in 1833. Artisans were brought from Madras to create images of the goddess Mariamman in all her aspects. Subsequently, a 23-ft (7-m) high *gopuram*

The ornate domes and graceful façade of Masjid Kapitan Kling

For hotels and restaurants in this region see pp276–7 and pp302–3

was added, with sculptures of about 38 Hindu deities. A statue of Lord Murugan, adorned with gold and diamonds, was also installed.

Several times a year, Sri Mariamman is taken out of the temple in a wooden chariot, and carried in procession through the streets of Little India. The most important occasion is Navaratri, a nine-night celebration in October or November when devotees worship female deities, such as Durga, Saraswati, Lakshmi, and Mariamman. Penang's annual Thaipusam *(see p29)* procession also begins here.

🏛 Little India

Lebuh Pasar. 🚌 🍴 www.tourism penang.gov.my

Penang's colorful and vibrant Little India, throbbing with antiquity and tradition, dates back to the early 19th century, when Indian migrants to Penang began to settle in and around Lebuh Pasar, then called Kadai Teru, or shop street. Since most of the early migrants were Tamils, the area was commonly known as Little Madras, but over the years other communities also moved in. Soon the enclave acquired a distinctive south Asian feel and gained its current sobriquet.

The narrow streets of Little India are lined with shops selling all kinds of south Asian produce, from saris and gold jewelry to flower garlands and images of Hindu deities. The wide range of shops and services includes astrologers, millers, grocers, fruit-sellers, herb dealers, and moneychangers. The aroma of spice, incense, and curry suffuses the air, while the bells of trishaw drivers and the constant bustle of the crowds make the ambience quintessentially Indian.

Although Bahasa Malaysia and English are the main spoken languages of Penang, here, the rolling, fast-paced southern Indian tongues of Malayalam and Tamil

predominate. With attractions that include mosques, Hindu temples, and Chinese clan enclaves, as well as a host of restaurants, Little India is now a great draw for food-lovers, heritage enthusiasts, and visitors who simply want to soak up the atmosphere.

🏯 Kuan Yin Temple

Jalan Masjid Kapitan Kling. 🚌

Dedicated to Kuan Yin, or the goddess of mercy, this temple was originally constructed as a shared Hokkien and Cantonese temple and community center. Its foundation stone was laid in 1800, making it one of the oldest Chinese temples in the province of Penang.

Kuan Yin is perhaps the most worshiped of Chinese deities, and also much revered by Buddhists and Taoists. Associated with peace, good fortune, and fertility, she is portrayed with 18 arms. Feast days are held to honor Kuan Yin's birthday, initiation, and attainment of *nirvana.* Even today, the temple bustles with worshipers carrying ritual offerings of flowers, oil, and food, especially on temple days. These fall on the first and 15th day of every lunar month, and on the 19th day of the second, sixth, and ninth lunar months. Puppet shows and Chinese opera performances are held on these days to honor the goddess.

Tourists on a trishaw ride

St. George's Church with its Doric columns and octagonal steeple

✝ St. George's Church

Lebuh Farquhar. **Tel** *(04) 261-2739.*
🚌 🕐 *8:30am–12:30pm and 1:30–4:30pm Tue–Sat, 8:30am–4:30pm Sun.* ♿ ✝ www.stgeorgespg.org

The oldest Anglican church in Southeast Asia, St. George's Church was constructed in 1818 to serve the growing Christian community of Penang. Designed by military engineer and painter Captain Robert Smith, it was built by the British East India Company using convict labor. In 1886, to mark the centenary of the founding of Penang and to honor Sir Francis Light, a small Greek-style domed pavilion was built on the church grounds. The tall octagonal steeple of the Neoclassical church once dominated the town, although today the graceful structure is overshadowed by towering commercial buildings. Farther west on Lebuh Farquhar is the **Protestant Cemetery**, where Sir Francis Light is buried in a gazebo-like tomb shaded by frangipani trees.

SIR FRANCIS LIGHT

Born in Suffolk, England, in 1740, Francis Light joined the British East India Company in 1765. Directed to find a suitable island base for their commercial activities in Southeast Asia, he chose Pulau Penang, which he then acquired from the Sultan of Kedah in 1786. Having successfully established a colony, he served as its superintendent until his death in 1794 of malaria. He was buried at the Protestant Cemetery at Lebuh Farquhar. As closely linked to Penang's growth as Sir Stamford Raffles is to Singapore's, Sir Francis Light is still honored as a founding father. His statue now stands at Georgetown's Fort Cornwallis.

Statue of Sir Francis Light

The stately gray exterior of the Cathedral of the Assumption

Penang Museum and Art Gallery

Lebuh Farquhar. *Tel* (04) 261-3144.
9am–5pm Sat–Thu.
Located next to St. George's Church in the former Penang Free School, this small museum houses an excellent collection of maps, records, and displays charting the growth of Penang since the arrival of Sir Francis Light. The first floor showcases the various ethnic groups that constitute the population of Penang, with exhibits of clothing, photographs, household items, and artifacts associated with the island's Peranakan, Malay, Chinese, and Indian communities. The second floor is devoted to Penang's history with special emphasis on the colonial era, the Japanese occupation, the Chinese and Indian settlements, and the gaining of independence. The adjacent art gallery features 19th-century paintings of Penang by Robert Smith, the architect of St. George's Church.

British East India Company insignia, Penang Museum and Art Gallery

Cathedral of the Assumption

Lebuh Farquhar.
The city's premier Catholic place of worship, the stately Cathedral of the Assumption was founded to serve the Eurasian Catholics who had moved to Penang following Sir Francis Light's establishment of a British colony here. The Eurasians, who were originally from Phuket, had fled to Kuala Kedah in 1781 with Bishop Garnault of Siam to escape religious persecution. In Kuala Kedah, they were joined by Catholics of Portuguese descent. The group, led by Garnault, arrived in Georgetown on the eve of the Feast of the Assumption in 1786. His mission was later relocated to Penang. Although this imposing gray structure, built along classical lines, was not erected at Lebuh Farquhar until 1857, it was nonetheless named in memory of the arrival of these first parishioners. The cathedral houses Penang's only pipe organ. In 1955, it was elevated by Vatican decree to the status of Cathedral of the Diocese of Penang.

100 Cintra Street

100 Cintra Street. *Tel* (04) 264-3581.
11am–6pm Tue–Sun.
www.100cintrastreet.com
Located in the heart of Chinatown, this is a Peranakan-influenced mansion that was built in 1897 by a local woman of Thai origin. Partially destroyed by fire in 1984, it was rebuilt using as much of the surviving structure as possible, and was reopened in 1999 as a shopping center specializing in antiques and artifacts. It also has a small tea shop.

Since then it has undergone several changes, and today the first floor of the three-story building functions as an antique and curio center offering a fascinating selection of 19th-century furniture, pictures, porcelain, brassware, calligraphy, paintings, and carpets. The second floor functions as a budget guesthouse, while the third floor has been converted into a folk museum, focusing on the history and culture of Penang, with special emphasis on the Peranakan, or Straits Chinese community. Indian and Malay items are also on display.

Hainan Temple

Lebuh Muntri.
Popularly known as the Hainan Temple, the bustling Thean Ho Keong, which means Temple of the Heavenly Queen, is dedicated to Mar Chor, the patron saint of seafarers. Commonly known as Matsu in China and Thien Hau in Vietnam, the

Chinese worshiper praying at the colorful altar at Hainan Temple

Cheong Fatt Tze Mansion, now a luxurious hotel

goddess is worshiped, in particular, wherever the Chinese settled throughout Southeast Asia. The temple was initially established as a clan house for overseas Chinese from Hainan Island in 1866, although the current building dates from 1895. During its centenary celebrations in 1995, the temple was carefully restored and a new frontage was added with ornate carvings and distinctive swirling dragon pillars.

🏛 Cheong Fatt Tze Mansion

14 Lebuh Leith. *Tel* (04) 262-5289. 🎫 for tours. 🕐 11am & 3pm Mon–Fri, 11am Sat & Sun. **www**.cheong fatttzemansion.com

This spectacular mansion was built by Cheong Fatt Tze, a young Hakka Chinese entrepreneur who eventually became one of Southeast Asia's richest businessmen. Although Cheong Fatt Tze built several grand houses, this 1904 mansion is considered the most magnificent. Fatt Tze lived here with three of his favorite wives, raising eight sons. The house fell into disrepair after his death in 1916, but it has since been beautifully restored, winning the prestigious UNESCO Asia Pacific Heritage Award for authentic restoration in 2000. Said to be the largest traditional courtyard house in the region, the building conforms to the principles of geomancy, and blends Chinese and Western architectural concepts. Painted a deep blue, the mansion features Qing dynasty latticework and

filigree ornamentation with louvered and stained-glass windows in the Western style, cast-iron balusters, and Stoke-on-Trent floor tiling. Today, the mansion functions as an opulent and unique homestay heritage hotel *(see p277)*.

🏛 E & O Hotel

10 Lebuh Farquhar. *Tel* (04) 222-2000. 🚗 🍴 🖥 📷 **www**.e-o-hotel.com

The grande dame of Penang's hotels, the Eastern & Oriental *(see p277)* is not just one of the most luxurious, but also one of the great historic hotels of Southeast Asia. Popularly called the E & O, it was established in 1884 by the Armenian Sarkies brothers, who went on to found Singapore's Raffles Hotel and Rangoon's famous Strand. A landmark in colonial architecture, it boasts a 830-ft (253-m) seafront lawn – the longest in the world – and its suites overlook manicured lawns and lush gardens with a panoramic view across the Strait of Malacca.

Long a center of Penang's social life, the hotel has hosted eminent guests such as Noel Coward, Rudyard Kipling, Herman Hesse, and Douglas Fairbanks. Somerset Maugham, another visitor, referred to the E & O in several of his writings. Today, it is a great place to eat a light tiffin lunch followed by afternoon tea, or to sip a cocktail at sunset under the rain trees on the hotel's private veranda.

Georgetown's historic Eastern & Oriental Hotel

FIVE FOOT WAYS

Originally used by builders from Guangdong in China, this style of Chinese shophouse has long been associated with the former Straits Settlements of Singapore, Penang, and Malacca. The widespread presence of Five Foot Ways in Singapore and urban Malaysia is attributed to Sir Stamford Raffles, who decreed that all shophouses should have verandas that form continuous and open passages.

Characterized by load-bearing gable walls and massive roof beams that span the building, these shophouses extend over the narrow sidewalks forming a sort of covered walkway and providing shelter from the sun and the monsoon rains. The sidewalk can be further shaded by lowering split bamboo blinds.

Shop signs over a Five Foot Way

Dhammikarama Temple ⑮

Burma Lane, off Jalan Burma, Pulau Tikus, 2 miles (3 km) NW of Georgetown. 🚌 🅿 *daily.* 📅 *Burmese New Year (Apr).*

The 200-year old Burmese enclave at Pulau Tikus is home to a spectacular Theravada Buddhist monastery, founded in 1803 and known originally as the Nandy Molah Burmese Temple. Now called the Dhammikarama Temple in honor of the *dhamma*, or corpus of Buddhist teachings, this is Penang's oldest Buddhist place of worship.

The temple gateway, well guarded by a pair of stucco elephants, leads to a compound shaded by a peepul tree and dotted with mythical figures and religious icons, among them myriad Buddhas, flying beings, and chimeras. The ornate red-tiled roof of the temple, embellished with gleaming gold filigree work, is Burmese in inspiration and visible from afar. The complex includes monks' quarters, a wishing pool where visitors toss coins that are later used towards temple maintenance, and a peaceful prayer hall housing a large Burmese-style image of the Buddha. Within the hall are rows of finely carved *arhat*, or spiritual practitioner who had attained nirvana, created by Burmese artisans. The temple also has a shrine

Detail on Wat Chayamangkalaram

to the Arahant Upagutta, an *arhat* widely revered in Burma for his powers. A mural depicts the renunciation of Siddhartha Gautama, the Historical Buddha.

Wat Chaya-mangkalaram ⑯

Burma Lane, off Jalan Burma, Pulau Tikus, 2 miles (3 km) NW of Georgetown. 🚌 🅿 *daily.* 📅 *Songkran (Apr).*

Popularly known as the Temple of the Reclining Buddha, this is the largest Buddhist temple in Penang. The name means temple of auspicious victory. The building dates from 1845, when the Thai community asked the government for land on which to build a monastery. The land was granted by the then Governor of Penang, W. L. Butterworth. The temple houses a Reclining Buddha statue, constructed in 1958 to mark the 2,500th anniversary of the birth of Gautama Buddha. Called Phra Chaiya Mongkol, the statue measures an impressive 108 ft (33 m) in length and is said to be the third-longest Reclining Buddha in the world. Besides the main shrine hall, the temple includes a Thai-style gilded stupa, or *chedi*, and fierce temple guardians called *yaksas*. The whole complex is distinctively central Thai in style, down to the gold-painted pagodas. The temple is

attended to by Thai monks and serves the small local Thai community, as well as both Theravada and Mahayana Buddhist devotees from across the island. Legend has it that the temple's first abbot, a monk named Phorthan Kuat, or honorable father Kuat, was fond of local *laksa* or spicy noodle soup, and even today devotees bring bowls of *laksa* to offer at his shrine.

The manicured grounds of the Penang Botanic Gardens

Penang Botanic Gardens ⑰

5 miles (8 km) W on the outskirts of Georgetown. 🚌 ℹ *(04) 227-0428.* 🅿 *5am–8pm daily.* 🎫 *by prior arrangement.* ♿ *special walkways.* 🖥 📱 **www.sukpp.gov.my/ KebunBunga/main.html**

Established by the colonial administration in 1884 on the site of a disused quarry, the beautifully landscaped Penang Botanic Gardens are undoubtedly the finest botanical gardens in Peninsular Malaysia. Spread across 72 acres (29 ha) of land dominated by an attractive waterfall, rain forest-covered hills, and a small river, the gardens provide protected habitat for rare species of plant and also serve as a green lung for Georgetown and its people.

The gardens owe their beauty to the untiring work of Charles Curtis, who was the first to nurture and transform the former granite quarry into a lush tropical garden and nursery. In 1946,

Ornate and colorful façade of the Buddhist Wat Chayamangkalaram

For hotels and restaurants in this region see pp276–7 and pp302–3

after World War II ended, the Penang Botanic Gardens were separated from their parent establishment in Singapore and began functioning as an independent entity.

Besides their educational and preservational role, the gardens are a popular spot for locals to exercise, jog, or walk in the refreshingly unpolluted air. There are two paved trails, the shorter Lower Circle and the longer Upper Circle. Surrounding these are less accessible forested areas. Botanical attractions include the Aroid Walkway, featuring plants of the philodendron family, the ornamental plant house, the fern house, the cactus house, and the lily pool. Among the species of rare trees seen here are the cannonball tree, the candle tree, the baobab, ebony, and the argus pheasant tree. The gardens also house a nursery of commercial plants, such as pepper, cloves, and nutmeg.

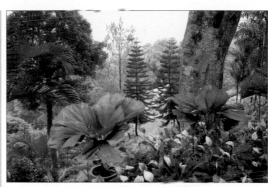

The rich variety of fauna that blankets the Penang Hill

Kek Lok Si Temple ⑱

Ayer Itam, 5 miles (8 km) W of Georgetown. 🚌 🛈 *(04) 828-3317.* ◻ *daily.* 🖼 🚌 🎫 🎦 *Loy Krathong (Nov).*

The largest and most celebrated Buddhist temple in Malaysia, Kek Lok Si, or the temple of supreme bliss, is spread across a hilltop overlooking the district of Ayer Itam. Long sacred to the island's Chinese residents, the hills of Ayer Itam are believed by locals to be geomantically fortuitous and a suitable retreat for Taoist devotees seeking immortality. This beautiful temple was initially envisioned by the head monk of the Kuan Yin Temple *(see p103)* on Jalan Masjid Kapitan Kling and supported by the Chinese consul in Penang. Later, the idea was backed by the Qing Emperor Guangxu, who gave its foundation an imperial tablet and 70,000 volumes of Buddhist sutras. Construction began in 1893

Bronze statue of Kuan Yin, Kek Lok Si Temple

and took Burmese, Chinese, and Thai artisans more than two decades to complete.

Kek Lok Si's most celebrated feature is the magnificent seven-tier **Pagoda of King Rama VI**, completed in 1930 and named after the Thai monarch who laid the foundation stone. Also known as the pagoda of ten thousand Buddhas, it stands at a height of 100 ft (30 m). This impressive pagoda was designed in three different styles, with an octagonal Chinese-style base, middle tiers of Thai architecture, and a Burmese-style crown, symbolic of the unity of Mahayana and Theravada Buddhism. The temple grounds contain lovely gardens and sacred ponds, including the Sacred Turtle Pond where the devout release captive turtles as an act of spiritual liberation. Dominating all is a massive bronze statue of Kuan Yin, the goddess of mercy.

Penang Hill ⑲

Ayer Itam. 🚞 *Funicular Railway, 6:30am–9pm Mon–Fri, 6:30am 11:15pm Sat–Sun.* 🚌 *to Funicular Railway terminal.* 🖼

Malaysia's oldest hill station, Penang Hill, also known as Bukit Bendera or Flagstaff Hill, was first developed in 1897. Although only one hotel functions today, the 2,720-ft

(830-m) hill still offers a refreshing retreat from the tropical heat of Georgetown.

Sir Francis Light, the founder of Penang, is said to have ordered the construction of a horse track to the top of the hill in 1788. Today, however, visitors can ride up the hill in a more spectacular and comfortable manner on the **Penang Hill Railway**, a steep funicular line built in 1923. Enthusiastic walkers can opt for a 3-hour hike up a tarred track that begins at the quarry at the entrance of the Penang Botanic Gardens.

The hill is an area rich in biodiversity and has a number of rare endemic species. Dipterocarp and coniferous trees are common, as are tree ferns. The summit offers panoramic views across the nearby Strait of Malacca to Penang Bridge, the mainland, and Butterworth. Also on the summit are a colorful Hindu temple and a mosque.

Carriage being pulled up the steep funicular Penang Hill Railway

Boats and jet-skis off the beaches of Batu Ferringhi

Batu Ferringhi ⑳

9 miles (14 km) NW of Georgetown.
🚌 93 from Georgetown. 🍴 🏨

Also known as Foreigner's Rock, Batu Ferringhi is Penang's premier beachside destination and one of the most developed beach strips anywhere in Malaysia. Facing northwest into the Strait of Malacca, the shore at Batu Ferringhi was once a delightful coconut-lined sandy strand and a popular destination for hippies in the 1970s.

However, over the past three decades, it has changed dramatically into a bustling coastal strip, lined with high-rise hotels and a wide range of restaurants and shops. Although the beach is clean, the sea is a little murky and filled with jellyfish. The waves are not high enough for surfing, but this is a good place to sunbathe and relax.

The beach was hit by the 2004 tsunami, but has since completely recovered. Today, Batu Ferringhi's easy accessibility from Georgetown means that it is popular with day visitors and usually busy, especially at weekends. Prices are especially low on weekdays and off-season months (from around March to October).

Just a mile (2 km) west of Batu Ferringhi is the **Tropical Spice Garden**, where visitors can view more than five hundred species of plants from Malaysia, Thailand, and

Indonesia. Three specially designed garden trails lead to 11 separate gardens that feature special plant collections with signboards indicating their common and botanical names and their various uses.

🌿 **Tropical Spice Garden**
🕐 daily. 📷 free for children below 4 years. 🖥️ 🏨

Teluk Bahang ㉑

12 miles (19 km) NW of Georgetown.
🚌 93 from Georgetown. ⛺

At the western end of Penang's northern beaches sits the small fishing village of Teluk Bahang, or sunburned bay. The detritus of an active fishing industry litters the sand, and while the beach is not suitable for swimming, it is an excellent place to stop and enjoy fresh seafood. Several tracks lead westward

from the village to the rocky promontory of **Muka Head**, passing the scenic Ailing and Duyong Bays, heading southwest into the Pantai Aceh Forest Reserve and beyond to Kerachut Beach.

On the eastern side of Teluk Bahang is the **Penang Cultural Center**, which offers a glimpse of the diverse cultures of Malaysia through daily performances of traditional music and dance. Just south of the bus station, **Craft Batik** is a handicraft workshop and showroom where visitors can observe *batik* being made and also shop for sarongs and *batik* paintings. Nearby, the **Teluk Bahang Orchid Garden** is a cozy place that displays a fine selection of Southeast Asian orchids. Next door is the **Penang Butterfly Farm**, where more than 100 species of butterflies, along with spiders and other insects, are on view amid attractive

Fishing boats moored along the shores of Teluk Bahang

gardens with varied flora, waterfalls, and ponds. South of Teluk Bahang, the well-maintained **Forest Recreation Park** offers further good opportunities for trekking and camping in relative comfort of the lush jungle.

🎪 Penang Cultural Center
(04) 885-1175. ⬭ *9:30am–10pm daily.* 📷 📹

🦋 Penang Butterfly Farm
⬭ *9am–5pm Mon-Fri, 9am–5:30pm Sat–Sun.* 📷

🌺 Teluk Bahang Orchid Garden
⬭ *8am–7pm daily.* 📷

Universiti Sains Malaysia Museum and Art Gallery ㉒

4 miles (6 km) S of Georgetown. *Tel (04) 657-7888.* ⬭ *from Georgetown.* ⬭ *9am–4:30pm Sun-Thu, 10am–1pm Sat.* ⬤ *12:15–2:45pm Fri.* 📷 📹

Situated on the campus of Universiti Sains Malaysia, near the western end of Penang Bridge, is the well-presented Universiti Sains Malaysia Museum and Art Gallery. Exhibits on display highlight various aspects of Malay, Peranakan, Sarawak, and Sabahan cultures. Collections of textiles, traditional jewelry, musical instruments, and *keris,* or Malay daggers, are also exhibited. A section of the museum is devoted entirely to ethnography and the performing arts. The art gallery displays both contemporary Malaysian paintings and items from the university's fine arts collection.

Snake Temple ㉓

Bayan Lepas, 7 miles (12 km) S of Georgetown. ⬭ *66 from Komtar in Georgetown.* ⬭ *7am–7pm daily.* 📷 *anniversary of the birth of Chor Soo Kong, 6th day of First Lunar month (Jan/Feb).*

Named Ban Kah Lan, meaning the temple of the azure clouds in the Hokkien dialect, this highly unusual temple was built in 1850 by Chinese migrants. It honors the memory of a venerated Chinese Buddhist monk named Chor Soo Kong who is said to have had healing powers. He was born in China's Fujian Province during the reign of the 11th-century Song Emperor Renzong. Chor Soo Kong later became an ascetic seeking spiritual enlightenment, which he attained under the guidance of Zen master Ming Song. Soon after he practiced as a doctor, catering to the needs of the poor. Chor Soo Kong retired to a monastery on Peng Lai Mountain, where he was sanctified after his death.

According to folklore, the statue of the deified Chor Soo Kong was brought to Penang by a monk from China in 1850, and was enshrined in a temple at Bayan Lepas. When the temple was complete, the pious monk allowed snakes from the surrounding jungle to take shelter there. The snakes were venomous Wagler's pit vipers called *ular kapak tokong* in Malay. Today, these vipers still inhabit the temple, and are its main attraction, especially during the festival season. About 3ft (1m) long in maturity, they are dark green with wide yellow bands. Devotees regard them as harmless guardian angels of the temple. Although rarely fatal, the bite of the vipers is painful. Fortunately, they are sluggish during the day, perhaps dulled by the incense smoke, but are active at night, when they descend from their perches in the eaves to consume offerings left by the pious.

Offerings at the Sam Poh Footprint Temple at Batu Maung

Batu Maung ㉔

9 miles (15 km) S of Georgetown.
⬭ 📷 🍴 ⬜ 📷

A Chinese fishing village in the southeast of Pulau Penang, Batu Maung is known for its fine fresh seafood restaurants. It is also famous for the **Sam Poh Footprint Temple,** named for a strange footprint-shaped indentation in a rock. This footprint reportedly belongs to 15th-century Chinese Admiral Zheng He, who was locally known as Sam Poh.

He visited Pulau Penang during his exploration of Southeast Asia, the Indian Ocean, and the Red Sea. The footprint is said to mark the spot where he first stepped ashore. The rock is enshrined in the temple, which is surrounded by lush, well-maintained gardens close to the shore, overlooking the harbor and the jetty.

A Buddhist monk praying at the Snake Temple

Archaeological remnants, main temple Candi Bukit Batu Pahat

Lembah Bujang ㉕

16 miles (26 km) NW of Sungai Petani. 🚌 ✔ www.mykedah.com

Peninsular Malaysia's most important archaeological site, the Hindu-Buddhist remains at Lembah Bujang, or Bujang valley, reveal significant aspects of a major pre-Islamic civilization. First excavated by the British archaeologist H.G. Quaritch-Wales in 1936, this archaeological site stretches over a vast 87-sq mile (225-sq km) area extending from Gunung Jerai to Kuala Muda.

Bujang, which derives its name from a legendary winged dragon, was a notable kingdom and port in the 5th century AD. It had trade relations with India, Srivijaya (on Sumatra), and Cambodia, and was visited by the Chinese Buddhist monk I-Ching in AD 672. In the 7th century, it was absorbed into the Srivijaya Empire, and reached its zenith between the 9th and 10th centuries, before Islam gained a foothold on the peninsula.

Over 50 sites have been excavated in the valley. Among the finds, the most impressive are the *candi*, or two tomb-temples, which have been transported and reassembled at the **Lembah Bujang Archaeological Museum** in nearby Merbok. The 7th-century Candi Bukit Batu Pahat has a *vimana*, or inner sanctuary, with images of Hindu deities, and a *mandapa*, or open hall,

with a stone roof supported by pillars. The *candi* performed the function of temples for Hindu or Buddhist religious activities, and honored the deceased rulers and members of the royal family. The museum preserves, chronicles, and explains the various excavations as well as displays collections of artifacts discovered at the site. These include Chinese porcelain, Shiva *lingas*, statues of the Hindu god Ganesh and goddess Durga, terra-cotta statues, and a bronze Buddhist image discovered here in 1976. It is possible to see the excavated sites through privately arranged guided tours from the museum. The neighboring waterfall is also a favorite picnic spot. At some point in the future, the whole area is scheduled to become an archaeological park.

Fragment of a stone lintel at Lembah Bujang

🏛 **Lembah Bujang Archaeological Museum**
Jalan Tanjung Dawai, Merbok.
Tel (04) 457-2005. ⬜ *daily.*
🔴 *noon–2:45pm Fri (for prayers).*
✔ www.jmm.gov.my

Gunung Jerai ㉖

19 miles (30 km) N of Sungai Petani.
🚌 ⬜ *daily.* ✔ 🍴 △

Rising sharply out of the surrounding Kedah plains is the imposing 3,993-ft (1,217-m) Gunung Jerai. Formerly known as Kedah Peak, this

massive forest-clad limestone outcrop that is a part of the Titiwangsa Mountain Range is clearly visible from the sea. It adds a touch of variety to the scenic flat plains visible throughout the area. In the past, it acted as a navigation point for sailors from southern India, and was considered sacred by the Hindu kingdom of Bujang. It marked the start of a cross-peninsula portage route between the Indian Ocean and the South China Sea that avoided the long voyage around the Strait of Malacca. Today, the peak is visited for its pristine splendor and panoramic view of rhododendron and pine-covered forests. On the summit is a dilapidated 6th-century Hindu shrine and bath called **Candi Telaga Sembilan**, or nine pool temple, which was discovered in 1884.

Another attraction on the mountain is the Muzium Perhutanan, or **Forestry Museum**, which is saturated with delicious balsamic fragrances from various types of coniferous and oak trees. Run by the Malaysian Forestry Commission, the museum has exhibits on trees of the surrounding **Sungai Teroi Forest Recreation Park**, which houses rare orchids and wildlife.

🏛 **Forestry Museum**
Gunung Jerai. ⬜ *9am–3pm daily.*
🦌 **Sungai Teroi Forest Recreation Park**
Gunung Jerai. 🏞 ✔ *compulsory.*

Misty view above the treetops at Gunung Jerai

The elegant Masjid Zahir, or state mosque, in Alor Star

Alor Star ②

59 miles (95 km) N of Georgetown.
🏛 *205,000.* ✈ ⓘ *179B Kompleks Alor Star, Lebuhraya Darul Aman, (04) 730-1322.* **www**.tourism.gov.my

Kedah's state capital, Alor Star, is mainly a transit point to Thailand and a junction for the road west to Kuala Kedah, the ferry port for Pulau Langkawi. However, it also has several attractions. Among these is the **padang**, a lovely old colonial town square surrounded by a number of royal and religious buildings. Among these is the **Balai Besar**, or the royal audience hall, which stands on tall pillars embellished with Victorian iron lacework. The unique **Balai Nobat**, or drum hall, is an eight-sided tower topped by an onion-shaped dome. The building houses the Kedah Royal Orchestra. **Masjid Zahir**, or state mosque, incorporates elegant Moorish designs in its five black domes and slender minarets. Also by the padang are two municipal buildings that are open to the public. These are the **Balai Seni Lukis Negeri**, or state art gallery, which exhibits modern Malaysian art, and the Muzium Di Raja, or **Royal Museum**, featuring royal paraphernalia.

More interesting is the Muzium Negeri, or the **State Museum**, located a mile (2 km) north of the Padang. It displays exhibits dating back to the 19th century when Kedah was a tributary of neighboring Siam (now known as Thailand). Another reminder of the state's Siamese connections is **Wat Syam Nikrodharam**, a Theravada Buddhist temple which was built in the unmistakable Thai style, located at Kampung Telok Sena. Today, the city's considerably vast Chinese Buddhist population worships here.

🅒 Masjid Zahir
Jalan Sultan Muhamad Jiwa.
◻ *daily.* ● *noon–3pm Fri (for prayers).*

🏛 State Museum
Lebuhraya Darul Aman.
Tel *(04) 733-1162.* ◻ *Sat–Thu.* ● *noon–3pm Fri (for prayers).*

🏛 Royal Museum
Next to Balai Besar. ***Tel*** *(04) 732-7937.* ◻ *daily* ● *noon–3pm Fri (for prayers).*

Kuala Kedah ②

7 miles (12 km) W of Alor Star.
🏛 *220,000.* 🚌 ⚓

As Kuala means river mouth in Malay, Kuala Kedah is an aptly named fishing port that is located at the northern bank of its namesake river. This small town serves as the convenient southern ferry point for travelers sailing to Pulau Langkawi. The crowning glory of the town is **Kota Kuala Kedah**, a fort dating to the mid-18th century standing on the right bank of Sungai Kedah. The structure was originally built to protect the kingdom against naval attacks by Siam (Thailand). However, the Thais invaded and captured the fort in the early 19th century. The town is guarded by thick walls and a moat, and comprises a number of buildings including the Royal Audience Hall. Six of the 19th-century British cannons are on display, resting on the crumbling walls, facing the river estuary. Today, Kuala Kedah is famous for the variety of delectable seafood, especially *laksa*, served at the numerous eateries that have cropped up at this ancient historic site.

ORANG SYAM

Malaysians of Thai ethnic origin, known in Malay as Orang Syam, have lived in northern Malaysia for centuries. When and how they came to settle in this predominantly Malay-speaking region remains unclear. Their dialect suggests that their roots go back at least four centuries to the Narathiwat province which neighbors Thailand. The Orang Syam are recognized as *bumiputras*, or indigenous Malaysians, having the same rights and status as Muslim Malays. They settled primarily in prosperous kampung syams, or Siamese villages in Kedah, Kelantan, Perak, Penang, and Perlis, dwelling harmoniously with their Muslim neighbors. One easy way to identify a kampung syam is the presence of elaborately sited Buddhist temples. They have quintessentially Thai curved roofs, lavishly gilded pagodas, tinkling wind-chimes, and edifices of the Buddha in various postures. The five-centuries old temple at Kampung Jubakar claims to have the largest Seated Buddha image in Southeast Asia.

Orang Syam people working in the fields

Pulau Langkawi ㉙

Set in the heart of an archipelago of some 100 islands and islets in the Andaman Sea, Pulau Langkawi is one of Malaysia's most popular destinations. Fringed with sandy beaches and forested hills in the interior, it is also one of the most beautiful. A number of idyllic resorts and spas offer soothing retreats, while a range of sporting activities, such as waterskiing, diving, and trekking, attract adventurous visitors. Kuah, the small bustling capital, is a good jumping-off point for Langkawi's other sights.

Langkawi Crocodile Farm, home to more than 1,000 crocodiles

Telega Tujuh Falls
Literally meaning seven wells, Telega Tujuh is a cascading waterfall – an ideal site for bathing and picnics.

The **Ibrahim Hussein Museum** exhibits works by the Malaysian artist.

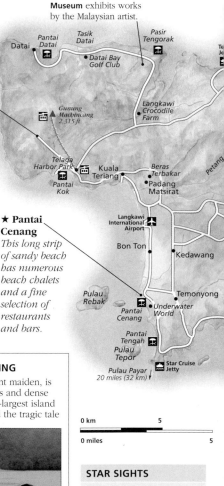

★ Pantai Cenang
This long strip of sandy beach has numerous beach chalets and a fine selection of restaurants and bars.

THE LEGEND OF TASIK DAYANG BUNTING

Tasik Dayang Bunting, or lake of the pregnant maiden, is a freshwater lake set amid the limestone cliffs and dense forests of Pulau Dayang Bunting, the second-largest island in the archipelago. A legend revolves around the tragic tale of Princess Mahsuri who claimed she became pregnant by drinking from the lake. She was then falsely accused of adultery and executed. The legendary crocodile which inhabits the lake is said to be Mahsuri's child. Local women still come here to pray for children.

A boat on Tasik Dayang Bunting

0 km — 5
0 miles — 5

STAR SIGHTS

★ Pantai Cenang

★ Gunung Raya

★ Tomb of Mahsuri

The Langkawi Birds Paradise
Located at Belanga Pecah, this lush tropical garden is home to at least 150 species of birds, including hornbills, toucans, and flamingos.

The Durian Perangin Waterfall cascades through 14 levels and is a popular picnic spot.

VISITORS' CHECKLIST

19 miles (30 km) W of Kuala Perlis. 120,000. Jalan Persian Putra, Kuah; (04) 966-7789. **www**.langkawi-online.com

★ **Gunung Raya**
Literally the great mountain, Gunung Raya is the highest peak in the archipelago. Its summit offers fine views across the Andaman Sea.

Masjid al-Hana
The largest mosque on Pulau Langkawi, the golden domes of Masjid al-Hana tower over Kuah, the island's capital.

★ **Tomb of Mahsuri**
This quiet shrine was built in memory of Princess Mahsuri who was executed at this spot after being unjustly accused of adultery.

KEY

═══	Major road
══	Minor road
---	Ferry route
⊢⊣	Cable car route
✈	International airport
🚢	Ferry port
🚡	Cable car
🏖	Beach
ℹ	Visitor information
▲	Peak

Exploring Pulau Langkawi

The largest among a cluster of tropical islands, Pulau Langkawi is a mountainous, palm-fringed island peppered with paddy fields and sandy coves. In 1986, Pulau Langkawi was transformed from an isolated, overwhelmingly Malay rural area, into a duty-free zone in a successful attempt to make it a holiday destination, wooing backpackers and upmarket visitors alike. Access to the archipelago by air and ferry has never been easier, and Langkawi's excellent road network makes exploring the island convenient. Once-sleepy Kuah, Langkawi's capital, now boasts a slew of shopping centers, supermarkets, resorts, and luxury hotels catering to rising tourist demands.

Main street in Kuah lined with shops and cafés

Kuah

SE Pulau Langkawi. 🏙 *94,000.*
🚌 🚤 🛈 *Jalan Persiaran Putra, (04)
966-7789.* 🛒 *Wed & Sat.* **Langkawi
History Garden** Jalan Persiaran
Putra, near Kuah Jetty. *Tel (04) 966-
4223.* ⬭ *8am–11pm daily.* 🅿️
Skirting a large bay on the southeastern tip of the island, Kuah is Langkawi's main town. Originally a small fishing village, Kuah is undergoing rapid development as a result of the island's growing tourism industry.

The most distinguished building in town is the Friday Congregational Mosque, **Masjid al-Hana**, located next to the tourist office. Built in 1959, the mosque incorporates Uzbek and Moorish elements along with traditional Malay design. The **Langkawi History Garden**, a theme park by the seafront, features sculptures and exhibits that recount the archipelago's history. The garden overlooks Dataran Lang, a landscaped square with a prominent statue of an eagle. Kuah is the best place on Langkawi to shop, change

money, and rent vehicles for sightseeing. It also has a vibrant *pasar malam*, or night market. For those arriving by sea, Kuah is a useful transit point to Kuala Perlis, Kuala Kedah, and Penang.

🛕 Tomb of Mahsuri

7 miles (12 km) W of Kuah.
⬭ *tomb: 7:30am–6pm daily;
show: 11am.* 🅿️
Dedicated to the memory of a Malay princess, the tomb of Mahsuri is a simple white structure. According to legend, Mahsuri was unjustly accused of adultery and sentenced to death. Mahsuri was stabbed by the executioner with her own *keris.* Her blood flowed white as an indication of her purity, and with her dying breath she cursed the island to seven generations of bad luck. A tomb of fine marble was built on the spot where she was killed. Today, this is honored as a shrine by the islanders. Every day a cultural show depicting the legend is staged at the tomb, along with displays of traditional dancing and Malay *silat,* or martial arts.

🌴 Langkawi Rain Forest Canopy Adventure

9 miles (15 km) NW of Kuah.
🚌 🍴 🖼️
One of Malaysia's most exhilarating outdoor activities, the Langkawi Rain Forest Canopy Adventure allows visitors to pass high above the rain forest floor on the Gunung Raya mountainside. This adrenalin-charged experience features a 492-ft (150-m) slide along metal cables and a 98-ft (30-m) vertical rappel. It is both exciting and safe as it is operated by skilled professionals and pre-activity training is provided on site.

🌴 Pantai Cenang

10 miles (16 km) W of Kuah.
🚌 🚤 🍴 🖼️ 🛈 **Underwater
World** *Tel (04) 955-6100.*
⬭ *10am–6pm daily.* 🅿️
A sweep of dazzling white sand, Pantai Cenang is the most popular and developed beach on Pulau Langkawi. Fortunately, largely due to a local government prohibition on building anything higher

Plaque narrating the story of Princess Mahsuri at the site of her death

For hotels and restaurants in this region see pp276–7 and pp302–3

Visitors taking a closer look at marine life at Underwater World

than a coconut palm, it has not been overshadowed by high-rises. Small restaurants, bars, and chalets line the beach. At its southern end are a number of entertainment projects, including the vast **Underwater World**. This spectacular aquarium is among the largest in Malaysia, with over 5,000 marine species on display. The aquarium also boasts a walkthrough tunnel and 3D cinema. Nearby, **Pantai Tengah** beach is a southward continuation of Cenang. With several restaurants to choose from, Tengah is a great place for a quiet evening meal accompanied only by the sound of waves gently crashing on the shore.

⛰ Telaga Tujuh Falls
14 miles (22 km) W of Kuah. **Langkawi Cable Car** ◯ 10am–7pm daily. 🖼

Set in an attractive spot on the west coast of Langkawi, Telaga Tujuh or seven wells, is ideal for freshwater bathing and picnics. Located west of Pantai Kok, it is a 30-minute walk to the seven waterfalls, which are joined by smooth, slippery stone sills that bathers can slide down. Legend has it that fairies bathe at these wells when humans are not present, which may account for the pleasantly sweet perfume that suffuses the air.

In the vicinity is the **Langkawi Cable Car**, which carries passengers over ancient rain forests to the summit of Gunung Machincang, at 2,315 ft (706 m), for fabulous views

across the island to the sea and neighboring Thailand. At an incline of 42 degrees, with a vertical rise of 2,231 ft (680 m), the ride is among the steepest in the world. There are two stops, Middle and Top stations, where visitors can alight. The rocks here are some of Malaysia's oldest at 450 million years. The area is now a UNESCO Geopark.

⛰ Teluk Datai
22 miles (35 km) NW of Kuah.
🍴 🖼 **Ibrahim Hussein Museum** Pasir Tengkorak. *Tel (04) 959-4669.* ◯ daily. 🖼 **Kompleks Budaya Kraf** Teluk Yu. *Tel (04) 959-1913.* ◯ daily. 🖼

Well off the beaten track, Teluk Datai on the island's north coast offers the most stunning vistas on the island, with several beautiful beaches scattered along the shore. The lovely bay is home to exclusive resorts and a golf course.

Among the many nearby attractions is the **Ibrahim Hussein Museum**, housed in a modern, light-filled building perched on a cliff. Part of a non-profit cultural organization, the museum exhibits works by, among others, Ibrahim Hussein, one of Malaysia's best-known artists. Farther along the coast, the **Kompleks Budaya Kraf**, or craft cultural complex, showcases Malay handicrafts, such as *batik*, *ikat*, pottery, paintings, and woodcarvings.

On the way to Teluk Datai is the **Langkawi Crocodile Farm**. The reptiles can be viewed during their hourly feedings and daily shows.

Basketwork at
Kompleks Budaya Kraf

⛰ Pulau Payar Marine Park
20 miles (32 km) S of Langkawi.
🛥 🛖 *with prior arrangement.*

An hour's boat ride from Kuah, the tropical island of Pulau Payar is popular with keen divers and snorkelers. Payar and the smaller islands of Lembu, Segantang, and Kaca cluster around coral reefs that teem with marine life, such as moray eels, large groupers, and black-tipped reef sharks.

The **Coral Garden** in the sheltered, clear waters off Pulau Payar is enduringly popular and is said to have the largest number of coral species in Malaysia. Here visitors can also feed baby sharks under the supervision of experts. To visit, it is best to book a day in advance with a tour group.

⛰ Pulau Dayang Bunting
3 miles (5 km) S of Kuah.
🛥 🍴 🖼

Lying across the Kuah Straits, Dayang Bunting is the second largest island in the Langkawi archipelago. Covered with rain forest and mangroves, the island boasts over 90 species of birds, including hornbills, kingfishers, and woodpeckers. The highlight here is the freshwater Tasik Dayang Bunting, or lake of the pregnant maiden, surrounded by limestone cliffs and dense forests. A legend holds that the waters of the lake bestow fertility, and local women come to the lake to pray for children. Visitors can swim in the lake, explore it by pedalo, or simply picnic by its shores.

Boats anchored in the waters off Pulau Dayang Bunting

SOUTHERN PENINSULA

*T*he southern tip of Peninsular Malaysia is also the southernmost extremity of continental Asia, encompassing the country's largest state, Johor, and the often overlooked state of Negeri Sembilan, stronghold of the Minangkabau culture. Cosmopolitan Malacca, the capital of the historically significant state of the same name, is on every tourist's itinerary, while on the east coast, the sandy beaches and colorful reefs of Pulau Tioman are a magnet for visitors from around the world.

With only the narrow Strait of Malacca dividing this side of Malaysia from Sumatra, there have always been close relations between the two cultures. Negeri Sembilan was settled by the Minangkabau people from Sumatra in the 15th century and their unique style of architecture, with upswept roofs imitating buffalo horns, is still seen across the state.

Malacca, too, was founded by an exiled Sumatran prince who introduced Islam to the peninsula in the 15th century. The city's strategic location on the busy trade routes between China and India made it phenomenally wealthy, as everything from tea, silks, and spices to gold, opium, and slaves was bought and sold here. Such riches attracted the attention of the Portuguese who captured the city in 1511. They were followed by Dutch and then British colonists, alongside Chinese and Indian ethnic groups who intermarried with Malays to create the distinct Baba-Nonya and Chitty communities.

Malacca is famous today for its colonial architecture and an eclectic cuisine that draws on its multicultural influences.

After the fall of Malacca to the Portuguese, Johor became the most powerful state on the peninsula. Facing threats from the Minangkabau, Johor was forced to cede Singapore to Sir Stamford Raffles in 1819. Today, the hectic state capital, Johor Bahru, is Malaysia's second-largest city, but the islands of the Seribuat Archipelago hold more appeal, offering some of the very best diving and snorkeling in the country.

Colorful trishaws decorated with flowers outside Christ Church, Malacca

◁ Volcanic peaks rising above the lush forested landscape on Pulau Tioman

Exploring the Southern Peninsula

Bounded on the west by one of the world's busiest shipping lanes, the Strait of Malacca, on the east by the open South China Sea, and on the south by the island city-state of Singapore, the Southern Peninsula offers everything from bustling cities to great tracts of jungle, lazy seaside resorts, and deserted islands. The top draw is historic Malacca, home to some of Malaysia's best museums, most varied cuisine, and earliest European buildings. The beautiful old palace, Istana Lama, in Sri Menanti is a prime example of Minangkabau craftsmanship, while Seremban, the capital of Negeri Sembilan, makes the ideal base for exploring the state. Johor's main attractions are its beach resorts and the beautiful islands of the Seribuat Archipelago off the east coast.

Inside the royal throne room at Istana Lama, Sri Menanti

SIGHTS AT A GLANCE

Towns
Desaru Beach ❽
Johor Bahru ❼
Kuala Pilah ❸
Kukup ❻
Malacca pp122–7 ❹
Mersing ❾
Muar ❺
Seremban ❶
Sri Menanti ❷

Islands
Pulau Tioman pp130–31 ⓫
Seribuat Archipelago ❿

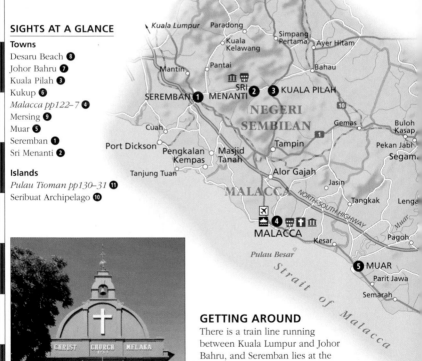

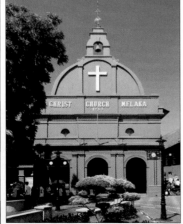

The colorful façade of Christ Church, Malacca

GETTING AROUND

There is a train line running between Kuala Lumpur and Johor Bahru, and Seremban lies at the end of the KTM line from the capital. However, the quickest and easiest way of getting around the region is by bus and there are regular services between all the main urban centers. Smaller towns, such as Kukup, are best reached by taxi while Pulau Tioman has an air link to Kuala Lumpur and Singapore and a ferry link from Mersing.

KEY

═══ Highway

─── Major road

═══ Minor road

─── Railroad

▬▬▬ International border

─── State border

△ Peak

SEE ALSO

- **Where to Stay** pp278–9

- **Where to Eat** pp303–4

0 km ═══════════ 40

0 miles ═══════════ 40

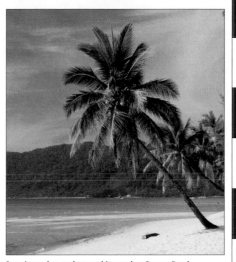

Swaying palms and pure white sand on Desaru Beach

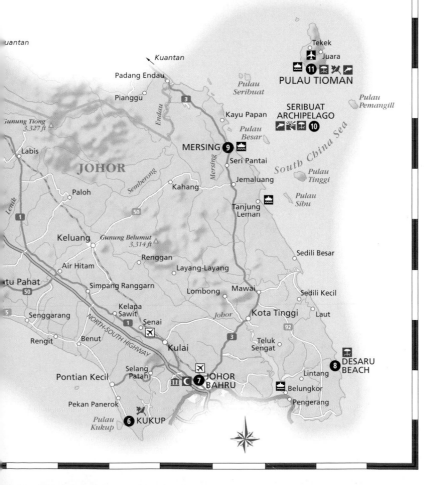

uantan

Kuantan

Padang Endau

Pianggu

Endau

Gunung Tiong
3,327 ft

Labis

JOHOR

Paloh

Semberong

Lenuk

Keluang

Gunung Belumut
3,314 ft △

Air Hitam

Renggan

atu Pahat

Simpang Ranggarn

Kelapa
Sawit

Senai

Senggarang

Rengit

Benut

Kulai

Selang
Patah

Pontian Kecil

Pekan Panerok

*Pulau
Kukup*

6 KUKUP

Tekek

Juara

11 PULAU TIOMAN

*Pulau
Seribuat*

Kayu Papan

**SERIBUAT
ARCHIPELAGO 10**

*Pulau
Pemangill*

*Pulau
Besar*

MERSING 9

Seri Pantai

Mersing

Jemaluang

South China Sea

*Pulau
Tinggi*

Kahang

Tanjung
Leman

*Pulau
Sibu*

Sedili Besar

Layang-Layang

Lombong

Mawai

Sedili Kecil

Johor

Kota Tinggi

Laut

NORTH-SOUTH HIGHWAY

Teluk
Sengat

**DESARU
8 BEACH**

**7 JOHOR
BAHRU**

Lintang

Belungkor

Pengerang

The peaceful Lake Gardens in Seremban

Seremban ●

42 miles (67 km) S of Kuala Lumpur. 👥 700,000. 🚆 KTM Komuter Seremban. 🚌 from Kuala Lumpur and Malacca. 🎭 Negeri Sembilan Cultural Carnival (Jun). **www**.tourismnegerisembilan.com

The capital of Negeri Sembilan state, Seremban is a busy and largely modern town that at first glance seems much like any other provincial Malaysian city. Although low on sights, Seremban is a center for the unique Minangkabau culture. The most obvious expression of this is found in the local architecture, such as the **State Secretariat Building** with its striking, traditional pointed roof made to resemble a pair of buffalo horns. Some original, relocated Minangkabau buildings are on show at the **State Museum**. These include the Istana Ampang Tinggi, with its beautiful carvings, built for a sultan's daughter in the 1860s, and the less ornate Rumah Negeri Sembilan. The State Museum also hosts exhibitions of costumes, musical instruments, weaponry, and stamps.

East of the town center are the attractively landscaped **Lake Gardens** and the circular State Mosque.

Environs
Port Dickson is a small port town 20 miles (32 km) south-west of Seremban. It is the main base for the 11-mile (18-km) beach strip running south to **Tanjung Tuan**, also known as Cape Rachado. As the nearest beach resort to Kuala

Lumpur, it is hugely popular with locals at weekends so the beaches can get crowded. The water quality in the Strait of Malacca is not great, but there's always something going on, with several festivals and sporting events taking place throughout the year.

🏛 **State Museum**
Cultural Handicrafts Complex, Jalan Sungei Ujong. **Tel** (09) 731-149. 🕐 10am–6pm daily. ● noon–2:45pm Fri. ♿ grounds only. 📷 📱

Sri Menanti ●

19 miles (30 km) E of Seremban. 👥 6,000. 🚌 from Seremban. 🎭 Sultan's Birthday Celebrations (Jul).

The old royal capital of Negeri Sembilan, Sri Menanti is today little more than a rustic village. The Old Palace, or **Istana Lama**, was used as the royal residence until 1931 and is a fine example of Minangkabau architecture. Now a museum, this magnificent wooden edifice was completed in 1908 without the use of a single

nail. The palace stands upon 99 pillars representing the royal warriors, while the façade is decorated with elegant carvings of foliage and animals. The royal bedchambers and banquet hall can be viewed inside, along with displays of costumes and photographs. Balconies on the upper floors offer panoramic views over the neat palace gardens.

🏛 **Istana Lama**
Tel (06) 497-0242. 🕐 10am–6pm daily. ● 12:15–2:30pm Fri.

Kuala Pilah ●

25 miles (40 km) E of Seremban. 👥 154,000. 🚌 🚗 ⛲

In the heart of Minangkabau territory, Kuala Pilah is a small provincial center with little to interest tourists, but it has an attractive collection of 1930s shophouses and a handful of minor sights. Among the most interesting is the Martin Lister Memorial Arch located just behind the bus station. This grandiose classical arch, topped with a Chinese roof, commemorates the state's first British Resident, Martin Lister, and dates from 1897. Nearby is the blue clapboard St. Joseph's Catholic Church.

The center of town hosts a number of temples, including the multicolored **Sri Kanthaswamy Hindu Temple**, filled with ornate statues of various deities.

🛕 **Sri Kanthaswamy Hindu Temple**
Jln Melang. 🕐 6am–7pm daily. ♿

Detail of a frieze at the Sri Kanthaswamy Hindu Temple in Kuala Pilah

Minangkabau Architecture

Negeri Sembilan is a stronghold of the Minangkabau people who originally came from the highlands of western Sumatra and settled here in the 15th century. Their name comes from *minang* and *kerbau*, translating as victorious buffalo and, according to legend, derives from a war with the Javanese in which the final battle was decided by a fight between two water buffalos. The Minangkabau won and adopted the buffalo horns as their national symbol. These stylized horns are used in traditional female headwear and, more notably, in their houses, which are supported on pillars and are always topped with an elaborate roof with pointed, upswept gables reminiscent of a pair of horns. These family homes are known as *rumah gadang*, or big house, and, as the Minangkabau are a matrilineal society, belong to the women and are passed down the female line.

The central tower once held the royal records and functioned as a look-out post. It is reached via steep wooden stairs.

Roof tiles are made from expensive, and now scarce, ironwood specially imported from Sarawak.

ISTANA LAMA, SRI MENANTI

The Old Palace is the most impressive example of Minangkabau architecture in Malaysia. Built between 1902 and 1908, it remained the royal residence until 1931 and has been a museum since 1992.

The palace is supported on 99 pillars, each hewn from a *cengal* tree trunk. Many are carved with elaborate designs.

The dramatic upswept gables *of the State Museum in Seremban, erected in 1984, are typical of Minangkabau architecture. Older reconstructed houses can also be seen within the grounds.*

Istana Ampang Tinggi, *with its* attap *(thatched) roof, was built for a local 19th-century princess. It originally stood near Sri Menanti but is now at Seremban's State Museum.*

The magnificent gateway *straddling the main road into Sri Menanti has dramatic horn-shaped pillars.*

Malacca ❹

With its colorful, cosmopolitan heritage, the town of Malacca (also known as Melaka) is one of Malaysia's biggest tourist draws. According to legend, it was founded by the Sumatran Prince Parameswara in 1400 and named by him for the local malacca tree. The city grew quickly and by the 15th century it was one of the richest trading empires in the East. In 1511, it fell to the Portuguese, who in turn gave way to the Dutch in 1641 and the British in 1795. The influences of all the city's rulers can still be seen in its historic core around St. Paul's Hill. The city is known for its multicultural population, including Portuguese Eurasians and, most notably, the Baba-Nonyas who are descendants of early merchants from China who intermarried with local Malay women.

Stadthuys, the former hub of Dutch colonial administration

⛪ Stadthuys

Town Square. *Tel (06) 284-1934.*
◯ daily. ◉ 12:15–2:45pm Fri. 🗾
🗾 10:30am & 2:30pm Sat & Sun.
This magnificent, sturdy old building looming over the town square was built by the Dutch in the 1650s as the seat of colonial administration.

Today, it houses the city's **Museum of History and Ethnography**. Nonya tableware, Ming ceramics, Dutch furniture, pistols, and swords are among the exhibits, alongside dioramas illustrating the wedding ceremonies of local ethnic groups and a full-size replica of a traditional wooden Malay house.

Behind the Stadthuys, and included in the same entry ticket, are a number of small museums including the **Museum of Literature**, dedicated to Malaysian writers, and the **Democratic Government Museum**, hosting displays on the political history of post-independence Malaysia. Also included is the **Seri Melaka**, an impressive colonial mansion, which was the official residence of Dutch and British colonial governors, and, until 1996, was the home of local chief ministers.

⛰ St. Paul's Hill

Occupying a commanding site in the heart of town overlooking the sea, St. Paul's Hill was the site of the now almost entirely vanished Portuguese **A'Famosa** fortress. Its last remnant, Porta de Santiago, stands sentinel at the bottom of the mount.

At the summit of the hill is **St. Paul's Church**, originally erected in 1521 and then known as Nossa Senhora da Annunciada, or Our Lady of the Annunciation. Under Dutch rule the church was renamed St. Paul's, but was abandoned after Christ Church was built.

Sadly, St. Paul's Church is now a ruin, but it still holds a fascinating collection of elaborate 17th-century Dutch tombstones, as well as the empty tomb of St. Francis Xavier, the founder of the Jesuit order in the 16th century.

Outside the main entrance is an abandoned 19th-century lighthouse and a marble statue of St. Francis Xavier, erected in 1952. From here, a path leads down to the Dutch Cemetery at the bottom of the hill. Only five of the 38 tombs here belong to 17th-century Dutchmen; the rest are 19th-century British residents. Most are in a bad state of disrepair but an information board at the entrance lists the names of those who lie here.

⛩ Porta de Santiago

Jalan Kota.
One of four main gateways into the Portuguese A'Famosa fortress, the Porta de Santiago is the sole surviving remnant of those once massive defenses. It was built in 1512 by Alfonso de Albuquerque, the Portuguese viceroy, and the fortress was reused and redeveloped by the Dutch in the 17th century. The squat stone archway, now standing in isolation at the bottom of St. Paul's Hill, bears the coat of arms of the Dutch East India Company on both sides and there are several Dutch cannons on display in front.

The fortress, with its 10-ft (3-m) thick walls, was demolished by the British in 1807 in case the city fell into the hands of the French. It was only the intervention of Sir Stamford Raffles *(see p38)*, the founding father of Singapore, that saved this small section for posterity.

The ruins of Porta de Santiago, all that remains of A'Famosa fortress

Plinth and gardens in front of the Muzium Budaya, a replica Malay palace

VISITORS' CHECKLIST

SW Malacca. 720,000. ✕
Tampin, 24 miles (38 km) N.
Dumai, Sumatra. Jalan
Kota, (06) 281-4803.
Dragon Boat Festival (Jul).
www.melaka.gov.my

♦ Muzium Budaya

Jalan Kota. **Tel** (06) 282-7484.
daily. free admission to
the garden.

At the base of St. Paul's Hill is the Muzium Budaya, an impressive re-creation of a traditional Malay palace based closely on descriptions of the original 15th-century Malacca Sultanate Palace that once stood in this area. It houses the **Cultural Museum**, which displays life-sized dioramas of the sultan's court in session and the *nobat*, or royal orchestra. Also on show are scale models of other royal palaces from across Malaysia and displays of costumes and weaponry, including the fearsome *tombak* spears.

Upstairs is the sultan's bedchamber and another flight of stairs leads to a small room housing a display of *keris*, or traditional curved Malay daggers.

In front of the palace is the so-called Forbidden Garden, a pleasant, formal space, laid out with fountains and pools, and shaded by bamboo, palm trees, and magnolia trees.

♦ Christ Church

Town Square. **Tel** (06) 284-8804.
17. daily. 8:30am
English Eucharist.

This striking, bright red church is one of the iconic symbols of Malacca. It was built by the Dutch in 1753 to celebrate the centenary of their rule over the city, and consecrated for Anglican worship in 1838. Built of local red laterite stone, the building is now painted red and the color scheme continues on the neighboring Stadthuys and Clock Tower. A three-arched porch runs along the front of the church, while inside there are numerous Dutch and British tombstones. Look out too for the gigantic ceiling beams, each cut from a single tree trunk, the hand-carved pews, and the frieze of the Last Supper over the altar.

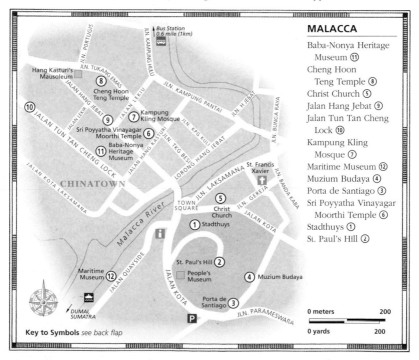

Key to Symbols *see back flap*

0 meters 200
0 yards 200

🗿 Sri Poyyatha Vinayagar Moorthi Temple

Jalan Tukang Emas. *Tel* (06) 288-3599.

This unassuming structure is the oldest surviving Hindu temple in Malaysia. It was built in 1781 on the site of the city's first Chitty, or Indian Peranakan, settlement.

The temple is dedicated to the deity Vinayagar, also known as Ganesh, the elephant-headed god of wisdom. An image of Vinayagar stands on the main altar in the back of the temple, and his younger brother, Lord Murugan, appears at a side altar. The temple is a popular venue for weddings.

🕌 Kampung Kling Mosque

Jalan Tukang Emas.
Tel (06) 283-7416. ♿

Founded in 1748, this is one of the oldest mosques in the country, although the present buildings date largely from 1872 when the old wooden structure was replaced with brick in the original design.

Like Malacca itself, the mosque draws influences from other cultures and its unique architectural features are based on Sumatran, Chinese, Malay, and European styles. The peculiar pyramidal roof with its green tiling shows a strong Hindu influence, while the striking pagoda-like minaret has recognizably Chinese and Moorish origins.

The main prayer hall, which is closed to non-Muslims, is surrounded by Ionic columns, ironwork, and English ceramic tiles.

🏮 Cheng Hoon Teng Temple

Jalan Tokong 25. *Tel* (06) 282-9343.
⊙ 7am–7pm daily. ♿
www.chenghoonteng.org.my

Also known as the temple of the green clouds and Kuan Yin Teng, this venerable building is the oldest Chinese temple in Malaysia. Founded in the mid-17th century and dedicated to Kuan Yin, the goddess of mercy, it is a superb example of southern Chinese architecture, and is still a vital focus for the local Chinese community. Taoism, Confucianism, and Chinese Buddhism are given equal status within the temple. Restoration work on the main complex was completed in 2005, and its elaborate decorations can now be seen to their full effect. The main hall is richly adorned with beautiful paintings and symbolic carvings, with lions, golden phoenix, and other mythical creatures gracing the interior. There are also scenes from Chinese legend and literature including a prayer screen depicting the life of the Buddha, and a watercolor of Lao Tzu, the Chinese philosopher and founder of Taoism. Religious ceremonies take place here every day, and visitors are welcome to come in and watch.

Mausoleum of Hang Kasturi on Jalan Hang Jebat

🚏 Jalan Hang Jebat

Tamil Methodist Church 🏛 9:30am Sun (English service). **Jonker Walk Night Market** ⊙ Fri–Sun evenings.

Better known by its old name of Jonkers Street, busy Jalan Hang Jebat is the main thoroughfare of Malacca's Chinatown. It is famous for its many antique and curio shops, bars, and restaurants, although prices here tend to be higher than elsewhere. The street is especially lively on weekend evenings when the **Jonker Walk Night Market** gets going. There are stalls selling Chinese food, clothes, and souvenirs, while Chinese opera takes place on outdoor stages. Unfortunately, rapid tourist-oriented development has forced many traditional businesses out and historic buildings have been demolished. There are still some points of interest, including the **Mausoleum of Hang Kasturi**, dedicated to a local 15th-century hero, and the **Tamil Methodist Church** dating from 1908.

Sri Poyyatha Vinayagar Moorthi Temple

Detail from an intricately carved frieze at the Cheng Hoon Teng Temple

For hotels and restaurants in this region see pp278–9 and pp303–4

🐟 Jalan Tun Tan Cheng Lock

8 Heeren Street 8 Jalan Tun Tan Cheng Lock. *Tel* (06) 281-1507. ◯ 11am–4pm Tue–Sat. 🖼 10:30am Tue & Thu. www.badanwarisan.org.my
Tham Siew Inn Artist Gallery 49 Jalan Tun Tan Cheng Lock. *Tel* (06) 281-2112. ◯ Tue–Sun. 🖼 🔥
Malaqa House 70 Jalan Tun Tan Cheng Lock. *Tel* (06) 281-4770. ◯ daily. 🖼 🔥

Formerly known as Heeren Street, and still referred to as such by many locals, Jalan Tun Tan Cheng Lock has retained much more of its original character than nearby Jalan Hang Jebat. The long, narrow street is now lined with shops, cafés, hotels, restaurants, and several art galleries.

The townhouses here date from the 18th century, and the narrow façades are a result of the tax on house widths that was imposed by the Dutch colonial authorities at that time. To make up for this, they also tend to have very deep interiors. The houses, with their colorful tiles, stucco work, and painted plaster, were once the homes of rich Baba-Nonya families and most are still in private hands.

A few of the historic buildings along this road are in a very poor state of repair. However, one of these townhouses, known simply as **8 Heeren Street**, has been restored and now functions as a resource center. In the few rooms on show here, there

The decorated façade of a townhouse on Jalan Tun Tan Cheng Lock

are displays that explain the conservation and restoration processes, and document the traditional techniques and materials used by the artisans who worked on the project.

Farther along Jalan Tun Tan Cheng Lock is the Baba-Nonya Heritage Museum *(see pp126–7)*, a preserved townhouse that provides a glimpse into a wealthy Malaccan home. One of the street's best art galleries is the **Tham Siew Inn Artist Gallery**, which displays beautiful watercolors by local artist Tham Siew Inn. Another gallery worth visiting is **Malaqa House**, a grand Baba-Nonya mansion with large rooms filled with Oriental furniture, carvings, paintings, and bric-a-brac.

🏛 Baba-Nonya Heritage Museum

See pp126-7.

🏛 Maritime Museum

Jalan Quayside. *Tel* (06) 282-6526. ◯ daily. 🖼 one ticket for both museums. 🔥 modern building only.
Royal Malaysian Navy Museum ◯ 9am–5:30pm Mon–Thu, 9am–9pm Fri.

The Maritime Museum is Malacca's most visually arresting museum, located on board an impressive, full-scale replica of the 16th-century Portuguese galleon *Flora de la Mar*, which sank in the Strait of Malacca overburdened with looted treasure. Displays recount the city's seafaring past from the time of the 15th-century Malacca Sultanate through the ensuing Portuguese, Dutch, and British colonial periods. Exhibits include dioramas depicting bustling dock scenes, cases containing scale-model ships and weapons, maps, and other nautical artifacts.

A modern building next to the galleon houses the second part of the museum's collection. On show here are traditional fishing boats, more model ships, and displays on Malaysian maritime life.

The museum ticket includes entry into the **Royal Malaysian Navy Museum** on the opposite side of the road, which has a specialist collection showing numerous uniforms, insignia, model ships, and photographs, as well as a naval helicopter. The collection continues in the garden outside, where the star exhibit, a 1960s British-built patrol craft, the *Sri Terengganu*, is on show. It is possible to climb aboard and look around the upper deck, although the vessel suffers from a lack of maintenance.

BETEL, "THE NUT OF LOVE"

Betel nuts, the dried seeds of the Areca or Pinang palm tree, are prized for their mildly narcotic and supposed aphrodisiac qualities. The ritual chewing of this nut was once common across Malaysia but the practice is now mainly confined to rural areas. The nut is prepared during courtship rituals by combining it with herbs, cloves, tobacco, and ground lime, which are then wrapped in betel leaves. Chewing releases a sticky substance said to freshen the breath, relax the mind, and stimulate passion. In the past, brides would chew betel nut to blacken their teeth, considered an attractive sign of status. Today, a betel-nut decoration is still presented as a gift at weddings and festivals.

Betel nuts, thought to be an aphrodisiac, growing in the wild

Malacca: Baba-Nonya Heritage Museum

This absorbing museum is dedicated to the unique culture of Malacca's Baba-Nonya, also known as Straits Chinese or Peranakan, community, who were born through the intermarriage of Chinese traders and local Malay women. The house dates from 1896 when three older houses were combined to create a grand home for a wealthy Baba-Nonya family. Opulent decor with gold leaf, mother-of-pearl, and exotic hardwoods is used throughout the house. The eclectic design incorporates traditional Chinese wall-hangings and woodcarvings alongside English tilework, heavy Dutch furniture, Italian marble, and colorful Baba-Nonya porcelain.

Hand-painted lantern, a typical decoration in Chinese homes

Bedroom
The four-poster bed in the master bedroom is decorated with elaborate gilded carvings of foliage and mythological scenes. A hidden peephole in the floor overlooks the guest hall.

Second floor

The atrium allows natural light and cool air into the house.

First floor

House no. 52

House no. 50 (entrance)

★ Glass Partition
This screen allowed young unmarried women, hiding in the Dark Chamber, to peer through the etched panels at male visitors in the Guest Hall without being seen themselves.

House no. 48

★ Wooden Staircase
This highly ornate wooden staircase, constructed without the use of a single nail, is decorated with gilded carvings and is the only one of its kind in Malacca.

STAR EXHIBITS

- ★ Glass Partition
- ★ Wooden Staircase
- ★ Ancestral Altar

Baba-Nonya Shutters
These elegant louvered shutters, made of overlapping movable wooden slats, draw on European design and are a common feature of 19th-century Baba-Nonya architecture.

VISITORS' CHECKLIST

50 Jalan Tun Tan Cheng Lock.
Tel *(06) 283-1273.* ☐ *10am–12:30pm & 2–4:30pm daily.*
♿ Ⓟ ♿ 🎥 *free for children up to five years.* 🎥 *1:30pm daily; reservations are recommended.*

Baba-Nonya Porcelain
This distinctive pink and green porcelain, decorated with floral motifs and Buddhist symbols, was made to order in China for wealthy Baba-Nonya customers.

MUSEUM GUIDE
After walking through the impressive Guest Hall, continue beyond the glass partition into the living area. Take the stairs to the master bedroom and the funerary room on the first floor. Descend at the rear of the building to the kitchen area and return to the main entrance passing the ancestral altar en route.

KEY

☐	Bedroom
☐	Kitchen
☐	Ancestor worship
☐	Guest hall
◼	Dark chamber
☐	Funerary room
☐	Bathroom
☐	Exhibition space
☐	Non-exhibition space

The kitchen is perfectly preserved and stocked with traditional objects, including a noodle press.

★ Ancestral Altar
A common feature of Chinese homes, this family altar has Ming dynasty-style carvings of dragons and bats. The bronze cherub lamps show a strong European influence.

Façade
The façade is typical of the ornate and eclectic styles favored by the 19th-century Baba-Nonyas. It incorporates Chinese style with elements of European design, such as stucco pilasters, Rococo plasterwork, and louvered windows.

Boats moored at jetties in the old port town of Muar

Muar ❺

28 miles (45 km) SE of Malacca.
🏘 329,000. 🚌 from Malacca
and Kuala Lumpur. 🚢 from Dumai,
Sumatra. 🎏 Water Sports Festival
(Sep). **www**.johortourism.com.my

The bustling riverside town of
Muar, also known as Bandar
Maharani or Empress Town, is
bypassed by most tourists, but
its colorful history and elegant
colonial architecture make it a
pleasant stopover.

The town was once a major
trading port, and its former
status can be seen in the
collection of impressive colonial buildings standing close
to the waterfront on Jalan
Maharani, including the grand
**Royal Customs and Excise
Building**, dating from 1909.
Also here is a row of early
20th-century shophouses, and
nearby is the magnificent
Sultan Ibrahim Mosque, with
its soaring four-story minaret,
completed in 1930.

Muar is renowned as a
center of Malay culture and
the local dialect is considered
to be the purest form of
Malay in the country. The
town is famous for the local
ghazal music, which is sung
by a female chorus. However,
Muar is best known for its
food, in particular the popular
mee bandung Muar, a tasty
concoction of noodles, eggs,
prawns, and chili in beef
broth, and *ikan asam pedas*,
a sour and spicy fish dish.
There is no shortage of *kedai
kopis* (coffee shops) where
these dishes can be sampled.
Muar is also, allegedly, the
only place in Malaysia where
satay is served for breakfast.

Kukup ❻

25 miles (40 km) SW of Johor Bahru.
🏘 3,000. 🚌 from Johor Bahru to
Pontian Kecil, then taxi.
ℹ️ (07) 223-4935.

Sitting on the southwestern
tip of Johor close to the southernmost point of continental
Asia, Kukup is a traditional
fishing village, complete with
old-fashioned kampung-style
wooden houses on stilts
strung along the waterfront.

The village is famous for
its seafood, with chili crabs
being the local specialty, and
the many seafront restaurants
do a roaring trade with weekend visitors, many coming
from Singapore. Although this
one-street town offers no
other tourist attractions, just

offshore lies **Pulau Kukup**, one
of the world's largest uninhabited mangrove islands. Once
the haunt of pirates, it has
been declared a national park
and wetland area of international importance. A regular
ferry service to the island
allows visitors a glimpse of
this fascinating protected eco-
system. Its wildlife includes
wild pigs, crabs, and numerous species of birds.

🦌 **Pulau Kukup**
🚤 from Kukup jetty. ℹ️ Pulau
Kukup Johor National Park, 1319
Mukim Air Masin, (07) 696-9355.
www.johorparks.com

Johor Bahru ❼

2 miles (3 km) N of Singapore; 124
miles (200 km) SE of Malacca.
🏘 1,065,000. ✈️ Senai. 🚉 🚌
🚢 ℹ️ 2 Jalan Air Molek, (07) 223-
4935. 🎏 Johor Cultural Festival (Jul).
www.johortourism.com.my

The capital city of Johor state,
commonly known as "JB,"
sprawls across the southern
tip of the peninsula facing
Singapore over the narrow
strait. Most visitors pass
quickly through this big
traffic-clogged border town
after getting their passports
stamped, but some sights are
worth seeing. Chief among

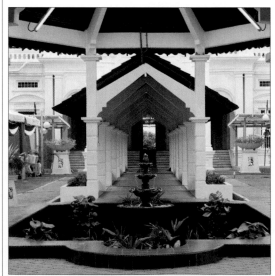

Fountain in the Royal Sultan Abu Bakar Mosque, Johor Bahru

these is the **Royal Sultan Abu Bakar Museum**, housed in the sparkling white Victorian Istana Besar, or Great Palace, west of the city center. Built in 1866, it is one of the oldest buildings in Johor Bahru and is set in extensive landscaped grounds overlooking the Strait of Singapore. The palace is now a museum devoted to the royal family and is still used for occasional official ceremonies. Photographs, costumes, weapons, and other royal mementos are on show in the lavishly furnished rooms, such as the Hunting Room featuring stuffed tigers, elephant-foot umbrella stands, and suchlike.

Also of interest nearby is the **Sultan Abu Bakar Mosque**, an Anglo-Malay edifice that was erected in 1893 and can hold up to 2,000 worshipers. The **Sultan Ibrahim Building** with its 210-ft (64-m) high Mughal-style tower dominates the skyline. During World War II, it was used by the Japanese but today houses state government offices.

🏛 **Royal Sultan Abu Bakar Museum**
Jalan Ibrahim. **Tel** (07) 223-0222.
⭘ 8am–5pm Sat–Thu daily. 🈳 US$ for foreigners. 🚻 limited.

Desaru Beach ❽

55 miles (88 km) E of Johor Bahru. 🚌 from Johor Bahru to Kota Tinggi, then taxi. 🚤 from Singapore to Tanjung Belungkor, then bus. **www**.desaru.com.my

The seaside resort of Desaru boasts over 15 miles (25 km) of fine, white sandy beaches fringed with casuarinas, and is particularly popular with weekend trippers from nearby Singapore. Most visitors come on package deals and the beach is dominated by hotel and restaurant developments. Sunbathing, swimming, and snorkeling are the main activities here, and the sea is clean and shallow close to shore. There is also an onsite golf course and horse-riding, while fishing and jungle-trekking are other possibilities for active vacationers.

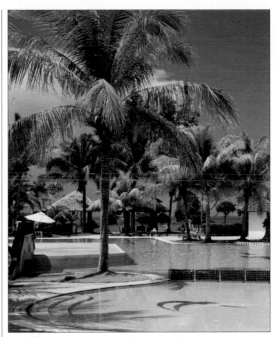
Luxurious swimming pool at one of Desaru Beach's hotel resorts

Mersing ❾

124 miles (200 km) N of Johor Bahru. 👥 68,000. 🚤 to Pulau Tioman. ℹ Jalan Abu Bakar, (07) 799-5212. **www**.mersing.com.my

This fishing town is the main access point for Pulau Tioman (*see pp130–31*) and the islands of the Seribuat Archipelago. Many people opt to spend a night here en route but there is little inducement to linger. Mersing is known for its *kerepok* (fish crackers) and these are sold all around the town center.

Seribuat Archipelago ❿

59 miles (95 km) S of Kuantan. 🚤 from Mersing; each of the private resorts runs a ferry service for guests.

Off the east coast of Johor lies the Seribuat Archipelago, made up of 64 volcanic islands, the largest being Pulau Tioman (*see pp130–31*). Most are tiny and uninhabited and can only be reached by chartering a private boat, but they are among the most beautiful islands in Malaysia.

Just a handful of the islands are big enough to support tiny villages and some secluded beach resorts, which range from simple beach huts to smart hotels with restaurants and swimming pools. The larger and more developed islands are Pulau Besar, Sibu, and Tinggi, renowned for their fine sandy beaches and excellent snorkeling and diving opportunities among the abundant coral reefs. Smaller islands provide a more sedate experience, such as Pulau Rawa, which has just one resort. The remote islands, including Pulau Pemanggil, Dayang, and Aur, have only basic facilities, but are rich in marine life and popular with more intrepid divers.

Tour operators in Mersing run island-hopping trips stopping off at a few of the islands, but otherwise access is restricted to guests at the private resorts. Ferries to Pulau Sibu depart from Tanjung Leman, 37 miles (60 km) south of Mersing, and take about an hour to reach the island.

Pulau Tioman ⑪

The largest of Malaysia's east coast islands, Tioman is famed for its soft, sandy beaches, warm waters, and coral reef. Its past is shrouded in myth – it is said that a dragon princess stopped here to break a long journey. She loved it so much that she stayed and her body was transformed into Pulau Tioman. Most of the resorts are strung out on isolated bays along the western coast. Diving and snorkeling opportunities in the protected marine park are superb, but jungle hiking and sunbathing are also popular activities. The island is a haven for wildlife – more than 140 different bird species live here. Monitor lizards, snakes, monkeys, and porcupines thrive in the jungle interior thanks to the absence of large predators, while the sea teems with countless varieties of tropical fish.

★ Snorkeling
Easy to arrange either alone or on organized trips, snorkeling is a captivating way to observe coral life.

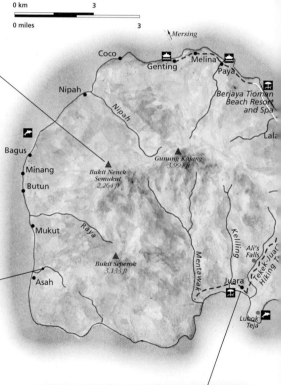

Twin Peaks
The twin peaks of Bukit Nenek Semukut are often shrouded in mist. Legend has it they are the horns of the dragon princess.

★ Asah Waterfall
A short walk from Kampung Asah is this picturesque waterfall, which was once used as a backdrop in the 1958 film South Pacific.

Juara
The only large resort on the east coast, secluded Juara is located in a beautiful curving bay. It has the finest white-sand beach on Tioman but the sea can be rough.

For hotels and restaurants in this region see pp278–9 and pp303–4

★ **Tekek-Juara Hiking Trail**
This sometimes challenging 5-mile (8-km) trail cuts across the island through jungle that is full of wildlife, streams, and waterfalls. It takes about three hours to reach Juara from Tekek.

VISITORS' CHECKLIST

19 miles (30 km) NE of Mersing. 🚶 🚢 *from Mersing.* ℹ️ *Mersing Tourist Information Center, Jalan Abu Bakar, (07) 799-5212.* 🍴 🛏️ 🚻 **Note** *water taxis and round-island boat trips are available.* **www**.tioman.com.my

Pulau Tulai

Pulau Tulai has reefs that are popular with snorkelers and divers.

Monkey Beach is a secluded cove with deep, clear water – ideal for diving.

Air Batang Panuba Salang

Tekek

Salang Beach
Tioman's most northerly resort, Salang has a short, sandy beach and shallow waters. There are plenty of budget accommodations and seafront bars providing low-key nightlife.

KEY

✈️	Domestic airport
🚢	Ferry
🏖️	Beach
🤿	Diving
═══	Minor road
– –	Trail
– –	Ferry route
▲	Peak

STAR SIGHTS

★ Snorkeling

★ Asah Waterfall

★ Tekek-Juara Hiking Trail

Air Batang
Popularly known as ABC, this lively resort is a favorite backpacker hangout, although better beaches can be found elsewhere.

Coral Reef
With more than 180 coral species, Tioman's waters offer some of the most rewarding diving in Malaysia.

EASTERN AND CENTRAL PENINSULA

The Eastern and Central Peninsula is blessed with some of the most beautiful natural features in Malaysia. Rising in the west are the lush forested Titiwangsa mountains, to the east of which lie Kelantan, Pahang, and Terengganu. Dominated by a vast rainforest and flanked by an unbroken coastline with delightful beaches and islands, the region is considered the heartland of Muslim Malay culture.

The three states of this region share a similar early history, having been vassals of Siam (now Thailand) and under the rule of the Sultanate of Malacca in the 14th and 15th centuries. Thereafter, Pahang was ruled by the Sultans of Johor until the British took control and made it one of the Federated Malay States. Terengganu and Kelantan continued to be under Siamese rule through the 19th century. In 1909, they became part of the Unfederated Malay States. In 1963, all three states were incorporated into the Federation of Malaysia.

Physically cut off from the west coast by the jungle interior, and free from British control until the 19th century, the eastern and central states developed at a different pace, commercially and culturally. Separated from the tin and rubber boom of the 19th century, which attracted Asian immigrants, they retained a rural and predominantly Malay character. These states are still considered the conservative Malay Muslim heartland of the country. The interior regions are inhabited by Orang Asli and Orang Syam people.

The east coast possesses a rural tranquility and offers spectacular natural scenery. Pahang is home to Taman Negara, the country's premier national park, as well as a host of offshore islands and some of Malaysia's best beaches. While the towns and villages of Terengganu are centers for Malay handicrafts, those of Kelantan are the best places to see traditional activities, such as fishing. Trips along the east coast may become difficult during the rainy season, between November and March.

The colorful fishing boats on Sabak Beach, Kelantan

◁ The unbroken coastline of the beach at Perhentian Besar, the largest of the Perhentian Islands

Exploring the Eastern and Central Peninsula

This region offers spectacular natural beauty with the magnificent Taman Negara and Endau-Rompin national parks located in its forested interiors and an endless coastline of white sand beaches and stunning offshore islands. Pulau Redang, Pulau Tenggol, and the Perhentian Islands are home to a fascinating underwater world and offer some of Malaysia's top diving and snorkeling. While Kuantan, the capital of Pahang, is a transport hub for the region and used mostly as a transit point, especially for nearby beaches and the picturesque Tasik Chini, the two other state capitals, Kuala Terengganu and Kota Bharu, are rich in Malay culture.

SIGHTS AT A GLANCE

Towns and Cities
Cherating **5**
Kota Bharu pp146–7 **14**
Kuala Terengganu **11**
Kuantan **1**
Pekan **4**
Tumpat **15**

Parks and Preserves
Endau-Rompin National Park **6**
Taman Negara pp138–9 **7**

Places of Worship
Wat Machimmaram **18**
Wat Phothivihan **17**

Areas of Natural Beauty
Gua Charas **2**
Tasik Chini **3**
Tasik Kenyir **10**

Islands and Beaches
Pantai Dasar Sabak **16**
Perhentian Islands **13**
Pulau Kapas **9**
Pulau Redang **12**
Pulau Tenggol **8**

Tour
The Jungle Railway p149 **19**

0 km   25

0 miles   25

PAN
DA
TUMPAT **15**   SAI
KOTA BHARU
WAT MACHIMMAR
17
WAT
PHOTHIVIHAN
Ketare

Jeli   Macang
Banding Batu
Melintang
Kuala
Kerai
Jerimbong

Kemubu

Gunung Camah 7,099 ft   Bertam

KELANTAN

THE JUNGLE RAILWAY **19**

Sungai Kemudu

Gua Musang

Gunung Taban 7,085 ft
Merapoh

Cegar Perah

Jelai

Kuala Lipis

Beluan   Ku
Tembel
Sega   **8**

Jeran

Raub

Bentong
Karak

Kuala
Lumpur

Bahau

Fishermen and women drying their catch by the sea in Kuantan

GETTING AROUND

Kuantan, Kuala Terengganu, and Kota Bharu are served by domestic airports. Route 3, a major national road, runs the length of the three states, and a good bus network serves the region. While the condition of the major roads is good and traffic is safe, the quality of the minor roads that branch off to the interior tends to deteriorate, necessitating 4WD vehicles. It is easiest to visit the national parks with a tour group. The railroad is a pleasant travel option. Regular ferries connect the mainland with the offshore islands.

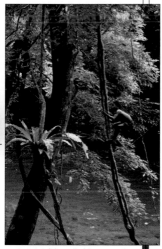

An Orang Asli boy climbing a tree in Taman Negara

KEY

▬▬	Major road
═══	Minor road
┄┄	Railroad
▬▬	International border
▬▬	State border
△	Peak

SEE ALSO

• **Where to Stay** pp280–81

• **Where to Eat** pp304–5

Ferries docked in Kuantan, capital of Pahang

Kuantan ❶

160 miles (259 km) E of Kuala
Lumpur. 🚶 315,000. ✈ 🚌 🚆
ℹ Jalan Makhota, (09) 517-8113.
www.pahangtourism.com.my

The capital of Pahang, Kuantan
is a commercial town and a
major transport hub, located at
the mouth of Sungai Kuantan.
The town has a few sites of
interest and is visited mostly
by travelers en route to the
attractive beaches and riverside villages nearby.
Overlooking the padang at
the heart of town is the stunning Moorish-style **Masjid
Negeri**, or state mosque. It
is crowned with a blue and
white dome and is surrounded by four Ottoman-style
minarets. It also features
stained-glass windows, a rare
feature in Malaysian Islamic
architecture. The mosque
is illuminated every night,
lending it a magical quality.
The town also has several
streets of old Chinese shophouses. The redeveloped
riverfront of Kuantan offers
pleasant views and has shops
that sell excellent local handicrafts. From the jetty, boat
trips take visitors to the
nearby fishing village of
Tanjung Lumpur as well as
to a mangrove forest reserve.

Environs
Just 3 miles (5 km) east of
the capital, **Teluk Chempedak**,
or jackfruit bay, is Kuantan's
main attraction. It marks the
beginning of the splendid
beaches on the east coast and
is famous locally for its sands
and waves. The coastal strip
is dotted with hotels and
restaurants and also has a

popular handicraft center
specializing in *batik*. Besides
an array of watersports, there
are several walking trails, all
leading south to the headland
of Tanjung Tembeling.

Gua Charas ❷

15 miles (25 km) NW of Kuantan.
🚌 from Kuantan.

Near the small settlement
of Panching, a short distance
from Kuantan, Gua Charas is
a series of deep caves set
dramatically in a mas-
sive limestone karst
outcrop. In 1954, the
Sultan of Pahang
granted permission
to a Thai Buddhist
monk to convert the
main cave into a
Buddhist shrine. A
steep ascent up 200
steps leads to the enormous
cave, which contains several
religious images carved out
of stone. Dominating the cave
is a 30-ft (9-m) long Sleeping
Buddha. Next to it are shrines
dedicated to Kuan Yin, the
Chinese goddess of mercy,

and to several bodhisattvas.
There is always a monk in
residence at the temple
who occasionally shows
visitors around.

Tasik Chini ❸

85 miles (138 km) SW of Kuantan
on Federal Hwy 82. 🚌 to Felda
Chini – 3.1 miles (5 km) S of Tasik
Chini, then taxi; to Maran, then taxi
to Kampung Belimbing, then boat.
🏞 treks organized by Lake Chini
Resort and Kampung Gumum. 🚤

Nestled in the hills, deep in
Malaysia's forested interior,
Tasik Chini is a collection of
beautiful lakes connected by
waterways teeming with fish
and birds and framed by giant
trees. The best time to visit is
between June and September
when the lakes are covered
with red and white lotus
blooms. Around the shores
live the indigenous Jakun
people, belonging to the
Orang Asli community.
Kampung Gumum is a small
Orang Asli settlement at the
northern end of the
lakes, where friendly
locals show visitors
around their homes
and display their
traditional handi-
crafts. At the village,
accommodation is
also available offering
an alternative to the
resort at the edge of the
main lake. Although public
transport to the lakes is not
conveniently accessible, once
there, the entire lake system
can be explored by boat,
organized by the resort and
the village. Several trails of

**Lotus blossom
at Tasik Chini**

The enormous Sleeping Buddha enshrined at Gua Charas

For hotels and restaurants in this region see pp280–81 and pp304–5

Boats moored at a jetty on one of the lakes at Tasik Chini

varying lengths weave through the area. Day tours to Tasik Chini can be arranged from Kuantan and Cherating.

Pekan ❹

27 miles (44 km) S of Kuantan on Federal Hwy 3. 🏘 30,000. 🚌 from Kuantan.

Located on the south bank of Sungai Pahang, the longest river in Malaysia, is the town of Pekan, the former royal capital of Pahang.

Scattered along the busy riverfront street at the town's northern edge are many of its attractions, including a row of beautiful Chinese shophouses and the **Sultan Abu Bakar Museum**. The museum collection contains royal regalia, weapons, instruments, and Chinese porcelain. Nearby are two white marble mosques, the blue-domed **Masjid Abdullah**, which dates back to the 1920s, and the newer **Masjid Abu Bakar**. Farther away from the river is the royal quarter, with its lavish **Istana Abu Bakar**, or royal palace, overlooking a polo ground. As the residence of the royal family, the palace is not open to the public. About 3 miles (5 km) south of the town is a silk-weaving center **Kampung Pulau Keladi**, built in the traditional Malay style on stilts with wooden walls.

🏛 **Sultan Abu Bakar Museum**
⬜ 9:30am–5pm Tue–Sun, 12:15–5pm Mon, 9:30am–2:45pm Fri.
🖼 donations.

Cherating ❺

29 miles (47 km) N of Kuantan on Federal Hwy 3. 🏘 2,000. 🚌 from Kuantan. 🟥

Occupying a windswept bay facing the South China Sea, the palm-fringed fishing village of Cherating is, quite simply, one of the best and most tranquil beaches on Malaysia's lovely east coast. Well-provided with accommodation of all types, from budget guesthouses to high-end resorts, Cherating is an extremely popular destination. The waters here are ideal for surfing, especially during November and December. It is also an excellent base from which to explore the surrounding areas of Tasik Chini, Gua Charas, and the various points north of Kuala Terengganu. Another area of interest close by is **Cendor Beach** for sightings of green turtles, which come ashore to lay their eggs during the nesting period.

Endau-Rompin National Park ❻

35 miles (57 km) S of Kuantan. 🚌 to Endau; to Kuala Rompin, then 4WD to park boundary. 🚢 from Endau. 🛈 (07) 223-7471. 🖼 🗹 guides mandatory. 🟥 🍽 🅰

Named for the two rivers that mark its northern and southern frontiers, the 336-sq mile (870-sq km) Endau-Rompin National Park is among the last remaining stretches of lowland forest in Malaysia. It nurtures a splendid variety of flora and fauna and is one of the few habitats of the Sumatran rhinoceros. The park's varied landscape allows for a variety of activities, such as trekking, rafting, mountain climbing, and abseiling.

At the confluence of Sungai Endau and Sungai Jasir is the base camp, **Kuala Jasin**, 9 miles (15 km) from the park headquarters. From here, a 4-hour trail leads to **Janing Barat Plateau** while two other routes trace the Sungai Jasin leading to the park's most spectacular waterfall, **Buaya Sangkut**. Visitors are also welcome at the Orang Asli villages that dot the area.

All visitors must carry entry permits, which can be obtained for free from Kuala Rompin or the park headquarters, or for a fee from Johor Bahru. Paid daily permits are required to visit certain sites within the park. Although it is possible to visit the park independently, complicated travel arrangements mean that it is best to visit on an organized tour. Allow a period of three days to cover the park.

The sky-blue domed Masjid Abdullah at the former royal capital of Pekan

Taman Negara ●

Established in 1938, Taman Negara is Malaysia's oldest and largest national park. Extending across 1,660 sq miles (4,300 sq km) of pristine rain forest, the park encompasses parts of three states, Pahang, Kelantan, and Terengganu. A profusion of birdlife can be spotted here, along with rare animals such as the Indochinese tiger, Sumatran rhinoceros, Malayan gaur, and Asian elephant. Access to the park is spectacular, involving a 37-mile (60-km) boat journey along the lovely Sungai Tembeling, passing Orang Asli villages en route.

KEY

☐ Taman Negara

Four Steps Waterfall

Gunung Tahan
7,152 ft   Padang

Gunung Gedong
6,752 ft

Kuala Teku

GUNUNG TAHAN TRAIL

Kuala Pute

Tenor

RENTIS TENO

Bukit G
Gende
1,864

Atok

★ **Gunung Tahan**
The 7,175-ft (2,187-m) high Gunung Tahan is the highest peak in Peninsular Malaysia. The long trek to the summit is very demanding with the route passing rivers and undulating ridges before finally reaching the peak.

Boat Trips
At the Mutiara Taman Negara Resort park headquarters, boats can be hired for trips to the Lata Berkoh rapids, as well as for fishing trips to the Taban and Kenyam rivers.

KEY

– –	Trail
= =	Park boundary
✈	Domestic airport
ℹ	Visitor information
⛺	Campsite
▲	Peak

STAR SIGHTS

★ Gunung Tahan

★ Bukit Teresek

★ Canopy Walkway

Bukit Guling Gendang, at a height of 1,864 ft (568 m), offers panoramic views across virgin rain forest from its summit.

Hornbills
For many the main attraction of Taman Negara is its abundant birdlife. The park is home to rare hornbills, including the wreathed hornbill, great hornbill, Indian pied hornbill, and the rhinoceros hornbill.

For hotels and restaurants in this region see pp280–81 and pp304–5

Asian Elephants
Taman Negara is a haven for endangered species such as the Asian elephant. Wild elephants are often relocated here from the surrounding region.

VISITORS' CHECKLIST

106 miles (170 km) W of Kuantan. 🚌 to Kuala Tembeling, *then boat to Kuala Tahan.*
ℹ️ *Kuala Tahan, (09) 266-1122.*
Permits *available at Department of Wildlife and National Parks.*
www.taman-negara.com

★ **Bukit Teresek**
The climb up to the summit of Bukit Teresek along a muddy track takes over an hour but is well worth the effort for the great views across the valley to Gunung Tahan and Gunung Perlis.

Gua Telinga, a limestone cave, is one of the most easily accessible in the park. Guided by a rope, visitors can follow a stream through the cavern.

EXPLORING THE PARK

All trails start from or near park headquarters and have been marked or signposted. The two main trails in the park are the 9-day, 34-mile (55-km) trek to Gunung Tahan and the 4-day, 10-mile (16-km) Rentis Tenor loop trail. However, the most heavily used trail in the park is the short 1.6-mile (2-km) route to Bukit Teresek, which also leads on to Bukit Indah. Guides are compulsory for the longer, more strenuous treks.

★ **Canopy Walkway**
A 1,673-ft (510-m) walkway, one of the world's longest, runs through the canopy at Kuala Tahan. Suspended 147 ft (45 m) above the ground, it enables visitors to explore the rain forest from a novel perspective.

Clear blue waters lapping the pristine shore of Pulau Tenggol

Pulau Tenggol ⑧

8 miles (13 km) E of Kuala Dungun.
🚤 from Kuala Dungun. ⌐

Part of a group of 12 small and remote islands, Pulau Tenggol is a renowned diving destination on the east coast of Malaysia. Uninhabited until the 1970s, the island was developed into a dive site *(see 326)* and is now part of the Terengganu Marine Park.

The blue waters around the densely forested islands harbor spectacular underwater cliffs, boulders, and coral reefs that shelter a variety of colorful marine life. A ban on fishing,

spear-fishing, and any other form of marine life harvesting ensures a rewarding underwater diving experience. There are at least ten dive sites in this group of islands, but most of them are deep water and suitable only for divers with prior experience.

Pulau Kapas ⑨

4 miles (6 km) E of Marang. 🚤 from Marang. 🚼 🏠 ⌐

A small, beautiful island with white sand beaches and dazzling waters, Pulau Kapas, or cotton island, is a designated marine park and promoted as a diving and snorkeling paradise. Located to the north is the much smaller islet of **Pulau Gemia**, which can only be visited by guests of its resort.

The best sites for snorkeling on Pulau Kapas are found around its northern shore as well as around Pulau Gemia. North of Gemia, a sunken World War II shipwreck is one of the most popular sites. All the resorts on Kapas can arrange diving trips. There is also a professional scuba diving center that offers training programs. The island

is an excellent place for swimming, windsurfing, and sea kayaking or just relaxing under the palm trees. A walking track that cuts across the island to its isolated eastern shore offers panoramic views.

Tasik Kenyir ⑩

34 miles (55 km) SW of Kuala Terengganu. 🚌 from Kuala Terengganu. 🛥 boat tours. ⌐

Extending over 100 sq miles (260 sq km) and containing around 350 small islands, Tasik Kenyir is the largest man-made lake in Southeast Asia. It was created by the construction of a dam on the Sungai Kenyir in 1985. Surrounded by lush tropical jungle, which is home to a number of wildlife species, Tasik Kenyir has been developed as an ecotourism destination. Today, there are some 15 resorts around the lake, offering quiet and comfortable retreats. Other options include houseboats and floating chalets. Among the highlights of the lake are 14 picturesque waterfalls, which cascade down into natural pools. These can be reached by boat from the lake's main jetty. Boat trips can also be taken to the limestone Bewah Caves at the southern end of the lake. Fishing is a popular activity here, as the lake teems with an abundance of freshwater fish. The best time to visit is between February and June when the water level is high.

A trained monkey selecting a ripe coconut

COCONUT-COLLECTING MONKEYS

It is common practice in Peninsular Malaysia to train monkeys to shin up palm trees, twist off the coconuts, and throw them to the ground where they are gathered up by the tree's owner. It has been estimated that coconut-collecting monkeys can harvest at least five times as many nuts per day than a human collector, chiefly due to their speed, agility, and ease with heights. **Kampung Jenang**, near Marang in Terengganu, has made a thriving business out of this technique. A monkey training school established almost three decades ago by Muda Mamat, a local villager, now even tutors monkeys belonging to coconut plantation owners from neighboring states for a steep fee.

One of the 14 beautiful waterfalls at Tasik Kenyir

Exquisite traditional Malay houses in the grounds of Terengganu State Museum Complex

Kuala Terengganu ⓫

138 miles (220 km) N of Kuantan.
🏚 275,000. ✈ 🚌 🚢 ℹ *Plaza
Padang Negara, (09) 617-3553.*
www.tourism.terengganu.gov.my

The state capital and the seat of the sultans of Terengganu, Kuala Terengganu is a former fishing village that was transformed into an affluent city from the revenue of its South China Sea oilfields.

The city remains to this day a stronghold of Malay culture, with colorful markets and vibrant traditional handicraft workshops where visitors can buy *batik*, brocade, *songket*, brassware, and basketware. The busiest spot in town is the **Pasar Payang**, or central market. All kinds of foods including fresh fish, fruit, and vegetables are available here. It also has a number of craft shops. South of the market is the compact **Chinatown**. Its crescent-shaped street is lined with restored shophouses and restaurants, as well as a Buddhist temple.

Just a short walk away from the market, in the opposite direction, is the colonial-style, apricot-colored **Istana Maziah**, which is the sultan's palace. It is closed to the public except for some ceremonial occasions. Nearby is the beautiful **Masjid**

Zainal Abidin, with golden domes and a single, towering minaret. A number of fascinating sights are within easy reach of the capital, including the **Terengganu State Museum Complex**, the **Masjid Tengku Tengah Zaharah**, and the island of Pulau Duyung *(see p143)*, which is host to the prestigious Monsoon Cup yachting race.

⛫ Terengganu State Museum Complex

Losong, 2 miles (3 km) SW of Kuala Terengganu. *Tel (09) 622-1444.*
⏰ 9am–5pm Sat-Thu. ⬤ *Fri.* 📷
Said to be one of the largest museums in Southeast Asia, Kompleks Muzium Negeri Terengganu, or Terengganu State Museum Complex, consists of several buildings sprawled across landscaped gardens. The main building, which is a reproduction of a

traditional Malay stilt house, contains displays of textiles, handicrafts, Islamic artifacts, and a gallery dedicated to the state's petroleum industry. Within the grounds are several traditional Malay boats and houses as well as a maritime museum. The highlight of the complex, however, is the **Istana Tengku Long**, a wooden palace that dates back to 1880, with exhibits of royal artifacts.

⛫ Masjid Tengku Tengah Zaharah

3 miles (5 km) SE of Kuala Terengganu.
Owing to its location by the water, Masjid Tengku Tengah Zaharah is also referred to as the Floating Mosque. This sparkling white mosque is set in a park and combines modern and traditional Moorish architecture. The mosque is closed to non-Muslims.

Colorful fresh vegetables at the Pasar Payang in Kuala Terengganu

Holidaymakers relaxing on one of the quiet, beautiful beaches of Pulau Perhentian Besar

Pulau Redang ⑫

38 miles (62 km) N of Kuala Terengganu. ✈ *from Kuala Lumpur.* ⛴ *from Merang and Kuala Terengganu.* 🍴 🛏 ◈

One of the largest and most beautiful of the east coast islands, Pulau Redang is also the most developed. It is set at the center of the Redang Archipelago, a group of nine islands that together constitute a protected marine park. With crystal clear waters and a wealth of marine life sustained by some of Malaysia's best coral reefs, the island offers excellent diving and snorkeling opportunities. Sadly, silt and building waste have damaged the coral, but active efforts are being made to prevent further damage and even snorkeling has been restricted to certain parts of the reef. The permitted areas do, however, offer superb opportunities for underwater exploration. The waters also contain the historic wrecks of two British warships, HMS *Repulse* and HMS *Prince of Wales*, which were sunk off Pulau Redang by the Japanese during World War II.

The island's beaches are set against a backdrop of verdant jungle-clad hills. **Pasir Panjang** and **Teluk Dalam Kecil**, two of the best beaches, occupy the eastern coast and have most of the resorts. Kampung Air, Pulau Redang's main village, sits at the center of the island.

Most travelers visit the island on a package tour but dive trips can also be arranged from the Perhentian Islands.

Perhentian Islands ⑬

12 miles (20 km) NW of Kuala Terengganu. ⛴ *from Kuala Besut.* 🍴 🛏 ◈

Located off the Terengganu coast, **Pulau Perhentian Besar** and **Pulau Perhentian Kecil** together comprise the Perhentian Islands, which means stopping-place islands. Breathtakingly beautiful, the islands have inevitably attracted a great deal of development in recent years but still retain their appeal. Both islands feature white sand beaches and an aquamarine sea that is home to spectacular coral reefs teeming with an astounding variety of marine life. Besides diving and snorkeling, other activities available on the islands include sailing, windsurfing, and jungle walks.

Among the beaches on Pulau Perhentian Besar is the exquisite **Three Coves Bay**, a group of three beaches

Snorkeling in the crystal clear waters off the east coast islands

separated by rocky outcrops. This sheltered spot is where green and hawksbill turtles lay their eggs between May and September, when the bay is closed to visitors.

Pulau Perhentian Kecil is smaller than Pulau Perhentian Besar, but is otherwise an exact replica of it, with beautiful beaches, coconut palms, and azure waters. A small village on its southeastern coast is inhabited by people originally from Sulawesi in Indonesia. The island's main attraction is the east-facing **Pasir Panjang**, or Long Beach.

Of the two islands, the more expensive accommodations, with quieter ambience, are available in Perhentian Besar. Dozens of resorts and guesthouses are clustered around the southwestern shore. With the vast abundance of cheaper hotels and restaurants, Perhentian Kecil attracts backpackers.

The islands are usually packed during the peak season between late May and September, and finding accommodation is difficult. It is worth exploring options on both islands since the narrow strait separating them is easily crossed by boat. Getting around the islands is simple. There are some good walking trails but the best way to hop between beaches is by boat, which can be arranged by most resort and chalet owners.

Northwest of these islands lie the smaller, uninhabited **Pulau Susu** group covered in virgin forests. They provide one of the best diving sites in the region.

Boatbuilders of Pulau Duyung

Just off the western waterfront of Kuala Terengganu lies Pulau Duyung where an ancient tradition of boatbuilding still thrives. Decorated vessels, called *bangau*, were once made all along the east coast, from Kota Bharu to Kuantan and beyond. Primarily used as fishing boats, these wooden craft are constructed by master boatbuilders using techniques

Carved and painted prow

passed down through many generations and it is believed that they are built entirely from memory. Each boat is painted in bright colors and painstakingly decorated with individual designs, making them unique. The island is accessible via a causeway from Kuala Terengganu and by ferry from a jetty near the Seri Malaysia Hotel (*see p279*).

Local shipyards and workshops *are scattered throughout the island and visitors are usually welcome to see the boatbuilders at work. Most of the boats are used by local fishermen, but their exquisite craftsmanship has won them international acclaim.*

BOAT DESIGN

Most boat designs feature representational characters, often derived from Hindu mythology. However, these are becoming rarer as boat designers are increasingly turning to non-representational Islamic art such as the elaborate geometric arabesque pattern.

Stylized prows *are carved and painted to represent shadow puppets, birds, and Garuda, a bird from Hindu mythology.*

Rows of vibrant fishing boats *line the beaches of Pulau Duyung. Originally propelled by oars or sails, many of the boats today are fitted with removable motor engines, both for convenience as well as modernity.*

Mythical creatures, *such as dragons and demons, appear to be derived from Hindu epics such as the* Ramayana.

The boats *need to be brought ashore every day, far away from treacherous waves and close to the tree line. Therefore, they are created with an expert blend of functionality and aesthetics: sturdy in order to withstand the strongest of storms, yet light enough to be easily pulled out of the water.*

Traditional kite-making at Kota Bharu ▷

Kota Bharu ⑭

Situated in the northeast corner of the peninsula, near the mouth of Sungai Kelantan, Kota Bharu, or new fort in Malay, is the state capital of Kelantan, and perhaps the most traditional Malay and predominantly Muslim city in the country. A modern city on the surface, Kota Bharu is a repository of culture, crafts, and religion. It is rich in palaces, museums, and mosques, and offers a fine regional cuisine. Traditional skills and customs such as kite-flying, silver-working, and weaving thrive here. Prayer times are rigorously observed, when all activity comes to a standstill, especially on Fridays, the Muslim holy day. Most of the city's attractions lie in its northeast section, at the heart of which is the Pasar Besar, one of the most vibrant markets in the country. Kota Bharu is also a good base to explore the surrounding region.

impressive among all the exhibits is the *singakerti*, an impressive royal carriage shaped in the form of a mythical beast.

The towering State Mosque, northwest of the city center

Elegantly furnished dining room at Istana Batu, now the Royal Museum

🏛 Istana Batu
Jalan Hilir Kota. **Tel** *(09) 748-7737.*
⭕ *8:30am–4:45pm Sat–Thu.* 📷
The sky blue Istana Batu, or stone palace, completed in 1939 by Sultan Ismail, was given by him as a wedding gift to his nephew Sultan Yahya. Once used as a guesthouse for visiting royalty and a wedding venue for the sultan's family, it has now been converted into the Royal Museum. Rooms preserved in their original state display royal artifacts such as old family pictures and glassware.

🏛 Istana Balai Besar
Jalan Hilir Kota. ⭕ *to public*
Standing at the very center of town, surrounded by a wooden fort, Istana Balai Besar is a traditional Kelantan palace. Built in 1844 by Sultan Muhammad II, it served as the official residence of the royal family of Kelantan for many

years. This unique Malay palace has Thai architectural influences in its design. The throne room and the audience hall are used on important royal occasions and official state functions. The palace is closed to the public but visitors can view the beautiful façade.

🏛 Istana Jahar
Jalan Hilir Kota. **Tel** *(09) 744-4666.*
⭕ *8:30am–4:45pm Sat–Thu.* 📷
Built by Sultan Ahmad in 1887 for his son Long Kundur, Istana Jahar remains an outstanding example of traditional Kelantan wooden architecture, with delicately carved beams, panels, and iron grilles. In 1991 it was made the **Museum of Royal Traditions and Custom**. Its collections include textiles, brass and silverware, and artifacts related to various royal rituals and ceremonies, such as weddings and births. The Weapons Gallery displays, spears, old *keris*, and other weapons. Perhaps the most

ⓒ State Mosque
Jalan Sultanah Zainab.
Near the palaces, which are clustered near Padang Merdeka, the imposing State Mosque was built in 1926 during the reign of Sultan Ismail IV. Known locally as the Brick Mosque, the State Mosque serves as the center for Muslim *dawah*, or missionary activity in Kelantan. Visitors should dress conservatively, ensuring that their arms and legs are covered. Non-Muslims are not allowed to enter during prayer times.

🏛 Islamic Museum
Jalan Sultan. **Tel** *(09) 744-0102.*
⭕ *8:30am–4:45pm Sat–Thu.* 📷
Close to the State Mosque is the beautiful old wooden building of the Islamic Museum decorated with fine carvings. Formerly known as the Serambi Makkah, or

The green and white façade of the Islamic Museum

veranda to Mecca, it functioned as a religious college, the first of its kind in Kelantan. It also symbolized the prominence of Islam in the state. The museum now houses a display of photographs and artifacts that give an account of the history of Islam in the state.

🏛 World War II Memorial Museum

Jalan Sultan. 🕐 *8:30am–4:45pm Sat–Thu.* 🚫

Located in the old Bank Kerapu, the World War II Memorial Museum contains more than 1,000 exhibits, pictures, and guns that document the Japanese occupation of Kelantan during the Second World War. Kota Bharu was the landing point for the Japanese forces in Malaysia, on December 8, 1941. During the invasion the bank also functioned as the headquarters of the Japanese secret police, or *kempetai*. Another display of photographs and arms dates from the years of the Emergency, when British and Malay troops fought a long-running struggle against the Chinese Communist Party of Malaya between 1948 and 1960. An upstairs gallery describes the history of prewar Kelantan.

🏛 Gelanggang Seni

Jalan Mahmud. ***Tel*** *(09) 744-3124.* 🕐 *timings vary, call to confirm; free shows Mon, Wed, Fri afternoons and evenings Mar–Oct, except during the Ramadan period.*

The city's premier cultural center, Gelanggang Seni organizes cultural shows and exhibitions to showcase a wide variety of traditional Kelantan arts and sports, many of which are in danger of dying out. There are free performances of *silat*, a Malay martial art form, and *mak yong* and *manohra*, traditional dance-dramas accompanied by *gamelan* music. Drummers perform on huge *rebana* drums made out of hollowed logs, and *kertok*, smaller coconut drums. The center presents displays of *gasing*, the traditional game of wooden top-spinning, and kite-flying using huge Kelantan moon kites called *wau bulan*. Spellbinding shadow-puppet plays called *wayang kulit* are also performed, using characters and stories from the Hindu epics of the *Ramayana* and the *Mahabharata*.

VISITORS' CHECKLIST

NE Kelantan. 👥 *1,310,000.* ✈ 🚆 🚌 ℹ *Jalan Sultan Ibrahim, (09) 748-5534.* 🎉 *Kite Festival (May/Jun), Drum Festival (Jul), Sultan's Birthday (Jul).*

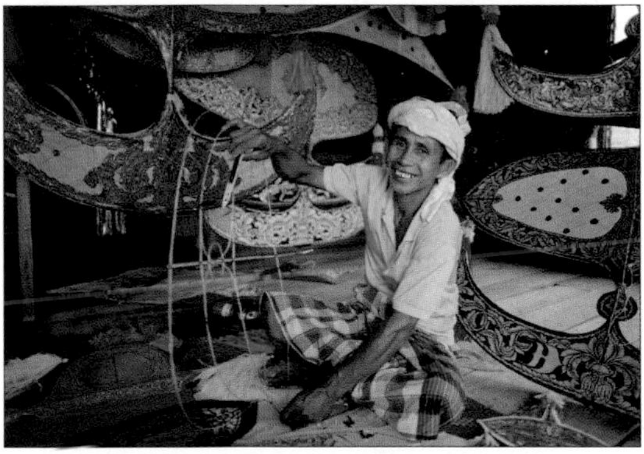

A traditional kite-maker surrounded by colorful kites in Kota Bharu

KOTA BHARU CITY CENTER

Gelanggang Seni 7
Islamic Museum 5
Istana Balai Besar 2
Istana Batu 1
Istana Jahar 3
State Mosque 4
World War II Memorial Museum 6

0 meters 500
0 yards 500

Key to Symbols *see back flap*

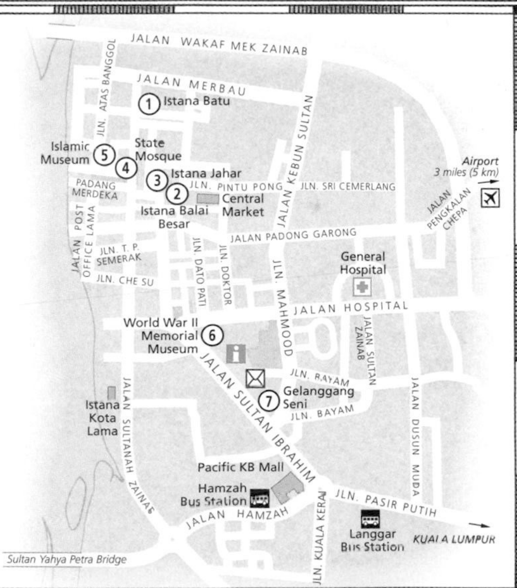
JALAN WAKAF MEK ZAINAB
JALAN MERBAU
JLN. ATAS BANGGOL
1 Istana Batu
Islamic Museum 5
4 State Mosque
3 Istana Jahar
PADANG MERDEKA
JLN. PINTU PONG
JLN. SRI CEMERLANG
2 Istana Balai Besar
Central Market
JALAN KEBUN SULTAN
Airport 3 miles (5 km)
JALAN PENGKALAN CHEPA
JALAN POST OFFICE LAMA
JLN. T. P. SEMERAK
JLN. CHE SU
JLN. DATO PATI
JLN. DOKTOR
JALAN PADONG GARONG
JLN. MAHMOOD
General Hospital
JALAN HOSPITAL
JALAN SULTAN ZAINAB
World War II Memorial Museum 6
JALAN SULTAN IBRAHIM
JLN. BAYAM
7 Gelanggang Seni
JALAN DUSUN MUDA
Istana Kota Lama
JALAN SULTANAH ZAINAB
Pacific KB Mall
Hamzah Bus Station
JALAN HAMZAH
JLN. PASIR PUTIH
JLN. KUALA KERAI
Langgar Bus Station
KUALA LUMPUR
Sultan Yahya Petra Bridge

The elaborate temple roof of Wat Phothivihan

Tumpat ⑮

9 miles (15 km) NW of Kota Bharu.
🚉 🚌 from Kota Bharu.

Located in a predominantly
agricultural region, the little
town of Tumpat in Kelantan
is a center of the Orang Syam
people. It is also an important
transport hub for southbound
travelers on the Jungle Railway
track or northbound travelers
to nearby Thailand.

Tumpat is a good place to
start exploring the region's
numerous Thai Buddhist temples, always a surprising and
colorful sight in the otherwise
strictly Islamic Kelantan.

Pantai Dasar Sabak ⑯

8 miles (13 km) NE of Kota Bharu.
🚌 from Kota Bharu.

To the north and east of Kota
Bharu are several attractive
beaches overlooking the
South China Sea. One of
the most easily accessible is
Pantai Dasar Sabak. Situated
near the Malay fishing village
of Sering, it is a dazzling
stretch of palm-lined beach
and has a significant history.
On December 8, 1941, the
Imperial Japanese Navy
troops landed here in one of
Japan's first acts of aggression
during World War II.

It is possible to combine
an excursion to the beach
with an opportunity to watch
the return of the local fishing
fleet in the afternoon, and
perhaps to buy some fresh

seafood for cooking on the
spot. Visitors should bear in
mind that the east coast of
Kelantan is predominantly
Malay Muslim, and dressing
modestly is advisable.

Wat Phothivihan ⑰

2 miles (3 km) S of Chabang Empat,
near Tumpat. 🚌 from Kota Bharu or
Tumpat. ⬡ 7am–5pm daily.
🎎 Vesak Day (Apr/May).

Within Kelantan, the lives of
Thai Buddhists are organized
around 20 or so monasteries.
One of the most interesting
of these, Wat Phothivihan is
worth visiting for its elaborate
temple roof and saffron-clad
monks, both of which form
a marked contrast to the surrounding Muslim villages.

Built in 1973 by chief abbot
Phra Krurasapia Chakorn, the
monastery attracts thousands
of Thai pilgrims every year.
As with most Thai temples,

the buildings and grounds
are large and imposing.
The main attraction here is
a 131-ft (40-m) long *phra
non*, or Reclining Buddha
that was built in 1975.

Wat Phothivihan is a social,
cultural, and spiritual center
for Thai, Chinese, and Indian
worshipers. Its monks are
always eager to show vistors
around. The temples and
groves also elicit the secular
interest of Muslims who view
it as a tourist attraction.

Wat Machimmaram ⑱

Kampung Jubakar, near Tumpat.
🚌 from Kota Bharu or Tumpat.
⬡ 7am–5pm daily. 🎎 Vesak Day
(Apr/May).

One of the many Buddhist
temples in the Thai villages of
Kelantan, Wat Machimmaram
is located in the village of
Kampung Jubakar on the
main road between Kota
Bharu and the Thai border.
As in neighboring Thailand,
the *ketek*, or temple, has
familiar lotus-shaped corner
stones, gilded spires of venerable *chedi*, or stupas, lac-
quered doors, and shuttered
windows. Its most outstanding feature is a statue of the
Seated Buddha, constructed
by local Thai Buddhists and
said to be the largest in Southeast Asia. At about 105 ft (32
m), the statue towers over the
surrounding Kelantan plains,
making a definite statement
about the presence of
Theravada Buddhism in this
predominantly Islamic state.

A golden seated Buddha and ornate pillars at Wat Machimmaram

The Jungle Railway [19]

One of the most delightful ways of exploring the wild interior of Peninsular Malaysia is by the Jungle Railway, officially called the East Coast Line. Considered an engineering marvel when it was completed in 1931, it created links between the east coast state of Kelantan with the west coast states of Kedah, Perak, and Penang. This line winds its way south from Kelantan through the spectacular jungle gorges of Kuala Lipis to join the main line from Singapore to Kuala Lumpur at Gemas.

TIPS FOR TRAVELERS

Starting point: *Tumpat, 9 miles (15 km) from Kota Bharu.*
Getting there: *by taxi, or by bus no. 27, 27A, and 43 from Central Bus Station, Kota Bharu.*
Duration: *15 hours by daytime slow train from Tumpat to Gemas; 10 hours by overnight express train.*

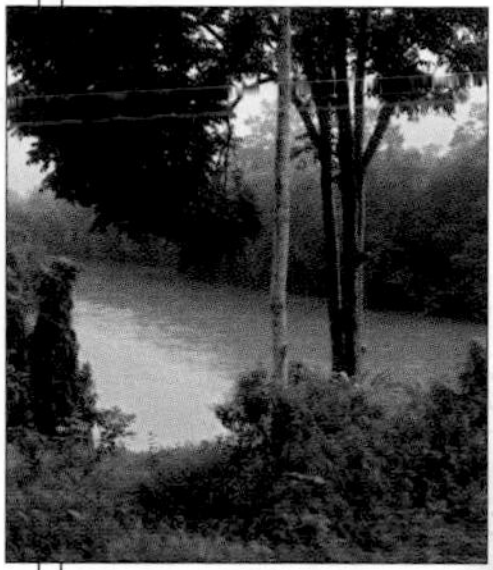

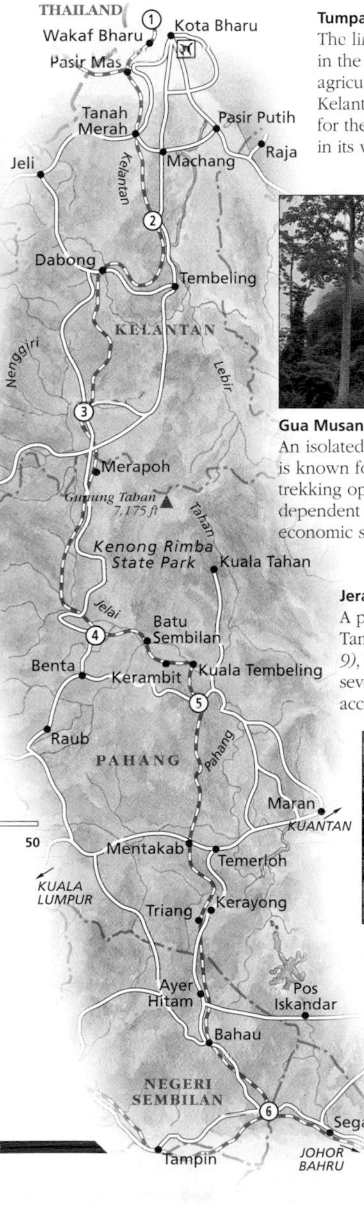

KEY

- Minor road
- Railroad
- International border
- State border
- Domestic airport
- ▲ Peak

Tumpat ①
The line starts at Tumpat in the north, a small agricultural town in rural Kelantan that is chiefly noted for the several Thai temples in its vicinity.

Kuala Krai ②
The Railway passes by the banks of the Sungai Kelantan near the settlement of Kuala Krai, which is surrounded by rubber plantations and dense rainforest.

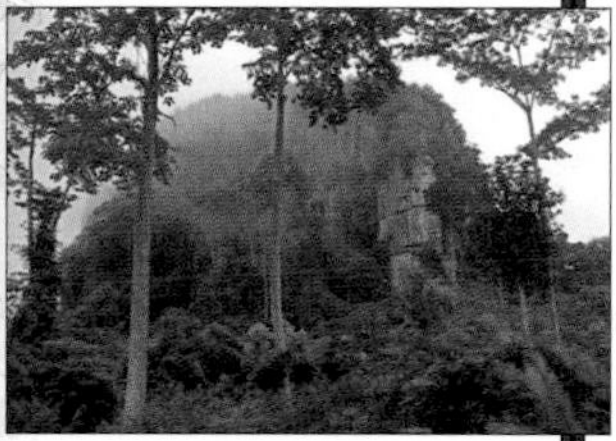

Gua Musang ③
An isolated town, Gua Masang is known for its caves and trekking opportunities, but is dependent on timber for its economic survival.

Kuala Lipis ④
Located at the confluence of Jelai and Lipis rivers, this former gold-mining town is known for its tranquility and lovely colonial architecture.

Jerantut ⑤
A popular gateway to Taman Negara *(see pp138–9)*, this small town has several restaurants and accommodation options.

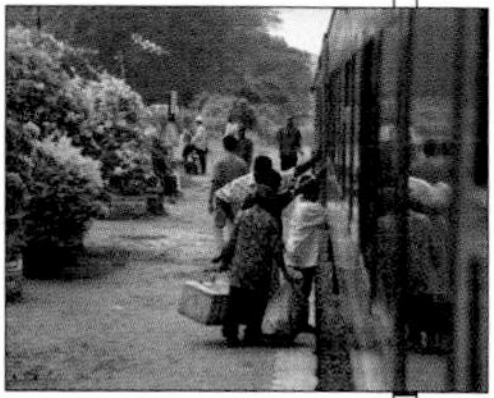

Gemas ⑥
The Jungle Railway ends at Gemas, a busy junction town with excellent road and rail links to Kuala Lumpur and Johor Bahru.

SARAWAK

Teeming with natural wonders, including precipitous mountains, lush rain forests, abundant wildlife, and some of the world's largest caves, Sarawak is nicknamed the Land of the Hornbill. This diversity of flora and fauna, along with Sarawak's swashbuckling history and the cultural heritage of its indigenous people, attracts increasing numbers of visitors to the state.

Sarawak's first inhabitants were cave dwelling hunter-gatherers who lived here about 40,000 years ago. Evidence of the existence of early settlements was discovered in 1958 at Niah Caves in the northeast of the state, testifying to Sarawak's long, although largely unwritten, history of human habitation.

Until the mid-19th century, the region was governed by the Sultan of Brunei whose imposition of heavy taxes led to frequent rebellions by local indigenous groups. During one such outbreak in 1839, the English adventurer James Brooke entered the service of the Sultan and subdued the rebels. For this, he was rewarded with the title of Rajah, becoming the first of the White Rajahs *(see p157)* who ruled an area the size of Britain as their private kingdom for over a century. Sarawak joined the Federation of Malaysia in 1963. The state is blessed with an abundance of natural resources, and petroleum and forestry have been the mainstay of Sarawak's economy in the 20th century. Sarawak's population of 2.2 million largely comprises the indigenous people known collectively as Dayaks, while the remaining minority are the Orang Ulu. Most people live in the southwest of the province, in and around the historic capital of Kuching. The city is an excellent base for visiting the traditional Dayak longhouses, wildlife reserves, and national parks scattered throughout the province. The breathtaking ancient limestone pinnacles at Mulu National Park are excellent for trekking and rock climbing. These, together with Niah Caves and Bako National Park – one of Sarawak's oldest national parks – are the highlights of a visit to the state.

Mother and baby orangutan scavenging for food at Semenggoh Nature Reserve

◁ The Niah Caves, one of Sarawak's most spectacular attractions and home to bats and swiftlets

Exploring Sarawak

Located in northwest Borneo, Sarawak
is the largest state in Malaysia and is famous
for its diversity of flora and fauna. Within easy
reach of its capital, Kuching, are beautiful
national parks and scenic beaches. Flanked
by longhouse settlements of the Dayaks, the
Batang Rajang meanders through the heart of
the state as the main channel of communication
with the towns of Sibu, Kapit, and Belaga. In
the northeast of the state, the Niah Caves are
a site of archaeological significance, while the
limestone outcrops at Mulu National Park are
a climber's dream. To the northeast lies Brunei,
one of the smallest countries in the world.

**The opulent facade of Masjid Jamek, or
Friday Mosque, Brunei**

SIGHTS AT A GLANCE

*South
China
Sea*

MUKAH ✕🚁 ⑰   Balingiar

Sirik

Matu   Kut   Narub   Rum
Daro   Nanga   Chang
                  Tamin   Mamb
                         Sekuau   Mu

Belawai ○   ✕🚁 ⑭ SIBU
      Sarikei Binatang *Rajang*   BATAN
Grigat ○   RAJAN
                  Julau   ⑬
Roban ○   Pakan Kanowit
               ○   Uka   Rumah Be

✕🚁 ❽ TANJUNG DATU
    NATIONAL PARK
SEMATAN   DAMAI
❼ 🏕   BEACH
  SARAWAK ❹ ✕🏖 BAKO NATIONAL
  CULTURAL ❺ ⑫ PARK
❾ VILLAGE   ❸ SANTUBONG
GUNUNG   ❻ ✕🚁   Rumah
GADING NP ② SUNGAI SANTUBONG Layang   Rumah
KUBAH ⛰   ❶ KUCHING   Beladin ○ Pusa   Tungku
NP 🏛🏕 Simunjan ○ Debak ○
  ⑩   *Lupar* ○
WIND CAVE Siburan ⑪   Betong ○
AND FAIRY CAVE ⑪   *Lupar*
SEMENGGOH Gedong ○ Bandar   *Batang Ai
NATURE   Sri Aman ○ Reservoir*
RESERVE   Ensabang ○   Engkilili ○
                      Lubok Antu ○

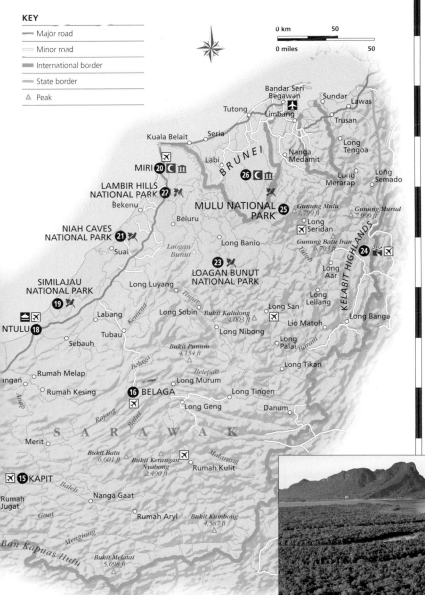

KEY

— Major road

═ Minor road

▬ International border

— State border

△ Peak

0 km 50

0 miles 50

Bandar Seri Begawan
Sundar
Lawas
Tutong
Limbang
Trusan
Kuala Belait
Seria
Long Tengoa
MIRI **20** Ⓒ 🏛
Labi
Nanga Medamit
26 Ⓒ 🏛
BRUNEI
Long Merarap
Long Semado
LAMBIR HILLS NATIONAL PARK **22**
Bekenu
MULU NATIONAL PARK **25**
Gunung Mulu 7,799 ft
Gunung Murud 7,999 ft
Beluru
Long Seridan
NIAH CAVES NATIONAL PARK **21**
Long Banjo
Gunung Batu Iran 6,703 ft
24
Suai
Laogan Bunut
KELABIT HIGHLANDS
LOAGAN BUNUT NATIONAL PARK **23**
Long Aar
SIMILAJAU NATIONAL PARK **19**
Long Luyang
Long Lellang
Long Banga
NTULU **18**
Labang
Long Sobin
Bukit Kalulong 4,003 ft
Long San
Lio Matoh
Sebauh
Tubau
Long Nibong
Long Palai
Rumah Melap
Bukit Punum 4,154 ft
Long Tikan
Rumah Kesing
Belepah
Long Murum
BELAGA **16**
Long Tingen
Danum
Long Geng
Merit
S A R A W A K
Bukit Batu 6,601 ft
Bukit Kerangan Nyabong 2,490 ft
Rumah Kulit
Malarang
15 KAPIT
Nanga Gaat
Rumah Jugat
Rumah Aryl
Bukit Kumbong 4,587 ft
Ban Kapuas Hulu
Mengiong
Bukit Melatai 5,098 ft

GETTING AROUND

Domestic flights connect most towns in Sarawak and are ideal for visitors with limited time. For those with a more leisurely schedule, boat rides are an exciting way of getting to the remote villages and national parks and are the most common mode of local transport. There are speedy passenger *ekspres* boats as well as longboats for long- and short-haul journeys. Because of the rugged terrain, the road network in Sarawak is limited to a highway between Kuching and the Brunei border, plus a few short routes from Kuching to places such as Bako and Semantan.

Aerial view of mangrove forests surrounding Sungai Sarawak

Kuching ❶

The capital of Sarawak, Kuching is one of Malaysia's most attractive cities with historic buildings juxtaposed against modern high-rises and restaurants. It became the capital of Rajah James Brooke's empire in the mid-19th century and was known as Sarawak until 1872 when its name was officially changed to Kuching. Long a confluence of Malay, Chinese, Indian, and indigenous people, such as the Iban and Bidayuh, Kuching reflects its varied cultural influences. Although the city sprawls both to the north and south of Sungai Sarawak, the main sights of interest, such as the waterfront, colonial buildings, and ethnic souvenir shops, are all concentrated around the south bank of the Kuching waterfront.

Sungai Sarawak meandering through the city of Kuching

🏛 Sarawak Museum
Jalan Tun Haji Openg. **Tel** (082) 244-232. ⬤ daily. ⬤ public hols. ◻◻
www.museum.sarawak.gov.my
Perhaps one of Malaysia's finest museums, the Sarawak Museum provides an overview of the province's history and ethnography. The artifacts of the museum are housed in two buildings. The older section of the main building is a colonial mansion opened in 1891 at the suggestion of naturalist Alfred Wallace who discovered many of Sarawak's endemic species of flora and fauna. The natural science section, on the first floor, includes stuffed specimens of many of Sarawak's best-known species, such as rhinoceros hornbills, hawksbill turtles, and proboscis monkeys. On the upper floor is an introduction to the traditional lifestyles of Sarawak's main indigenous groups, with displays of handicrafts, traditional dress, ceremonial artifacts,

Detail of a burial pole at Sarawak Museum

musical instruments, and various tools such as the three-pronged pricker that is used by the Iban to create tattoos. Among the highlights on display are a replica of an Iban longhouse, Iban war totems, and early 20th-century Chinese glazed jars. Rotating art exhibitions are held in the new Tun Abdul Razak Hall, opposite the old wing, which is accessible by a footbridge.

🏛 Islamic Museum
Jalan P. Ramlee. **Tel** (082) 244-232. ⬤ 9am–6pm Sat–Thu. ⬤ Fri, public hols. ◻ www.museum. sarawak.gov.my
Housed in a restored colonial building that was constructed in 1930 and once functioned as a school, the Islamic Museum presents the history of Islam and its spread in Sarawak as well as the rest of the Malay-Indonesian archipelago. Its seven galleries, each with a different theme, contain displays on

traditional Islamic design, architecture, costumes, coins, jewelry, weapons, ceramics, and weights and measures. The last gallery gives an insight into the ability of Arab seafarers to navigate accurately in uncharted waters long before the Christian world developed the capacity. There is also a display of navigational techniques using the astrolabe.

🏛 Textile Museum
Jalan Tun Haji Openg. ◻ www.museum.sarawak.gov.my
Located in the heart of the city, it is hard to miss the Pavilion, a building decorated with ornate ironwork. Built in 1907 as a hospital, it was used as a propaganda center by the invading Japanese army during World War II. Today, the Pavilion is home to Kuching's Textile Museum. Its two floors contain exhibits of everyday clothes worn by the various indigenous groups of Sarawak, as well as the costumes worn for weddings and other ceremonies. There are also models of women engaged in activities such as cloth spinning, weaving, and dyeing. Traditional *songket* and *ikat* are also on display.

🏯 Round Tower
Jalan Tun Haji Openg. **Tel** (082) 245-652. ⬤ 8:30am–12:30pm, 2–5pm Mon–Fri; 8:30am–noon Sat & Sun. www.sarawakhandicraft.com
Built in the 1880s, the Round Tower was originally intended to be a fort, but functioned instead as a dispensary in its early days. It now houses the **Sarawak Crafts Council**, which has showrooms that feature some of the province's finest handicrafts. Regular demonstrations of weaving and basket-making skills are also held here.

🏯 Jalan India
Near the waterfront. **Masjid Bandaraya** ⬤ 9am–3pm Sat–Thu. ⬤ Fri.
Located on the western edge of the city center, near the river and the city's main fresh market on Jalan Gambier, the pedestrianized Jalan India is one of Kuching's most popular shopping streets. The majority of shops here, most

Colonial buildings with ironwood roofs in the Courthouse Complex

VISITORS' CHECKLIST

SW Sarawak. 🏠 *500,000.* ✈
🚌 ℹ *Courthouse Complex,*
(082) 410-944; National Parks
and Wildlife Booking Desk,
(082) 248-088.
www.sarawaktourism.com

of which are fronted by colonial-style arches, sell textiles, shoes, brassware, and household goods, but there are also several souvenir shops and food stalls.

Dominating the western end of the street is the large and impressive **Masjid Bandaraya**, or City Mosque, topped with gilded cupolas. Built in 1968 to replace an old wooden mosque, it quickly became one of the city's most distinctive landmarks. Non-Muslims, dressed appropriately, are allowed to enter the mosque except during prayer

times. The mosque has now been superseded in size by the **State Mosque**, located across the river at Petrajaya, which can accommodate up to 14,000 worshipers.

🛕 Courthouse Complex
Junction of Main Bazaar and Jalan Tun Haji Openg.

A splendid example of Kuching's colonial heritage, the Courthouse Complex is a cluster of buildings covered with ironwood roofs that are supported by Romanesque and regal columns. It was built in 1871 as the seat of

Sarawak's government, which remained its function until 1973. The state's law courts continue to operate from here, and the main court chamber, with walls and ceiling covered with murals depicting rural life in Sarawak, is worth visiting. The **Clock Tower** at the front of the complex was added in 1883 and the granite **Charles Brooke Memorial** in 1925. At the four corners of the memorial are stone figures representing the principal ethnic groups of Sarawak – the Dayaks, Malays, Chinese, and Orang Ulu. The complex houses the Sarawak Tourism Board's **Visitor Information Center**, which has a booking desk for the National Parks and Wildlife office. Retail outlets and restaurants are also being developed here.

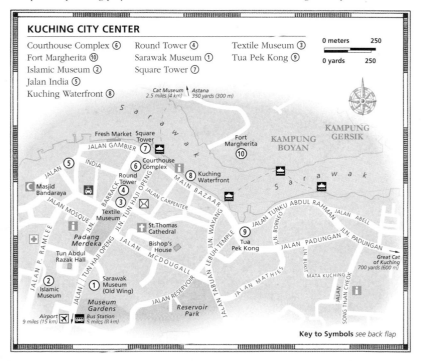

KUCHING CITY CENTER

Courthouse Complex ⑥
Fort Margherita ⑩
Islamic Museum ②
Jalan India ⑤
Kuching Waterfront ⑧
Round Tower ④
Sarawak Museum ①
Square Tower ⑦
Textile Museum ③
Tua Pek Kong ⑨

0 meters   250
0 yards   250

Cat Museum 2.5 miles (4 km) \ Astana 350 yards (300 m)

KAMPUNG GERSIK

Fresh Market Square Tower
JALAN GAMBIER ⑦
Fort Margherita ⑩
KAMPUNG BOYAN

JALAN ⑤ INDIA
Courthouse Complex ⑥
Round Tower ④
Kuching Waterfront ⑧
MAIN BAZAAR

Masjid Bandaraya
JALAN MOSQUE
Textile Museum ③
JALAN CARPENTER

St. Thomas Cathedral
Padang Merdeka
Bishop's House
JLN. WAYANG
Tua Pek Kong ⑨
JALAN TUNKU ABDUL RAHMAN
JALAN ABELL

Tun Abdul Razak Hall
MCDOUGALL
JALAN PADUNGAN
JLN PADUNGAN

② Islamic Museum
① Sarawak Museum (Old Wing)
Museum Gardens
JALAN RESERVOIR
LEBUH TABUAN
LEBUH TEMPLE
JALAN MATHIES
MATA KUCHING

Airport 9 miles (15 km) Bus Station 5 miles (8 km)
Reservoir Park
SONG THIAN CHEOK

Great Cat of Kuching 700 yards (600 m)

Key to Symbols see back flap

The historic Square Tower, today a multimedia information center

Square Tower

Main Bazaar. **Tel** (082) 426-093.
◐ 10am–4pm daily.

In 1879, the Square Tower was built by Rajah Charles Brooke just north of the Courthouse to replace a wooden fort that had been burnt down by Chinese gold-miners during a rebellion in 1857. However, the tower was never again needed as a defensive structure and over the years it was put to other uses, including a brief role as a prison and later even as a ballroom. The Square Tower, which marks one end of Kuching's beautiful waterfront, has now been converted into a tourist information center.

Kuching Waterfront

Between Square Tower and Hilton Hotel. ☐ ◢ stalls in the evening.
Sarawak Steamship Building Main Bazaar. ◐ daily. **Chinese History Museum** Main Bazaar. **Tel** (082) 231-520. ◐ 9am–6pm Sat–Thu.

A stroll along the Kuching waterfront is one of the high-lights of a visit to the city. In the mid-1990s, several dilap-idated warehouses along the waterfront were demolished and an extensive renovation project transformed this stretch into a lovely riverside promenade. Landscaped gardens, sculptures, cafés, food stalls, and benches now embellish this strip. Several plaques along the path mark historical spots. It also offers spectacular views of the Astana and Fort Margherita on the north bank of Sungai

Sarawak, and has rapidly grown into one of the city's most popular spots for jog-ging, dining, strolling, and enjoying a spectacular sunset over the river.

Set back a little from the waterfront, the Main Bazaar is the city's oldest street and is packed with shops. Two of the most significant build-ings on this street, both carefully restored, are the **Sarawak Steamship Building** and **Chinese History Museum**. The former, built in 1930, is now home to the Kuching Waterfront Bazaar, which has several souvenir and handi-crafts stalls. The museum was built by Rajah Charles Brooke in 1911 and once functioned as the Chinese Chamber of Commerce. Today, however, the museum provides an overview of the evolution of the Chinese community in Sarawak through photographs,

artifacts, documents such as maps of early trade routes, and information about their traditional trading activities.

Tua Pek Kong

Jalan Tuanku Abdul Rahman.
◐ 6am–10pm daily. ✿ Chinese New Year (Feb).

Located opposite the Chinese History Museum and over-looking the river, Tua Pek Kong is the oldest Taoist temple in Kuching, dating back to 1876. It is thought that the current structure was preceded by a Chinese temple that existed here in the late 18th century. Vibrantly colored and intricately decorated, the temple is dedicated to Tua Pek Kong, the patron saint of merchants, and is always very busy. It is built on a site carefully chosen for its geo-mancy, according to Chinese tradition. The Wang Kang festival to commemorate the dead is also held here.

Fort Margherita

North bank of Sungai Sarawak.
◢ from the jetty near the Square Tower. ◐ Tue–Sun. ◑ Mon.

Close to the Astana, along the riverbank to the east, is Fort Margherita, with crenellated, whitewashed walls and large cannon. This structure, built in 1879 by Rajah Charles Brooke and named for his wife, was the second fort to be built on the site. The first, built by his uncle, James Brooke, was burnt to the ground by rebel Chinese gold-miners in 1857. Commanding a sweeping view of Sungai

An early morning view of the Kuching waterfront

For hotels and restaurants in this region see pp282–3 and p306

Sarawak, Fort Margherita was built to protect Kuching against attack from pirates and other enemies approaching the town by the river route. However, it never fulfilled its intended purpose as Kuching did not come under attack until World War II when the Japanese took control of the entire city.

For many years, the fort was open to the public but it is currently under renovation and its future use is uncertain.

The stately Astana on the north bank of Sungai Sarawak

An imposing watch tower at Fort Margherita in Kuching

THE WHITE RAJAHS

Sir James Brooke

In 1839, British explorer James Brooke found Sarawak in the grip of a rebellion by the local Dayaks against the rule of the Sultan of Brunei. After his success in quelling the uprising, he was granted the title of Rajah of Sarawak in 1841, establishing an empire that was to last for over a century. At the time of James Brooke's death in 1868, his territory only covered what is now the southwest corner of Sarawak – the area around Kuching. It was his successor and nephew, Charles Brooke, who was responsible for expanding Sarawak to the current size, and also for commissioning most of the town's colonial buildings. A stickler for detail, he made frequent unannounced inspections of his officers, and any slack conduct was severely punished. Upon his death in 1917, Charles was succeeded by his son, Charles Vyner Brooke, and for a while Sarawak was run as a personal fiefdom. This ended with the Japanese invasion in 1941. After World War II, Vyner Brooke ceded the territory to Britain, and in 1963 it became part of the Federation of Malaysia.

🏯 Astana

North bank of Sungai Sarawak.
🛥 from the jetty near the Square Tower. **Note** only open to public on Hari Raya Puasa.

On the north bank of the river lies Kuching's most important historical building, the impressive Astana. The name is a local version of the Malay word istana, meaning palace. The Astana was built in 1870 by Rajah Charles Brooke as a gift to his bride, Margaret. She later reminisced about her time here in her 1913 memoir, *My Life in Sarawak*.

Set among manicured lawns and offering a lovely view of the Courthouse on the south bank, the palace consists of three elegant bungalows with wooden shingle roofs. Charles Brooke is said to have grown betel nut on the palace grounds so that he could offer it to visiting Dayak chiefs. The Astana still functions as the official residence of the governor of Sarawak.

🏯 Cat Statues

Kuching means cat in Malay and although the origin of the city's name is uncertain, there are several statues of cats around the town, giving it a unique identity. The statues are all located on the south bank of Sungai Sarawak, and include a small statue on the waterfront just east of the Chinese History Museum, a larger one opposite the Hilton Kuching *(see p283)* on Jalan Tun Abdul Rahman, and a third at the base of a pillar farther east along Jalan Pandungan. The biggest statue, the 5-ft (1.5-m) tall **Great Cat of Kuching**, sits at the junction of Jalan Padungan and Jalan Central.

🏛 Cat Museum

North of Kuching City Hall. *Tel* (082) 446-688. 🚌 Petra Jaya bus 2C or 2D. 🕐 Tue–Sun. 🔴 Mon & public hols. 📷 RM3 for use of camera, RM5 for use of video.

Located in the new town of Petra Jaya, on the north bank of the river, the Cat Museum moved here in 1993 and claims to be one of the few such museums in the world dedicated exclusively to cats. It covers everything to do with cats, and the exhibits include cat-related art, stamps, photographs, music, movies, and even Garfield comic strips.

Sungai Santubong ❷

12 miles (20 km) N of Kuching.
🚌 tour bus to Santubong jetty.
🚤 tour boats between 4 and 5pm.
🚩 from Kuching.

After meandering through the plains around Kuching, Sungai Santubong flows through Sarawak into the South China Sea. During the dry season, between March and October, groups of the rare Irrawaddy dolphin are sometimes seen feeding and playing around the mouth of the river. These small, snub-nosed dolphins are often difficult to spot as they do not leap out of the water like their better-known seafaring cousins. Nevertheless, the experience of watching these unusal creatures is a major draw on the popular boat trips along the river.

Some cruises continue down the adjoining Sungai Salak to **Kuching Wetlands National Park**. Covering a vast expanse of saline mangrove swamps and patches of scrubland, the wetlands also include a network of small water channels and tidal creeks. The swamps are inhabited by a variety of wildlife, including proboscis monkeys, lorises, and colorful birds. In the evenings, large groups of fireflies illuminate the riverside trees. River cruises are the only way to explore the wetlands, and a number of tour operators in Kuching offer trips.

🌲 Kuching Wetlands National Park
9 miles (15 km) N of Kuching.
🚤 🏞 🚩

Lagoon-style pool at the Holiday Inn Resort at Damai Beach

Santubong ❸

19 miles (32 km) N of Kuching.
🏔 800. 🚌 Petra Jaya bus 2B.

This fishing village sits near Sungai Santubong in the shadow of the 2,657-ft (810-m) Gunung Santubong. During the Tang and Sung dynasties, which lasted from the 9th century to the 13th century, Santubong was an important trading center. Today, it is merely a small village but it is worth visiting for the colorful wooden houses built on stilts and fishing boats on the beach, which are very photogenic. The morning is the liveliest time in Santubong when the fishermen sell their daily catch at the quay. The cafés nearby are well known for their excellent seafood.

From the main road into Santubong is a small turning which leads to **Sungai Jaong**, one of the most important archaeological sites in Sarawak. Among its artifacts are ancient Buddhist and Hindu rock carvings, thought to be about 1,000 years old. A reclining human figure is still well-defined, but many other carvings have eroded.

Damai Beach ❹

21 miles (35 km) N of Kuching.
🚌 Petra Jaya bus 2B. 🍴 🏖 🎿

On the west coast of the Santubong Peninsula, Damai is one of Sarawak's prettiest beaches. Only a short journey from Kuching, and featuring some beautifully designed resorts, the beach is a popular tourist destination and can get quite crowded on weekends. There is a wide selection of watersports on offer, including sailing, snorkeling, and windsurfing, as well as other activities such as mountain biking and golf. Cafés and restaurants here have gained a reputation for their superb fresh seafood dishes.

Picturesque trails around Gunung Santubong begin here and trekking is a popular activity for visitors to Damai Beach. The Santubong Jungle Trek, with blue trail markers, is an easy, circular 1-mile (1.6-km) walk that starts at the Holiday Inn Resort Damai Beach (see p282). A more challenging route that also begins here is the Gunung Santubong Summit Trek, winding up to the top. The trail, with red markers, takes 5- to 7-hours to complete. It also requires a good level of fitness, sturdy hiking shoes, and plenty of drinking water. The resorts at Damai can arrange for guides.

Gunung Santubong towering over Sungai Santubong

For hotels and restaurants in this region see pp282–3 and p306

Sarawak Cultural Village ❺

21 miles (35 km) N of Kuching. *Tel (082) 846-411.* 🚌 *tour bus and Petra Jaya bus 2B.* ⭘ *9am–5:15pm daily; cultural shows at 11:30am and 4:30pm daily.* 🖼 🚻 📷 🛍 *Harvest Festival (May), Rainforest World Music Festival (Jul).* **www**.scv.com.my

Located at the foot of Gunung Santubong, Sarawak Cultural Village serves as an excellent introduction to the cultural traditions of Sarawak. Erected by the Sarawak Development Corporation in the early 1990s to give visitors a taste of indigenous lifestyles, the village comprises seven houses clustered around a lake, each a good example of the traditional dwellings built by the main indigenous groups. Iban, Bidayuh, and Orang Ulu longhouses sit side by side with a Melanau tall-house, a Penan hut, a Chinese farmhouse and a Malay house. Women and men of respective groups live in these dwellings and also demonstrate art and craft skills, such as wood carving, textile and basket-weaving, swordmaking, and beadwork. Outside the Melanau tall-house is a demonstration of a traditional sago press, while the process of blowpipe-making can be seen at the Penan hut. Visitors can take part in 3- to 4-day courses to learn a particular ethnic skill or craft. A cultural show featuring traditional music and dancers in elaborate costumes is also held daily at the indoor theater located in the village.

RAINFOREST WORLD MUSIC FESTIVAL

In July each year, Sarawak Cultural Village hosts this festival, which celebrates music from around the world. This 3-day event, which has been held every year since 1998, previously featured musicians from as far away as Mali, Mongolia, and Madagascar. The festival now also provides a rare opportunity to hear indigenous musicians from various regions of Malaysia. Seminars and workshops are held during the day, spontaneous jam sessions take place in the longhouses, and artistes perform on outdoor stages in the evenings. The exotic setting around a lake against the backdrop of Gunung Santubong makes for an electric atmosphere. Accommodation is available at the resorts on Damai Beach, and frequent buses run from Kuching for those who prefer to stay in town. It is advisable to check the official website (**www.** rainforestmusic-borneo.com) for information on events.

Jerry Kamit, a *sape* (lute-like instrument) virtuoso

All traditional artifacts that are produced at the village can also be purchased from the handicraft shop as souvenirs.

Kubah National Park and Matang Wildlife Center ❻

12 miles (20 km) W of Kuching. *Tel (082) 231-044.* 🚌 *from Kuching.* 🖼 🍴 🅰 **www**.sarawakforestry.com

Encompassing 9 sq miles (22 sq km), Kubah National Park is one of the smallest parks in Sarawak. A sandstone plateau and three peaks – the 2,990-ft (911-m) Gunung Serapi and the smaller Gunung Selang and Gunung Sendok – form the backdrop to this wildlife haven. Among the dipterocarp (hardwood) forests and gentle waterfalls and streams are more than 90 species of palms and a wide variety of orchids. Although there are bearded pigs, mouse deer, and other wildlife, these are rarely seen. Visitors are more likely to spot birds such as the maroon woodpecker or the rufus-collared kingfisher.

Several trails crisscross the park and the mountains including the beautiful Waterfall Trail that leads through split-level falls and a 2- to 3-hour hike to the mist-shrouded peak of Gunung Serapi. The Rayu Trail links Kubah to the adjacent **Matang Wildlife Center**, a rehabilitation center for endangered species such as orangutans, sambar deer, hornbills, and proboscis monkeys. Along the Pitcher Trail are several varieties of the carnivorous pitcher plant. Accommodation for the parks may be booked in advance at the Visitor Information Center in Kuching (*see p155*).

🦧 **Matang Wildlife Center**
8 miles (13 km) N of Kubah. *Tel (082) 225-012.* 🚌 *to Kubah or Matang Polytechnic, then local minibus.* 🖼 🏠 🍴 🅰

A Bidayuh woman weaving rattan baskets at the Sarawak Cultural Village

Sematan ⓿

100 km (62 miles) W of Kuching.
🚶 2,300. 🚌 from Kuching to
Lundu, STC 17 from Lundu.
🎭 Sematan Carnival (Aug).

The coastal village of Sematan
is a popular weekend retreat
for Kuching residents. There
is a long, quiet beach lined
with coconut palms and colorful fishing boats are harbored
in the bay. The village itself is
small, consisting of a few rows
of shophouses, a local market
with food stalls that serve
delicious fish dishes, a busy
timber dock, and a jetty. Boats
go from Sematan to Teluk
Melano, a Malay fishing village nestled in a pretty bay
on the Datu Peninsula.
The village has a home-
stay program that is
organized by the
Malaysian Fisheries
Board, which enables
visitors to stay with local
families. Boat trips to Teluk
Melano are not possi-
ble in the monsoon
season, from October to
March, as the sea is too rough.

**Flowers at
Tanjung Datu**

Providing a boost to local
tourism is the annual Sematan
Carnival that takes place here
in August. The 3-day event
hosts a music festival, beach
games, and an exhibition of
local products.

Tanjung Datu National Park ⓿

14 miles (23 km) from Sematan.
🚤 chartered from Sematan or
Teluk Melano. 🌐 Apr–Sep. 🎭
www.sarawakforestry.com

Occupying just 14 sq km
(5 sq miles) on the western-
most tip of the state, Tanjung
Datu is one of Sarawak's
smaller national parks. It has
two beautiful beaches, Pasir
Antu and Pasir Berunpu,
backed by towering peaks.
The real highlight of the park
are the beautiful coral reefs,
visible in the crystal-clear
water and close enough to
the shore to walk around.
Artificial reefs farther out in
the sea are accessible
by boat. The park's
lush rainforest is
home to varied
wildlife, so visitors
are likely to hear
gibbon-cries and may
even spot dolphins and
turtles near the shore.
Tanjung Datu has four
trails of varying lengths leading through an unspoilt forest
and coastline. There are currently no facilities for visitors
at the park, but given its natural beauty and the idyllic
landscape, a day trip to
the park is worth the effort.

**Trekking through a lush trail at
Gunung Gading National Park**

Permits for the park and entry
tickets should be obtained
from the Visitor Information
Center in Kuching *(see p155)*.

Gunung Gading National Park ⓿

50 miles (80 km) W of Kuching.
🚌 STC 17 from Lundu. 🛈 **Tel** (082)
735-714 (Park HQ). 🕗 8:30am–
12:30pm, 2–5pm daily. 🎭 🎭 🎭
🅰 www.sarawakforestry.com

In 1983, Gunung Gading
National Park was established
as a conservation area for the
world's largest flower, the
rafflesia. Visitors can view the
flowers from walkways which
have been designed to prevent
people from treading on the
fragile young buds that sprout
inconspicuously. The bud
grows into a foul-smelling red
flower with white specks, and
reaches a width of up to 3 ft
(1 m). This rare parasitic plant
blooms at unpredictable times
and lasts only a few days,
therefore it is advisable to call
the park ahead to check if
one is in bloom. Visitors can
also see *Amorphophallus*, a
gigantic herbaceous plant of
the aroid family.
The park sprawls across
four jungle-clad mountains,
Gunung Gading, Gunung
Perigi, Gunung Lundu, and
Gunung Sebuloh. Color-coded
trails of varying levels of dif-
ficulty crisscross the park. The
easiest is the Waterfall Trail
which passes through seven
cataracts. The challenging

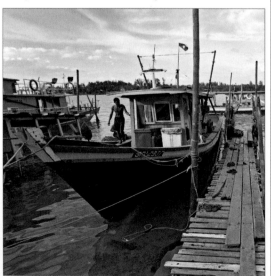

Fishing boats docked at the Sematan jetty

For hotels and restaurants in this region see pp282–3 and pp306

Gunung Gading Trail leads up to the summit of the 2,985-ft (910-m) hill. Visitors will also find a natural pool near the Park Headquarters.

Wind Cave and Fairy Cave ⑩

31 miles (50 km) SW of Kuching.
STC 2 to Bau from Kuching, then taxi. from Kuching.
www.sarawakforestry.com

Two caves formed in a range of limestone cliffs located near the former gold-mining town of Bau make an interesting day trip from Kuching. Wind Cave, 2 miles (3 km) west of Bau, is made up of a network of underground streams that pass through the cave before joining Sungai Kayan. The cave's smooth, tubular interior is filled with stalagmite and stalactite pillars. A boardwalk passes right through the cave to the river at the other end, which is a popular spot for picnics and swimming. To protect the cave and its surrounding limestone forest, which is home to a number of rare plant species, including some types of palms, Wind Cave has been designated as a nature reserve.

Fairy Cave, 3 miles (5 km) farther south, is larger and accessed by a flight of steps leading up to the cave mouth. Its main chamber also contains a series of stalagmite formations. One of these, thought to resemble Kuan Yin, the Chinese goddess of mercy,

Mother and baby orangutans at Semenggoh Nature Reserve

has transformed the chamber into a popular shrine. Neither of the two caves is illuminated and flashlights are essential in the dark interior.

Semenggoh Nature Reserve ⑪

15 miles (24 km) SW of Kuching.
Tel (082) 618-325. STC 6 from Kuching. 8am–12:45pm, 2–4:15pm daily. **www**.sarawak forestry.com

This reserve functions as a rehabilitation center for honey bears, orangutans, crocodiles, monkeys, gibbons, hornbills, and porcupines, all of which were either orphaned due to hunting or rescued from cages where they were kept illegally as pets. Reintroducing

orangutans to their natural habitat is the primary aim of this nature reserve and its orangutan rehabilitation program has been particularly successful, resulting in a thriving population of semi-wild orangutans inhabiting the surrounding forest. With the forest having reached its capacity to hold the primates, the program has now been transferred to the Matang Wildlife Center *(see p159)*. Since the orangutans roam freely, spotting them is not guaranteed. The best chance to see them is at feeding time, around 9am and 3pm.

There are also pleasant walking trails around the reserve. A Botanical Research Center here is dedicated to analysing jungle plants with medicinal properties.

THE BIDAYUH

The Bidayuh are one of the largest indigenous Dayak groups living in Sarawak and have traditionally been farmers and hunters. Concentrated in the area west of Kuching, their longhouses dot the slopes of Anna Rais. Unlike other Dayak groups of Sarawak, they build their longhouses at the foot of hills rather than on riverbanks. The British referred to them as "Land Dayaks" to distinguish them from the "Sea Dayaks" – such as the Iban – who traveled everywhere by boat. The Biyaduh are particularly skilled at bamboo-carving, basket-weaving, and beadwork. Women can be seen sitting on the *ruai*, or communal veranda, making bead-covered hats that are used for special occasions. Among these is the Gawai Padi festival, held in early June, when Bidayuhs give thanks to the rice goddess for a bountiful harvest. The celebration involves singing, dancing, and drinking.

The terrace, *ruai*, of a Bidayuh longhouse

Bako National Park ⑫

Established in 1957, Bako was Sarawak's first national park. Spread across 10 sq miles (27 sq km), it nurtures vegetation that ranges from rain forest to swampland and mangrove forests to *kerangas*, or scrubland. With steep rocky cliffs punctuated by deep bays, white sandy beaches, and a mangrove-fringed coastline, Bako is a nature-lover's paradise. It is also one of the best parks in Malaysia for spotting rare animals, such as proboscis monkeys, bearded pigs, sambar deer, and macaques, which makes it a popular destination for wildlife enthusiasts. Though the park can be visited on a day trip, the chances of wildlife sightings are higher in the early morning and in the evening, so an overnight trip is advisable.

South China Sea

Area of map
Illustrated

KEY

☐ Bako National Park

★ **Sea Stacks**
These towering rock formations are a peculiar characteristic of Bako's coastline. They were formed by the action of the sea on the softer sandstone at the base of the cliffs, which eroded, leaving behind pillars of harder limestone.

South China Sea

Teluk
Pandan
Kecil

Teluk
Pandan
Besar

Teluk Batu
Belah

Teluk Paku

TELUK PANDAN BESAR T.

KAMPUNG
BAKO   Teluk
Assam

Bako Park
Headquarters

Bukit
Tambi

Tanjung
Sapi

ULU ASSAM

Teluk
Delima

SERAIT TRAIL

LINTANG TRAIL

★ **Bako's Wildlife**
Bako offers opportunities to spot a diverse range of wildlife, including flying lemurs, monitor lizards, and 150 species of birds. However, the stars of the park are the endangered proboscis monkeys, named for their prominent nose, who forage in groups for mangrove leaves.

Teluk Delima Trail is one of the best trails in Bako for spotting proboscis monkeys.

Lintang Trail is a 3-mile (5-km) long loop route that climbs to a sandstone plateau before plunging down to the coast.

0 km   1

0 miles   1

STAR SIGHTS

★ Sea Stacks

★ Bako's Wildlife

★ Tajor Waterfall

Sundew Plant
With much of the soil in Bako lacking nutrients, carnivorous plants such as the pitcher and sundew plants must attract and trap insects to derive sustenance from their victims.

VISITORS' CHECKLIST

25 miles (40 km) N of Kuching.
🚌 to Bako village, then boat to the Park. *Tel* (011) 225-049 (Park HQ). 🔲 🅰
Permits for camping should be booked in advance in Kuching at the Visitor Information Center (see p155).
www.sarawakforestry.com

Tajor Trail, 2 miles (3 km) long, includes a brisk climb up to *kerangas* scrubland before descending into a shady forest.

EXPLORING THE PARK

There are several trails in the park, and each one is color-coded with splashes of paint on trees, making it easy to explore without a guide. Viewpoints along the trails offer great views. There are lodges and a campsite near the Park Headquarters but bookings should be made well in advance.

★ **Tajor Waterfall**
A popular picnic spot, Tajor Waterfall is 2 miles (4 km) down the Tajor Trail. The waterfall is quite small and has a dip pool. The best time to visit is after a heavy rainfall. It takes about two hours to get to the waterfall from the Park Headquarters.

KEY

—— Trail

－－ Park boundary

- - Ferry route

🛳 Ferry port

ℹ Visitor information

🅰 Campsite

▲ Peak

MONKEY BUSINESS IN BAKO

Relatively accustomed to the presence of visitors, long-tailed macaques are easy to spot as they scavenge for food near the Park Headquarters. While a close sighting can initially be thrilling, macaques can be intimidating and are likely to snatch bags or possessions if left unguarded for a moment. Even the garbage disposal system has to be specially designed to keep the macaques out.

A female macaque carrying an infant

Colorful longboats moored on the banks of the Batang Rajang

Batang Rajang ⑬

From Kuching. 🚢 *Bintawa Wharf,*
daily boat from Kuching to Sibu at
8:30am. 🚌 *daily.* 🎏 *Gawai Padi*
Festival (May–Jun).

Flowing 348 miles (560 km)
through the heart of Sarawak,
the vast Batang Rajang is
Sarawak's longest river and
the main artery of trade for
towns in the central and
southern parts of the province. The upper reaches are
the heartland of the timber
industry, and the river is often
muddy with topsoil and
littered with debris from
various logging operations.

This region is populated
largely by the indigenous
people, and the banks of the
river and its tributaries are
scattered with longhouses.
The lower reaches of the river
are inhabited predominantly
by the Iban people, while the
upper section mostly contains
the dwellings of the Kayan
and Kenyah. Trips up the
river to these longhouses can
be arranged through tour
operators in Kuching, Sibu,
and Kapit. Independent travel
is also possible, but it is
essential that visitors wait to
be invited in before entering
a traditional longhouse.

Boats are a major form of
transportation between the
towns that flank the Batang

Rajang. The jetties of all the
towns teem with huge *ekspres*
boats as well as the smaller,
motorized longboats. It is
possible to travel the entire
distance from Kuching to
Belaga by boat. The first leg
of this journey is up to the
town of Sibu, the principal
transport hub on the Batang
Rajang. The jetties are divided
between upriver and
downriver traffic, which
provides easy access to
Kanowit and Kapit.

The journey from
Kapit to the town of
Belaga, a further six
hours away, passes
through the treach-
erous Pelagus
Rapids, a 1.5-mile
(2.5-km) stretch of
cataracts and whirl-
pools caused by a
sudden drop in the
riverbed. Boats may
not run at all on
this stretch when
the water level in
the rapids is dangerously low,
usually between May and
August. Beyond Belaga, the
Rajang divides into Sungai
Belaga and Batang Balui.

The best time for a trip up
the Batang Rajang is between
late May and early June to
coincide with the Gawai
Padi *(see p51)* festival celebrated by the Dayak people
in their longhouses.

**Temple guardian,
Tua Pek Kong Temple**

Sibu ⑭

120 miles (193 km) NE of Kuching.
🏠 200,000. ✈ 🚌 *Sungei Antu.*
🚢 *Jalan Khoo Peng Loong.* ℹ *32*
Jalan Cross, (084) 340-980. 🚌 *daily.*

The capital of Sarawak's
largest district, Sibu is also the
major port of the province
and an important economic
center, managing trade
between the coast and the
hinterland. The town's
early growth was
funded by the rubber
industry, run mostly
by Chinese mer-
chants who were
encouraged by Rajah
Charles Brooke to
set up businesses
here. Later, they
also established a
thriving timber trade.

Among the sights
of Sibu is the 100-
year-old temple dedi-
cated to Tua Pek
Kong, the patron
saint of merchants. Located
on the western end of the
waterfront, the temple has a
beautiful seven-story pagoda
with fantastic views of the
town and river.

North of the city center is
the **Sibu Civic Center Heritage
Museum**, which traces the
town's history through old
photographs and artifacts.
The museum also has a rich

collection of white ceramics that dates back to the 10th and 12th centuries.

Environs
Located about 40 miles (65 km) upriver of Sibu, **Kanowit** is a small place with few sights of interest. The main highlight is Fort Emma, built by Rajah James Brooke in 1859 and named after his sister. Constructed of bamboo and timber, it was an attempt to prevent Iban raids on Melanau tribes on the Batang Rajang. Eventually, the place became key to the success of the Rajahs' rule. The fort is not open to the public.

🏛 Sibu Civic Center Heritage Museum
Jalan Tun Haji Openg. ☐ 3–8pm Tue–Sat, 9am–noon & 2–8pm Sun.

Kapit ⓯

124 miles (200 km) E of Sibu.
🏠 99,840. ✈ 🚢 from Sibu.
ℹ (084) 796-445.

Kapit is a small but bustling riverside town, with an attractive waterfront lined with trees and plants. The town's main landmark is the historic **Fort Sylvia**, a whitewashed ironwood structure named after the wife of Vyner Brooke, the third of the White Rajahs. It was built in 1880 in an effort to control Iban head-hunting parties in the region. In 1997 the fort was listed as a historical monument, and now houses a museum and a

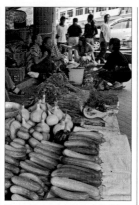

Vegetable vendor at the colorful daily market in Kapit

training center for artisans. There is also an interesting museum at the town's civic center, which has displays of Iban and Orang Ulu long-houses as well as photo-graphs of the early days.

Kapit is also a trading center for the indigenous people that inhabit the upriver areas. A lively market sets up daily, near the center of town, packed with vendors selling an assortment of jungle pro-duce, such as vegetables, tropical fruits, and beeswax. A major draw for most visitors to Kapit is a chance to visit the remote longhouses along the upper tributaries of the mighty Batang Rajang.

Environs
Located just 6 miles (10 km) from Kapit, **Rumah Seligi** is an authentic Iban longhouse that is the home to about 40

families. The best time to visit is in the late afternoon, as most longhouse residents work in the fields through the day. Guests are usually shown around and often offered a glass of *tuak*, the potent rice wine.

🏰 Fort Sylvia
Jalan Kubu. *Tel* (084) 799-171. ☐ 10am–noon, 2–5pm Tue–Sun.

🏰 Rumah Seligi
🚌 irregular service from Jalan Airport, Kapit.

Belaga ⓰

93 miles (150 km) NE of Kapit.
🏠 25,300. ✈ to Bintulu. 🚢 from Kapit. 🚢 daily. **Belaga Hotel** 14 Belaga Bazaar. *Tel* (086) 461-244.

The last settlement of any significant size on the Batang Rajang, Belaga has a wider mix of ethnic groups than any other town in Sarawak. Apart from Iban, Kayan, Kenyah, and Penan people, who bring their jungle produce to sell at the Belaga bazaar, the town is also visited by seasonal collectors of wild honey from Kalimantan. Few foreign visitors make it so deep into Sarawak, but if they do, it is one of the best places to arrange visits to Kenyah and Kayan longhouses, common to this section of the river. These longhouses feature *salong*, or intricately carved tomb mark-ers, which can be seen from a distance. Arrangements for a longhouse visit can be made at the **Belaga Hotel**.

The bright, whitewashed exterior of Fort Sylvia on the Kapit waterfront

Mukah

112 miles (180 km) NE of Kuching.
🏠 55,000. ✈️ 🚌 🎭 Pesta Kaul
(2nd week of Apr).

Located on the coast north of Sibu *(see p164)*, Mukah is a quiet fishing town that offers a glimpse into the lifestyle of the Melanau, the indigenous group that predominates in this region. A few of their traditional tall-houses can still be seen in the area, although most Melanau prefer simple Malay dwellings now. The majority of the town's sights are clustered along the south bank of Sungai Mukah, and include the market and Tua Pek Kong Temple, whose walls are adorned with well-executed murals of Buddhist and Taoist deities.

Mukah springs to life in mid-April to celebrate the Pesta Kaul *(see p51)* festival, held annually to appease the sea spirits and mark the beginning of a new fishing season. As part of the festivities, the Melanau dance to folk rhythms on the beach and sway back and forth on a *tibau*, a tall swing used as part of a fertility rite.

A short distance from town is Kampung Tellian, a fishing village with colorful boats, winding lanes, and narrow bridges. Here, the **Lamin Dana** museum is dedicated to the preservation of Melanau culture with exhibits of textiles, betel nut boxes, and rattan baskets. Traditional tall-houses are available for overnight stays.

🏛 **Lamin Dana**
Kampung Tellian. 📞 *(082) 241-735.*
🕘 9am–5pm Mon–Sat.
www.lamindana.com

Bintulu ⑱

221 miles (356 km) NE of Kuching.
🏠 100,000. ✈️ 🚌 🚢 **www.**
bintulu.net.my

Originally a fishing and farming center on Sungai Kemena, Bintulu experienced a period of intense development in the late 1970s when Malaysia's largest natural gas reserves were discovered just

offshore. This led to the construction of an oil terminal and Bintulu Port, Malaysia's second-largest deep-sea port.

Among the prominent buildings in town is a tower called the **Council Negeri Monument**. Located in the western part of town near the river, the monument commemorates the first meeting of the Legislative Council of Sarawak during September 1867. Also worth visiting are **Masjid Assyakirin**, a Moorish-style mosque bearing a distinctive blue dome and set in well-landscaped grounds, and **Kuan Yin Tong Temple**, which features a beautiful rock garden and an artificial waterfall.

Across the river, Kampung Jepak features Melanau stilt houses and is famous for its *belacan*, a pungent shrimp paste used in Malay cooking. **Taman Tumbina**, a short distance north of town, is a compact recreational park, the ideal place to escape the bustle of town.

Monument marking the founding of the Sarawak Legislative Council

A boardwalk across a small stream in Similajau National Park

Similajau National Park ⑲

13 miles (21 km) NE of Bintulu.
Tel (086) 391-284. 🚌 🚢 *speedboat from Bintulu.* 🕘 *daily.* 🎭 🌿 🅰
www.sarawakforestry.com

Occupying just 27 sq miles (70 sq km), Similajau National Park was established in 1976 to create a protected habitat for the green turtles that nest on its beaches each year. Visitor facilities were added only in the 1990s and Similajau is still one of Sarawak's least visited parks.

A 19-mile (31-km) strip of coastline lined by trees and punctuated by rocky headlands offers visitors some of the country's best beaches. The park's main walking trail is well marked and follows the coast. Interesting routes branch off from it, including the **Viewpoint** and the **Selansur Rapids Trails**. The path ends at Golden Beach, which is great for swimming. Walkers can look out for gibbons and banded langurs, as well as flying foxes, which are under threat in other regions due to excessive hunting. The park supports over 180 bird species, including the hook-billed bulbul and the wrinkled hornbill. Saltwater crocodiles live in some of the larger rivers and signs posted in the park warn against swimming here.

Dolphins and porpoises are occasionally found swimming in groups close to the shore, and are best viewed from a boat trip along the coast.

Iban Longhouses

Traditionally, all indigenous groups of Sarawak lived in communal longhouses that reflected the tight-knit nature of tribal culture. One of the largest Dayak groups, the Iban migrated to Sarawak from Kalimantan's Kapual River basin (now in Indonesia) between the 16th and 18th centuries. Most Iban longhouses, called *rumah panjang,* or *rumah panjai,* are located in the Skrang, Lemanak, Batang Ai, and Batang Rajang

A traditionally tattooed Iban man

areas, and visiting them often involves a longboat trip. Generally erected next to rivers, most longhouses are stilt dwellings built of timber, with thatched roofs and bamboo or rattan woven walls tied together with fiber from creepers. Staying in a longhouse is the highlight of a visit to the province as the Iban make excellent hosts, often welcoming visitors with *tuak,* or rice wine, a meal, and providing a longhouse tour.

Traditional thatched roofs are now often replaced by the more durable corrugated iron.

Stilts support the structure, which is accessed by steps made of steeply-angled tree trunks.

Private rooms, or *bilek,* line the *ruai,* a long, covered communal veranda.

A TRADITIONAL LONGHOUSE

The main internal division of the longhouse is created by a wall through the center of the building. On one side is a wide communal veranda, while on the other is a row of *bilek,* or private rooms, each entered by a single door. The kitchen area is inside the *bilek.*

The area beneath the living quarters has chickens and pigs, rooting for scraps which fall through the bamboo slats.

An outdoor veranda *called* tanju *fronts the longhouse and runs along the length of the building. The veranda's split-bamboo floor is exposed to rain and sun. This area is used mainly for drying rice, coffee, cocoa beans, pepper, and even clothes.*

A wide public veranda, *or* ruai, *runs down the middle of the longhouse, with all* bilek *facing out onto it. The* ruai *is used for socializing and making handicraft items.*

Miri ⑳

516 miles (830 km) NE of Kuching.
🏠 *300,000.* **Tel** *(082) 764-231.*
✈ 🚌 🚢 *Sat & Sun.* 🎷 *Miri International Jazz Festival (May), Hari Gawai (Jun).* **www**.*miri.net.my*

Originally a quiet fishing village, Sarawak's second largest city Miri emerged as a major commercial center when Malaysia's first oil well was drilled here in 1910. In the 1970s, the onshore oil-fields closed down and Miri shifted its focus to developing its tourism industry.

Packed with markets and cafés, the atmospheric old town around Jalan China is the liveliest part of the city. Among the most interesting markets is Tamu Muhibba, or local market, where upriver indigenous people come to sell jungle produce such as tropical fruits, rattan mats, and Bario rice. The city's biggest wet market on the northern end of Jalan China borders the simple red-and-yellow building of the Tua Pek Kong temple. The **Al Taqwa Mosque**, with its whitewashed arches and a huge golden dome framed by palm trees is also worth a visit. Perhaps Miri's most significant site, perched atop Canada Hill, is Oil Well No. 1. The site of Malaysia's first oil excavation, it is now a National Monument. Close to it, the new **Petroleum Museum** documents the growth of this industry. The discovery of a number of

Vegetables for sale in the Tamu Muhibba Market

superb reefs around Miri's coast, teeming with electric-blue angel fish, and blue-spotted sting rays, has been a boost to its tourism industry.

⊂ Al Taqwa Mosque
Jalan Merpati. **Tel** *(085) 412-291.*
⊙ *non-Muslims welcome outside prayer times.*

🏛 Petroleum Museum
Canada Hill. ⊙ *9am–5pm daily.* 📷

Niah Caves National Park ㉑

71 miles (115 km) S of Miri. 🚹 *park headquarters, Pengkalan Batu, Miri;* (085) 737-450. 🚌 *from Miri to Batu Niah, then taxi.* ⊙ *8am–5pm daily.*
📷 🚫 💻 🚻 ♿ 🅰 *may be booked in advance at Miri's Visitor Information Center.* **www**.*sarawakforestry.com*

Considered by many to be the most important archaeological site in Southeast Asia, the Niah caves are among Sarawak's most spectacular attractions. In 1958, Tom Harrison, curator of the Sarawak Museum in Kuching, discovered skulls and tools at the mouth of the Great Cave – evidence that the caves had been inhabited by humans 40,000 years ago. With the enormous Great Cave as its centerpiece, the national park was established in 1975, covering 12 sq miles (32 sq km) of dense rainforest and limestone outcrops

From the Park Headquarters, a short boat ride across Sungai Niah takes visitors to the board-walk that links the caves. The first is Traders' Cave, named for the guano and birds' nest collectors who once sold their harvest here. Farther along is the Great Cave, one of the world's largest caves. It measures a staggering 820 ft (250 m) in width and has a 196-ft (60-m) high cave mouth. It is home to several species of swiftlets and bats, and during the harvest season, nest and bat guano collectors camp inside the cave. From within the Great Cave, the trail continues to the Painted Cave, where ancient rock paintings made with red hematite stone cover a narrow 98-ft (30-m) strip on the back wall. Several small boat-shaped coffins called death-ships were also found in the cave, indicating that it may have been used once as a burial chamber. The paintings and the coffins are protected by a fence. The caves are dimly lit so it is wise to carry a flashlight.

Rock formations in the Painted Cave at Niah Caves National Park

For hotels and restaurants in this region see pp282–3 and p306

Pantu waterfall at Lambir Hills National Park

Lambir Hills National Park ⓒ

20 miles (32 km) S of Miri. **i** *park headquarters, (085) 491-030.* 🚌 *from Miri.* ⏰ *8am–5pm daily.* 🎫 🖥 🔗 🅰 *may be booked in advance at the Visitor Information Center in Kuching or Miri.* **www** sarawakforestry.com

With its range of rugged sandstone hills, mixed dipterocarp (hardwood) forest, low-lying *kerangas*, or scrubland, and teeming wildlife, Lambir Hills National Park is a popular weekend getaway from Miri. Among its main attractions are sparkling waterfalls that cascade into natural swimming pools. There are also some excellent jungle trails that lead to the falls, ranging from easy 15-minute strolls to all-day hikes. The longest is the 4-hour trek to the summit of Bukit Lambir for a scenic view of the park. Closest to the park headquarters is the Latak waterfall, with an enticing pool and sandy beach, while deeper into the jungle are the Pantu and Pancur waterfalls.

Although the animals here may be difficult to spot, the national park is home to flying squirrels, gibbons, pangolins, clouded leopard, and barking deer, as well as numerous species of birds. There are several Iban longhouses, including Rumah Nakat, which has an interesting traditional handicraft center.

Loagan Bunut National Park ⓒ

81 miles (130 km) SE of Miri. **Tel** *(085) 779-410.* 🚌 *from Miri to Lapok, then taxi.* ⏰ *8am–5pm daily.* 🎫 🔗 *Entry permits must be booked in advance at the Visitor Information Center in Kuching or Miri.* **www**.sarawakforestry.com

Consisting of Bunut Lake, Sarawak's biggest freshwater lake, and the surrounding dense peat swamp and dipterocarp forest, Loagan Bunut National Park is a birdwatcher's paradise. A profusion of bird species inhabit this park, including herons, darters, kingfishers, egrets, magpies, robins, and hornbills. The lake is dependent on the water levels of the Bunut and Tinjar rivers, and often dries up completely for a few weeks in February, May, and June. At this time, the local fishermen practice a unique type of fishing called *selambau* to catch fish that are stranded in the receding waters. The fish are scooped up in huge nets mounted on spoon-shaped wooden frames. Boat cruises on the lake's tranquil waters, especially rewarding in the early morning and dusk, can be arranged at the park headquarters. A few trails, lined with *tapang* and *belian* trees, lead through the forest. Limited access makes this a seldom-visited park, but new roads and visitor facilities are being planned to attract tourists to the park.

Kingfisher at Loagan Bunut

Kelabit Highlands ⓒ

116 miles (190 km) SE of Miri. ✈ *from Miri to Bario.* 🎫 *from Miri.*

One of Borneo's most isolated and unspoilt regions, Kelabit Highlands is a 3,281-ft (1,000-m) high plateau that is home to the hospitable Kelabit people. A visit to one of their longhouses is a highlight of a trip to this spectacular region. Among the most populous of the highland settlements is **Bario**, which nestles in a lush valley. The village has a small airport and a few lodging houses, and these make it a good base for exploring the region. Day trips from Bario include a visit to the beautiful longhouse at Pa Umor. A longer and much more challenging outing is the 5-day trek along the Bario Loop. The trail offers some delightful views, and trekkers have the option of making overnight stays at the Ramudu, Pa Dalih, or Long Dano longhouses. For serious mountain climbing head to **Gunung Murud**, located 12 miles (20 km) north of Bario. At 7,999 ft (2,438 m), Murud is Sarawak's highest peak and is regarded as a holy mountain by the indigenous people of the highlands. Scaling its sheer walls should only be attempted by fit and experienced climbers. There are two main trails up the mountain and having a guide is advisable. All the treks can be arranged through the lodges at Bario.

Lush paddy fields near Bario in the Kelabit Highlands

Mulu National Park ㉕

Listed both as a UNESCO World Heritage Site and a Rainforest Conservation Area, Mulu National Park is one of Sarawak's premier tourist destinations. Named for the sandstone peak of Gunung Mulu, it is a region of great natural beauty. The park encompasses over 200 sq miles (500 sq km) of rain forest and has two mountain ranges and some of the largest caves in the world. Gorges, valleys, and underground passages in the park provide the ideal habitat for an abundance of flora and fauna, including several species of orchids and hornbills. Trekking up to the limestone pinnacles of Gunung Api, exploring Clearwater and Deer Caves, and traversing the Canopy Skywalk are among the park's highlights.

BRUNEI

Area of map Illustrated

MALAYSIA

KEY

☐ Mulu National Park

★ **Clearwater Cave**
Thought to be the longest in Southeast Asia, the 62-mile (100-km) long Clearwater Cave features spectacular natural formations of helictites and photokarsts.

Mulu Trail, a 4-day guided trek to the summit of Gunung Mulu, is tiring but exhilarating, and passes through some of the park's wildest terrain.

Park Headquarters, located to the south-west of the park, is the starting point for all explorations of Gunung Mulu.

Lutut

Melinau

MELINAU TRAIL

Kuala Birar

Melinau

Wind Cave

GUNUNG MULU TRA

Mulu Airport ✈

ⓘ

Mulu Rainforest Resort

Lang's Cave

★ **Deer Cave and Bat Exodus**
The 571-ft (175-m) high cave mouth of Deer Cave is the largest in the world. At sunset, millions of freetail bats stream out of it in a writhing spiral as they fly off to look for food.

VISITORS' CHECKLIST

93 miles (150 km) E of Miri.
[X] to Mulu. [🚌] from Miri.
[ℹ] Lot 452, Jalan Melayu, Miri;
(085) 434-181. [📷] [📹] Wind
and Clearwater Caves: 9:30–
10:30am; Deer and Lang's Caves:
3:30–4:30pm. [💻] [☕] available
at Park Headquarters. [⛺]
www.mulupark.com. **Permits**
for trekking are available at
Park Headquarters.

★ **The Pinnacles**
One of the park's most memorable sights, these 147-ft (45-m) high razor-sharp spikes of rock on Gunung Api were formed by erosion, and can only be reached by a steep climb.

0 km   3
0 miles   3

EXPLORING THE PARK

Mulu National Park has exceptional facilities with well-maintained wooden walkways and a good network of paths. Most visitors arrive by plane and have accommodation options such as the four-star Mulu Rainforest Resort, chalets, and dormitories in the park. The Bat Exodus and the view from the Canopy Skywalk are fascinating. There are regular tours of the main caves.

Headhunters Trail is named for local indigenous people who used this route on raiding expeditions.

Gunung Mulu, at a height of 7,799 ft (2,377 m), is the second-highest peak in Sarawak.

KEY

═══	Minor road
– –	Trail
▬ ▬	Park boundary
[X]	Airport
[⛺]	Campsite
[ℹ]	Visitor information
▲	Peak

A visitor braving the Canopy Skywalk

CANOPY SKYWALK

Mulu National Park's newest attraction is the 1,575-ft (480-m) long Canopy Skywalk, which is among the longest in the world. A series of swaying walkways is held aloft by steel cables about 66 ft (20 m) above the ground, offering visitors the chance to explore the forest canopy, to get close up to the several species of birds that inhabit the park, and provides an aerial view of the swamp below. The 2-hour walk can be arranged at the Park Headquarters.

STAR SIGHTS

★ Clearwater Cave

★ Deer Cave and Bat Exodus

★ The Pinnacles

Brunei 26

Located on the northwest coast of Malaysian Borneo and hemmed in by the borders of Sarawak, the Sultanate of Brunei Darussalam is among the world's smallest countries. It played a pivotal role in Borneo's history, with its sultans having once controlled vast tracts of the island's north and west. Today, Brunei occupies a modest 2,226 sq miles (5,765 sq km). Most of the country is a low-lying coastal plain backed by rain forest and hills. Off the west coast lie vast oil fields, which are responsible for the country's affluence. It is divided into four districts: Brunei Muara which includes Bandar Seri Begawan, the capital; Tutong, an agricultural region; Belait, the center of the oil industry; and Temburong, an area of natural beauty.

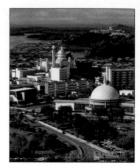
A panoramic view of the capital, Bandar Seri Begawan

Tasek Merimbun
Brunei's largest lake, this tranquil expanse of water is a popular spot for picnics and bird-watching. A wooden walkway leads to a tiny wooded island where eagles and falcons are commonly spotted.

Pantai Seri Kenangan is a beautiful strip of beach separating the Tutong River from the South China Sea.

Labi
This quiet agricultural town relies mainly on the harvest of fruits such as durian and rambutan. The 31-mile (50-km) long Labi Road is dotted with Iban longhouses.

SULTAN OF BRUNEI

Head of the world's oldest hereditary monarchy, Sultan Hassanal Bolkiah is Brunei's reigning sultan and prime minister, as well as its defense and finance minister. Best known for his legendary personal fortune and vast car collection, the sultan has attempted to share his nation's oil wealth by providing free education and healthcare for his people.

Sultan Hassanal Bolkiah, the reigning Sultan of Brunei

KEY

✈ Airport
▬ Major road
═ Minor road
– – International border
– ‑ State border
⊞ Beach
▲ Peak

★ Sultan Omar Ali Saifuddien Mosque

Built in 1958 and named for Brunei's 28th sultan, this mosque is a classic example of Islamic architecture. With its minarets and 171-ft (52-m) high golden dome reflected in the surrounding lagoon, it makes an impressive sight.

VISITORS' CHECKLIST

120 miles (193 km) NE of Miri.
🚏 380,000. ✈ 🚢 from Miri.
🛈 Jalan Menteri Besar, Bandar
Seri Begawan; (673) 238-2822.
📅 Islamic New Year (Jan),
National Day (Feb).
www.tourismbrunei.com

★ Kampung Ayer

Built entirely on stilts along the Brunei River, Kampung Ayer is a cluster of 28 villages housing an estimated 30,000 people. The community is a reflection of the country's traditional way of life.

★ Istana Nur-ul-Iman

The world's largest residential palace, the Istana Nur-ul-Iman is the official home of the Sultan of Brunei. It contains nearly 2,000 rooms, a sumptuous throne room, and a banquet hall for 4,000 diners.

Bukit Pagon, at a height of 6,070 ft (1,850 m), is the highest peak of Brunei and is located in Ulu Temburong National Park.

STAR SIGHTS

- ★ Sultan Omar Ali Saifuddien Mosque
- ★ Kampung Ayer
- ★ Istana Nur-ul-Iman

Ulu Temburong National Park

Covering about 10 percent of Brunei, this national park is the country's foremost nature preserve. Its canopy walkway gives visitors a chance to spot the flying lizards, hornbills, and gibbons that inhabit the park.

SABAH

alaysia's second largest state, Sabah sits on the northeastern tip of Borneo. Located just south of the typhoon belt, this Land below the Wind is geographically stunning, with magnificent caves, coral reefs, forests, and mountains. The state is also the ideal destination for a range of adventure activities including mountain climbing, white-water rafting, and diving.

Archaeological excavations reveal evidence of prehistoric human habitation in eastern Sabah approximately 40,000 years ago. This remote province, with over 30 indigenous groups, as well as immigrants from China, Indonesia, and the Philippines, was nominally ruled by the sultans of Brunei for centuries until the British negotiated the rights to exploit the region's reserves of rubber, tobacco, and timber in the late 19th century. Although the British never had a stable leadership over Sabah, they clung on to power, with the region continuing to be known as North Borneo until it joined the Federation of Malaysia in 1963.

Today, Sabah's economy lags behind that of other states in Malaysia because of an inequitable distribution of wealth between the state and federal governments, and an influx of immigrants from neighboring countries. However, with ecotourism contributing to the state's economy, and abundant agricultural produce, such as palm oil, Sabah is starting to catch up.

Sandakan, the administrative capital between 1883 and 1942, and Kota Kinabalu, the present state capital, were both almost completely destroyed during World War II, but today they have been rebuilt and are charming destinations. From Kota Kinabalu it is an easy journey north to the Tip of Borneo, south to the Padas River for white-water rafting, and northeast to Gunung Kinabalu for a challenging trek. Sandakan is a good base from which to visit the dive sites that lie off the east coast and the nature reserves at Sukau and Danum Valley. Sabah also offers visitors a cultural experience with its vibrant *tamus* held weekly, and fascinating longhouses.

Rafflesia, one of Sabah's most unusual and pungent attractions

◁ The towering peak of Gunung Kinabalu, a favorite among trekkers

Exploring Sabah

The state is characterized by steep mountains and lush valleys teeming with magnificent wildlife and marine life. The highlights of a visit to Sabah are a trek up Gunung Kinabalu, diving trips from the islands of Sipadan and Lankayan, and white-water rafting on the Padas River. Danum Valley is excellent for wildlife spotting while the villages of Kota Belud, Gombizau, Bavanggazo, and Sumangkap offer an opportunity to interact with indigenous groups in exciting and memorable ways.

KEY

— Major road

═ Minor road

⌐ Railroad

▬ International border

— State border

△ Peak

SIGHTS AT A GLANCE

Towns and Villages

Bavanggazo ❿

Gombizau ❽

Kota Belud ❼

Kota Kinabalu ❶

Kudat ⓫

Sandakan ⓮

Semporna ㉒

Sumangkap ❾

Tawau ㉔

Areas of Natural Beauty

Danum Valley ㉑

Gomantong Caves ⓳

Klias Wetlands ❹

Tip of Borneo ⓬

Parks and Preserves

Kinabalu National Park pp184–7 ⓭

Kinabatangan Wildlife Sanctuary ⓲

Sepilok Orangutan Rehabilitation Center ⓯

Tabin Wildlife Reserve ⓴

Tambunan Rafflesia Forest Reserve ❸

Tawau Hills State Park ㉕

Tunku Abdul Rahman National Park ❷

Turtle Island National Park ⓰

River

Padas River ❻

Islands and Beaches

Pulau Labuan ❺

Pulau Lankayan ⓱

Pulau Sipadan pp194–5 ㉓

TIP
BOR

KUDA

BAVANGGAZO ❿

SUMANGKAP ❾

GOMBIZAU ❽

South China Sea   Rampayan

KOTA BELUD ❼

TUNKU ABDUL RAHMAN NATIONAL PARK ❷

KOTA KINABALU ❶

GUNUNG KINAB
NATIONAL P
⓭
Gunung Kinabalu 13,455 ft
Ra

TAMBUNAN RAFFLESIA FOREST RESERVE ❸

Papar   Bid

Gunung Trus Maa 8,570 ft △

Kimanis

Illanum

Mansud

Klias

Menumbok

Membakut

Beaufort

Keningau

Lanas

❺ PULAU LABUAN

❹ KLIAS WETLANDS

❻ PADAS RIVER

Crocker Mountains

Tenom   Sook

Pingas

Nabawan

Bandar Seri Begawan

Sipitang

Malaman

Pendawang

Gunung Napotong 4,888 ft

Maligan   Melutut   Rundum   Sapulut

Gunung Antulai 5,620 ft

Gunung Muruk Miau 6,834 ft △

Sigattal

Lush tropical rainforest at Kinabalu National Park

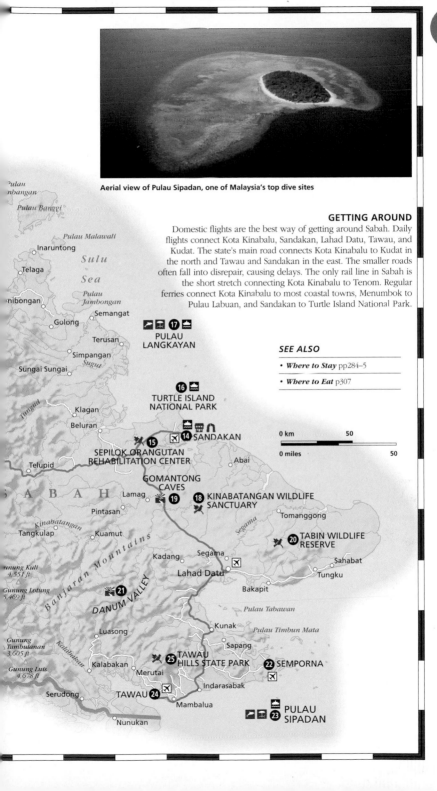

Aerial view of Pulau Sipadan, one of Malaysia's top dive sites

GETTING AROUND

Domestic flights are the best way of getting around Sabah. Daily flights connect Kota Kinabalu, Sandakan, Lahad Datu, Tawau, and Kudat. The state's main road connects Kota Kinabalu to Kudat in the north and Tawau and Sandakan in the east. The smaller roads often fall into disrepair, causing delays. The only rail line in Sabah is the short stretch connecting Kota Kinabalu to Tenom. Regular ferries connect Kota Kinabalu to most coastal towns, Menumbok to Pulau Labuan, and Sandakan to Turtle Island National Park.

SEE ALSO

- **Where to Stay** pp284–5
- **Where to Eat** p307

Map labels:

Pulau nbangan
Pulau Banggi
Pulau Malawali
Inaruntong
Telaga
Sulu
Sea
nibongan
Pulau Jambongan
Golong
Semangat
Terusan
Simpangan
Sungai Sungai
Sugur
Klagan
Beluran
17 PULAU LANGKAYAN
16 TURTLE ISLAND NATIONAL PARK
15 SEPILOK ORANGUTAN REHABILITATION CENTER
Telupid
14 SANDAKAN
Abai
19 GOMANTONG CAVES
Lamag
Pintasan
18 KINABATANGAN WILDLIFE SANCTUARY
Tomanggong
S A B A H
Tangkulap
Kinabatangan
Kuamut
Kadang
Segama
Segama
20 TABIN WILDLIFE RESERVE
Sahabat
Lahad Datu
Tungku
unung Kuli 4,551 ft
Bakapit
Gunung Lotung 5,469 ft
Banjaran Mountains
21 DANUM VALLEY
Pulau Tabawan
Luasong
Kunak
Pulau Timbun Mata
Gunung Tambulanan 3,605 ft
Sapang
Kalabakan
25 TAWAU HILLS STATE PARK
22 SEMPORNA
Gunung Luis 4,678 ft
Merutai
Indarasabak
Serudong
24 TAWAU
Mambalua
23 PULAU SIPADAN
Nunukan

0 km   50
0 miles   50

Stilt village and State Mosque in Kota Kinabalu, the fastest growing city and capital of Sabah

Kota Kinabalu ❶

190 miles (300 km) NE of Miri.
🏃 350,000. ✈ 🚉 ⛴ 🛈 *Sabah Tourism Board, 51 Jalan Gaya; (088) 212-121.* 🗓 *Sun.*
www.sabahtourism.com

The capital of Sabah, Kota Kinabalu occupies a narrow stretch of land between the western seafront and a range of forested hills. Formerly known as Jesselton, it became the provincial capital after World War II, and was renamed Kota Kinabalu in 1967. Most of its historic buildings were destroyed by bombing during the war and the city had to be completely rebuilt. Only three structures remain of the old town – the Land and Survey building, the General Post Office, and the Atkinson Clock, a 49-ft (15-m) tall timepiece built in 1905 and named for the city's first district officer. Despite the lack of historical landmarks, the city has charm, with friendly people, bustling streets, and a good range of accommodations, restaurants, and bars. The city center is small and easy to explore around on foot. The city's main attractions include the lively seafront *tamus*, or markets, such as the Filipino Market, as well as the Sabah Museum, and the State Mosque. The new and larger City Mosque, often referred to as the Floating Mosque, was built in 2000 beside Likas

Bay. Also overlooking the bay is the magnificent 31-story glass building of the Sabah Foundation. An observatory on Signal Hill offers a sweeping view of the city and offshore islands. Kota Kinabalu is the best base from which to explore Sabah's northwest coast, including the magnificent Gunung Kinabalu *(see pp184–7)* and Tunku Abdul Rahman National Park.

🏛 Sabah Museum

Jalan Muzium. **Tel** *(088) 253-199.*
🚌 🕐 *9am–5pm Sat–Thu.* 📷
📹 ♿ 🚫 🖥 www.mzm.sabah.gov.my

Opened in 1985, the Sabah Museum is set amid spacious grounds, and is designed in the style of a Rungus longhouse. The museum has several floors, with sections on ethnography, natural history, ceramics, history, and archaeology. The ethnographic exhibits are among the

highlights of the museum, and include examples of musical instruments, swords, spears, and blowpipes, ethnic costumes, and displays on the various uses of bamboo. The archaeology gallery displays intricately carved coffins. A "time tunnel" exhibit documents the arrival of Filipino and Indonesian immigrants, the colonial era, the Japanese occupation, and the incorporation of Sabah into the Federation of Malaysia in 1963. In front of the museum is a small but interesting collection of vintage cars.

The museum grounds also contain a Heritage Village, which has excellent examples of houses of Sabah's main indigenous groups. The Murut house features an unusual bouncing platform that is used for communal dances. Talks on a range of topics can be arranged for visitors by prior request.

The majestic façade of the Sabah State Mosque

Sabah State Mosque

Jalan Sembutan. 8–11am & 2–4:30pm Mon–Thu, 8–10:30am & 2:30–4:30pm Fri, 8–11am & 2–4pm Sat & Sun.

Located close to the museum, southwest of the city center, this mosque is a striking example of contemporary Islamic architecture. Though set away from the bustle of the city center, its golden dome is visible from many parts of town. The mosque, built in the late 1970s, is one of the largest in Malaysia. It has a capacity of over 5,000 worshipers, and has a separate section for women to pray. While non-Muslims are permitted to go inside (except during prayer times), they should dress appropriately and remove their shoes before entering.

Bright exterior of the popular Filipino Market

Filipino market

Jalan Tun Fuad Stephens. Central Market Jalan Tun Fuad Stephens.

Several bustling markets line the city's waterfront, the most interesting of which is the Filipino Market, also known as the Handicrafts Market, named for the Filipino immigrants who run most of the stalls. A huge variety of souvenirs, shells, baskets, and bags are available, though these are not exclusively from the Philippines. The market is also a good place to buy cultured pearls and traditional medicines. Visitors should beware of pickpockets in the market. Farther north is the Central Market, where vendors sell a range of snacks such as grilled chicken and the local favorite *murtabak*, a stuffed pancake.

Visitors arriving on Pulau Sapi in the Tunku Abdul Rahman National Park

Tunku Abdul Rahman National Park ②

2 miles (3 km) W of Kota Kinabalu. Sabah Parks Office, Block K, Sinsuran Complex, Kota Kinabalu; (088) 211-881. on Pulau Manukan. on Pulau Gaya and Manukan. permits from Sabah Parks Office.

A short boat ride away from Kota Kinabalu, Tunku Abdul Rahman National Park is made up of five beautiful islands that cover an area of 19 sq miles (50 sq km). Named for the country's first prime minister, the park was established in 1974 to protect the fragile coral reefs around **Pulau Gaya**, **Pulau Sapi**, **Pulau Manukan**, **Pulau Mamutik**, and **Pulau Sulug**. Several varieties of marine life thrive in these reefs, including parrotfish, clownfish, batfish, and lionfish. Wildlife on the islands include long-tailed macaques, bearded pigs, pangolins, and pied hornbills.

Pulau Gaya is the biggest of the five islands. Covered in dense forest, it has about 12 miles (20 km) of trails and dazzling white sand beaches such as Police Beach on the northeast coast. Although much of the coral around Pulau Gaya has been destroyed by dynamite fishing, the rest of the islands have reefs teeming with marine life.

Just off the southwest tip of Pulau Gaya, and linked to it by a sandbar at low tide, Pulau Sapi is tiny in comparison but has some lovely waters that are ideal for swimming and

snorkeling, as well as a short nature trail. The three other islands are clustered together a little farther south. Pulau Manukan, where the park headquarters is located, is the most popular of the five islands, especially for day trips. This crescent-shaped island's facilities include a resort and restaurant. Among the many activities on offer are snorkeling, glass-bottomed boat rides, sea kayaking, and parasailing. Scuba gear and underwater scooters can be hired on the island. Pulau Manukan has particularly good beaches on its eastern shore, but the large number of visitors and constant movement of boats sometimes cause the reefs to become murky.

The last two islands are very small and attract fewer visitors, and are therefore quieter. Pulau Mamutik is the smallest of the five islands, while Pulau Sulug is the farthest, but both have beautiful coral reefs and are popular with snorkelers.

Sunbathers on Pulau Manukan, Tunku Abdul Rahman National Park

Tambunan Rafflesia Forest Reserve ❸

37 miles (60 km) E of Kota Kinabalu.
🚐 ℹ️ *(088) 774-691.* ⏰ *8am–12:45pm, 2–5pm Mon–Fri; 8am–5pm Sat–Sun.* 📷

Located near the top of the 5,410 ft (1,649 m) high Sinsuron Pass in the Crocker Mountain Range, the Tambunan Rafflesia Forest Reserve was set up to protect the unique rafflesia flower. The botanical name of the commonest rafflesia, *Rafflesia arnoldi*, is derived from Sir Stamford Raffles, founder of Singapore, and naturalist Dr. Joseph Arnold, who discovered it in Sumatra in 1818. A 15-lb (7-kg) specimen was immediately sent back to the Royal Society in London. This parasitic plant is pollinated by carrion flies and emits a smell of rotting flesh to attract them. Its natural habitat is in moist, shaded areas. The flower takes about nine months to bloom into the world's largest flower, with brick-red petals and white dots. The display is short-lived as the petals begin to wilt within a few days.

As the blooming season is unpredictable and the rafflesia flowers only for a few days in a year, visitors are advised to enquire in advance if one is in bloom. The reserve has comprehensive information on the rafflesia and its habitat.

Guides are available at the information center, but are mostly not necessary, since the paths are well marked and staff can give directions.

Proboscis monkeys, named for their long, drooping noses

Klias Wetlands ❹

62 miles (100 km) SW of Kota Kinabalu. 🚐 *to Kota Klias jetty.* ⛴️ *tour boats from Kota Klias jetty.* 📷 *from Kota Kinabalu.*

Located on a peninsula south of Kota Kinabalu, the Klias Wetlands are a mangrove forest interspersed with countless channels of the Sungai Klias. It is among Sabah's relatively new attractions. Wildlife here is rich and diverse so visitors might spot several species of monkey, such as the silver-leaf and long-tailed macaque, an amazing variety of birds, and swarms of fireflies that illuminate the riverside trees in the evenings. The real highlight of the wetlands, however, is the chance to see the unique proboscis monkey, a species native to Borneo. They are timid but can be seen feeding on tender leaves near the edge of the water. The monkeys are named for their long, drooping noses that are particularly prominent in males, often twice as large as the females. The males also have a bulbous belly. These distinctive features have earned the monkey the nickname *orang belanda*, meaning Dutchman, in some parts of Borneo. The Klias Wetlands are a relatively new attraction, but most tour companies in Kota Kinabalu now offer boat trips to these wetlands. Although independent travel is possible, joining a tour group is a preferred option.

Pulau Labuan ❺

5 miles (8 km) W of the Klias Peninsula. 🏘️ *86,000.* ✈️ ⛴️ ℹ️ *(087) 423-445.*

Located off the southwest coast of Sabah, Pulau Labuan is a small island with a significant history. In 1846, the Sultan of Brunei ceded the island to the British who were particularly keen to mine the island's large coal deposits to provide fuel for passing steamships. The island remained a British territory for almost 100 years, until it was overrun by the Japanese at the beginning of their occupation of Borneo during World War II. A few years later the Japanese surrendered here at the end of the war. In 1963, Pulau Labuan joined the Federation of Malaysia. Today, the island is a quiet, pleasant place, with nice beaches and popular as a duty-free shopping haven.

Labuan Town is the main settlement on the island. Just north of Labuan is the **An-Nur Jamek Mosque**, a distinctive, futuristic structure. The **Peace Park** at Layang Layangan, 2 miles (4 km) north of town, contains a war memorial which marks the site of the

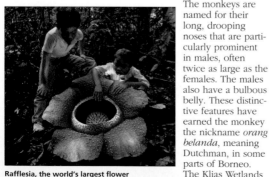

Rafflesia, the world's largest flower

Japanese surrender. An Allied war cemetery on the east coast has nearly 4,000 graves of Allied soldiers who lost their lives in Borneo.

The island's waters are particularly popular among divers, especially for wreck-diving. Several World War II and other shipwrecks lie in the waters off Labuan's coast. Dive operators organize visits to these interesting sites. The **Labuan Marine Park** is centered around Pulau Kuraman, a small island near the south coast, accessible by boats from the Labuan jetty. A number of activities such as diving, sailing, fishing, and organized short jungle walks are offered at the park. It also has some beautiful beaches, perfect for picnics and sun-bathing.

Padas River ⑥

Pangi, near Tenom 🚃 to Beaufort from Kota Kinabalu, then by train. 🚗 from Kota Kinabalu.

The Padas River weaves through the southwest region of Sabah, linking the small, quiet towns of Tenom and Beaufort. Known to be a turbulent river, it has flooded Beaufort several times. As a result, shophouses in the town are now built on stilts. Early photographs show Beaufort resembling the canal city of Venice. The Padas River is popular as a destination for great white-water rafting *(see p327)*. The boulder-strewn river cuts through lowland rainforest, and between April and July,

White-water rafting down the turbulent Padas River

the water level of the river creates Grade II and III rapids. The access point for rafting trips on the Padas River is at the town of Pangi, near Tenom, which can be reached by train from Beaufort. From Pangi, challenging rapids, with names such as Merry-Go-Round, Washing Machine, and Headhunter, tumble downstream. The river has several gentle stretches as well, where it is possible to hop out of the raft and float downstream with the current.

Rafting trips can be organized by tour companies in Kota Kinabalu who brief visitors well on safety procedures. As well as rafting trips, there is also the opportunity to take a tour of the southwest region of the state and ride on Borneo's only railway line from Beaufort to Tenom, tracing the Padas River and meandering through jungles.

Headstones of World War II soldiers at the Allied war cemetery in Labuan

THE NORTH BORNEO RAILWAY

When the British-run North Borneo Chartered Company began operating in the late 19th century, its managing director, William Cowie, developed a plan for a trans-Borneo railway stretching from Brunei Bay beside Pulau Labuan to Sandakan in the east of the province, cutting through steep ranges and uncharted jungles. Construction began in 1896 and by 1905 a line had been built from Weston, on Brunei Bay, to Beaufort in the southwest, and from there to both Jesselton, now known as Kota Kinabalu, and to Tenom, east of Beaufort. From Tenom it was extended a further 10 miles (16 km) to Melalap, where work came to a halt and was never continued. Cost of construction was high, and the rice tax levied on locals to pay for it resulted in rebellions against the British. The Chartered Company then ensured that the train paid for itself by refusing to build roads connecting Tenom, Beaufort, and Jesselton. The line still exists today, though more as a curiosity. Trains from Kota Kinabalu to Beaufort take about three hours, but it is the stretch from Beaufort to Tenom that is worth taking. Most trains are pulled by diesel engines, though the Sutera Harbour Resort *(see p285)* has put an old steam train in service.

Tourists enjoying the view while on a train trip

A stall displaying plants at the
weekly *tamu* in Kota Belud

Kota Belud ❼

47 miles (75 km) N of Kota Kinabalu.
🏛 *73,000.* 🚌 🛥 *Sun.* 🎎 *Tamu
Besar (Oct/Nov).*

Located on fertile alluvial
plains, Kota Belud is a quiet
town inhabited mainly by
Bajau people, famed for their
skill with horses. Gunung
Kinabalu dominates the landscape to the east.

The town itself is small
and unassuming, except on
Sunday mornings when it
springs to life during the
weekly *tamu*, or market. Held
at Jalan Hasbollah, a short distance from the town center,
the *tamu* is the hub of local
trade and is as much a social
event as a commercial one.
Local people from diverse
ethnic groups such as Chinese,
Indians, and Malay, come
together to sell their goods
while visitors soak up the
atmosphere and enjoy a
hearty breakfast at one of
the many stalls.

Just about anything one
can imagine is on sale, from
livestock, fruit, vegetables,
and meat to hand-crafted
knives, musical instruments,
bark waistcoats, and local
textiles. Tempting snacks
and drinks are also on offer.
Vendors are very friendly,
and expect potential buyers
to haggle for their goods.
The weekly *tamu* is busy
from around 6am until
early afternoon.

Tamu Besar, or the big
market, is an annual festive
event at Kota Belud which
is celebrated amid cultural
festivities and handicraft
demonstrations. The highlight
of the market are the stalls of
horses for sale.

Traditionally-dressed Bajau
horsemen, commonly called
Cowboys of the East, pose for
the crowds. The Bajau with
their resplendently dressed
horses also display their
unrivaled horse-riding skills
at the Tamu Besar.

Gombizau ❽

56 miles (90 km) N of Kota Kinabalu.
🏛 *140.* 🚌 ℹ️ *(013) 854-9188
(cell).* ⏲ *8:30am–5:30pm daily.*
📷 ✉️ 🏛

Located up the coast from
Kota Belud on the Kudat
Peninsula in the north of
the province, Kampung
Gombizau is one of several
smaller villages in the area
that are taking part in the
local government's scheme
of One Village, One Product.
The program encourages the
communities to produce and
market unique handmade
products and handicrafts
made from locally available
material. The villagers, most
of whom are part of the
Rungus minority, dedicate
their time to the industry of
beekeeping and the sale of
honey and beeswax. Royal
jelly, a bee secretion which
is a good dietary supplement
and an ingredient in several
beauty products, is also
cultivated and sold here.
Visitors are shown around
the carefully-tended beehives
and can see how the bees
are smoked out for the
honeycombs to be removed.

Sumangkap ❾

57 miles (92 km) N of Kota Kinabalu.
🏛 *431.* 🚌 ℹ️ *(088) 615-714.*
⏲ *8am–6pm daily.* 📷 ✉️ 🏛

A short drive from Gombizau
is the village of Sumangkap,
which resounds with the
beating of metal being made
into gongs and can thus
boast the highest decibel
count in Sabah. One of the
most important elements of
Sabahan music, the gongs
feature in all traditional
celebrations. These gongs
are skilfully crafted by local
artisans. Set horizontally in
frames or suspended verti-
cally, gongs come in all sizes,

Striking a massive gong in Kampung Sumangkap

For hotels and restaurants in this region see pp284–5 and p307

from massive ones that are 6 ft (2 m) in diameter and meant for use in temples, to tiny ones sold as souvenirs. Visitors can watch the gongmakers at work, as they beat out the raised center of an aluminum sheet to give the instrument its particular resonance and timbre.

Symbolic globe at the Tip of Borneo marking the island's northernmost point

Bavanggazo ⑩

61 miles (98 km) N of Kota Kinabalu.
🏯 *250.* 💺 🏨 *(088) 621-971*
💺 🗂 📷

The Rungus people, who live in the region around Kudat, have managed to maintain more of their traditions and culture than many other indigenous groups. A visit to a longhouse in the village of Bavanggazo, just off the road from Kota Belud to Kudat, is an excellent opportunity to appreciate Rungus heritage.

The longhouses are aligned in an auspicious east-west direction, with outward sloping walls to allow for maximum ventilation. One such longhouse is **Matunggung**, which features traditional bamboo-slatted sides and a thatched roof, and contains the living quarters of approximately 100 families.

The Rungus are famed for their beadwork, and visitors to the longhouse can usually see women sitting on the communal veranda crafting shoulder bands, necklaces, and bracelets from multicolored beads, using motifs from Rungus folklore. The older Rungus women wear brass coils as jewelry. They are also skilled textile weavers, and use locally grown, hand-spun cotton on simple looms for their clothes.

Organized tours, which can be booked in Kota Kinabalu, include a visit to the villlages of Gombizau and Sumangkap as well as lunch at Bavanggazo. These tasty meals are made with fresh vegetables from adjoining fields. Visitors have the option of staying overnight to attend a cultural performance of traditionally dressed dancers and gong players.

Kudat ⑪

118 miles (190 km) N of Kota Kinabalu. 🏯 *75,000.* ✈ 💺 *Ekspress minibus service from Kota Kinabalu.* 📅 *Sun.* 🎉 *Pesta Kelapa.*

A small port sitting at the northern tip of Sabah, Kudat is inhabited by a large number of Chinese and Filipino traders. Sheltered by the Marudu Bay, the Kudat Peninsula was deemed suitable enough to be selected as the administrative capital of British North Borneo in 1882. However, the town's era of importance was short-lived, as frequent pirate attacks and a lack of fresh water forced the provincial capital to be shifted in 1883 to Sandakan *(see p190)*.

There are not many sights in town, although a stroll around the harbor, watching fishing boats come and go, can be refreshing. A walk along the Sidek Esplanade around the bay is also rejuvenating. Kudat's main street,

Rock pools at Bak Bak Beach, north of Kudat

Jalan Lo Thien Chock, has some attractive shophouses and a colorful Chinese temple. About 4 miles (7 km) north of town, the beach at **Bak Bak** is a popular picnic spot.

Tip of Borneo ⑫

124 miles (200 km) N of Kota Kinabalu. 💺 *Ekspress minibus service from Kota Kinabalu.* 🗂 📷

The northernmost tip of Borneo, known locally as Tanjung Simpang Mangayau, which means battle junction, makes an excellent day trip from Kota Kinabalu. Located in the Kudat district, the tip can be reached after stopping off at the Gombizau bee farm, at the gong village of Sumangkap, and along the way at the Rungus longhouse at Bavanggazo.

A few miles before Kudat, a branch of the road forks to the left, passing under towering coconut palms and leading directly to a lovely windswept promontory that looks out over the South China Sea to the west and the Sulu Sea to the east.

Just before the headland, the road passes behind a sandy crescent shaded by casuarinas to Kalampunian Beach, where the Irranun people sell colorful shells. At the Tip of Borneo itself, a flagpole stands beside a giant globe of the world. An inscription on the globe recounts that Ferdinand Magellan spent 42 days here repairing his ship during his circumnavigation of the world between 1519 and 1522.

Kinabalu National Park ⓭

A UNESCO World Heritage site, the 754-sq km (291-sq mile) national park protects the environment around Gunung Kinabalu. Popular for its trails and wildlife, the park is home to 4,500 species of plants, including 1,500 varieties of orchids and nine types of pitcher plants. Also found here are large mammals such as orangutans, gibbons, and clouded leopards, unusual birds such as the Kinabalu friendly warbler and the Bornean mountain whistler, and a dazzling variety of butterflies and insects. At its southeast corner lies Poring Hot Springs, the ideal place to relax after the rigors of the park's trails.

Area of map Illustrated

Kiau · Lohan

Kundasang ·

KEY

☐ Kinabalu National Park

Low's Peak 13,455 ft

Laban Rata Rest House

Layang Layang

Power Station

Park Headquarters

Bundu Tuhan

Kundasang

★ Gunung Kinabalu
At a towering 13,455 ft (4,101 m), the mountain offers unrivaled views from its summit. A reasonable degree of fitness is essential for attempting the climb (see pp186–7). Kiau

The Bukit Tupai Trail, an easy 30-minute walk, leads up to a ridgetop with excellent views of Kinabalu's summit.

Kinabalu Botanical Garden
The botanical garden behind the Park Headquarters features many varieties of plants from the mountain's middle ranges. All species are labeled, making a stroll around the grounds both informative and enjoyable.

0 km — 3

0 miles — 3

★ Silau Silau Trail
This 50-minute walk along the length of the Silau Silau stream, from its source to its confluence with Sungai Liwagu, is excellent for bird-watching.

STAR SIGHTS

★ Gunung Kinabalu

★ Silau Silau Trail

★ Poring Hot Springs

★ **Poring Hot Springs**
Fed by mineral waters, these springs have been developed into public and private baths. The site also features a short but exciting canopy walkway, an orchid farm, and a butterfly farm.

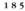

VISITORS' CHECKLIST

37 miles (60 km) NE of Kota Kinabalu. 🚌 🛈 *Kota Kinabalu Resorts, 15 First Floor, Wisma Sabah (088) 243–629.* 📷 🍴 🛍
Kinabalu Botanical Garden
⭕ *daily.* 📷 *9am, 12noon, 3pm.*

EXPLORING THE PARK

There are several trails around the park along its ridgetops and streams, all of which pass through delightful terrain where quiet and observant walkers may see some of the region's mammals, such as bearded pigs and mouse deer. Popular walks include the Liwagu Trail, Mempening Trail, and Bukit Tupai Trail, which take anywhere between 20 minutes and three hours to complete.

KEY

═══	Major road
══	Minor road
‒ ‒	Summit Trail
‒ ‒	Mesilau Trail
‒ ‒	Liwagu Trail
‒ ‒	Bukit Tupai Trail
——	Mempening Trail
‒ ‒	Silau Silau Trail
‒ ‒	Park boundary
🅐	Campsite
🛈	Visitor information
▲	Peak

The alternative route to the summit of Gunung Kinabalu begins 11 miles (17 km) east of Park Headquarters at Mesilau.

Poring Hot Springs

Mesilau

LOHAN

The canopy walkway is only 490 ft (150 m) long, but it gives a splendid bird's-eye view of the surrounding forest.

FLORA AND FAUNA

One of the richest areas in species diversity, the park's attractions include such mammals as tarsiers, squirrels, and tree shrews, birds such as hornbills, partridges, and mountain blackbirds, as well as a long list of colorful butterflies and beetles. The park is also home to several varieties of rare and exotic flora, including the extraordinary rafflesia (*see p180*).

Tarsiers *are easily recognized by their long feet and large eyes. They are nocturnal primates that feed on insects, birds, and snakes.*

Pitcher plants, *which are one of the prime attractions of Kinabalu National Park, are carnivorous plants that attract and trap insects with their bright pigments and sweet nectar.*

Slipper orchids *are named for their bright slipper-shaped pouches that attract pollinating insects. These delicate plants are fast becoming an uncommon sight.*

Climbing Gunung Kinabalu

The climb to the summit of Gunung Kinabalu begins at the power station, just above Park Headquarters. There is an alternative route, longer but less steep, which starts at Mesilau Nature Resort, 11 miles (17 km) to the east. The two trails meet at Layang Layang and continue to the Laban Rata Rest House, where most climbers break for the night. Some, however, travel another hour to the more basic rest house at Sayat Sayat, which has the benefit of a shorter clamber to the summit the next morning. The last, and toughest, part of the hike begins well before dawn to allow climbers to view the sunrise from Low's Peak. The descent takes five hours, so it is best to start back by noon to reach the base before dark.

The mighty Gunung Kinabalu rising above the clouds

The Summit Trail
From the power station to the summit at Low's Peak, this trail takes at least two days to traverse. Handrails are erected along the trickier stretches to help climbers.

South Peak, as its name suggests, is the southernmost of Kinabalu's peaks. A near-perfect pinnacle, it provides lofty views of the surrounding area.

Layang Layang, at 8,599 ft (2,621 m), has a staff base and is the first rest stop for most climbers.

Low's Peak 13,455

St John's Peak 13,438 ft

South Peak 12,9...

Villo Shelt...

Mempening Shelter

Kamborangoh Telekoms Station

Ubah Shelter

Power Station

Tropical montane rainforests, typically composed of oak, birch, and pine, as well as fern and moss, are found between 2,953 ft (900 m) and 5,900 ft (1,800 m), including the area around Park Headquarters.

Kandis Shelter

Timpohon Gate

Rhododendron Forests
Found between 5,900 ft (1,800 m) and 8,530 ft (2,600 m), these forests comprise 26 varieties of rhododendron, including the beautiful copper-leaved rhododendron.

Park Headquarters
The jumping-off point for walks along trails, Park Headquarters has accommodations, restaurants, and a shop selling provisions for climbers.

For hotels and restaurants in this region see pp284–5 and p307

Summit Peaks of Kinabalu
St. John's Peak, Donkey's Ears, and the Ugly Sisters are just a few of the peaks that soar near the summit of Gunung Kinabalu.

LOW'S PEAK

Sir Hugh Low

The highest peak of Gunung Kinabalu, Low's Peak is named for Sir Hugh Low, a naturalist and British Colonial Secretary on Pulau Labuan. Ironically, he never stood on its summit despite three attempts during the 1850s. On his second attempt, in 1858, he was accompanied by Spencer St. John, the British Consul in Brunei, who made it to the top of South Peak only to see other peaks around it that stood still higher. It was not until 1888 that John Whitehead, a zoologist, conquered the highest peak while collecting new species of birds and mammals, some of which are also named for Sir Hugh Low.

y Sisters
3,228 ft
▲

▲ *Donkey's Ears*
   13,300 ft

● *Sayat Sayat*
  Rest House

i Rata
House

ka Cave
elter/Helipad

Gunting Lagadan Hut
Situated just above Laban Rata, this simple rest house can sleep up to 60 people in dormitories. It also has sweeping views of the mountain's upper reaches, with Donkey's Ears as a backdrop.

od
ter

● *Chempaka*
  Shelter

Mesilau Gate

● *Nepenthes*
  Shelter

● *Mesilau*

CLIMBING THE SUMMIT TRAIL

Climbing the mountain is more fun when traveling light, but a few items are essential, including a hat, suntan lotion, sunglasses, and a flashlight. Warm, waterproof clothing is a must. Sleeping bags are provided free of charge at Laban Rata and Sayat Sayat rest houses, and the shop at Park Headquarters sells basic food. Allow a day for booking accommodation at Laban Rata and arranging a climbing permit (RM100), guide (RM60 for a small group), and porters (RM6 per kilo).

0 km   1

0 miles   1

KEY

-- Summit Trail

-- Mesilau Trail

△ Campsite

ℹ Visitor information

▲ Peak

Mesilau Trail
Located 11 miles (17 km) east of Park Headquarters, Mesilau provides a quieter base for the climb. The trail from here is longer, quieter, and offers a particularly good display of several species of pitcher plants.

Sandakan ⑭

250 miles (400 km) E of Kota
Kinabalu. 🏠 *12,500*. ✕ 🚌
ℹ *(089) 229-751*.

Lying on the northern edge
of Sandakan Bay, Sandakan is
sandwiched between a steep
escarpment and the Sulu Sea.
During the late 18th century,
exports of timber, pearls, birds'
nests, and hornbill ivory made
Sandakan a wealthy town. It
became the administrative
capital of North Borneo
between 1884 and 1942, but
was bombed out of existence
by the end of World War II,
like Kota Kinabalu. Much of
the modern town is built on
reclaimed land, but its indis-
criminate architecture of concrete grids lacks the sense of
space of Kota Kinabalu. These
days, trade is focused on palm
oil and cocoa crops.

There is little to interest
visitors in the center of town,
though the waterfront is lively
with the constant movement
of barges and ferries, and a
daily fish market which is
the biggest in Sabah. On the
escarpment behind the town
center is an Observation
Pavilion that offers a spectacular view across the town
and the harbor front.

Overlooking the pavilion
is a well-preserved colonial
building known as **Agnes
Keith's House**. An American
author who lived here in the
1930s, Agnes Keith wrote
several books on Sabah and its
culture. The house has ornate
furnishings and wooden flooring, and the author's study still
exudes an aura of tranquility.

Next door, another slice of
colonial memorabilia, the
English Tea House is a refreshing stop for tired visitors.

For many, the most moving
sight in town is the **Sandakan
Memorial Park**, about 7 miles
(12 km) east of the town center. In 1944, over 2,000 Allied
British and Australian prisoners
of the Japanese POW camp
were marched to Ranau near
Gunung Kinabalu. Only six
Australians survived. The small
museum in the park, built by
the Australian government, is a
grim reminder of the tragedy.

> 🏛 **Agnes Keith's House**
> Jalan Istana. ○ *daily*. 🎟
>
> 🏛 **Sandakan Memorial Park**
> 7 miles (12 km) E of Sandakan.
> ○ *daily*. 🎟

Sepilok Orangutan Rehabilitation Center ⑮

14 miles (23 km) E of Sandakan.
Tel *(089) 531-180*. 🚌 ○ *9am–
12:30pm, 2–4:30pm daily. Feeding
times are 10am–3pm*. 🎟 🖥 🎫 🅰

One of only four orangutan
sanctuaries in the world,
Sepilok was established in
1964 and is today one of
Sabah's most popular attractions. Occupying 17 sq miles
(43 sq km) of lowland rain
forest, the center was set up to
care for orphaned and injured
animals, and teach them the
skills needed to survive independently. The center aims to
eventually reintroduce the
orangutans into their natural
habitat. Located at the

Orangutans at the Sepilok
Orangutan Rehabilitation Center

entrance to Sepilok is the
Nature Education Center
which provides an insightful
introduction to all that goes
on behind the scenes, and
also periodically screens a
short video on orangutans.
A short walk from here are
two feeding stations where
the animals are fed fruit and
milk twice a day.

After registering at the reception, visitors can follow several
walking trails that lead through
the forest. But there are strict
restrictions against approaching or touching the animals.

Turtle Island National Park ⑯

25 miles (40 km) N of Sandakan.
🚤 *from Sandakan*. ℹ *Crystal
Quest, 12th floor, Wisma Khoo
Siak Chiew, Sandakan,
(089) 212-711*. 🎟 🎫 🍴 🎫 *on
Pulau Selingan*. 🅰
www.sabahparks.org.my

The three small islands of
Selingan, Bakungan Kecil,
and Gulisan constitute this
turtle sanctuary, commonly
known as the Pulau Penyu
National Park, where green
and hawksbill turtles come
ashore to nest.

The most rewarding time
to visit the Turtle Island
National Park is between July
and October when visitors
are most likely to see these
creatures lay their eggs in
the sand. Booking in advance
is necessary. Vigilant rangers
transfer the hatchlings to
nurseries, from where they

The impressive Agnes Keith's House, home of the American writer

For hotels and restaurants in this region see pp284–5 and p307

are regularly released into the sea. Sadly, the chance of survival for each hatchling is only about one in a clutch of 100 eggs, as they often fall prey to poachers as well as natural predators.

The park also nurtures an interesting variety of flora such as mangroves, lantana, the yellow-flowered sophora, and the furry-leaved tournefortia among others.

Pulau Lankayan ⑰

50 miles (80 km) N of Sandakan. *from Sandakan.* ⛳ *Pulau Sipadan Resorts, 484 Bandar Sabindo, Tawau; (089) 765-200.* 🏨 💧 🅰 www.lankayan-island.com

Just a 90-minute boat ride from Sandakan, Lankayan is a teardrop-shaped island, surrounded by dazzling white beaches and stunning coral reefs. It is visited mostly by divers for its colorful world of marine life, and, with only one resort, the place is rarely crowded. Some of the species that divers might spot around the Lankayan shipwreck, one of the many dive sites near the island, are glassfish, painted frogfish, and marble stingrays. Gazing into the waters from the jetty, visitors can often see black-tip sharks, especially in the months of April and May. Lankayan is a part of the Sugud Islands Marine Conservation Area, and its lush tropical vegetation is also worth a mention. The island is covered with screwpine *(Pandanus amaryllifolins)*, which has a bloom resembling a pineapple.

Kinabatangan Wildlife Sanctuary ⑱

84 miles (135 km) S of Sandakan. *from Sandakan.* 🛥 *along Sungai Kinabatangan.* 🏨 *in Sukau.* 🅰

Sungai Kinabatangan is Sabah's longest river at 348 miles (560 km) and its lower reaches, bordered by dense forests, provide the largest corridor for wildlife in the country. A unique feature of the river are the oxbow lakes set back from the main course, creating abundant habitats for the diverse flora and fauna. Much of this area has been designated as the Kinabatangan Wildlife Sanctuary. It is easily visited on a day trip from Sandakan, but staying overnight in the nearby town of Sukau enables visitors to take a boat ride along the river in the early morning, the best time to spot wildlife. Sungai Menungal, a small tributary that joins the Kinabatangan just above Sukau, is a particularly successful spot for wildlife sightings. Proboscis monkeys, a species common in Borneo, and macaques that feed high up in the trees, are among the highlights. Visitors are almost certain to see a wide range of reptiles such as crocodiles, and birds such as the hornbill, oriental darter, and the blue-eared kingfisher.

Gomantong Caves ⑲

68 miles (110 km) S of Sandakan. *from Sandakan.* 🏨 *(089) 230-189.* ⬜ *8am–noon, 2–4:30 pm.* 🎦 📷 📧

The limestone caves of Gomantong are the largest caves in Sabah and home to a remarkable population of swiftlets and bats. Locals clamber up slender bamboo poles to harvest swiftlet nests, which are the prime ingredient for bird's-nest soup, a delicacy in Chinese cuisine.

The two main caves are **Simud Hitam**, or black cave, and **Simud Putih**, or white cave, both of which are difficult to get to. However, visitors can venture into Simud Hitam aided by a boardwalk to avoid wading through ankle-deep bat guano which collects on the cave floor. Most tours of the caves include a trip down Sungai Kinabatangan.

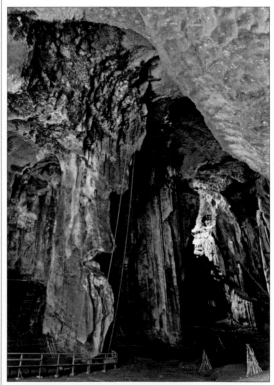

The entrance into Simud Hitam at Gomantong Caves

Tabin Wildlife Reserve ⑳

137 miles (220 km) SE of Sandakan.
🚌 *from Lahad Datu.* ℹ️ (089) 821-
060. ⏰ 8am–6pm daily. 📷
🎫 *organized by Tabin Wildlife
Resort,* **Tel** (088) 261-558. ✉️
www.tabinwildlife.com.my

Established as a protected
area in 1984, the 473-sq mile
(1,225-sq km) Tabin Wildlife
Reserve is one of the last
remaining habitats of the
critically endangered Sumatran
rhinoceros. Comprised mostly
of secondary growth rain
forest, this is a conservation
zone for several other wildlife
species as well, including
endangered Borneo pygmy elephants, giant flying squirrels,
orangutans, and several bird
species including hornbills.
Activities organized by the
reserve in collaboration with
Tabin Wildlife Resort are exciting ways to spot wildlife and
include jungle walks, night
safaris, and bird-watching trips.
    The reserve offers visitors
challenging walking trails, one
of which leads to a waterfall
that plunges into a river which
is good for a swim. Another
trail leads to a cluster of low,
mud volcanoes.

Danum Valley ㉑

50 miles (80 km) W of Lahad Datu.
🚗 *from Lahad Datu.* ℹ️ (088)
881-092. 🎫 *mandatory.* ✉️

Covering an area of 168 sq
miles (438 sq km), Danum
Valley is a conservation area
that consists of primary

**Wild bearded pigs rooting for food
in the Danum Valley**

lowland rainforest, one of the
most complex ecosystems,
which is why it features high
on most nature-lovers' itineraries on their visit to Sabah.
    The surrounding logging
concession, run by the Sabah
Foundation, which has now
been mostly reforested, acts
as a buffer zone for the fantastic range of wildlife. Visitors
are likely to spot elephants,
barking deer, and slow loris
on several guided walks along
nature trails. Among the birds
that are visible in this region
are the great argus pheasant,
the rhinoceros hornbill, and
the crimson sunbird. Most
visitors stay at the Borneo
Rainforest Lodge *(see p284)*,
by Sungai Danum, where a
network of trails offer multiple
options for exploring the area.
The ideal time to observe
wildlife is early morning and
evening, when even the most
cautious of animals, such as
bearded pigs, emerge to root
for food, while orangutans
and Bornean gibbons can be

spotted often rustling about
in treetops by the lodge. A
steep 2-mile (3-km) climb
leads to an ancient Kadazan
Dusun burial site, high up in
a cliff-top cave. The site
contains old coffins and offers
a spectacular view over the
Segama River Valley.

Semporna ㉒

209 miles (336 km) SE of Sandakan.
🏘️ 150,000. 🚌 🎉 *Regatta
(Mar/Apr).*

With most of its houses
perched on wooden piles
over the water, Semporna is
a town juxtaposed between
land and sea. This picturesque fishing town hovers
over an ancient coral reef that
supports a diverse variety of
fish, soft corals, sponges,
anemones, echinoderms,
and mollusks.
    The inhabitants are mainly
the Bajau, a seafaring people
who fish in the Celebes Sea
to earn their living using delicately carved, traditional boats
called *lipa lipa,* which they
adorn with bright sails and
colorful festoons.
    Semporna is frequented by
visitors who use it as a base
for diving and snorkeling day
trips to the offshore islands of
Mabul and Sipadan *(see pp194–
5).* Of the many island destinations that skirt the town of
Semporna, the volcanic island
of Pulau Bohey Dulang, also
the site of a Japanese pearl
culture station, is popular. The
cliff-fringed Bohey Dulang is
frequented by adventure
lovers who trek up its highest

Traditional stilt buildings in the harbor in Semporna

For hotels and restaurants in this region see pp284–5 and p307

Ferry passengers disembarking at Tawau

peak for stunning views of the surrounding islands. The area around Semporna has intrigued archaeologists since the discovery of stone tools at nearby Tingkayu, which predate similar implements found in the region by 10,000 years.

Pulau Sipadan ㉓

See pp194–5.

Tawau ㉔

223 miles (360 km) S of Sandakan. 🏠 178,000.
✕ 🚍 🅰 Tawau Central Market, daily. 🎭 Tawau Cultural Carnival (Mar).
www.sabahtourism.com

Tawau sits on the coast in the extreme southeast of Sabah. It is a transport hub and a transit point for visitors heading toward Semporna and the offshore islands of Sipadan (see pp194–5).

This bustling port began life as a modest Bajau settlement, but in 1878 the British North Borneo Company, attracted by the fine natural harbor and rich volcanic soil found in the region, settled in Tawau. They shipped in elephants from Burma to assist with logging in the forest.

Timber has always been the prime produce of this town, although the rich soil also sustains plantations of rubber, coconut, cocoa, and palm oil. In fact, Tawau is the cocoa capital of Borneo, and the cocoa estate at nearby Quoin Hill admits

visitors to see the stages of processing cacao beans to chocolate. Palm oil is cultivated even more extensively in Tawau, and plantations of its fan-like fronds are scattered around the state of Sabah.

Tawau faces Kalimantan across the strait and has a high percentage of Indonesian and Filipino residents. While there are some squalid areas, the town center is a tidy blend of traditional wooden shophouses and modern concrete blocks. The cheerful street markets offer a wide mix of goods such as herbs, vegetables, clothes, and toys sold by mobile traders. Tawau's fish market is always busy, and exotic seafood is available at the open-air stalls seen all over town.

Tawau is the jumping-off point for trips to the Maliau Basin to the west, which is dubbed "Sabah's lost world"

Cacao pod

due to its inaccessibility and diversity of plant and animal life. This is a trip for enthusiasts as facilities offered to visitors are very basic.

Tawau Hills State Park ㉕

15 miles (24 km) N of Tawau.
🚍 from Tawau. 🛈 (089) 753-564.
🕐 7am–6pm daily. 🎭 🐾 🏕

A lush stretch of low hills and thick mossy rainforest, Tawau Hills State Park was established here in 1979 to protect the watershed of the Tawau, Merotai, Kinabutan, Mantri, and Balung rivers.

Occupying about 104 sq miles (270 sq km), the park is a favorite among birders. The blue-banded kingfisher, wattled pheasant, blue-headed pitta, and the Bornean wren-babbler can be spotted here. Sightings of monkeys are also common.

The highest hill is the 4,268 ft (1,300 m) high Gunung Magdalena. A lower peak, Bombalai Hill, just 1,739 ft (530 m) high, is an extinct volcano that can be reached following a half-hour trail from the park headquarters. A 3-hour trek leads to some hot springs and Table Waterfall, where the crystal clear river makes for a good swimming spot.

Being so close to a big town, this park is very popular and gets crowded during weekends, making a mid-week visit advisable.

Air Tejun Galas Falls, Tawau Hills State Park

Pulau Sipadan ㉓

Rated among the world's top five dive sites, Pulau Sipadan is a limestone spire rising about 1,970 ft (600 m) from the sea-bed. Fringed with white and sandy beaches, the island is surrounded by a stunning coral reef teeming with over 3,000 species of marine life, including colorful butterflyfish, angelfish, and bright orange and electric blue damsel-fish. Sightings of sharks, barracudas, turtles, and manta rays are also common in the waters around the reef.

SEMPC
MABU,
KAPAL
ISLAND

★ Turtle Cavern
The eerie Turtle Cavern is an underwater cave stacked with the skeletal remains of green and hawksbill turtles that drifted into it and never found their way out.

★ The Drop Off
Just east of the Sipadan jetty, the Drop Off is a seemingly endless wall of rock covered with several species of corals and sponges.

Diving Trips
Several tour operators arrange all-day dives as well as night diving expeditions. Qualified personnel accompany visitors on each diving trip.

Hanging Gardens
The reef descends gradually to a depth of 230 ft (70 m), where terraces covered with alcyona-rian and gorgonian fan corals form the Hanging Gardens.

0 meters | 300
0 yards | 300

Lobster Lairs is a good place for spotting lionfish, lobsters, scorpionfish, and pipefish. This shallow dive site is an ideal spot for beginners.

STAR SIGHTS

★ Turtle Cavern

★ The Drop Off

★ White-Tip Avenue

Barracuda Point
The site is named for the spectacular spirals of blacktail and chevron barracuda that come here to feed along a wall that harbors turtles and parrotfish.

VISITORS' CHECKLIST

21 miles (35 km) S of Semporna. 🚢 from Semporna. 🛈 **Borneo Sea Adventures** 8A Karamunsing Warehouse, Kota Kinabalu; (088) 230-000. 🚤 available at Semporna, and Mabul and Kapalai islands. **Best time to visit** Apr –Aug, when visibility is up to 98 ft (30 m).

Coral Garden, where almost every species that inhabits these waters can be viewed, is a haven for the underwater photographer.

★ White-Tip Avenue
A gap in the coral reef, White-Tip Avenue is frequented by white-tip sharks and gray reef sharks. Divers may encounter a school of bigeye trevallies and bumphead parrotfish.

Mid Reef

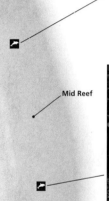

Turtle Patch
This site offers frequent sightings of hammerhead and thresher sharks, triggerfish, bumphead parrotfish, and the green and hawksbill turtles that are commonly seen around Sipadan.

South Point, a site for experienced divers, is popular for frequent sightings of hammerhead sharks and turtles.

KEY

– –	Ferry route
🚢	Ferry port
🏖	Beach
🐟	Dive sites

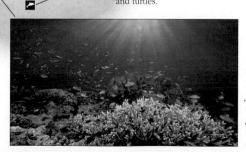

Staghorn Crest
This is a drop-off dive site with a fabulous garden of giant staghorn corals teeming with shoals of gobies, groupers, angelfish, and triggerfish. Currents can be strong here and divers need to be careful.

SINGAPORE AREA BY AREA

A PORTRAIT OF SINGAPORE

*T*he *small city-state of Singapore is bustling, cosmopolitan, trendy, modern, and plays a part on the world's financial and political stage that seems disproportionate to its size. Its varied traditions and intriguing mix of the old and new (in its people and way of life) make Singapore a great multicultural city in the truest sense.*

Located at the tip of the Malay Peninsula on the Strait of Malacca, Singapore consists of one large island encircled by several smaller islets. Gleaming high-rise buildings and a fascinating diversity of foliage are crammed into a tiny area of just 269 sq m (697 sq km), some of it reclaimed land. Humidity and heavy downpours define its climate; showers are so sudden that the umbrella is a regular accessory.

Pink orchid Vanda Miss Joaquim, the national flower of Singapore

When Sir Stamford Raffles of the British East India Company landed on its shores in 1819, Singapore was little more than a nondescript fishing village. However, the town soon went on to become a British stronghold. After gaining independence from the British, Singapore was incorporated into the Federation of Malaysia in 1963, and went on to become a wholly independent nation in 1965.

Kuan Yew from its inception in the 1960s right up to the 1990s. Even with the presence of an active opposition, a one-party system has prevailed on the whole. While critics deem it autocratic, the party is seen as having been instrumental in helping Singapore become the super-developed, modern nation that it is today. Singaporeans give credit to Lee Kuan Yew who has enjoyed unrivaled popularity as a nation builder.

THE ECONOMY

Singapore has a highly successful and transparent economy. Despite accusations of the government having too many stakes in the market, the economy is believed to be among the most powerful in the world, chiefly because of government efficiency, the exceptional infrastructure, minimal corruption, and a skilled workforce.

GOVERNMENT AND POLITICS

Singapore is a democratic republic that follows the British parliamentary system, with a government led by a prime minister. Political affairs have long been dominated by the People's Action Party, which was led by statesman Lee

Towering skyscrapers dominate Singapore's skyline

◁ Singapore city's business district with SIngapore River in the foreground

Singapore's economy thrives on the electronics and chemical sectors, as well as business and financial services. Due to its strategic location linking the mainland and the islands of Southeast Asia with the rest of the world, Singapore has the busiest port in the region. Canned food, biotechnology, rubber processing, and, lately, tourism have emerged as other key revenue generating industries.

Ornately dressed performers of the Chinese opera

PEOPLES, LANGUAGES, AND RELIGIONS

Singapore is a country of immigrants, with a multiracial ethnicity comprising mainly 77 percent Chinese, 14 percent Malay, and 7.6 percent Indians, with a small number of Western expatriates. Ethnic neighborhoods, the norm in the 19th century, have given way to government-provided public housing. Old enclaves that have been left behind are now used only for shopping or entertainment that is unique to that particular community. The cultural heritage of the British colonialists is also deeply woven into the Singaporean lifestyle.

Malay, Chinese, English, and Tamil are all official languages in Singapore. The unique "Singlish" – a patois that combines English with Malay and Chinese words and intonation – is understood by most resident Singaporeans but rarely by visitors.

Except for certain radical groups that are banned, religion is freely practiced. Mahayana Buddhism is the most common, followed by Islam, Christianity, and Hinduism. Since the

Worshipers at Sri Mariamman Temple

racial riots of the 1960s, society has been considerably harmonized, with the government making every possible effort to keep it so.

CULTURE AND THE ARTS

The arts flourish in this diverse city. Chinese opera and drama, Western classical music, Indian classical dance forms, and English theater are all part of local culture, and several theater and dance ensembles keep Malay culture alive. However, government censorship is rigid; each performance needs a seal of approval before being shown to the public. A plethora of museums, festivals, and religious places complement the visual arts.

Food is an integral part of Singaporean culture, and eating out is considered the best way of socializing. Although Chinese, Indian, and Malay flavors dominate, international cuisine ranging from African to Eastern European is also widely available. Being a food haven has added to the popularity of this gateway between the East and the West, and it remains as alluring today as it was centuries ago.

SINGAPORE THROUGH THE YEAR

Singapore's multicultural heritage has resulted in a calendar studded with holidays and vibrant festivals, both secular and religious. Many of the religious festivals are based on the lunar calendar *(see p333)*, so their dates vary annually. Check with the Singapore Tourism Board for exact timings. While some festivities, such as Chinese New Year and Hari Raya Puasa, are celebrated with pomp and pageantry all over the island, others are quieter local market and temple affairs. Visitors are welcome in temples and mosques as long as customs are respected. Other cultural events such as the Singapore Arts Festival further add to the year's festivities.

Paying respect to elders on Hari Raya Puasa

JANUARY TO MARCH

Ponggal *(Jan/Feb)*. A Tamil (south Indian) harvest festival celebrated at temples such as the Sri Srinivasa Perumal Temple *(see pp230–31)*. Rice is cooked in new pots and allowed to boil over to symbolize prosperity. It is then offered to the gods as thanksgiving.
Thaipusam *(Jan/Feb)*. A Hindu festival of penance in honor of Lord Murugan. Male devotees carry *kavadis,* or steel arches, anchored to their skin with hooks, in a long colorful procession from the Sri Srinivasa Perumal Temple to the Chettiar Temple *(see p217)*.
Chinese New Year *(Jan/Feb)*. This vibrant Chinese festival is a two-week celebration culminating with Chap Goh Mei, marked by a final dinner and prayers. Chinatown is ablaze with lights and packed with shoppers.
Chingay Parade *(Jan/Feb)*. Part of the New Year festivities, a grand, colorful parade of stiltwalkers, lion

dancers, floats, and other multicultural performers travels down Orchard Road.
Qing Ming Festival *(Mar/ Apr)*. Chinese families visit temples and ancestral graves to clean and restore them. Red candles and joss sticks are lit and offerings of rice, wine, and flowers are made.

Lion dance performance during the Chinese New Year

APRIL TO JUNE

Vesak day *(May/Jun)*. Buddhists commemorate the birth, enlightenment, and death, of the Buddha on this day. Monks chant prayers at packed Buddhist temples and caged birds are set free to symbolize kindness. In the evening, candlelit processions set out from the temples. Thian Hock Keng Temple *(see pp222–3)* is a good place to see celebrations.
Singapore Arts Festival *(May/ Jun)*. Organized by the National Arts Council, this premier arts festival has a captivating program of local, regional, and international art, drama, dance, and music.
Dragon Boat Festival and Boat Race *(Jun)*. This festival commemorates the death of the 4th-century Chinese poet Qu Yuan, who drowned himself in protest against political corruption. It is said that people searched for him in boats, beating drums and throwing rice dumplings into the water to distract the fish from attacking his body. Today, international teams compete in dragon-shaped boats to honor this event. Drums are still beaten and rice dumplings wrapped in bamboo leaves are the festival's traditional snack.

JULY TO SEPTEMBER

Great Singapore Sale *(May/ Jun)*. Shops throughout the island hold sales during this period – the discounts can be extremely enticing *(see p247)*.
National Day *(Aug 9)*. Singapore's Independence Day is celebrated with a spectacular show at the Padang. The highlights include military parades, an airforce flypast, and cultural

performances, with a laser and fireworks display as a final flourish.

Festival of the Hungry Ghosts *(Aug/Sep).* The Chinese believe that during the seventh lunar month, souls of the dead return to earth to feast. Joss sticks, red candles, and paper money are burnt, and lavish feasts and dramatic Chinese street operas, *wayang (see p254),* are held to appease the spirits.

Mid-Autumn Festival *(Aug/Sep).* The full moon on the 15th day of the eighth month in the Chinese calendar is celebrated with mooncakes and lanterns. Traditionally a thanksgiving for a bountiful harvest, the festival also commemorates a 14th-century Chinese patriot who is said to have hidden notes to his companions in mooncakes while trying to overthrow the Yuan Dynasty.

Mooncakes, pastries filled with lotus seeds or red bean paste, and sometimes a duck egg, are sold in hotels and in Chinatown, and children parade with brightly-colored lanterns. A lantern display and competition are held at the Chinese Garden.

Lantern competition at the Chinese Garden during Mid-Autumn Festival

OCTOBER TO DECEMBER

Hari Raya Puasa *(variable).* A day of celebration for the Muslim community to mark the end of Ramadan, the Muslim holy month. Areas such as Sultan Mosque and Arab Street *(see p228)* come alive with festivities.

Deepavali *(Oct/Nov).* The Hindu festival of lights marks Lord Krishna's victory over Narakasura – a triumph of good over evil. Homes and temples are decorated with oil lamps to attract Lakshmi, the goddess of prosperity, and Little India dazzles with lights and decorations. The precise date is established each year according to the Indian almanacs.

Thimithi Festival *(Oct/Nov).* A festival procession begins at the Sri Srinivasa Perumal Temple and makes its way to the Sri Mariamman Temple *(see p218)* where devotees prove the strength of their faith by walking barefoot across a stretch of burning hot coals.

Festival of the Nine Emperor Gods *(Oct/Nov).* A nine-day festival in honor of the Nine Emperor Gods, thought to bring good luck and longevity, is celebrated at Kiu Ong Yiah Temple on Upper Serangoon Road. Prayers, feasts, and Chinese opera performances are followed by a procession of the nine gods seated on elaborate chairs, led by temple mediums with swords and whips.

During this festival, many devotees also make a pilgrimage to the temple of Tua Pek Kong on Kusu Island (Turtle Island).

Christmas *(25 Dec).* From November onwards, Orchard Road is transformed into a stunning stretch of fairy lights and Christmas decorations. Shops and hotels join in the festivities. Christmas is celebrated in the traditional way, with late-night mass, carols, and presents.

Hari Raya Haji *(variable).* A festival in honor of those Muslims who have made the pilgrimage to Mecca. It is marked by animal sacrifices and prayers at mosques.

PUBLIC HOLIDAYS

Local festivals follow the lunar calendar, and the dates are variable.

New Year's Day (Jan 1)

Hari Raya Puasa (variable)

Chinese New Year (Jan/Feb)

Hari Raya Haji (variable)

Good Friday (Mar/Apr)

Labor Day (May 1)

Vesak Day (May/Jun)

National Day (Aug 9)

Deepavali (Oct/Nov)

Christmas Day (Dec 25)

Offerings at the family altar during Deepavali

SINGAPORE AT A GLANCE

hile most of Singapore's attractions lie at the heart of the city, south of the island, its compactness and efficient infrastructure make it easy to visit the outer reaches. The north, west, and east are studded with older suburbs, nature reserves, and historic sites. Despite being a model modern metropolis with skyscrapers, glitzy shopping malls, museums, and contemporary entertainment, a traditional Singapore survives beneath its glossy exterior. At its core is a multicultural heritage, revealed in the timeless elegance of colonial architecture, Chinatown's shophouses, and the uniquely juxtaposed temples, mosques, and churches.

SINGAPORE'S TOP TEN ATTRACTIONS

Raffles Hotel
See pp214–15

Orchard Road
See pp232–5

Chinatown
See pp218–23

Little India
See pp224–31

Singapore Botanic Gardens
See pp240–41

Singapore Zoological Gardens
See p238

Sentosa
See pp244–5

Chijmes
See p212

Boat Quay
See p221

Fort Canning Park
See p217

◁ The unmistakable colonial architecture and simple elegance of Raffles Hotel

The Singapore River

Botero's *Bird* sculpture

The Singapore River winds through the heart of the main city and has long been the hub of its life and commerce. Flanked by the towering skyscrapers of the financial district on the southern bank and the stately colonial buildings on the northern bank, the river is lined with leafy walkways, shops, and eateries. River cruises depart from several piers along the bank.

UOB Plaza's entrance lobby is embellished with sculptures by Dali and Botero.

Cavenagh Bridge
Signs restricting horse-drawn carriages still stand at the city's only suspension bridge.

The Fullerton Hotel's colonial façade dominates the entrance to the river. The present building replaced Fort Fullerton in 1925.

Asian Civilizations Museum II *(see p210)*

Merlion
This mythical half-fish, half-lion symbol of Singapore guards the river as it opens into Marina Bay.

Raffles' Landing Site
A plaque below a poly-marble statue of Raffles marks the site of his original landing in 1819.

Anderson Bridge
This bridge was built in 1910 to relieve the increasing traffic on Cavenagh Bridge.

Parliament Complex
Opened in 1999, the new Parliament House complements the Victorian style of the original parliament building (see p211), dating to 1827.

Boat Quay
Bars and restaurants bring new life to the restored row of old trading houses lining the southern bank of the river (see p221).

Elgin Bridge
The present bridge was built in 1929 on the site of the first one across the river, and is named for Lord Elgin, then Governor General of India.

Clarke Quay
Refurbished warehouses form a colorful backdrop to this lively shopping and eating area (see p217).

Swissotel Merchant Court Hotel

Riverside Point is a shopping mall that leads to Merchant Square and Central Mall.

Riverwalk Galleria is a shopping complex. A sculpture of a boy and his cat sits on the river's edge.

River taxi kiosk

Read Bridge

To Robertson Quay

Hill Street Building

0 meters 100
0 yards 100

Coleman Bridge
This bridge was named for George D. Coleman, the architect who designed much of Singapore's urban landscape.

THE COLONIAL CORE AND CHINATOWN

Sir Stamford Raffles' city plan of 1822 designated the south of the river as the commercial district, and reserved the north for administrative offices. This northern area is known today as the Colonial Core. It is the heart of downtown Singapore and is dotted with historical landmarks. The Padang and Fort Canning Park are focal points of this area and have witnessed major events in Singapore's history. To the south of the river lies the flourishing Central Business District, also known as the Golden Shoe due to its shoe-shaped district boundary. Adjoining the business district lies Chinatown. As trading houses grew along the south bank in the 19th century, coolies and Chinese merchants settled in the area and Raffles officially allocated it to the community. It is characterized by distinctive shophouses, temples, and markets.

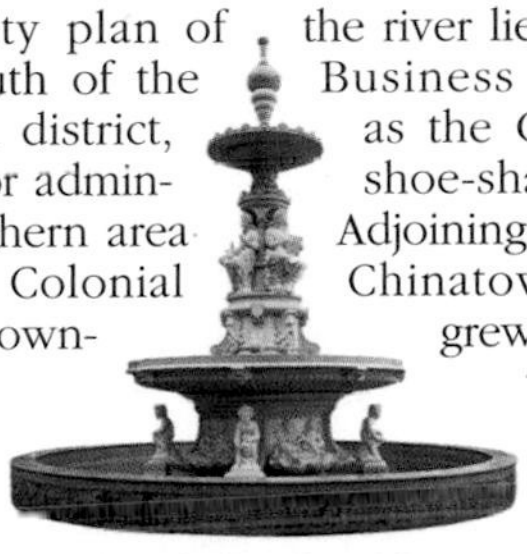

Tan Kim Seng fountain

SIGHTS AT A GLANCE

Historic Streets, Buildings, and Monuments

Ann Siang Hill 23
Boat Quay 28
Chijmes 9
Chinatown Heritage Center 18
Clarke Quay 17
Lau Pa Sat 25
Old Parliament House 5
Raffles Hotel pp214–15 8
Raffles' Landing Site 1
Raffles Place 27
Tanjong Pagar Conservation Area 22
Telok Ayer Street 24
Temple Street 20
Victoria Theater and Concert Hall 4

Museums and Galleries

Asian Civilizations Museum II 2
National Museum of Singapore 12
Peranakan Museum 13
Singapore Art Museum 10

Parks and Gardens

Esplanade Park 3
Fort Canning Park 15

Shopping

Chinatown Complex 21
Raffles City 7

Churches and Temples

Armenian Church 14
Cathedral of the Good Shepherd 11
Chettiar Temple 16
St. Andrew's Cathedral 6
Sri Mariamman Temple 19
Thian Hock Keng Temple pp222–3 26

GETTING THERE

The MRT goes to both the Colonial Core and Chinatown. Take bus numbers 7, 14, 16, 106 or 111 to the Colonial Core. Bus numbers 124, 143, 174 and 190 go to Chinatown.

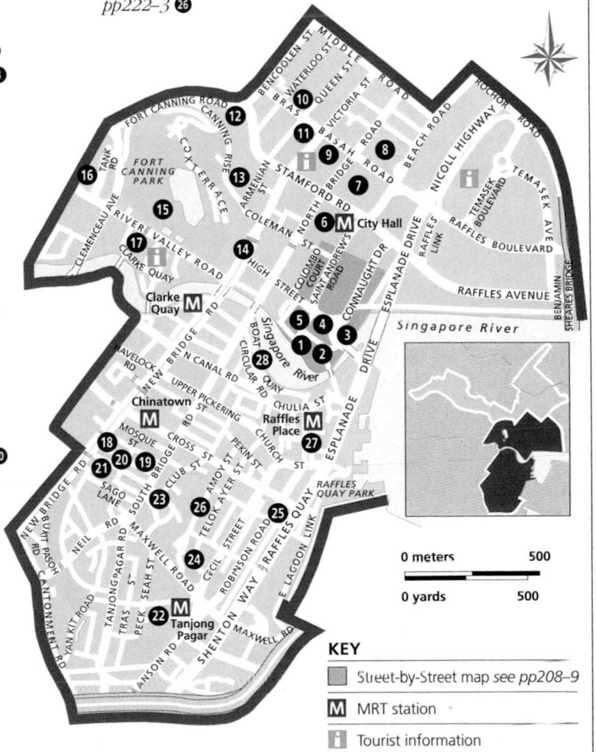

KEY

Street-by-Street map *see pp208–9*
[M] MRT station
[i] Tourist information

◁ **A refurbished shophouse on Duxton Road, Tanjong Pagar Conservation Area**

Street-by-Street: Around the Padang

The heart of Singapore's colonial district is the Padang, or square, which was once used by the 19th-century colonials as a site for big sporting events as well as National Day parades. Sporting activities from cricket and field hockey to soccer and rugby still take place here on a weekly basis. The square is flanked by grand structures such as the domed Supreme Court, the Neo-Classical City Hall, the Parliament House, and the exclusive Singapore Cricket Club. Also of interest here is Esplanade Park, which lies on the eastern side of the Padang. One of the oldest parks in Singapore, it is home to many historical landmarks.

★ Supreme Court
The courthouse was the last Classical building to be erected in Singapore.

HIGH STREET

★ Victoria Theater and Concert Hall
Built in 1862, the Victoria Theater was originally the Town Hall. The Victoria Memorial Hall was added in 1905 to commemorate the death of Queen Victoria. Its name was later changed to the Victoria Concert Hall ❹

PARLIAMENT LANE

Asian Civilizations Museum II

Raffles' Landing Site

To the Boat Quay

Old Parliament House
Constructed in 1827, this building was originally commissioned as a private residence for a Scottish merchant, John Argyle Maxwell ❺

STAR SIGHTS

- ★ Supreme Court
- ★ Victoria Theater and Concert Hall
- ★ City Hall

The Pyramid
Located in front of Empress Place, the Pyramid contains a time capsule which will be opened in 2015 to celebrate Singapore's silver jubilee.

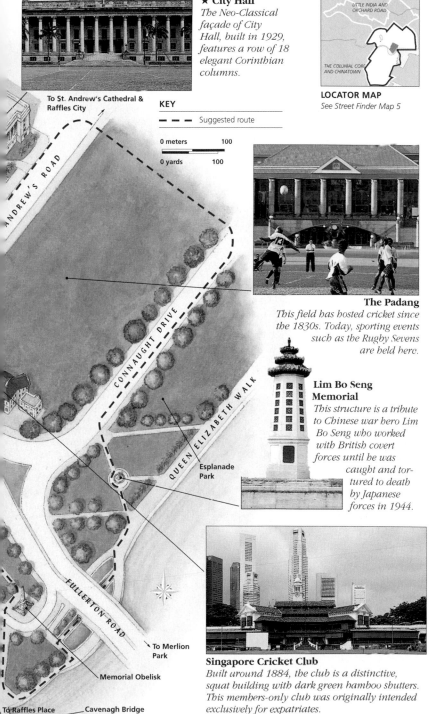

★ City Hall
The Neo-Classical façade of City Hall, built in 1929, features a row of 18 elegant Corinthian columns.

LOCATOR MAP
See Street Finder Map 5

KEY

– – – Suggested route

0 meters 100
0 yards 100

The Padang
This field has hosted cricket since the 1830s. Today, sporting events such as the Rugby Sevens are held here.

Lim Bo Seng Memorial
This structure is a tribute to Chinese war hero Lim Bo Seng who worked with British covert forces until he was caught and tortured to death by Japanese forces in 1944.

Singapore Cricket Club
Built around 1884, the club is a distinctive, squat building with dark green bamboo shutters. This members-only club was originally intended exclusively for expatriates.

Statue of Sir Stamford Raffles at the original landing site

Raffles' Landing Site ❶

North Boat Quay. **Map** 5 D3.
Ⓜ *Raffles Place, City Hall.* 🚌 *7, 32, 51, 81, 124, 145, 197, 603, 851.*

A statue of Sir Stamford Raffles gazing upon the flourishing Central Business District, complete with a plinth, marks the spot where he first set foot on Singapore soil, on the morning of January 29, 1819 *(see p204)*. The modern poly-marble statue is a replica of the original bronze work cast by British sculptor-poet, Thomas Woolner, which was unveiled on the Padang on June 27, 1887. The original statue, which narrowly escaped being melted down during the Japanese invasion, now stands in front of the Victoria Concert Hall.

Asian Civilizations Museum II ❷

1 Empress Place. **Map** 5 D3.
Tel *6332-7798.* Ⓜ *Raffles Place, City Hall.* 🚌 *75, 540, 608.* ⏱ *1–7pm Mon, 9am–7pm Tue–Sun, 9am–9pm Fri.* 🎟 *free entry after 7pm.* 📷 *2pm Mon, 11am & 2pm Tue–Fri, also at 3:30pm Sat & Sun.* ♿ 🍴 🌐 www.nhb.gov.sg/acm

Home to over 1,600 artifacts that trace the history of the varied cultures and civili-zations of Asia, the second wing of the Asian Civilizations Museum is housed in the Empress Place Building. Named in honor of Queen Victoria and completed in 1867, the Palladian structure was built by convicts and first functioned as a courthouse. Over the years, the build-ing housed many colonial administra-tive departments.

Today, this Neo-Classical structure showcases a wealth of exhibits in 11 themed gal-leries and four ACE (Asian Civilizations Education) Zones: South Asia, West Asia/Islam, Southeast Asia, and China. There is also a fascinating Singapore River Interpretive Gallery where the story of generations of immigrants who settled and worked on the banks of the Singapore River is told using old photographs.

Mythological mask, Asian Civilizations Museum II

Esplanade Park ❸

Connaught Drive. **Map** 5 E3.
Ⓜ *City Hall.* 🚌 *10, 70, 75, 82, 97, 100, 130, 131, 167, 196, 608.*

Running along Connaught Drive from the underpass at Anderson Bridge to Stamford Road, Esplanade Park was one of the most popular outdoor spots for both the European and Asian commu-nities during the colonial era.

The park contains Queen Elizabeth Walk and several landmarks, including the Cenotaph, which commemo-rates those who lost their lives during the two World Wars; the **Lim Bo Seng Memorial**, which eulogizes the World War II hero who died in Japanese captivity; and the Tan Kim Seng Fountain, which was built in honor of the philan-thropist who set up Singapore's first freshwater supply.

In 2002, the park was the center of controversy when **Esplanade – Theaters on the Bay** was built, sparking debate over the radical archi-tecture of the new building. Located on the waterfront, the huge, spiked shells of the complex contain a plethora of performing arts venues, including a concert hall, the-ater, outdoor theater, and recital studio, as well as gal-lery space, a performing arts library, and a shopping mall.

The massive riverside complex of Esplanade – Theaters on the Bay

For hotels and restaurants in this area see pp286–8 and pp308–11

The Neo-Palladian façade of the Old Parliament House

Victoria Theater and Concert Hall ❹

9 Empress Place. **Map** 5 E2.
Tel 6338-8283 (theater); 6338-6124,
6339-6120 (concert hall). Ⓜ Raffles
Place, City Hall. 🚌 75, 540, 608.
◯ 10am–7pm Mon–Sat, later for
performances. ♿ 🖥 🏛

A splendid example of
colonial architecture, Victoria
Theater was built in 1862
by the British to showcase
amateur dramatic productions
and Gilbert and Sullivan
operettas. The Victoria
Memorial Hall was added in
1905 to celebrate Queen
Victoria's jubilee. The
Memorial Hall was
renamed Victoria
Concert Hall in 1980
when it became home
to the Singapore
Symphony Orchestra
(see p254).
   Over the years,
the hall has been
put to a variety
of uses. During
World War II, it
was converted into a hospital.
Its clock tower was set to
Tokyo time when Japan occupied the island, and after the
Japanese surrender, it was
here that the war crimes
tribunals were held.
   The two buildings are the
venue for a range of concerts,
performances, and multi-
cultural extravaganzas (see
pp252–5). Details of events
held here are posted on the
billboards, and tickets can be
obtained at the box office or
at outlets in Singapore's main
shopping areas.

Old Parliament House ❺

1 High Street. **Map** 5 D3. **Tel** 6332-
6900. Ⓜ City Hall, Raffles Place.
🚌 7, 32, 51, 81, 124, 145, 197,
603, 851. ◯ 10am–9pm Mon–Fri,
11am–9pm Sat. Box office opens 90
mins before Sunday events. 📷 only
for tours. 🎟 11am & 3pm daily. 🏛
🖥 🏛 www.theartshouse.com.sg

Singapore's oldest surviving
government building, the Old
Parliament House was originally built as the residence of
Scottish merchant John Argyle
Maxwell in the late 1820s. It
was designed in Neo-
Palladian style by G.D.
Coleman, an architect
who was to shape
much of Singapore's
urban landscape.
Maxwell leased it to
the government for
use as a courthouse. In
the 1950s, it became
the colonial
government's
Assembly House,
and, in 1962, the
Parliament House of the independent state. The bronze
elephant outside the building
was a gift from the Thai
monarch, Rama V, after his
1871 visit to Singapore.
   A new Parliament House
was built nearby in 1999.
In 2004, after careful
restoration, the old building
was converted into The Arts
House, an elegant arts and
heritage space. The center
offers a range of contemporary visual and performance
arts, art house movies, and
improvisational theater.

Elephant sculpture, Old
Parliament House

St. Andrew's Cathedral ❻

Coleman Street. **Map** 5 E2.
Tel 6337-6104. Ⓜ City Hall. 🚌 7,
32, 51, 81, 124, 145, 197, 603, 851.
◯ daily. 🎟 ♿ 🕇 7am, 8am,
11am, 2pm, 5pm, 7:30pm Sun.
🏛 www.livingstreams.org.sg

Although an Anglican church,
St. Andrew's was named for
the patron saint of Scotland
in recognition of the Scottish
merchants who contributed
funds to build it. The gleaming cathedral of today is
actually the second ecclesias-
tical building to be built on
this site. The first church,
designed and built by G.D.
Coleman in the late 1830s,
was declared unsafe and
closed in 1852 following two
lightning strikes. In 1862, it
was replaced by the present-
day cathedral. Designed by
Colonel MacPherson in Early
Gothic style and built using
convict labor from India, its
lancet windows, turret-like
pinnacles, and decorated
spire are reminiscent of
England's Salisbury Cathedral.
The exterior was coated with
chunam plaster, a mixture of
eggwhite, shell, lime, sugar,
coconut husk, and water,
which was molded into the
ornate façade and polished
to a smooth finish.
   Within the church are brass
plaques dedicated to families
of past congregations, and
memorials to soldiers who
lost their lives in the Sepoy
Mutiny of 1915 and in the
two World Wars.

Graceful spire of the Victorian-era
St. Andrew's Cathedral

The soaring silver blocks of the Raffles City complex

Raffles City ❼

2 Stamford Road. **Map** 3 D5, 5 E2.
Tel 6433-2238. Ⓜ City Hall. 🚌 7,
36, 77, 97, 103, 124, 131, 147, 162,
166, 174, 190, 501, 511, 603.
◯ 10am–9:30pm daily. 🍽 🛍 🏛
www.rafflescity.com

Raffles Institution, a school
founded by Sir Stamford
Raffles and built in 1835 by
G.D. Coleman, was demol-
ished in 1984 to make way
for Raffles City, a huge complex comprising a shopping
mall, high-rise offices, and
two hotels – Raffles the Plaza
and Swissôtel the Stamford,
which was the world's tallest
hotel when it was completed
in 1985. Perched atop the
Stamford are lavish bars and
restaurants, including The
Equinox on Level 69, which
offers stunning panoramic
views of the city and parts
of Malaysia.

Popularly dubbed the
Tin Can for its metallic
appearance, Raffles City
was designed by I.M. Pei,
the Chinese-American
architect who is famous
for his designs of the
glass pyramid in front
of the Louvre in Paris
and Bank of China
skyscraper in
Hong Kong. Four

levels of stores at the complex
offer everything from electronics and premier labels such
as Mont Blanc and Armani
Exchange to cafés and specialty stalls selling Thai silk
and Chinese handicrafts. There
is also a shop of New York
City's Metropolitan Museum of
Art. To the east of Raffles City
stand the four dignified 229-ft
(70-m) high white columns of
the Civilian War Memorial.

Raffles Hotel ❽

See pp214–15.

Chijmes ❾

30 Victoria Street. **Map** 3 D5, 5 E1.
Tel 6332-6273. Ⓜ City Hall. 🚌 2, 7,
12, 33, 81, 107, 130, 133, 147, 190,
520, 851, 960. ◯ 11am–3am daily.
🍽 🛍 🏛 www.chijmes.com.sg

Chijmes (pronounced
"chimes"), an elegant walled
complex of shops, restaurants,
bars, and gallery spaces, was
once the Convent of the Holy
Infant Jesus. Founded by a
French Jesuit priest in 1854
and run by nuns, the convent
functioned as a school and a
women's refuge, as well as
a home for babies who were
abandoned at its gates. In
1983, when the convent was
relocated to the suburbs, the
buildings, including a school,
a chapel, and a private residence, were redeveloped
into what is now one of
Singapore's most beautiful
public spaces.

Quiet courtyards, cobbled
paths, fountains, and covered Italianate walkways
encircle shops that sell
arts and crafts from China,
the Philippines, Thailand,
Malaysia, and India, as
well as restaurants
that serve everything
from *sushi* to tapas.
The most striking
building in the
complex is the

Façade of the chapel of Chijmes, now an arts and dining venue

former chapel, designed in
Neo-Gothic style by Jesuit
priest Father Nain. Most of
this historic building has been
restored, including the beautiful 19th-century stained-glass
windows. The chapel's lofty
columns are decorated with
intricate plasterwork and it
is capped with a magnificent
spire. It is now Chijmes Hall,
a venue for art exhibitions,
recitals, and weddings.

Singapore Art Museum, a former Catholic boys' school

Singapore Art Museum ❿

71 Bras Basah Road. **Map** 3 D5,
5 D1. **Tel** 6332-3222. Ⓜ City Hall,
Dhoby Gaut. 🚌 7, 14, 16, 36, 77,
97, 131, 167, 171, 518, 602, 603,
605, 607, 700. ◯ 10am–7pm Mon–
Sun, 10am–9pm Fri. 🎟 free for
children under 6 years. 🎟 ♿ 🛍
🏛 www.nhb.gov.sg/sam

A bronze statue of two
schoolboys with 17th-century
saint John Baptiste de la Salle
stands above the porch of
the Singapore Art Museum, a
reminder that until 1987 this
was St. Joseph's Institution,
a Catholic boys' school.

Today, the building is a
showcase for contemporary
Asian art. Since the museum's
opening in January 1996, its
permanent collection has
grown from under 2,000 works
of art to over 7,000 pieces,
making it one of the world's
largest public collections of
modern and contemporary
Southeast Asian art. The core

of the museum's art, which includes sculptures, installations, and paintings, is richly supplemented by a regular roster of local and international traveling exhibitions, featuring 20th-century art from American and European compilations. Works from the museum's own collection are loaned out to international exhibitions.

Usually only a selection of works are on display at any given time. There are works by artists such as Georgette Chen, Liu Kang, Chen Chong Swee, Lim Tze Peng, and Huang Yao from Singapore, and those by regional artists such as Wong Hoy Cheong from Malaysia, Affandi from Indonesia, and Bui Xian Phai and Tran Trong Vu from Vietnam.

The old Classical-style building has been restored and skillfully converted for use as a museum. The former school chapel is used as an auditorium. While the chapel's original character has been retained, its central window has been replaced with a modern stained-glass work by Filipino artist Ramon Orlina. The building's two courtyards are used as exhibition spaces, arranged on either side of the Glass Hall, which is a glass-enclosed converted veranda decorated with blown-glass installations by American artist Dale Chihuly. The old classrooms are now galleries. The state-of-the-art E-mage Multimedia Gallery provides information on the history and techniques of contemporary Southeast Asian art. The museum also has a library and a shop which sells souvenirs showcasing the works of renowned artists.

The Dome Café, ensconced in one of the naves of the museum, serves excellent sandwiches, cakes, and coffee drinks. There is also the Venezia restaurant, which serves excellent fusion cuisine and offers set dinners. A trendy alfresco wine bar adds to the pleasant ambience.

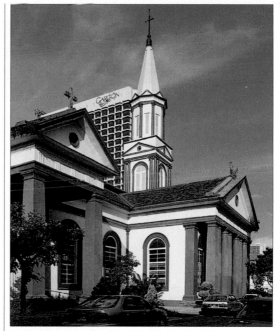

Renaissance-style exterior of the Cathedral of the Good Shepherd

Cathedral of the Good Shepherd ⓫

4 Queen Street. **Map** 3 D5, 5 D1.
Tel 6337-2036. Ⓜ City Hall. 🚍 7, 14, 16, 36, 77, 97, 131, 167, 171, 501, 700, 957, 960. ◯ daily.
✝ 8am, 10am, 6pm Sun; 7am, 1:15pm Mon–Fri; 7am, 6:30pm Sat.
⛪ www.veritas.org.sg

Singapore's oldest Catholic place of worship, this cathedral was built between 1843 and 1847. It was administered by French missionary Father Jean-Marie Beurel, who also established the Convent of the Holy Infant Jesus and St. Joseph's Institution. Designed by noted colonial architect D.L. McSwiney in a Latin-cross pattern, the church combines a Renaissance-style exterior with Doric columns, Palladian porches, and a beautifully crafted timber ceiling. The octagonal steeple was a later addition by Charles Dyce.

The church, which was accorded cathedral status in 1897, served as an emergency hospital during World War II, and was listed as a national monument in 1973.

Three interesting buildings stand within the church compound. The **Archbishop's House**, a 19th-century double-story bungalow with a projecting portico, casement windows, and enclosed verandas, is a simple structure in contrast to the cathedral. The **Resident's Quarters**, a U-shaped single-story building with Doric columns, and the **Priest's House** are more ornate and decorated with elaborate plasterwork.

Sculpture, Singapore Art Museum

Stained glass in the Cathedral of the Good Shepherd

Raffles Hotel ❽

Singapore Sling

A legendary hotel and a national monument, Raffles, which opened in 1887, is a tranquil haven of white, veranda-enclosed, colonial-style buildings with terra-cotta tiled, pitched roofs. It was once the venue for grand colonial balls and dances, and its guest list boasted such names as Noel Coward, Somerset Maugham, Rudyard Kipling, Joseph Conrad, Charlie Chaplin, and Michael Jackson. The cool, calm refuges of its court-yards, gardens, and covered walkways can still be enjoyed by residents and visitors alike.

★ **Long Bar**
The Singapore Sling, the pink drink originally intended for women, was created in 1915 by Hainanese bartender Ngiam Tong Boon.

★ **Ornamental Fountain**
Made in Scotland in the early 1890s, the 20-ft (6-m) high cast-iron fountain was donated to the hotel in 1990 and now stands in the Palm Garden.

Raffles Hotel souvenir shop

Bar and Billiard Room

Tiffin Room

★ **Lobby**
The lobby, home to the Writers' Bar, features photo-graphs of some of the writers who have stayed at Raffles.

Writers' Bar

Palm Court
This area is a beautifully restored space lined with palm and frangipani trees. Collectively, the hotel's gardens house over 50,000 plants representing about 80 different species.

The Raffles Grill is one of Singapore's most prestigious restaurants *(see p310)*, serving fine French cuisine. The French doors of the Grill overlook the Palm Court.

For hotels and restaurants in this area see pp286–8 and pp308–11

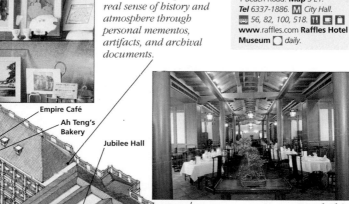

★ Raffles Hotel Museum
The museum imparts a real sense of history and atmosphere through personal mementos, artifacts, and archival documents.

Empire Café

Ah Teng's Bakery

Jubilee Hall

VISITORS' CHECKLIST

1 Beach Road. **Map** *5 E1.*
Tel *6337-1886.* **M** *City Hall.*
🚌 *56, 82, 100, 518.* 🚻 🖥 🛍
www.raffles.com **Raffles Hotel Museum** ◯ *daily.*

Royal China
Replacing the old Empress Room in 2003, this restaurant offers its signature dishes in an "old-world" atmosphere.

The Seah Street Deli specializes in New York-style delicatessen food. The portions are authentic, large, and reasonably priced.

The Raffles Culinary Academy is where the hotel holds cooking classes conducted by renowned visiting chefs.

The lawn's tropical foliage combined with a gazebo provides the setting for garden receptions.

Doc Cheng's
This award-winning, themed restaurant offers an exciting fusion of Western and Oriental cuisines (see p309).

STAR FEATURES

★ Long Bar

★ Ornamental Fountain

★ Lobby

★ Raffles Hotel Museum

The grand Neo-Palladian exterior of the National Museum of Singapore

National Museum of Singapore ⑫

93 Stamford Road. **Map** 3 D5, 5 D1. **Tel** 6332-3659. Ⓜ City Hall, Dhoby Ghaut. 🚌 7, 14, 16, 36, 77, 97, 131, 166. ⭘ 9am–7pm Tue–Sun, 9am–9pm Wed. 🎫 🎦 11am, 2pm daily, also 3:30pm Sat & Sun. 🎟 **www**.nationalmuseum.sg

Housed in a Neo-Palladian structure and crowned with a stunning stained-glass dome, the island's oldest museum opened in 1887. Known as the Raffles Museum and Library, it was famed for its remarkable collections of natural history, ethnology, and archaeology.

Following Singapore's independence in 1965, the museum was renamed the National Museum to reflect its new role and altered its focus to exhibitions that concentrated on the history and peoples of Singapore. The museum has a permanent collection and various exhibitions on a range of subjects from Chinese secret societies to botany, but the highlights of the museum are the 11 artifacts that have collectively been christened the "Treasures of the National Museum." Among these rare pieces are 14th-century east Javanese-style gold ornaments excavated at Fort Canning, the 20th-century Xin Sai Le Puppet Stage, and William Farquhar's collection of 477 natural history drawings. Other exhibits include a Peranakan house exhibit, a Children's Discovery Gallery, and a History of Singapore Gallery, which displays a series of 20 model dioramas.

Peranakan Museum ⑬

39 Armenian Street. **Map** 2 C5, 5 D2. **Tel** 6332-7798. Ⓜ City Hall. 🚌 7, 14, 16, 36, 77, 97, 131, 166. ⭘ 1–7pm Mon, 9am–7pm Tue–Sun, 9am–9pm Fri. 🎫 🎦 🍴 🎟 **www**.acm.org.sg

This museum was originally the Tao Nan School, established in 1910 by three Chinese philanthropists for the education of boys from the Hokkien region of China. In 1997, this Neo-Classical building was opened as the first wing of the Asian Civilizations Museum. Having undergone a recent overhaul, it is now a Peranakan-themed museum representing a pan-Southeast Asia perspective of Peranakan culture with a focus on its main centers, which include Singapore, Malacca, and Penang.

The museum explores the history and ethnology of the culture of these regions and also provides an interesting glimpse into their heritage, including language and religious customs. Exhibits include silver artifacts, porcelain, jewelry, and textiles.

Armenian Church ⑭

60 Hill Street. **Map** 3 D5, 5 D2. **Tel** 6334-0141. Ⓜ City Hall. 🚌 2, 12, 32, 33, 51, 103, 124, 147, 174, 190, 197, 851. ⭘ 9am–5pm Mon–Fri, 9am–noon Sat. ⭘ Sun.

The Armenian Church of St. Gregory the Illuminator was the first permanent place of Christian worship in Singapore. The church was built in 1835 and the spire was added later, in 1850. It was able to seat a congregation of only 50 people, a reflection of the minority status of the local Armenian community then.

Designed by G.D. Coleman, the architect responsible for other landmarks of early Singapore such as St. Andrew's Cathedral (see p211), the church is an elegant example of tropical Neo-Classical architecture. The interior contains a photograph of the Armenian community from around 1917, as well as

Interior of the Armenian Church

portraits of the patriarchs of the Armenian Church. In the church's compound is the grave of Agnes Joaquim, who discovered an orchid hybrid in 1893. The flower was later named Vanda Miss Joaquim for her and adopted as Singapore's national flower *(see p198)*.

Fort Canning Park ⑮

51 Canning Rise, Singapore, 179872. **Map** 2 C5, 4 C2. *Tel* 6332-1200. Ⓜ Dhoby Ghaut. ⬛ 14, 32, 54, 77, 124, 139, 195. ⭕ 8am–noon, 5:30–8:30pm daily.

Once the seat of Temasek, a 14th-century Malay kingdom *(see p34)*, Fort Canning Park is now a verdant, tranquil oasis in the heart of the city. Because of the lovely view the site commands, Raffles built his bungalow here, and until the mid-19th century, it was home to Singapore's governors. The park was also the first site of Raffles' botanical garden.

In 1860, Fort Canning was built here; only the fort gate still stands. Nearby is the Fort Canning Center, formerly a barracks that now serves as a performance space and gallery. Another historic landmark is the Battle Box, a World War II bunker containing a museum that uses animatronics to recreate the 1942 surrender of the city to the Japanese. Also worth a visit is the ASEAN (Association of Southeast Asian Nations) sculpture park.

Sculpture, Fort Canning Park

Chettiar Temple ⑯

Crossing of Tank Road and River Valley Road. **Map** 4 C2 *Tel* 6737-9393. Ⓜ Dhoby Ghaut. ⬛ 14, 32, 54, 65, 139, 195. ⭕ 8am–noon, 5–8:30pm daily.

Built in 1984, this Shaivite Hindu temple replaced a much older one, founded in 1860 by wealthy Indian Chettiars (moneylenders). Dedicated to Lord Subramaniam (also known as Murugan), the colorful temple is believed to be one of the wealthiest and grandest in Singapore.

Craftsmen from southern India were specially brought in to create the temple's distinctive architectural features, which include a striking five-tiered *gopuram*, or entrance archway, massive patterned rosewood doors, and columns and prayer halls richly decorated with sculptures of Hindu deities. The ceiling has 48 etched-glass panels of gods that are angled to catch the rising and setting sun. Another feature, a rarity for Hindu temples, is the presence of a *thoonganai maadam*, a representation of the rear of an elephant at rest. The dominance of the temple's main deity is apparent throughout the temple, with Lord Murugan represented in six of his holy abodes. Inside the temple are two connected rooms, the *mandapam* and the *antarala*, through which worshipers move to perform their devotions. The *antarala* leads to the innermost sanctum, the *garbhagraha*, which only priests may enter.

The Chettiar Temple plays an important role in the life of Hindu Shaivites as it is the culmination point of a spectacular procession that begins at Sri Srinivasa Perumal Temple *(see pp230–31)* during the annual Thaipusam festival, which occurs between January and February and honors Lord Murugan *(see p200)*.

The colorful *gopuram* of the Hindu Chettiar Temple

Clarke Quay ⑰

3 River Valley Road, Singapore 179019. **Map** 4 C2. Ⓜ Clarke Quay. ⬛ 14, 32, 54, 65, 139, 195, or 3 min. walk from Hill Street. 🚹 ⬛ 🛗 🏬 ⬛ flea market on Sat&Sun. **www**.clarkequay.com.sg

Named for Sir Andrew Clarke, the second governor of Singapore, Clarke Quay is an upscale area along the banks of the Singapore River with waterfront shops and eateries. Lying near the mouth of the Singapore River, the site of Clarke Quay was a commercial hub during the late-19th century, containing warehouses run by Chinese traders. It was redeveloped in the early-1990s into an entertainment precinct offering restaurants, wine bars, retail stores, craft stalls, street performers, and cruises in authentic bumboats (boats that bring provisions and commodities to ships at port). While it is relatively quiet during the day, Clarke Quay offers a lively atmosphere at night.

The wide frontage of the Fort Canning Center, now a performance space

Figurines adorning the *gopuram*, or gateway, of Sri Mariamman Temple

several times over the years. In its early days, the temple gave shelter to new immigrants and also served as a social center for the community.

Although many of the splendid friezes and statues depict the Hindu divine trinity of Brahma, Vishnu, and Shiva, as well as other Hindu deities, the temple is dedicated to the goddess Sri Mariamman (an incarnation of Shiva's wife Parvati), known for her power to cure disease. The temple is famous for the annual Thimithi festival *(see p201)* in autumn, during which devotees walk on hot coals as a sign of faith.

Temple Street ⑳

Map 4 C4. Ⓜ *Chinatown.* 🚌 *51, 80, 124, 145, 174, 197, 608.* 🔟 🔳 📷

The area bounded by Mosque, Pagoda, Temple, Terengganu, and Smith Streets is the place that Sir Stamford Raffles had first earmarked for the Chinese community. It grew into the hub of Chinese life and culture, with streets that were lined with temples, traditional craft stores, *kongsi*, or clan houses, restaurants, and shophouses, shuttered buildings where the ground floor was occupied by a shop while families lived on the upper floor. Some shophouses contained opium dens and brothels, giving the area a somewhat colorful reputation.

Sensitive restoration has meant that much of the original character of these shophouses has been

Chinatown Heritage Center ⑱

48 Pagoda Street. **Map** 4 C3.
Tel *6325-2878.* Ⓜ *Chinatown.* 🚌 *61, 80, 197.* ◯ *daily.* 📷
www.chinatownheritage.com.sg

A superb museum housed in three restored shophouses, the center provides one of the most vivid accounts of the history and culture of Chinese immigrants. Three levels of galleries recreate their living conditions and, together with first-hand accounts of former residents and a variety of artifacts, trace the lives of early settlers and evoke different periods of Chinatown's history.

Sri Mariamman Temple ⑲

244 South Bridge Road. **Map** 4 C4.
Tel *6223-4064.* Ⓜ *Chinatown.* 🚌 *51, 80, 124, 143, 174, 197.* ◯ *7am–1:30pm, 6–8:30pm daily.*

The southern end of South Bridge Road is dominated by the *gopuram*, or entrance gateway, of the Sri

Mariamman Temple, vividly decorated with about 72 Hindu deities. The complex is encircled by a boundary wall topped with figures of sacred cows.

The oldest Hindu place of worship on the island, Sri Mariamman dates back to 1827 when the first temple, a simple wood and *attap*, or thatched-roof, was built on this site. The land belonged to an Indian merchant, Narain Pillai, who arrived in Singapore on the same ship as Sir Stamford Raffles. It was replaced by the present structure in 1843. The temple has been repaired

The entrance to a shop on Temple Street, Chinatown

retained. Many are painted in bright, contemporary colors. While escalating rents have driven out some of the traditional businesses, the area still features a variety of shops selling souvenirs, antiques, porcelain, and clothing. There are also several pleasant restaurants and cafés The surrounding housing blocks also offer an authentic flavor of the old Chinatown. These streets come alive during Chinese New Year, with festivities, vibrant decorations, and food and gift stalls.

Chinatown Complex ㉑

New Bridge Road. **Map** 4 C4.
Ⓜ *Outram Park, Chinatown.* 🚌 2, 12, 33, 54, 62, 63, 81, 124, 147, 961. ◯ *10am–10pm daily.* 🎫
🏪 🏛

On the corner of Terengganu Street and Sago Street, the Chinatown Complex houses one of the most boisterous wet markets in the city, where a bewildering variety of fresh produce is on sale, including fruit, vegetables, and seafood. The most startling meat and fish, including freshly skinned frogs, is on sale in the mornings. Above the wet market are stalls offering silk sarongs, jade jewelry, DVDs, and more.

Next door is Sago Street, named for its factories that once produced sago, starchy granules obtained from palm. The street was also infamous for its "Death Houses," hospices where the terminally ill came to die. Today, rattan mat-makers and paper kite sellers operate here.

Tanjong Pagar Conservation Area ㉒

Map 4 B5. Ⓜ *Tanjong Pagar.* 🚌 80, 145. 🎫 🏪 🏛

Once a nutmeg plantation, this area at the southern tip of South Bridge Road boasts some of Singapore's most elegant stretches of renovated

Restored double-story shophouses along Duxton Road

shophouses, especially along the impressive sweep of Tanjong Pagar Road and around Duxton Road. One of the first of the old neighborhoods to be renovated, Tanjong Pagar is now home to many lively restaurants, bars, and hotels including the beautiful Berjaya Duxton Hotel *(see p288)*.

At the corner of Neil Road and Tanjong Pagar Road is the former Jinrickshaw Station, built in 1903. Jinrickshaws

were first imported from Shanghai in the 1880s. By 1919 there were about 9,000 rickshaws and 20,000 rickshaw-pullers. The rickshaws were phased out by legislation after World War II and soon disappeared from the streets of Singapore.

A highlight of Tanjong Pagar is a visit to one of the traditional tea houses on Neil Road, where visitors can take part in the rituals of tea-drinking.

SHOPHOUSE STYLES

The shophouse is a memorable feature of Singapore's local architecture. Five styles, roughly chronological, have been identified – the Early, First Transitional, Late, Second Transitional, and Art Deco styles.

The Early Style (1840–1900) shophouse is a squat, two-story building. The windows and façade are plain.

The First Transitional Style (early 1900s) shophouse is three stories high, such as this unit at Telok Ayer Street.

The Late Style (1900–1940) shophouse is flamboyantly ornamented with eclectic styles, as seen in this unit (No. 21) on Bukit Pasoh Road.

The Second Transitional Style (late 1930s) shophouse, such as this unit (No. 10) on Stanley Street, is much simpler and less ornate.

The Art Deco Style (1930–1960) shophouse is typified by classical geometric motifs, as illustrated by this unit (No. 30) located on Bukit Pasoh Road.

The distinctive architecture of Lau Pa Sat's food court

Ann Siang Hill ㉓

Map 4 C4. Ⓜ *Tanjong Pagar, Chinatown.* 🚌 *51, 61, 63, 80, 103, 124, 145, 174, 197, 603, 608, 851.* 🍴 🖥 📷

Once a clove and nutmeg plantation, Ann Siang Hill and its neighboring streets are today a hub of Chinese life and activity. The gently curving street, flanked by shophouses, makes for an interesting walking tour. Some of the shophouses feature *pintu pagar*, or half doors, reflecting Malay influence. Club Street nearby is noted for its dining and upmarket boutiques. It is also famous for its temple-carving shops and the clan associations and guilds that gave the street its name. Some, such as the **Victorian Chinese Weekly Entertainment Club**, still survive on the hill, their walls plastered with photographs of former members. Also striking are house numbers 33 and 35, designed by architect Frank Brewer, famed for his skilled plasterwork.

Telok Ayer Street ㉔

Map 5 D4. Ⓜ *Tanjong Pagar, Raffles Place.* 🚌 *10, 70, 75, 82, 97, 100, 107, 130, 167, 186.* 🍴 🖥 📷

Originally located on the seafront before modern land reclamation, Telok Ayer Street, which means water bay in Malay, retains much of the feel of 19th-century Singapore. On the street are a number of traditional businesses, as well as temples and mosques where early immigrants gave thanks for their safe passage. One of the most famous is the Hokkien **Thian Hock Keng Temple** (*see pp222–3*), the city's oldest Chinese temple. The neighboring **Al Abrar Mosque** was built between 1850 and 1855 by Indian Muslims, who also built the nearby **Nagore Durgha** in the 1820s, a blend of Classical architecture and Indian-Islamic details such as arches and perforated grills. All three are national monuments. Farther down the street is the **Fuk Tak Ch'i**

Museum, standing on the site of the Hock Teckk Ch'i Temple. Among its display of Chinese artifacts is a diorama depicting Telok Ayer Street as it would have been in the 1850s. **Far East Square**, on Amoy Street, offers a variety of shops and restaurants housed in renovated shophouses.

Lau Pa Sat ㉕

18 Raffles Quay. **Map** 5 D4. Ⓜ *Raffles Place.* 🚌 *10, 70, 75, 82, 97, 100, 107, 130, 131, 167, 186.* ⏰ *24 hours.* 🍴 🖥 📷

Singapore's first municipal market, Telok Ayer Market, now renamed Lau Pa Sat, is an architecturally impressive food court offering an extensive variety of Asian cuisines and is a favorite lunch venue for locals. Originally commissioned by Raffles in 1822 on reclaimed land, the elegant octagonal cast-iron structure was designed by James MacRitchie and shipped over from a Glasgow foundry in 1894. It was declared a national monument in 1973. The market was dismantled during MRT tunnel construction and was later painstakingly reassembled. The adjacent Boon Tat Street is closed off to traffic in the evenings for traditional hawker stalls to set up shop.

Thian Hock Keng Temple ㉖

See pp222–3.

Row of restored shophouses on Ann Siang Hill

For hotels and restaurants in this area see pp286–8 and pp308–11

Raffles Place ㉗

Map 5 D3. [M] *Raffles Place.* [🚌] *10, 70, 75, 82, 97, 100, 107, 130, 131, 167, 196.* [🚻][🛒][📷]

Nowhere is Singapore's transition from a colonial backwater to a cutting edge, booming economy more apparent than in the gleaming skyscrapers of Raffles Place. This is the heart of the city's financial world, packed with well-known multinational corporations and financial institutions. Among the first banks to open here were the Hong Kong and Shanghai Bank and Standard Chartered Bank. The three tallest buildings in Singapore are located here – UOB Plaza, OUB Center, both designed by renowned Japanese architect Kenzo Tange, and Republic Plaza. All the buildings are 920 ft (280 m) high. The Bank of China building is one of Southeast Asia's earliest skyscrapers.

Dotted around the area are installations of modern sculpture, including Salvador Dali's *Homage to Newton* (1985) and Fernando Botero's *Bird* (1990). The Merlion statue, symbol of the city, is also located nearby. **Clifford Pier**, which provided a location for Conrad's *Lord Jim*, is the departure point for a number of excellent sightseeing cruises on the Singapore River.

Dali's *Homage to Newton*, Raffles Place

CONRAD'S LORD JIM

Born to Polish parents in what is now Ukraine, Teodor Josef Konrad Korzeniowski sailed to many places, including the Malay states, between 1874 and 1894, becoming a mariner and a British subject in 1886. Joseph Conrad is perhaps the most celebrated English writer on late 19th-century Southeast Asia, and Singapore figures prominently in his works, especially in the novel *Lord Jim*. It was in this region that he heard of an English merchant navy officer, Austin Podmore Williams, who earned lasting disgrace by abandoning the steamer *Jeddah*, along with 953 Muslim pilgrims, in the Red Sea in 1880, dooming himself to a life of exile. He became the tragic model for Conrad's *Lord Jim*.

Joseph Conrad

Boat Quay ㉘

Map 5 D3. [M] *Raffles Place.* [🚌] *2, 12, 33, 51, 54, 61, 81, 103, 145, 147, 166, 174, 190.* [🚻][🛒]

A thriving strip of restored shophouses converted into restaurants, shops, and bars, Boat Quay today is very different from the riverfront area of a century ago. The center of the city's commercial activities in the 1860s, most of its trading was handled from here. Shophouses crowded the curve of the south bank, the shape of which was thought to resemble the belly of a carp, an indicator of prosperity according to Chinese belief. The river teemed with bumboats, which were used to load and unload ships anchored on the river. By the 1960s, however, technological advances had changed the face of the shipping industry. New, high-tech container ports opened up farther up the river, claiming Boat Quay's role in the river's trade. Trading houses moved out and the area slowly declined. The government embarked upon a river-cleaning program which cleared out all the bumboats and the barges, leaving Boat Quay a desolate region.

In 1986, the government started restoring the area as part of a conservation project, renovating the old shophouses and godowns (warehouses) and revitalizing the riverfront area by pedestrianizing it. Today, there are plenty of little shops and restaurants with enchanting views of the river. A taxi service also plies between Boat Quay and Clarke Quay.

Bars and restaurants lining the riverbank at Boat Quay, once a busy trading center

Thian Hock Keng Temple ㉖

Carving of a gilded Buddha
on the temple's roof

Built in 1839, Thian Hock Keng Temple is the oldest Chinese temple in Singapore. Constructed by Hokkien sailors on the site of a joss house, it was the most important center of worship for immigrants from their community. It was also where seafarers gave thanks for a safe passage to Singapore. Construction was paid for by individual donors, the main one being Hokkien leader Tan Tock Seng (1798–1850). The temple itself is laid out along a traditional north-south axis and has shrines dedicated to several deities. Today, people of all ages come to this temple to give their thanks to Ma Zhu Po, the goddess of the sea.

★ **Roof Decorations**
On the temple's roof ridge stand twin dragons that embody the principles of yin and yang. Between them is the "night-shining pearl," a glass globe that represents the sun.

Rear Hall
Dedicated to the moon goddess, Yue Gong Niang Niang, Rear Hall houses a shrine to the goddess. She is worshiped alongside Kuan Yin, the goddess of mercy. The sun god, Ri Gong Tai Zi, is also worshiped here.

★ **Secondary Shrines**
In the side hall to the left of the main courtyard stand shrines to Kai Zhang Shen Wang, an early immigrant, and Cheng Hang, a local deity.

STAR FEATURES
★ Roof Decorations
★ Secondary Shrines
★ Ceiling of Main Hall

The pagoda, which used to house Chong Wen Ge, the first Chinese school in Singapore, was built in 1849.

Gift shop

VISITORS' CHECKLIST

158 Telok Ayer Street. **Map 5**
D4. *Tel* 6222-8212. Ⓜ️ *Tanjong
Pagar.* ⬜ *8:30am–5:30pm daily.*

Ancestor Tablets
*The spirits of ancestors are
believed to reside in these
venerated tablets.*

The roof ridge is
decorated with glazed
tile chips.

The furnace is where
paper money offerings
and other gifts are
burned to placate the
spirits of the dead.

The door at the
main entrance is
decorated with
temple guardians
from Chinese
mythology.

Granite Pillars
*The intricate
columns which
support the roof,
made of granite
from China, are
carved with
entwined dragons.*

The main hall contains the
image of Ma Zhu Po, the sea
goddess. She is flanked by
Guan Gong, the god of war,
and Pao Sheng Da Di, the
protector of life.

★ Ceiling of Main Hall
*Gilded carvings on the temple's ceiling
depict stories from Chinese folklore. These
carvings have been restored by artisans
from China. The gray pillars supporting the
ceiling are made of granite from China.*

LITTLE INDIA AND ORCHARD ROAD

Originally occupied by Europeans and Eurasians, Little India was settled by the Indians when they set up brick-kilns and cattle yards in the latter half of the 19th century. Packed with lively restaurants, shops, and ornate temples, the area is a heady mix of sights, scents, and sounds. With colonial architecture and a Middle Eastern ambience, Kampong Glam provides some of the best insights into Singapore's Malay community. Arab traders were the earliest settlers,

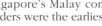

Stone guardian at Ngee Ann City

joining Buginese, Boyanese, and Javanese arrivals, to create a Muslim enclave. The ethnic area of Little India is the spiritual heart and commercial center of the local Indian community. Orchard Road lies to the north-west of the Colonial Core. In the 1840s it was a dirt road, lined with orchards and nutmeg plantations, but today it constitutes Singapore's most famous shopping district. Lavish hotels, cafés, pubs, and shopping malls with a tempting array of luxury brands are located here.

SIGHTS AT A GLANCE

Historic Streets and Buildings
Arab Street ❸
Dhoby Ghaut ❾
Istana Kampong Glam ❷
Serangoon Road ❼

Mosques and Temples
Goodwood Park Hotel ⓮
Leong San See Temple ❹
Peranakan Place and Emerald Hill ❿
Sakya Muni Buddha Gaya ❺
Sri Srinivasa Perumal Temple pp230–31 ❻
Sri Veeramakaliamman Temple ❽
Sultan Mosque ❶

Shopping
Centerpoint ⓫
Ngee Ann City ⓬
Tanglin Shopping Center ⓯
Tangs ⓭

KEY

Street-by-Street maps
see pp226–7 and 232–3

Ⓜ MRT station

Bus station

GETTING THERE
The MRT goes to Little India, Bugis, and Orchard Road. Bus numbers 7, 107, 111 go to Little India. Bus numbers 7, 77, 14, 106, 111 or 143 go to Orchard Road.

◁ **Mythological carving at Sri Srinivasa Perumal Temple**

Street-by-Street: Kampong Glam

Kampong Glam is the focal point of Muslim life in Singapore. Its name is derived from the Malay words *kampung*, or village, and *gelam*, a tree that once grew abundantly in the area. In 1819, the area was given to Sultan Hussein Shah as part of a treaty by which Singapore was ceded to the British. The Sultan built his palace, the Istana Kampong Glam, and the stunning Sultan Mosque here and soon the area was filled with Muslims from diverse ethnic backgrounds. This early impact is reflected in the distinct Islamic flavor of its street names, shops, buildings, and restaurants. Arab Street is a major draw, with its intricate textiles, fine leather, and caneware. Good Malay food stalls can be found on Kandahar Street.

Alsagoff Arabic School
Built in 1912, this was the first girls' school and the first Muslim school to be built in Singapore. It was named for a prominent Arab trader and philanthropist.

To Malabar Jama-Ath Mosque and old Malay cemetery

★ Istana Kampong Glam
Malay motifs combine with Palladian style in this former royal residence, now a Malay cultural center ❷

★ Sultan Mosque
Designed by Irishman Denis Santry, the Sultan Mosque dominates the skyline with its golden domes and four corner minarets ❶

NORTH BRIDGE ROAD

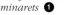
KANDAHAR STREET

MUSCAT STREET

ARAB STREET

Bendahara House
This yellow mansion, erected in the 1920s by Sultan Ali Iskandar Shah, is an example of Palladian-inspired architecture.

To Bugis MRT Station

Hajjah Fatimah Mosque
Named for a female Malaccan merchant, it was built in 1846, with an eclectic mix of European, Chinese, and Middle Eastern architectural styles.

Sultan Plaza

To Lavender MRT Station

LOCATOR MAP
See Street Finder Map 2

Jalan Sultan Center

0 meters	100
0 yards	100

JALAN SULTAN

ALIWAL STREET

PAHANG STREET

SULTAN GATE

BAGHDAD STREET

BEACH ROAD

BUSSORAH STREET

Pondok Java used to be a theater for Javanese immigrants but now lies derelict.

Bussorah Mall
This street leads to the Sultan Mosque, and comes to life during the Muslim fasting month. Religious items and a variety of food are sold here.

KEY

— — — Suggested route

★ Arab Street
Rows of shops line Arab Street, selling fine textiles, cane, rattan, and straw products.

STAR SIGHTS

★ Istana Kampong Glam

★ Sultan Mosque

★ Arab Street

Main prayer hall inside the Sultan Mosque

Sultan Mosque ❶

3 Muscat Street. **Map** 3 E4.
Tel 6293-4405. M Bugis. 🚌 7,
32, 124, 145, 166, 174, 195, 197.
⏰ 11am–7pm daily. 🎫 voluntary.
Note visitors can only view the prayer
hall from the foyer.

Named for Sultan Hussein
Shah of Johor, the mosque was
originally built in 1827 with the
aid of a grant from the British
East India Company, the
result of a treaty between the
Sultan and Stamford Raffles.
It was replaced a century
later by the present structure,
designed by Irish architect
Denis Santry. Arabesque in
style with Moorish overtones,
golden domes, balustrades,
and arches, as well as a minaret at each corner, Singapore's
largest mosque accommodates
5,000 worshipers in its main
hall. Visitors are welcome
in the lobby except during
Friday prayers.

Istana Kampong Glam ❷

Sultan Gate. **Map** 3 F4. **Tel** 6390-
0450. M Bugis. 🚌 107, 961, 980.
⏰ 9am–7pm daily. 🎫

Istana Kampong Glam was
the official royal residence of
Sultan Hussein Shah who
ceded the sovereign rights of
Singapore to the British. As
part of this historic agreement,
the Sultan built a wooden
palace in 1820 and named the
area Kota Raja, or the King's
Enclave. In 1840, his son,
Sultan Ali Iskandar Shah, the
last Sultan of Singapore, built
the present palace. The Istana

presides over extensive
grounds. Several smaller
Malay village-style houses
were built within the walled
compound. These housed
the Sultan's large entourage
which included his family of
hundreds of relatives and
servants. Also on the premises
was the Kota Rajah Club, a
sports club founded by one
of the descendants of the
Sultan, where young men of
good breeding could enjoy
recreational activities such
as badminton.

According to the provisions
of the 1904 Sultan Hussein
Ordinance, enacted by the
British Government, the
Sultan's descendants were
entitled to live in the palace
and receive an annual government stipend. Over the years,
however, disputes and dwin-
dling fortunes led the palace
to gradually fall in ruins.

The Istana Kampong Glam
has now been reclaimed by
the government, which has
compensated the Sultan's
descendants for their displace-
ment. The palace has been
transformed into the **Malay
Heritage Center**, to celebrate
Malay history, culture, and arts.

Arab Street ❸

Map 3 E4. M Bugis. 🚌 2, 7, 12,
32, 33, 51, 61, 62, 63, 125, 130,
145, 197, 520, 851, 960.
🍴🛍️📷

Located within the smallest of
Singapore's ethnic quarters,
this street acquired its name
from the Arab merchants who
settled here when they came
to trade in the 19th-century.
The vibrant colors of Arab
Street are striking. It is a maze
of shops that sell all manner
of Middle Eastern and Islamic
wares. Religious items such
as prayer mats, holy beads,
copies of the Koran, and skull
caps jostle for space with
excellent basketware, rattan,
cane and straw work, leather
products, jewelry, precious
and semi-precious gems, and
perfumes. Visitors should be
prepared to bargain. The
majestic Sultan Mosque looms
over this pedestrianized
tourist market strip.

Arab Street is most famous
for its textile stores. Bales of
colorful cotton, chiffon,
organza, and silk cloth cram
the shopfronts and spill onto
the pavement. *Batik* from
Indonesia and Malaysia,
handmade or machine-printed
with traditional designs, is
typically sold in *sarong*
lengths of 6 ft (2 m). Shops
also sell readymade *batik*
shorts, shirts, dresses, ties, and
table linen. To complement
the fabric sellers, specialist
shops sell ostrich feathers,
dazzling lamé in several
shades, various types of
sparkling sequins, and thread
in a profusion of colors.
Traditional Malay wedding
outfits can also be found
in shops on Arab Street.

Baskets and leather bags for sale on Arab Street

Leong San See Temple ❹

Race Course Road. **Map** 3 E1.
Ⓜ *Farrer Park.* 🚌 *23, 64, 65, 111, 130, 131, 133, 139, 147.* ⭘ *6am–6pm daily.*

Situated across the road from the dazzling Sakya Muni Buddha Gaya Temple, the Leong San See Temple honors Kuan Yin, the goddess of mercy and compassion, and Sakyamuni Buddha. Leong San See, or dragon mountain temple, was built in 1917 by a Buddhist monk. Today, both Taoists and Buddhists worship here. The temple is beautifully decorated with timber beams and intricate carvings of phoenix, dragons, chimeras, and flowers. A courtyard in the temple contains many ancestral tablets.

Large gilded Buddha at Leong San See Temple

Sakya Muni Buddha Gaya ❺

366 Race Course Road. **Map** 3 E2.
Tel 6294-0714. Ⓜ *Farrer Park.* 🚌 *23, 64, 65, 106, 111, 125, 130, 131, 142, 147, 151, 857.* ⭘ *7:30am–5pm daily.* ♿

Popularly known as the Temple of a Thousand Lights, Sakya Muni Buddha Gaya was built by Vuttisasara, a Thai monk. The temple has a Thai *wat* design, embellished with a mix of Chinese and Indian influences. To the left of the entrance is an ebony

and mother-of-pearl replica of what is believed to be the footprint of the Buddha. Beyond, a 50-ft (15-m) seated statue of the Buddha is illuminated by the colored electric lights that give the temple its popular name.

Another relic that draws devotees here is a branch believed to be from the *bodhi*, or peepul, tree under which the Buddha gained his enlightenment. In a chamber behind the Seated Buddha is a statue of the Reclining Buddha. About 25 scenes from the Buddha's life are portrayed on the base of the statue. Visitors can have their futures foretold at a wheel of fortune near the prayer hall.

Sri Srinivasa Perumal Temple ❻

See pp230–31.

Serangoon Road ❼

Map 3 F1. Ⓜ *Little India.* 🚌 *23, 64, 65, 106, 111, 125, 130, 131, 142, 147.* ♿ 🚻 📷

The early Indian migrants to Singapore in the 19th century settled along the banks of the Rochor Canal. The area eventually became a trading and cattle-breeding center, evident from street names such as Kerbau Road, which means Buffalo Road in Malay. Over time, as more Indians arrived, Serangoon Road became the heart of "Little India," the religious, cultural, and economic center for the local Indian community.

One of the oldest roads in Singapore, Serangoon Road is a kaleidoscope of quintessential Indian life. Vying for attention are elaborate Hindu temples and ornate shophouses. The shopkeepers hang mirrors above their doors to ward off evil influences and sell jewelry, textiles, and

Bollywood movie soundtracks. The area is full of restaurants, such as the Komala Villas Restaurant for vegetarian food. The noise of fortune-telling parrots, street pedlars, and a heady aroma of spices and flowers fill the air.

Sri Veeramakali-amman Temple ❽

Serangoon Road. **Map** 3 D3.
Tel 6293-4634. Ⓜ *Dhoby Ghaut, Bugis.* 🚌 *23, 64, 65, 103, 106, 111, 125, 130, 131, 142, 147, 151, 857.* ⭘ *6am, 1pm, 4pm, 7:30pm daily.* 🚻 📷

This temple, built in 1881 by Bengali laborers, is dedicated to the Hindu goddess Kali, who epitomizes the struggle of good over evil and is the consort of Shiva, the god of destruction. The name of the temple means Kali the Courageous.

The main altar of the temple has a black statue of Kali with each of her many arms and legs holding a weapon. She is flanked by her two sons Ganesh, the elephant god, and Murugan, the child god riding a peacock. The temple is especially crowded on Tuesdays and Fridays, which are Hindu holy days when devotees throng the temple to worship.

Sri Veeramakaliamman Temple, a temple in honor of the Hindu goddess Kali

Sri Srinivasa Perumal Temple 🟆

Lotus symbol on ceiling

One of the most important religious buildings in Singapore, this Hindu temple is devoted to the worship of Lord Vishnu (also known as Perumal). It is also one of the oldest temples in Singapore. Built in 1854, the temple was originally a simple structure with a *mandapam,* or a prayer hall, and the area around the temple had many ponds and vegetable gardens. In 1966, when the temple was consecrated, a six-tiered *gopuram*, or entrance tower, was built, funded by one of the earliest Indian migrants, P. Govindasamy Pillai. The temple is the starting point of the annual Thaipusam festival parade.

★ Mandapam
The main mandapam *or prayer hall has a decorated ceiling that is supported by ornately carved columns.*

The inner sanctum is where the main idol lies. Only priests can enter.

★ Subsidiary Shrines
Several subsidiary shrines are dedicated to different deities. This shrine is in honor of Ganesh, the elephant-headed god who removes obstacles.

STAR FEATURES

- ★ Mandapam
- ★ Subsidiary shrines
- ★ Gopuram

Vimanams
Decorated vimanams, *or domes, mark the position of the temple's subsidiary shrines.*

THAIPUSAM FESTIVAL

This Hindu festival begins at dawn at the temple. Male devotees enter a trance-like state, carrying ornately decorated *kavadis*, or steel arches, attached by metal hooks to their torsos, with skewers pierced through their tongues and cheeks. Devotees take part in this act in penance for their sins and in honor of Lord Murugan, the god of bravery, power, beauty, and virtue. Women carry coconut milk pots, also fulfilling vows relating to penance. Accompanied by chanting and singing, they walk to Sri Thendayuthapani Temple on Tank Road, about 2 miles (3 km) away.

Devotee carrying an ornately decorated *kavadi*

Main Shrine
*Here, devotees make offerings
of ghee, flowers, and fruit, to
the accompaniment of music
and chanting. They also sprin-
kle their heads with holy water.*

Vishnu
*This sculpture of Vishnu
shows him with four
sacred instruments –
the conch shell, club,
lotus, and saber.*

VISITORS' CHECKLIST

397 Serangoon Road. **Map** 3 E2.
Tel 6298-5771. Ⓜ *Little India.*
🚌 *23, 64, 65, 111, 130, 131,
139, 147, 857.* ⏲ *6:30am–
noon, 6–9pm daily.* ♿
📷 *on request.*

★ Gopuram
*The 60-ft
(20-m) high
entrance tower
has six tiers of
sculptures.*

The office provides
information on temple
activities.

Main Entrance
*Statuary stands guard on
either side of the massive
wooden door. Devotees
ring the bells before
entering, asking the gods
to grant their prayers.*

Hanuman
*This shrine is dedicated to Hanuman,
the monkey god. In the Hindu epic,
the Ramayana, he helped rescue Sita
from the demon, Ravana.*

Street-by-Street: Orchard Road

A local cheongsam

Stretching from Tanglin Mall to Plaza Singapura, the range and scale of retail outlets on Orchard Road make it not just an exemplary shopping experience but a tourist marvel as well. Shady trees dot the road between malls and department stores, including Singapore's oldest, Robinson's at Centerpoint and the historic Tangs. These large, glitzy buildings are interspersed with smaller designer boutiques, antique stores, cafés, and food courts. Crowds throng the streets, especially on weekends.

★ **Ngee Ann City**
With seven floors, Ngee Ann City is one of the largest malls in Southeast Asia. It has numerous restaurants, a post office, banks, a Japanese department store, and more than 120 shops (see pp234–5) ⑫

Wheelock Place
Shaped like a steel and glass Christmas tree, Wheelock Place houses a major bookshop and a few restaurants.

Delfi Orchard

Paragon shopping center boasts a vast, shop-lined atrium. It houses five floors of gift, fashion, and lifestyle stores.

Forum is packed with shops selling clothes and children's toys.

Liat Towers

Tangs (see p235)

```
0 meters        200
0 yards         200
```

★ **Tanglin Shopping Center**
A paradise for antique lovers, Tanglin Shopping Center is a treasure-house for old maps, bric-à-brac, books, furniture, carpets, and art ⑮

Wisma Atria
The blue Wisma Atria houses Isetan, a Japanese department store. A range of merchandise from fashion to electronics can be found here.

LOCATOR MAP
See Street Finder Map 3

★ Peranakan Place
Beyond Peranakan Place's Baroque Chinese shophouse façade are cafés, pubs, and restaurants (see p234) ❿

STAR SIGHTS

★ Ngee Ann City

★ Tanglin Shopping Center

★ Peranakan Place

Centerpoint
Centerpoint's flagship store, Robinson's, has an excellent range of household goods. Cold Storage in the basement has one of the best supermarket selections (see p234) ⓫

The Heeren

Plaza Singapura
One of the earliest malls on Orchard Road, Plaza Singapura was refurbished in the 1990s. As well as a department store, it houses a number of specialist outlets.

Cuppage Center

To Park Mall

Specialist Shopping Center
The mainstay of this mall is the John Little Department Store.

Park Mall
Furniture and interior decoration are the themes of Park Mall. From the traditional to the avant garde, displays include state-of-the-art kitchens and furniture from Europe and Asia.

Dhoby Ghaut ➒

Map 2 C4, 4 C1. Ⓜ *Dhoby Ghaut.*
🚌 *7, 14, 16, 36, 64, 65, 77, 85,
106, 111, 123, 124, 139, 143, 167,
171, 174, 190, 502, 518.* 🔲 ▢

The area known as Dhoby
Ghaut takes its name from the
dhobies, or Indian laundrymen,
who worked here many
years ago, and *ghaut,* which
means landing place in Hindi.
Dhobies used to go door-to-
door, collecting clothes from
residents and recording the
items in a book. They washed
the clothes in the nearby
stream, which ran down the
side of Orchard Road, and
dried them on land that is
now occupied by the YMCA.
This land was also once the
site of detention and interro-
gation rooms used by the
Japanese during World War II.
Next to the YMCA is a white
Presbyterian church established by Scottish settlers in 1877.
It was once used as a supply
base for Japanese civilians.

Peranakan Place and Emerald Hill ➓

Emerald Hill Road. **Map** 2 B4.
Ⓜ *Somerset.* 🚌 *7, 14, 16, 65, 77,
106, 111, 123, 124, 143, 167, 171,
174, 190.* ♿ 🔲 ▢ ▢

An upscale neighborhood of
traditional residences, plush
boutiques, and pricey eateries
today, Peranakan Place and
Emerald Hill were orginally
granted in 1845 to Englishman
William Cuppage, an officer
in the postal service. Emerald
Hill was later acquired by

the Peranakans *(see p20).*
Between 1900 and 1930,
30 different owners built
residential units along
Emerald Hill Road resulting
in a street lined with unique
Peranakan architecture.
Interesting features include
the wooden *pintu pagar,* or
half doors, often elaborately
carved, across unconventional
doorways. Also visible are
richly colored ceramic tiles,
shuttered windows, mirrors
above doors to ward off evil
spirits, and animal reliefs
across brightly-painted façades
to invite good luck. Toward
Orchard Road, these typical
terrace houses were converted into shophouses, with the
first floors occupied by small
provision stores, seamstresses,
and dry-goods stores. Other
roads on Emerald Hill that
developed between 1900 and
1930 were Hullet Road and
Saunders Road.

In 1984, the buildings on
Peranakan Place were carefully restored to their former
glory, making this area the
only stretch of old shophouse
architecture left on Orchard
Road. Peranakan Place now
comprises a group of modern
air-conditioned shops with an
eclectic mix of retailers offering Eastern and Western
goods. A French café, Chinese
barbecue shop, Mediterranean
restaurant and wine cellar,
and an outdoor pub and
restaurant combine to offer
a varied streetscape. Farther
along, a row of shophouses
at the pedestrianized Cuppage
Terrace have become flou-
rishing bars and interesting
sidewalk cafés.

The multicolored shophouses near Peranakan Place

For hotels and restaurants in this area see pp288–91 and pp311–12

**Centerpoint shopping center,
Orchard Road**

Centerpoint ⓫

176 Orchard Road. **Map** 2 B4.
Tel 6235-6629. Ⓜ *Somerset.* 🚌 *7,
14, 16, 65, 77, 106, 111, 123, 124,
143, 167, 171, 174, 190.*
🕐 *10:30am–8:30pm Sun–Thu,
10:30am–9:30pm Fri & Sat.* 🔲 ▢

The large shopping center,
Centerpoint, is dominated by
the Robinson's Department
Store, which first opened in
1858. The store claims to
have the best seasonal sales
in Singapore, one of which
coincides with the Great
Singapore Sale held in June
(see p247). There is a host
of other shops from branded
Western retailers such as
Marks & Spencer and Lacoste
to Singaporean and Hong
Kong fashion outlets, jewelry
shops, interior decoration,
and furniture shops. The
basement has a supermarket
and quick-service outlets.

Ngee Ann City ⓬

391A Orchard Road. **Map** 2 A4.
Tel 6738-1111. Ⓜ *Orchard.* 🚌 *7,
14, 16, 65, 77, 106, 111, 123, 124,
143, 167, 171, 174, 190.* 🕐 *10am–
9:30pm daily.* 🔲 ▢

Easily the most imposing mall
on Orchard Road, Ngee Ann
City has marble twin towers
and a main entrance that has
two silver columns and is
guarded by two hand-carved
foo dogs imported from China
to bring prosperity. The building's atrium is five floors high,
crisscrossed by escalators, and
packed with over 100 local
and international specialty

Modern sculpture and fountain in front of Ngee Ann City

stores. The dazzling array of some of the world's prestigious retailers includes Gucci, Chanel, Tiffany, Cartier, Tod's, Wedgwood, Burberry, Kenzo, Waterford, Bulgari, Louis Vuitton, Loewe, and Takashimaya, a Japanese department store.

Other facilities at the mall include a post office, a ticket-booking office, a bookstore, a library, various banks, a private health club, a night-club – Sparks – on the top floor, and a café with a great view over the Civic Plaza.

Tangs ⓭

310 & 320 Orchard Road. **Map** 2 A3. **Tel** 6737-5500. Ⓜ Orchard. ▥ 7, 14, 16, 36, 64, 65, 77, 106, 111, 123, 124, 132, 139, 143, 167, 171, 174, 190, 502, 518, 700. ◯ 11am–9pm Mon–Fri, 11am–9:30pm Sat, noon–8:30pm Sun. ⏸

The growth of Singapore's most famous department store reflects the vision of a young Chinese immigrant of

Entrance to Tangs department store

the 1920s. From selling his wares on an old cart, the dynamic C.K. Tang nurtured his business into a store that rivals all others on Orchard Road. From under its distinctive pagoda-style roof, Tangs now sells everything from cosmetics to rice cookers.

The distinctive tower of the elegant Goodwood Park Hotel

Goodwood Park Hotel ⓮

22 Scotts Road. **Map** 2 A3. **Tel** 6737-7411. Ⓜ Orchard. ▥ 54, 105, 124, 132, 143, 167, 171, 190, 518, 700. ⏸ ▢ www.goodwoodparkhotel.com

Originally the Teutonia Club for German expatriates in the early 1900s, the Goodwood Park Hotel was declared enemy property and seized by the government when World War I broke out in 1914. In 1929, the club was converted into a hotel.

Designed by J. Bidwell, the architect who also designed its famous rival, Raffles Hotel, Goodwood competed furiously for famous guests – Charlie Chaplin stayed at Raffles while Goodwood boasted the Duke of Windsor as a patron.

When World War II broke out, Goodwood was again seized, this time by the occupying Japanese forces. After the war, it was chosen to be the venue of a court dealing with war crimes.

Today, this landmark, the only colonial hotel apart from Raffles, has returned to its former incarnation. Its elegant corridors are lined with art and antique furniture and in 1989, the Tower Wing of the hotel, distinguished by its gable ends with ornamental plaster work, was selected as a national monument. The hotel has also grown from its original 60 rooms into a 234-room luxury retreat with a fantastic range of restaurants.

Tanglin Shopping Center ⓯

19 Tanglin Road. **Map** 1 E2. **Tel** 6737-0849. Ⓜ Orchard. ▥ 7, 77, 105, 106, 111, 123, 132, 174, 502. ◯ 11am–7pm Mon–Fri, 10:30am–9pm Sat, 10:30am–8pm Sun. ⏸ ▢ ▢

Tucked away at the far end of Orchard Road and removed from the bustle is the quiet Tanglin Shopping Center, unrivaled for its array of collectibles, antiques, and art. Shop after shop offers a veritable treasure of Persian rugs, tapestries, curios made of jade and brass, and contemporary Southeast Asian art.

Tanglin, a favorite haunt of expatriates, is home to some of the "firsts" and "bests" of Singapore shopping. **Antiques of the Orient**, the best-stocked antique map and secondhand bookseller in Singapore, sells fascinating prints, postcards, and photographs. **Apsara** offers a good collection of Chinese and Burmese antiques, and **Select Books** has a range of Southeast Asia titles. Also on offer are impeccably tailored men's suits.

FARTHER AFIELD

Some of Singapore's most interesting sights lie outside the city limits. Though much of its west is dominated by industrialized towns such as Jurong, it still contains some major tourist attractions including the theme park Haw Par Villa, the Singapore Discovery Center, the Singapore Science Center, and the fascinating Jurong Bird and Reptile Parks. The central north area retains the island's spectacular primary rainforests and mangrove swamps and is dedicated to most of its nature reserves, such as Bukit Timah and the

Camping tents at Pasir Ris

Singapore Zoological Gardens. The Singapore Botanic Gardens is a treasure-house of rare orchids. Other sights of historic and religious significance include the museum at Changi village and Kusu Island. The island is famous for its turtle legend and is popular with Taoists and Muslims. To the south, Sentosa, full of attractions and activities, is the city's favorite getaway spot. East Coast Park offers a range of outdoor and indoor activities. The rustic island of Pulau Ubin is a peaceful retreat.

SIGHTS AT A GLANCE

Parks, Gardens, and Nature Preserves
Bukit Timah Nature Reserve **2**
East Coast Park **10**
Jurong Bird and Reptile Parks **4**
Singapore Botanic Gardens pp240–41 **6**

Singapore Zoological Gardens **1**

Museum
Changi Museum **11**

Themed Attractions
Haw Par Villa **7**

Singapore Discovery Center **3**
Singapore Science Center **5**

Outlying Islands
Kusu Island **8**
Pulau Ubin **12**
Sentosa pp244–5 **9**

KEY

▨ Street Finder	⚓ Ferry port	— Railroad
Built-up area	▬ Highway	
✈ International airport	▬ Major road	

◁ **Vibrant mythological figures at Haw Par Villa**

The endangered Malayan tiger in Singapore Zoological Gardens

Singapore Zoological Gardens ❶

80 Mandai Lake Road. *Tel 6269-3411.* M *Ang Mo Kio, Choa Chu Kang.* 138 from Ang Mo Kio, 927 from Choa Chu Kang, 926 from Woodlands bus interchange (Sun & public hols), or 171 from the city (alight at Mandai Road, then take 138 from across the road). ◯ daily. ▧ ♿ ▣ optional. ▮ ▯ www.zoo.com.sg **Night Safari** ◯ 7:30pm–midnight daily (last adm 11pm). ▧ ⊘

Set in refreshingly green and peaceful surroundings, the Singapore Zoo is one of the world's few open zoos, where animals roam freely in landscaped enclosures that simulate their habitats. Dry and wet moats camouflaged by waterfalls and vegetation separate the animals from visitors. While some animals, such as leopards, jaguars, and pumas still have to be kept in glass enclosures, others such as monkeys and peahens roam freely.

The zoo houses about 3,000 animals, representing 290 species. Several of them are rare such as the white (Bengal) tiger and clouded leopard, while others are endangered species such as the Komodo dragon and the Malayan tiger.

Major exhibits include Wild Africa with its white rhinos and magnificent lions, and the Fragile Forest, which is a walk-through rain forest filled with butterflies, bats, and birds, and the Primate Kingdom featuring lion-tailed macaques, brown capuchins, and golden-lion tamarins. There is also a children's petting zoo and aquariums offering clear underwater views of sea lions and penguins. The zoo's breeding program is well-known and it has the distinction of fostering the world's first tropical birth of a polar bear cub. There are daily animal shows and feeding times featuring sea lions, elephants, primates, and reptiles. Visitors also have the opportunity to have breakfast or tea with the orangutans, which makes it a wonderful and memorable visit.

The **Night Safari**, sprawled over 100 acres (40 ha) of lush secondary forest next to the zoo, is a night zoo and a wildlife park combined. This unique sight allows visitors to observe the nocturnal activities of over 1,200 animals belonging to over 110 different species. A 45-minute guided tram ride (with a hop-on-hop-off option) takes visitors through eight habitats designed to resemble the Himalayan, Indian, Nepalese, African, Indo-Malayan, Southeast Asian, South American, and Burmese geographical regions. Those who prefer to walk can choose from three designated walking trails for a closer, moonlit encounter with the park's inhabitants.

Bukit Timah Nature Reserve ❷

177 Hindhede Drive. *Tel 6468-5736.* M *Newton.* 171. ◯ 8am–6pm daily. ▮

One of the only two rain forests in the world that are within city limits, Bukit Timah was established as a reserve in Singapore in 1883 to protect the native biodiversity. Today, about 410 acres (164 ha) of the verdant rain forest, which once covered the entire island, still exist, containing a cornucopia of flora and fauna, and providing a refuge for a variety of mammals, birds, and reptiles. The view from the disused quarry lake is not to be missed. Bukit Timah has cycling and walking trails, one of which leads to the highest point, **Bukit Timah Hill**, 540 ft (164 m) above sea level. Free trail maps are available at the visitor center.

Cycling on the bike track at the Bukit Timah Nature Reserve

Singapore Discovery Center ❸

510 Upper Jurong Road. *Tel 6792-6188.* M *Boon Lay.* 193 from Boon Lay. ◯ 9am–6pm Tue–Sun, 9am–8pm Sat. ▧ ♿ ▮ ▯ www.sdc.com.sg

Originally intended as a museum to showcase the history of Singapore Armed Forces (SAF), the Singapore Discovery Center today gives an interesting glimpse into Singaporean history. Recently,

Green iguana at Jurong Bird and Reptile Parks

the center has undergone a major expansion and redevelopment of its exhibition space. Located on the Singapore Armed Forces Training Institute's (SAFTI) grounds, the center is about 48,500 sq ft (4,500 sq m), with five main galleries and eight different themes.

The center has a spectacular light and sound show with kaleidoscopic images of Singapore. For a truly sensory experience, a visit to Singapore's largest flat screen theater with 2D and 3D movies is a must. The center also offers a bus tour to army, navy, and airforce grounds.

Jurong Bird and Reptile Parks ❹

2 Jurong Hill, off Ayer Rajah Expressway. *Tel* 6265-0022. Ⓜ *Boon Lay.* 🚌 *194, 251 from Boon Lay.* ◷ *9am–6pm Mon–Fri, 8am–6pm Sat, Sun & public hols.* 🎥 🎫 🍴 🛍 www.birdpark.com.sg **Jurong Reptile Park** 241 Jalan Ahmad Ibrahim/Ayer Rajah Expressway. *Tel* 6261-8866. Ⓜ *Boon Lay.* 🚌 *194, 251 from Boon Lay.* ◷ *daily.* 🎥 🎫 🎬 *10am, 11am, 3pm, and 4pm.* 🍴 🛍

Over 8,000 birds of more than 600 species from all over the world, including exotic and endangered birds, can be seen at Jurong Bird Park. The park has four aviaries, including the Waterfall Aviary, the world's largest walk-in aviary. Here, visitors can walk among 1,500 free-flying birds against the backdrop of the world's tallest man-made waterfall. Other highlights include the

Southeast Asian Birds Aviary, where a tropical thunderstorm is simulated daily at noon. This enclosure showcases one of the largest collections of Southeast Asian birds in the world. The penguin enclosure has a recreated Antarctic environment. Daily birdshows include the World of Hawks, which features a demonstration of the hunting skills of birds of prey.

Not far from Jurong Bird Park is the Jurong Reptile Park. Previously a crocodile park, the area now houses over 50 different species of reptiles and amphibians from around the world in a lush natural environment. The park's inhabitants include giant tortoises, 15–18 ft (4.6–5.5 m) crocodiles, king cobras, chameleons, iguanas, and anacondas.

Both children and adults enjoy the thrilling reptile shows and feeding sessions daily, when crocodiles leap up to snatch their food from the keepers.

Singapore Science Center ❺

15 Science Center Road, off Jurong Town Hall Road. *Tel* 6425-2250. Ⓜ *Jurong East.* 🚌 *66, 178, 198, 335.* ◷ *10am–6pm Tue–Sun & public hols.* 🎥 🍴 🛍 🛍 www.science.edu.sg **Omnimax Theater** ◷ *9:30am–8:30pm Tue–Sun and public hols. Regular screenings.* 🎥

Acclaimed as one of the world's top ten science museums, the Singapore Science Center has over 850 hands-on exhibits in eight galleries that are dedicated variously to aviation, space science, ecology, biotechnology, and IT among other disciplines. Visitors can explore innumerable scientific phenomena, and the Center aims to make even the most complex of principles more accessible and easier to understand. The emphasis here is on fostering the learning of science and technology in a creative, entertaining, and interactive way.

Exhibits at the Science Center include one that enables visitors to experience the world from within a fishbowl. There is also a mock television studio, where children are encouraged to become journalists for a day.

Next door, the **Omnimax Theater** features spectacular educational movies on science, technology, history, adventure sports, space, and the universe. The movies are projected on gigantic hemispherical screens in a 276-seat theater.

Singapore Science Center, a place to explore science and technology

Singapore Botanic Gardens ❻

Dendrobium sonia

The Singapore Botanic Gardens are located close to the bustling city and serve as a peaceful sanctuary. This idyllic garden sits on 130 acres (52 ha) of land and is dotted with lakes inhabited by swans, ducks, and turtles. The park is excellent for a stroll around its pretty waterfalls, landscaped fountains, and well-situated rest spots. Refrains of orchestral music can at times be heard from outdoor concerts. It has both primary jungle and manicured lawns. The gardens' orchid breeding program, begun in 1928, has produced more than 2,000 hybrids, with more being added each year. The garden has a reference library containing journals, rare books, and botanical illustrations dating back to 1875.

★ National Orchid Garden
With over 1,000 species, this beautifully landscaped garden has the largest display of tropical orchids in the world.

VIP Orchid Garden
In 1928, the government started breeding hybrid orchids, and after 1957 started naming selected ones for distinguished guests.

Burkill Hall was home to many of the Garden's past directors, including Isaac Henry Burkill and his son.

Bandstand
This octagonal bandstand was popular in the 1860s, when promenading in the gardens while listening to music played by a band was a fashionable pastime.

Swan Lake is home to a host of swans as well as a variety of pond flora.

Sculptures
Girl on a Swing *(1984) is the first of a series of works created by Sydney Harpley.*

★ Yuen-Peng McNeice Bromeliad Collection

The collection of 20,000 bromeliads, which come from the forests of Central and South America, was donated by Lady Yuen-Peng McNeice. More than 700 species and 500 hybrids can be seen.

VISITORS' CHECKLIST

Cluny Road. **Map** 1 D1.
Tel 6471-7361. M Orchard.
7, 105, 106, 123. Visitors'
Center, Evans Road. 5am–
midnight daily. optional.
Outdoor concerts some
weekends. **www**.sbg.org.sg

| 0 meters | 100 |
| 0 yards | 100 |

Towards Eco Lake

EJH Corner House

This colonial bungalow has been converted into a restaurant with a pleasant view of the idyllic surroundings.

The Tan Hoon Siang Mist House contains rare orchid blooms. Cultural artifacts particular to the orchid's country of origin are displayed alongside.

Visitors' Center

The center has an information counter, a café, a shop, and restrooms, as well as ample parking space. It has its own main entrance access from Evans Road.

Symphony Lake

On an islet in the middle of Symphony Lake is the Shaw Foundation Symphony stage. Concerts and performances are regularly held in the pavilion.

STAR SIGHTS

★ National Orchid Garden

★ Yuen-Peng McNeice Bromeliad Collection

Exhibit from Chinese folklore at Haw Par Villa

Haw Par Villa 7

262 Pasir Panjang Road. **Tel** 6339-6833. M Buona Vista. 10, 30, 51, 143, 200. 9am–6pm daily. 🟥 ◻ **Hua Song Museum** ● Mon. 📷

This landscaped park has picturesque surroundings, carp ponds, and statues depicting aspects of Chinese folklore. Established by the Haw brothers with the fortune they made from Tiger Balm, their camphor and menthol remedy, this theme park is based on Chinese legends and myths and aims to teach traditional values. Over 1,000 statues and tablets show mythical creatures and tell stories from Chinese folklore. The Ten Courts of Hell section graphically portrays the punishment for sins such as gambling and theft, and the **Hua Song Museum** displays the lifestyles and clothing artifacts of ethnic Chinese communities.

Kusu Island 8

Tel 6275-0388 for ferry times. 🛳 from Marina South Pier. 📷 Includes ferry ticket.

According to legend, Kusu Island, otherwise known as Turtle Island, was actually a giant turtle which transformed itself into land to save two shipwrecked sailors, one Chinese and one Malay.
Kusu Island receives most of its visitors during the ninth lunar month (October or November), when Taoist and Muslim devotees flock to the island on an annual pilgrimage. Taoists visit the Tua Pek Kong Temple located on the island. The temple is dedicated to Tua Pek Kong, the patron saint of merchants. Devotees pray for prosperity, good luck, and wealth, light joss sticks, and make offerings of flowers and food.
Muslim devotees climb 122 steps up a steep hill to visit a Malay shrine of Keramat Kusu. Childless couples mark their prayers by tying pieces of cloth around trees on their way up to the shrine.
The island is known for its two blue lagoons, its vast pristine beaches, and a wishing well. It has undergone much development and has a pleasant spot for picnics. However, overnight stays are not permitted on the island.

Sentosa 9

See pp244–5.

East Coast Park 10

Off East Coast Parkway (ECP). 🚌 13, 15, 16, 31, 196, 197 to Marine Terrace and take underpass across ECP. 🟥 ◻ ◻

The stretches of beach along East Coast Park are considered among the best in the country. The park stretches for more than 6 miles (10 km) along the coast from Changi Airport to Marina Bay. The seafront is lined with palm trees, shady rest areas, and park benches. For the fitness-conscious there are walking and jogging paths, as well as well-marked cycling and in-line skating tracks. Bicycle hire shops in the area offer a choice of racers and mountain bikes or tandems for couples. There is also an in-line skate rental and repair store.
Fishing enthusiasts can set up their rods; picnickers can pitch tents on the beach; health buffs can work out at the outdoor fitness stations, and bird-watchers can take a walk through designated bird sanctuaries.
The pleasing sea breezes and scenic views of the East Coast Park make this a very fashionable place to live. The area is well-provided with bars, chic restaurants, and a host of recreational facilities. The food on offer ranges from fast food and hawker fare to seafood and Western snacks. At the East Coast Recreation Center, indoor activities such as bowling, snooker, and children's games can be enjoyed. For watersports, the Pasta Fresca

Taoist Tua Pek Kong Temple on Kusu Island

Seasports Center offers windsurfing and sailing (see p256). Holiday chalets can be rented for short-term stays. These chalets on the beachfront also provide facilities such as swimming pools, spas, and barbecue pits. The East Coast Park is a local favorite, especially for weekend family outings.

Families cycling along well-marked tracks at East Coast Park

Changi Museum ⓫

1000 Upper Changi Road North. **Tel** 6214-2451. M Tanah Merah, Tampines. 🚌 2, 29. 🕒 9:30am–5pm (4:30pm last admission). ⬆ 5:30pm Sun. 🎫 🖥 🖨 *Chalets available for rent.* **www**.changimuseum.com

Changi Prison, which once served as a World War II prisoner-of-war camp for Allied troops, is still in use. Changi Museum is located just up the road from the prison, at the site of the Old Changi Prison Chapel. The museum is dedicated to all those who lived and died in Singapore, in particular the prisoners who suffered unspeakable torture at the hands of Japanese jailers during their internment here.

Over the years, the museum has amassed a valuable collection of photographs, paintings, and personal effects donated by former POWs and their families. A selection of photographs by George Aspinall, then a young Australian trooper, and more than 400 sketches by W.R.M. Haxworth are among the works of art by various prison artists that are showcased here. Replicas of the Changi

Murals, which were originally drawn by prisoner Stanley Warren on the walls, are also on display.

In the museum's courtyard is a replica of the simple thatched-roof wooden chapel built by the POWs. The brass cross at the wreathed altar was crafted out of spent artillery casings.

Tour groups of ten or more people are required to inform the museum of their visit, at least three days in advance.

Pulau Ubin ⓬

M Tanah Merah, Tampines. 🚌 2, 29. 🚤 from Changi Village. 🕒 daily. 🍴 🖥 🖨 ♻

Singapore's second largest offshore island, Pulau Ubin, which sits in the Johor Strait between Changi and the mouth of the Johor River, is perhaps the last place left for a peek into the rustic atmosphere of Singapore as it was in the 1960s. A Malay and Chinese community once engaged in farming, granite quarrying, and fishing on the island. Today, only about 200 people live on Pulau Ubin. Measuring only 5 miles (8 km) across and 1 mile (1.5 km) wide, Pulau Ubin is the site of a traditional Malay fishing village. The remnants of rural kampung life can still be seen here: *attap,* or thatched-roof, and zinc-roofed wooden houses stand on stilts; *sampans,* or

Jackfruit grown in Pulau Ubin

wooden fishing boats, line the beach; and fishing nets spread out to dry in the sun.

The island has a variety of flora and fauna and includes species that once existed on the mainland but now can only be found here. These include various fruit trees such as coconut, durian, rambutan, and jackfruit, wild berries, wild orchids, the insect-trapping pitcher plant, several medicinal plants and herbs, and mangrove flora. The island's wildlife includes monkeys, monitor lizards, water hens, squirrels, fruit bats, and snakes such as pythons and cobras. The waters around the island teem with fish, crabs, and prawns. Pulau Ubin is also a good spot for bird-watchers as birds of prey such as eagles, kites, and hawks, and migratory birds nest here during the northern winter months. Bicycles can be rented from the jetty. The community center nearby has a good collection of photographs of life on the island during its heyday. There are also a few seafood restaurants, old-style coffee shops, and sundry shops that offer necessities for the visitor, such as insect repellent, sun-block, hats, canned drinks, and snacks. A couple of taxis ply the gravel tracks. Campsites, chalets, and lodges provide overnight accommodation on the island.

Rustic Malay kampung house on Pulau Ubin

Sentosa 9

Sentosa Island was once called Balakang Mati, which means "behind the dead" in Malay. One of the theories about the origins of this name speaks of a mysterious disease that claimed the lives of nearly all the original settlers. The British used the island as a military base until 1967. Today, Sentosa, which means "peace" in Malay, has been transformed into a recreational playground with attractions that include museums, historical sights, theme parks, nature trails, and sporting activities. All the sights can be reached by the island's monorail, beach trams, or internal bus network. Sentosa has two major hotels *(see p291)* as well as chalets.

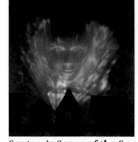

Sentosa's Songs of the Sea
This musical extravaganza on Silosa Beach features giant water screens, spectacular pyrotechnics, a live cast, and an open-air viewing gallery.

Cable car from Mount Faber.

Carlsberg Sky Tower gives a bird's-eye view of Singapore's skyline.

Dragon Trail nature walk.

★ **Underwater World**
In this tropical fish oceanarium, a moving walkway transports visitors through a 274-ft (83-m) tunnel to view 2,500 species of marine life.

Shangri-La's Rasa Sentosa *(see p291)*

★ **Fort Siloso**
The last bastion of the British during World War II, this fort was built in the 1880s and is an intriguing complex of bunkers, cannons, and underground passageways.

★ **Images of Singapore**
Using lifelike wax figures, this museum showcases Singapore's diverse cultures and explores the country's unique history.

Sentosa Express

A monorail network, Sentosa Express links Harbor Front, Vivocity, and St James Powerhouse MRT stations on the mainland to Beach and Imbiah stations. It also links sights within the island.

VISITORS' CHECKLIST

1.3 miles (2.1 km) S of Singapore. **Tel** 6275-0388. to Sentosa; or to Mount Faber or Harborfront Center, then cable car. Sentosa Express. 9am–9pm daily. www.sentosa.com.sg

Dolphin Lagoon
Visitors can observe dolphins at training and feeding times, and can wade in for a closer look during "Meet-the-Dolphin" sessions.

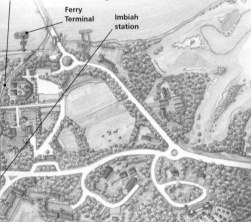

Ferry Terminal

Imbiah station

Merlion Walk

Sentosa's Songs of the Sea

Beach station

The Sentosa Golf Club has two 18-hole championship golf courses and excellent facilities including chipping and putting greens, as well as a pro shop.

```
0 meters        200
0 yards         200
```

STAR SIGHTS

★ Underwater World

★ Fort Siloso

★ Images of Singapore

Palawan Beach
A suspension bridge links Palawan Beach to a small islet that is believed to be the southernmost tip of continental Asia.

SHOPPING IN SINGAPORE

Singapore is a shopper's paradise. Scores of shops at every turn offer almost unlimited choices. Whether you want to immerse yourself in the plush shopping arcades of Orchard Road or Raffles City, or scour the flea markets and back alleys of the ethnic quarters, Singapore caters to all tastes and budgets. Best known for its array of attractively priced electronic goods, such as computers, mobile phones, and cameras, Singapore also offers a tantalizing choice of luxury brands, art,

antiques, curios, jewelry, and more. Away from the exclusive stores and boutiques, some of the most exciting shopping can be found in Little India, Chinatown, and Arab Street. A rich selection of traditional Southeast Asian handicrafts, such as fine caneware, *batik*, and textiles, is sold from stalls and specialist stores. Singapore is also famous for its bargains and sales, especially on electronic goods, but do spend some time browsing to find the best deals and only buy from reputable dealers.

A traditional
Oriental happy coat

The upmarket Tanglin Mall on Orchard Road

DEPARTMENT STORES AND MALLS

Orchard Road (see pp232–3), with its vast stretch of glitzy department stores and malls, such as **Tanglin Shopping Center**, **Ngee Ann City**, and **Wisma Atria**, is packed with just about everything one could want – shoes, clothes, books, music, jewelry, carpets, curios, and especially branded luxury items. **Tangs** (see p234) and **Robinsons** at Centerpoint are two of the oldest department stores on Orchard Road. **Park Mall** specializes in furniture and interior decoration. Major shopping malls can be found in the city center, including **Parco Bugis Junction**, **Raffles Hotel Shopping Arcade**, and **Raffles City Shopping Center**. **Suntec City Mall** is farther out near Marina Bay. For electronic goods, head to **Sim Lim Square** or **Funan Digitalife Mall**. Little India's **Mustafa Center**, a Singapore favorite, sells every conceivable item, from

electrical to household goods. Japanese chain stores **Isetan**, **Takashimaya**, and **Seiyu** are very popular, as is the British retail outlet **Marks & Spencer**. Singapore's department stores and malls are well organized, with obliging staff, and usually an informative help desk.

SHOPPING HOURS

Most shops and malls are open every day from 10am to 9pm, though a few stay open until 10pm or later. Mustafa Center in Little India is an exception – it is open 24 hours a day, making it great for a midnight shopping excursion. The revamped Clarke Quay opens around 5pm and stays open until midnight. Little India and Arab Street are best avoided on Fridays as several shops may be closed for the Muslim holy day. All 7-Eleven convenience stores are open 24 hours a day.

HOW TO PAY

International credit cards are accepted at most shops – MasterCard, VISA, American Express, Diners Club, and Citibank. If a surcharge is charged by the shop for the use of credit cards, the customer is often allowed to call the local office of the card company for a discount. However, some of the smaller shops and the hawker stalls insist on being paid in cash.

Bargaining is an accepted practice in Singapore. Department stores generally have fixed prices, but most other shops, even in high-end malls, may be open to bargaining. It is best to be knowledgable about the correct value of a product. Start by asking the shopkeeper for his best price and then negotiate a suitable deal. Keep the exchange good-natured. Though several high-end shopping centers may accept traveler's checks

The Alessi Shop, a designer furnishing store in Park Mall

One of the many Southeast Asian handicrafts shops

in major currencies, it is always preferable to use the Singapore dollar. Traveler's checks can be cashed at a number of banks, which are open from 9:30am to 3:30pm on weekdays, and 9:30am to 11:30am on Saturdays. Currency can be exchanged at all banks and hotels which display the "Licensed Money Changer" sign.

SALES

Daily newspapers such as *The Straits Times* have listings of all current sales. The free monthlies, *Where Singapore* and *Singapore Shopping Guide*, published by the Singapore Tourism Board, also give details on shopping options. But for the true thrill of Singapore's best bargains, time your trip during the Great Singapore Sale, held every year in June and July and promoted by the Singapore Tourism Board. This super-sale offers discounts of up to 80 percent on almost all goods and is the perfect chance to strike off all those things crowding your wish list. Visitors from neighboring countries are known to fly in just for this sale.

GOODS RETURN POLICIES

Most large stores provide shoppers with a receipt, and accept returns of unused goods in original condition within three days of purchase. Of course it is better to be sure of a purchase to avoid complications later. Keep all receipts until the end of your

stay. Ensure that a warranty card that is recognized internationally is provided with any electronic product and is properly dated and stamped.

CONSUMER CLAIMS

Several stores display the "Gold Circle" which means they have been certified by the Singapore Tourism Board for the quality of goods and services they offer visitors. Hotels, tourist offices, and the airport can provide a free listing of these stores. The country has an excellent redress policy for tourist complaints, such as being cheated by a retailer or finding that an international guarantee card has not been properly filled out. Advice and assistance are available from the **Retail Promotions Center**. Visitors' complaints against retailers can also be registered at the **Consumer Association of Singapore**. The **Small Claims Tribunal** has a fast-track

Interior of Ngee Ann City, one of Singapore's premier shopping malls

system for visitors, where claims can be filed for a fee of S$10 up to 1 percent of the claim amount. Visitors can avail themselves of the "electronic mediation" service at the **E@DR Centers** in the subordinate courts. Claims can be filed with this center by email at any time during the trip or after returning home.

PERMITS AND LAWS

Singapore has a reputation for stringent laws against the purchase and transport of weapons, endangered species, and narcotics. Even the smallest offence is not overlooked and can result in a fine, caning, or brief imprisonment. Visitors should be very careful about what they buy and where they make their purchases.

A busy Sunday flea market in Singapore

TAXES AND REFUNDS

In Singapore, a 7 percent Goods and Services Tax (GST) is levied on most goods and services. A tax refund can be claimed on purchases worth S$100 or more made at shops that display a "Tax Free Shopping" logo. Claims can be made at GST counters at **Changi International Airport** and cash refund centers across the country, including those at **Funan Digitalife Mall**, **Sim Lim Square**, and **Wisma Atria**. Receipts and purchased items should be retained as they will be needed for verification before a refund is given. Refunds are limited to S$500 per person, and a credit card will be required as proof of identity.

Where to Shop

Malls and shopping centers are considered convenient places to shop, as an extensive range of products is available under one roof. Some malls have become popular for a particular product, such as Sim Lim Square and Funan Digitalife Mall, which are known for electronic goods. There are several smaller boutiques and specialist outlets to choose from. Many warehouses and traditional shophouses throughout the city, such as those that line the river, have been renovated into shopping venues. Little India, Chinatown, and Arab Street brim with shops and galleries that sell handicrafts from their respective regions as well as from other Asian countries.

CLOTHES AND FABRICS

In Singapore, you will find international designer brands, such as **Gucci**, **Calvin Klein**, **Burberry**, **Emporio Armani**, **Hugo Boss**, **Giordano**, and **Chanel**, located along Orchard Road and at the other major shopping areas. Local designers, including **Vera Wang**, stock a blend of contemporary Chinese and Western fashion. The latest collections from top Indian fashion designers are displayed at the upscale **Mumbai Se**.

For a great selection of textiles, the best areas are **Arab Street** (see p228) and **Serangoon Road** (see p229) in Little India. Indonesian and Malaysian *batik* silks are available on Arab Street, sold mostly by the meter. *Batiks* are also sold in *sarong* lengths (about 6 ft/2 m) and as readymade garments. Indian *saris* (a 6 yard/5.5 m length of cloth) can be found in Little India. **Chinatown** (see pp218–21) specializes in Chinese silk and traditional garments such as *cheongsam*

and *samfoo*, which can be bought readymade. Chinese silk garments are available at Tangs. Sizes of readymade garments are in keeping with the petite Asian body frame.

JEWELRY

For exclusive platinum and 18-carat gold jewelry, luxury brands such as **Bulgari** and **Tiffany** have outlets at Raffles Hotel Shopping Arcade, Orchard Road, and Raffles City Shopping Center. Local jewelers **Larry Jewelry** and **Lee Hwa** are reputed for their excellent craftsmanship. For antiques or gold fashioned in ethnic designs, such as Chinese ornaments and Indian jewelry, Chinatown and Little India offer the best selection. Cheaper imitations of the gold jewelry are available as well. Chinatown is also a good place to buy Chinese jade jewelry. The hawker stalls at **Clarke Quay** (see p217) offer a good range of trendy silver pieces.

SHOES AND BAGS

All the international designer labels offer a superb selection of shoes and bags at their stores on Orchard Road and other upmarket shopping arcades. **Louis Vuitton**, **Fendi**, and **Ferragamo** are popular with shoppers. **Charles & Keith** and **Substance** are among the sought-after brands for shoes. Singapore is also known for its wide range of footwear at affordable prices especially at Tangs and **On Pedder**. Arab Street is the place to head to for fine leather products.

ANTIQUES AND CRAFTS

Antiques and handicrafts available in Singapore are predominantly Southeast Asian. **Tanglin Shopping Center** (see p235) is the popular place for

Handmade mask

antiques and crafts. Old maps and curios from the Southeast are stocked at **Antiques of the Orient**. The many shops at Clarke Quay, the renovated warehouses along Dempsey Road, and **Lim's Arts & Crafts** are also good places. For good handmade Kashmiri, Persian, and Turkish carpets, **Amir & Sons** in Kampong Glam, the oldest carpet shop in Singapore, is worth a visit. Arab Street is known for Southeast Asian crafts such as fine cane products. Chinatown offers religious and architectural artifacts. Brass statues and lamps can be found both in Little India as well as in Chinatown.

Stacks of traditional Oriental textiles in vivid colors and patterns

DIRECTORY

DEPARTMENT STORES AND MALLS

Funan Digitalife Mall
109 North Bridge Road.
Map 3 E4.
Tel 6336-8327.
www.funan.com.sg

Isetan Scotts
350 Orchard Road. **Map** 1 F2. *Tel 6733-1111.*
www.isetan.com.sg

Marks & Spencer
501 Orchard Road. **Map** 1 F2. *Tel 6733-8122.*
www.marksandspencer. com

Mustafa Center
145 Syed Alwi Road. **Map** 3 E2. *Tel 6295-5855.*
www.mustafa.com.sg

Ngee Ann City
391 Orchard Road. **Map** 2 A4. *Tel 6739-9323.*
www.ngeeanncity.com.sg

Parco Bugis Junction
200 Victoria Street. **Map** 3 D5. *Tel 6557-6557.*
www. bugisjunction-mall. com.sg

Park Mall
9 Penang Road. **Map** 3 C5 *Tel 6339-4031.*

Raffles City Shopping Center
252 North Bridge Road. **Map** 5 E2.
Tel 6338-7766.
www.rafflescity.com

Raffles Hotel Shopping Arcade
328 North Bridge Road. **Map** 5 E1. *Tel 6337-1886.* www.raffleshotel. com/arcade

Robinsons
176 Orchard Road. **Map** 2 B4. *Tel 6733-0888.*
www.robinsons.com.sg

Seiyu
230 Victoria Street. **Map** 3 D5. *Tel 6223-2222.* www.bhg
singapore.com.sg

Sim Lim Square
1 Rochor Canal Road.
Map 3 E4.
Tel 6338-3859.

Suntec City Mall
3 Temasek Boulevard.
Map 5 F1. *Tel 6825-2667.*
www.sunteccity.com.sg

Takashimaya
391 Orchard Road. **Map** 2 A4. *Tel 6738-1111.*
www.takashimaya-sin. com

Tanglin Shopping Center
163 Tanglin Road. **Map** 1 E2. *Tel 6736-4922.*
www.tanglinmall.com.sg

Tangs
310/320 Orchard Road. **Map** 2 A3. *Tel 6737-5500.* www.tangs.com

Wisma Atria
435 Orchard Road. **Map** 2 A4. *Tel 6235-2103.*
www.wismaonline.com.

CONSUMER CLAIMS

Consumer Association of Singapore
170 Ghim Moh Road.
Tel 6463-1811.
www.case.org.sg

E@DR Centers
www.e-adr.gov.sg

Retail Promotions Center
Blk 1 Thomson Road.
Map 2 B1.
Tel 6352-9909.
www.rpc.com.sg

Small Claims Tribunal
1 Havelock Square.
Map 4 C3. *Tel 6435-5937.* www.smallclaims.
gov.sg

TAXES AND REFUNDS

Changi International Airport
50 Airport Boulevard.
Tel 6542-1122.
www.changiairport.com.
Open 24 hours.

Funan Digitalife Mall
109 North Bridge
Road. **Map** 3 E4.
Tel 6336-8327.
www.funan.com.sg.
Open 11am–8pm daily.

Sim Lim Square
1, Rochor Canal Road.
Map 3 E4. *Tel 6338-3859.* www.simlim.net.
Open 11am–8pm daily.

Wisma Atria
435 Orchard Road. **Map** 2 A4. *Tel 6235-2103.*
www.wismaonline.com.

CLOTHES AND FABRICS

Burberry
01-28 Ngee Ann City.
Map 2 A4.
Tel 6735-1283.

Calvin Klein
01-32 Ngee Ann City.
Map 2 A4.
Tel 6887-5981.

Chanel
01-25 Ngee Ann City.
Map 2 A4. *Tel 6733-5120.* www.chanel.com.

Emporio Armani
508 Orchard Road. **Map** 1 F2. *Tel 6735-8063.*

Giordano
B2-28 Ngee Ann City.
Map 2 A3.
Tel 6736-4302.

Gucci
01-40 Paragon, 290 Orchard Road. **Map** 2 A4.
Tel 6734-2528.

Hugo Boss
01-03 Ngee Ann City, 391 Orchard Road. **Map** 2 A4.
Tel 6735-0233.

Mumbai Se
02-03 Palais Renaissance, 390 Orchard Road. **Map** 1 F2. *Tel 6733-7188.*

Vera Wang
390 Orchard Road.
Map 1 F2. *Tel 6235-4648.*
www.verawang.com

JEWELRY

Bulgari
02-1/3 Ngee Ann City.
Map 2 A4. *Tel 6735-6689.* www.bulgari.com

Larry Jewelry
02-12 Ngee Ann City.
Map 2 A4.
Tel 6732-3322.
www.larryjewelry.com

Lee Hwa
01-23, 200 Victoria Street. **Map** 3 D5.
Tel 6334-2838.
www.leehwa.com.sg

Tiffany
01-05 Raffles Hotel Shopping Arcade, 328 North Bridge Road. **Map** 3 E4. *Tel 6334-0168.*
www.tiffany.com/
locations

SHOES AND BAGS

Charles & Keith
01-05 Wisma Atria, 435 Orchard Road. **Map** 2 A4. *Tel 6238-3312.*
www.charleskeith.com

Fendi
01-32 Ngee Ann City.
Map 2 A4. *Tel 6733-0337.*

Ferragamo
290 Orchard Road. **Map** 1 F2. *Tel 6738-3206.*

Louis Vuitton
01-20/24 Ngee Ann City, 391 Orchard Road. **Map** 2 A4. *Tel 6734-7760.*
www.louisvitton.com
one of several branches

On Pedder
02-12 P/Q, Tower B, Ngee Ann City. **Map** 2 A4.
Tel 6835-1307.

Substance
02-12 Wheelock Place, 501 Orchard Road. **Map** 1 F2. *Tel 6836-0111.*

ANTIQUES AND CRAFTS

Amir & Sons
Lucky Plaza, 304 Orchard Road. **Map** 1 F2.
Tel 6734-9112.

Antiques of the Orient
02-40 Tanglin Shopping Center. **Map** 1 D3.
Tel 6734 9351.
www.aoto.com.sg

Lim's Arts & Crafts
Holland Road Shopping Center. *Tel 6467-1300.*

A display of high-end audio equipment

ELECTRONIC GOODS

The absence of import duties makes Singapore one of the most popular places to buy electronic gadgets. Several stores stock the latest high-tech audio-visual products. Latest models are available at specialist centers such as **The Sony Center**. Sim Lim Square and **Mustafa Center** are the best for music systems, televisions, and DVD players. The **Adelphi Shopping Center** is good for audio products. Make sure a worldwide guarantee is provided and that your purchase is compatible with the voltage system in your country.

CAMERAS AND WATCHES

Most electronics shops and dedicated camera shops stock brands such as Nikon, Canon, and Olympus. **Cathay Photo Store** and **Mustafa Center** have a good range of all the popular camera brand names. The shops also offer equipment for professional photographers. A huge range of watches is available at most shopping centers. Many companies such as **Rolex** and **Swatch** have their own outlets, while **The Hour Glass** stocks an expensive range, including the exquisite Gerald Genta, De Bethune, and steely Daniel Roth pieces. The bustling **Lucky Plaza** is known for cameras and watches. Branded second-hand watches can also be bought at **Peng Kwee**. The **Camera Workshop** at Peninsula Shopping Center sells second-hand cameras and collector's models.

COMPUTERS

Funan Digitalife Mall, the main computer shopping center in Singapore, also claims to be the largest computer store in Asia. Located between the Excelsior and Peninsula Hotels in the Colonial Core, it has five floors packed with shops selling computers, software, and other electronic equipment. The prices here are somewhat lower than those elsewhere and a number of special deals and offers are available so it is a good idea to compare prices. Two popular computer shops are **Proton-Wisma Computers** and **The Mac Shop** at the Funan Center. Other good places to buy computers include Suntec City Mall and Sim Lim Square *(see p249)*. As with many stores, bargaining is an accepted practice.

BOOKS AND MUSIC

HMV has the most extensive selection of music with over 200,000 CD titles. Separate floors are dedicated to different genres of music, including sections on classical music, jazz, rock, and pop. **Borders** also has a good selection. It is also popular for its excellent children's books section. For the best range of titles on Southeast Asian subjects visit **Select Books**. Japanese bookstore **Kinokuniya** stocks a number of titles in several languages. They sell Chinese books and also have a bargain section. **Times the Bookstore** is another favorite.

SINGAPORE MEMORABILIA

The ubiquitous Merlion, the half-fish, half-lion symbol of Singapore, is the most popular souvenir. A wide range of items sporting the symbol is available, including coffee mugs, T-shirts, pendants, stuffed toys, musical trinket boxes, china plates, key rings, and much more. There are gift shops at most Singapore national gardens and museums, which also offer an interesting collection of mementos. Museum shops such as those at the **National Museum of Singapore** offer an array of products inspired by the collections on display. **The Garden Shop** at the Singapore Botanic Gardens *(see pp240–41)* stocks an eclectic range of books on natural history. Raffles Hotel has an excellent **Raffles Hotel Gift Shop**.

ORCHIDS

Orchids are the country's national flower and more than 3,000 varieties of this exotic flower are grown at the **National Orchid Garden** and the **Mandai Orchid Garden**. The 5-acre (2-ha) Mandai Orchid Garden has a vintage garden and even a tropical orchid fruit garden. Part of Singapore Botanic Gardens, the National Orchid Garden has over 1,000 species and 2,000 hybrids. Every year new hybrids are added to the garden's collection. The gardens have gift shops where the orchids can be packed and shipped home upon

Orchids at Mandai Orchid Garden

request. Unique gold-plated orchids can be purchased at the **RISIS Store** at Suntec City Mall or the Mandai Orchid Gardens gift shop.

GOURMET FOOD

Singapore is a renowned gourmet destination and a number of specialty foods are available as gifts and souvenirs. Aromatic ground spices from Little India can be used to flavor curries and marinades. Singaporean delicacies such as *kaya*, a toast spread, and the Hainan chicken-rice paste mix, along with other ready-to-serve foods are available at all **Bee Cheng Hiang** outlets, Kee's Gourmet Boutique, **Chinatown Heritage Center** *(see p218)*, and **Faber Forest Gift Shop**. **The Tea Chapter** in Chinatown has a delightful selection of teapots, cups, accessories, and fine teas for sale. **Brown Rice Paradise** and **Tierney's Gourmet** are also worth a visit. Handmade chocolates and premium quality caviar are some of the gourmet foods from around the world stocked at **Thos. S.B. Raffles**.

DIRECTORY

ELECTRONIC GOODS

Adelphi Shopping Center
1 Coleman Street. **Map** 5 D2. *Tel 6339-9179.*

The Sony Center
04-01 Wisma Atria, 435 Orchard Road. **Map** 2 A4. *Tel 6473-6500.*

CAMERAS AND WATCHES

Camera Workshop
Peninsula Shopping Center, 3 Coleman Street. **Map** 5 D2. *Tel 6336-1956.*

Cathay Photo Store
01-11-14 Peninsula Plaza, 111 North Bridge Road. **Map** 3 E4. *Tel 6337-4274.* www.cathayphoto.com. sg

The Hour Glass
01-02 Takashimaya Shopping Center, 391 Orchard Road. **Map** 2 A4. *Tel 6734-2420.* www.thehourglass.com

Lucky Plaza
304 Orchard Road. **Map** 1 F2. *Tel 6235-3294.* www.luckyplaza.com.sg

Peng Kwee
01-45A Peninsula Plaza, 111 North Bridge Street. **Map** 3 E4. *Tel 6334-0155.* www.pengkwee. com.sg

Rolex
1-01 Tong Building, 302 Orchard Road. **Map** 1 F2. *Tel 6737-9033.* www.rolex.com

Swatch
81-27 Plaza Singapura, 68 Orchard Road. **Map** 1 F2. *Tel 6334-8042.* www.swatch.com

COMPUTERS

Proton-Wisma Computers
109 North Bridge Road. **Map** 3 E4. *Tel 6338-3066.*

The Mac Shop
4–11 Funan Digitalife Center. **Map** 5 D2. *Tel 6334-1633.*

BOOKS AND MUSIC

Borders
1–00 Wheelock Place, 501 Orchard Road. **Map** 1 F2. *Tel 6235-7146.* www. bordersstores.com/stores

HMV
1–11 The Heeren, 260 Orchard Road. **Map** 1 F2. *Tel 6733-1822.*

1 Raffles Link, B1–47 CityLink Mall.
Map 3 E2.
Tel 6238-7218.
www.hmvgroup.com

Kinokuniya
03-10 Ngee Ann City, 391 Orchard Road. **Map** 2 A4. *Tel 6737-5021.* www.kinokuniya.com.sg *One of several branches.*

Select Books
03-15 Tanglin Shopping Center, 19 Tanglin Road. **Map** 1 D3. *Tel 6732-1515.* www.selectbooks.com.sg

Times the Bookstore
04-08 Centerpoint, 176 Orchard Road. **Map** 1 F2. *Tel 6734-9022.* *One of several branches.*

SINGAPORE MEMORABILIA

The Garden Shop
Singapore Botanic Gardens, 1 Cluny Road. **Map** 1 D1. *Tel 6475-2319.* www.natures niche.com

National Museum of Singapore Shop
93 Stamford Road. **Map** 3 D5. *Tel 6332-3251.* www.museum shop.com.sg

Raffles Hotel Gift Shop
01-01 Raffles Hotel, 1 Beach Road. **Map** 3 F4. *Tel 6412-1143.* www.raffleshotelgifts.com

ORCHIDS

National Orchid Garden
1 Cluny Road. **Map** 1 D1. *Tel 6471-7361.* www.sbg.org.sg

Mandai Orchid Garden
200 Mandai Lake Road. *Tel 6269-1036.* www.mandai.com.sg

RISIS Store
01-084 Suntec City Mall, 3 Temasek Blvd.
Map 3 E5. *Tel 6338-8250.* www.risis.com

GOURMET FOOD

Bee Cheng Hiang
1359 Serangoon Road. **Map** 3 E1. *Tel 6291-5753.* www.bch.com.sg

Brown Rice Paradise
03-15 Tanglin Mall, 163 Tanglin Road. **Map** 1 D3. *Tel 6738-1121.*

Chinatown Heritage Center
48 Pagoda Street. **Map** 4 C3. *Tel 6325-2878.* www.chinatown heritage.com.sg

Faber Forest Gift Shop
109 Mount Faber Road. *Tel 6377-9670.*

The Tea Chapter
9–11 Neil Road, Tanjong Pagar. **Map** 4 C4. *Tel 6226-3026.* www.tea-chapter.com.sg

Thos. S.B. Raffles
01-30 Raffles Hotel Arcade, 1 Beach Road. **Map** 3 F4. *Tel 6412-1148.* www.raffleshotelgifts. com

Tierney's Gourmet
02-01/04 Serene Center, 10 Jalan Serene. *Tel 6466-7451.*

ENTERTAINMENT IN SINGAPORE

In its endeavor to become a regional center for the arts, Singapore delights visitors with a diverse array of entertainment, ranging from classical to contemporary. Professional and amateur theater groups, dance troupes, and orchestras offer Asian performances and Western productions. The lively scene is enhanced by the presence of international artists, who come to participate in the many arts festivals

A Chinese dancer performing at full stretch

held throughout the year. Performance venues are scattered throughout the island, but among those that hold pride of place are the Riverside Arts District, the striking Esplanade – Theaters on the Bay, and the open-air Fort Canning Park. Singaporeans love their nightlife and its increasingly eclectic mix of venues – jazz clubs, blues bars, nightclubs, karaoke lounges, and traditional pubs – will satisfy all tastes.

INFORMATION

Daily newspapers, such as **The Straits Times**, carry comprehensive listings of current and upcoming events. Brochures at hotels and free publications including Where Singapore, **Juice Magazine**, **Think Magazine**, and I-S (Inside Singapore) also carry detailed listings and reviews. Internet websites, such as singaporetheatre.com, are also an excellent resource for all the latest information.

TICKETS

It is best to purchase tickets at least two days in advance at the venue itself, though some shows may be totally booked out months ahead. Internet booking is now a convenient option. **TicketCharge** and **SISTIC** are two outlets that handle tickets for most events. Check the schedules on their websites, by telephone, or by visiting one of their many locations across the island. Tickets, once purchased, are not usually refundable or exchangeable. For Indian cultural shows, the **Annalakshmi Restaurant** hands out free tickets at the restaurant.

DISABLED ACCESS

Although most entertainment venues are located in heritage buildings or renovated warehouses, several of them have added disabled access. In newer venues, such as the Esplanade, such facilities have been provided. It is always

best to call ahead and confirm. **Access Singapore**, run by the National Council of Social Services has a detailed list of venues with amenities.

VENUES

Ever since its opening, **Esplanade – Theaters on the Bay** has been the focal point for the performing arts, though the elegant **Chijmes Hall**, **Jubilee Hall**, and **Victoria Theater & Concert Hall** are still traditional favorites for theater and musical performances. **Cox Terrace at Fort Canning Park** and the **Shaw Foundation Symphony Stage**, perched on a lake at the Singapore Botanic Gardens, are popular outdoor venues. **Singapore Indoor Stadium**, **Kallang Theater**, and the **University Cultural Center** are preferred for large concerts, especially for visiting international artists, while the **DBS Arts Center**, **The Room Upstairs**, and **The Substation** specialize in more offbeat acts.

FESTIVALS

Singapore hosts several performing arts festivals throughout the year. The riveting **Singapore Arts Festival**, held every June, is one of the highlights, drawing international acts, as does the four-day, open-air **WOMAD** (World of Music, Arts, and Dance). The **Buskers' Festival** for street performers is held by the riverside every November. The **Singapore International Film Festival**, which screens about 300 movies, has been held every April for over 15 years. It showcases mainstream cinema, documentaries, and animation from around the world. More recently, **The Substation** has been organizing an alternative Singapore Short Film Festival. The most popular, and allegedly Asia's largest, outdoor cinema festival is held by **Starlight Cinemas** every June at the Fort Canning Park. The **Singapore Piano Festival** also draws crowds.

Musicians at WOMAD, at Fort Canning Park

FREE PERFORMANCES & OPEN AIR SHOWS

Free events are held regularly at Esplanade – Theaters on the Bay. A list of the frequently changing performances, including world music and drama, is available on their website *(see Directory)*. Indian classical music and dance shows, such as Bharatnatyam and Odissi, are organized at different venues by the **Temple of Fine Arts**, a non-profit making arts organization. Tickets for shows hosted by Temple of Fine Arts are also available at Annalakshmi Restaurant. The **Singapore Dance Theater**'s "Ballet under the Stars" is a delightful event at Fort Canning Park. Classical music concerts, including performances by the **Singapore Symphony Orchestra**, are held at the Singapore Botanic Gardens, while street musicians often play by the Singapore River. Every Sunday, the **Chijmes Lawn and Fountain Court** hosts jazz and Latin music recitals.

The Singapore Symphony Orchestra in concert, Botanic Gardens

DIRECTORY

INFORMATION

Juice Magazine
Tel 6733-1111.
www.juiceonline.com

The Straits Times
Tel 6319-5397.
www.straitstimes.asia1.com.sg

Think Magazine
Tel 9880-6520.
www.think.cz

TICKETS

Annalakshmi Restaurant
133 New Bridge Road,
B1-02 Chinatown Point.
Tel 6339-9993. www.annalakshmi.com.sg

SISTIC
Tel 6348-5555.
www.sistic.com.sg
Several locations from Raffles City; Victoria Concert Hall Box Office.

TicketCharge
Tel 6296-2929.
www.ticketcharge.com.sg
Several locations from Tanglin Mall; Centerpoint.

DISABLED ACCESS

Access Singapore National Council of Social Service
150 Pandan Gardens.
Tel 6899-1220.
www.dpa.org.sg/access

VENUES

Chijmes Hall
30 Victoria Street. **Map** 3 D5. *Tel 6334-3801.*
www.chijmes.com.sg

Cox Terrace at Fort Canning Park
Fort Canning Road. **Map** 2 C5. *Tel 6332-1200.*
www.nparks.gov.sg

DBS Arts Center
20 Merbau Road. **Map** 4 C2. *Tel 6733-8166.*
www.srt.com.sg

Esplanade – Theaters on the Bay
1 Esplanade Drive,
Marina Bay. **Map** 5 E2.
Tel 6828-8222.
www.esplanade.com

Jubilee Hall
Raffles Hotel.
Map 3 E5. *Tel 6412-1319.* www.raffles.com

Kallang Theater
1 Stadium Walk.
Map 5 D2. *Tel 6345-8488.* www.nac.gov.sg

The Room Upstairs
42 Waterloo Street.
Map 3 D4.
Tel 6837-0842.

Shaw Foundation Symphony Stage
Botanic Gardens,
1 Cluny Road.
Map 1 D2. *Tel 6471-7361.* www.sbg.org.sg

Singapore Indoor Stadium
2 Stadium Walk.
Tel 6344-2660.

The Substation
45 Armenian Street.
Map 3 D5.
Tel 6337-7535.

University Cultural Center
50 Kent Ridge Crescent.
Tel 6516-2492.
www.nus.edu.sg

Victoria Theater & Concert Hall
9 Empress Place.
Map 5 D3. *Tel 6338-8283.* www.nac.gov.sg

FESTIVALS

Buskers' Festival
www.singapore-buskers.com

Singapore Arts Festival
Map 5 D2. *Tel 6345-8488.* www.nac.gov.sg

Singapore International Film Festival
www.filmfest.org.sg

Singapore Piano Festival
www.pianofestival.com.sg

Starlight Cinemas
www.starlightcinema.com

WOMAD

35 A Duxton Road.
Map 4 C4.
Tel 6220-2676.
www.womadsingapore.com

FREE PERFORMANCES & OPEN AIR SHOWS

Chijmes Lawn and Fountain Court
30 Victoria Street.
Map 3 D5.
Tel 6336-1818.
www.chijmes.com.sg

Singapore Dance Theater
2nd Story,
Fort Canning Center,
Cox Terrace. **Map** 5 D1.
Tel 6338-0611. www.singaporedancetheatre.com

Singapore Symphony Orchestra
Victoria Concert Hall,
11 Empress Place.
Map 5 D3
Tel 6338-1230.
www.sso.org.sg

Temple of Fine Arts
133 New Bridge Road,
B1-02 Chinatown Point.
Tel 6535-0509.
www.templeoffinearts.org/sg

Wayang (Chinese Opera) performance on an elaborate stage on Teochew street

WESTERN CLASSICAL MUSIC & DANCE

The **Singapore Symphony Orchestra** *(see p253)* was founded in 1979 and performs regularly at its home base, the Esplanade, and the Victoria Concert Hall. The concerts often feature special guest conductors, composers, and soloists. The **Singapore Dance Theater** *(see p253)*, the state's foremost dance company, presents classic and contemporary Western ballet, while the **Odyssey Dance Theater** and **Ecnad** stage contemporary and fusion dance performances.

CHINESE OPERA, MALAY & INDIAN MUSIC

Traditional Chinese opera, or *wayang,* is a cultural street event best seen during the Festival of the Hungry Ghosts *(see pp200–201)*. The **Chinese Opera Institute** and the Chinese Theater Circle also stage a two-hour opera every Friday and Saturday, complete with explanations. The **Singapore Chinese Orchestra**, the island's only professional Chinese orchestra, plays Indian and Malay music as well as Chinese pieces.

For traditional Malay culture, the **Malay Village** has a program on weekends, which includes the traditional Kudu Kepang dance. Other features include the Orchestra Melayu and the Malay opera, *Bangasawan*, based on folktales. The rich repertoire

of Indian classical dance and music is presented by the **Temple of Fine Arts** *(see p253)*, as well as the **Nrityalaya Aesthetics Society**.

THEATER & MUSICALS

Singapore's vibrant theater scene ranges from runaway Broadway and West End hits on international tour to local groups performing contemporary productions by local playwrights. Well-known companies are the **Action Theater**, **Singapore Repertory Theater**, **TheaterWorks**, **Toy Factory**, and **The Necessary Stage**. While most productions are in English, albeit with an all-Asian cast, vernacular Chinese dialects, as well as Malay and Tamil theater, are represented too. Troupes such as **The Singapore Stage Club**, set up in 1945, with members from around the world, perform pantomimes, especially at Christmas.

CINEMA

Most of the films shown in Singapore are in English, with Chinese subtitles. Other language films have both English and Chinese subtitles. Hollywood blockbusters and Indian films are extremely popular and there are many multiplex cinemas to choose from, such as the **Golden Village** and **Shaw Beach Road** theaters. Art-house films in European languages are screened by the **Singapore**

Film Society at the **Alliance Français**, or **Goethe Institute**. The **British Council** organizes regular shows of critically acclaimed movies. Local cinema's popularity gained momentum after the success of the comedy *Money No Enough* in 1998. Today, films by young directors such as Royston Tan and Kelvin Tong draw large audiences. Special midnight showings are also held.

NIGHTLIFE

Orchard Road is the mainstay of nightlife on the island, while some pubs, clubs, and bars on the riverside quays are more suited for cozy get-togethers, and are largely frequented by young professionals in the evening. Swing to the blues and rock and roll at **Crazy Elephant** and **Harry's Bar**. Singapore's first Irish pub that plays Irish music, **Molly Malone's**, is located by the riverside. **Sanctuary Bar** on Orchard Road, **Bar Sa Vanh** in Chinatown, and **Sunset Bay** on Sentosa Island are a few of the favorite venues. The wine bars offer friendly service and

Local rock band playing at the Crazy Elephant

intimate ambience. Most of them are located in renovated shophouses. Though all are fairly popular, the ones that attract the most crowds are **No. 5**, the city's first wine bar which has a rustic feel to it with unpolished wooden floors and Persian carpets, **Barcelona**, and the busy **Bisous**. Karaoke rooms (also known as KTV stations) are hugely popular, and even the smallest pub will feature a karaoke station.

Dance clubs are always packed and tend to play alternative music – trance, progressive trance, and garage. **Dbl O** has one of the largest dance floors in Singapore and its resident DJs dominate the scene. For a mind-thumping dance night, **Thumper** is also one of the venues that top the list of favorites. The trendy **Zouk** complex houses **Velvet Underground** and **Phuture**. The Velvet Underground has

a main dance floor and a separate bar for chilling out. Enter a futuristic world with trendy murals on **Phuture**'s walls and enjoy all sorts of hip music, hip-hop, and drum 'n' bass at the club. The Ministry of Sound establishment, famous for featuring electronic music, has an avant-garde super-club at Clarke Quay.

The majority of these clubs charge a cover price between S$20–30.

DIRECTORY

MUSIC & DANCE

Chinese Opera Institute
111 Middle Road.
Map 3 D4. **Tel** 6339-1292. ww.chineseopera-institute.com.sg

Ecnad
04–05 182 Cecil Street.
Map 5 D4. **Tel** 6226-6772. www.ecnad.org

Malay Village
39 Geylang Road.
Tel 6748-4700.

Nrityalaya Aesthetics Society
Stamford Arts Center, 155 Waterloo Street.
Map 3 D4. **Tel** 6336-6537. www.nas.org.sg

Odyssey Dance Theater
04–04, 182 Cecil Street.
Map 5 D4.
Tel 6221-5516.
www.odysseydance-theatre.com

Singapore Chinese Orchestra
7 Shenton Way, Singapore Conference Hall.
Map 5 D5. **Tel** 6440-3839. www.sco.org.sg

THEATER

Action Theater
42 Waterloo Street.
Map 3 D4. **Tel** 6837-0842. www.action.org.sg

Chinese Theater Circle
5 Smith Street. **Map** 4 C4.
Tel 6323-4862.
www.ctcopera.com.sg

The Necessary Stage
278 Marine Parade Road. **Tel** 6440-8115.
www.necessary.org

Singapore Repertory Theater
DBS Arts Center, 20 Merbau Road.
Map 4 C2.
Tel 6733-8166.
www.srt.com.sg

The Singapore Stage Club
24 Whitchurch Road.
Tel 6251-1350.
www.stageclub.com

TheaterWorks
72–13 Mohamed Sultan Road. **Map** 2 B5.
Tel 6737-7213.
www.theatreworks.org.sg

Toy Factory
15 A Smith Street. **Map** 4 C4. **Tel** 6222-1526.
www.toyfactory.org.sg

CINEMA

Alliance Français
1 Sarkies Road.
Map 2 A2. **Tel** 6737-8422. www.alliance francais.org.sg

British Council
30 Napier Road.
Map 1 D2.
Tel 6473-1111.
www.britishcouncil.org/sg

Goethe Institute
05–01,163 Penang Road, Winsland House II.
Map 2 B4.
Tel 6735-4555.
www.goethe.de/ins/sg

Golden Village
Marina Leisureplex, Raffles Avenue. **Map** 5 F2.
Tel 1900 912-1234.
www.gv.com.sg
One of several branches.

Shaw Beach Road Cineplex
Shaw Tower, 100 Beach Road.
Map 3 F4.
Tel 6738-0555.
www.shaw.com.sg
One of several branches.

Singapore Film Society
03–01 Marina Leisureplex, 5A Raffles Avenue.
Map 5 F2.
Tel 90-170-160.
www.sfs.org.sg

NIGHTLIFE

Barcelona
01–30 Robertson Walk, 11 Unity Street.
Map 4 C2.
Tel 6235-3456.
www.uno-restaurant.
com.sg

Bar Sa Vanh
49 Club Street.
Map 4 C4.
Tel 6323-0145.

Bisous
25 Church Street.
Map 5 D3.
Tel 6226-5505.
www.bisous.com.sg

China Jump Bar & Grille
Fountain Court, Chijmes, 30 Victoria Street.
Map 3 D4.
Tel 6338-9388.

Crazy Elephant
Clarke Quay, 3E River Valley Road.
Map 1 E4.
Tel 6337-7859.
www.crazyelephant.com

Dbl O
01–24 Robertson Walk, 11 Unity Street. **Map** 4 C2. **Tel** 6735-2008.

Harry's Bar
28 Boat Quay. **Map** 5 D3.
Tel 6538-3029.
www.harry's-bar.com

Molly Malone's
56 Circular Road.
Map 5 D3. **Tel** 6536-2029. www.molly-malone.com

No. 5
5 Emerald Hill.
Tel 6732-0818.

Sanctuary Bar
Wisma Atria, 435 Orchard Road. **Map** 1 F2. **Tel** 6238-3473.

Sparks
150 Orchard Road. **Map** 1 F2. **Tel** 6735-6133.

Sunset Bay
Fort Siloso Beachwalk, Sentosa Island.
Tel 6275-0668.
www.sunsetbay.com.sg

Thumper
22 Scotts Road. **Map** 1 F2.
Tel 6735-0827. www.
thumper.com.sg

Zouk, Velvet Underground, and Phuture
17 Jiak Kim Street.
Tel 6738-2988.
www.zoukclub.com.sg

OUTDOOR ACTIVITIES IN SINGAPORE

Singapore is not only a place for shopping and dining, but also for a range of exciting outdoor activities. Being a tropical island, all the favorite watersports such as diving, sailing, water-skiing, and wakeboarding are available throughout the year. The most popular spots for these are the Kallang River located to the east of the city, East Coast Park, and Sentosa. Ample cycling trails are provided around the outer reaches of the island and within its beautiful nature reserves. Golf and fitness activities are widely enjoyed here. Tennis is also a popular sport but can be strenuous and it's best to play early in the day. The tropical sun can be strong, so adequate protection is required.

Golf driving range at East Coast Park

GOLF

Singapore has a number of beautifully kept golf courses. Visitors are permitted to play at most clubs, but only on weekdays. However, the **Seletar Country Club** is open to non-members on the weekends. The other popular golf clubs include **Laguna National Golf & Country Club**, **Sentosa Golf Club**, and the **Raffles Country Club** where there is a spectacular view of the South China Sea.

DIVING

Singapore is one of the most economical places in the world for diving lessons. PADI (Professional Association of Diving Instructors) courses for beginners as well as advanced divers are available. There are a number of reputable dive schools to choose from, including the **Big Bubble Center**, **Blue Wave Sports**, **Waikiki Dive Center**, **Scuba Corner**, **Scuba Connection**, **Friendly Waters Seasports Services**, **Sentosa Water Sports Center**, and **Marsden Brothers** which has the only custom-made dive boat in Singapore. Besides offering dive lessons, most schools also rent out equipment and organize dive trips. These excursions range from a day's outing to explore local Singapore waters to longer dive tours and live-aboard trips that cover popular dive spots off Malaysia's east coast, Thailand, or Indonesia's Riau Archipelago.

WATER-SKIING AND WAKEBOARDING

Several individual operators rent out equipment and offer professional instruction. The facilities of the **Cowabunga Ski Center** are among the best in Singapore. **William Water Sports Center** offers waterskiing every day and conducts all-day wakeboarding lessons every Tuesday and Thursday.

SAILING AND WINDSURFING

Most sailing and windsurfing facilities are located on the east coast of the island. Among these are the **Pasta Fresca Seasports Center**, **National Sailing Center**, **Keppel Marina**, **Raffles Marina**, **Republic of Singapore Yacht Club**, **SAFRA Seasports Center**, and **Changi Sailing Club**, which offer various marine activities, including sail boat charters (permits may be required), windsurf boards for hire, and boat berthing docks. Some hold large regattas and many conduct training courses. Call or check websites for details.

ADVENTURE SPORTS CLUBS

Singapore Adventurers' Club organizes a range of exciting activities such as trekking, cycling tours, canoeing, and sailing. Most of its activities are open to all, with the exception of a few members-only events. Intensive courses in kayaking, rock climbing, and abseiling are offered all year round by **Outward Bound Singapore** located at Pulau Ubin and East Coast Park.

Diving, a popular activity in SIngapore

NATURE WATCH

Nature Society (Singapore) organizes bird-watching trips twice each month to various locations. Call or check its website for more details. In addition, spotting the diverse species of animals, birds, and plants protected within Singapore's stunning nature reserves can be a truly rewarding experience.

CYCLING

Cycling is an excellent way to explore the attractions that lie outside Singapore's city limits. Hiring a bike on Sentosa is a good alternative to the island's monorail system. For a leisurely ride along the seashore of the East Coast Park, bikes can be rented at the **Sunsport Center** or **SDK Recreation**. The varied landscape of the tracks at the Bukit Timah Nature Reserve *(see p238)* offers a more challenging experience, but you will need to bring your own bike. Pulau Ubin *(see p243)* off the northeastern coast is a favorite cycling destination. With its maze of trails, it is particularly good for mountain biking. Bikes can be hired on the island near the dock or from Changi Village.

TENNIS

Tennis courts can be booked every day between 7am and 10pm at various centers, such

A game in progress at Singapore Tennis Center

as the **Kallang Squash and Tennis Center**, and **Farrer Park Tennis Court**, The **Singapore Tennis Center** offers one-on-one coaching, and you can put your name on a partner list and hire a court. An Instant Tennis course for beginners is available at a very reasonable fee.

DIRECTORY

GOLF

Laguna National Golf & Country Club
11 Laguna Golf Green.
Tel 6542-6888.

Raffles Country Club
450 Jalan Ahmad Ibrahim.
Tel 6861-6888.

Seletar Country Club
101 Seletar Club Road,
Seletar Airbase.
Tel 6481-4812.

Sentosa Golf Club
27 Bukit Manis Road.
Tel 6275-0022.

DIVING

Big Bubble Center
57 Cantonment Road.
Map 4 B4. *Tel 6222-6862.* www.bigbubble.com

Blue Wave Sports
02–29 Riverside Point,
30 Merchant Road.
Map 4 C3.
Tel 6557-2702.

Friendly Waters Seasports Services
01-36 The Riverwalk,
20 Upper Circular Road.
Tel 6557-0016.

Marsden Brothers
113 Holland Road.
Tel 6475-0050.

Scuba Connection
Blk 261, Waterloo Street.
Map 3 D4. *Tel 6337-0700.* www.scubaconnection.com

Scuba Corner
Blk 809 French Road. **Map** 3 F3. *Tel 6338-6563.* www. scubacorner.com.sg

Sentosa Water Sports Center
1 Garden Avenue, Sentosa.

Waikiki Dive Center
298 Beach Road. **Map** 3 F4. *Tel 6291-1290.* www.waikikidive.com

WATER-SKIING & WAKEBOARDING

Cowabunga Ski Center
10 Stadium Lane.
Tel 6344-8813. www.extreme.com.sg

William Water Sports Center
60 Jalan Mempurong.
Tel 6257-5859.

SAILING AND WINDSURFING

Changi Sailing Club
32 Netheravon Road.
Tel 6545-2876. www.csc.org.sg

Keppel Marina
Lot 1016 and 2003,
Bukit Chermin Road.
Tel 6270-6665. www.keppelmarina.com

National Sailing Center
1500 East Coast Parkway.
Map 5 F4. *Tel 6444-4555.* www.sailing.org.sg

Pasta Fresca Seasports Center
1212 East Coast Parkway.
Map 5 F4.
Tel 6449-5118.

Raffles Marina
10 Tuas West Drive.
Tel 6861-8000. www.rafflesmarina.com.sg

Republic of Singapore Yacht Club
52 West Coast Ferry Road.
Tel 6768-9288. www.rsyc.org.sg

SAFRA Seasports Center
10 Changi Coast Walk.
Tel 6546-5880,

ADVENTURE SPORTS CLUBS

Outward Bound Singapore
9 Stadium Link, Pulau Ubin. *Tel 6545-9008.* www.obs.pa.gov.sg

Singapore Adventurers' Club
74B Lorong 27, Geylang.
Tel 6749-0557. www.sac.org

NATURE WATCH

Nature Society
02-05 The Sunflower,
510 Geylang Road.
Tel 6741-2036. www.nss.org.sg

CYCLING

SDK Recreation
1000 East Coast Parkway.
Map 5 F4.
Tel 6445-2969.

Sunsport Center
East Coast Parkway.
Map 5 F4.
Tel 6440-9827.

TENNIS

Farrer Park Tennis Court
Rutland Road.
Tel 6299-4166.

Kallang Squash & Tennis Center
Stadium Road.
Tel 6348-1291.

Singapore Tennis Center
1020 East Coast Parkway.
Map 5 F4.
Tel 6442-5966.

SINGAPORE STREET FINDER

The key map below shows the area of Singapore covered in this Street Finder. Map references given for sights, shops, and entertainment venues described in the Singapore section of this guide refer to the maps on the following pages. Map references are also given for Singapore hotels *(see pp286–91)* and restaurants *(see pp308–13)*. Major sights are also marked. A complete index of street names and places of interest shown on the maps follows on pages 264–7. The first figure in the map reference indicates which Street Finder map to turn to, and the letter and the number which follow refer to the grid on the map. The key, below, indicates the scale of the maps and other features marked on them, including post offices and tourist information centers.

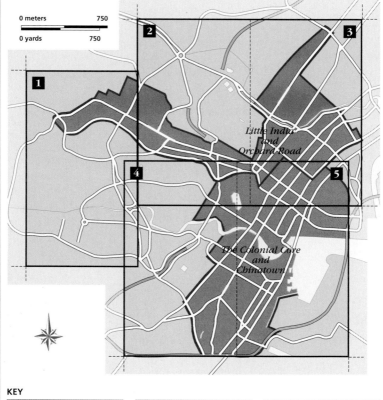

| 0 meters | 750 |
| 0 yards | 750 |

KEY

▪ Major sight	🅿 Parking	═ Railroad
▪ Place of interest	🚓 Police station	▤ Expressway
▪ Other buildings	ℹ Tourist information	— Pedestrian bridge
Ⓜ MRT station	🛕 Indian temple	
🚇 Railroad station	✝ Church	
🚌 Bus station	🔶 Buddhist temple	**Scale of map pages**
⊠ Post office	☪ Mosque	0 meters 250
✚ Hospital	✡ Synagogue	0 yards 250

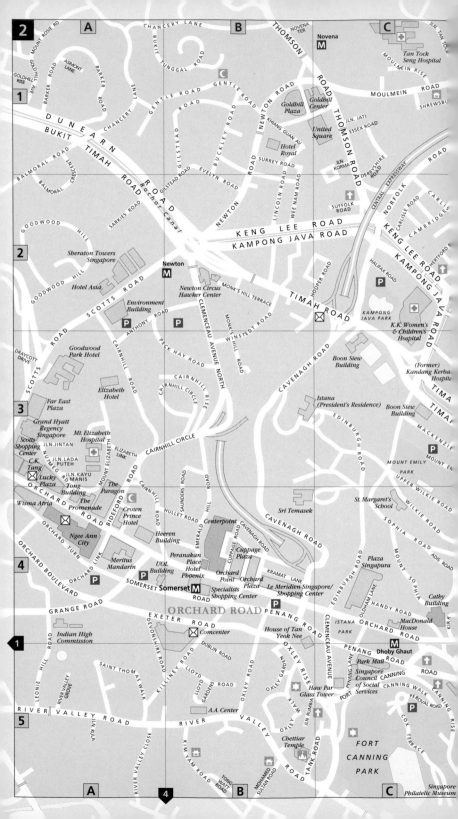

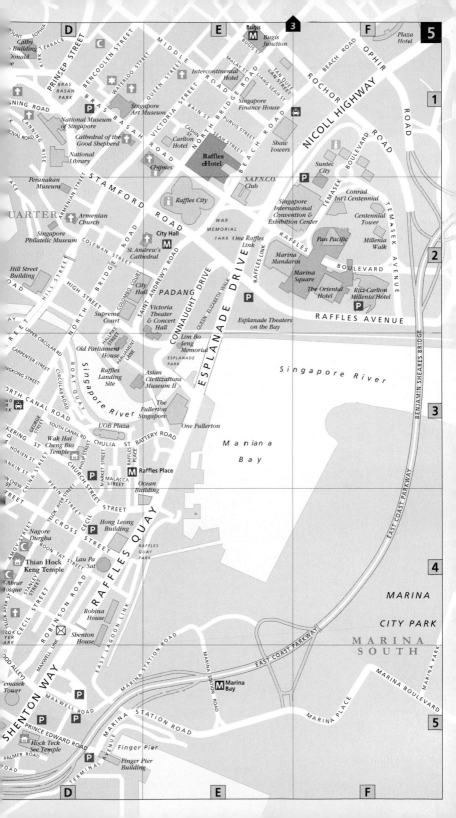

Street Finder Index

TRAVELERS' NEEDS

WHERE TO STAY

Both Malaysia and Singapore offer a variety of accommodations, from luxury hotels to simple guesthouses. Prices are fairly reasonable, although Malaysian Borneo and Singapore tend to be more expensive than Peninsular Malaysia. Top international hotel chains are well-represented, and there are some beautiful resorts in idyllic settings. Mid-range options include government rest houses, an echo of the countries' colonial past, and some lovely boutique hotels. Budget travelers will find excellent guesthouses offering dormitory beds, and in some parts of the country, homestays can be arranged. An overnight stay in a longhouse is a wonderful way of experiencing Dayak culture. Malaysia's national parks provide cabins and campsites, making it possible to stay in the heart of the rain forest. For more information, refer to the detailed listings on pages 272–91.

Doorman at the Raffles Hotel

The well-designed Sutera Harbour Resort, Sabah (see p285)

RATINGS

All hotels in Malaysia and Singapore follow the star grading system. Top- and mid-range hotels are accredited with star ratings according to the level of luxury, facilities, and services they offer but guesthouses have no such ratings. While these ratings help in selecting accommodations, it is wise to visit the official websites of individual hotels for the best deals.

INTERNATIONAL AND RESORT HOTELS

Several of the world's best known international hotel chains are represented in Malaysia and Singapore, offering luxurious rooms and impeccable service. Many of them incorporate features of local architecture in an effort to make their rooms more personal. The resorts, located in beautiful surroundings, have spas, watersports and fitness facilities, golf courses, and a range of shops, restaurants, and bars, giving guests no reason to step out of the resort during their stay.

MID-RANGE HOTELS

Some of the mid-range hotels have facilities comparable to top-end hotels, but with the opening of a slew of international chains, they have had to reduce their prices to stay competitive and now provide extremely good value for money. This category includes boutique hotels, which focus on generating an exotic and relaxing ambience. They are usually more intimate than the chain hotels, and can offer personalized services. Also in this category are former government rest houses, which once lodged colonial officials. Most of them have now been renovated and are managed by **Seri Malaysia Hotels**, and are good options for visitors keen to get a sense of heritage during their stay.

BUDGET HOTELS AND HOMESTAYS

All the cities and towns of Malaysia have budget hotels and guesthouses in tourist areas. Not only are these economical, but they can also be a good source of local information. While the facilities offered by most guesthouses are basic, some include free breakfast and Internet access. Homestays are becoming increasingly popular as they present an opportunity to get to know Malaysians outside the tourist industry. The local tourist offices always have a list of homestay programs.

LONGHOUSES

Travelers to Malaysian Borneo, particularly Sarawak, can experience a night in a longhouse, the traditional dwelling of many indigenous groups, such as the Bidayuh (see p161) and the Iban (see p167). The majority of visitors to longhouses organize their trips through tour agents, such as

The Planters Inn restaurant, Crowne Plaza, Kuala Lumpur (see p274)

◁ White sand beaches set against the emerald seas in Pulau Perhentian Kecil, off Terengganu

Suite at Royal Mulu Resort, Sarawak *(see p282)*

Borneo Adventures *(see p329)* and **Sabah Tourism Board** *(see p335)*, who arrange stays at working longhouses. Facilities provided are generally very basic, consisting of little more than a floor mattress and mosquito net, although some longhouses have now installed western-style toilets to make the stay a little more comfortable for their guests.

Some top-end international hotels are also constructed in the form of longhouses, duplicating the traditional structure while including a range of urban luxuries and comforts.

NATIONAL PARKS AND CAMPING

National Parks and reserves throughout Malaysia offer reasonably comfortable accommodations in lodges or cabin-style huts, usually located around the Park Headquarters. They also have campsites where visitors may either rent a tent or pitch their own. Few other campsites in Malaysia or Singapore permit travelers to put up a tent on a beach, but facilities are basic. For information, bookings, and permits, it is wise to contact the **Department of Wildlife and National Parks**, **Sarawak Forestry Corporation**, and **Sabah National Parks**.

RATES AND RESERVATIONS

Room rates tend to remain steady throughout the year, increasing only slightly during festivals such as Hari Raya Puasa, Chinese New Year *(see pp28–9)*, and Christmas, when all levels of accommodations

fill up and advance booking also becomes necessary. At quieter times of the year, especially during the monsoon season between November and February, rates drop significantly and discounts can be obtained on the east coast of the peninsula. Prior reservations are essential at top-end hotels, for the best prices.

HIDDEN COSTS

Most budget and mid-range hotels quote net prices that include all taxes. However, top-end hotels in Malaysia display a price amount with the symbol "++" after the rate, which means that 10 percent service charge and 5 percent government tax will be added to it. In Singapore, this symbol becomes "+++", which refers to 10 percent service charge, 17 percent Goods and Services Tax, and 1 percent government tax. Food and beverage items in luxury hotels and restaurants also have taxes and service charges added on.

Cabin-style huts, Sepilok Nature Resort, Sandakan *(see p285)*

TRAVELING WITH KIDS

Hotel staff in both Malaysia and Singapore tend to indulge younger guests, and will occasionally also give preferential treatment to their parents. Even at basic hotels, children under the age of 12 years can often stay for free in their parents' room. Not all hotels have playgrounds and other special facilities for kids, but most are very flexible about providing extra beds in rooms and arranging special meals. Baby cots and high chairs are available with some notice. Some resort hotels organize activities for kids and offer babysitting services.

SPECIAL NEEDS

Apart from top-end hotels, few places offer special facilities for the disabled in Malaysia or Singapore *(see p334)*. For the mobility impaired, facilities are limited to ramps for wheelchairs and lifts to all floors. Some five-star hotels have rooms fitted with wider doors, low-level light switches, and wheelchair access. It is rare for budget hotels and dormitories to have any such provisions.

DIRECTORY

MID-RANGE HOTELS

Seri Malaysia Hotels
Tel (03) 2300-2777.
www.serimalaysia.com.my

NATIONAL PARKS AND CAMPING

Department of Wildlife and National Parks
KM 10 Jalan Cheras, Kuala Lumpur.
Tel (03) 9075-2872.
www.wildlife.gov.my

Sabah National Parks
Kota Kinabalu.
Tel (088) 212-508.

Sarawak Forestry Corporation
Level 12, Office Tower, Hock Lee Center, Jalan Datuk Abang Abdul Rahim, Kuching.
Tel (082) 348-001.
www.sarawakforestry.com

Choosing a Hotel

These hotels have been selected for their good value, facilities, and location. The prices listed are those charged by the hotel, although discounts may be available. Price bands for Singapore are given on pages 287, 289, and 291. Map references for Kuala Lumpur refer to maps on pp78–85 and for Singapore to maps on pp258–67.

PRICE CATEGORIES
The price ranges are for a standard double room, inclusive of breakfast for two and service (10%) and government tax (5%) during peak season.

(RM) Under RM100
(RM)(RM) RM100–RM200
(RM)(RM)(RM) RM200–RM300
(RM)(RM)(RM)(RM) RM300–RM400
(RM)(RM)(RM)(RM)(RM) Over RM400

KUALA LUMPUR

AMPANG SuCasa Service Apartments
222 Jalan Ampang, Kuala Lumpur, 50450 **Tel** *(03) 4251-3833* **Fax** *(03) 4252-1096* **Rooms** *180*

Shielded from the bustle of city life, this service apartment property has a tranquil charm providing quiet accommodations. The long-term rates are substantially cheaper than the daily tariffs. The apartments are well-equipped and fully furnished. **www.sucasa.com.my**

BANGSAR Cititel Mid Valley
Mid Valley City, Kuala Lumpur, 59200 **Tel** *(03) 2296-1188* **Fax** *(03) 2283-5551* **Rooms** *646*

This hotel is conveniently situated for the Mid Valley Megamall and is a favorite with shopaholics. The rooms are simple, compact, and well-equipped. Though the hotel is a little out of the city center, it is self-sufficient with its own complex of shops, services, restaurants, fitness center, and bars. **www.cititelhotel.com**

BUKIT BINTANG Bintang Warisan Hotel
68 Jalan Bukit Bintang, Kuala Lumpur, 55100 **Tel** *(03) 2148-8111* **Fax** *(03) 2148-2333* **Rooms** *97* **Map** *5 C3*

This is a good budget hotel situated in the center of the Bukit Bintang shopping and entertainment district. The rooms are clean and comfortable with double-glazed windows to eliminate street noise. There is an atmospheric coffeehouse that opens onto the street. **www.bintangwarisan.com**

BUKIT BINTANG Hotel Agora
106–110 Jalan Bukit Bintang, Kuala Lumpur, 55100 **Tel** *(03) 2142-8133* **Fax** *(03) 2142-7815* **Rooms** *48* **Map** *5 C3*

Located in the busiest part of Kuala Lumpur, close to the Bukit Bintang monorail station, this compact hotel is well-suited for budget travelers. The rates do not include breakfast, but within walking distance is Kuala Lumpur's main entertainment district, with myriad dining options, including food stalls on Jalan Alor. **www.agorahotel.net**

BUKIT BINTANG Hotel Nova Kuala Lumpur
16–22 Jalan Alor, Kuala Lumpur, 50200 **Tel** *(03) 2143-1818* **Fax** *(03) 2142-9985* **Rooms** *154* **Map** *5 C2*

Located on Jalan Alor, Hotel Nova is a bargain, especially for visitors eager to sample local hawker food. The hotel's Casanova Kafe serves delicious breakfasts, evening snacks, and Jalan Alor's cheapest beer during happy hours between 5:30 and 9:30pm. **www.novahtl.com**

BUKIT BINTANG Radius International Hotel
51A Changkat Bukit Bintang, Kuala Lumpur, 50200 **Tel** *(03) 2715-3888* **Fax** *(03) 2715-1888* **Rooms** *433* **Map** *5 B2*

This is one of the city's modest international hotels with reasonable facilities. It is popular with tourist groups and budget travelers because of its proximity to Bukit Bintang and Jalan Alor's food hawkers. The premier floor offers special services such as cable TV and in-room Internet access. **www.radius-international.com**

BUKIT BINTANG Capitol Hotel
Jalan Bulan, Kuala Lumpur, 55100 **Tel** *(03) 2143-7000* **Fax** *(03) 2143-0000* **Rooms** *225* **Map** *5 C3*

In the thick of Kuala Lumpur's busy shopping district is the Hotel Capitol. With contemporary decor and well-ventilated rooms, it offers facilities of international standards, at reasonable tariffs. Guests have access to the pool at the adjoining Federal Hotel. **www.fhihotels.com**

BUKIT BINTANG The Federal Kuala Lumpur
35 Jalan Bukit Bintang, Kuala Lumpur, 55100 **Tel** *(03) 2148-9166* **Fax** *(03) 2148-2877* **Rooms** *431* **Map** *5 C3*

Enjoying an excellent location along busy Bukit Bintang, this is among the city's oldest hotels and still retains a strong appeal especially for those interested in the hotel's 50-year heritage. The Mandarin Palace offers ornately-carved wooden features and fine *dim sum*. **www.fhihotels.com**

BUKIT BINTANG Swiss-Garden Hotel Kuala Lumpur
117 Jalan Pudu, Kuala Lumpur, 55100 **Tel** *(03) 2141-3333* **Fax** *(03) 2141-5555* **Rooms** *310* **Map** *5 B3*

The hotel, located equidistant from Chinatown, Times Square, and Bukit Bintang, is remarkably peaceful with well-appointed rooms. Broadband Internet access is available for an additional fee. The Samsara Spa offers a tranquil retreat, while the Blue Chip Bar livens up the atmosphere in the evenings. **www.swissgarden.com**

Key to Symbols *see back cover flap*

BUKIT BINTANG The Royale Bintang Kuala Lumpur

17–21 Jalan Bukit Bintang, Kuala Lumpur, 55100 **Tel** *(03) 2143-9898* **Fax** *(03) 2142-1807* **Rooms** *418* **Map** *5 C3*

Tucked away in the quieter recesses of Kuala Lumpur's busy shopping precinct, this hotel offers contemporary facilities. The rooms are well-equipped, with facilities such as in-room Internet and double-glazed windows. There is a club floor for executive guests. **www.royale-bintang-hotel.com.my**

BUKIT BINTANG JW Marriott Hotel Kuala Lumpur

183 Jalan Bukit Bintang, Kuala Lumpur, 55100 **Tel** *(03) 2715-9000* **Fax** *(03) 2715-7000* **Rooms** *561* **Map** *5 C3*

The JW Marriott is an incredibly well-located luxury hotel in the middle of the bustling Bintang Walk. The classic rooms exude comfort and convenience. Its chic Third Floor restaurant *(see p298)* is a gourmet's paradise serving an array of international cuisines with a hint of Asian flavors. **www.ytlhotels.com**

BUKIT BINTANG The Ritz-Carlton

168 Jalan Imbi, Kuala Lumpur, 55100 **Tel** *(03) 2142-8000* **Fax** *(03) 2143-8080* **Rooms** *248* **Map** *5 C3*

This is Kuala Lumpur's first boutique hotel with a retro European club-like ambience and an emphasis on discreet personalized service, including a 24-hour butler service. Its well-equipped Spa Village is an urban oasis and the hotel's Li Yen Chinese restaurant is superb. **www.ritzcarlton.com**

BUKIT BINTANG The Westin Kuala Lumpur

199 Jalan Bukit Bintang, Kuala Lumpur, 55100 **Tel** *(03) 2731-8333* **Fax** *(03) 2773-8406* **Rooms** *452* **Map** *5 C3*

The pulsating Bintang Walk is home to the Westin Kuala Lumpur, one of the city's trendiest hotels. The decor is stylish and the all-white signature beds are ideal for a good night's sleep. Several chic restaurants, including Eest *(see p298)*, and bars serve a range of the world's finest cuisines. **www.westin.com/kualalumpur**

CHINATOWN Ancasa Hotel

Jalan Cheng Lock, Kuala Lumpur, 50768 **Tel & Fax** *(03) 2026-8322* **Rooms** *300* **Map** *4 F3*

Formerly known as Impiana Hotel Kuala Lumpur, the Ancasa Hotel is ideal for budget travelers who arrive at Puduraya Bus Station, which is within walking distance of the hotel. It is located just around the corner from Chinatown's bargain streetside shops and eateries. The in-house Sesame Fun Bar is a great place to unwind. **www.udaancasa.com**

CHINATOWN Hotel Malaya Kuala Lumpur

Jalan Hang Lekir, Kuala Lumpur, 50000 **Tel** *(03) 2072-7722* **Fax** *(03) 2070-0980* **Rooms** *238*

Strategically located in the middle of Kuala Lumpur's Chinatown, Hotel Malaya is a popular choice with international budget travelers seeking shopping and dining bargains. The rooms have been recently refurbished and are well-equipped. Easy access to most intra-city public transport adds to its appeal. **www.hotelmalaya.com.my**

CHINATOWN Swiss-Inn Kuala Lumpur

62 Jalan Sultan, Kuala Lumpur, 50000 **Tel** *(03) 2072-3333* **Fax** *(03) 2031-7799* **Rooms** *110* **Map** *4 F3*

Providing comfortable accommodations in the thick of all the Chinatown action, this hotel is small but well-equipped and offers good value for money. However, not all the rooms have windows and some feel a bit cramped. Its Terrace Café has great views of Chinatown's streetlife. **www.swissgarden.com**

CHOW KIT Cititel Express

Jalan Tuanku Abdul Rahman, Kuala Lumpur, 50100 **Tel** *(03) 2691-9833* **Fax** *(03) 2691-9839* **Rooms** *168* **Map** *1 B3*

For those fascinated by local streetlife, the former Stanford Hotel, now called the Cititel Express, located near Chow Kit is ideal. The rooms are well-equipped and prices are reasonable. The Terrace Coffeeshop of Cititel Express serves good food. The nearby Chow Kit monorail station provides access to other parts of the city. **www.cititelexpress.com**

CHOW KIT Hotel Grand Continental

Jalan Raja Laut, Kuala Lumpur, 50350 **Tel** *(03) 2693-9333* **Fax** *(03) 2694-8429* **Rooms** *194* **Map** *1 A3*

Although some distance away from the city center, this hotel is located conveniently close to the Putra World Trade Center as well as to monorail and LRT stations, offering easy access to the rest of the city. The hotel has a mini-gym for guests. **www.ghihotels.com**

CHOW KIT Quality Hotel City Center

Jalan Raja Laut, Kuala Lumpur, 50750 **Tel** *(03) 2693-9233* **Fax** *(03) 2693-9634* **Rooms** *250* **Map** *1 A3*

Strategically located near Central Market and Little India, this was once one of the city's finest accommodations. The rooms are clean and comfortable with warm, welcoming tones. The Quality Club Floor has been recently refurbished. **www.quality.com.my**

CHOW KIT Best Western Premier Seri Pacific Kuala Lumpur

Jalan Putra, Kuala Lumpur, 50746 **Tel** *(03) 4042-5555* **Fax** *(03) 4041-7236* **Rooms** *556* **Map** *1 A2*

Situated adjacent to the Putra World Trade Center, this lavish luxury hotel was once the Pan Pacific. Stylishly furnished, it has several restaurants and facilities such as a pool and gym. The hotel is close to various transport hubs and located next to a shopping mall and business center. **www.seripacific.com**

CHOW KIT Sheraton Imperial Kuala Lumpur

Jalan Sultan Ismail, Kuala Lumpur, 50250 **Tel** *(03) 2717-9900* **Fax** *(03) 2717-9999* **Rooms** *398* **Map** *1 A4*

Beautifully decorated, this hotel is a member of the elite Sheraton Luxury Collection. The rooms are plush and fully-equipped with modern amenities, and the spa is a haven of relaxation and rejuvenation. The hotel's Celestial Court restaurant *(see p299)* has fabulous Chinese food. **www.luxurycollection.com/kualalumpur**

DAMANSARA The Royale Bintang Damansara

6 Jalan PJU 7/3, Petaling Jaya, Selangor, 47800 **Tel** *(03) 7843-1111* **Fax** *(03) 7843-1122* **Rooms** *145*

This is one of several hotels in the city attached to a shopping mall called the Curve. Among the suburban shopping delights are furniture outlets such as IKEA and bookstores such as Borders. Visitors can enjoy a drink in the hotel's dramatic Mystery Bar and Café or unwind by the poolside. **www.royale-bintang-hotel.com.my**

GOLDEN TRIANGLE Concorde Hotel Kuala Lumpur

2 Jalan Sultan Ismail, Kuala Lumpur, 50250 **Tel** *(03) 2144-2200* **Fax** *(03) 2144-1628* **Rooms** *570*   **Map** *1 A4*

A modern hotel, conveniently located in the Golden Triangle, the Concorde Hotel Kuala Lumpur is within walking distance of the city's major attractions. The hotel's 24-hour coffeeshop, the Melting Pot Café, is very popular with clubbers and party-hoppers, and the famous Hard Rock Café is next door. **www.concorde.net**

GOLDEN TRIANGLE Pacific Regency Hotel Apartments

Jalan Punchak, Kuala Lumpur, 50250 **Tel** *(03) 2332-7777* **Fax** *(03) 2381-2085* **Rooms** *153*   **Map** *5 B1*

This is one of a growing number of service apartment properties near Kuala Lumpur's business district. The rooms are spacious and include full kitchens, dining and lounge areas, home entertainment systems, and Internet access. There is a fabulous Thai restaurant and a chic rooftop bar with a spectacular view of the cityscape. **www.pacific-regency.com**

GOLDEN TRIANGLE Parkroyal Kuala Lumpur

Jalan Sultan Ismail, Kuala Lumpur, 50250 **Tel** *(03) 2147-0088* **Fax** *(03) 2141-5524* **Rooms** *348*   **Map** *1 A4*

Set back from the busy Bintang Walk, this hotel is a quiet retreat and exudes warm comfort. Recent renovations have given it a contemporary appeal. Chatz Brasserie and the hotel's Chinese restaurant, Si Chuan Dou Hua, are atmospheric. Adjoining the hotel is an Irish pub, ideal for a cool ale. **www.parkroyalhotels.com**

GOLDEN TRIANGLE Renaissance Kuala Lumpur Hotel

Corner of Jalan Sultan Ismail and Jalan Ampang, Kuala Lumpur, 50450 **Tel** *(03) 2162-2233* **Rooms** *921*   **Map** *1 A4*

The hotel complex has two wings, a West Wing tastefully furnished with contemporary facilities at affordable rates, and an East Wing exuding opulence. It is well-equipped with an Olympic-sized swimming pool, 24-hour gym, Dynasty restaurant *(see p299)*, Med@Marche *(see p300)*, and a European-style club. **www.renaissance-kul.com**

GOLDEN TRIANGLE Crowne Plaza Kuala Lumpur

Jalan Sultan Ismail, Kuala Lumpur, 50250 **Tel** *(03) 2148-2322* **Fax** *(03) 2144-2157* **Rooms** *577*   **Map** *1 A4*

Originally the Hilton Kuala Lumpur, this hotel has been recently rebranded and renovated. The rooms are stylish although somewhat noisy. The hotel offers an array of food and beverage outlets such as the immensely popular Ishq *(see p299)*. Limited shopping facilities are also available within the hotel premises. **www.crowneplaza.com**

GOLDEN TRIANGLE Hotel Equatorial Kuala Lumpur

Jalan Sultan Ismail, Kuala Lumpur, 50250 **Tel** *(03) 2161-7777* **Fax** *(03) 2161-9020* **Rooms** *300*   **Map** *1 A4*

Part of a well-established regional chain of business hotels, the hotel is well-situated and offers state-of-the-art facilities and specially designed rooms for the physically impaired. A pre-dinner drink at Flo, the hotel's chic bar, can be followed by a sumptuous dinner at Chalet *(see p299)* or the Golden Phoenix. **www.equatorial.com**

GOLDEN TRIANGLE Hotel Istana

73 Jalan Raja Chulan, Kuala Lumpur, 50200 **Tel** *(03) 2141-9988* **Fax** *(03) 2141-0111* **Rooms** *516*   **Map** *4 F2*

Convenient for visiting Bukit Bintang, the Moorish-inspired Hotel Istana is located in the middle of the prestigious Golden Triangle. The hotel has an extravagant lobby and rooms with good views. The recently opened Urban Bistro serves excellent "Mod Oz" Australian food and wines. **www.hotelistana.com.my**

GOLDEN TRIANGLE Novotel Hydro Majestic Kuala Lumpur

2 Jalan Kia Peng, Kuala Lumpur, 50450 **Tel** *(03) 2147-0088* **Fax** *(03) 2147-0889* **Rooms** *291*   **Map** *6 D1*

This hotel is relatively new and within easy reach of the Kuala Lumpur Convention Center and the Raja Chulan monorail stop. Although well-provided with facilities, such as broadband Internet, the rooms are often small. The hotel's restaurant, Qing Zhen, serves Chinese-Muslim cuisine. **www.novotel-asia.com**

GOMBAK Jungle Lodge

Jalan Gombak, Batu Caves 52100 **Tel & Fax** *(03) 6187-0840* **Rooms** *6*

For a tryst with adventure, the Jungle Lodge on the outskirts of Kuala Lumpur is a suitable choice. Built by Asia Overland Services, a leading inbound tour operator, it is more for corporate training and kids' camps but individual travelers are welcome. The cabin-style accommodations are comfortable with basic amenities. **www.summercamp.com.my**

KLCC Corus Hotels

Jalan Ampang, Kuala Lumpur, 50450 **Tel** *(03) 2161-8888* **Fax** *(03) 2161-2393* **Rooms** *378*   **Map** *1 C5*

One of the city's oldest premier hotels, this was formerly called the Ming Court Vista. The rooms are well-appointed with contemporary decor and modern facilities. The hotel also has restaurants serving Chinese and Japanese food. The Hainanese chicken rice served in the Dondang Sayang Coffeehouse is fabulous. **www.corushotelkl.com**

KLCC Hotel Nikko Kuala Lumpur

165 Jalan Ampang, Kuala Lumpur, 50450 **Tel** *(03) 2161-1111* **Fax** *(03) 2161-1122* **Rooms** *470*   **Map** *1 C5*

This is a charming hotel with a well-heeled international clientele. Business guests feel at home in the 26th-floor Executive Club, and leisure travelers can relax by the pool or be pampered in the spa. Bentley's Pub and Benkay Japanese Restaurant entice guests to dine in-house. **www.hotelnikko.com.my**

Key to Price Guide *see p272* **Key to Symbols** *see back cover flap*

KLCC MiCasa All Suite Hotel
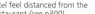

368B Jalan Tun Razak, Kuala Lumpur, 50400 **Tel** *(03) 2179-8000* **Fax** *(03) 2161-1186* **Rooms** *242* **Map** *1 A1*

This is one of the best serviced apartment properties in the city. The rooms are ideal for long-term stays or for families as there are facilities to prepare light meals. However, guests will be tempted to dine at Cilantro *(see p300)*, one of the city's leading restaurants and the sports bar, Tapas, both within the hotel premises. **www.micasahotel.com**

KLCC Ascott Kuala Lumpur

9 Jalan Pinang, Kuala Lumpur, 50450 **Tel** *(03) 2142-6868* **Fax** *(03) 2142-9888* **Rooms** *225* **Map** *2 F5*

A cluster of sophisticated service apartments of up to three bedrooms, ideal for long-stay guests. The views of the Petronas Towers from the pool on the 22nd floor are unbeatable. The Ascott offers luxuriously furnished modern rooms, with fully-stocked kitchens and home entertainment systems. **www.theascottkualalumpur.com**

KLCC Hotel Maya Kuala Lumpur

138 Jalan Ampang, Kuala Lumpur, 50450 **Tel** *(03) 2711-8866* **Fax** *(03) 2711-9966* **Rooms** *206* **Map** *1 C5*

A boutique resort, with a well-provided and relaxing spa, helps visitors staying in the hotel feel distanced from the stresses of urban life. The rooms are Bohemian in their decor. The hotel's Still Waters Restaurant *(see p300)* specializes in Japanese cuisine infused with European flavors. **www.hotelmaya.com.my**

KLCC Mandarin Oriental
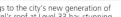

Kuala Lumpur City Center, Kuala Lumpur, 50088 **Tel** *(03) 2380-8888* **Fax** *(03) 2380-8833* **Rooms** *643* **Map** *2 F5*

Located close to the Petronas Towers and boasting a spacious club floor, this ultra-chic hotel is popular with business travelers. Leisure guests are equally well served with an infinity pool that appears to flow into the KLCC parklands. The hotel's Li Po Heen restaurant *(see p300)* specializes in Chinese delicacies. **www.mandarinoriental.com**

KLCC Traders Hotel

Kuala Lumpur City Center, Kuala Lumpur, 50088 **Tel** *(03) 2332-9888* **Fax** *(03) 2332-2666* **Rooms** *571* **Map** *2 F5*

Well-situated in KLCC, Traders Hotel is the epitome of discreet elegance. It belongs to the city's new generation of technology-savvy hotels offering the latest hotel gadgetry. The Sky Bar on the hotel's roof at Level 33 has stunning views of the cityscape. The KLCC parklands at the hotel's doorstep offer jogging tracks. **www.tradershotels.com**

PETALING JAYA Eastin Hotel
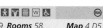

13 Jalan 16/11, Selangor, 46350 **Tel** *(03) 7665-1111* **Fax** *(03) 7665-9999* **Rooms** *388*

The Eastin Hotel has won several awards as Malaysia's best four-star business hotel and its prime location in the suburbs of Kuala Lumpur in a commercial complex gives the hotel a competitive edge. Some rooms overlook a picturesque golf course. The in-house restaurant serves exquisite Cantonese cuisine. **www.eastin.com**

PETALING JAYA Pyramid Suites and Studios

Persiaran Lagoon, Bandar Sunway, Selangor, 46150 **Tel** *(03) 7492-8000* **Fax** *(03) 7492-8001* **Rooms** *764*

This smart, seamlessly designed hotel is part of an integrated complex of hotels, theme park, restaurants, ice-skating rink, and shopping mall. Removed from the city center, it is popular with families as there is literally something for everyone. The rooms are simple, with modern self-contained facilities. **www.kl-hotels.com/sunway**

SENTRAL YMCA Kuala Lumpur

95 Jalan Padang Belia, Kuala Lumpur, 50470 **Tel** *(03) 2274-1439* **Fax** *(03) 2274-0559* **Rooms** *58* **Map** *4 D5*

The YMCA offers simple, basic, but clean rooms with either attached or communal bathrooms to accommodate individuals, families, or groups. The tariffs are inclusive of breakfast and there are extensive sporting facilities. The LRT Stesen Sentral and the monorail station are both accessible. **www.ymcakl.com**

SENTRAL Hilton Kuala Lumpur

3 Jalan Stesen Sentral, Kuala Lumpur, 50470 **Tel & Fax** *(03) 2264-2266* **Rooms** *510* **Map** *3 C5*

The dazzling new Hilton Kuala Lumpur has made a striking impression on travelers as well as locals. The rooms are contemporary and the showers come with their own mini TV. Its restaurants are among Kuala Lumpur's most popular venues. The LRT Stesen Sentral and the express rail link to KLIA are close by. **www.kuala-lumpur.hilton.com**

SUBANG JAYA Sheraton Subang Hotel and Towers

Jalan SS12/1, Subang Jaya, Selangor, 47500 **Tel** *(03) 5031-6060* **Fax** *(03) 5031-9446* **Rooms** *502*

This is an excellent suburban hotel situated in a quiet area. There are some good meal options, and The Emperor, one of the city's finest Cantonese eateries *(see p301)*, is within the hotel premises. There is a free shuttle bus service to shops, transport nodes, and the Sunway Lagoon *(see p321)*. **www.sheraton.com**

TASIK PERDANA Heritage Station Hotel Kuala Lumpur

Jalan Sultan Hishamuddin, Kuala Lumpur, 50050 **Tel** *(03) 2273-5588* **Fax** *(03) 2273-7566* **Rooms** *160* **Map** *4 E4*

Housed in the Moorish-style Kuala Lumpur Railway Station *(see p65)*, this hotel has an exotic charm. Day rooms are available for those awaiting trains. The ground-floor restaurant Charlis, serves delicious meals at reasonable prices. The hotel is an excellent bargain in terms of functionality. **www.heritagehotelmalaysia.com**

TASIK PERDANA Carcosa Seri Negara

Jalan Mahameru, Kuala Lumpur, 50480 **Tel** *(03) 2295-0888* **Fax** *(03) 2282-7888* **Rooms** *13* **Map** *3 B3*

Standing in manicured grounds, this boutique property *(see p67)* offers discreet accommodations for heritage-lovers as well as the elite, with Queen Elizabeth having stayed here in 1989. Refined elegance best describes the rooms. The hotel's plush Dining Room *(see p301)* has won several awards. **www.carcosa.com.my**

img_4

NORTHWEST PENINSULA

ALOR STAR Holiday Villa

Jalan Tunku Ibrahim, 05000 **Tel** *(04) 734-9999* **Fax** *(04) 734-1199* **Rooms** *160*

The tastefully furnished Holiday Villa is a business hotel with a great range of facilities including a gymnasium, Jacuzzi, sauna, spa, a business center, and two restaurants. The hotel also has a bowling alley and karaoke lounge. The rooms are immaculate and have cable TV and minibars. **www.holidayvillaalorstar.com**

CAMERON HIGHLANDS The Bala's Holiday Chalet

Lot 55, Tanah Ratah , 03900 **Tel** *(05) 491-1660* **Fax** *(05) 491-4500* **Rooms** *30*

Set in one of the oldest mock-Tudor buildings in the Cameron Highlands, this chalet retains its colonial country charm. The small rooms are neat and cozy. The hotel's British-Indian restaurant specializes in curries and afternoon cream teas with strawberry jam and scones. There is also a decent library for residents. **www.balaschalet.com**

CAMERON HIGLANDS Ye Olde Smokehouse

Jalan Jeriau, 49000 **Tel** *(05) 491-1215* **Fax** *(05) 491-1214* **Rooms** *13*

Perhaps the most celebrated of all Malaysia's hill station colonial-style hotels, Ye Olde Smokehouse has a classic appeal, consciously striving to be as British as possible. Residents can enjoy a drink by the fireplace in the well-appointed bar or sample traditional English cuisine at the in-house restaurant *(see p302)*.

FRASER'S HILL Fraser's Pine Resort

Jalan Pecah Batu, 49000 **Tel** *(09) 362-2122* **Fax** *(09) 362-2288* **Rooms** *132*

Attractively placed amid lush pine forests, this large, well-appointed apartment hotel offers a range of facilities from satellite TV, minibar, medical care, dry cleaning, laundry, and currency exchange to creche service for families with children. There are banqueting and business rooms, as well as a restaurant and coffee shop.

GENTING HIGHLANDS Resort Hotel Genting Highlands

Pahang Darul Makmur, 69000 **Tel** *(03) 2070-8667* **Fax** *(03) 2031-9698* **Rooms** *838*

Amid the cool comfort of nature, the Resort Hotel Genting Highlands is a massive luxury hotel. It offers every facility on a visitor's wish list, from in-house movie channels to non-smoking rooms. It also has handicapped facilities, Internet access, and restaurants. It is advisable to book in advance.

IPOH Grand View Hotel

36, Jalan Horley, 30300 **Tel** *(05) 243-1488* **Fax** *(05) 243-1811* **Rooms** *62*

This is a reasonably priced, clean, and conveniently located hotel catering mainly to business class travelers. All rooms have a television set and minibar. It is usually possible to negotiate a discount on room prices. A car rental service is available in the hotel's lobby.

IPOH Majestic Station Hotel

Jalan Panglima, 30000 **Tel** *(05) 255-2605* **Fax** *(05) 255-3393* **Rooms** *100*

This quaint heritage hotel designed in Moorish style is set in the splendid colonial-era building of the Ipoh Railway Station. There is a wide range of rooms, all of which have cable TV as well as a minibar. The hotel also has a coffee shop and restaurant. **www.majesticstationhotel.com**

KUALA KANGSAR Rumah Rehat Kuala Kangsar

Bukit Chandan, 33000 **Tel** *(05) 776-3872* **Rooms** *17*

Sprawling across parklands by the Bukit Chandan, this hotel is situated on the banks of Sungai Perak. It is a pleasant Malay *rumah rehat*, or resthouse. The large, well-appointed rooms are clean with en suite bathrooms. It also has a good Malay restaurant set on a riverside terrace.

KUALA SELANGOR De Palma Inn

Jalan Tanjung Keramat, 45000 **Tel** *(03) 3289-7070* **Fax** *(03) 3289-7080* **Rooms** *48*

Set amid lush surroundings, the De Palma Inn offers chalet accommodations with modern facilities and comfort. All rooms have air conditioning, color TVs, coffee- and tea-making facilities, and minibars. It also has a swimming pool and tennis court. Boating, camping, and fishing trips can be arranged by the hotel.

MAXWELL HILL Bukit Larut Guesthouse

Bukit Larut Guesthouse, 34000 **Tel** *(05) 807-7241* **Rooms** *21*

Always full during school and public holidays, these comfortable bungalows have pleasant gardens for picnics. The Bukit Larut Guesthouse is fully equipped with cooking facilities, but simple meals are available on request. As the hotel is very popular among locals, be sure to book in advance.

PENANG Golden Plaza Hostel

Lebuh Acheh, Georgetown, 10200 **Tel** *(04) 263-0560* **Fax** *(04) 263-2388* **Rooms** *20*

A long-time budget traveler favorite, the Golden Plaza Hotel offers friendly services at reasonable rates. The rooms are clean and well-appointed. Its restaurant serves Western and local cuisine. There is a laundry service, free locker facilities, and a useful information and onward travel service.

Key to Price Guide *see p272* **Key to Symbols** *see back cover flap*

PENANG Bayview Hotel

*25A Lebuh Farquhar, Georgetown, 10200 **Tel** (04) 263-3161 **Fax** (04) 263-4124 **Rooms** 320*

This high-rise hotel *(see p105)* is reasonably priced for the elegant facilities offered. Among the several restaurants on the premises is a revolving rooftop dining area with stunning views across Georgetown. Its services include a gymnasium, spa, hair salon, shopping complex, pharmacy, business center, and wireless broadband Internet access.

PENANG Cheong Fatt Tze Mansion

*Lebuh Leith, Georgetown, 10200 **Tel** (04) 262-0006 **Fax** (04) 262-5289 **Rooms** 16*

The prestigious Cheong Fatt Tze Mansion *(see p105)* is a homestay heritage hotel, as well as Georgetown's prime historical attraction. Furnished with antiques, the individually designed suites cluster around five distinct and airy courtyards. Personal butler services are available. **www.cheongfatttzemansion.com**

PENANG Lone Pine Hotel

*Batu Ferringhi, 11100 **Tel** (04) 881-1511 **Fax** (04) 881-1282 **Rooms** 97*

Batu Ferringhi's oldest hotel, the Lone Pine Hotel is most distinguished and offers fine views across the Strait of Malacca. The hotel's emphasis is on elegance and colonial charm. It is adequately provided with all essential amenities such as an in-house Chinese restaurant specializing in Hainanese cuisine. **www.lonepinehotel.com**

PENANG Eastern and Oriental Hotel

*10 Lebuh Farquhar, Georgetown, 10200 **Tel** (04) 222-2000 **Fax** (04) 261-6333 **Rooms** 101*

The grandest hotel in Penang and perhaps in all of Malaysia, the Eastern and Oriental *(see p105)* is a historic site in Georgetown. Lavishly decorated, the E&O has plush rooms and also offers a 24-hour private butler service. There are six separate bars and restaurants serving Malay, Chinese, Indian, and Western cuisine. **www.e-o-hotel.com**

PENANG Shangri-La's Rasa Sayang Resort and Spa

*Batu Ferringhi Beach, 11100 **Tel** (04) 888-8888 **Fax** (04) 881-1800 **Rooms** 304*

This is a plush resort at the northern end of Batu Ferringhi nestled between the sea and emerald hills. The hotel's restaurants and bars offer Southeast Asian cuisine as well as international fare. A lavish spa, large wine cellar, and cigar humidor rounds off the luxury. **www.shangri-la.com/penang/rasasayang/en**

PULAU LANGKAWI City Bayview Hotel

*Pusat Bandar Kuah, 07000 **Tel** (04) 966-1818 **Fax** (04) 966-3888 **Rooms** 282*

Set against a backdrop of glimmering seas, the City Bayview Hotel is the largest and best hotel in Langkawi's modest capital Kuah. It is the best choice for visitors who use Kuah as a stopover before heading for the island's beaches. Facilities on offer balance leisure with entertainment and a grand ballroom is the hotel's highlight.

PULAU LANGKAWI The Frangipani Resort and Spa

*Jalan Teluk Baru, Pantai Tengah, 07100 **Tel** (04) 952-0000 **Fax** (04) 952-0001 **Rooms** 117*

Formerly known as the Langkawi Village Resort, The Frangipani Resort and Spa is a friendly and small family resort. Located across a fine strip of golden beachfront at Pantai Tengah, the hotel has recently been refurbished. Accommodations are in isolated bungalows set in tropical gardens and offer excellent facilities.

PULAU LANGKAWI Beach Garden Resort

*Pantai Cenang, 07000 **Tel** (04) 955-1363 **Fax** (04) 955-1221 **Rooms** 12*

A German-managed resort, doubling as a bistro and a beer garden, Beach Garden Resort also has a restaurant serving dishes of international quality. Imported German beers feature prominently at the bar. The hotel offers lovely views across the Andaman Sea. **www.beachgardenresort.com**

PULAU LANGKAWI Meritus Pelangi Beach Resort and Spa

*Pantai Cenang, 07000 **Tel** (04) 952-8888 **Fax** (04) 952-8899 **Rooms** 350*

Styled as a Malay village, the Meritus Pelangi Beach Resort and Spa offers fantastic beachside views. The hotel has well-appointed rooms, excellent facilities, and restaurants serving Malay, Chinese, Thai, and Western fare. There are babysitting services and a special Kiki club for children. **www.pelangibeachresort.com**

PULAU PANGKOR Nipah Bay Villa

*Teluk Nipah, 32300 **Tel** (05) 685-2198 **Fax** (05) 685-2386 **Rooms** 16*

Relaxed and homely chalet-style accommodations with friendly services; perfect for a laid-back stay. Its restaurant serves Malay and Western dishes. Buffet lunches are available and barbecues can be organized on request. The hotel offers a number of different tours of Pangkor Island as well as jungle trekking trips. **www.pulau-pangkor.com**

PULAU PANGKOR Pangkor Island Beach Resort

*Teluk Belanga, 32300 **Tel** (05) 685-1091 **Fax** (05) 685-1852 **Rooms** 240*

Formerly known as Pan Pacific Resort, this is a luxurious hotel set on Pangkor's Golden Sands Bay. Just about every facility is available including shopping, emergency medical care, and a business center. In addition there are good restaurants as well as volleyball and tennis courts, and an eight-hole golf course. **www.pangkorislandbeach.com**

TAIPING Panorama Hotel

*61–79 Jalan Kota, 34000 **Tel** (05) 808-4111 **Fax** (05) 808-4129 **Rooms** 79*

This is a well-furnished business hotel in the heart of Taiping. All rooms have attached bathrooms, cable TV, minibar, and coffee-making facilities. The hotel's conference center is spacious and there is a good restaurant serving Malay and Western dishes. There is also an in-house supermarket. **www.pinganchorage.com.my**

SOUTHERN PENINSULA

DESARU Golden Beach Hotel
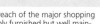
Desaru, 81907 **Tel** *(07) 822-1101* **Fax** *(07) 822-1480* **Rooms** *220*

This sprawling beach resort is especially popular with families and has a variety of accommodation options ranging from standard rooms to garden villas and large suites. The recreational options include a fantastic swimming pool and a cocktail lounge. The hotel is attached to the nearby Desaru Golf & Country Resort. **www.desaruresort.com**

DESARU The Pulai

Desaru, 81900 **Tel** *(07) 822-2222* **Fax** *(07) 822-2223* **Rooms** *200*

Occupying an uninterrupted stretch of pristine beachfront, The Pulai is an award-winning resort. The rooms are bright and spacious, and all have private balconies with great views. There is also a spa and a Kids' Club. The hotel offers a wide choice of activities such as waterskiing, jet skiing, snorkeling, and diving. **www.thepulai.com.my**

JOHOR BAHRU A Vista Melati

16 Jalan Station, 80000 **Tel** *(07) 222-2888* **Fax** *(07) 224-9292* **Rooms** *119*

Located in the heart of Johor Bahru's Central Business District, this hotel is within easy reach of the major shopping malls and eateries, making it an option for budget travelers. The rooms are plain and simply furnished but well maintained, and all have private bathrooms. Free daily newspapers are provided. **www.avistamelatihotel-johorbahru.com**

JOHOR BAHRU Hotel Selesa

Corner of Jalan Tebrau and Jalan Dato, 80300 **Tel** *(07) 332-3999* **Fax** *07) 332-1999* **Rooms** *288*

A soaring four-star business hotel, Hotel Selesa is the tallest in Johor Bahru and offers stunning views of the city. The rooms are spacious and attractively furnished. The excellent amenities include a pool, gym, and a cocktail lounge. It is within walking distance of several malls. **www.johorhotels.com**

JOHOR BAHRU New York Hotel

22 Jalan Dato Abdullah Tahir, 80300 **Tel** *(07) 331-1588* **Fax** *(07) 331-8588* **Rooms** *413*

Situated opposite the busy Plaza Pelangi shopping mall, this towering glassy hotel is a chic place with great facilities. The rooms come with coffee-making facilities and a minibar. There are a few decent restaurants, nightclubs, and bistros as well as a small indoor pool on-site.

JOHOR BAHRU Grand Blue Wave Hotel

9R Jalan Bukit Meldrum, 80300 **Tel** *(07) 221-6666* **Fax** *(07) 222-9473* **Rooms** *184*

This all-suite hotel is perfectly placed for exploring both Johor Bahru and Singapore and offers long-stay deals. Studios as well as one and two-bedroom apartments are available, all fitted with kitchens, refrigerators, and TVs. There are some great restaurants and also a pool, squash court, gym, and sauna. **www.bluewavehotels.com**

MALACCA The Baba House

125-127 Jalan Tun Tan Cheng Lock, 75200 **Tel** *(06) 281-1216* **Fax** *(06) 281-1217* **Rooms** *82*

Situated in the heart of Chinatown this elegant Baba Nonya mansion has been restored and converted into an attractive and reasonably priced boutique hotel. There are some beautiful original wooden screens and tilework in the hotel. The simple rooms have private bathrooms. **www.melaka.net/babahouse**

MALACCA Heeren Inn

23 Jalan Tun Tan Cheng Lock, 75200 **Tel & Fax** *(06) 288-3600* **Rooms** *6*

This historic house overlooks the riverfront and is ideally situated for exploring Chinatown. Dating back to the 18th century, the Heeren Inn has been modernized and offers small but neat and tidy rooms with river views. There is a café and courtyard garden. Sizeable discounts are often available. **www.melaka.net/heerenhouse**

MALACCA Hotel Puri
118 Jalan Tun Tan Cheng Lock, 75200 **Tel & Fax** *(06) 282-5588* **Rooms** *50*

Built in the 1870s, this traditional Baba Nonya townhouse has been carefully restored and retains its original features such as the elaborate stucco façade and mosaic-tiled floors. The rooms are pleasant and comfortable, while the suites are more stylishly designed. **www.hotelpuri.com**

MALACCA The City Bayview Hotel

Jalan Bendahara, 75100 **Tel** *(06) 283-9888* **Fax** *(06) 283-6699* **Rooms** *192*

Located north of the city center next to the historic St. Peter's Church, this international chain hotel offers comfort and excellent services. The large rooms are furnished in contemporary style with televisions and minibars, while the luxury suites come with kitchens and Jacuzzis. The lounge features live music every night. **www.bayviewintl.com**

MALACCA Renaissance Melaka Hotel

Jalan Bendahara, 75100 **Tel** *(06) 284-8888* **Fax** *(06) 284-9269* **Rooms** *300*

This towering 24-story hotel seamlessly blends old-world charm with modernity. The rooms are spacious and the plushest in town offering views of the Strait of Malacca. There are excellent restaurants such as the Capers Restaurant *(see p304)*, an English-style bar. There is a helpful concierge service. **http://marriot.com**

Key to Price Guide *see p272* **Key to Symbols** *see back cover flap*

MERSING Hotel Timotel

839 Jalan Endau, 86800 **Tel** *(07) 799-5888* **Fax** *(07) 799-5333* **Rooms** *44*

The Timotel Hotel is one of the better mid-range hotels in central Mersing, offering simple but adequate rooms. It is a quiet place just across the bridge on the northern side of the River Mersing, and is a 10-minute walk from the town center. There is a decent in-house café and pub. **www.timotel.com.my**

MUAR Hotel Sri Pelangi

79 Jalan Sisi, 84000 **Tel** *(06) 951-8088* **Fax** *(06) 952-2786* **Rooms** *82*

A trendy hotel providing mid-range comforts at a reasonable price. There are also a couple of bigger suites on offer. Children under 12 years can stay free of charge in their parents' room. The on-site Galaxy Lounge is one of the hottest night spots in Muar, with regular live band performances. **www.sripelangi.com**

PORT DICKSON Corus Paradise Resort

Jalan Pantai, 71000 **Tel** *(06) 647-7600* **Fax** *(06) 647-7630* **Rooms** *201*

This resort hotel occupies a prime beachfront location, south of Port Dickson. The rooms are spacious and stylishly furnished. The facilities include tennis courts, a large pool, and gym. It caters especially well for children, having a separate kids' pool, playground, and free stays for children under 12 years. **www.corusparadisepd.com**

PULAU BESAR Aseania Resort

Pulau Besar, Johor **Tel** *(07) 797-0059* **Fax** *(07) 799-1413* **Rooms** *49*

This resort, located on the west coast of the island, is a cluster of identical wooden chalets with a kampung ambience. All the chalets have twin beds, hot showers, and verandas and a choice of either sea or jungle view, and the price varies accordingly. There is an outdoor pool and Jacuzzi, as well as a restaurant. **www.pulaubesar.net**

PULAU RAWA Rawa Safaris Island Resort

Pulau Rawa, 86800 **Tel** *(07) 799-1204* **Fax** *(07) 799-3848* **Rooms** *72*

The only resort on this tiny island, Rawa Safaris Island Resort offers a range of huts, chalets, and suites across different price ranges. While the better accommodations are perched on the beach, all rooms have bathrooms and balconies. The charges are inclusive of overnight stay and return ferry from Mersing. **www.rawasfr.com**

PULAU SIBU Sea Gypsy Village Resort

Pulau Sibu, 86800 **Tel** *(07) 222-8642* **Fax** *(07) 221-0048* **Rooms** *28*

Set in a jungle clearing just off a dazzling beach, this tranquil eco-friendly resort has 22 traditional wooden chalets and six backpacker huts with basic facilities. It is family-run and offers a basic diving center, Kids' Club, and a range of water sports. The price includes meals and return ferry from Johor. **www.siburesort.com**

PULAU TIOMAN Panuba Inn

Kampung Panuba, 86800 **Tel** *(09) 777-9865* **Fax** *(09) 419-1092* **Rooms** *30*

Located in an isolated bay on the northwest coast of the island, Panuba Inn is a peaceful spot that is popular among divers and accessible only by boat. Guests can pick from chalets ranging from fan-cooled huts to those with air conditioning, hot showers, and refrigerators. All accommodations have sea-facing balconies. **www.panubainn.com**

PULAU TIOMAN Puteri Salang Inn

Salang **Tel** *(13) 788-0075* **Rooms** *12*

One of the cheaper options in Salang, this quiet inn has a clutch of wooden huts set in an isolated jungle clearing a short walk from the beach. The huts are either fan-cooled or air-conditioned and they all have mosquito nets and private showers. The Puteri Salang Inn offers atmospheric accommodations, perfect for wildlife watching.

PULAU TIOMAN Berjaya Tioman Beach, Golf and Spa Resort

Tekek, 86807 **Tel** *(09) 419-1000* **Fax** *(09) 419-1718* **Rooms** *96*

This is the only luxury resort on Tioman and offers an array of airy studios and suites with kitchenettes. This resort has its own spa, 18-hole golf course, dive center, and tennis courts, all set on well-tended grounds near the beach. Discounts and special packages are also available. **www.berjayaresort.com**

SEREMBAN Hotel Seri Malaysia

Jalan Sungai Ujong, 70200 **Tel** *(06) 764-4181* **Fax** *(06) 764-4179* **Rooms** *49*

This dependable nationwide chain is a popular choice as it offers standard comfort at affordable rates. The hotel has an interesting Minangkabau-style roof and comfortable rooms. Though slightly away from the city center, Hotel Seri Malaysia is conveniently placed to visit the Muzium Negeri. **www.serimalaysia.com.my**

SEREMBAN Royal Adelphi Hotel

Jalan Dato AS Dawood, 70100 **Tel** *(06) 766 6666* **Fax** *(06) 766-6000* **Rooms** *345*

On the edge of the idyllic Lake Gardens, this five-star hotel promises a rejuvenating experience. The rooms are spacious and attractively furnished. Facilities include a swimming pool, tennis court, and the popular Han Pi Yuen Restaurant *(see p304)*. Being close to the city center, it is popular with business travelers. **www.royaladelphi.com**

SEREMBAN Allson Klana Resort

Jalan Penghulu Cantik, 70100 **Tel** *(06) 762-7888* **Fax** *(06) 767-7788* **Rooms** *228*

A haven of tranquility, this hotel is tucked away on the far edge of the Lake Gardens. The rooms on offer include private two- and three-bedroom condominiums with balconies. There are basketball and tennis courts and a huge lagoon-style pool, as well as a chic Japanese restaurant, Yuri *(see p304)*. **www.allsonklana.com.my**

EASTERN AND CENTRAL PENINSULA

CHEMPEDAK Hillview Hotel
Teluk Chempedak, 25050 **Tel** *(09) 567-0600* **Rooms** *45*

This budget hotel with basic facilities is almost the only option in Chempedak. A small in-house coffeeshop serves breakfast and snacks, but there is easy access to a number of beachside bars and restaurants on Chempedak which offer delectable seafood, Chinese food, and Malay snacks.

CHEMPEDAK Hyatt Regency Kuantan Resort
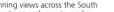
Teluk Chempedak, 25050 **Tel** *(09) 566-1234* **Fax** *(09) 567-7577* **Rooms** *330*

Styled as a Malay stilt house, this chic resort on the Malaysian east coast boasts stunning views across the South China Sea. It offers extravagant facilities such as multiple swimming pools, tennis courts, and a choice of stylish Malay and Chinese restaurants. **http://kuantan.regency.hyatt.com/hyatt/hotels**

CHERATING Ranting Resort
Kampung Budaya Cherating, 26080 **Tel** *(09) 581-9068* **Fax** *(09) 581-9208* **Rooms** *15*

Close to the South China Sea, this is a relaxed Malay kampung-style resort. Accommodation is in chalets set around lotus ponds. The restaurant serves different local specialties each night. Friendly service makes the Ranting Resort a good place to relax.

CHERATING The Legend Resort
Mukim Sungai Karang, 26080 **Tel** *(09) 581-9818* **Fax** *(09) 581-9400* **Rooms** *250*

This is a compact resort set amid tropical gardens with great views across the South China Sea. It offers a choice of restaurants and a remarkable range of activities including tennis, squash, windsurfing, jet skiing, sailing, canoeing, snorkeling, fishing, and jungle trekking. There is also a stylish swimming pool. **www.kl-hotels.com/legend-cherating**

KOTA BHARU Crystal Lodge
Jalan Che Su, 15000 **Tel** *(09) 747-0888* **Fax** *(09) 747-0088* **Rooms** *50*

Located in central Kota Bharu, Crystal Lodge is a friendly and well-maintained hotel offering a wide range of services. Besides in-room television, broadband Internet, and complimentary daily newspapers, it has a karaoke bar and mini-cinema hall for entertainment. **http://www.crystallodge.com.my**

KOTA BHARU Renaissance Kota Bharu Hotel

Jalan Sultan Yahya Petra, 15150 **Tel** *(09) 746-2233* **Fax** *(09) 746-1122* **Rooms** *298*

This is the only five-star world-class hotel in the city. All the rooms are spacious, elegantly designed, and stylishly furnished for ultimate comfort. Rooms include IDD, telephones, high-speed Internet access, voice mail, tea- and coffee-making facilities, and a well-equipped mini-bar.

KUALA BESUT Bubu Inn
Pasir Panjang, 22300 **Tel** *(09) 690-3080* **Fax** *(09) 697-5080* **Rooms** *14*

This is an excellent mid-range resort for an overnight stay. Usually, a stay at the Bubu Inn is part of a pre-booked diving package which includes meals. The inn offers activities such as diving, snorkeling, sea-kayaking, and deep-sea fishing. The hotel serves Malay, Chinese, and Western cuisine, specializing in fresh seafood. **www.buburesort.com.my**

KUALA DUNGUN Tanjong Jara Resort
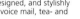
Jalan Dunggun, 23000 **Tel** *(09) 845-1100* **Fax** *(09) 845-1200* **Rooms** *100*

Tastefully furnished, the Tanjong Jara Resort's chalet accommodations are typically Malay. Set in lush tropical gardens, the resort has panoramic views of the South China Sea and is one of the best hotels in Malaysia. Three restaurants serve innovative and authentic Malay, Chinese, and international cuisine. **www.tanjongjararesort.com**

KUALA TERENGGANU Ping Anchorage Travelers Inn
Jalan Sultan Sulaiman, 20000 **Tel** *(09) 626-2020* **Fax** *(09) 626-2022* **Rooms** *28*

The oldest budget hotel in Kuala Terengganu, the Ping Anchorage Travelers Inn is simple and clean. There is a restaurant on the first floor and a rooftop beer garden. The management is involved in making bookings and organizing tours all over Malaysia, so this is a place to book onward travel. **www.pinganchorage.com.my/backpacker.htm**

KUALA TERENGGANU Primula Beach Resort
Jalan Persinggahan, 20400 **Tel** *(09) 622-2100* **Fax** *(09) 623-3360* **Rooms** *249*

The Primula Beach Resort is a spacious and well-equipped beachfront hotel on the east side of town. The hotel has cozy rooms, a large business center, and some excellent restaurants such as the Rhu-Sila Coffee House, which offers an elaborate international buffet, and the alfresco Pelangi restaurant. **http://www.primulaparkroyal.com**

KUANTAN Citiview Hotel Kuantan

Jalan Haji Abdul Aziz, 25000 **Tel** *(09) 555-3888* **Fax** *(09) 555-2999* **Rooms** *90*

These spacious, clean, and reasonably priced accommodations in the heart of Kuantan are exceptionally hospitable with special emphasis on disabled facilities. All rooms have en suite bathrooms, cable TV, and minibars. The facilities include a well-equipped business center, health center, travel agency, and car hire, as well as a restaurant and coffee shop.

Key to Price Guide *see p272* **Key to Symbols** *see back cover flap*

KUANTAN MS Garden Hotel Kuantan

Lorong Gambut, 25300 **Tel** *(09) 517-7899* **Fax** *(09) 517-7558* **Rooms** *202*

This is a comfortable hotel with Chinese decor including replica terra-cotta warriors in the foyer. It is attached to a large shopping mall. Its Yuen Yuen Chinese restaurant specializes in Cantonese cuisine and *dim sum*. The hotel has the largest pillarless ballroom in east coast Malaysia.

MERANG Hotel Seri Malaysia

Jalan Kampung Paya, 21600 **Tel** *(09) 618-2889* **Fax** *(09) 618-1285* **Rooms** *47*

The Hotel Seri Malaysia offers unsurpassable hospitality and the best rooms, services, and restaurant in town. The facilities include shopping, traditional massage, and a business center. The hotel also organizes day-trips to nearby Pulau Kapas, and deep-sea fishing and cruising on the Merang and Terengganu rivers. **www.serimalaysia.com.my**

MERANG Kembara Resort

Pantai Peranginan Merang, 21010 **Tel** *(09) 653-1770* **Fax** *(09) 653-1900* **Rooms** *19*

Kembara Resort is a simple and unpretentious establishment with a selection of rooms and air-conditioned chalets which offer the best value for money in Marang. There are facilities for beach volleyball, football, and bicycle hire. The hotel also arranges island cruises, river cruises, fishing trips, trekking, and camping. **http://kembararesort.tripod.com**

PULAU KAPAS Kapas Island Resort

Pulau Kapas **Tel** *(09) 618-1976* **Fax** *(09) 614-4386* **Rooms** *50*

Fashioned as a bungalow, this resort has a mix of air-conditioned and fan-cooled rooms as well as dormitory beds. The in-house restaurant is a culinary extravaganza featuring local and Western fare, and specializing in seafood. Activities include water sports such as scuba-diving, sea kayaking, snorkeling, deep sea fishing, and sailing.

PULAU KAPAS Gem Island Resort

Pulau Gemia **Tel** *(09) 669-5910* **Fax** *(09) 772-79661* **Rooms** *45*

This is a luxurious offshore spa and resort set on a privately-owned island. The management offers an all-inclusive package. The in-house restaurant serves a delectable mix of national and international cuisine. Attractions include a turtle conservation sanctuary close by. **www.gem-travel.com.my/gemisland/**

PULAU PERHENTIAN BESAR Paradise Island Resort

Northwest coast of Perhentian Besar, 22300 **Tel** *(09) 697-4095* **Fax** *(09) 697-8679* **Rooms** *23*

This modest accommodation has clean rooms and basic facilities and is good value for money. The only television set on the resort is at the restrobar which serves good local and international food. Attached to the resort is the Watercolor Dive Center, which provides diving lessons. **www.pulauperhentian.com.my/paradise.php**

PULAU PERHENTIAN BESAR Tuna Bay Resort

West coast of Perhentian Besar, 22300 **Tel** *(09) 697-7779* **Fax** *(09) 697-8769* **Rooms** *44*

Tuna Bay Resort is a simple resort overlooking the narrow passage between the islands Perhentian Besar and Perhentian Kecil. The hotel's Tuna Bay Restaurant *(see p305)* serves both local and Western food. Barbecue dinners by the beach are available. The resort offers thrilling activity packages of diving, sea kayaking, snorkeling, fishing, and trekking.

PULAU PERHENTIAN KECIL Suria Perhentian Dive Resort

Pasir Panjang **Tel** *(09) 697-7960* **Fax** *(09) 7806-4753* **Rooms** *50*

This is a charming resort offering several types of accommodation from air-conditioned chalets to fan-cooled beach huts overlooking the emerald seas. Targeting young executives, the hotel focuses on adventure activities such as kayaking, diving, and island-hopping, which are used for team-building courses. **www.suriaresorts.com**

PULAU PERHENTIAN KECIL Watercolors Impiani Resort and Restaurant

Near Pasir Petani beach, 08000 **Tel & Fax** *(09) 697-7346* **Rooms** *40*

Attractive chalet accommodations with beach, garden, and hillside options. The restaurant specializes in seafood barbecues and is open from early morning until midnight. Package deals of diving and snorkeling around the island are organized by the resort, prices of which are negotiable. **www.watercoloursworld.com**

PULAU REDANG Coral Redang Island Resort

Pantai Pasir Panjang, 20100 **Tel** *(09) 630-7110* **Fax** *(09) 630-7112* **Rooms** *40*

Set amid dazzling beaches and overlooking the sea, this island resort offers a wide range of diving and snorkeling packages. There are two restaurants, Matahari *(see p305)*, which offers a daily buffet as well as three *a la carte* meals daily, and Chicack Poolside Bar. **www.coralredang.com.my**

PULAU TENGGOL Tenggol Island Resort

Jalan Yayha Ahmad, 23000 **Tel** *(09) 848-4862* **Fax** *(09) 845-7302* **Rooms** *21*

This privately owned offshore resort on Pulau Tenggol focuses on diving activities with more than 20 dive sites in the area. It offers special package rates that include three meals a day and diving with all equipment provided and experienced diving instructors. **www.tenggolisland.com**

TASIK CHINI Lake Chini Resort

Tasik Chini, 26690 **Tel** *(09) 477-8000* **Fax** *(09) 477-2008* **Rooms** *10*

Rural tranquility envelops this resort by Tasik Chini with chalet, dormitory, and camping options fitting every budgetary need. The restaurant serves local and international delights, and barbecues can be requested *(see p305)*. The resort organizes tours of Tasik Chini, as well as visits to local Orang Asli homes. **www.lakechini.com**

SARAWAK

BINTULU Regency Plaza

116 Taman Sri Dagang, Jalan Abang Galau, 97000 **Tel** *(086) 335-111* **Fax** *(086) 332-742* **Rooms** *161*

Probably Bintulu's most pleasant and convenient choice, the Plaza Regency is located fairly close to the town center. The hotel has an impressive lobby and large, elegantly furnished rooms with large beds. There is also a swimming pool and bar on the top floor. **www.plazabintulu.com.my**

BRUNEI Brunei Hotel

Jalan Pemancha, Bandar Seri Begawan, 8670 **Tel** *(0673) 224-2372* **Fax** *(0673) 222-6196* **Rooms** *105*

This hotel is centrally located in Bandar at the heart of its business district. The rooms are large and carpeted, with en suite bathrooms, satellite TVs, and minibars. The hotel also has a grand conference room, and a restaurant serving both Asian and Western dishes. **www.bruneihotel.com.bn**

BRUNEI Sheraton Utama

Jalan Tasek Lama, Bandar Seri Begawan, 8674 **Tel** *(0673) 224-4272* **Fax** *(0673) 222-1579* **Rooms** *155*

Located north of the city center, Sheraton Utama is the first chain hotel in Bandar Seri Begawan. Its facilities include a business center and a choice of restaurants. Rooms are well-furnished with Internet access, minibars, and tea- and coffee-making facilities. **www.starwooodhotels.com/sheraton**

DAMAI BEACH Holiday Inn Resort Damai Beach

Teluk Badung, Santubong, Kuching , 93756 **Tel** *(082) 846-999* **Fax** *(082) 846-777* **Rooms** *320*

Occupying a prime section of Damai Beach, this resort blends with its surroundings and has a beach shaded by coconut palms. There are two swimming pools and an outdoor massage center. The choice of accommodations ranges from chalets set in the hills to enormous poolside rooms. **www.ichotelsgroup.com**

DAMAI BEACH Permai Rainforest Resort

Jalan Sultan Tengah, Pantai Damai Santubong, 93050 **Tel** *(082) 846-490* **Fax** *(082) 846-486* **Rooms** *34*

This is an eco-friendly resort with large tree houses and cabins surrounded by pristine rain forest. The tree houses have fabulous views across the sea. Adventure activities offered include mountain climbing and rappeling. The hotel also has a swimming pool, restaurant, and campsites. **www.permairainforest.com**

DAMAI BEACH Holiday Inn Resort Damai Lagoon

Jalan Teluk Penyuk, Santubong, Kuching, 93762 **Tel** *(082) 846-900* **Fax** *(082) 846-901* **Rooms** *253*

This place manages to outdo the competition particularly in terms of surrounding landscape. It sits in a private cove where guests can indulge in water sports. The facilities include a health center, sauna, Jacuzzi, and a number of restaurants and pools, one with a sunken bar. **www.asiatravel.com/malaysia**

GUNUNG MULU Royal Mulu Resort
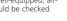

CDT 62, Sungai Melinau, Baram, 98000 **Tel** *(085) 790-100* **Fax** *(085) 790-101* **Rooms** *188*

Situated on the banks of the Sungai Melinau, just upstream from Mulu National Park, this resort is ideal for exploring the province's most popular national park. The rooms, though fashioned as longhouses, are spacious with parquet flooring and rattan furnishings. Activities include all-terrain vehicle (ATV) jungle safaris. **www.royalmuluresort.com**

KAPIT Meligai

Jalan Airport Kapit, PO Box 212, Kapit, 96807 **Tel** *(084) 799-304* **Fax** *(084) 798-103* **Rooms** *45*

Although not comparable to the premier hotels in Sarawak's bigger towns, this is the plushest place in the remote town of Kapit. It has large, well-appointed rooms and a good restaurant. Conveniently located in the town center, it is particularly popular with businessmen.

KUCHING Borneo Hotel

30 C-F Jalan Tabuan, 93100 **Tel** *(082) 244-122* **Fax** *(082) 254-848* **Rooms** *65*

Kuching's oldest hotel, Borneo Hotel appears slightly dated. However, it remains popular for the well-equipped, air-conditioned rooms, with polished floors and television sets, at competitive prices. Still, a room should be checked before accepting as some seem dingy.

KUCHING Singgahsana Lodge

1 Temple Street, 93000 **Tel** *(08) 242-9277* **Fax** *(082) 242-9267* **Rooms** *18*

This guesthouse, located just a few steps from the Kuching waterfront, is a budget traveler's dream. Immaculate rooms and friendly staff make it welcoming. There is a cozy communal area with free Internet access. Reasonably priced dormitories are also available. **www.singgahsana.com**

KUCHING Harbor View Hotel

Lorong Temple, 93100 **Tel** *(082) 274-666* **Fax** *(082) 274-777* **Rooms** *245*

A reliable hotel, Harbor View is particularly popular among business travelers for its services, convenient location in Kuching's business center, and competitive rates. The rooms are clean and comfortable and some have good views across the Kuching waterfront. Buffet breakfasts are included in the room rate. **www.harbourview.com.my**

Key to Price Guide *see p272* **Key to Symbols** *see back cover flap*

KUCHING Telang Usan

Lot 340-345, Jalan Ban Hock, 93124 **Tel** *(082) 415-588* **Fax** *(082) 425-316* **Rooms** *66*

Run by people of the Kenyah community, this hotel is embellished with Kenyah artwork. It has good facilities in addition to a convenient and quiet location in Kuching. The hotel's bars and café are ideal for soaking up local ambience. **www.telangusan.com/kuchinguk.htm**

KUCHING Kingwood Inn
Lot 618, Section 62, Jalan Padungan, 93100 **Tel** *(082) 330-888* **Fax** *(082) 332-888* **Rooms** *315*

Tucked away from the town center, the Kingwood Inn offers good services. The rooms are of decent size and all have television and the additional benefit of late check-out. The hotel has a pool, coffee house, and a convivial bar. **www.kuchinghotels.net**

KUCHING Hilton Kuching
Jalan Tunku Abdul Rahman, 93756 **Tel** *(082) 248-200* **Fax** *(082) 428-984* **Rooms** *315*

Despite tough competition, Hilton Kuching stands out as Kuching's finest hotel. The rooms are well-furnished and offer fantastic views of the Kuching waterfront. It also has a good choice of restaurants on-site such as The Steakhouse *(see p306)*. There is also a traditional handicrafts shop. **www.kuching.hilton.com**

KUCHING Merdeka Palace Hotel
Jalan Tun Abang Haji Openg, 93804 **Tel** *(082) 258-000* **Fax** *(082) 425-400* **Rooms** *214*

This hotel is reasonably priced with spacious rooms equipped with minibar, satellite TV, and tea- and coffee-making facilities. It also has a pool, business center, and health club. Guests have a choice of six restaurants and bars on the premises. **www.merdekapalace.com**

KUCHING Crowne Plaza
Jalan Tunku Abdul Rahman, 93756 **Tel** *(082) 247-777* **Fax** *(082) 425-858* **Rooms** *253*

Occupying a prime riverside site, the Crowne Plaza is one of Kuching's best hotels. The well-furnished rooms are equipped with modern amenities and offer great views of the river. The hotel has several bars and restaurants, as well as a fitness club, a business center, and an adjoining shopping complex. **www.crowneplaza.com**

MIRI Brooke Inn
14 Jalan Brooke, 98007 **Tel** *(085) 412-881* **Fax** *(085) 420-899* **Rooms** *15*

A clean and reliable option for budget travelers, this inn is conveniently located near places of interest in the town center. The rooms have all the basics, such as hot water in bathrooms, air conditioning, television, and telephone. The hotel's helpful and friendly staff makes the stay enjoyable. **brookeinn@hotmail.com**

MIRI Park City Everly

279 Block 11, Jalan Temenggong, 98008 **Tel** *(085) 418-888* **Fax** *(085) 419-999* **Rooms** *168*

With a beachfront location in the Brighton district of Miri, just off the town center, this hotel offers lovely seaside walking trails. The rooms are well-appointed with minibars, complimentary newspapers, and tea- and coffee making facilities. The hotel also has a restaurant, coffee house, and a poolside bar. **www.pinganchorage.com.my**

MIRI Dynasty
Lot 683, Block 9, 98009 **Tel** *(085) 421-111* **Fax** *(085) 422-222* **Rooms** *132*

The rooms of this three-star hotel are elegantly and tastefully furnished with all necessary comforts. The hotel has conference facilities, a pool, a health center, and several bars. It is strategically situated for exploring Miri and the Oil Town Shopping Complex is close by. **www.dynastyhotelmiri.com**

MIRI Mega Hotel
Lot 907, Jalan Merbau, 98000 **Tel** *(085) 432-432* **Fax** *(085) 433-433* **Rooms** *228*

As its name suggests, the Mega Hotel is one of Miri's biggest and is located in the business district in the city center. Among the facilities are a pool and Jacuzzi, a health center, and a business center. Within walking distance of the hotel are banks, restaurants, parks, and a shopping complex. **www.megahotel.com.my**

MIRI Miri Marriott Resort and Spa

Jalan Temenggong Datuk Oyong Lawai, 98000 **Tel** *(085) 421-121* **Fax** *(085) 421-099* **Rooms** *220*

Sprawling across lush tropical gardens, the Marriott Resort and Spa has a range of deluxe rooms and suites, and boasts five-star luxury. Although located at the outskirts of town, it is equipped with restaurants, recreational facilities, and the extremely rejuvenating Mandara Spa. **www.marriotthotels.com**

SIBU Kingwood
12 Lorong Lanang 4, 96000 **Tel** *(084) 335-888* **Fax** *(084) 846-777* **Rooms** *168*

Sibu's only four-star hotel, Kingwood is also the largest, offering idyllic views of the Batang Rajang. The large rooms have king-size or twin beds and all the bathrooms have bathtubs. The conference rooms are big, and there is also a health and fitness center. The hotel has a choice of stylish eateries.

SIBU Premier
Jalan Kampong Nyabor, 96008 **Tel** *(084) 323-222* **Fax** *(084) 323-399* **Rooms** *48*

This small hotel is probably Sibu's second-best option, and appears to be popular with tour groups. All rooms are spacious and tastefully decorated, and include a minibar and satellite TV. The room rates include a good buffet breakfast. The evenings are enjoyable with a Filipino band performing in the lounge. **www.premierh.com.my**

SABAH

DANUM VALLEY Borneo Rainforest Lodge

Lot 20, Block 3, MDLD 3285, Fajar Center, 91120 **Tel** *(089) 880-207* **Fax** *(089) 885-051* **Rooms** *32*

The charges here are per person sharing a double room. The comfortable rooms have panoramic views across the Danum Valley. A complete package of room along with food and drinks includes jungle trips for bird-watching from the lodge's canopy walkway with nature guides.

GUNUNG KINABALU Kinabalu Pine Resort

Kundasang Ranau Highway, 89300 **Tel** *(088) 243-629* **Fax** *(088) 259-552* **Rooms** *64*

Located just outside the Kinabalu National Park, this resort offers spectacular views of Gunung Kinabalu from the timber chalets with wide verandas. The site is steeped in pine aroma and has a children's playground and outdoor barbecue pits, making it popular with families. **www.kinabalupineresort.com**

GUNUNG KINABALU Sutera Sanctuary Lodges

G15, Wisma Sabah, 88000 **Tel** *(088) 889-077* **Fax** *(088) 889-091* **Rooms** *34*

The Sutera Sanctuary Lodges have several lodges around the Park Headquarters at Kinabalu National Park, some resorts, and chalets scattered on the hike up the Gunung Kinabalu. Accommodations range from basic dormitory rooms to luxury lodges. The website should be consulted before booking. **www.suterasanctuarylodges.com**

KOTA KINABALU Backpacker Lodge

Lot 25, Lorong Dewan, Australia Place, 88000 **Tel** *(088) 261-495* **Rooms** *10*

Also known as Lucy's Homestay, the Backpacker Lodge is one of the cheapest accommodations available in Kota Kinabalu. Facilities offered are basic, and dormitories have shared bathrooms. There is a communal area for chatting and watching television. The hotel owner can help arrange climbing trips.

KOTA KINABALU Mandarin

138 Gaya Street, 88820 **Tel** *(088) 225-222* **Fax** *(088) 225-481* **Rooms** *52*

One of Kota Kinabalu's smaller hotels, the Mandarin is worth considering for its reasonable facilities and competitive rates. Well located in the downtown area, it has big, comfortable rooms with marble flooring. During low seasons, discounts on room prices are available.

KOTA KINABALU Trekker's Lodge

30 Jalan Haji Saman, 88803 **Tel** *(088) 252-263* **Fax** *(088) 258-263* **Rooms** *12*

Conveniently located in the heart of Kota Kinabalu, this place is popular with budget travelers. The lodge offers decent rooms with shared bathrooms, and a fan-cooled dormitory. Free breakfast and all-day coffee and tea are offered. The management helps with arranging out-of-town trips. **www.trekkerslodge.com**

KOTA KINABALU Beverly Hotel

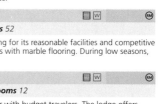

Lorong Kemajuan, 88000 **Tel** *(088) 258-998* **Fax** *(088) 258-778* **Rooms** *200*

The Beverly Hotel offers elegantly furnished rooms equipped with a minibar, free in-house movie viewing facilities, and Internet access. This comfortable hotel has a business center, health center, swimming pool and several restaurants including the Bamboo Restaurant and the Oriental Café.

KOTA KINABALU Hyatt Regency Kinabalu

Jalan Datuk Salleh Sulong, 88991 **Tel** *(088) 221-234* **Fax** *(088) 218-909* **Rooms** *288*

Located on the waterfront in the city center, this trendy hotel offers all the comforts provided by an international chain hotel. There are Chinese and Japanese restaurants in-house. The staff is efficient and helpful. **www.kinabalu.regency.hyatt.com**

KOTA KINABALU Jesselton Hotel

69 Jalan Gaya, 88000 **Tel** *(088) 223-333* **Fax** *(088) 240-401* **Rooms** *31*

Originally built in the 1950s, this is the oldest hotel in Kota Kinabalu. It was refurbished in the 1990s as a boutique hotel. The rooms boast comforts such as satellite TV, a minibar, and coffee-making facilities. The in-house Gardenia Grill Room *(see p307)* offers fine dining. **www.jesseltonhotel.com**

KOTA KINABALU Le Meridien Kota Kinabalu

Jalan Tun Fuad Stephens, Sinsuran, 88000 **Tel** *(088) 322-222* **Fax** *(088) 322-223* **Rooms** *306*

Among Kota Kinabalu's new generation of chic hotels, the Le Meridien Kota Kinabalu offers services to pamper guests. The rooms enjoy great views of the offshore islands and have king-size beds and luxurious bathrooms. The eateries include The Circle, Bamboo Chic, Rumba, and a Latin bar and grill. **www.kotakinabalu.lemeridien.com**

KOTA KINABALU Nexus Resort Karambunai

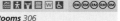

Kampung Karambunai, 88450 **Tel** *(088) 411-222* **Fax** *(088) 411-020* **Rooms** *490*

Sprawling across a stretch of pristine beaches to the northeast of Kota Kinabalu, this exclusive five-star hotel offers fantastic rooms. Activities such as golf, kayaking, windsurfing, and boat rides are also provided. The room rates include airport transfers as well as complimentary breakfasts and dinners. **www.nexusresort.com**

Key to Price Guide *see p272* **Key to Symbols** *see back cover flap*

KOTA KINABALU Shangri La Tanjung Aru

Tanjung Aru, Locked Bag 174, 88995 **Tel** *(088) 225-800* **Fax** *(088) 217-155* **Rooms** *495*

Located at Tanjung Aru close to Kota Kinabalu Airport, this five-star resort is luxurious with a delightful beachfront. It has well-equipped rooms and offers a range of activities to guests, such as horse riding, bird-watching, water volleyball, and a pool, as well as eight in-house restaurants and bars. **www.shangri-la.com**

KOTA KINABALU Sutera Harbour Resort

1 Sutera Harbour Boulevard, 88100 **Tel** *(088) 318-888* **Fax** *(088) 317-777* **Rooms** *956*

Located just south of the city center, this massive complex consists of two separate properties – the Pacific Sutera and Magellan Sutera – as well as a vast marina and a golf course. The rooms have fantastic views of the sea. The hotel's spa offers rejuvenating aromatherapy treatments. **www.suteraharbour.com**

LAHAD DATU The Executive Hotel

Jalan Teratai, MDLD No. 0852, Lahad Datu, 91121 **Tel** *(089) 881-333* **Fax** *(089) 881-777* **Rooms** *50*

These are the best accommodations in Lahad Datu with well-equipped rooms and attentive service, which includes free drops at the airport. The hotel's eateries, including the Spring Palace restaurant *(see p307)* and the Plantation Coffee House, serve excellent food.

PULAU LABUAN Tiara Labuan Hotel

Jalan Tanjung Batu, Labuan, 87015 **Tel** *(087) 414-300* **Fax** *(087) 410-195* **Rooms** *71*

Adjacent to the Labuan Golf Club and a short distance from the airport and town center, the Tiara Labuan Hotel is well located. There are well-equipped chalets and suites surrounded by tropical vegetation. Also on-site are The Grill, offering Western and local cuisine, the Blue Bayou Lounge, and Cheers Pub. **www.tiaralabuan.com.my**

PULAU LABUAN Sheraton Labuan Hotel

Lot 462, Jalan Merdeka, Labuan, 87029 **Tel** *(087) 402-677* **Fax** *(087) 425-176* **Rooms** *178*

This hotel offers all the comforts typical of this international chain, such as spacious carpeted rooms with balconies, minibars, and satellite TV. The in-house Victoria's Brasserie and Somewhere Else are good restaurant options. The botanical gardens are close by. **www.sheraton.com/labuan**

PULAU LANKAYAN Pulau Sipadan Resort and Tours

484 Bandar Sabindo, Tawau, 91021 **Tel** *(089) 765-200* **Fax** *(089) 763-575* **Rooms** *15*

A delightful resort on Pulau Lankayan, it consists of chalets and apartments. The package price includes accommodation, meals, and three dives a day. Located an hour and a half by boat from Sandakan, it is one of the most isolated and tranquil spots imaginable. **www.sipadan-resort.com**

SANDAKAN Hotel Sabah

Jalan Utara, 90703 **Tel** *(089) 213-299* **Fax** *(089) 271-271* **Rooms** *120*

This premier hotel situated just outside the town center provides one of the best accommodation options. The rooms have every conceivable comfort, and facilities include a large pool, jogging track, spa and massage services. The hotel's location is convenient for trips to the Sepilok Orangutan Rehabilitation Center *(see p190)*.

SANDAKAN Hotel Sandakan

Block 83, Town Center, Lebuh 4, 90007 **Tel** *(089) 221-122* **Fax** *(089) 221-100* **Rooms** *105*

This is the most convenient place to stay in Sandakan because of its location in the town center and all the sights worth visiting are close by. The rooms are tastefully decorated and well equipped. The restaurants serve local and international cuisine. Banquet facilities are also available. **www.hotelsandakan.com.my**

SANDAKAN Sepilok Nature Resort

Labuk Road, **Tel** *(089) 228-081* **Fax** *(089) 271-777* **Rooms** *17*

Encircling an attractive lake, the timber bungalows of this resort enjoy some idyllic views of lush forests. The rooms are fitted with overhead fans or air conditioners, televisions, and a minibar. It is located right next to the Sepilok Orangutan Rehabilitation Center *(see p190)*. **http://sepilok.com/index.html**

SEMPORNA Seafest Hotel

Jalan Kastam, 91308 **Tel** *(089) 782-333* **Fax** *(089) 782-555* **Rooms** *63*

Located an hour's drive from Tawau Airport and within a short boat ride of the offshore islands, this is Semporna's fanciest hotel. The rooms have televisions, and coffee- and tea-making facilities. There are also good fitness and business centers along with a restaurant serving local and international cuisine.

SEMPORNA Sipadan Water Village Resort

TB226, Lot 3 Wisma MAA, Tawau, 91000 **Tel** *(089) /97-006* **Fax** *(089) 784-228* **Rooms** *45*

Built on stilts over the pristine waters that lap Pulau Mabul, this resort is for divers and the package includes all meals, though dive charges are extra. Each chalet has its own private deck with panoramic views over coral reefs, while inside the rooms have polished wood floors and rattan furniture. **www.swvresort.com**

TAWAU Belmont Marco Polo

3 Jalan Clinic, Tawau, 91008 **Tel** *(089) 777-988* **Fax** *(089) 763-739* **Rooms** *146*

This is by far the best place to stay in Tawau since the rooms are large with good facilities. There is a business center, coffee shop, and a Chinese restaurant. The hotel also operates a shuttle bus to the airport, making it a convenient stopover for visitors heading off to the dive sites around Pulau Sipadan.

SINGAPORE

COLONIAL CORE Bugis Backpackers ▤ [W] $

162B Rochor Road, 188437 ***Tel*** *6338-5581* ***Fax*** *6338-8192* ***Rooms*** *12* ***Map*** *3 E4*

A clean and comfortable hotel with extremely helpful staff. Situated in the colorful, bustling Bugis Village with a popular nightlife scene, this hotel might not be the best option for those looking for quiet accommodation. Co-ed dormitories as well as shared women-only rooms are available. **www.hostelsclub.com**

COLONIAL CORE New 7th Story Hotel 🍸 ▤ [W] $

229 Rochor Road, 188452 ***Tel*** *6337-0251* ***Fax*** *6334-3550* ***Rooms*** *40* ***Map*** *3 E4*

Despite its name, this hotel actually has nine floors including a rooftop area. The facilities here are excellent, and include clean and well-furnished rooms complete with a business center, garden patio, and bicycle rentals. Staff are friendly and the manual lift is perhaps the last of its kind in Singapore. **www.nsshotel.com**

COLONIAL CORE YWCA Fort Canning Lodge ▣ 🏊 ▤ [W] ♿ $

6 Fort Canning Road, 179494 ***Tel & Fax*** *6338-4222* ***Rooms*** *175* ***Map*** *5 D1*

Part of the international chain of hostels, the YWCA occupies a wonderful location near the historic city center and Fort Canning Park. The rooms are basic but comfortable, and some have a view of the park. A simple breakfast buffet is also offered. The hostel is a favorite with backpackers and visitors on a budget. **www.ywcafclodge.org.sg**

COLONIAL CORE Carlton Hotel 🏊 🏋 🍸 ▤ [W] ♿ $$

76 Bras Basah Road, 189558 ***Tel*** *6388-8333* ***Fax*** *6399-6866* ***Rooms*** *630* ***Map*** *5 D1*

Situated in the colonial district, within walking distance of many major attractions, the 26-story Carlton Hotel offers smart and contemporary accommodations. It has two wings, main and premier. Rooms in the latter feature broadband Internet access and marble-floored bathrooms. Breakfast is included in the tariff. **www.carlton.com.sg**

COLONIAL CORE Hotel Rendezvous 🏊 🏋 🍸 ▤ [W] ♿ $$

9 Bras Brasah Road, 189559 ***Tel*** *6336-0220* ***Fax*** *6337-3773* ***Rooms*** *300* ***Map*** *5 D1*

Blending old-world colonial elegance with sleek modern decor, this hotel has efficient service and a number of amenities for extended-stay travelers such as safe-deposit boxes and luggage rooms. There is a relaxing Balinese-style pool on the third floor, complete with tropical greenery. **www.rendezvoushotels.com/singapore**

COLONIAL CORE Novotel Clarke Quay Hotel 🏊 🏋 🍸 ▤ [W] ♿ $$

177A River Valley Road, 179031 ***Tel*** *6338-3333* ***Fax*** *6339-2854* ***Rooms*** *398* ***Map*** *5 D2*

A fabulous riverfront location and views of Clarke Quay and the surrounding areas make up for the hotel's small rooms. A short boat ride can transport guests to many of the quayside bars and restaurants. There is a pleasant alfresco dining area. **www.accorhotels.com**

COLONIAL CORE Grand Copthorne Waterfront 🏊 🏋 🍸 ▤ [W] ♿ $$$

392 Havelock Road, 169663 ***Tel*** *6733-0880* ***Fax*** *6737-8880* ***Rooms*** *550* ***Map*** *4 A2*

The parquet-floored rooms at this hotel are small and furnished with rattan, although some of them are a bit worn out. Still, all of them offer wonderful views of the Singapore River. There are good tennis courts on the sixth floor together with a gym and pool. This hotel is very popular with large tourist groups. **www.grandcopthorne.com.sg**

COLONIAL CORE Conrad International Centenniel 🏊 🏋 🍸 ▤ [W] ♿ $$$$

2 Temasek Boulevard, 038982 ***Tel*** *6334-8888* ***Fax*** *6333-9166* ***Rooms*** *509* ***Map*** *5 F2*

Close to the Central Business District, this luxurious business hotel offers impeccable service and special touches in the guest rooms such as teddy bears, rubber ducks in the bathtub, and chocolate and fruit platters. They even have a pillow menu from which guests can choose their pillows. **www.conradhotels.com**

COLONIAL CORE Grand Plaza Parkroyal 🏊 🏋 🍸 ▤ [W] ♿ $$$$

10 Coleman Street, 179809 ***Tel*** *6336-3456* ***Fax*** *6339-9311* ***Rooms*** *326* ***Map*** *5 D2*

Set in refurbished shophouses and retaining many of its architectural details, this hotel has a huge lobby, rooms with floor to ceiling windows that overlook the pool, and the posh St. Gregory Spa. Among the spa's specialties are hydrotherapy, and Chinese and Balinese massages. **www.parkhotelsgroup.com**

COLONIAL CORE Pan Pacific 🏊 🏋 🍸 ▤ [W] ♿ $$$$

7 Raffles Boulevard, Marina Square, 039595 ***Tel*** *6336-8111* ***Fax*** *6339-1861* ***Rooms*** *775* ***Map*** *5 F2*

A 35-story atrium, with a striking Italian glass mural of the Vanda Miss Joachim orchid, Singapore's national flower, is one of the highlights of this luxury hotel. Plush rooms, with butler service for guests in the suites, business facilities, and six award-winning restaurants are among its amenities. **www.panpacific.com**

COLONIAL CORE The Fullerton Singapore 🏊 🏋 🍸 ▤ [W] ♿ $$$$$

1 Fullerton Square, 49178 ***Tel*** *6733-8388* ***Fax*** *6735-8388* ***Rooms*** *400* ***Map*** *5 E3*

This former government building, a grand 1920s structure complete with Doric columns, vaulted ceilings, and an astounding sunlit atrium lobby, was beautifully renovated in 2001 and converted into a luxury hotel. Its waterfront location at the junction of Marina Bay and Singapore River adds to its appeal. **www.fullertonhotel.com**

Key to Symbols *see back cover flap*

COLONIAL CORE Marina Mandarin

$$$$$

*6 Raffles Boulevard, Marina Square, 039594 **Tel** 6845-1000 **Fax** 6845-1001 **Rooms** 575* **Map** 5 F2

Featuring a beautiful atrium believed to be the largest in Southeast Asia, the Marina Mandarin is noted for its sleek decor and personalized attention. They even have Venus rooms which cater exclusively to solo women travelers. Unfortunately the nearest MRT station is a 15-minute walk away. **www.marina-mandarin.com.sg**

COLONIAL CORE The Oriental Singapore

$$$$

*5 Raffles Avenue, Marina Square, 039797 **Tel** 6338-0066 **Fax** 6339-9537 **Rooms** 527* **Map** 5 F2

Black marble, leather seats, and hand-woven carpets are some of the luxurious touches in this otherwise subdued hotel. Vibrant paintings and pictures of old Singapore embellish the entire property. Some rooms look out onto the harbor and there is an elaborate breakfast buffet. **www.mandarinoriental.com**

COLONIAL CORE Peninsula Excelsior Hotel

$$$$$

*5 Coleman Street, 179805 **Tel** 6337-2200 **Fax** 6339-3847 **Rooms** 271* **Map** 5 D2

Popular with tourists for its excellent services, this hotel comprises two towers and a food court. Despite being quieter, with panoramic views of the Singapore River, the rooms in the Peninsula Tower are priced lower than those in its twin. A glass-sided pool adjoins the lobby. **www.ythotels.com.sg**

COLONIAL CORE Raffles Hotel

$$$$$

*1 Beach Road, 189673 **Tel** 6337-1886 **Fax** 6339-7650 **Rooms** 103* **Map** 5 E1

One of the world's most exclusive hotels, Raffles *(see pp214–15)* exudes colonial elegance and is renowned for its exquisite facilities and flawless hospitality. The rooms are stylish and there are nine superb restaurants, five bars, a Culinary Academy, and a luxurious spa, as well as the Raffles Hotel Arcade. **www.raffleshotel.com**

COLONIAL CORE Raffles the Plaza

$$$$$

*80 Bras Brasah Road, 189560 **Tel** 6339-7777 **Fax** 6337-1554 **Rooms** 769* **Map** 5 D1

Consistently rated among the best hotels in the world, Raffles the Plaza is a renowned luxury hotel occupying a prime location between Singapore's business and cultural districts. It boasts exquisitely furnished rooms, impeccable service, distinguished restaurants, and a superb spa among its array of facilities. **www.singapore-plaza.raffles.com**

COLONIAL CORE Ritz-Carlton Millenia

$$$$$

*7 Raffles Avenue, 39799 **Tel** 6337-8888 **Fax** 6338-0001 **Rooms** 608* **Map** 5 F2

Home to one of the finest ballrooms in Singapore and a remarkable collection of contemporary art, this stunning hotel is set amid sprawling tropical gardens, and offers fantastic views of the harbor and city skyline. There are hot and cold plunge pools located in a pleasant landscaped area. **www.ritzcarlton.com**

CHINATOWN A Travellers Rest-Stop

$

*5 Teck Lim Road, 088383 **Tel** 6225-4812 **Fax** 6225-4813 **Rooms** 12* **Map** 4 C4

This small but clean, comfortable, and conveniently located hostel is housed in a colorful building with equally vibrant rooms and dormitories. It has basic amenities such as lockers, a guest kitchen, self-service laundry, and bicycle rental. There are plenty of restaurants within walking distance. **www.atravellersreststop.com.sg**

CHINATOWN Damenlou Hotel

$

*12 Ann Siang Road, 069692 **Tel** 6221-1900 **Fax** 6225-8500 **Rooms** 12* **Map** 4 C4

Taking its name from the Chinese nickname for the area, which referred to the gates that stood at the entrance of Ann Siang Road in the 1930s, Damenlou, meaning the Big Gate House, is a small family-run hotel noted for its friendly service. The comfortable rooms have basic facilities but deluxe rooms are offered. **www.damenlou.com**

CHINATOWN Royal Peacock

$

*55 Keong Saik Road, 89158 **Tel** 6223-3522 **Fax** 6221-1770 **Rooms** 74* **Map** 4 C4

This vibrantly colored hotel, with painted wooden shutters, is housed in a row of 10 converted shophouses and is on the infamous Keong Saik Road, a former red light area. The rooms are small but guests still like it for the historic feel. The hotel also has an excellent in-house restaurant. **www.royalpeacockhotel.com**

CHINATOWN Holiday Inn Atrium

$$

*317 Outram Road, 169075 **Tel** 6733-0188 **Fax** 6733-0989 **Rooms** 515* **Map** 4 A3

The dominating feature of this hotel, located in a quieter part of the city, is its spectacular 27-story glass atrium. Rooms are comfortable and spacious. Staff are multilingual and very polite. The popular club complex Zouk *(see p255)* is nearby. **www.holiday-inn.com/atrium-sin**

CHINATOWN Hotel 1929

$$

*50 Kong Siak Road, 089154 **Tel** 6347-1929 **Fax** 6327-1929 **Rooms** 32* **Map** 4 C4

This hip, retro hotel takes its name from its setting in a renovated 1929 shophouse. Although the rooms are small, they are well-appointed and feature beautiful vintage chairs from the owners' private collection. The suites have a lovely terrace with an outdoor bathtub. **www.hotel1929.com**

CHINATOWN The Inn at Temple Street

$$

*36 Temple Street, 058581 **Tel** 6221-5333 **Fax** 6225-5391 **Rooms** 42* **Map** 4 C4

Among the best budget accommodations in the area and the recipient of several awards, this inn occupies five renovated shophouses and features lovely Peranakan decor. Although some rooms are without windows, the service is fast and efficient. **www.theinn.com.sg**

$ under S$100 $$ S$100–200 $$$ S$200–300 $$$$ S$300–400 $$$$$ over S$400

CHINATOWN Amara $$$
165 Tanjong Pagar Road, 88539 **Tel** *6879-2555* **Fax** *6224-3910* **Rooms** *380*   **Map** *4 C5*

Located 15 minutes from the international airport, this stylish hotel has spacious rooms, tastefully done in sober colors, and bathrooms fitted with bathtubs and marble-top sinks. Business travelers will find impressive facilities. The hotel has several good restaurants, a spa, and an outdoor pool fed by water spouts. **www.amarahotels.com**

CHINATOWN Berjaya Duxton $$$
83 Duxton Road, 089540 **Tel** *6227-7678* **Fax** *6227-1232* **Rooms** *48*   **Map** *4 C4*

Singapore's first boutique hotel, this fine accommodation has a traditional Straits Chinese façade with an interior that blends modern decor with old-world features, such as spiral wooden staircases. A range of plush rooms are available; the garden rooms open onto a private courtyard and garden. **www.berjayaresorts.com**

CHINATOWN Miramar Singapore Hotel $$$
401 Havelock Road, 169631 **Tel** *6733-0222* **Fax** *6733-4027* **Rooms** *342*   **Map** *4 A2*

Sitting between Clarke and Robertson Quays, this hotel is perfectly located near some of the city's best nightlife and the shopping paradise of Orchard Road. In addition to pleasant rooms and efficient service, the hotel has food and beverage outlets, a business center, an outdoor pool, and fitness facilities. **www.miramar.com.sg**

CHINATOWN Furama City Center $$$$
60 Eu Tong Sen Street, 059804 **Tel** *6533-3888* **Fax** *6534-1489* **Rooms** *354*   **Map** *4 B4*

Designed in a contemporary, minimalist style, this hotel is housed in a distinctive, curved building in the heart of Chinatown. It is a favorite with business travelers for its excellent amenities including personalized stationery and accessibility to the Central Business District. **www.citycenter.furama.com**

CHINATOWN Swissotel Merchant Court $$$$
20 Merchant Road, 058281 **Tel** *6337-2288* **Fax** *6334-0606* **Rooms** *476*   **Map** *4 C3*

Enjoying an excellent location, close to the financial center as well as shopping and entertainment venues, this hotel offers pleasantly appointed rooms, modern business meeting services, and a lovely rooftop pool with slides and a separate Jacuzzi with a fabulous view of the Singapore River. **www.swissotel-merchantcourt.swissotel.com**

CHINATOWN Copthorne King's Hotel $$$$$
403 Havelock Road, 169632 **Tel** *6733-0011* **Fax** *6732-5764* **Rooms** *314*   **Map** *4 A2*

This business hotel is within walking distance of the popular nightlife venue of Mohammad Sultan Road, and within easy reach of the Central Business District and Orchard Road. The deluxe rooms have a private balcony. Among the hotel amenities is a mini putting green, sauna, steam room, and outdoor Jacuzzi. **www.copthornekings.com.sg**

CHINATOWN Furama Riverfront $$$$$
405 Havelock Road, 169633 **Tel** *6333-8898* **Fax** *6733-1586* **Rooms** *525*   **Map** *4 A2*

Stylish, contemporary decor defines the Furama Riverfront. Suites have kitchenettes, and guests can use facilities such as a business center, fitness center, outdoor pool and Jacuzzi, tennis court, and restaurants. A complimentary shuttle-bus service to Chinatown and Orchard Road is offered to guests. **www.riverfront.furama.com**

LITTLE INDIA Claremont Hotel $
301 Serangoon Road, 218224 **Tel** *6392-3933* **Fax** *6392-7833* **Rooms** *90*   **Map** *3 E1*

Proximity to the bazaars of Little India makes this hotel a popular choice. Although the amenities are basic, a range of rooms are offered, which are airy and comfortable. A conference room and business center is also available. The tour desk is efficient and helpful. **www.claremont.com.sg**

LITTLE INDIA The Inncrowd Hostel $
73 Dunlop Street, 209401 **Tel** *6396-6694* **Fax** *6296-9169* **Rooms** *35*   **Map** *3 D3*

This budget hostel is noted for its immaculately clean and comfortable rooms, friendly owners, and excellent facilities, which include a well-stocked library and a modern kitchen with a washing machine. The bathrooms are communal, large, and airy. Bus stops and MRT stations are within walking distance. **www.the-inncrowd.com**

LITTLE INDIA Perak Hotel $
12 Perak Road, 208133 **Tel** *6299-7733* **Fax** *6392-0919* **Rooms** *35*   **Map** *3 D3*

This modest but exceptionally well-maintained hotel in a renovated Peranakan-style building is the best option for those who want to explore the back lanes of Little India or for travelers on a budget. The rooms, although tiny, are extremely clean and the service is personalized. Public transport is within easy reach. **www.peraklodge.net**

LITTLE INDIA Albert Court $$
180 Albert Street, 189971 **Tel** *6339-3939* **Fax** *6339-3253* **Rooms** *210*   **Map** *3 D4*

Bright Peranakan colors, traditional teak wood furnishings, antique china, and old-fashioned brass fittings in the bathrooms blend seamlessly in this atmospheric hotel. The courtyard rooms are an especially pleasant option. Colorful shops and the numerous restaurants of Little India are just across the street. **www.albertcourt.com.sg**

LITTLE INDIA New Hotel Park Royal on Kitchener Road $$
181 Kitchener Road, 208533 **Tel** *6428-3000* **Fax** *6297-2827* **Rooms** *527*   **Map** *3 E2*

The hotel's best feature is its efficient travel desk, offering booking services and arranging local tours. Rooms are comfortable and equipped with modern facilities. The hotel is also popular for its location right behind the electronics haven at the Mustafa Shopping Center. **www.kitchener.singapore.parkroyalhotels.com**

Key to Price Guide *see p289* **Key to Symbols** *see back cover flap*

LITTLE INDIA Summerview Hotel 📄 [W] $$

173 Bencoolen Street, 189642 ***Tel*** *6338-1122* ***Fax*** *6336-6346* ***Rooms*** *86* ***Map*** *3 D4*

A budget hotel that exceeds expectations in value for money, service, and facilities. Despite being small, the rooms are well-ventilated and extremely clean. Breakfast is included in the room tariff. Sim Lim Square *(see p251)*, one of the most popular electronics malls, is just around the corner. **www.summerviewhotel.com.sg**

LITTLE INDIA Copthorne Orchid 🏊 🏋 🍴 📄 [W] ♿ $$$

214 Dunearn Road, 299526 ***Tel*** *6415-6000* ***Rooms*** *440* ***Map*** *2 A1*

Located a little away from the city, this hotel has spacious rooms decorated in pastel shades with large windows and balconies. Hotel amenities include a brasserie, two lounge bars including a karaoke lounge, fitness facilities, a business center, and an outdoor pool. **www.copthorneorchid.com.sg**

LITTLE INDIA Plaza Park Royal 🏊 🏋 🍴 📄 [W] $$$

7500A Beach Road, 199591 ***Tel*** *6298-0011* ***Fax*** *6296-3600* ***Rooms*** *341* ***Map*** *3 F4*

This hotel, located in the Arab quarter, has spacious rooms with wooden floors. The pool complex is excellent, with a waterfall, sundeck, and a well-manned spa, offering traditional Indonesian and aromatherapy treatments. There is also a Chinese restaurant that serves good Sichuan cuisine. **www.plaza.singapore.parkroyalhotels.com**

LITTLE INDIA InterContinental 🏊 🏋 🍴 📄 [W] ♿ $$$$

80 Middle Road, Bugis junction 188966 ***Tel*** *6338-7600* ***Fax*** *6338-7366* ***Rooms*** *409* ***Map*** *3 D4*

Impeccable service, beautiful interiors featuring Straits Chinese artifacts, and a great location in the historic Bugis district at the edge of the Colonial Core set this hotel apart. The large breakfast buffet at the Olive Tree restaurant features Western dishes, as well as Chinese and Japanese choices. **www.intercontinental.com**

ORCHARD ROAD Hotel Asia 🏋 🍴 📄 [W] ♿ $$

37 Scotts Road, 228229 ***Tel*** *6737-8388* ***Fax*** *6733-3563* ***Rooms*** *146* ***Map*** *2 A3*

Within walking distance of the major shopping and entertainment districts as well as the famed Newton Food Center, this is a comfortable hotel. Rooms and suites are fitted with all conveniences such as in-room Internet access, and a minibar. For travelers using the hotel as a base, extra luggage can be stored for no charge. **www.hotelasia.com.sg**

ORCHARD ROAD SHA Villa 🏋 📄 [W] ♿ $$

64 Lloyd Road, 239113 ***Tel*** *6734-7117* ***Fax*** *6736-1651* ***Rooms*** *40* ***Map*** *2 B5*

This hotel is the training center for the city's hotel industry staff, run by the SHA or Singapore Hotel Association. The villa's colonial architecture, polished wooden flooring, teakwood framed beds, and rich Oriental rugs exude an old-world elegance. The Rosette restaurant has an all-day dining menu. **www.sha.org.sg**

ORCHARD ROAD YMCA International House 🏊 🍴 📄 [W] $$

1 Orchard Road, 238834 ***Tel*** *6336-6000* ***Fax*** *6336-8003* ***Rooms*** *111* ***Map*** *2 A4*

The YMCA is popular not just for being one of the rare budget options in the Orchard Road area but also for its clean rooms fitted with the latest modern facilities and extremely friendly staff. Rooms and dormitories are available and the breakfast is included in the room tariff. **www.ymcaih.com.sg**

ORCHARD ROAD Holiday Inn Park View 🏊 🏋 🍴 📄 [W] ♿ $$$

11 Cavenagh Road, 229616 ***Tel*** *6733-8333* ***Fax*** *6734-4593* ***Rooms*** *315* ***Map*** *2 B4*

Popular with travelers making a brief halt in Singapore, this hotel has well-appointed rooms with extremely comfortable beds and attentive hotel staff. Guests are also provided with disposable slippers. The rooftop pool is beautifully lit at night. **www.singapore.holiday-inn.com**

ORCHARD ROAD Le Grove Serviced Apartments 🏊 🍴 📄 $$$

32 Orange Grove Road , 258354 ***Tel*** *6732-2212* ***Fax*** *6738-9281* ***Rooms*** *97 units* ***Map*** *1 E1*

Surrounded by greenery, these serviced apartments are a popular choice for travelers on extended stays as well as with families traveling with children. Guests can choose to stay in furnished singles, doubles, and three-bedroom units. Each unit has a fully-equipped kitchen and is attended daily by housekeeping staff. **www.cdl.com.sg**

ORCHARD ROAD Negara on Claymore 🏊 🏋 🍴 📄 [W] ♿ $$$

10 Claymore Road, 229540 ***Tel*** *6737-0811* ***Fax*** *6737-9075* ***Rooms*** *200* ***Map*** *1 F2*

Unassuming and sparsely furnished in a blend of Italian and Oriental decor, the rooms at this hotel are comfortable and scrupulously clean. Most rooms have large bathrooms. Business travelers will be impressed by the excellent office facilities. The hotel's swimming pool is filled with mineral water. **www.negara-claymore.com.sg**

ORCHARD ROAD Park Hotel Orchard 🏊 🏋 🍴 📄 [W] ♿ $$$

270 Orchard Road, 238857 ***Tel*** *6732-1111* ***Fax*** *6732 7018* ***Rooms*** *302* ***Map*** *2 A4*

This hotel's location on Orchard Road, the shopping hub of Singapore, close to business and entertainment venues, is its greatest draw. It has a wide variety of rooms, all large and airy, as well as other standard facilities such as a business center, restaurants, and a swimming pool. **www.crownhotels.com.sg**

ORCHARD ROAD Traders Hotel 🏊 🏋 🍴 📄 [W] ♿ $$$

1A Cuscaden Road, 249716 ***Tel*** *6738-2222* ***Fax*** *6831-4314* ***Rooms*** *546* ***Map*** *1 E2*

One of the best features of Traders Hotel is the fully-equipped hospitality lounge that guests can use even after check-out. All of the rooms are well-equipped. A special package is offered to extended-stay guests along with discounts at the nearby Tanglin Shopping Center *(see p249)*. **www.shangri-la.com/singapore/traders**

$ under S$100 $$ S$100–200 $$$ S$200–300 $$$$ S$300–400 $$$$$ over S$400

ORCHARD ROAD York Hotel Singapore 　🖼🏃🖼📄Ⓦ　$$$

21 Mount Elizabeth Road, 228516 **Tel** *6737-0511* **Fax** *6732-1217* **Rooms** *406*　**Map** *2 A3*

Despite its proximity to the shopping district, this hotel is calm and quiet. The staff are particularly accommodating of large families, and can provide adjoining rooms or arrange for extra space, if required. The hotel has a grand pool along with cabana rooms and a palm-fringed sundeck facing a garden. **www.yorkhotel.com.sg**

ORCHARD ROAD The Elizabeth 　🖼🏃🖼📄Ⓦ♿　$$$$

24 Mount Elizabeth Road, 228518 **Tel** *6738-1188* **Fax** *6732-3866* **Rooms** *256*　**Map** *2 A3*

Nestled amid tranquil, leafy surroundings in a residential district close to Orchard Road, this hotel has Neoclassical architecture and decor accented with contemporary European design. The glass-panelled lobby looks out onto a landscaped garden studded with water features that cascade over a rockery. **www.fareast.com.sg**

ORCHARD ROAD Le Meridien Singapore 　🖼🏃🖼📄Ⓦ♿　$$$$

100 Orchard Road, 238840 **Tel** *6733-8855* **Fax** *6732-7886* **Rooms** *407*　**Map** *2 A4*

Simple but stylish rooms in warm earth tones are fitted with the latest amenities and most rooms feature balconies. A delicious high tea can be enjoyed on weekends. The reception staff are very helpful, particularly for early check-ins or late check-outs. **www.lemeridian.com.sg**

ORCHARD ROAD Meritus Mandarin 　🖼🏃🖼📄Ⓦ♿　$$$$

333 Orchard Road, 238867 **Tel** *6737-4411* **Fax** *6732-2361* **Rooms** *1051*　**Map** *2 A4*

Situated in the middle of Orchard Road, this hotel is home to the city's popular revolving restaurant Top of the M *(see p312)* and its lobby features an attractive marble mural depicting 87 Taoist Imperials. Rooms on the higher floors have fantastic views of the Strait of Malacca and Malaysia on clear days. **www.mandarin-singapore.com**

ORCHARD ROAD Orchard Hotel 　🖼🏃🖼📄Ⓦ♿　$$$$

442 Orchard Road, 238879 **Tel** *6734-7766* **Fax** *6733-5482* **Rooms** *653*　**Map** *2 A4*

Situated on a quieter section of Orchard Road, yet close to all the malls, this hotel features rooms that reflect a mix of Western and Oriental decor with rosewood bedstands and silk lampshades. The hotel has a beautiful ballroom and an attached shopping mall. Several embassies are close by. **www.orchardhotel.com.sg**

ORCHARD ROAD Orchard Parade 　🖼🏃🖼📄Ⓦ♿　$$$$

1 Tanglin Road, 247905 **Tel** *6737-1133* **Fax** *6733-0242* **Rooms** *387*　**Map** *1 D3*

Maintaining a Mediterranean theme throughout the space, this hotel, on a quiet end of Orchard Road, is decorated in earthy shades with terra-cotta artifacts, wrought-iron railings, and chandeliers. It is preferred by families with children as the rooms are spacious and include extra beds. **www.orchardparade.com.sg**

ORCHARD ROAD Phoenix 　🏃🖼📄Ⓦ　$$$$

277 Orchard Road, 238858 **Tel** *6737-8666* **Fax** *6732-2024* **Rooms** *394*　**Map** *2 A4*

Although primarily a business hotel, the Phoenix is also suitable for leisure travelers. Rooms are equipped with computers, and some have computerized massage chairs and exercise equipment such as stair climbers. Guests have free entry to the disco and wine bar in the basement. **www.hotelphoenixsingapore.com**

ORCHARD ROAD Four Seasons 　🖼🏃🖼📄Ⓦ♿　$$$$$

190 Orchard Boulevard, 248646 **Tel** *6734-1110* **Fax** *6733-0682* **Rooms** *254*　**Map** *2 A4*

One of the world's most luxurious hotel chains, the Four Seasons offers exquisite accommodation and impeccable service and facilities. In-room fitness equipment, surround sound systems, babysitting facilities, and complimentary baby toiletries are just a few of the amenities guests can expect. **www.fourseasons.com**

ORCHARD ROAD Goodwood Park Hotel 　🖼🏃🖼📄Ⓦ♿　$$$$$

22 Scotts Road, 228221 **Tel** *6737-7411* **Fax** *6732-8558* **Rooms** *232*　**Map** *2 A3*

Built in 1900, this historic hotel *(see p235)*, now a designated National Monument, often hosts international dignitaries and celebrities. The hotel is surrounded by a lovely garden and has elegant rooms, decorated in either colonial or modern style, facing the beautifully landscaped pool area. **www.goodwoodparkhotel.com**

ORCHARD ROAD Grand Hyatt 　🖼🏃🖼📄Ⓦ♿　$$$$$

10 Scotts Road, 228211 **Tel** *6738-1234* **Fax** *6732-1696* **Rooms** *663*　**Map** *2 A3*

A free-form pool surrounded by a lush garden and a cascading four-story waterfall are the spectacular features of this luxury hotel. The interiors sport dark wood and leather. Rooms on the terrace wing have glass niches overlooking the garden. The hotel also has a popular bar and a restaurant, Mezza9 *(see p312)*. **www.hyatt.com**

ORCHARD ROAD Hilton International 　🖼🏃🖼📄Ⓦ♿　$$$$$

581 Orchard Road, 238883 **Tel** *6737-2233* **Fax** *6732-2917* **Rooms** *422*　**Map** *2 A4*

This hotel is perhaps best known for the many international designer stores such as Gucci, Louis Vuitton, and Donna Karan housed in its shopping arcade. Rooms have superb city views as does the rooftop pool. Also on the hotel premises is the excellent Harbor Grill and Oyster Bar. **www.singapore-hilton.com**

ORCHARD ROAD Royal Plaza on Scotts 　🖼🏃🖼📄Ⓦ♿　$$$$$

25 Scotts Road, 228220 **Tel** *6737-7966* **Fax** *6737-6646* **Rooms** *511*　**Map** *2 A3*

A splendid lobby with two grand staircases and a magnificent stained-glass dome greets guests upon arrival. The service is exceptional and rooms have free broadband access and a complimentary minibar stocked with water and soft drinks. Some rooms have a separate dressing area. **www.royalplaza.com.sg**

Key to Price Guide *see p289* **Key to Symbols** *see back cover flap*

ORCHARD ROAD Shangri-La Singapore
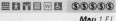 $$$$$

22 Orange Grove Road, 258350 **Tel** *6737-3644* **Fax** *6737-3257* **Rooms** *760*   **Map** *1 E1*

One of the most expensive hotels in Singapore, the beautiful Shangri-La is an oasis of luxury and tranquility in the heart of the city. Sheer glass walls throughout the hotel overlook a lush tropical garden with walking paths and an outdoor ground floor pool. The staff are very attentive. **www.shangri-la.com**

ORCHARD ROAD Sheraton Towers
$$$$$

39 Scotts Road, 228230 **Tel** *6737-6888* **Fax** *6737-1072* **Rooms** *413*   **Map** *2 A3*

Named as one of the top 10 business hotels in the world, the Sheraton Towers offers its signature brand of luxury, service, and amenities. The glass lobby features a grand staircase, and rooms have exceptionally soft and luxurious beds. Live music is performed in the lobby and piano bar every evening. **www.sheratonsingapore.com**

ORCHARD ROAD Singapore Marriott
$$$$$

320 Orchard Road, 238865 **Tel** *6735-5800* **Fax** *6735-9800* **Rooms** *392*   **Map** *2 A4*

This green pagoda-roofed hotel is a landmark in Singapore. Its lavish rooms are decorated in floral themes. It also houses the very popular alfresco Crosswards Café. The rooftop swimming pool, where attendants greet guests with orchids and cold towels, is particularly luxurious. **www.singaporemarriott.com**

FARTHER AFIELD Fern Loft Backpacker Hostel
$

693 A East Coast Road, 459058 **Tel** *6449-9066* **Fax** *6449-9066* **Rooms** *22 beds, 4 dorms*

Located 10 minutes from the Changi Airport, this cozy hostel is run like a homestay. Free breakfast, a reading room, a restaurant, and a pub are some of its in-house facilities, while within walking distance are a beach and some of Singapore's best seafood restaurants. **www.fernloft.com**

FARTHER AFIELD One Florence Close
$

1 Florence Close, Upper Serangoon Road, 549588 **Tel** *6289-9005* **Rooms** *26 beds, 10 rooms*

Featuring hip, minimalist decor, this small budget hotel occupies a serene location, away from the city center. Rooms are equipped with all the basic facilities and are scrupulously clean. The common bathrooms are tiny but sport modern showers. Children below 4 years are not accepted here. **www.oneflorenceclose.com**

FARTHER AFIELD Hotel Royal
$$

36 Newton Road, 307964 **Tel** *6253-4411* **Fax** *6253-8668* **Rooms** *331*   **Map** *2 B2*

This budget hotel offers spacious rooms, restaurants, bars, shops, and efficient service. It is particularly popular with large tourist groups and guests keen on sampling local flavors at the adjacent Newton Food Center and Circus, which is famous for its hawker stalls. **www.hotelroyal.com.sg**

FARTHER AFIELD Grand Mercure Roxy
$$$

50 East Coast Road, Roxy Square, 428769 **Tel** *6344-8000* **Fax** *6344-8010* **Rooms** *539*

This modest hotel, with all the basic facilities, suits travelers looking for a quiet escape and also those with children. It is located away from the bustle of the city and is close to East Coast Parkway which has beaches, restaurants, shops, and recreational facilities such as cycling and hiking. **www.mercure.com**

FARTHER AFIELD Hotel Changi Village
$$$

1 Netheravon Road, Changi Village, 508502 **Tel** *6379-7111* **Fax** *6545-0112* **Rooms** *380*

Although set away from the city center, the Hotel Changi Village lies close to the airport and includes an array of attractions to keep guests engaged. Leisurely strolls along scenic trails, kayaking, a beach, a golf course, and the Changi Chapel and Museum are some of the highlights here. **www.changivillagehotel.com.sg**

FARTHER AFIELD Treasure Resort Sentosa
$$$

23 Beach View, Sentosa, 98679 **Tel** *6271-2002* **Fax** *6274-0220* **Rooms** *63*

Housed in a pre-war colonial building at the heart of a theme park, this is the only budget hotel on Sentosa (see pp244–5). Most rooms and suites have private balconies with lovely views of the sea or the enormous Merlion statue which stands opposite the park. Facilities include a football pitch and mini golf course. **www.sijoriresort.com.sg**

FARTHER AFIELD M-Hotel
$$$$

81 Anson Road, 079908 **Tel** *6224-1133* **Fax** *6222-0749* **Rooms** *413*

A well-priced hotel with office suites for business travelers. The rooms, categorized into standard, superior, club, and suite, are slightly larger than those on offer at most other places and tastefully furnished. The hotel's contemporary Café 2000 serves all-day Western and Asian cuisine. **www.millenniumhotels.com/**

FARTHER AFIELD Shangri-La Rasa Sentosa Resort
$$$$

101 Siloso Road, Sentosa, 98870 **Tel** *6275-0100* **Fax** *6275-1055* **Rooms** *459*

Located on the western tip of the island, on a quiet, palm-lined beach with white sands, this resort has an option of sea-facing rooms with large balconies and exceptional views. Activities such as nature walks and cycling tours are organized by the resort. **www.shangri-la.com**

FARTHER AFIELD The Sentosa Resort and Spa
$$$$$

2 Bukit Manis Road, Sentosa, 99891 **Tel** *6275-0331* **Fax** *6275-0228* **Rooms** *215*

The resort is superbly situated with its pool facing the Strait of Malacca. There is a great outdoor restaurant, beautiful tropical gardens with cozy nooks, covered walkways, and peacocks. The luxurious rooms have large balconies. A 130-step beach stairway leads directly to the serene Tanjong Beach. **www.thesentosa.com**

$ under S$100 $$ S$100–200 $$$ S$200–300 $$$$ S$300–400 $$$$$ over S$400

WHERE TO EAT

With their clever combinations of textures and flavors, the cuisines of Malaysia and Singapore offer exciting dining discoveries for the visitor. Dishes of Malay, Chinese, and Indian origin are widely available, reflecting the three major communities that make up the population of the two countries. The type of restaurant varies but the quality is usually good, whether it is a sumptuous restaurant in a top hotel or a simple street stall in a local market. Major centers such as Kuala Lumpur, Singapore, Kota Bharu, Georgetown, and Malacca usually offer a good variety, including Italian, French, Mexican, Vietnamese, and Japanese eateries. However, even the smaller towns have a decent choice of cuisines at remarkably cheap prices.

TYPES OF RESTAURANTS

Though the cuisines available in Malaysia and Singapore are amazingly varied, eateries are essentially of three types: street hawker stalls, *kedai kopi*, or coffee shops, and restaurants that range from the simple to the lavish.

Street hawker stalls are not only the cheapest, with food often as good as the best eateries, but also a real cultural experience as this is where most locals eat. *Kedai kopi* are no-frills neighborhood cafés that usually offer a limited range of dishes at cheap prices, but are not much by way of service and ambience. However, culinary standards are reasonably high.

Restaurants vary from simple shopfronts to establishments that serve gourmet food in elegant surroundings. The most expensive are the restaurants in Kuala Lumpur and Singapore. Some excellent seafood restaurants can be found in beach resorts and big cities, serving superb local delicacies, such as fish head curry, shark's fin soup, and freshly-caught fish.

In the bigger tourist centers, such as Singapore, Kuala Lumpur, Sarawak, and Penang, visitors can often combine a meal with a cultural show. The shows feature traditional musicians and dancers, who perform during peak dinner hour. Although some visitors may not enjoy watching a performance while dining, these shows offer short-stay travelers a chance to experience a bit of the local culture. Prices at such dining establishments tend to be higher than budget restaurants with regular meal options.

Satay, a popular Malay delicacy

READING A MENU

Virtually all restaurants and coffee shops, and many hawker stalls, display the names of the dishes they offer in English. If they don't have English menus, it is acceptable to just point at your

Customers relaxing in a *kedai kopi*, or traditional coffee shop

choice of dish. The problem is not so much finding out what is on offer but what to select.

Menus are often organized according to the main ingredient, such as chicken, beef, pork (though Muslim restaurants do not serve pork at all), seafood, and vegetables. There is usually a small selection of individual meals, but most people tend to eat in groups and choose a variety of food in order to sample more dishes. Portions are relatively generous and for a couple, three dishes will usually suffice.

TABLE ETIQUETTE

Eating in restaurants where food is not served on a single plate in front of them may be uncomfortable for some people, but adapting to the dining customs of Malaysia and Singapore is not difficult. Generally a fork and spoon are the preferred eating utensils, although chopsticks are useful for noodle dishes. Most Malay, Chinese, and Indian food is cut into small pieces, so a knife is not required. Diners are presented with an individual plate or bowl of rice, and expected

Lunchtime patrons at a food stall in Chinatown, Kuala Lumpur

to help themselves, a spoonful at a time, from the bowls of stir fried dishes, curries, soups, and salads in the center of the table. Seniority is important, so when eating with locals, it is advisable to wait for the oldest member of the group to help himself first.

Fine dining in The Steakhouse, Hilton Kuching (see p306)

RESERVATIONS

Reservations are not generally necessary except at the most popular or upscale restaurants. Weekends can be busy, when most families go out for a meal. People with special dietary needs should mention it to the restaurant manager before making a reservation.

WINE AND DRINK

With the growth of tourism in Malaysia and Singapore, many restaurants are beginning to serve alcoholic drinks. Muslim restaurants, however, serve no alcohol at all. It is generally easy to get a beer or fresh fruit juice at hawker stalls. The variety of exotic tropical fruits has an irresistible appeal, and many restaurants and food stalls use them to concoct shakes and smoothies. *Tuak*, or rice wine, is brewed in the longhouses of Sabah and Sarawak, but visitors should note that it is extremely potent.

Champagne and wine

PAYMENT AND TIPPING

Few restaurants, apart from mid-range and top-end hotels, accept credit cards, so it is best to carry sufficient cash to pay the bill. While tipping is not common among locals in Malaysia and Singapore, as the bill almost always includes service tax and government tax, staff at restaurants in tourist areas have become used to the custom.

STREET FOOD

Sampling street food is one of the highlights of a visit to Malaysia and Singapore, not just because many dishes served at hawker stalls are unfamiliar to foreign visitors, but also because the food is generally prepared with great expertise. Another advantage of hawker stalls is that it is possible to sample Malay, Chinese, and Indian cuisine in just one sitting. Most of the stalls are inexpensive and specialize in just one rice or noodle dish, along with *satay*. Those called *cze char*, or pick-and-mix, however, offer a range of items on their menu, including meatballs, spring rolls, tofu, and stuffed chilies.

Hawkers displaying a variety of food at a *cze char* in Sibu, Sarawak

VEGETARIANS

Despite the abundance of fresh fruit and vegetables available in markets throughout the region, it can often be difficult for vegetarians to find items on a menu that do not contain meat or seafood. However, authentic Indian restaurants serve vegetarian dishes and all Chinese restaurants have at least one dish of mixed vegetables on their menu. Little India in both Singapore and Kuala Lumpur have a wide range of meal options for vegetarians. Most hawker stalls prepare food on the spot, so dishes can be cooked without meat upon request.

EATING WITH CHILDREN

There are no restrictions on children entering restaurants in Malaysia and Singapore; in fact, in most places they are welcome. Some restaurants offer special children's meals. Mild Chinese soups and rice dishes are best for those unaccustomed to spicy food. High standards of food preparation and quality control are maintained, yet care should be taken as children traveling here could be prone to food and water-related ailments.

SMOKING

Smoking is prohibited in enclosed, air-conditioned environments, which comprise two-thirds of the restaurants in Malaysia and Singapore. However, about one-third of the eateries have a terrace or outdoor smoking area.

The Flavors of Malay Cuisine

Malaysians and Singaporeans live to eat, so it is not surprising that markets offer an abundance of fresh tropical fruit and vegetables, meat, and seafood. Mounds of cabbages, eggplants, mangoes, and pineapples are stacked up beside bowls of dried shrimp and fresh crabs, slabs of beef, and marinated ducks. Some stalls specialize in types of rice, the staple of Malay cuisine; others in flavorings and pastes, such as *rempah* and *belacan*, essential to Malay cooking. Though many dishes are unknown outside the region, *satay* has become a worldwide favorite.

Galangal, lemongrass, and bird's-eye chilies

Stall at the Chow Kit fish market, Kuala Lumpur

NASI AND MEE

Rice *(nasi)* and noodles *(mee)* form the basis of any Malay meal, though the preparation of both is almost as varied as the sauces, broths, and curries that accompany them.

Rice may be served fried, steamed, glutinous, or boiled into *bubur*, a savoury soup or porridge. It is commonly steamed, and eaten with a selection of toppings *(nasi campur)*. It is also sometimes enhanced with coconut milk *(santan)*, in *nasi lemak*.

Noodles may be made from wheat, wheat and egg, rice, or mung beans and are served fried or as a soup with vegetables and meat or seafood. Typical Malay noodle dishes are *laksa* and *mee rebus*, both of which are usually served with scrumptious spicy sauce.

REMPAH AND SAMBAL

The carefully blended seasoning pastes are the secret to the mouth-watering flavors of Malay food. The most widely used paste is

Jambu air (water apple)   Betik (papaya)   Limau (pomelo)   Kaktus madu (dragon fruit)

Durian   Nenas (pineapple)

Mangga (mango)

Belimbing (star fruit)

Tropical fruits of the region

MALAY DISHES AND SPECIALTIES

Chicken *satay*

Breakfast can be almost anything in Malaysia and Singapore, but a couple of favorites are *laksa* (spicy noodle soup) and *nasi lemak* (a rice dish). Lunch is usually a one-dish meal, which might easily be *nasi campur* or *mee goreng*. Dinner generally brings family groups or friends together to share a variety of classic Malay dishes, such as *satay* (spicy meat skewers with a peanut sauce), *rendang,* and *ayam panggang* (chicken marinated with garlic and lime, grilled and served with a hot *sambal*). This is likely to be followed by an *ais kacang* or a plate of fresh fruit. Constantly passionate about food, locals don't miss out on a late-night supper, indulging in anything from a steaming hot bowl of rice soup to a plate of barbecued chicken wings.

Mee goreng *are yellow noodles, stir-fried with vegetables and meat, fish, or tofu, and garnished with lime.*

A woman selling fruit and other produce at a market in Kota Belud

ingredients that are usual in Malay food, such as pork and duck, using Chinese cooking techniques but adding elements of Portuguese, Indian, and Thai cuisine. A typical Peranakan dish is *mee siam*, or fine rice noodles in a spicy, sweet-sour gravy.

Visitors to Malaysian Borneo can sample local specialties such as *linut* (in Sarawak) and *ambuyat* (in Sabah), both translucent pastes made of sago starch, *paku* (jungle ferns), and *jaruk* (wild boar mixed with salt and rice and cooked in a bamboo tube).

rempah, for which garlic, lemongrass, shallots, galangal, and ginger are pounded in a mortar. Cinnamon, coriander seeds, cloves, and peppercorns are added to thicken curries, or are fried in oil until fragrant before being added to meat or vegetables.

Sambal is a chili paste that is served as a side dish. *Sambal ulek* is a blend of chili, salt, and vinegar, while the hugely popular *sambal belacan* is made of chili, salt, and sugar pounded with fermented shrimp paste, and served with a wedge of lime.

PERANAKAN AND BORNEAN CUISINE

Malay cuisine is influenced by Chinese, Indian, Thai, Indonesian, and other cultures, but there are several regional variations, of which Bornean and Peranakan, or Straits Chinese, food are the most distinctive. In Malaysia, Peranakan cuisine came into existence when Chinese traders settled in the region and married local Nonya women. They combined spicy Malay pastes with

Grilling *satay* at the Gurney Drive hawker center in Penang

REGIONAL LAKSAS

Every state has its own version of this noodle soup, a national favorite, including:

Asam laksa From the Penang region, this uses tamarind to give a sour edge, as well as flaked fish, wild ginger buds, and *belacan*. Pineapple is shredded for a sweet garnish.

Laksa Johor A very rich fish *laksa* flavored with coconut milk, cumin, coriander seeds, and turmeric. It is garnished with cucumber, bean sprouts, and Vietnamese mint.

Sarawak laksa This features chicken, and prawns in tangy *kalamansi* lime. Toasted rice and coconut give the soup a brownish color.

Singapore laksa Deep-fried anchovies, *belacan*, and coconut milk are used to make a rich, sour soup that is topped with fish cakes.

Rendang, *influenced by Indonesian cuisine, is a fiery, dry curry made with chicken, mutton, or beef.*

Laksa lemak, *found around Kuala Lumpur and known as curry laksa, features prawns, tofu, and egg.*

Ais kacang *is a vivid dessert concoction of shaved ice with syrup, jelly, corn, red beans, and evaporated milk.*

The Flavors of Malay-Chinese Cuisine

The Chinese had been trading in the region for centuries, but it was not until the 19th century that immigrants began settling in large numbers, attracted by tin- and gold-mining, and plantation agriculture. The greatest concentration of settlers was in Singapore, where Chinese cuisine still predominates, though its influence is apparent throughout Malaysia. In Malay cuisine, rice and noodles are a staple in most meals, of which the latter is a major Chinese import. Key elements in all regional variations of Chinese food are the use of fresh produce and the balance of tastes and textures.

Dried shiitake mushrooms

Frying street snacks in Chinatown, Kuala Lumpur

REGIONAL INFLUENCES

The Chinese food found in Malaysia and Singapore is usually Cantonese, which is noted for its mild flavorings and specialties such as *dim sum* (steamed or fried filled dumplings).

Hakka cuisine, from the provinces of Guangdong and Fujian, mixes fresh and preserved ingredients.

Deep-fried bean-curd is a Hakka specialty, and pork (especially belly) is the preferred meat.

Hainanese food features fresh ingredients and the sparing use of spices. It has given Malaysia and Singapore one of their most common dishes – Hainanese chicken rice, garnished with cucumber, and chili and ginger dips. Hokkien, sometimes called peasant food, is still the source of delicate spring rolls. Noodles are found in many dishes, such as *Hokkien mee*, thick wheat noodles stir-fried with seafood or pork.

Teochew cuisine, from Chiuchow, is famed for *muay* porridge – a pale rice broth served with side dishes of crayfish, salted eggs, and vegetables.

"Long" buns
Coriander dumplings
Prawn and bamboo dumplings
Chive dumplings
Pork buns
Open-faced dumplings
Seafood dumplings

Selection of steamed dumplings that make up a typical *dim sum*

ON THE CHINESE MENU

Aromatic soup of pork ribs, shiitake mushrooms, and coriander

Bak kut teh (Hokkien) Pork rib soup.

Cao fan (Cantonese) Fried rice.

Char kway teow (Hokkien) Spicy flat rice noodles with cockles, sausage, and egg in soy sauce.

Cha siew mee (Cantonese) Egg noodles in soup with minced pork dumplings.

Chee cheong fun (Hokkien) Rice flour rolls stuffed with shrimp or pork.

Hay mee (Hokkien) Prawn and pork rib noodle soup.

Lou ark (Teochew) Braised duck.

Lui char fan (Hakka) Rice porridge with ground peanuts, sweet potato leaves, peppercorns, and mint.

Pai quat (Cantonese) Steamed pork ribs with black beans.

Sek bak (Hokkien) Pork belly in spicy black bean sauce.

Sha bou fan (Cantonese) Rice in a claypot with chicken, sausage, salted fish, and soy sauce.

Siew mai (Cantonese) Minced pork wrapped in dumplings.

The Flavors of Malay-Indian Cuisine

The main period of Indian immigration was the 19th century, when laborers were shipped across to work on rubber plantations operated by the British. Most were Hindus from southern India and, like the Chinese, they became a major influence on Malay cuisine. Although rice is a staple, Indian food is also characterized by its use of pulses and various types of flatbread, such as *roti, naan,* and *chapati.* The most commonly used flavorings are chili, cumin, garam masala, coriander, mustard seed, turmeric, yogurt, coconut, and ghee.

***Naan* bread**

Baskets of chilies in the market at Langkawi, Malaysia

NORTH AND SOUTH

Northern Indian cuisine is characterized by the use of dairy products to make rich, thick sauces. Many dishes are baked in a cylindrical clay oven called a tandoor; these include *naan* breads and the famous Tandoori chicken, now enjoyed worldwide. Breads are eaten in preference to rice.

In contrast to the emphasis on bread and meat in the northern Indian diet, southern Indian food is always accompanied by rice and many vegetarian dishes. Despite the hotter climate, dishes from south India tend to be spicy and are distinguished by the liberal use of coconut milk, lentils, and curry leaves. The *thali* is a popular southern Indian meal, comprising small portions of a variety of dishes and condiments.

MAMAK CUISINE

A third type of Indian food frequently found in Malaysia is that produced by Indian Muslims. These dishes are mostly sold at hawker stalls, and include *mee goreng* (spicy-fried noodles), *rojak* (deep-fried vegetables and seafood in a sweet and spicy sauce), and *mee rebus* (a mix of yellow noodles and beansprouts in a sweet potato gravy, topped with a boiled egg).

Fish in coconut tamarind sauce | Mung bean *dal* | Chickpea masala | Coconut chutney | Banana chutney | Raita | Lemon pickle
Prawn curry | Pilau | *Roti canai*

Example of a *thali*, laid out on a banana leaf

INDIAN FAVORITES IN MALAYSIA

Red lentils

From early morning, cooks at *roti* stalls throughout Malaysia can be seen spinning dough into a flat disk, folding it in on itself, then frying it on a griddle to make *roti canai,* which can either be dipped in a bowl of curry sauce or sprinkled with sugar for a less spicy breakfast.

At lunchtime, one of the most popular dishes sold at Indian Muslim hawker stalls is the vegetarian *mee rebus.* For dinner, among the many delicious and filling options are *biryani* and a *thali.* The former has a base of seasoned rice cooked with saffron, nuts, and vegetables, and is served with meat or seafood, and vegetables. The latter consists of a tray or banana leaf, laden with vegetable, fish, or meat curries, pulses *(dal)*, pickles, and yogurt (raita), as well as rice, breads, or poppadoms.

Lamb *biryani*, fragrant with saffron and other spices

Choosing a Restaurant

These restaurants have been selected for their food, good value, and location. They are listed alphabetically by region, beginning with Kuala Lumpur, and then by price. Price bands for Singapore are on pages 308, 311, and 313. Map references for Kuala Lumpur refer to maps on pp78–85 and for Singapore to maps on pp258-67.

PRICE CATEGORIES
The prices are based upon a three-course meal for one and a non-alcoholic drink, and are inclusive of service charges (10%) and taxes (5%).
RM Under RM25
RM RM RM25–RM50
RM RM RM RM50–RM100
RM RM RM RM RM100–RM150
RM RM RM RM RM Over RM150

KUALA LUMPUR

AMPANG Tamarind Springs

   RM RM RM

Jalan 1, Taman Tun Abdul Razak, Ampang, Selangor, 68000 **Tel** *(03) 4256-9300*

A scented candle-lit path leads up to this delightful restaurant, which may be a little difficult to find as it is set at the edge of a jungle. Delicious Lao, Vietnamese, and Cambodian dishes are served in an intimate environment. There is another branch of the restaurant in Tamarind Hill, also in Ampang, and one on Pulau Tioman.

BANGSAR La Bodega

   RM RM RM

16 Jalan Telawi Dua, Bangsar Baru, Kuala Lumpur, 59100 **Tel** *(03) 2287-8318*

Started as a tapas bar, La Bodega has expanded to include a bistro, deli, and a cigar lounge. The excellent Spanish menu offers an extensive array of tapas, paellas as well as a selection of contemporary Catalan dishes. Sangrias and a comprehensive wine list complement the food. There are a number of branches throughout Kuala Lumpur.

BANGSAR Opus Bistro

RM RM RM

67 Jalan Bangkung, Bukit Bandaraya, Near Bangsar, Kuala Lumpur, 59100 **Tel** *(03) 2092-4288*

Situated in a quiet suburban location, close to Bangsar's entertainment hub, Opus Bistro offers a healthy selection of Italian and Pan-European dishes. The grilled cod, served with a variety of sauces, is one of the specialties. Desserts are mostly Italian cakes and pastries and there is a variety of well-chosen wines with several available by the glass.

BANGSAR Telawi Street Bistro

RM RM RM RM

1–3 Jalan Telawi 3, Bangsar Baru, Kuala Lumpur, 59100 **Tel** *(03) 2284-3168*

Located in one of Kuala Lumpur's trendiest suburbs, this restaurant, with a dining area on the lower floor and a bar upstairs, is very popular with the young crowd. The menu comprises contemporary Western cuisine with dishes such as rocket salad, prawn bisque, cod with *nori* (seaweed) wrap, and rack of lamb.

BUKIT BINTANG Sao Nam

RM RM RM

25 Tengkat Tong Shin, Kuala Lumpur, 50200 **Tel** *(03) 2144-1225*   **Map** 5 B2

The contemporary Sao Nam is arguably one of the best venues in Kuala Lumpur for Vietnamese cuisine. It is so popular with the city's chic urban crowd that guests not only reserve tables but also specific dishes, such as the prawn and mangosteen salad. A second branch has opened in Plaza Damas, Jalan Sri Hartamas.

BUKIT BINTANG Prego

   RM RM RM RM

The Westin Kuala Lumpur, 199 Jalan Bukit Bintang, Kuala Lumpur, 55100 **Tel** *(03) 2731-8333*   **Map** 5 C3

To sample modern interpretations of Italian favorites, Prego at The Westin *(see p273)* is a good option. There are two levels of indoor dining, with a wood-fired pizza oven on the ground floor, as well as tables set out on the pavement. There is also a well-balanced wine list. The Sunday champagne brunch is one of the best in the city.

BUKIT BINTANG Shook!

   RM RM RM RM

1st Floor, Starhill Gallery, 181 Jalan Bukit Bintang, Kuala Lumpur, 55100 **Tel** *(03) 2719-8535*   **Map** 5 C3

Located in the chic Starhill shopping mall, Shook! has a hip, minimalist ambience, good food, and live jazz. The menu features four types of cuisine that are prepared in four separate show kitchens. A dazzling array of Japanese, Chinese, Italian, and Western grilled dishes are offered with an equally extensive wine list.

BUKIT BINTANG Eest

RM RM RM RM RM

The Westin Kuala Lumpur, Jalan Bukit Bintang, Kuala Lumpur, 55100 **Tel** *(03) 2773-8013*   **Map** 5 C3

Hailed by the Condé Nast *Traveler* magazine as one of the world's trendiest restaurants, Eest at The Westin *(see p273)* is a pan-Asian restaurant, which features Japanese, Chinese, Thai, Vietnamese, and Malaysian cuisine. The dishes have a seafood emphasis and a good *dim sum* selection is offered.

BUKIT BINTANG Third Floor

RM RM RM RM

3rd Floor, JW Marriott Hotel, 183 Jalan Bukit Bintang, Kuala Lumpur, 55100 **Tel** *(03) 2141-3363*   **Map** 5 C3

This restaurant at the JW Marriott Hotel *(see p273)* has established itself as a must visit for those seeking fine food. Great care is taken to prepare exquisite dishes that include quail stuffed with prawn mousse, snow crab wrapped in brick pastry, and date and pecan pie. Excellent wines complement the food.

Key to Symbols *see back cover flap*

CHINATOWN Old China Café

*11 Jalan Balai Polis, Kuala Lumpur, 50000 **Tel** (03) 2072-5915* **Map** 4 F4

Tucked away from the main action of Jalan Petaling is this historic Chinese café that was once the headquarters of the laundrymen's association. Sepia photographs and bric-à-brac add to the old-world charm at this eatery. Hearty Nonya food is served here, including *ayam pong teh*, a chicken and potato dish in fermented soya bean gravy.

CHOW KIT Celestial Court

*Sheraton Imperial Kuala Lumpur, Jalan Sultan Ismail, Kuala Lumpur, 50250 **Tel** (03) 2717-9900* **Map** 1 A4

This stylish Chinese restaurant at the Sheraton Imperial *(see p273)* with a grand pagoda-style façade offers fantastic Cantonese food. Seafood dishes dominate the menu and the *dim sum* is considered not only one of the city's best but also one of the most imaginative. The restaurant does not serve any pork.

CHOW KIT CoChine

*Asian Heritage Row, Jalan Doraisamy, Kuala Lumpur, 50300 **Tel** (03) 2697-1180* **Map** 1 B4

Located in a renovated shophouse, CoChine offers splendid Vietnamese, Lao, and Khmer cuisine. A must-have is the CoChine Platter, which consists of fried spring rolls and uncooked rice-paper duck rolls. There is an extensive salad selection including the popular pomelo and prawn salad. There is also a smart bar downstairs.

CHOW KIT Villa Danieli

*Sheraton Imperial Kuala Lumpur, Level 5, Jalan Sultan Ismail, Kuala Lumpur, 50250 **Tel** (03) 2717-9922* **Map** 1 A4

An elegant trattoria at the Sheraton Imperial *(see p273)*, Villa Danieli serves traditional Italian cuisine with many dishes prepared in a wood-fired oven to maintain the authentic flavor. The restaurant's poolside location makes outdoor dining an attractive option. Wines are taken seriously, with one table even situated within the open cellar.

DAMANSARA Sandias

*44 Plaza Damansara, Jalan Medan Setia 2, Bukit Damansara, Damansara, 50490 **Tel** (03) 2095-8431*

With its cozy atmosphere Sandias provides the ideal setting for savoring traditional homestyle Mexican cooking. Among the top choices in the appetizer selection is the starter platter with *tortillas* and *quesadillas* accompanied by guacamole and several dipping sauces. For the main course, try the turkey served with chilli chocolate sauce.

DAMANSARA SOULed Out

*20 Jalan 30/70A, Desa Sri Hartamas, Kuala Lumpur, 50480 **Tel** (03) 2300-1955*

Flourishing for over a decade, SOULed Out is a winning combination of a restaurant and a bar, offering a fantastic atmosphere, hearty cuisine, and excellent beverages. It is a sprawling venue and attracts an eclectic mix of patrons. Tables under the aerodynamic white canopies are the best in the house.

THE GOLDEN TRIANGLE Hakka

*6 Jalan Kia Peng, Kuala Lumpur, 50450 **Tel** (03) 2143-1907* **Map** 6 D1

A 50-year old veteran of the Kuala Lumpur food scene, this eatery serves Hakka cuisine which is originally from China's Guangdong and Fujian provinces, and is typically home-cooked, simple, and satisfying. The service might not be fancy but well-prepared dishes such as country chicken and *yong tau foo* make for a pleasant meal.

THE GOLDEN TRIANGLE Bijan

*3 Jalan Ceylon, Kuala Lumpur, 50200 **Tel** (03) 2031-3575* **Map** 5 A2

This is one of the few upscale restaurants in the capital to serve Malay cuisine. It stands out among the hawker stalls that are usually the venues to savor Malay food. Housed in a bungalow with bright burgundy walls, Bijan serves innovative dishes and creative desserts such as *cendol* ice cream. They also have a reasonable wine list.

THE GOLDEN TRIANGLE Chalet

*Hotel Equatorial Kuala Lumpur, Jalan Sultan Ismail, Kuala Lumpur, 50250 **Tel** (03) 2161-7777* **Map** 1 A4

Furnished in alpine wood, the Chalet at Hotel Equatorial *(see p274)* exudes elegance and serves fine Swiss cuisine. The menu includes hot and cold hors d'oeuvres, soups, and fondue, as well as classic meat, poultry, and seafood dishes. An extensive beverage selection, especially wines, complements the food.

THE GOLDEN TRIANGLE Dynasty

*Renaissance Kuala Lumpur Hotel, Jalan Ampang, Kuala Lumpur , 50450 **Tel** (03) 2162-2233* **Map** 1 C5

This is the Chinese restaurant at the Renaissance Hotel *(see p274)*. Dynasty serves authentic Cantonese food and their signature dish is suckling pig. Other delicacies, such as abalone, shark-fin soup, and bird's-nest soup are also available, but tend to be expensive. *Dim sum* lunch is served during the day and on weekends, and queues are not uncommon.

THE GOLDEN TRIANGLE Ishq

*Main Lobby, Crowne Plaza Kuala Lumpur, Jalan Sultan Ismail, Kuala Lumpur, 50250 **Tel** (03) 2144-3440* **Map** 1 A4

This contemporary eatery in the Crowne Plaza Hotel *(see p274)* serves modern Asian food with an emphasis on Thai, Cambodian, Lao, and Kashmiri cuisine. Diners can eat indoors or alfresco in a secluded garden area. There is also an adjoining bar, comfortably furnished in a blend of French-Colonial and Indo-Chinese styles.

THE GOLDEN TRIANGLE Lafite

*Shangri-La Hotel Kuala Lumpur, 11 Jalan Sultan Ismail, Kuala Lumpur, 50250 **Tel** (03) 2032-2388* **Map** 1 A4

This is arguably one of the city's best French *nouvelle cuisine* restaurants. Glamorous interiors and impeccable service perfectly complement the innovative fare. An extensive wine list, featuring premium and reserve vintages, and cigars from around the world are also offered.

THE GOLDEN TRIANGLE La Terrasse
33 Jalan Berangan, Kuala Lumpur, 50200 **Tel** *(03) 2145-4964* **Map** *5 C2*

For traditional home-style French food, served in a relaxed, casual atmosphere, La Terrasse is the ideal venue. Classic dishes such as braised pork and *coq au vin* are just some of the specialties on offer. Wines can be selected from a superb collection at the adjoining Tastevin Cellars. They also have a great Sunday champagne brunch.

THE GOLDEN TRIANGLE Le Bouchon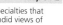
14 and 16 Changkat Bukit Bintang, Kuala Lumpur, 50200 **Tel** *(03) 2142-7633* **Map** *5 B2*

Traditional and authentically prepared French food and a high level of service are the hallmarks of this fine restaurant. The ambience is elegant and cozy, reminiscent of a rustic French country home. Wines are taken seriously here and a wide range, from Margaux to Margaret River, is available. Le Bouchon does not serve any pork.

THE GOLDEN TRIANGLE NiroVivo
3A Jalan Ceylon, Kuala Lumpur, 50200 **Tel** *(03) 2070-3120* **Map** *5 A2*

This trendy Italian eatery has an extensive menu featuring authentic and creative regional Italian specialties that include salads, pastas, and main courses of meat and fish. An option of alfresco dining offers splendid views of Menara KL *(see p74)*. There is a superb selection of well-priced wines with an Italian bias.

KLCC Bombay Palace
215 Jalan Tun Razak, Kuala Lumpur, 50450 **Tel** *(03) 2145-4241* **Map** *1 A1*

Superb northern Indian cuisine, including a range of tandoori dishes, such as *tikkas*, tandoori chicken, and tandoori prawns, are featured at this restaurant. Regular diners rave about the *biryani*, a seasoned rice dish, Kashmiri *naan*, a type of bread stuffed with dried fruit, and the garlic *kulcha*, a deep-fried bread.

KLCC Chinoz on The Park
Suria KLCC, Kuala Lumpur City Center, Kuala Lumpur, 50200 **Tel** *(03) 2166-8277* **Map** *2 F5*

A landmark restaurant within a landmark building, Chinoz was once the pinnacle of high society cafés. It still remains one of the most upmarket eateries in Kuala Lumpur where patrons order from an extensive menu of international dishes including steaks, pasta, seafood, and gourmet sandwiches. They also feature a good wine list.

KLCC Prime Grill Room
11th Floor, Crown Princess Hotel, Jalan Tun Razak, Kuala Lumpur, 50400 **Tel** *(03) 2162-5522* **Map** *1 A1*

Classic international favorites, including steaks and oysters as well as dishes prepared with seasonal ingredients, define the Prime Grill Room. The restaurant has a retro ambience and the show kitchens offer a glimpse of the chefs at work. The Australian wine list is excellent and reasonably priced.

KLCC The Taj
Crown Princess Hotel, Jalan Tun Razak, Kuala Lumpur, 50400 **Tel** *(03) 2162-5522* **Map** *1 A1*

This is one of the best formal northern Indian restaurants in the city and has won many awards. The large bay windows offer a wonderful view of the city and it is worth reserving a window table. Among the popular northern Indian food served here are delectable tandoori dishes.

KLCC Top Hat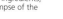
7 Jalan Kia Peng, Kuala Lumpur, 50450 **Tel** *(03) 2142-8611* **Map** *6 D1*

Located in a 1930s bungalow set in sprawling gardens, Top Hat offers delightful views of the Petronas Towers, especially in the evening. The menu features *à la carte* and set Nonya, Malay, Thai, and Western meals, as well as a selection of vegetarian dishes. The wine list is very good and the delicious desserts are not to be missed.

KLCC Cilantro
MiCasa All Suite Hotel, Jalan Tun Razak, Kuala Lumpur, 50400 **Tel** *(03) 2179-8000* **Map** *1 A1*

Possibly the city's finest restaurant, housed in the MiCasa Hotel *(see p275)*, Cilantro's tranquil atmosphere is perfect for enjoying a Japanese or French meal. Their signature dishes include steamed seabass with prawns and *nantua* sauce, a rich cream sauce, and pan-fried *unagi*, or eel, with *foie gras*. Friday's set lunch requires early reservations.

KLCC Lai Po Heen
Mandarin Oriental Kuala Lumpur, Kuala Lumpur City Center, Kuala Lumpur, 50088 **Tel** *(03) 2179-8883* **Map** *2 E5*

Located in the Mandarin Oriental *(see p275)*, Lai Po Heen echoes the hotel's opulent decor and serves classic Cantonese cuisine. Creatively presented dishes are prepared in glass-fronted kitchens and include *e-fu* noodles, steamed rice-paper chicken, and durian pancakes. The pork-free *dim sum* is very popular.

KLCC Still Waters
Hotel Maya Kuala Lumpur, 138 Jalan Ampang, Kuala Lumpur, 50450 **Tel** *(03) 2711-8866* **Map** *1 C5*

This restaurant at Hotel Maya *(see p275)* serves contemporary Japanese cuisine with a modern interpretation that borrows from other Asian as well as Western cuisines. Dishes such as grilled lamb chops with truffle *miso* exemplify the restaurant's signature style. They also have a good wine list and there is an adjoining martini bar.

KLCC Med@Marche
Renaissance Hotel Kuala Lumpur, Jalan Ampang, Kuala Lumpur, 50450 **Tel** *(03) 2162-2233* **Map** *1 C5*

Mediterranean dishes with a modern twist is the theme at Med@Marche at the Renaissance Kuala Lumpur Hotel *(see p274)*. Enjoy creations such as *foie gras* with aniseed and peppercorns and venison cooked in brown ale. They also have a smart bar playing great music. A walk-in cellar stocks wines from Europe, America, and Australia.

Key to Price Guide *see p298* **Key to Symbols** *see back cover flap*

PETALING JAYA Suchan

1 Jalan Dato Mahmud (11/4), off Jalan University, Petaling Jaya, Selangor, 46200 **Tel** *(03) 7957-9908*

Although the restaurant may be a little difficult to find, its good-value food makes it worth seeking out. The cuisine is a fusion of Eastern and Western flavors, and the menu also offers set meals. The afternoon teas, coffees, and cakes are delicious. Although alcohol is not served here, guests can bring their own wine.

PETALING JAYA Out of Africa

1 Lorong Sultan (inside Kelab Syabas), Petaling Jaya, Selangor, 46200 **Tel** *(03) 7955-3432*

This restaurant offers the experience of the hearty home-style food of South Africa. For over a decade it has built its reputation on superb creations, especially its authentic *braai* dishes, a type of South African barbecue. They have a good selection of South African wines and also an in-house bar, the Kudu Bar.

PETALING JAYA Avanti

Sunway Resort Hotel and Spa, Bandar Sunway, Petaling Jaya, Selangor, 46150 **Tel** *(03) 7492-8000*

The menu at this Italian restaurant includes favorites, such as pizzas and pasta dishes, as well as novel preparations such as the signature dish *maltagliati* with lobster ragout. A reasonable wine selection is offered. There is a good Sunday brunch and Avanti's location within a water theme park also makes it an enjoyable family day out.

PETALING JAYA Genji

Hilton Petaling Jaya, 2 Jalan Barat, Petaling Jaya, Selangor, 46200 **Tel** *(03) 7955-9122*

A well-known Japanese restaurant, Genji offers a good balance of traditional and creative dishes. A *teppan* suite and six *tatami* rooms offer the option of private dining. The sushi bar is good for quick meals of beef rolls, noodle dishes, and black codfish. A good variety of sake, beer, and wine is available.

SENTRAL Al Nafourah

Le Meridien Kuala Lumpur, Jalan Stesen Sentral, Kuala Lumpur, 50470 **Tel** *(03) 2263-7888*   **Map** *3 C5*

Stylish Arabian-inspired decor, including private dining tents, provides an exotic ambience. An extensive menu of Lebanese, Middle Eastern, and Mediterranean dishes is served here, including enormous hot and cold *mezze* dishes, which are almost a meal in themselves. Belly dancers provide nightly entertainment.

SENTRAL Prime

Le Meridien Kuala Lumpur, Level 5, 2 Jalan Stesen Sentral, Kuala Lumpur, 50470 **Tel** *(03) 2263-7555*   **Map** *3 C5*

This is the premier international beef restaurant in the city. Although it resembles a traditional steakhouse, it has some nice contemporary touches, such as high-backed leather chairs. Wines are taken seriously and aged beef from Argentina, Australia, and the USA are the specialties. Try the Kobe and Wagyu for a truly subliminal culinary journey.

SENTRAL Senses

Hilton Kuala Lumpur, 3 Jalan Stesen Sentral, Kuala Lumpur, 50470 **Tel** *(03) 2264-2264*   **Map** *3 C5*

For anyone who enjoys creative cuisine, Senses offers a fusion of Eastern and Western cuisine based on guidance of their famous consultant chef, Cheong Liew. The signature dish is Cheong's legendary creation – Four Dances of the Sea. The wine list is superb and the current direction in the kitchen is molecular gastronomy.

SERI KEMBANGAN Kim Ma

Palace of the Golden Horses, Mines Resort City, Jalan Kuda Emas, Selangor, 43300 **Tel** *(03) 8943-2333*

The restaurant has been decorated in Tang Dynasty style with splashes of red, the Chinese color of prosperity. Good Cantonese cuisine is served here and while the menu is predominantly traditional, a few contemporary interpretations, such as stir-fried tiger prawns with coconut milk and cheese, are also included.

SUBANG JAYA The Emperor

Sheraton Subang Hotel and Towers, Jalan SS12/1, Subang Jaya, Selangor, 47500 **Tel** *(03) 5031-6060*

Classy and spacious surroundings combined with outstanding food makes this restaurant at the Sheraton Subang Hotel and Towers *(see p275)* worth a visit. While most dishes are cooked in Cantonese style, a few Szechuan options are also available. The menu also includes some unique ostrich and venison preparations.

TASIK PERDANA Ka Soh

136 Jalan Kaah, Medan Damansara, Kuala Lumpur, 50490 **Tel** *(03) 2093-0905*

This no-frills Chinese restaurant has a bustling atmosphere and offers value-for-money meals. Guests can choose from an extensive non-*halal* menu featuring over 100 items, which includes the unmissable butter prawns and honey pork. Ka Soh has a branch on Jalan Bukit Bintang and one in the Mid Valley Megamall.

TASIK PERDANA Klimt's House

6–5 Jalan Balai, Damansara Heights, Kuala Lumpur, 50490 **Tel** *(03) 2092-1978*

A small Austrian restaurant tucked away in Damansara, Klimt's House is a family-run establishment that offers personalized service and hearty food. The menu features home-cooked Continental cuisine and includes mushroom soup, schnitzel, rainbow trout, and strudel. Colorful prints of Gustav Klimt's work decorate the restaurant.

TASIK PERDANA The Dining Room

Carcosa Seri Negara, Lake Gardens, Kuala Lumpur, 50480 **Tel** *(03) 2295-0888*   **Map** *3 B3*

Situated in the historic Carcosa Seri Negara *(see p275)*, this majestic restaurant offers a dining experience in unrivalled colonial elegance. The cuisine is French, and there is a tasting menu as well as an international *à la carte* selection. The English afternoon teas are very popular with Kuala Lumpur's high society.

NORTHWEST PENINSULA

CAMERON HIGHLANDS Bunga Suria

Jalan Camellia 3, Tanah Rata, 39000 **Tel** *(05) 491-4343*

This is a friendly and clean south Indian restaurant serving both vegetarian and non-vegetarian cuisine. The *masala dosa*, a crispy pancake, and *rava dosa* are delicious, as are the mutton and chicken samosas. *Thalis*, a selection of small dishes, are excellent value for money. Soft *idlis*, steamed rice cakes, with spiced tea make a good breakfast.

CAMERON HIGHLANDS Ye Olde Smokehouse

Tanah Rata, 39007 **Tel** *(05) 491-1215*

The in-house restaurant of the Ye Olde Smokehouse hotel *(see p276)* serves traditional English fare such as roast beef, Yorkshire pudding, steak and kidney pie, and Cornish pasties. Apple pie and pudding with custard and other classic desserts round off a splendid meal. Afternoon teas include scones with fresh cream and strawberry jam.

GENTING HIGHLANDS Kampung

Genting Hotel, Pahang, 69000 **Tel** *(03) 2718-1118*

Located in Malaysia's most expensive hill station, this enduringly popular Malay restaurant offers surprisingly good value for money. An excellent *à la carte* menu is available, but the real draw are the reasonably priced buffet lunch and dinner that allow guests to sample an extensive array of traditional delicacies.

IPOH FMS Restaurant

Jalan Sultan Idris Shah, 30000 **Tel** *(05) 253 7678*

This is one of the best Chinese restaurants in Ipoh. Set in an attractive old shoplot, FMS's specialties are its seafood dishes. Choices include prawns, soft shell crab, rock lobster, and squid. They also serve tofu dishes. Wine is available at the small bar although the selection is limited.

PENANG Nyonya Baba Cuisine

Nagore Road, Georgetown, 10050 **Tel** *(04) 227-8035*

Well-known for its authentic Nonya cuisine, this restaurant is run out of the front room of a traditional Penang home. The meals are prepared by the owner while the family helps with the service. Recommended dishes include the Kapitan curry with a crunchy texture from fried shallots, and *otak otak*, a fish soufflé steamed in a banana leaf.

PENANG Restoran Kapitan

Lebuh Chulia, Georgetown, 10200 **Tel** *(04) 264-1191*

This busy 24-hour Indian restaurant with highly efficient service is very popular with the locals. Their distinctive menu includes northern Indian *biryani*, and tandoori dishes, as well as *naans*, *parathas*, and other Indian breads. The Kapitan curry, a rich chicken dish, is recommended, as is the *lassi*, a yogurt drink.

PENANG Secret Garden

Lebuh Chulia, Georgetown, 10200 **Tel** *(04) 262-9996*

This restaurant offers healthy international cuisine at budget prices. Only natural ingredients are used to prepare the food. Everything on the menu is made from scratch, including the wholemeal bread and cakes. Big Western breakfasts are available all day. Diners have free Internet access and a free movie is shown every night.

PENANG Hong Kong Restaurant

Lebuh Cintra, Georgetown, 10100 **Tel** *(04) 261-5409*

A very popular place, this restaurant specializes in seafood and a wide selection of *dim sum*. Most of the seafood, which can be selected live from fish tanks, is familiar but there are also some less common types such as abalone and dragon prawns. Drinks include Guinness and iced beer.

PENANG Ferringhi Garden

Jalan Batu Ferringhi, Batu Ferringhi, 11100 **Tel** *(04) 881-1193*

One of the most upmarket restaurants in Batu Ferringhi *(see p108)*, Ferringhi Garden serves Western and Asian dishes. While the chef's expertise lies in seafood and steaks, they also serve Malay cuisine, including Penang chicken curry and spicy Malay king prawns. There is a reasonable selection of wine and tempting international desserts.

PULAU LANGKAWI Matahari

Pantai Tengah, 07000 **Tel** *(04) 995-6200*

An elegant Malay restaurant, Matahari, meaning the sun, serves a wide range of authentic local specialties, said to be prepared by local village cooks. Diners may eat their meal sitting cross-legged on rustic mats, which is the traditional practice. Western dishes and seafood are also available.

PULAU LANGKAWI Prawn Village

Kuah, 07000 **Tel** *(04) 966-6866*

Catering mainly to visitors from the mainland, this Kuah eatery serves tasty Cantonese food. Seafood dishes are the specialty here and among the signature dishes listed on the menu are crab, prawn, lobster, and imported abalone. The sweet and sour seabass is good enough to receive praise from *The Guardian*, a British newspaper.

Key to Price Guide *see p298* **Key to Symbols** *see back cover flap*

PULAU LANGKAWI Bon Ton

Pantai Cenang, 07000 **Tel** *(04) 955-6787*

The uber-chic restaurant within this intimate resort offers creative "west meets spice" cuisine. Nothing is left to chance – stylish cocktails, designer ambience, imaginative wines, and hip cuisine, all combine to make a visit to Bon Ton one of Malaysia's most enjoyable experiences.

PULAU PANGKOR Takana Juo
Teluk Nipah, 32300 **Tel** *(05) 685-4733*

Simple and friendly, this Indonesian restaurant appeals to budget travelers and young locals from the mainland who visit the island on the weekends. Excellently prepared Indonesian favorites such as *nasi goreng*, or fried rice, chicken and beef *satay*, *gado gado* salad with peanut sauce, and *mee goreng*, or fried noodles, can be savored here.

PULAU PANGKOR Uncle Lim's
Pangkor Laut, 32200 **Tel** *(05) 699-1100*

This restaurant occupies a beautiful spot atop a rocky outcrop overlooking the Strait of Malacca. Chef Uncle Lim has been creating fine Nonya as well as Hockchew dishes, a cuisine from China's Fuzhou province, at this eponymous restaurant, since its inception. Fresh seafood dishes are particularly good here.

TAIPING Tops Thai
Jalan Boo Bee, 34000 **Tel** *(05) 808-6296*

Both Thai and Chinese cuisine are served at this restaurant. The Thai food is standard fare from central Thailand, with highlights including delicious *tom yam gung*, or prawns in a spicy sauce, and *gai pat met mamuang*, or chicken with cashew nuts. As with most non-Malay establishments, alcohol, mainly beer, is served here.

SOUTHERN PENINSULA

JOHOR BAHRU IT Roo Café
17 Jalan Dhoby, 80000 **Tel** *(07) 222-7780*

This is a simple, bright, and modern café that serves cheap but delicious Chinese and Western dishes. It claims to cook the best chicken in town along with a variety of quick but satisfying meals, including soups, sandwiches, sweet and sour chicken, and various rice and noodle options.

JOHOR BAHRU Restoran Alif Laila
57 Jalan Meldrum, 80000 **Tel** *(07) 226-0445*

This excellent-value, 24-hour Indian-Muslim restaurant is crowded with locals throughout the day, occasionally making it difficult to find a seat, especially at lunch. The air-conditioned interior has a pleasing old-fashioned look, with wooden paneling and wicker furniture. Tandoori chicken, *naans*, and *biryani* are some of the best dishes.

JOHOR BAHRU House of Sundanese Food
Level 3 City Square Shopping Mall, Jalan Wong Ah Fook, 80000 **Tel** *(07) 226-6788*

Decorated with wooden screens and Javanese art, this attractive restaurant serves West Javanese cuisine, which has an emphasis on charcoal grilling and seafood. Sundanese (Indonesia) delicacies include *cumi cumi bakar*, or squid basted in sweet sauce, and deep-fried chicken. Pork dishes are available at the restaurant.

JOHOR BAHRU Stonegrill
Level 3 Plaza Pelangi Shopping Mall, Jalan Tebrau **Tel** *(07) 335-1133*

A fair distance from the city center, but convenient for those staying at nearby hotels, Stonegrill specializes in a unique style of cooking which uses heated natural volcanic stones. Steaks, mixed meat platters, and prawns, all served with vegetables, are brought to the table on sizzling stone, where they simmer away until tender.

JOHOR BAHRU Grand Straits Garden Restaurant

3 Jalan Persiaran Danga, Kawasan Danga Bay, 81200 **Tel** *(07) 238-8118*

This is one of the biggest and busiest seafood restaurants in Johor Bahru despite its inconvenient location west of the city center. All the favorites, including lobster, king crab, and fish-head curry, are served here along with rarer items such as shark's fin soup, abalone, and chilled duck tongue. Reservations are essential.

MALACCA Discovery Café

3 Jalan Bunga Raya, 75100 **Tel** *(06) 292-5606*

This eatery is a long-standing favorite especially among backpackers for its simple meals of curries, fish and chips, and steaks. Located beside the river in the city center, it has a terrace with pleasant views, a library, pool table, dartboard, and Internet access. The café also features occasional live music.

MALACCA Restoran De Lisbon

18 Medan Portugis, 75050 **Tel** *(06) 284-8067*

This is one of the best places to sample authentic Malaccan-Portuguese cuisine, and the only restaurant on Medan Portugis open for both lunch and dinner. Chili crabs, prawns, and devil's curry, a spicy curry flavored with vinegar and ginger, are popular dishes. There are plenty of outdoor tables but weekend evenings get very busy.

MALACCA Harper's Restaurant

2 Lorong Hang Jebat, 75200 **Tel** *(06) 282-8800*

One of the smarter eateries in Chinatown, Harper's Restaurant is housed in a beautifully renovated building with high ceilings and a narrow outdoor terrace overlooking the river. The menu is a mixture of mild Malay, Straits Chinese, and Western cuisine with dishes such as deep-fried chicken, salads, and pastas. The service tends to be slow.

MALACCA Nancy's Kitchen

7 Jalan Hang Lekir, 75200 **Tel** *(06) 283-6099*

This tiny, unassuming, family-run restaurant on a Chinatown side street is a great place to try authentic Straits Chinese cooking. A lengthy menu features traditional favorites such as *otak otak*, a fish soufflé steamed in a banana leaf, *sotong sambhol*, or spicy squid, and duck in Peranakan spices. It is closed on Tuesdays.

MALACCA Nya Nya Restoran

Jalan PM3, Plaza Mahkota, 75000 **Tel** *(06) 283-6327*

Located in the southern quarter of the city, away from the main tourist area, Nya Nya is a small, intimate restaurant which specializes in Peranakan cuisine. Staple dishes are offered along with delicacies such as *lemak nanas*, a pineapple and coconut rice dish, *udang goreng assam*, or fried shrimps, and chicken curry. It is closed on Monday.

MALACCA Capers Restaurant
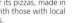

Renaissance Melaka Hotel, Jalan Bendahara, 75100 **Tel** *(06) 284-8888*

Housed in the five-star Renaissance Melaka Hotel *(see p278)*, this is the city's finest restaurant. Gleaming crystal, crisp linen tablecloths, and silver flatware create a sophisticated ambience which is complemented by faultless service. Eastern and Western fusion cuisine is accompanied by an excellent wine list. Open only for dinner.

MALACCA Coconut House
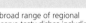

128 Jalan Tun Tan Cheng Lock, 75200 **Tel** *(06) 282-9128*

With its original tiled floors and wooden ceiling beams, this cozy little restaurant is famous for its pizzas, made in an authentic wood-fired oven. Classic options, such as the margarita, can be enjoyed along with those with local flavors, such as the chicken *satay* pizza. Pasta dishes are also available. Closed on Wednesdays.

MERSING Mersing Seafood Restaurant

56 Jalan Ismail, 86800 **Tel** *(07) 799-2550*

This busy restaurant is one of the better places in town to sample a broad range of local seafood. Fried squid, coconut prawns, and steamed fish are among the more popular orders. Diners can also try some unique preparations, such as drunken prawns, which are cooked in rice wine, and cuttlefish rings stuffed with egg.

SEREMBAN Han Pi Yuen Restaurant

Mezzanine Level, Royal Adelphi Hotel, Jalan Dato AS Dawood, 70100 **Tel** *(06) 766-6666*

This upmarket restaurant, located in the five-star Royal Adelphi Hotel *(see p279)*, offers a broad range of regional Chinese cuisines, including Szechuan, Cantonese, and Shanghainese food. Attentive staff serve tasty dishes including steamed fish, prawns, *dim sum*, and tofu preparations in a refined atmosphere.

SEREMBAN Yuri Restaurant

Allson Klana Resort, Jalan Penghulu Cantik, 70100 **Tel** *(06) 762-9600*

Ensconced in the luxurious Allson Klana Resort *(see p279)* but also open to non-guests, this is a high-end Japanese restaurant, which features a range of popular Japanese dishes. A sushi bar serves expertly prepared fish creations and a *teppanyaki* counter offers a variety of sizzling chicken, prawn, beef, and vegetable concoctions.

EASTERN AND CENTRAL PENINSULA

CHEMPEDAK Restoran Pattaya

Teluk Chempedak, 25050 **Tel** *(09) 567-4437*

One of the most lively eateries in Chempedak, Restoran Pattaya serves Chinese as well as international dishes. Fresh seafood is an attraction here and the house specialties include barbecued tiger prawns and locally caught lobster. There is plenty of ice-cold beer and they also have happy hours. Live music is organized on most evenings.

CHERATING Duyong Restaurant

Main Road East, 26080

Occupying a beautiful location at the Eastern end of Cherating Beach with fine sea views, Duyong specializes in seafood cooked in spicy central Thai style. The *tom yam kung*, or prawn with chili in coconut milk, is outstanding, as is the *gaeng karee gai*, or green chicken curry. There is live music every night.

CHERATING Payung Café

Main Road West, 26080 **Tel** *(09) 581-9658*

This Italian restaurant is aimed mainly at foreigners and young Malays. An extensive menu features numerous pasta dishes with many seafood options, pizza, steak, salad, and Italian desserts. Hearty breakfasts are served everyday. Cold beer is available everywhere, but not so frequently in the predominantly Muslim east coast.

KOTA BHARU Muhibah
Jalan Datok Pati, 15000 **Tel** *(09) 748-3808*

A rarity in meat-loving Kota Bharu, this vegetarian restaurant serves a wide range of Malay and Chinese dishes. The latter, interestingly, are sometimes prepared to resemble meat dishes but are nonetheless strictly vegetarian. Beverages include fresh fruit juices and soft drinks but no alcohol.

KOTA BHARU Four Seasons
Jalan Dusan Raja, 15300 **Tel** *(09) 748-6666*

A dependable Kota Bharu restaurant, this place offers a variety of predominantly Chinese dishes, specializing in Cantonese cuisine. The seafood steamboat is highly recommended and there is an array of freshly made *dim sum*. Since this is a Chinese establishment, it is one of the few places in Muslim Kelantan where alcohol is served.

KUALA TERENGGANU MD Curry House
Jalan Kampung Dalam, 20100

A south Indian restaurant, MD Curry House is well-known for its huge rice dishes served on banana leaves, *samosas*, tasty *dals*, or lentil soups, mutton or chicken *biryani*, a seasoned rice dish, and other south Asian treats. There is also a good range of Indian breads including *roti canai*, and *lassis*, or yogurt drinks. The spiced tea is hot and refreshing.

KUALA TERENGGANU Restoran Ocean
Sultan Zainal Abidin, 20000 **Tel** *(09) 623-9156*

This is possibly the best Chinese restaurant in Terengganu. Being in a Muslim state, there are few pork dishes, but cold beer is always available, except during Ramadan. Among the best dishes are the curry *mee* noodles, steamed pomfret in plum sauce, and Chinese kale with oyster and sesame sauce.

KUANTAN Restoran Patani
Jalan Tun Ismail, 25000 **Tel** *(09) 515-7800*

Almost always crowded, this is perhaps the best Malay restaurant in Kuantan. A good selection of superbly prepared traditional Malay dishes including *nasi goreng*, *roti canai*, and beef *rendang* are offered here. Delicious freshly grilled beef and chicken *satay* are also among the top draws. No alcohol is served.

KUANTAN Tjantek Art Bistro
Jalan Besar, 25000 **Tel** *(09) 967-2021*

A surprisingly sophisticated venue for conservative Kuantan, this little bistro, set in a tastefully restored 1928 Chinese shophouse, serves good Italian dishes including pasta, pizza, steak, seafood, and salad. Some dishes, notably the pizza toppings, reflect a Malay influence. The art on the walls, painted by local artists, is for sale.

PEKAN Restoran Islamiza
Jalan Sultan Ahmad, 26600

This restaurant makes a great lunch stop en route from Pekan to Tasik Chini or other destinations. It is a simple place, with superb *roti canai*, *samosas*, north and south Indian curries, and spiced tea served in a friendly atmosphere. It is *halal* so no beer or alcohol is served, but refreshing *lassis* are an appealing alternative.

PULAU PERHENTIAN BESAR Watercolours
Paradise Beach **Tel** *(019) 981-1852*

A combination of local and international dishes, with particularly good pizzas, is served at this 24-hour restaurant, but like most eateries on the Perhentian Islands, seafood is the highlight. Watercolours offers "red-hot barbecues" every evening. Vegetarian dishes are also available.

PULAU PERHENTIAN BESAR Tuna Bay Restaurant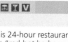
West Coast of Perhentian Besar **Tel** *(09) 697-7779*

One of the best restaurants on Perhentian Besar, located in the Tuna Bay Resort *(see p281)*, it serves a mix of international, Chinese, Malay, and Thai food. The restaurant excels in seafood dishes, and has a fresh seafood barbecue almost every evening. Beer, cocktails, and a limited selection of wines are also on the menu.

PULAU PERHENTIAN KECIL Tussy Café
Pasir Panjang, 22300

Simple and friendly, this beachside café offers good sea views and is especially popular with budget travelers for the Western-style breakfasts that include pancakes and fruit shakes. The Malay dishes are also good, with the stir-fried beef with ginger and garlic highly recommended. Barbecued seafood is occasionally available in the evenings.

PULAU REDANG Matahari
Coral Redang Island Resort **Tel** *(09) 630-7110*

This is a comfortable restaurant with a menu ranging from large Western breakfasts and steaks to lighter seafood and salad lunches, with barbecued prawns, crabs, and other seafood. There is a good selection of cold drinks, including imported beers and spirits. For guests at the resort *(see p281)*, the meals are usually part of a package deal.

TASIK CHINI Lake Chini Resort
Tasik Chini, 26690 **Tel** *(09) 477-8000*

This is the in-house restaurant of the Lake Chini Resort *(see p281)* and has something of a monopoly on dining facilities in the area. The restaurant overlooks the lake and the menu features freshwater fish dishes. Most dishes are Malay, although Western breakfasts are also served.

SARAWAK

BINTULU Riverfront Inn

256 Jalan Masjid, 97000 **Tel** *(086) 333-557*

Located on the bank of the Sungai Kemena, this Chinese restaurant has a refined atmosphere and is one of Bintulu's top dining venues. While the specialties include local favorites such as shark's fin soup with scrambled egg, the inn also serves Thai, Malay, and Western dishes.

BRUNEI Tasek Brasserie

Sheraton Utama Hotel, Jalan Tasek Lama, Bandar Seri Begawan, BS8674 **Tel** *(0673) 224-4272*

With its teak floors and panoramic glass windows, the Tasek Brasserie provides a bright and breezy place to enjoy a good meal of Asian or Western cuisine. The lunch and dinner buffets are particularly recommended and American breakfast is served as well. All food is *halal* and the dress code is smart casual.

KUCHING Hornbill's Corner

85 Jalan Ban Hock **Tel** *(082) 252-670*

Steamboat is the specialty of this place, which is hugely popular with locals and visitors to Kuching. Diners can select seafood and meat from a display, and then cook it in a pot at the table with vegetables and sauces. Cool draft beer is available and the TV screens live sports shows.

KUCHING The Junk

80 Jalan Wayang **Tel** *(082) 259-450*

The ideal place for a romantic dinner, this restaurant is located in an atmospheric old Chinese building, with intriguing art objects decorating the dining area. The signature dish here is lamb shanks with mashed potatoes, served in huge portions, so work up a good appetite before you go.

KUCHING Khatulistiwa Café

Jalan Tunku Abdul Rahman, 93100 **Tel** *(082) 248-896*

One of Kuching's most atmospheric restaurants, this place has a fantastic location right on the riverfront, making it an ideal place to watch local *tambangs*, or river ferries, sail past. The café serves a good variety of both local and international dishes and is open 24 hours. There are DJs playing music in the evenings.

KUCHING Jambu

32 Jalan Crookshank, 93100 **Tel** *(082) 235-292*

Located in a spacious colonial mansion, Jambu is beautifully decorated with European and local antiques. It serves Mediterranean dishes cooked with local ingredients as well as modern Bornean cuisine. Jambu also has an interesting selection of wines. There is a garden terrace with a *tapas* bar and live jazz on Friday evenings.

KUCHING See Good Food Center

53 Jalan Ban Hock, 93100 **Tel** *(082) 251-397*

This is probably the best place for seafood in Kuching. The owners are friendly and happy to advise. Although this is a Chinese restaurant, there are many local dishes on the menu, such as lobster in pepper sauce, and *midin*, a type of jungle fern, cooked until crispy. There is also an extensive wine list.

KUCHING The Steakhouse

Hilton Kuching, Jalan Tunku Abdul Rahman, 93100 **Tel** *(082) 248-200*

Located in the Hilton *(see p283)*, The Steakhouse is the classiest place to eat in Kuching, and does not disappoint. The portions are generous and presentation is attractive. There is an all-you-can-eat buffet at lunch, and in the evening diners can choose from the three- or four-course meals that are sure to satisfy.

MIRI Wheels Pub & Bistro

Lot 1271, Ground Floor, Block 9, MCLD, Miri Waterfront, 98000 **Tel** *(085) 419-859*

This friendly and inviting Western-style bar located in the new development on Miri's Waterfront offers a limited but tasty range of Western dishes, as well as draft beer, wine, and cocktails. They also have a pool table and good music, making it a popular gathering spot for travelers.

MIRI Maxim Delicious Food

1063 Jalan Miri Pujut, 98000 **Tel** *(085) 413-329*

Southeast of the city center, Maxim is one of Miri's most popular seafood restaurants, so arrive early to avoid disappointment. Grilled fish with *belacan*, a shrimp paste, is the highlight of the menu, but there are plenty of other dishes to choose from. Given the distance from the center of town, a taxi is the best way to get here.

SIBU Peppers Café

Tanah Mas Hotel, Lot 277, Block 5, Jalan Kampung Nyabor, 96000 **Tel** *(084) 333-188*

Serving international and Malay cuisine of a very high standard, Peppers Café is particularly popular for business lunches and dinners. The menu features a good range of fruit juices, beers, and spirits. It gets very crowded during weekends, so reservations are recommended.

Key to Price Guide *see p298* **Key to Symbols** *see back cover flap*

SABAH

GUNUNG KINABALU Fairy Garden Resort

Jalan Ranau-Tuaran, Kundasang, 88100 **Tel** *(088) 889-688*

Located on the main road, a short walk east of the entrance to Kinabalu National Park *(see pp184–7)*, this place is an excellent dining option, not only for its delicious array of reasonably priced Malay and Chinese dishes, but also for its panoramic views over the lush hillsides.

GUNUNG KINABALU Liwagu

Park Headquarters, Gunung Kinabalu National Park, 88100 **Tel** *(088) 889-077*

There are limited dining options for those staying in accommodations within Gunung Kinabalu National Park. Liwagu is one of the better eateries and although it may be a slightly expensive option, it has a wider range of both Western and Asian dishes which are all well prepared.

KOTA KINABALU Sinario Café

25 Bandaran Berjaya, 88000 **Tel** *(088) 246-286*

A simple but spotlessly clean café, Sinario turns out delicious northern Indian and Malay food at very cheap prices. With its central location, it is a convenient place to stop off during a walk around town to sample the tasty curries. The place is almost always busy, packed with local workers, especially at lunchtime.

KOTA KINABALU Sri Melaka

9 Jalan Laiman Diki, Kampung Air, 88000 **Tel** *(088) 224-777*

Although the decor and ambience of this restaurant are not exceptional, Sri Melaka serves some of the tastiest Malay food in Sabah's capital. Enormous portions of fish-head curry and a number of dishes prepared with seasonal vegetables are among the favorites that draw the crowds.

KOTA KINABALU Gardenia Grill Room

Jesselton Hotel, 69 Jalan Gaya, 88000 **Tel** *(088) 223-333*

Housed in the stylish Jesselton Hotel *(see p284)*, this international grill is one of the fanciest restaurants in Malaysia. Excellent beef cuts and delicious fresh fish are cooked to perfection, and the presentation is attractive. Attentive service and a good wine list make it an ideal choice for business lunches or a romantic dinner.

KOTA KINABALU Luna Rossa

Lot 6, Tanjung Lipat, Jalan Gaya, 88000 **Tel** *(088) 266-882*

One of Kota Kinabalu's newest restaurants, Luna Rossa is run by an enterprising Italian owner who has tastefully converted a former warehouse on the northeastern fringe of the city into a unique venue. The menu includes a good range of Italian dishes and wines, and there are daily specials as well.

KOTA KINABALU Port View

Jalan Haji Saman, 88000 **Tel** *(088) 252-813*

Located on the seafront, right next to the market, the cavernous Port View is equally popular among locals and tourists for its excellent and inexpensive seafood. The restaurant stages a cultural show every evening, with traditional dance performances by various indigenous groups.

KOTA KINABALU XO Steakhouse

54 Jalan Gaya, 88000 **Tel** *(088) 237-077*

Located to the northeast of the city center, this is perhaps Kota Kinabalu's best steakhouse outside of the top hotels. All the meat is imported and there are many seafood options on the menu. A good range of wine and cocktails plus excellent service make it a reliable choice.

LAHAD DATU Spring Palace

The Executive Hotel, Jalan Teratai, 91121 **Tel** *(089) 881-333*

Considering how far off the beaten track Lahad Datu is, it comes as a surprise to find this tastefully designed restaurant with attentive, smartly dressed staff serving a variety of Chinese and international dishes. Good *dim sum* are served at lunchtime. They also have delicious desserts and a good range of beer, wine, and spirits.

SANDAKAN Supreme Garden Vegetarian

Block 30, Jalan Leila, Bandar Ramai Ramai, 90000 **Tel** *(089) 213-292*

Located just west of the night market in Sandakan, this friendly place serves a bewildering range of vegetarian dishes at very competitive prices. Among these is the vegetarian steamboat, which consists of various types of vegetables cooked in a boiling broth. There are also several unusual dishes including a vegetarian version of fried frog.

SANDAKAN English Tea House and Restaurant

2002 Jalan Istana, 90716 **Tel** *(089) 222-544*

This smart restaurant, on a hill overlooking Sandakan, offers a slice of colonial life. Savor Continental classics, and Malay, and Indian dishes, all served by traditionally dressed staff. English tea is available in the tea house or on the lawn, where guests can also enjoy a game of croquet.

SINGAPORE

CHINATOWN Gorkha Grill
21 Smith Street, 058935 **Tel** *6227-0806*   **Map** *4 C4*

This authentic Nepalese restaurant offers great food at an affordable price. The signature dish here is the traditional Nepalese *momo* – a soft dumpling stuffed with seasoned minced chicken. *Jheenge papita,* a papaya stuffed with prawns in a wine sauce, is one of the best dishes.

CHINATOWN Imperial Hot Wok
1–1 Far East Square, 72 Telok Ayer Street, 048460 **Tel** *6438-8918*   **Map** *5 D4*

This is a tiny, sunlit restaurant that serves authentic Chinese food. Fragrant Hakka rice seasoned with dried shrimp and served with pickled vegetables and beancurd is their house specialty. They also serve excellent stir-fried vegetables. For dessert the fresh homemade coconut ice-cream garnished with sweet red beans is popular.

CHINATOWN Blue Ginger
97 Tanjong Pagar Road, 088518 **Tel** *6222-3928*   **Map** *4 C5*

To experience traditional Nonya cooking, a unique blend of Malay and Chinese flavors, visit the Blue Ginger, located in a picturesque shophouse. Sample the distinctive *ayam buah keluak*, chicken with tamarind paste and chocolatey *keluak* nuts, and a range of desserts made with the unique durian fruit.

CHINATOWN Da Paolo e Judie
81 Neil Road, 88905 **Tel** *6225-8306*   **Map** *4 B5*

Set in a converted shophouse, this tranquil Italian restaurant serves delightful homemade pasta with earthy sauces, homemade ice-cream, and authentic Italian espresso. Adding to this is the friendly service, which makes for a truly memorable evening.

CHINATOWN Casa Mediterranean
Berjaya Duxton Hotel, 83 Duxton Road, 089540 **Tel** *6221-8485*   **Map** *4 C4*

Fine dining in an elegant ambience is the hallmark of this restaurant located at the chic Berjaya Duxton *(see p288)*. Along with classic French fare, their extensive selection of cheeses and wines is exceptional. *Foie gras,* either glazed or accompanied by sauces and broth, is the restaurant's specialty. The menu is seasonal.

CHINATOWN Senso Ristorante and Bar
21 Club Street, 069410 **Tel** *6224-3534*   **Map** *4 C4*

Housed in a former colonial convent, this sophisticated restaurant serves excellent Italian food prepared with ingredients flown in from Italy. The delicious coffee ice-cream sprinkled with nuts is a must. Guests can opt to dine in the covered courtyard, which is complete with pillars and statues. The menu changes every month.

COLONIAL CORE Annalakshmi
 # B1-2 Chinatown Point, 133 New Bridge Road, 059413 **Tel** *6339-9993* **Fax** *6337-0861*   **Map** *4 B4*

Named for the Hindu goddess of food, Annalakshmi is unique in many ways – it is run entirely by volunteers of the Temple of Fine Arts, Indian vegetarian meals are served on silverware or banana leaves, and you can eat all you want and pay what you think is the fair amount for a meal. The proceeds go to various charitable projects.

COLONIAL CORE Bukhara
1–44 Clarke Quay, Block 3A River Valley Road, 179022 **Tel** *6338-1411*   **Map** *4 C2*

Northwest Indian frontier food is served at this colorful restaurant which is decorated with stone and wooden accents. Try the succulent tandoori lamb kebabs, fish, and chicken, while vegetarians can eat the stuffed tandoori potatoes and peppers. Opting for the buffet enables diners to sample most of the dishes for a reasonable price.

COLONIAL CORE House of Sundanese Food
55 Boat Quay, 049844 **Tel** *6534-3775*   **Map** *5 D3*

Renowned for its ethnic Indonesian food, this restaurant offers a menu comprising regional specialties. Among the dishes most recommended are barbecued seafood such as charcoal-dried squid or snapper with *sambhol.* Also try their freshly-made barley water. A buffet spread including traditional desserts is on offer too.

COLONIAL CORE Doc Cheng's
Raffles Hotel Arcade, 1 Beach Road, 189673 **Tel** *6431-6156*   **Map** *5 E1*

Internationally acclaimed Doc Cheng's at the Raffles Hotel Arcade is named for a legendary 1920s physician whose story appears on the menu. The restaurant's decor and food offer the best of East-West fusion. The desserts are exquisite and unique herbal cocktails are served at the bar. Closed for lunch on Saturdays, Sundays, and public holidays.

COLONIAL CORE Empire Café
Raffles Hotel Arcade, 1 Beach Road, 189673 **Tel** *6412-1101*   **Map** *5 E1*

Designed to resemble a *kopi tiam* (old-fashioned street-side coffee houses that were common in 1920s Singapore), Empire Café at the Raffles Hotel Arcade serves all the international favorites as well as local staples including *roti, paratha, laksa,* and Hainan chicken rice. The café is ideal for a quick bite.

Key to Symbols *see back cover flap*

COLONIAL CORE Father Flanagan's

B1–6, Chijmes, 30 Victoria Street, 187996 **Tel** *6333-1418* — **Map** *3 D5* — $$$

Hearty Irish and English fare such as stews, cottage pie, and Guinness pie are served in a traditional pub setting. Also try Monk's Brew, the in-house ale. Irish radio plays in the background adding to the authentic atmosphere. The restaurant is especially popular with the expatriate community.

COLONIAL CORE Flutes at the Fort

23B Coleman Street, 179290 **Tel** *6338-8770* — **Map** *2 C5* — $$$

This hilltop restaurant is ideal for a romantic, frangipani-scented dinner. Outdoor seating on the wooden veranda offers a view of sparkling city lights at night. Among the Australian fare served here, prepared with seasonal ingredients, are the highly recommended homemade breads and cheese platter with quince paste.

COLONIAL CORE Golden Peony

Level 3, Conrad International Centennial Hotel, 2 Temasek Boulevard, 038982 **Tel** *6332-7488* — **Map** *3 E5* — $$$

This swanky Chinese restaurant at the Conrad International Centennial Hotel *(see p286)* is popular for business lunches. The restaurant serves Cantonese-Hong Kong cuisine, made using only the seasonal ingredients flown in from China. A variety of *dim sum* and glutinous rice balls filled with vanilla ice-cream are its premier dishes.

COLONIAL CORE Imperial Herbal

3–8 Vivocity, 188396 **Tel** *6337-0491* — **Map** *3 E5* — $$$

Before placing their order, guests are checked by a resident Chinese herbalist who then makes suggestions from a menu comprising more than 100 dishes, each prepared with Chinese medicinal herbs to combat various ailments. Specialties at this restaurant in the Metropole Hotel include the braised codfish and Imperial chicken.

COLONIAL CORE Min Jiang at One-North

5 Rochestor Park, 139216 **Tel** *6774-0122* — $$$

Set in a beautiful colonial bungalow, this restaurant offers excellent Sichuan cuisine. The lobster medallion and tea-smoked duck are highly recommended. The crispy yet tender traditional Peking duck tastes slightly different here as it is roasted in authentic Chinese wood-fired ovens.

COLONIAL CORE The Moomba

52 Circular Road, Boat Quay, 049407 **Tel** *6438-0141* — **Map** *5 D3* — $$$

This restaurant, decorated with vibrant Aboriginal art, features contemporary Australian cuisine, such as barbecued kangaroo loin, squid cakes, and traditional sticky date pudding. Classic grilled steaks and vegetarian dishes are also on the menu. Some of the best Australian wines are served here. Closed on Sundays and public holidays.

COLONIAL CORE Pierside Kitchen and Bar

One Fullerton, 1 Fullerton Road, 049214 **Tel** *6438-0400* — **Map** *5 E3* — $$$

Located at the spot where the Singapore River meets Marina Bay, this waterfront restaurant offers a beautiful view of the ocean. A superb seafood menu includes pan-seared king scallops and fresh oysters on ice. The bar boasts an extensive collection of vintage wines. Alfresco dining is also available. Closed for lunch on Saturday and Sunday.

COLONIAL CORE Rang Mahal

Pan Pacific Hotel, 7 Raffles Boulevard, 039595 **Tel** *6333-1788* — **Map** *5 F2* — $$$

The oldest and most popular Indian restaurant in the city, situated at the Pan Pacific hotel *(see p286)*, Rang Mahal features stylish interiors and good North Indian food that is cooked over slow flames for extra taste. Try the *rogan josh* (spicy mutton dish) with *biryani* or *rotis*. Desserts such as *kheer* (milk pudding) are served.

COLONIAL CORE Ristorante Bologna

Marina Mandarin, 6 Raffles Boulevard, Marina Square, 039594 **Tel** *6845-1123* — **Map** *5 F2* — $$$

Established almost two decades ago, this chic restaurant at the Marina Mandarin *(see p286)* serves classic northern Italian fare. The menu features an extensive antipasti selection followed by pasta dishes served with rich sauces. Patrons can also mix and match ingredients and request the chef to tailor a dish to their taste.

COLONIAL CORE Sun with Moon

2–1 Chijmes, 30 Victoria Street, 187996 **Tel** *6336-3166* — **Map** *3 D5* — $$$

This is a contemporary Japanese restaurant, which features an open Zen kitchen. House specials are the traditional *kamameshi* or rice casserole, a savory black sesame pudding, and green tea ice-cream for dessert. Other unique dishes include half-broiled *sushi* and vitamin cocktails. Try the eight-dish buffet for lunch.

COLONIAL CORE The Tapas Tree

1–8, Block 3D, Shophouse Row, Clarke Quay, River Valley Road, 179023 **Tel** *6837-2938* — **Map** *5 D2* — $$$

Occupying a scenic riverside location, this Spanish *tapas* bar offers soups, salads, desserts, 70 different types of hot and cold *tapas*, and six types of *paella*. The beverage menu features sangria and wines. Live nightly music by a three-man guitar band or visiting artists enhances the ambience.

COLONIAL CORE Tiffin Room

Raffles Hotel, 1 Beach Road, 189673 **Tel** *6431-6156* — **Map** *5 E1* — $$$

Raffles Hotel's *(see p287)* main dining room is named after the simple midday meals eaten by Indians that also became a tradition for colonial rulers. The delectable lunch and dinner buffet serves all the staple tiffin dishes such as chicken curry in an atmosphere reminiscent of the early 20th-century colonial era.

$ under S$20 $$ S$20–30 $$$ S$30–50 $$$$ S$50–70 $$$$$ over S$70

COLONIAL CORE   Equinox The Restaurant $\textcircled{S}\textcircled{S}\textcircled{S}\textcircled{S}$

Level 70, Swissôtel the Stamford, Raffles City, 2 Stamford Road, 178882 **Tel** *6431-5669*   **Map** *3 D5*

This three-story restaurant offers the most panoramic views of Singapore and across the Strait to Malaysia and Indonesia. Service is gracious and guests can choose from a Western or Asian menu. The seafood buffet at lunch is excellent, but to make the most of its peerless views, visit the restaurant for dinner.

COLONIAL CORE   Fish Tales $\textcircled{S}\textcircled{S}\textcircled{S}\textcircled{S}$

1–7 Clarke Quay, Block 3D River Valley Road, 179024 **Tel** *6837-3251*   **Map** *4 C2*

Sitting on a jetty and with decor befitting its name, including fishing traps and fish hooks, this restaurant has a great selection of fresh seafood. Although the prices are on the high side, and the appearance of the dishes sometimes differs from that described on the menu, the preparation is delicious. Wednesdays are oyster nights.

COLONIAL CORE   Hai Tien Lo $\textcircled{S}\textcircled{S}\textcircled{S}\textcircled{S}$

37th Floor, Pan Pacific Hotel, 7 Raffles Boulevard, 039595 **Tel** *6826-8338*   **Map** *5 F2*

Fabulous Cantonese food, pleasant waitresses dressed in traditional Chinese *cheongsams,* and sweeping views of the city and Marina Bay makes a visit to Hai Tien Lo at the plush Pan Pacific Hotel *(see p286)* an enjoyable experience. Baked codfish in Champagne sauce, king crabs, and wok-fried lobster are among the specialties.

COLONIAL CORE   Inagiku $\textcircled{S}\textcircled{S}\textcircled{S}\textcircled{S}$

Level 3, Swissôtel the Stamford, Raffles City, 2 Stamford Road, 178882 **Tel** *6431-5305*   **Map** *3 D5*

A branch of the original Inagiku that opened in Japan in 1866, this upscale Japanese restaurant features some of Singapore's best *sushi*, *tempura*, and *sashimi*, complemented by an excellent wine list. There are also *tatami* rooms, or private dining areas, where food is prepared at the table. À *la carte* prices tend to be high, so try the set menu.

COLONIAL CORE   Indochine Waterfront $\textcircled{S}\textcircled{S}\textcircled{S}\textcircled{S}$

Asian Civilisations Museum, 1 Empress Place, 179555 **Tel** *6339-1720*   **Map** *5 D3*

Decorated with Shan antiques and Czech crystal chandeliers, this restaurant overlooking the Singapore River, serves Lao, Vietnamese, and Cambodian delicacies including beef stew, fish wrapped in banana leaf, and pungent Vietnamese coffee. Reservations are essential. No lunch service on weekends.

COLONIAL CORE   Jade $\textcircled{S}\textcircled{S}\textcircled{S}\textcircled{S}$

Lobby Level, The Fullerton Hotel, 1 Fullerton, 049178 **Tel** *6877-8188*   **Map** *5 E3*

Lofty ceilings and unobtrusive room dividers give this elegant restaurant, located on the lobby level of The Fullerton Hotel *(see p287)*, a spacious, airy feel. It serves modern Chinese cuisine along with one of the best selections of wine and champagne. Cocoa ribs – sweet chocolate-flavored pork ribs in raspberry dressing – is their signature dish.

COLONIAL CORE   Keyaki $\textcircled{S}\textcircled{S}\textcircled{S}\textcircled{S}$

4th Floor, Pan Pacific Hotel, 7 Raffles Boulevard, Marina Square, 039595 **Tel** *6826-8335*   **Map** *5 F2*

Set in a traditional Japanese garden on the rooftop of the Pan Pacific hotel *(see p286)*, complete with a carp pond and pavilion, this restaurant derives its name from the *keyaki* wood used to build it. Opt for the *robatayaki* form of eating where guests can choose fresh food from a display and have it barbecued before them.

COLONIAL CORE   Morton's of Chicago $\textcircled{S}\textcircled{S}\textcircled{S}\textcircled{S}$

4th Floor, The Oriental, 5 Raffles Avenue, 039797 **Tel** *6339-3740*   **Map** *5 F2*

Featuring dark wood panels and subtle lighting, this American steakhouse at The Oriental Singapore *(see p287)* is extremely popular although the prices are steep. Superior prime beef steaks, flown in all the way from Chicago, are the highlight of the restaurant. They also have a great selection of Napa Valley wines. No lunch service.

COLONIAL CORE   Tatsu Sushi $\textcircled{S}\textcircled{S}\textcircled{S}\textcircled{S}$

1–16 Chijmes, 30 Victoria Street, 187996 **Tel** *6332-5868*   **Map** *4 C2*

Personal service gets a whole new meaning here as the owners and chefs will plan a tailor-made meal if requested. The *sushi* counter is the main draw here, while cozy *tatami* rooms offer private dining. Guests can choose from an extensive menu of grilled, steamed, deep fried, or simmered dishes.

COLONIAL CORE   Viet Lang $\textcircled{S}\textcircled{S}\textcircled{S}\textcircled{S}$

1–3 Annex Building, Old Parliament House, **Tel** *6337-3379*   **Map** *5 D3*

For those craving authentic Vietnamese cuisine, this cozy restaurant is one of the best options in Singapore. The menu includes favorites such as beef wrapped in betel leaves, pork and coconut stews, roast suckling piglet, and rice vermicelli noodles. They also offer frog's legs dishes.

COLONIAL CORE   Au Jardin $\textcircled{S}\textcircled{S}\textcircled{S}\textcircled{S}\textcircled{S}$

EJH Corner House, Singapore Botanic Gardens, 1 Cluny Road, 259569 **Tel** *6466-8812*   **Map** *1 D1*

Housed in a plantation-style house, nestled in the lush Botanical Gardens, this is a celebrated French restaurant. It offers an extensive à *la carte* menu, but the real highlight is the seven-course meal accompanied by superb wines. Guests can choose to sit in the intimate dining room or outdoors on the cozy patio terrace.

COLONIAL CORE   Raffles Grill $\textcircled{S}\textcircled{S}\textcircled{S}\textcircled{S}\textcircled{S}$

Raffles Hotel, 1 Beach Road, 189673 **Tel** *6431-6156*   **Map** *5 E1*

The formal dining room of the Raffles Hotel *(see p287)*, Raffles Grill exudes elegance and sophistication. The service is discreet and the menu has classic as well as contemporary French cuisine including roast veal and pigeon. Wine from their impressive cellar and exquisite bitter chocolate tarts complete a superb meal. Closed on Sunday.

Key to Symbols *see back cover flap*

LITTLE INDIA Andhra Curry House

41 & 43 Kerbau Road, 219170 **Tel** *6293-3935* **Map** 3 D3

This unassuming restaurant specializes in cuisine from the South Indian state of Andhra Pradesh, which has the distinction of having the spiciest food in all of India. The fragrant Hyderabadi *biryani* and dry lamb dishes are delicious. The food is fiery so keep some water at hand.

LITTLE INDIA Banana Leaf Apollo

58 Race Course Road, 218564 **Tel** *6293-8682* **Map** 3 D3

This is a traditional South Indian restaurant, popular with the locals. A standard meal here involves being given a huge banana leaf on which a large mound of piping hot rice is served together with poppadoms, curries, vegetables, and yoghurt. Try eating the spicy food with your fingers the way the locals do.

LITTLE INDIA Delhi

60 Race Course Road, 218567 **Tel** *6296-4585* **Map** 3 D3

This multi-award-winning restaurant, filled with antiques, is one of the best options for authentic North Indian food in Little India. Favorites here include the tandoori mixed meat sizzlers, *rogan josh* (spicy mutton dish), and butter chicken. Among the excellent vegetarian options are spinach with cottage cheese and spicy mushrooms

LITTLE INDIA Komala Vilas

76 Serangoon Road, 217981 **Tel** *6293-6980* **Map** 3 E1

One of the oldest and best-known restaurants in Little India, Komala Vilas serves simple but outstanding South Indian vegetarian food that keeps it constantly crowded. Enjoy the crispiest of *dosas* (large, crisp pancakes), as well as an assortment of *dals*, curries, and condiments.

LITTLE INDIA Muthu's Curry

138 Race Course Road, 218591 **Tel** *6392-1722* **Map** 3 D3

This restaurant is synonymous with the legendary local fish-head curry. The dish essentially consists of a fish head cooked in a spicy gravy, which is best eaten with a portion of boiled rice. Besides this, the menu also includes other Indian treats such as chicken curry, *biryani*, and fish cutlets.

LITTLE INDIA Yhingthai Palace

36 Purvis Street, 198897 **Tel** *6337-1161* **Map** 3 E5

An unpretentious Thai restaurant, which is particularly popular for its variety of flavored rice dishes including olive, mango, and pineapple as well as chicken wings stuffed with spring onions and mushrooms. Excellent starters include the spicy mango salad and *otak otak* (fish soufflé). For dessert try the sticky rice with mango.

ORCHARD ROAD Lemongrass

5–2 The Heeren, 260 Orchard Road, 238879 **Tel** *6736-1998* **Map** 2 A4

Thai statues and artifacts and small waterfalls fill the interior of this restaurant located in one of the busiest malls on Orchard Road. It is known for authentic Thai dishes, most of which are dominated by three main ingredients – blue ginger, lemongrass, and rice. Guests can specify how spicy they like their food while ordering.

ORCHARD ROAD Mumtaz Mahal

5–22 Far East Plaza, 14 Scotts Road, 228213 **Tel** *6732-2754* **Map** 2 A3

Exceptionally friendly service sets this tiny, relatively uncrowded Indian restaurant apart. Their garlic, fruit, and onion *naans*, or bread with onion stuffing, are very popular as is the *raan aleshan* (spicy lamb curry). Indicate how spicy the food should be when placing the order and remember to leave room for the sinfully rich mango ice-cream.

ORCHARD ROAD The Rice Table

2–9 International Building, 360 Orchard Road, 238869 **Tel** *6835-3783* **Map** 1 F2

This is one of the rare restaurants that serves the Indonesian-Dutch *rijsttafel* (rice table) cuisine. The meals are enormous, comprising a portion of rice accompanied by as many as 20 side dishes of meat, poultry, seafood, and vegetables. The set lunches and dinners offer good value. They also have an all-you-can-eat buffet.

ORCHARD ROAD Stuart Anderson's Black Angus

1–8 Orchard Parade Hotel, 1 Tanglin Road, 247905 **Tel** *6734-1181* **Map** 1 F2

Housed in the Orchard Parade hotel *(see p290)*, Black Angus is a branch of the American chain that serves American fare. The menu has tender beef steaks and slow-roasted prime ribs with salads and mashed potatoes. The meat and vegetable gumbo is good too. Imported meat, US Department of Agriculture-approved, is used.

ORCHARD ROAD Aoki

2–17 Shaw Center, 1 Scotts Road, 228208 **Tel** *6333-8015* **Map** 1 F2

Zen-like interiors, smiling kimono-clad waitresses, saké sorbets, and fresh fish flown in from Japan are the highlights of this tiny Japanese restaurant. For the adventurous, the menu offers dishes with cod sperm or sea slug intestines. They also offer an elegant formal banquet known as *kaiseki*. No lunch on Sunday.

ORCHARD ROAD Chatterbox Coffeehouse

Meritus Mandarin Hotel, 333 Orchard Road, 238867 **Tel** *6831-6291* **Map** 2 A4

The Meritus Mandarin's *(see p290)* cozy, 24-hour coffee house, a favorite haunt of Orchard Road shoppers, is reputed to serve the best chicken rice in town. Specially bred chicken is used to prepare the dish and it is claimed that more than 1,000 portions are consumed in a day. *Nasi lemak* and carrot cake are other popular dishes.

$ under S$20 $$ S$20–30 $$$ S$30–50 $$$$ S$50–70 $$$$$ over S$70

ORCHARD ROAD Club Chinois $$$

Orchard Parade Hotel, 1 Tanglin Road, 247905 **Tel** *6834-0660*   **Map** *1 F2*

Illuminated in dazzling fuschia, purple, lime green, and other neon colors, Club Chinois at the Orchard Parade Hotel *(see p290)* is a popular restaurant serving modern Chinese food. The menu has an array of imaginative East-West fusion cuisine along with wines from Chile and Argentina. Choose from a range of private rooms for intimate dining.

ORCHARD ROAD Esmirada $$$

Orchard Hotel, 442 Orchard Road, 238879 **Tel** *6735-3476*   **Map** *1 F2*

A colorful Mediterranean restaurant at the Orchard Hotel *(see p290)* that serves an array of flavorful creations reflecting the diversity of the region. Favorites such as salads, couscous, paella, and hot garlic bread are served on Greek-style earthenware with iron cutlery. Wines can be selected from the adjoining bar.

ORCHARD ROAD Hard Rock Café $$$

2–1 HPL House, 50 Cuscaden Road, 249724 **Tel** *6235-5232*   **Map** *1 E2*

A 1961 Cadillac hangs over the entrance of this quick-service restaurant, part of an international chain famous for its signature display of rock-and-roll memorabilia. Hearty burgers, steaks, brownies, and beer make it a favorite for family outings. The Cecil iced tea with cinnamon and cloves is a specialty. A Filipino band plays music.

ORCHARD ROAD Teahouse $$$

Level 3, 2 China Square Food Center, 51 Telok Ayer Street, 238879 **Tel** *6533-0660*   **Map** *5 D4*

Hunan cuisine is served at this flashy restaurant, which is decorated with Red Army propaganda posters, party flags, and other political paraphernalia, and is serviced by staff dressed in Chairman Mao uniforms. Guests select ingredients of their choice which are cooked together in a hotpot at the table.

ORCHARD ROAD Mezza9 $$$

Grand Hyatt, 10 Scotts Road, 228211 **Tel** *6416-7189*   **Map** *2 A3*

Guests may have trouble choosing a meal at this 450-seat restaurant that serves Chinese, Thai, Japanese, European, and Italian cuisine prepared in nine separate kitchens. In addition, it boasts a superb wine cellar and swanky martini bar with over 30 mixers. The nine-dessert sampler platter is the signature dish. There is also a nine-course meal.

ORCHARD ROAD Blu $$$$

Shangri-La Hotel, 22 Orange Grove Road, 258350 **Tel** *6213-4598*   **Map** *1 E1*

With futuristic designer furnishings, contemporary cuisine with a French twist, and live jazz music, this restaurant reflects the stylish ambience of the Shangri-La Hotel *(see p290)*, enhanced by stunning views across the city. The bar features classic Napa Valley wines and superb Champagne cocktails.

ORCHARD ROAD Les Amis $$$$$

2–16 Shaw Center, 1 Scotts Road, 228208 **Tel** *6733-2225*   **Map** *2 A3*

Rated as the city's finest French restaurant, Les Amis is a favorite with Singapore's tycoons and celebrities. Exquisite meals are matched by a superb selection of vintage wines, including limited editions of Canadian ice wine. A *guéridon* service, in which skilled waiters prepare food at guests' tables, is also offered. Reservations essential.

ORCHARD ROAD Top of the M $$$$$

Meritus Mandarin Hotel, 330 Orchard Road, 238867 **Tel** *6831-6258*   **Map** *2 A4*

Savor a five-course French meal while enjoying a picturesque view of the Singapore skyline at this 567-ft (173-m) high revolving restaurant at the Meritus Mandarin *(see p290)*. Care has been taken to ensure that guests at each table have an unobstructed view. Musicians wander around the restaurant, stopping to play at individual tables.

FARTHER AFIELD Chilli Padi $

11 Joo Chiat Place, East Coast, 486350 **Tel** *6275-1002*

Nonya cooking uses generous amounts of fresh herbs and pungent spices, especially chili paste, so the food here is extremely spicy. Stir-frying and slow cooking result in remarkably flavorful dishes such as green bean *sambhol* and *udang mesak nanas*, prawns cooked with tamarind and pineapple. Dessert options include sago pudding with palm sugar.

FARTHER AFIELD Crystal Jade Kitchen $

2 Lorong Mambong, Holland Village, 277671 **Tel** *6469-0300*

The menu, a combination of Cantonese and Teochew cuisine, is extensive, with a huge variety of appetizing *dim sum*. They also serve the traditional Chinese *congee*, a rice porridge eaten plain or with condiments, and the popular Macau pork chop buns. The restaurant is noisy, but fun.

FARTHER AFIELD Jumbo Seafood $

1206 East Coast Parkway, 449883 **Tel** *6442-3435*

Located on the beach along the East Coast Parkway, with plenty of outdoor tables, Jumbo Seafood is always packed with noisy crowds. This is hardly surprising given the divine seafood served here. The Sri Lankan crab is succulent and well-seasoned, accompanied by tiny buns and thick chili sauces.

FARTHER AFIELD Long Beach Seafood $

1018 East Coast Parkway, 449877 **Tel** *6445-8833*

Every imaginable kind of seafood is served at this immensely popular restaurant. The restaurant's chili crabs are famous, but the real highlight is the dish the place claims to have invented – juicy black pepper crabs oozing with soy sauce. The seafood is sold by weight.

Key to Symbols *see back cover flap*

FARTHER AFIELD Original Sin ♿ ⛱ 🍷 [V] [$]

01–62 Chip Bee Gardens, 43 Jalan Merah Saga, 278115 ***Tel*** *6475-5605*

This is Singapore's first Mediterranean and Middle Eastern vegetarian food restaurant. A fabulous range of starters, salads, main dishes, pasta, and pizzas, with egg and dairy-free options, is complimented by divine desserts and an award-winning wine list. Don't miss the polenta tower and *moussaka*. Alfresco dining is also available.

FARTHER AFIELD Samy's Curry ♿ [V] [$]

Block 25, Dempsey Road, 249670 ***Tel*** *6472-2080*

Non-members will have to pay a S$2 entry fee to eat at this South Indian restaurant located in a private civil service clubhouse. There is no air conditioning, just a few old-fashioned fans turning overhead, and open windows. Hot rice, curries, and vegetables are served on a banana leaf by a long row of constantly moving waiters.

FARTHER AFIELD Trapizza ♿ ⛱ 🍸 [V] [$]

Siloso Beach, Sentosa Island, 099891 ***Tel*** *6376-2662*

A unique venue, Trapizza is a pizzeria as well as a trapeze school. Along with pizzas, a good choice of pastas, salads, and espressos are included on the menu. Unlike the other restaurants on Sentosa that are more suited for private dining, Trapizza is great for family outings. Seating is under pretty gazebos.

FARTHER AFIELD Au Petit Salut ♿ ⛱ 🍷 [V] [$][$]

01-54 Chip Bee Gardens, 44 Jalan Merah Saga, 278115 ***Tel*** *6475-1976*

Enjoy country-style cooking from southern France in a serene outdoor garden setting at this restaurant. The pan-fried *foie gras* accompanied by marinated dried apricots makes a delightful starter, followed by a main course of duck *cassoulet* or stuffed turkey among many others. A selection of wines is also available.

FARTHER AFIELD Mango Tree ♿ ⛱ 🍸 🍷 [$][$]

1000 East Coast Parkway, 449876 ***Tel*** *6442-8655*

This beachside restaurant specializes in Indian coastal food, featuring dishes from states such as Goa and Kerala. The Malabar seafood platter, tandoori lobster, and Kerala fish curry are all excellent choices. Book early to secure an outdoor table and sit back to enjoy a spectacular sunset over the ocean before dinner.

FARTHER AFIELD True Blue Cuisine ♿ [V] [$][$]

117 East Coast Road, 428805 ***Tel*** *6440-0449*

This is the best place in the Katong area for Nonya cuisine where the owner-chef prepares dishes from family recipes. Regulars swear by the *ayam buah keluak, or* chicken with tamarind paste, and chocolatey *keluak* nuts. Unusual for Nonya cuisine, all dishes here are pork-free. The dining room is beautifully decorated with *objets d'art*.

FARTHER AFIELD The Cliff ♿ ⛱ 🍸 🍷 [V] [$][$][$]

No.2, Bukit Mintang Road, Sentosa Resort & Spa, Sentosa 099891 ***Tel*** *6275-0331*

Occupying a fabulous clifftop location, this restaurant offers fantastic grilled seafood platters along with views of the South China Sea. There is also an extensive wine list. The fragrance of frangipani fills the air and visitors sitting out on the terrace can hear peacocks calling from the hotel grounds below.

FARTHER AFIELD Michelangelo's ♿ ⛱ 🍷 [V] [$][$][$]

01–60 Chip Bee Gardens, 44 Jalan Merah Saga, Holland Village 278115 ***Tel*** *6475-9069*

One of the best restaurants in the city, Michelangelo's has won almost every food and wine award in Singapore for its outstanding Italian creations, wine selection, and impeccable service. Among the unique dishes is the charred Australian outback ostrich in thick black pepper sauce. Reproductions of Michelangelo's friezes adorn the ceiling.

FARTHER AFIELD Olive Ristorante ⛱ 🍷 [$][$][$]

Labrador Park, Labrador Villa Road, 119187 ***Tel*** *6479-2989*

Set in a restored colonial mansion, this restaurant offers marvelous views of the sea and surrounding islands. Its main attraction lies in stylish outdoor dining amid pristine surroundings. The cuisine is predominantly Indonesian-Dutch, but Western dishes are also available. Light finger food and drinks are served at the café.

FARTHER AFIELD Tung Lok Seafood Gallery ♿ 🍷 [$][$][$]

1000 East Coast Parkway, 449876 ***Tel*** *6246-0555*

The Tung Lok Seafood Gallery is not as noisy as the neighboring seafood restaurants. Fresh catch is imported every day from all over the world, so diners can enjoy fish from Australia, king crabs from Alaska, or lobsters from Maine. *Wasabi* coated deep-fried prawns is the signature dish.

FARTHER AFIELD Vansh ♿ 🍸 🍷 [V] [$][$][$]

1–4 Singapore Indoor Stadium, 2 Stadium Walk, 397691 ***Tel*** *6345-4466*

Opt for a table looking out onto the Kallang River at this Indian restaurant or alternatively watch chefs create Indian delicacies in open stainless steel kitchens. Main dishes are accompanied by rice, *naan*, and *dal*. Some dishes take inspiration from other cultures, such as *kulchas* (deep-fried bread) topped with sundried tomatoes and honey.

FARTHER AFIELD Sky Dining at the Jewel Box, Mount Faber ⛱ 🍷 [$][$][$][$][$]

109 Mount Faber Road, Cable Car Station, Mount Faber Hill, 099203 ***Tel*** *6377-9688*

Dine on a three-course meal on board a cable car, from Mount Faber to Sentosa Island and enjoy breathtaking views from 230 ft (70 m) above sea level. The food is catered by award-winning restaurants and is therefore expensive. If planning to eat here, then it's worth making it in time for the gorgeous sunsets. Advance booking is advised.

[$] under S$20 [$][$] S$20–30 [$][$][$] S$30–50 [$][$][$][$] S$50–70 [$][$][$][$][$] over S$70

SHOPPING IN MALAYSIA

Malaysia is an affluent country with a rapidly developing economy. It has an astonishing variety of shopping options, from the latest electronic gadgets to a wealth of traditional art and handicraft items. Differences exist between the range, quality, and prices available in the various regions, with the large cities on the western coast of Peninsular

Woven bamboo products for sale

Malaysia, notably Kuala Lumpur, Penang, and Johor Bahru, offering sophisticated malls, and the smaller east coast cities, such as Kota Bharu and Kuala Terengganu, acting as the repository of Malay artistry, especially *batik*, colorful kites, and shadow puppets. Sarawak and Sabah in Malaysian Borneo are unrivaled for their array of ethnic products, skilfully crafted by the indigenous people.

DEPARTMENT STORES AND SHOPPING MALLS

Shopping malls, ranging from modest establishments to plush, air-conditioned, multistory buildings, are ubiquitous in Malaysian towns and cities. They contain a mix of large department stores that sell branded goods, supermarkets offering both local and imported food, and dozens of smaller shops that stock everything from mobile phones, computers, electronic goods, and English and Malay books, to a wealth of souvenirs, clothes, shoes, and accessories, such as bags and watches. Nearly all shopping malls have fast-food outlets, while the upmarket ones also feature expensive restaurants. Many have multiplex movie theaters, food courts, Internet cafés, and branches of banks with facilities such as money changing and ATMs. Malls in west coast cities, especially those in Kuala Lumpur, compare with the glitziest outlets in the Western countries and are an excellent source of a wide range of international luxury brands.

Besides those in the malls, there are several independent department stores, such as Kuala Lumpur's Isetan, which is part of a Japanese chain.

LOCAL MARKETS (TAMUS) AND STALLS

Malaysia is brimming with local markets, or *tamus*. Almost every town and village has at least one bustling central market, usually containing a multitude of stalls offering a bewildering selection of goods, from local crafts to clothes and household items. Very often there is also a wet market selling fresh meat, fruits, and vegetables. Numerous hawker stalls offer an array of local delicacies. Prices are reasonable, the quality is generally good, and standards of hygiene are very high, even in fish markets, which are regularly hosed.

Another enduringly popular feature and a highlight of a trip to Malaysia are its *pasar malams*, or night markets. The most fascinating of these are in Kuala Lumpur *(see pp56–77)*, Johor Bahru *(see p128)*, Penang *(see pp100–109)*, Kuching *(see pp154–7)*, and Kota Kinabalu *(see p178)*. Most state capitals and larger towns of Malaysia and Singapore often have ethnic enclaves, such as Chinatown and Little India, which are excellent places to buy Chinese and Indian products.

SHOPPING HOURS

Business hours for shops can vary substantially, but most establishments are open from

The Sungei Wang Plaza in Kuala Lumpur's Golden Triangle *(see p318)*

9am to 6:30pm, Monday to Saturday. Malls and major emporia open later, usually between 10 and 10:30am until 9:30 or 10pm. In most states in Malaysia, including Sabah and Sarawak, Saturday is a half day and Sunday a holiday. Shops in the conservative Islamic east coast states of Kelantan and Terengganu are closed on Friday, the Muslim Sabbath.

METHODS OF PAYMENT

Cash, preferably the Malaysian ringgit, is universally accepted although many places also take US dollars. However, money changers are found everywhere. Credit cards are widely accepted except in the smallest of stores. The preferred cards include VISA, MasterCard, and JCB, while larger establishments also accept American Express and Diners Club cards. A few shops levy a 3 percent service charge, but this tendency is becoming less common.

SALES TAX

Currently Malaysia does not impose a general sales tax on goods, but VAT, ranging from 5 to 10 percent, is being introduced on all types of imported goods. For food and accommodation, however, customers can expect to pay a service tax of 10 percent at luxury hotels and restaurants, in addition to the government tax of 5 percent. Malaysia has some designated duty-free areas, including Pulau Langkawi in the west and

Fresh fish sold at a market in Tawau, Sabah

Pulau Labuan in the east, designed to attract shoppers. There are also duty-free areas in Kelantan at Rantau Panjang and Pengkalan Kubur, as well as in Kedah at Padang Besar and Bukit Kayu Hitam.

BARGAINING

In Malaysia, bargaining is an accepted practice. However, whether to bargain or not depends on the kind of market shoppers are in. Top-end department stores, shopping malls, and government emporia have fixed prices, though the latter offer good fixed-price deals.

In most local markets and stalls, bargaining is not just accepted but is also expected. Buyers can often obtain a substantial reduction in the original price. Remember to keep the exchange polite and good-natured, and it is always a good idea to browse in several shops and know the fair price of a product before negotiating.

GUARANTEES

Buyers should always be careful with their selection at the time of purchase to avoid problems later. Most government shops and large department stores will accept the return of faulty goods, but it might not be as easily done for products bought at street stalls, especially antique shops that are not recommended or guaranteed by the government.

PHOTOGRAPHY

Malaysia, like Singapore, tends to be at the cutting edge of photographic technology. Deals are just as great as in Singapore, and sometimes better, due to good exchange rates. The range of products is excellent, though digital technology has swept aside slide film. Print film remains available, and film-developing facilities are ubiquitous, fast, and cheap.

IMITATIONS

Although the sale of imitation goods and knock-offs is illegal in Malaysia, and there is a growing clampdown on the sale of illicit goods, such products continue to be sold at small stores and stalls. Since most of these products are very cheap and of poor quality and because such trade breaches property rights, the purchase of fakes, such as faux designer bags, clothing, and illegal copies of VCDs and DVDs, although tempting, is best avoided.

A busy shopping street in Kuala Lumpur at night

What to Buy in Malaysia

Glitzy shopping malls, bustling local markets, vibrant *pasar malams* (night markets), and small craft shops across Malaysia offer a good range of souvenirs for visitors to take home. Traditionally-styled Malay, Chinese, and Indian artifacts are widely available; however, some craft items are restricted to specific regions. The country can boast an astonishing range of products, including antique furniture, *ikat* cloth, *batik* prints, wood carvings, and shadow puppets, besides handicraft items produced by indigenous people.

Visitors at a chic shopping mall in Kuala Lumpur

MALAY PRODUCTS

With the rising demand for ethnic Malay goods, aided by Malaysia's thriving tourism and patronage offered by the country's leading banks and oil companies, art in Malaysia is flourishing like never before. Malay goods are available almost everywhere, but are especially visible in Kuala Lumpur, Johor Bahru, Kelantan, and Terengganu.

Wayang Kulit
Shadow puppet theater, or wayang kulit, *is a Malay folk art whose traditions are passed on orally. These colorful leather puppets are available in Kelantan and Kuala Lumpur.*

Silverware
The best Malay silverware, with its hallmark filigree embellishments, is produced in Terengganu and Kelantan. These areas specialize in belt buckles and tobacco boxes.

Batik Fabric
Malay batik *uses wax and dyes to print on fabrics. Shirts, skirts, and sarongs in batik-print are best bought from Malaysia's east coast.*

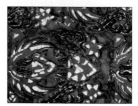

Songket Silk Fabrics
Belonging to the brocade family of textiles, songket *is handwoven on looms and features elaborate patterns created with a gold and silver weft.*

Kites
While the principal designs of traditional Malay kites are derived from nature, decorations are unique to each craftsman. Kite-making shops can be found in villages along the east coast of Peninsular Malaysia.

Ceramic Items
Shaped by hand, pottery is produced in Selangor and Perak. Ayer Itam, a small town in Peninsular Malaysia, is known for its pottery and porcelain crafts. The Cameron Highlands are also a good place to buy ceramics.

Masks
Traditionally, Malaysian and Southeast Asian masks represent people, demons, and deities. They are cultural icons that help preserve tradition, religion, and history. Malay ceremonial masks are commonly available in Malacca.

PRODUCTS FROM MALAYSIAN BORNEO

Sabah and Sarawak are unrivaled for items crafted by indigenous people and by Malay Christians, including fine *ikat* cloth, shamanistic religious paraphernalia, and wood carvings.

Ikat Design
Often a symbol of status and power, ikat, *meaning to tie in Malay, is a style of weaving created by dyeing the warp. The best* ikat *is produced in Sarawak.*

Bamboo Products
Items made of bamboo, palm leaf, and rattan, including finely woven baskets and hats, are available in bazaars throughout Sarawak and Sabah.

Wood Carvings
Wood carvings depicting people, spirits, and animals in the shamanistic tradition are widely available in Kuching, Kota Kinabalu, and at Selangor's small Orang Asli Museum.

CHINESE PRODUCTS

Malaysia is especially popular for locally produced Peranakan or Straits Chinese goods, including antique furniture and ceramics. Standard Chinese wares are imported from Hong Kong and the Chinese mainland.

Good Luck Charms
Chinese good luck charms in bright, attractive colors make cheap and fun purchases. They are available almost everywhere.

Chinese Antique Furniture
Antique furniture of the Baba Nonya tradition, made from hardwood with exquisite carvings, is available in Malacca, where Jalan Hang Jebat (see p124) is a treasure-house for antique lovers.

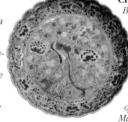

Chinese Ceramics
Baba-Nonya vases, which are unique to Malaysia, and imported chinaware are available in big retail outlets in Malacca, on the west cost of Peninsular Malaysia.

INDIAN PRODUCTS

Indian enclaves in Penang, Kuala Lumpur, and Johor Bahru exude a heady aroma of spices and have several authentic silk stores recreating an ambience similar to that in Southern Indian states.

Brassware
Fine brass goods, a Tamil tradition transplanted to Malaysia, comprise household objects, decoratives, and religious items.

Indian Silk Sarees
Traditional southern Indian kanchipuram *silk sarees are available in the fabric stores of Little India in Georgetown as well as in shopping malls across Malaysia.*

Indian Spices
Spices, such as pepper, cardamom, saffron, cloves, mace, nutmeg, and cinnamon, are widely available in Malaysia.

Where to Shop

There are good shops just about everywhere in Malaysia, from big cities on the peninsula to smaller towns and villages in Malaysian Borneo. The larger metropolises, especially Kuala Lumpur, Penang, Johor Bahru, and Kuching, have fantastic malls selling a fine range of products. The smaller east coast cities, such as Kota Bharu and Kuala Terengganu, are the center of traditional Malay arts and crafts, while Sarawak and Sabah are unrivaled for their ethnic goods.

KUALA LUMPUR

The main shopping areas in Kuala Lumpur are around Bukit Bintang and Jalan Sultan Ismail in the heart of the Golden Triangle. Major shopping malls here include **Bukit Bintang Plaza**, **Lot 10**, **Starhill Gallery**, and the huge new mall, **Berjaya Times Square**. **Sungei Wang Plaza** and **Low Yat Plaza**, also in the Golden Triangle, specialize in electronic goods. Among the upmarket malls, Suria KLCC inside the Petronas Towers *(see p73)* is stunning, and the **Mid Valley Megamall** is also worth visiting. Perhaps the best market in Malaysia is **Central Market**, which is the place to shop for local souvenirs. There is a great variety of *batik* and handicraft goods for sale at Kompleks Budaya Kraf *(see p75)*. The market at Jalan Tuanku Abdul Rahman *(see p70)* offers great bargains, with the **Globe Silk Store** popular for tailor-made clothes. The street springs to life at night with a *pasar malam*. Jalan Petaling *(see p64)* is great for DVDs.

PENANG

After Kuala Lumpur, the best place to shop is Penang, with outlets selling local crafts, antiques, and electronic items at competitive prices. Jalan Penang is the best shopping street in Georgetown, with **Komtar**, a shopping mall located in a massive 56-story building, and **Chowrasta Bazaar** for spices. 100 Cintra Street *(see p104)* has an interesting antique and curio center, while Little India *(see p103)* offers an array of southern Indian products. Batu Ferringhi *(see p108)* has a vibrant night market.

An antiques store displaying Peranakan artifacts, Malacca

PULAU LANGKAWI

One of the major attractions of Pulau Langkawi is its status as a duty-free shopping zone. The island's capital, Kuah, is where most duty-free shops are located. Popular outlets include the **Langkawi Fair Shopping Mall** and the **Jetty Point Duty-Free Complex**, both in Kuah. The **Zon DutyFree Shopping Paradise** at Pantai Cenang and **Sunmall** at Pantai Tengah are worth visiting, although they mainly stock cosmetics, cigarettes, and alcohol.

MALACCA

The restored Chinese district in Malacca is the place to look for antiques, both genuine and imitation, as well as all kinds of Chinese and Peranakan goods. Jalan Hang Jebat *(see p124)* sells beautiful porcelain, coins, old lamps, *songket* fabric, and antique furniture. There are a range of handicraft and souvenir shops in Taman Merdeka and a *pasar malam* on Jalan Paramesawara. The **Mahkota Parade** shopping complex on Jalan Merdeka is Malacca's largest shopping venue.

JOHOR BAHRU

Regarded as one of Malaysia's most prosperous towns, Johor Bahru is located across the causeway from Singapore, whose citizens often come to shop, notably at **Komplex Lien Hoe**, **Pelangi Leisure Mall**, **Perling Mall**, and **Plaza Pelangi** in Johor Bahru. All

Jalan Petaling, the commercial heart of Chinatown, Kuala Lumpur

these malls specialize in designer goods, clothing, luxury goods, and accessories. The Johor Area Rehabilitation Project on Jalan Sungai Chat sells handicrafts and furniture.

KOTA BHARU AND KUALA TERENGGANU

The east coast of Peninsular Malaysia abounds with shops selling traditional Malay crafts such as *batik* and *songket* fabric, silverware, wood carvings, and colorful kites. The handicraft workshops along the road to Pantai Cahaya Bulan and **Kompleks Bazaar Buluh Kubu** in Kota Bharu are good stops for their displays of *batik* items.

In Kuala Terengganu, Jalan Bandar near the Central Market has several small shops selling local handicrafts and *batik* cloth, which are open on all days except on Fridays. The **Noor Arfa Craft Complex** is also a favorite for traditional crafts, especially *batik* and *songket*.

KUCHING, SARAWAK

Kuching is one of Malaysia's best shopping destinations, rivaled only by Penang and Malacca. The city is filled with stores selling souvenirs, *ikat* cloth, and Asian antiques. It also specializes in artifacts made by indigenous peoples. Jalan Satok's Sunday market sells a variety of crafts and fresh produce. Demonstrations of these crafts are held daily at **Sarawak Handicraft Center**.

KOTA KINABALU, SABAH

The capital of Sabah, Kota Kinabalu, has several local handicraft shops selling goods of reasonable quality. The Filipino Market *(see p179)* at the waterfront is the best market and sells basketware and colorful woven ponchos. The products on display serve as a reminder of how much closer Sabah is to the Philippines than to Peninsular Malaysia.

Woman selling *batik* silk in the new Central Market in Kota Bharu

DIRECTORY

KUALA LUMPUR

Berjaya Times Square
1 Jalan Imbi. **Map** 5 C3.
Tel (03) 2144-9988.
www.timessquarekl.com

Bukit Bintang Plaza
Jalan Bukit Bintang.
Map 5 C3.
Tel (03) 4252-1781.
www.allmalaysia.info

Central Market
Jalan Hang Kasturi.
Map 4 E2. *Tel (03) 2274-6542.* www.central
market.com.my

Globe Silk Store
159 Jalan Tuanku Abdul
Rahman. **Map** 5 C3.
Tel (03) 2692-2888.
www.allmalaysia.info

Lot 10
Map 5 C3.
www.ytlcommunity.com

Low Yat Plaza
Lot 7, Jalan 1/77.
Tel (03) 2148-3651.
www.plazalowyat.com

Mid Valley Megamall
Federal Highway.
Tel (03) 7938-3333.
www.midvalley.com.my

Starhill Gallery
www.starhillgallery.com.

Sungei Wang Plaza
99 Bukit Bintang.
Map 6 D3.
Tel (03) 2144-9988.
www.sungeiwang.com

PENANG

Chowrasta Bazaar
Jalan Penang, Penang.

Komtar
Jalan Penang.
Tel (04) 269-9000.
www.allmalaysia.info

PULAU LANGKAWI

Jetty Point Duty-Free Complex
Kuah Jetty.
Tel (04) 966-5309.
www.jettypointlangkawi.
com/dutyfree_shops.htm

Langkawi Fair Shopping Mall
Persian Putra, Kuah.
Tel (04) 969-8100.

Sunmall
Jalan Teluk Baru. *Tel (07)
955-8300.* www.sun
grouplangkawi.com

Zon Duty Free Shopping Paradise
Pantai Cenang.
Tel (04) 955-6100.

MALACCA

Mahkota Parade
1 Jalan Merdeka.
Tel (06) 282-6151.
www. allmalaysia.info

JOHOR BAHRU

Komplex Lien Hoe
Jalan Sutera.
Tel (07) 334-0177.
www.allmalaysia.info

Pelangi Leisure Mall
Jalan Serampang
Teman Pelangi.
Tel (07) 335-2317.
www.allmalaysia.info

Perling Mall
Jalan Persisiran Perling.
Tel (07) 241-5058.
www.pelangi-bhd.com

Plaza Pelangi
Jalan Kuning.
Tel (07) 276-2216.
www.allmalaysia.info

KOTA BHARU AND KUALA TERENGGANU

Kompleks Bazaar Buluh Kubu
Central Market, Kota
Bharu. *Tel (09) 743-7302.*
www.allmalaysia.info

Noor Arfa Craft Complex
Chendering Terengganu.
Tel (09) 617-5700.
www.virtualmalaysia.com

KUCHING

Sarawak Handicraft Center
32 Jalan Tun Haji Openg.
Tel (082) 245-652. www.
sarawakhandicraft.com

ENTERTAINMENT IN MALAYSIA

Entertainment in Malaysia can range from a traditional dance performance by the indigenous Iban people to the hip nightclubs in Kuala Lumpur. As the capital, Kuala Lumpur boasts a wide choice of entertainment, including theater, concerts, and art exhibitions. However, state capitals such as Johor Bahru, Kuching, and Kota Kinabalu also cater for night-time revelry with a variety of nightclubs and karaoke bars. Malaysia's festivals through the year *(see pp50–53)* are often accompanied by traditional performing arts. Theme parks, such as the one at Genting Highlands, are a great way to enjoy an all-day outing with children, while cinema enthusiasts can watch the latest Hollywood films at multiplexes.

Male Iban dancer

Contemporary artwork at the National Art Gallery *(see p71)*, Kuala Lumpur

EVENT LISTINGS

For comprehensive listings of current and upcoming events including art exhibitions, theatrical performances, and concerts in Kuala Lumpur, check English-language dailies such as **The Sun**, **The Star**, and **New Straits Times**. Other useful publications are **KLUE**, a monthly arts review, and **Juice**, a monthly magazine that lists the trendiest clubs. Up-to-date listings from all these publications are also available on their official websites. In addition, the **Kakiseni** and **KL This Month** websites also offer a wealth of information regarding places to stay, restaurants, outdoor activities, and street maps.

There is no central ticket booking organization in Kuala Lumpur, so it is necessary to contact each venue directly or ask hotel staff for help with booking tickets. Unfortunately, not many entertainment venues are equipped with facilities for the disabled, although most

new establishments provide such amenities. Call individual venues in advance to check for details before booking.

ART EXHIBITIONS

There are several art halls in Kuala Lumpur, which host frequently changing exhibitions. The National Art Gallery *(see p71)* showcases works of over 2,500 artists and painters, especially works by contemporary Malaysian artists. The

gallery also hosts rotating exhibitions throughout the year. Another impressive art gallery is Galeri Petronas at Suria KLCC *(see p73)*, which has three separate halls of international standard. It houses Malaysia's largest private art collection. For detailed information on Kuala Lumpur's other art galleries it is best to visit the Kakiseni website.

THEME PARKS

Peninsular Malaysia has several theme parks that offer exciting all-day amusement for the entire family. Children especially enjoy the action-packed environment. One of the more popular venues is the Genting Theme Park *(see p90)*, Malaysia's first and biggest theme park, which has both indoor and outdoor activities. Among the extensive entertainment choices are roller-coaster rides, amusement arcades, a 32-lane bowling alley, the Awana Equestrian Ranch, and a cineplex, as well as music

Exciting rides at the Genting Theme Park *(see p90)*

The long-running Coliseum Cinema

Musicians playing a traditional Malay instrument

and theater performances. Another favorite hangout is the **Mines Wonderland**, which has a Snow House filled with ice sculptures, ice skating rinks, and exciting rides. It also presents Light Fantasy on Water, and a sound and light show. Wet World Water Park in Shah Alam *(see p76)* and **Sunway Lagoon** are water theme parks with water chutes and wave pools.

THEATER

Kuala Lumpur hosts a great variety of theatrical performances throughout the year. Apart from touring Broadway hits, traditional and experimental musicals, comedies, and tragedies written by international as well as local playwrights, are also staged. There is a particularly active fringe theater scene in Kuala Lumpur, with groups such as Instant Café producing thought-provoking plays. The venues are as varied as the productions, ranging from the state-of-the-art **Kuala Lumpur Performing Arts Center** to the simple **Old China Café**.

Traditional Malaysian theater is the shadow puppet play, or *wayang kulit*, accompanied by a *gamelan*, music played by a traditional Indonesian percussion orchestra. Once the main form of entertainment in Malay villages, it is now mostly performed in some rural parts of the east coast states of Terengganu and

Kelantan. One good place to catch a show is at Gelanggang Seni in Kota Bharu *(see pp146–7)* and a typical performance often lasts about 8 hours. Chinese opera, or *wayang*, a mix of dialog, dance, and music is also traditionally performed in the country. Street shows are held mostly during festivals such as the Chinese New Year *(see p28)*.

CINEMA

Kuala Lumpur and big towns around the country have numerous movie halls and multiplex cinemas, which screen the latest Hollywood releases, usually with the original soundtrack and subtitles in Malay and Chinese. Movies from China, India, and other Asian countries are also screened. Most cinemas have air conditioning. Some of the biggest cinema chains are **Golden Screen Cinemas**, **Tanjong Golden Village**, and **Cathay Cineplexes**. The oldest cinema in Kuala Lumpur, still functioning today, is the Coliseum Cinema *(see p70)*. Cinema listings, show times, and tickets are available on the **Cinema Online** website.

TRADITIONAL AND CLASSICAL MUSIC

Reflecting a blend of cultures, predominantly Indian, Chinese, Muslim, and Indonesian,

traditional Malaysian music is based largely around several types of drums – an influence of the *gamelan* – and other percussion instruments. Modern composers are constantly experimenting with a fusion of new and traditional instruments such as synthesizers in an attempt to keep classical music popular among the younger generation. Traditional music performances are frequently held at the Malaysian Tourism Information Complex *(see p74)* and the National Theater *(see p71)* both in Kuala Lumpur. Occasionally the National Theater hosts classical music concerts featuring the National Symphony Orchestra. The main classical venue in Kuala Lumpur is **Dewan Filharmonik Petronas**. This was Malaysia's first classical concert hall and is home to the Malaysian Philharmonic Orchestra. It stages classical concerts and hosts local and international cultural performances.

The grand auditorium at the Dewan Filharmonik Petronas

Hard Rock Café, one of the best venues in Kuala Lumpur for live bands

CONTEMPORARY MUSIC

Extremely popular among Malaysian youth, contemporary western music often provides inspiration for local groups who create songs in Malay that are set to pop, rock, hip-hop, or underground beats. Touring pop stars of international repute occasionally perform in Kuala Lumpur. The Arena of the Stars stadium in Genting Highlands (see p90) is a popular venue for such concerts. Some of the most popular contemporary live music venues in Kuala Lumpur are the **Hard Rock Café**, **No Black Tie**, and **Titus Blues**. Many famous DJs from Europe also visit Kuala Lumpur's hippest clubs.

TRADITIONAL DANCE

Like its music, Malaysia's traditional dances are strongly influenced by Islamic, Indian, and Chinese cultures, though they have evolved into their own unique styles. Many of these dance forms continue to enjoy widespread popularity in the country and are performed during special occasions and festivals. Perhaps the most popular traditional dance is *joget*, which has its origins in Portuguese folk dance and is performed by couples who blend fast and graceful movements with playful humor. *Mak yong* combines romantic

drama, dance, and operatic singing. Originally presented only in Kelantan's royal courts, it is now enjoyed by all. *Silat* is an elegant dance that developed from martial arts and is accompanied by percussion music. It is often performed at weddings and festivals. One of the most popular dances from Sarawak is the *datun julud*, or hornbill dance. Created by the Kenyah people, it is based on the story of a prince blessed with a grandson and involves a single female dancer who waves fans of hornbill feathers to the sound of a *sape*, or a traditional guitar. A good place to enjoy traditional music and dance in Sarawak is the Sarawak Cultural Village (see p159).

Dancer performing *datun julud*

In Kuala Lumpur, dance performances are held at the Malaysia Tourism Information Complex, as well as at the National Theater.

PUBS, BARS, AND KARAOKE

Kuala Lumpur has a dizzying range of nightlife haunts that cater to every taste. The greatest concentration of pubs and bars is in the Golden Triangle (see p74). Located here is **Planet Hollywood**, an international bar and restaurant chain that sprawls over three floors, as well as the **Beach Club Café**, which mostly plays old favorites and is often packed to the rafters. The capital's other pulsating nightspot is around Bangsar. Bars such as **Finnegan's** serving Kilkenny beer and **La Bodega** with its Spanish ambience infuse it with a cosmopolitan feel. Another bar worth a visit for lovers of rhythm and blues music is **Modesto's**.

Karaoke is hugely popular in most Asian countries, and Malaysia is no exception. Among Kuala Lumpur's chic, luxurious, and commonly visited karaoke bars are **Cherry Blossom**, **Deluxe Nite Club**, and **Club De Vegas**.

Other main towns in the country with a fair choice of pubs and bars are Kuching, Johor Bahru, Kota Kinabalu, and several in Penang. Since drinks can be expensive in Malaysia, it is worth looking out for places that offer happy hour prices, typically two drinks for the price of one. Generally, happy hour is between 5 and 8pm. Many bars feature live music, especially at weekends, for which there is usually a cover charge of around RM20.

Men performing *silat*, or a traditional martial art dance, in Kelantan

NIGHTCLUBS AND DISCOS

Although nightclubs and discos can be found in all large Malaysian towns, Kuala Lumpur has the widest choice of venues. Most places don't pick up pace until around 10pm, but are throbbing with life until the early hours of dawn. Several locations feature Ladies' Nights when women can get free entry. The popularity of individual clubs tends to fluctuate, but the hottest spots in town can usually be found around the junction of Jalan P. Ramlee and Jalan Sultan Ismail. Most places play European and British house music, and frequently feature well-known international DJs. Among the trendiest places are **Zouk**, **The Loft**, **Maison**, **Atmosphere**, and **Bliss**, the last two of which are situated in Twelve SI, Kuala Lumpur's biggest clubbing complex. Discos tend to be located in upmarket shopping malls or in hotels, and among the most popular clubs are **Liquid** and **Sugar Club**.

A crowded dance floor in a Malaysian club

DIRECTORY

EVENT LISTINGS

Juice
www.juiceonline.com

Kakiseni
www.kakiseni.com

KL This Month
www.klthismonth.com

KLUE
www.klue.com.my

New Straits Times
www.nst.com.my

The Star
www.thestar.com.my

The Sun
www.sun2surf.com

THEME PARKS

Mines Wonderland
Seri Kembangan, Selangor.
Tel (03) 8943-6688.
www.mineswonderland.
com.my

Sunway Lagoon
11/11 Bandar Sunway,
Petaling Jaya, Selangor.
Tel (03) 5635-8000.

THEATER

**Kuala Lumpur
Performing Arts
Center**
Jalan Strachan, Kuala
Lumpur. *Tel (03) 4047-
7000.* www.klpac.com

Old China Café
11, Jalan Balai Polis,
Kuala Lumpur.
Tel (03) 2072-5915.

CINEMA

Cathay Cineplexes
2 Selangor Darul Ehsan.
Tel (03) 7727-8051.

Cinema Online
www.cinemaonline.
com.my

**Golden Screen
Cinemas**
Mid Valley Megamall,
Bangsar.
Tel (03) 2938-3366.

**Tanjong Golden
Village**
Level 3 Suria KLCC. **Map**
2 F5. *Tel (03) 7492-2929.*

TRADITIONAL AND CLASSICAL MUSIC

**Dewan Filharmonik
Petronas**
Petronas Towers. **Map**
2 F4. *Tel (03) 2051-7007.*
www.
malaysianfilharmonik.com

CONTEMPORARY MUSIC

Hard Rock Café
Jalan Sultan Ismail,
Kuala Lumpur. **Map** 2 D5.
Tel (03) 2715-5555.

No Black Tie
17 Lorong Mesui,
Kuala Lumpur.
Tel (03) 2142-3737.

Titus Blues
7 Jalan Balai Polis,
Kuala Lumpur.
Tel (03) 2070-8191.

PUBS, BARS, AND KARAOKE

Beach Club Café
97 Jalan P. Ramlee,
Kuala Lumpur. **Map** 2 D5.
Tel (03) 2166-9919.

Cherry Blossom
Sun Kompleks, Off Jalan
Bukit Bintang, Kuala
Lumpur. **Map** 5 C5.
Tel (03) 2144-4895.

Club De Vegas
3 Jalan Imbi, Kuala
Lumpur. **Map** 5 C3.
Tel (03) 2141-3888.

Deluxe Nite Club
Ampang Park Shopping
Center, Jalan Ampang,
Kuala Lumpur.
Tel (03) 2162-1399.

Finnegan's
51 Jalan Sultan Ismail,
Kuala Lumpur.
Tel (03) 2145-1930.

La Bodega
31 Tengkat Tong Shin,
Kuala Lumpur.
Tel (03) 2142-6368.

Modesto's
Sri Hartamas, Kuala
Lumpur. **Map** 2 E5.
Tel (03) 6201-7898.

Planet Hollywood
Jalan Bukit Bintang, Kuala
Lumpur. **Map** 6 D2.
Tel (03) 244-6602.

NIGHTCLUBS AND DISCOS

Atmosphere
Jalan Sultan Ismail,
Kuala Lumpur.
Tel (03) 2145-9198.

Bliss
12 Jalan Sultan Ismail,
Kuala Lumpur.

Liquid
Jalan Hang Kasturi.

Maison
8 Jalan Yap Ah Shak,
Kuala Lumpur. **Map** 1 B5.
Tel (03) 2698-3328.

Sugar Club
Jalan Sultan Ismail,
Kuala Lumpur.
Tel (03) 2143-0020.

The Loft
Jalan Doraisamy, Kuala
Lumpur. **Map** 1 B4.
Tel (03) 2691-5668.

Zouk
Jalan Ampang, Kuala
Lumpur. **Map** 2 E4.
Tel (03) 2171-1997.

OUTDOOR ACTIVITIES IN MALAYSIA

From the summit of Gunung Kinabalu to the depths of the South China Sea, Malaysia offers an array of opportunities to enjoy the country's natural wonders. Pristine offshore islands such as Langkawi, Tioman, and Sipadan attract divers with their stunning coral reefs and rich marine life. Most beach resorts offer adventure sports such as windsurfing, parasailing, waterskiing and

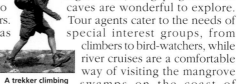

A trekker climbing Gunung Kinabalu

snorkeling. The oldest rain forests in the world with their towering trees, tangled vines, and gaping limestone caves are wonderful to explore. Tour agents cater to the needs of special interest groups, from climbers to bird-watchers, while river cruises are a comfortable way of visiting the mangrove swamps on the coast of Malaysian Borneo. The agreeable climate is perfect for golf enthusiasts.

Speedboat tour at Bako National Park *(see pp162–3)*, Sarawak

GUIDED TOURS

Tourism in Malaysia is well developed and tour operators, such as **CPH Travel Agency** and **Asian Overland Services**, offer a wide range of choices. Depending on a visitor's time and budget, everything from a half-day city tour to a 10-day tour of the country is available.

Independent travelers can join tour groups, such as **S.I. Tours** and **Exotic Adventure**, to visit sights and participate in activities that would otherwise be prohibitively expensive. For example, a tour is the best way to access Sarawak's Mulu National Park *(see pp170–71)*, hike up Gunung Kinabalu *(see pp184–7)* in Sabah, or join a whitewater rafting expedition down Sungai Padas *(see p181)*. The advantage of joining a guided tour is that the local guide's knowledge can enrich the experience of visiting a place you may never return to.

BOOKINGS AND PERMITS FOR NATIONAL PARKS

At most national parks and reserves in Malaysia, visitors can pay the entry fees at Park Headquarters within the reserve's boundaries or at the entrance. However, booking in advance is necessary for a few of the parks, such as Tanjung Datu National Park *(see p160)* and Semenggoh Nature Reserve *(see p161)*. Permits and entrance tickets can be obtained at the **National Parks Booking Office** in Kuching *(see pp154–5)* or at its branch in Miri. Visitors entering Endau-Rompin National Park *(see p137)* from Johor also have the option of buying a permit from the **Johor State Economic Unit**. Some parks require official

permits for professional filming and photography, as well as for activities such as trekking and fishing. These can be obtained either at the park itself or, if in Sarawak, from the National Parks Booking Offices. Many parks offer accommodations and, while it is not mandatory to book in advance for all, it is advisable to do so as preserves and parks tend to get busy, especially during weekends and holidays. Some parks may require permits for camping. The National Parks Booking Offices also handle accommodation bookings.

TREKKING

Malaysia's national parks are ideal for those wishing to trek through scenic landscape and observe the country's wildlife. At over 13,436 ft (4,095 m), Sabah's Gunung Kinabalu is one of the highest peaks in the world that can be climbed

Braving the Pinnacles at Mulu National Park

Following the jungle trail near Asah waterfall *(see p130)*, Southern Peninsula

without special climbing equipment, so it is not surprising that hundreds set out every day with the intention of standing on its summit. Park authorities advise against climbing Kinabalu independently and hiring a guide is recommended. A climbing permit can be purchased on arrival at Park Headquarters. Most climbers take two days to reach this summit with an overnight stay in one of the mountain huts, such as the one at Laban Rata, 10,738 ft (3,273 m) above sea level. It is essential to pre book, particularly in the peak season (April). Wear good walking boots and warm, waterproof clothing, and bring a sleeping bag, water, and high-energy food. A flashlight is invaluable since climbs can start early in the morning to catch the sunrise at the summit.

For less strenuous climbs, there are alternatives, ranging from a trek up Taman Negara's Gunung Tahan *(see pp138–9)* to the climb up Sarawak's Gunung Mulu *(see p171)* or the Pinnacles on Gunung Api *(see p171)*. Malaysia's terrain is challenging, and it is wise to trek with local tour companies, such as **Suniland Travel and Tours Sdn Bhd**.

In parks that lie within the protected area of **Sarawak Forestry Corporation**, such as Mulu National Park, guides are mandatory while trekking. Taman Negara is best for beginners as it has trails for every level of ability. Bako National Park *(see pp162–3)*

in Sarawak has several easy trails, while Gunung Mulu and Gunung Kinabalu test the fittest of walkers. Peradayan Forest Reserve in Brunei also offers many good trails.

Most of Malaysia's forests are ecologically fragile and protected by the **Department of Wildlife and National Parks**. While many visitors opt to trek on their own following color-coded trails, treks can be organized by the department or private companies, such as **Borneo Adventures** or **Utan Bara Adventure Team**.

Hikers should shield themselves from the sun and drink lots of water to avoid dehydration. Leech socks can also be very useful, especially during the wet season.

CAVING

Malaysia's landscape, riddled with some of the world's largest limestone caves, lures spelunkers from around the world. Many *guas*, or caves, such as Lang's Cave in Gulung Mulu, are covered with beautiful stalactites and stalagmites, while others, such as the nearby Deer Cave, offer opportunities for adventure caving, following rarely visited routes.

The caves at Niah *(see p168)* and Mulu National Park in Sarawak attract millions of bats and birds, which roost in their dank interiors. Sabah's Gomantong Caves *(see p191)* are famed for their swiftlet nests. Locals clamber up bamboo poles to retrieve the nests, considered a gastronomic delicacy by some. The best time to see the cave's wildlife is at dusk, during the changeover when bats come hurtling out for their night feeding and swiftlets return to their nests.

Though smaller than the caves in Borneo, the illuminated caverns at Tempurong in Selangor and the Hindu shrines at Batu Caves *(see p90)* are remarkable. For those intrigued by their hidden recesses, the **Malaysian Nature Society Caving Group** offers quick courses and arranges cave explorations.

Gua Kelam, or cave of darkness, in Kuala Perlis

Diving in Malaysia

The idyllic islands scattered around the coast of Malaysia provide easy access to the country's spectacular dive sites. While Malaysia is a strong draw for experienced divers, it is also a good training ground for amateurs, with numerous diving outfits offering lessons *(see p329)* in the waters around islands such as Pulau Tioman, Pulau Redang, and the Perhentian Islands. Some of the more common marine creatures that divers can hope to spot are whale sharks, manta rays, starfish, and a variety of sea turtles. The monsoon season reduces visibility and makes diving less rewarding. The best time to visit the west coast of Peninsular Malaysia is from November to May, while March to October are the ideal months for a trip to the east coast of the peninsula and around Sabah and Sarawak. The islands off the southwest coast of Sabah are suitable for diving all year round.

TYPES OF DIVING

Malaysia's coastline offers wreck diving, snorkeling, and coral reef diving. While wreck dives enable experienced divers to glimpse Malaysia's underwater treasures, coral reefs can be explored by snorkelers and scuba divers.

Wreck dives *allow divers to explore old shipwrecks. The easiest wreck to navigate is the Cement Wreck, which sank in 1980 off the coast of Labuan.*

MALAYSIA'S BEST DIVE SITES

- Miri *see p168*
- Perhentian Islands *see p142*
- Pulau Kapas *see p140*
- Pulau Labuan *see p180*
- Pulau Lankayan *see p191*
- Pulau Redang *see p142*
- Pulau Sipadan *see pp194–5*
- Pulau Sulug *see p179*
- Pulau Tenggol *see p140*
- Pulau Tioman *see pp130–31*

Scuba diving *in Malaysia offers the opportunity to experience its coral reef system, which supports aquatic organisms numbering up to at least 200 species.*

Snorkeling *needs only a mask and a snorkel. It is the best way to watch underwater life at close quarters.*

MARINE LIFE

The waters off Malaysia are a treasure trove of marine species. East coast islands such as Tioman are home to black marlin and yellowfin, schools of barracuda, and reef sharks.

Starfish, *also known as sea stars, are bright and vibrantly colored. These boneless species glide across the ocean floor.*

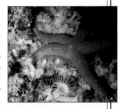

Whale sharks *are gentle and slow plankton-feeding sharks. The largest living fish species, they grow to 39 ft (12 m) in length.*

Green sea turtles *are an endangered species. The adult turtle's algae diet is responsible for its green color.*

White-water rafting along one of Malaysia's rivers

DIVING AND SNORKELING

Diving in Malaysia has grown in popularity in recent years. Numerous scuba diving and marine clubs as well as beach resorts offer equipment for hire. Most dive operators have five-day PADI courses leading to certification as a diver and also organize trips to dive sites. **Borneo Divers and Sea Sports, Pulau Sipadan Resort and Tours**, and **Borneo Sea Adventures** are some of Malaysia's best tour operators.

In several places, coral reefs are in shallow water, making it easy for snorkelers to get among them and explore the pristine vistas and vibrant corals. However, care should be taken not to touch the corals as they can sting and are easily damaged. The number of divers permitted at any one time in Pulau Sipadan *(see pp194–5)* is limited, and booking in advance is wise.

WATERSPORTS

Paragliding, windsurfing, waterskiing, wakeboarding, and jetskiing are just some of the watersports on offer at Malaysia's beach resorts. **Sea Quest Tours and Travel** organizes glass-bottom boat cruises along the coast. They also arrange sunset cruises and island-hopping tours.

Some travel insurance companies do not cover injuries sustained while indulging in watersports, so policies should be checked before signing up.

WHITE-WATER RAFTING

The frothing rivers that tumble out of Malaysia's rugged mountains become rapids en route to the sea. They once formed an impassable barrier for many explorers. Today, however, they form the perfect setting for a white-water rafting adventure. Rapids are graded from Class I to V, but anything above Class III will need an expert guide. One of the top sites is Sabah's spectacular Padas Gorge *(see p181)* with Class III–IV rapids that leave paddlers exhilarated. Sungai Sungkei and Sungai Kampar in Perak, north of Kuala Lumpur, feature gentler rapids.

No previous experience is necessary for white-water rafting, as tour operators such as **Nomad Adventure** and **Exotic Adventure** run through safety procedures before setting off. Rafters wear helmets and protective jackets and have to be good swimmers. The experience varies, as rivers offer a sedate drift in the drier months and a soaking roller-coaster ride after severe rain. Children above 12 are allowed on such trips provided they are good swimmers and are accompanied by parents or legal guardians.

RIVER CRUISES

A comparatively recent phenomenon on Malaysia's ecotourism scene is a cruise through lush rain forests and mangrove swamps. These cruises usually set out in the early mornings or late afternoons, and as the boat glides over the water, knowledgeable guides help spot long-tail macaques, silver langurs, and proboscis monkeys, as well as birds such as hornbills feeding in the trees close to the water's edge.

Such cruises are available in Pulau Langkawi *(see pp112–5)* and Taman Negara *(see pp170–1)* on the peninsula, or at the Klias Wetlands *(see p180)* and Kinabatangan Wildlife Sanctuary in Sabah *(see p191)*. Irrawaddy dolphins are occasionally seen splashing in the shallows around the mouth of the Sungai Santubong in Sarawak. On disembarking from the cruise, tour groups such as **S.I. Tours** and **Borneo Eco Tours** often treat their guests to a buffet dinner before driving them back to their hotels.

Kayaking tour in mangrove swamps

A golfer enjoying a round in a spectacular setting

GOLF

With affordable caddies, low green fees, and equipment hire at reasonable rates, the country's well-planned courses attract golfers from all over the world. Day visitors can usually enjoy a game of golf by paying a fee.

Almost 200 golf courses are currently available in the country, with locations ranging from the cool Fraser's Hill *(see p91)* to the sandy coastline of Borneo. A few of the most popular courses in Peninsular Malaysia include the **Royal Selangor Golf Club** and **Cameron Highlands Golf Club**. On the outskirts of Kuala Lumpur is the designer **Mines Resort Golf and Country Club** course. **North Borneo Tours and Travels Sdn Bhd** provides information about the Damai Golf Club and the Borneo Golf and Country Club.

WILDLIFE VIEWING

People visit Malaysia in great numbers to view its tropical biodiversity comprising over 200 kinds of mammals, many thousands of flowering plants, and a spectrum of butterflies. Malaysia's wildlife includes orangutans, Borneo gibbons, proboscis monkeys, and hornbills. It may be necessary to trek through jungles or climb up mountains to spot

rarer species. Fraser's Hill and Taman Negara *(see pp138–9)* are both easily accessible wild-life-spotting areas.

Another popular activity is an organized tour to spot orangutans in their natural habitat at Semonggoh Nature Reserve in Sarawak *(see p161)*, or at Sepilok Orangutan Rehabilitation Center *(see p190)* in Sabah. Wildlife enthusiasts can also see green and hawksbill turtles nesting and observe hatchlings being released by rangers on islands such as Gulisan, Bakungan Kecil, and Pulau Selingam, and on a trip to Turtle Island National Park *(see p190)*. **WWF**, the global conservation organization, plans events to support the terrain threatened by poaching and deforestation.

BIRD-WATCHING

With more than 600 identified species, Malaysia is a paradise for bird-watchers. Part of the reason for this great diversity is that Malaysia has many different habitats, including montane forests, lowland forests, mangrove swamps, and wetlands, which provide good nesting conditions for all kinds of birds. Apart from the eight varieties of hornbill that can be seen gliding over the rainforest canopy, crested serpent eagles, mangrove pittas, kingfishers, and trogons delight bird-watchers.

In Malaysian Borneo, Sarawak is the perfect place for a wildlife holiday and is often referred to as the Land of the Hornbill. Kinabalu National Park *(see pp184–5)* in Sabah has a fantastic variety of flycatchers and magpies. Among the best locations on Peninsular Malaysia for bird-watching are Kuala Selangor Nature Park and Fraser's Hill, where swiftlets and cuckoos predominate. Enthusiastic twitchers might like to join in one of many birding events, such as the Fraser's Hill International Bird Race *(see p90)* that takes place annually in June.

Borneo Mainland Travel and Tours, **Kingfisher Tours**, **Malaysian Nature Society Birding Group**, and **Wild Asia** are among the tour operators and groups that organize bird-watching. Binoculars, a good field-guide, and a hat will prove to be very useful on a bird-watching trip.

Enthusiastic bird-watchers on a jungle tour

DIRECTORY

GUIDED TOURS

Asian Overland Services
Ampang point,
Kuala Lumpur.
Tel (03) 4252-9100.
www.asianoverland.com

CPH Travel Agency
Kuching, Sarawak.
Tel (082) 243-708.
www.cphtravel.com.my

Exotic Adventure
Segama Complex,
Kota Kinabalu, Sabah.
Tel (088) 253-493.
www.exotic-adventure.
com

S.I. Tours
Wisma Khoo, Siak Chiew,
Sandakan, Sabah.
Tel (089) 673-502.
www.sitoursborneo.com

BOOKINGS AND PERMITS FOR NATIONAL PARKS

Johor State Economic Unit
Bangunan Sultan Ibrahim
Johor Bahru,Johor.
Tel (07) 223-7471.

National Parks Booking Office
Sarawak Tourism Complex,
Kuching, Sarawak.
Tel (082) 410-944/42.
www.sarawaktourism.
com

Lot 452, Jalan Melayu,
Miri, Sarawak.
Tel (085) 434-181.
www.sarawaktourism.
com

TREKKING

Borneo Adventures
Gaya Center, Jalan Tun
Fuad Stephens, Kota
Kinabalu, Sabah.
Tel (088) 238-731.
www.borneoadventure.
com

Department of Wildlife and National Parks
Jalan Charas,
Kuala Lumpur.
Tel (03) 9075-2872.
www.wildlife.gov.my

Sarawak Forestry Corporation
Hock Lee Center, Jalan
Datuk Abang Abdul
Rahim, Kuching, Sarawak.
Tel (082) 348-001.
www.sarawakforestry.
com

Suniland Travel and Tours Sdn Bhd
Rainfield Court Shop-
houses, Kota Kinabalu,
Sabah. *Tel (088) 702-188.*
www.sunilandtravel.
com.my

Utan Bara Adventure Team
The Heritage Unit,
Kuala Lumpur.
Tel (03) 4022-5142.
www.ubat.com.my

CAVING

Malaysian Nature Society Caving Group
641 JKR Jalan Kelantan,
Bukit Persekutuan,
Kuala Lumpur. **Map** 3 A4.
Tel (03) 2287-9422.
www.mns.org.my

DIVING AND SNORKELING

Borneo Divers and Sea Sports
Tel (088) 268-339.
www.borneodivers.info

Borneo Sea Adventure
1st floor, No. 8A
Karamunsing Warehouse,
Kota Kinabalu, Sabah.
Tel (088) 230-000.
www.borneosea.com

Pulau Sipadan Resort and Tours
1st floor, No. 484,
Block P, Bandar Sabindo,
Tawau, Sabah.
Tel (089) 765-200.
www sipadan-resort.com

WATERSPORTS

Sea Quest Tours and Travel
1 Sutera Harbour
Boulevard, Kota
Kinabalu, Sabah.
Tel (088) 248-006.
www.seaquesttours.net

WHITE-WATER RAFTING

Exotic Adventure
Lot 1, 1st Floor,
Block D, Segama Complex,
Kota Kinabalu, Sabah.
Tel (088) 253-493.
www.exotic-adventure.
com

Nomad Adventure
4.06B, 4th Floor,
The Summit Subang
USJ, Persiaran Kewajipan,
USJ 1, Subang Jaya,
Selangor.
Tel (603) 8024-5152.
www.nomadadventure.
com

RIVER CRUISES

Borneo Eco Tours
Pusat Perindustrian
Kolonbong Jaya,
Kota Kinabalu.
Tel (088) 438-300.
www.borneoecotours.
com

S.I. Tours
Lot 1002–1003,
Wisma Khoo Siak
Chiew, Sandakan,
Sabah.
Tel (089) 673-502.
www.sitoursborneo.com

GOLF

Cameron Highlands Golf Club
P.O. Box 66, 39007
Tanah Rata, Cameron
Highlands, Pahang.
Tel (05) 491-1126.
www.pahangtourism.
com.my

Mines Resort Golf and Country Club
The Mines Resort City,
Selangor Darul Ehsan.
Tel (03) 943-2288.
www.mines.com.my

North Borneo Tours and Travel Sdn Bhd
Lot E 3–1, Block E,
3rd Floor, Plaza Tanjung
Aru, Jalan Mat Salleh,
Kota Kinabalu.
Tel (088) 268-339.
www.golfbookingcentre.
com

Royal Selangor Golf Club
Jalan Kelab Golf,
Off Jalan Tun Razak,
Kuala Lumpur. **Map** G F4.
Tel (603) 9206-3333.
www.rsgc.com.my

WILDLIFE VIEWING

WWF (Worldwide Fund for Nature)
49 Jalan SS23/15 Taman
Sea, Petaling Jaya,
Selangor.
Tel (03) 7803-3772.
www.wwfmalaysia.org

Suite 1–6 W11 6th Floor,
CPS Tower, Center Point
Complex No. 1, Jalan
Center Point, Kota
Kinabalu, Sabah.
Tel (088) 262-420.
www.wwfmalaysia.org

BIRD-WATCHING

Borneo Mainland Travel and Tours
1081, 1st Floor,
Jalan Merpati, Miri,
Sarawak.
Tel (085) 433-511.
www.borneo
mainland.com

Kingfisher Tours
Suite 1107, 11th Floor,
Bangunan Yayasan,
Selangor Jalan Bukit
Bintang, Kuala Lumpur.
Tel (03) 2142-1454.

Malaysian Nature Society Birding Group
641 JKR Jalan Kelantan,
Bukit Persekutuan,
Kuala Lumpur.
Map 3 A4.
Tel (03) 2287-9422.
www.mns.org.my

Wild Asia
Upper Penthouse, No. 2
Jalan Raja Abdullah, Kuala
Lumpur. **Map** 1 C5.
www.wildasia.net

SURVIVAL GUIDE

PRACTICAL INFORMATION

Malaysia is one of Asia's top tourist destinations, appealing to package tourists and independent travelers alike. The government of Malaysia, long aware of the country's potential as a tropical paradise, has been promoting tourism for decades. Visitors will find that the tour operators are notably efficient, hotels are well maintained, traveling around is usually smooth, and local

Official logo of Tourism Malaysia

people are generally friendly in Singapore, Malaysia, and Brunei. Singapore is an exceptionally safe country, largely free of violent crime, dirt, and most tropical diseases. The Malaysian government is especially keen to demonstrate how the country has developed into a well-integrated and sophisticated modern society, offering all the conveniences that visitors are used to at home.

A percussionist at the Rainforest World Music Festival *(see p159)*

WHEN TO GO

Malaysia, Singapore, and Brunei fall entirely within the tropics, so all three countries have a hot and humid climate all year round, with temperatures hovering around 30° C (86° F) and rarely dipping below 20° C (68° F). Visitors keen to lounge on a beach or participate in adventure sports should avoid the monsoons. The rainy season affects the west coast of the peninsula between May and September. On the east coast and in Malaysian Borneo, the monsoon falls between November and February. It is worth timing a visit to coincide with one of the country's major festivals, such as the Merdeka Eve celebration *(see p60)* or the Rainforest World Music Festival *(see p159)*. Chinese and Hindu festivals in Singapore take place in January and February.

VISAS AND PASSPORTS

Visitors need a passport that is valid for at least six months from the date of arrival. A visa can be obtained overseas at Malaysian embassies, though many nationalities are granted one on arrival. Citizens of some European, African, South American, and ASEAN countries can stay in Malaysia for a month without a visa. Citizens of the UK, USA, New Zealand, Australia, Canada, and Ireland are automatically issued 3-month tourist visas on arrival which can be extended for another three months by applying to the Immigration Department. The Malaysian **Foreign Office** website has further details.

Although an integral part of Malaysia, Sarawak has its own immigration system, and officials stamp all passports granting a month's stay. A special permit required to travel in some remote parts of Sabah and Sarawak is generally

available from the Resident's office in the relevant areas.

Brunei issues visas on arrival to citizens of the UK, USA, Australia, Canada, and New Zealand. The initial stamp is valid for between two weeks and three months, and can be extended by applying to the Immigration Department in Bandar Seri Begawan, the capital of Brunei. Citizens of most other nationalities are given 72-hour transit visas.

Singapore stamps in citizens from the UK, USA, Australia, New Zealand, and Canada for an initial two weeks, although visitors can request a month.

CUSTOMS INFORMATION

Duty-free limits are 50 cigars, 200 cigarettes, or 250g of tobacco, as well as a liter of both wine and spirits in Malaysia. Duty is payable on all tobacco in Singapore. Visitors who are carrying over US$2,500 need to fill a Declaration Form on arrival.

Visitor's Center at Suntec City Mall, Singapore

◁ **Mass Rapid Transit (MRT) train in a station in Singapore**

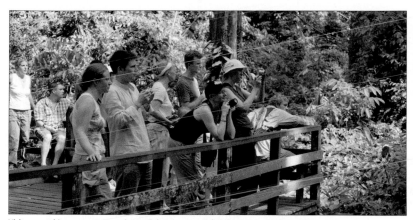

Visitors watching orangutans at the Sepilok Orangutan Rehabilitation Center *(see p190)*

Possession of illegal drugs can result in a prison term or the death penalty in Malaysia, Singapore, and Brunei.

VISITOR INFORMATION

Anyone considering a visit to Malaysia, Singapore, and Brunei will find useful information on the official websites of **Tourism Malaysia**, the **Singapore Tourism Board**, and **Tourism Brunei**. The websites provide details of festivals, hotels, and resorts. The tourist boards, aided by their efficient network of domestic and overseas offices, offer a wide range of pamphlets on the most attractive tourist destinations. For information on Malaysian Borneo, both the **Sabah Tourism Board** and the **Sarawak Tourism Board** have detailed websites. Most hotels operate a tour service or can make arrangements for guests while backpackers' lodges are generally excellent sources of local information.

Guide of Singapore Tourism Board

OPENING HOURS

Government offices in Malaysia are open between 7:30am and 5:30pm, Monday to Friday. Museums keep similar hours, though it is worth checking specific locations for details. In Malaysia's more devout Muslim states, such as Kedah, Terrangganu, and Kelantan, offices are closed on Friday. Post offices are generally open between 8am to 6pm, from Monday and Saturday.

In Singapore, government offices remain open between 8:30am and 5pm, Monday to Friday. In Brunei, government offices are open between 7:45am and 4:30pm and remain closed on Friday and Sunday. For details on the opening hours of banks see pp340–41, and for shops see pp314–5.

ADMISSION CHARGES

Most museums charge a nominal entry fee both in Malaysia and in Singapore. Most national parks charge RM10, except Kinabalu National Park, where the fee is RM15. Some of the more developed attractions charge a higher entry fee, including the Sepilok Orangutan Rehabilitation Center (RM30) and Sarawak Cultural Village (RM25). Night safaris tend to be expensive. Both countries have lower rates for children.

LOCAL TIME

Malaysia, Singapore, and Brunei are eight hours ahead of Greenwich Mean Time (GMT), 16 hours ahead of US Pacific Standard Time (PST) and 13 hours ahead of Eastern Standard Time (EST) in the USA. However, Malaysia does not have daylight saving time, and visitors should note that these differences will change when countries observing daylight saving time move their clocks forward.

LUNAR CALENDAR

Malaysia and Singapore use the Gregorian (Western) calendar for administrative purposes, but many of their festivals, particularly Islamic or Chinese, are celebrated according to the lunar calendar. This means they fall on a different day each year. The main difference between the Chinese and Islamic lunar calendars is that the former uses an intercalary month, so that festivals occur mostly at the same time each year, while Islamic festivals occur about 10 days earlier each year. Most festivals are planned to coincide with the night of the full moon. To find exact dates of any festival, it is best to check the tourist board website of the country concerned.

ELECTRICITY

The electrical current in the region is 220–240 volts at 50 hertz. Equipment using 110 volts requires a converter. Adaptors are cheap and available in most big towns. Most wall sockets accommodate three-pronged square pin plugs as used in the UK.

Family boat ride on Sungai Santubong

TRAVELING WITH CHILDREN

Many Asians are fond of children, and parents traveling with children will often be surprised and delighted to find that their children are usually treated with affection and care almost everywhere in Malaysia, Singapore, and Brunei. An example of this is in restaurants, where the staff are often helpful, and willing to occupy children while parents have their meal. Malaysia is particularly child-friendly, with lots of places to visit that interest people of all ages. Childcare products are available throughout the region except in rural areas and remote destinations. Children's health, however, requires protection, especially against exposure to heat, and food- and water-related ailments.

WOMEN TRAVELERS

Malaysia, Singapore, and Brunei are reasonably safe for women traveling alone. It is important to bear in mind, though, that due to the conservative nature of Malaysian culture, unaccompanied Western women may attract attention, particularly in rural districts and Muslim areas. Women travelers are unlikely to be harassed if they are considerate of local customs, wear modest clothing, and avoid taking risks such as hitchhiking and walking alone at night.

DISABLED TRAVELERS

Singapore provides the best facilities for the disabled, while Malaysia unfortunately offers little in the way of assistance. Many hotels, banks, cinemas, and shopping centers in Singapore provide ramps and other amenities for those with special needs, but these are less common in Malaysia. Facilities are slowly improving, but only at high-end hotels. Public transport lacks wheelchair accessibility, and towns have high kerbs and uneven pavements. *Access Singapore* is a free guide that gives a list of amenities. Travel websites for the disabled, such as **Global Access News**, also offer guidance.

GAY AND LESBIAN TRAVELERS

Officially, neither Malaysia nor Singapore welcomes gay and lesbian travelers, and delivers strict punishment for homosexual acts. Nevertheless, a number of bars and clubs in Singapore and Kuala Lumpur bolster a thriving gay scene. For more information on gay and lesbian issues and events across Asia consult the website **Utopia**.

WHAT TO WEAR

Light, casual clothes in cotton and other natural fibers are ideal for the tropical climate of Malaysia, Singapore, and Brunei, which are hot and humid year-round. Hats and sunglasses are also advisable. A sweater and windproof jacket are recommended for those visiting hill stations. As there is some rainfall throughout the year in Malaysia, a raincoat is handy. It is also important to carry a few long-sleeved shirts and pairs of trousers or full-length dresses, not just as protection from the sun, but also for visits to conservative rural areas and religious venues as well as visits to smart restaurants and hotels. As a rule, especially in Malaysia and Brunei, it is best to dress modestly at all times.

Since laundry services are available in most hotels and guesthouses and cheap clothing, such as T-shirts and *batik* shirts, can be bought everywhere, it is best to travel light.

PHOTOGRAPHY

Natural beauty, teeming wildlife, and stunning architecture ensure that most places in Malaysia, Singapore, and Brunei are extremely photogenic. People are generally quite happy to have their picture taken, but to avoid unpleasantness it is always best to request their permission first, especially while visiting the indigenous people. Similarly, it is advisable to ask a priest or *imam* at all temples and mosques before taking pictures there.

Photo shops in Malaysia's big cities and in Singapore are well-stocked with equipment, memory cards, and print film; prices are cheaper than in the West. Professional slide film is only available in big cities, and even then it might be better to

Stalls selling clothes and other wares at Jalan Petaling market

Arm wrestling between a tourist and a local

carry your own, as it tends to be improperly stored. It is worth using photographic services, such as film processing, before heading home. It is also easy and cheap to get images on a memory card transferred onto a DVD and to get prints from digital images.

SOCIAL CUSTOMS

The majority of the Malaysian population is conservative, but visitors will find most social customs flexible and generally easy to comply with. Loud behavior is considered rude. As a rule, do not point at people or objects using the index finger; instead indicate with the thumb or the whole hand. Although men shake hands, wait for a hand to be offered. Also note that in Muslim company it is impolite to touch people with the left hand or on the head. Public displays of affection such as hugging and kissing are also frowned upon. Topless sunbathing and nudity on beaches are taboo.

Before entering a Malaysian home, visitors should take their shoes off. Never help yourself to food without it being offered first and avoid eating with the left hand.

While most big cities have a modern outlook in terms of fashion, Muslim women still dress conservatively. Care must be taken to dress modestly, with arms and legs

covered, when visiting rural areas, temples, mosques, and other religious places, as well as in Muslim areas or homes. Non-Muslim women may be forbidden to enter mosques in some places.

LANGUAGE

Bahasa Malaysia, which means Malay language, is the official language of Malaysia and Brunei. In Singapore, English and Mandarin are widely spoken, though visitors may also hear Tamil, Cantonese, Hindi, or any number of indigenous languages that are still used by the multi-ethnic population. Visitors who learn even a few Malay phrases will endear themselves to their hosts.

CONVERSION CHART

Malaysia, Singapore, and Brunei use the metric system for weights and measures.
Imperial to Metric
1 inch = 2.5 centimeters
1 foot = 30 centimeters
1 mile = 1.6 kilometers
1 ounce = 28 grams
1 pound = 454 grams
1 US pint = 0.473 liter
1 US quart = 0.947 liter
1 US gallon = 3.6 liters
Metric to Imperial
1 centimeter = 0.4 inch
1 meter = 3 feet 3 inches
1 kilometer = 0.6 mile
1 gram = 0.04 ounce
1 kilogram = 2.2 pounds
1 liter = 2.1 US pints

DIRECTORY

EMBASSIES

Australia
Kuala Lumpur. *Tel* (03) 2146-5555. www.australia.org.my
Singapore. *Tel* 6836-4100. www.australia.org.sg

Canada
Kuala Lumpur. *Tel* (03) 2718-3333. www.dfait-maeci.gc.ca
Singapore. *Tel* 6854-5900. www.dfait-maeci.gc.ca

New Zealand
Kuala Lumpur. *Tel* (03) 2078-2533. www.nzembassy.com
Singapore. *Tel* 6235-9966. www.nzembassy.com

UK
Kuala Lumpur. *Tel* (03) 2170-2200. www.britain.org.my
Singapore. *Tel* 6424-4200. www.britain.org.sg

USA
Kuala Lumpur. *Tel* (03) 2168-5000. http://malaysia.usembassy.gov
Singapore. *Tel* 6476-9100. http://singapore.usembassy.gov

VISAS AND PASSPORTS

Foreign Office
www.kln.gov.my

VISITOR INFORMATION

Sabah Tourism Board
www.sabahtourism.com

Sarawak Tourism Board
www.sarawaktourism.com

Singapore Tourism Board
www.visitsingapore.com

Tourism Brunei
www.tourismbrunei.com

Tourism Malaysia
www.tourismmalaysia.gov.my

DISABLED TRAVELERS

Access Singapore
www.dpa.org.sg/access/contents.htm

Global Access News
www.globalaccessnews.com

GAY AND LESBIAN TRAVELERS

Utopia
www.utopia-asia.com

Personal Security and Health

Tourist police logo

Malaysia, Singapore, and Brunei are all relatively safe to travel in as crime rates are low. However, the same common-sense safety rules apply here as anywhere else and visitors need to be vigilant in big cities where pickpockets and bag-snatchers may operate. Avoid wearing expensive jewelry. There are no particular health dangers in these countries as the health and hygiene standards are among the highest in Asia. However, while hospitals in major cities are well equipped there are limited medical facilities in rural areas.

Singapore policeman and a patrol car

POLICE

Most visitors never have cause for dealings with the police, unless reporting a theft or loss. In Malaysia, areas with large numbers of tourists are also patrolled by special tourist police who offer extra protection.

Singapore has strict laws that prohibit smoking in public places, littering, and even chewing gum, for which steep fines ranging from S$50–1,000 are imposed. The police here are particularly vigilant. Although sometimes tourists may be let off with a warning for these offences, it is best to respect local laws.

GENERAL PRECAUTIONS

While traveling in the region is relatively safe, some basic precautions should be followed. Avoid carrying large sums of money or wearing expensive jewelry; leave them in your hotel safe. Keep

money and passports in a money belt beneath clothing to prevent the risk of pickpocketing. Valuables such as cameras and mobile phones should be hidden from view. Avoid walking along dimly-lit streets after dark or leaving purses unattended. It is a good idea to photocopy travel insurance papers, passport, and documents, in case of theft or loss.

LOST AND STOLEN PROPERTY

If you are robbed, report the theft immediately to the local police station. A police report will be necessary to make an insurance claim later. Lost or stolen credit cards and traveler's checks must be reported to the issuing bank to prevent withdrawals and cards must be cancelled thereafter for replacements. If a passport is lost or stolen, contact your embassy or consulate in order to obtain a replacement *(see p335)*.

Tourist police in Malaysia

NARCOTICS

Malaysia and Singapore are two of the strictest countries in the world when it comes to penalties for possessing or smuggling narcotics, and anyone caught carrying them can expect either a long time in prison or possibly the death sentence. Brunei, too, carries the death penalty for drug trafficking.

HEALTH PRECAUTIONS

Standards of health and hygiene are high in both Malaysia and Singapore, so visitors have little to fear. No inoculations are necessary, unless you have recently visited countries where yellow fever is prevalent. If so, you will be required to show proof of vaccination to immigration authorities on arrival.

Most areas of Malaysia have no risk of malaria. However, if visiting remote areas, it is advisable to begin a course of malaria tablets at least two weeks before traveling. Since these tablets are only partially effective, it is also advisable to use insect repellent and ensure that sleeping areas are equipped with mosquito screens on the doors and windows or mosquito nets over the beds.

The most common problem for travelers is diarrhea and stomach upsets caused by a change in diet, water, and climate. To reduce the risk of diarrhea, drink only bottled or boiled water, avoid ice in drinks and raw food, and eat only in clean places.

For people from temperate climates, the greatest danger of traveling to the tropics is the heat, which can easily cause dehydration and sunburn. Drink plenty of water, stay in the shade, and protect yourself from direct sunlight with a hat, sunscreen, and sunglasses. The tropical climate can also play havoc with open cuts and burns, so treat them immediately. Bring a well-stocked medical kit, which should include personal medication, painkillers, antiseptic, antibiotics, anti-diarrhea tablets, and insect

A private hospital in Singapore, a country with superb health care

sting relief to help tackle most minor problems. However, if a problem persists, seek medical advice immediately.

HOSPITALS AND MEDICAL TREATMENT

All large towns in Malaysia have a district hospital as well as private clinics. Most are clean and all doctors speak some English. These hospitals also have an emergency department, where foreigners are usually given priority. Clinics catering specifically for expatriates and tourists are usually more expensive than local facilities. However, while amenities in the major cities are well developed, with hospitals in Kuala Lumpur such as **Gleaneagles Medical Center** and **Pantai Medical Center** being among the best, reliable medical care can be

difficult to find in rural areas. Brunei has adequate health care facilities but serious health problems are better treated in Singapore, which has world-class medical facilities. Major hospitals here include **Raffles Hospital** and **Singapore General**.

PHARMACIES

Even the smallest towns in Malaysia have well-stocked pharmacies. The **Guardian Pharmacy** has a large number of outlets in Malaysia. The well-known pharmacies in Singapore include **Changi General Hospital Pharmacy** and **AM Pharmacy**. Medication may be bought over the counter in Malaysia without a doctor's prescription, but that is not possible in Singapore. When traveling, carry a good supply of your prescription medicines from home.

TRAVEL AND HEALTH INSURANCE

It is best to take out travel insurance before traveling to the region. Ensure that it covers you for injury, sickness, accident, emergency hospital treatment, and repatriation as well as medical assistance. You will need extra coverage if you participate in high-risk activities such as diving or mountain climbing.

Ambulance in Malaysia

Fire engine in Malaysia

Directory

EMERGENCIES

Ambulance and Fire (Nationwide)
Malaysia *Tel 994*.
Singapore *Tel 995*.
Brunei *Tel 238-0402*.

Police (Nationwide)
Malaysia *Tel 999*.
Singapore *Tel 999*.
Brunei *Tel 242-3901*.

HEALTH PRECAUTIONS

World Health Organization
www.who.int/ith

Malaysia Medical Association
www.mma.org.my

HOSPITALS AND MEDICAL TREATMENT

Gleneagles Medical Center
282 Jalan Ampang,
Kuala Lumpur.
Tel (03) 4257-1300.

Pantai Medical Center
Jalan Bukit Pantai,
Kuala Lumpur.
Tel (03) 2282-5077.

Raffles Hospital
585 North Bridge Road,
Singapore.
Map 3 E4.
Tel 6311-1555.

Singapore General
Outram Road.
Map 4 A3.
Tel 6222-3322.

PHARMACIES

AM Pharmacy
150 Orchard Road, 04–06
Orchard Plaza, Singapore.
Map 1 F2.
Tel 6737-4760.

Changi General Hospital Pharmacy
2 Simei Street 3,
Singapore.
Tel 6788-8833.
www.mypharmacy.com.sg

Guardian Pharmacy
Lot 89 & 91, Jalan Bukit Bintang, Kuala Lumpur.
Map 6 D2.
Tel (03) 2145-7553.
www.guardian.com.my

Banking and Currency

Banks are generally easy to find in Malaysia, Singapore, and Brunei. Commercial and merchant banks freely allow non-residents to open foreign currency accounts without too many restrictions on the movement of funds through these accounts. Visitors can bring any amount of foreign currency into or out of Malaysia or Singapore, although it must be declared at customs. However, there is a limit of RM1,000 on the amount of ringgit allowed into or out of Malaysia.

at major banks, and many hotels and shops will also accept them as cash on presentation of a passport. Lost or stolen traveler's checks and credit cards must be reported to the issuer.

CURRENCY

The Malaysian unit of currency is the ringgit, denoted by RM before the price of an item. Locals often refer to it, rather confusingly, as dollars. It is further divided into 100 sen although tourists are unlikely to need these small denomination coins unless shopping in a local market. In Singapore, the unit of currency is the Singapore dollar, written S$, which is made up of 100 cents. The Brunei dollar is at par with the Singapore dollar and is legal tender in Singapore.

Citibank, one of the many international banks in Singapore

BANKS

Maybank is Malaysia's largest bank. International banks, such as **Citibank**, are also established in all three countries. Malaysian banking hours are from 9:30am to 4pm from Monday to Friday and 9:30 to 11:30am on Saturday. In the Muslim states of Kedah, Terengganu, and Kelantan, however, the banks are open from 9:30am to 4pm from Saturday to Wednesday, and from 9:30 to 11am on Thursday; they remain closed on Friday. Banks in Singapore are open from 9:30am to 3pm from Monday to Friday, and from 9:30 to 11:30am on Saturday.

CHANGING MONEY

Cash and traveler's checks can be exchanged at large branches of all banks for a small service fee. Most major currencies such as dollars and euros are easily exchangeable, though outside the big cities, it can be difficult to exchange other currencies such as the Thai baht or the Indonesian rupiah. Top-end hotels will also exchange dollars and some common currencies, but

rates are usually less favorable than at banks. Licensed money-changers generally stay open until 6pm and often offer the best rates. Exchange facilities can be difficult to find in remote areas, especially in Sarawak and Sabah, so carry adequate cash at all times.

ATMS

Automatic teller machines (ATMs) are becoming ubiquitous in Malaysia, except in isolated areas, and have long been so in Singapore. ATMs only issue the currency of the respective country, and there is a daily withdrawal limit of around US$800. A fee is levied for each transaction, usually about US$3.

CREDIT CARDS AND TRAVELER'S CHECKS

Major credit cards can be used in most urban and tourist areas, with **VISA** and **MasterCard** being the most widely accepted. They can also be used at ATMs for withdrawals and at major banks for cash advances. Traveler's checks, commonly issued by **American Express** and VISA, can be exchanged

DIRECTORY

BANKS

Citibank
Menara Citibank, 165 Jalan Ampang, Kuala Lumpur.
Tel (03) 2380-1111.
www.citibank.com.my
40A Orchard Road 01-00, Singapore. **Map** 1 F2. **Tel** 6225-5225. **www**.citibank.com.sg

Maybank
3rd Floor (West Wing), 100 Jalan Tun Perak, Kuala Lumpur.
Map 4 E1. **Tel** (03) 2074-7266.
www.maybank.com.my
3 Battery Road, Singapore.
Map 5 E3. **Tel** 6550-7158.
www.maybank.com.sg

CREDIT CARDS AND TRAVELER'S CHECKS

American Express
Malaysia **Tel** (03) 2050-0888.
Singapore **Tel** 6297-7666.

MasterCard
Malaysia **Tel** 1-800 804594.
Singapore **Tel** 6533-2888.

VISA
Malaysia **Tel** 1-800 802997
(stolen cards).
Singapore **Tel** 1-800 110-0344
(stolen cards).

Malay Ringgit

Bank notes are issued in denominations of RM1, RM2, RM5, RM10, RM50, and RM100. All notes bear the image of Malaysia's first prime minister, Tunku Abdul Rahman. RM1 coins are rare. The ringgit is divided into 100 sen, available in coins of 1, 5, 10, 20, and 50 sen.

5 sen

10 sen

20 sen

50 sen

1 ringgit

2 ringgits

5 ringgits

10 ringgits

50 ringgits

Singapore dollar

The Singapore dollar is made up of 100 cents, and coins are minted in denominations of 1 (slowly being phased out), 5, 10, 20, and 50 cents. S$1 coins are also circulated. Singapore dollars are issued in notes of S$1, S$2, S$5, S$10, S$20, S$50, S$100, S$500, and S$1,000. There is a S$10,000 note, but it is rare.

1 cent

5 cents

10 cents

20 cents

50 cents

1 Singapore dollar

2 dollars

5 dollars

10 dollars

50 dollars

100 dollars

Communications and Media

The communications network in Malaysia, Singapore, and Brunei is fast and efficient, offering a variety of local, national, and worldwide services. Local and international calls can be made from public telephones in all but the smallest of islands. Mobile phone facilities and Internet access are particularly impressive, with networks that compete with the best in the West. The postal system is reliable and well organized. International publications and several locally published English newspapers and magazines are available in big cities.

messaging is cheap, and many local network companies offer a certain amount of free messages as promotions.

INTERNET FACILITIES

The entire region has fully embraced the use of the Internet and cheap Internet access is available even in remote locations. Internet cafés in Malaysia charge by the hour and most places offer broadband connections. Rates in Singapore are comparable, and broadband is even more widespread. Bigger hotels often have Internet access in rooms or in a business center, but this is usually more expensive than the Internet cafés. Many backpacker lodges offer free Internet access to their guests. For those traveling with laptops, Wi-Fi (wireless Internet connection) facilities are highly advanced in Singapore, but uncommon outside Kuala Lumpur in Malaysia. Note that wall sockets accommodate three-pronged, square-pin plugs, and adaptors are easily available in most big towns.

Conveniently located public telephone booths in Malaysia

INTERNATIONAL AND LOCAL PHONE CALLS

Public telephones can be found all over Singapore, Malaysia, and Brunei. They are both phonecard- and coin-operated, and most also accept credit cards. **Telekom Malaysia** is a national operator while **SingTel** is Singapore's main telephone company. Local calls in Malaysia cost 10 sen for unlimited time, and 10 cents for three minutes in Singapore. Public telephones in all three countries offer international direct dialing (IDD), and it is best to use a phonecard for these calls. Phonecards of several companies are available at petrol stations and convenience stores, such as 7-Eleven, in denominations of between RM5 and RM50 in Malaysia, S$2 and S$50 in Singapore, and B$10 and B$100 in Brunei. Collect calls from Malaysia can only be made from a Telekom Malaysia office, which can also be used for regular long-distance calls.

Most big hotels in the region also have IDD facilities, but this service is extremely expensive. Faxes can be sent from telecom offices in major cities and hotels.

Malaysian phone numbers generally consist of six or seven digits, except in Kuala Lumpur which has eight-digit phone numbers. All numbers are preceded by a two- or three-digit area code. Phone numbers all across Singapore consist of eight digits and there is no area code within the country.

CELL PHONES

Generally, cell phone network coverage is good in Malaysia, except in the remote regions of Sarawak and Sabah where some networks work better than others. There is complete coverage across Singapore. Cell phones with international roaming service will automatically tune into one of the local networks, but this service is very expensive. It is best to buy a local prepaid SIM card, such as **Maxis** and **Celcom** in Malaysia, or SingTel and **M1** in Singapore; these are all widely available. Text

POSTAL SERVICES

Post offices are found all over Malaysia and Singapore, and are generally very efficient. Each Malaysian town has a General Post Office (GPO) with poste restante, as do the GPOs in Singapore and Brunei. In Malaysia, post offices are open from 8am–5pm Monday to Friday, and some Saturdays, though in the states of Kedah, Terengganu,

A well-equipped Internet café in Malaysia

and Kelantan they close on Friday instead of Sunday. The opening hours in Singapore are from 8am to 6pm Monday to Friday, and from 8am to 2pm on Saturday. Brunei post offices open from 7:45am to 4:30pm Monday to Thursday and Saturday, and from 8 to 11am and 2 to 4pm on Friday.

Letters and parcels posted from Malaysian towns usually take a week to reach overseas destinations. Anything posted from remote places in Sabah and Sarawak may take a few weeks to reach its destination. Postcards and aerograms cost 50 sen from Malaysia, and 50 cents from Singapore for the same service. Postcards from Brunei to any destination cost 30 cents. Most major post offices in the region have fax facilities too. Several well-known international courier services such as **DHL**, **Federal Express**, and **United Parcel Service (UPS)** operate in both Malaysia and Singapore as do local courier companies such as **Nationwide Express**.

TELEVISION AND RADIO

Both Malaysia and Singapore have a huge selection of satellite television channels. Terrestrial TV stations are closely monitored for signs of criticism of the respective governments. RTM1 and RTM2 are Malaysia's government-run TV stations, which broadcast uncontroversial programs in Bahasa Malaysia. Commercial stations such as NTV7 feature English news, and international soaps and films.

Six government-run radio stations air programs in various languages including English. Singapore's television and radio channels offer a mixture of English, Tamil, Chinese, and Malay programs. Brunei has one TV channel with many imported programs and two radio channels.

NEWSPAPERS AND MAGAZINES

A wide range of international publications is available in most major hotels, bookstores, and newsstands in Singapore, and big cities in

The colorful *Virtual Malaysia*, packed with useful information

Malaysia, such as Kuala Lumpur. These include magazines such as *Newsweek* and *Time* and newspapers such as the *International Herald Tribune*. Both countries have local newspapers in English, though government censorship is strict, and dissenting views are rarely published. The leading English daily in Malaysia is *The Star*, besides *The New Straits Times*, *Sun*, and *The Malay Mail*. These are all good sources of information for upcoming events. In Sabah and Sarawak, the leading newspapers are *New Sabah Times* and the *Sarawak Tribune*. Malaysia also publishes some English magazines, including *Virtual Malaysia*. Singapore's main English papers are *Straits Times* and *New Paper*, while Borneo's main newspaper is *Borneo Bulletin*.

DIRECTORY

CELL PHONES

Celcom
www.celcom.com.my

M1
www.m1.com.sg

Maxis
www.maxis.com.my

SingTel
www.singtel.com

Telekom Malaysia
www.tm.com.my

POSTAL SERVICES

DHL
Malaysia *Tel (03) 7964-2800.*
Singapore *Tel 6880-6060.*
www.dhl.com

Federal Express
Malaysia *Tel (03) 2179-0370.*
Singapore *Tel 1 800 743 2626.*
www.fedex.com

Malaysian Postal Service
www.pos.com.my

Nationwide Express
Malaysia *Tel (03) 5512-7000.*
Singapore *Tel 6285-4223.*

Singapore Post
www.singpost.com.sg

United Parcel Service
Malaysia *Tel (03) 7784-1233.*
Singapore *Tel 6883-7000.*
www.ups.com/asia

USEFUL DIALLING CODES

- The country code for Malaysia is 60; Singapore 65; Brunei 673.
- To call these countries from abroad, dial your international access code, the country code, the area code minus the first 0 (except Singapore), and the number.
- For international calls from Malaysia dial 00, from Singapore dial 001, and from Brunei 01, followed by the country code, the area code minus the first 0, and the local number.
- Country codes: USA and Canada 1; Australia 61; UK 44; New Zealand 64; France 33.
- Calls between Malaysia and Singapore are considered long distance, not international calls.
- For interstate calls in Malaysia dial the area code followed by the number. For calls within a state, omit the area code.
- For directory enquiries in Malaysia and Singapore, dial 103; in Brunei, dial 0213.
- For the international operator in Malaysia, dial 108; in Singapore, dial 104.

TRAVEL INFORMATION

Most overseas visitors to Malaysia and Singapore arrive at Kuala Lumpur International Airport (KLIA) and Changi Airport, respectively. Many visitors prefer to arrive overland taking a train or a bus from Thailand, and a few opt for cruise ships. Although most towns in Malaysia are well-connected by domestic flights and buses, remote areas in Sarawak and Sabah suffer from poor road conditions. These days, increasing numbers of tourists opt for low-cost carriers, such as

Tiger Airways in Singapore and AirAsia in Malaysia, to make short hops within Southeast Asia from places like Bangkok and Hong Kong. Traveling by rail can be fun, with comfortable sleeper compartments for long journeys, though the network is limited to a couple of lines. Both Singapore and Kuala Lumpur have good public transport services, such as the Light Rail Transit (LRT) and the Mass Rapid Transport System (MRT), that make life easy for first-time visitors to these cities.

Singapore's MRT logo

Budget airline AirAsia at Kuala Lumpur's Low-Cost Carrier Terminal

ARRIVING BY AIR

Over 50 international carriers connect Singapore and Malaysia to most continents. Some of the international carriers that operate out of the two countries are **Air Canada**, **Cathay Pacific**, **China Airlines**, **Emirates Airlines**, **Japan Airlines**, **Garuda Indonesia**, **British Airways**, **KLM**, **Qantas**, **Thai Airways**, and **United Airlines**.

Low-cost carriers such as **AirAsia**, **Silk Air**, **Tiger Airways**, and **Jetstar** offer several options for passengers flying in from other Southeast Asian countries. There are flights from Singapore to Langkawi by Silk Air and to Kuching by Singapore Airlines as well.

Malaysia Airlines (MAS) and **Singapore Airlines**, the national carriers, are well-connected to most parts of the world. There is a regular service between Kuala

Lumpur and Singapore, operated by both official airlines, leaving at half-hour intervals during peak hours.

Many international airlines use either **KLIA** or **Changi Airports** as their gateways to Southeast Asia, or as stopover points from Europe to New Zealand and Australia. Both airports are super-modern and well equipped with all the facilities that travelers might need, such as shops, restaurants, and Internet access. Passengers arriving at Changi Airport, 10 miles (16 km) from central Singapore, have a choice of transport to reach the city, including MRT, limousine services, and airport shuttles.

Airport arrival hall sign

AIR FARES

There is a wide range of tickets available for travel to and around Singapore and Malaysia, but the prices vary

seasonally. During the peak months from July to August, and December to January, prices soar for flights from the USA and Europe.

With over 50 international carriers using the main airports there is stiff competition, and it makes sense to compare the rates of different airlines before booking a flight. For travelers already in Southeast Asia, it is worth considering budget airlines such as Tiger Airways and AirAsia, which offer fares comparable to those on buses and trains. The ticket price is usually exclusive of an international departure tax. It is best to book in advance and check with online booking services.

ARRIVING BY LAND

Traveling by train is a popular way for visitors from Thailand to enter Malaysia, crossing the border at Padang Besar. Passengers can change at Butterworth for Penang or continue to Kuala Lumpur's **Stesen Sentral** or **Singapore**

Luxurious interior of the Eastern & Oriental Express

Train Station. The **Eastern & Oriental Express (E & O)**, combining luxury with classic sightseeing, covers the route from Bangkok to Singapore, passing through Kuala Lumpur's Stesen Sentral.

The main route for buses and taxis from Thailand is via Bukit Kayu Hitam at the Malaysian border. A causeway connects Johor Bahru at the southern tip of Malaysia to Singapore. From Pontianak in Kalimantan (Indonesian Borneo), it is possible to enter Sarawak in Malaysian Borneo. The main terminals are **Puduraya Bus Station** in Kuala Lumpur and the **Singapore Bus Station**.

ARRIVING BY SEA

Both the countries can be reached by sea. Malaysia has several authorized entry points. Some cruise liners, such as **Star Cruises**, travel regularly between Singapore, Port Klang, Penang, Pulau Langkawi, and even Phuket in Thailand. A ferry link connects Penang and Malacca on the peninsula with Medan and Dumai in Sumatra (Indonesia). There are regular longboat services between Pulau Langkawi and Satun in South Thailand. Ferries and small boats also connect Singapore to Tanjung Belungkor in the state of Johor in Malaysia.

ORGANIZED TOURS

The most economical way to visit Malaysia and Singapore is via an organized tour. A package deal usually includes flights, hotels, road transport, guides, and admission fee to tourist sights for little more than the cost of a flight. Tour companies such as Borneo Adventures *(see p329)* and **Thomson Worldwide** offer exciting itineraries.

A cruise liner docked at Langkawi

DIRECTORY

AIRPORTS

Changi Airport
Singapore. *Tel* 6542-1122.
www.changiairport.com

Kuala Lumpur International Airport (KLIA)
Kuala Lumpur.
Tel (03) 8776-4386.
www.klia.com.my

ARRIVING BY AIR

AirAsia
Kuala Lumpur.
Tel (03) 8775-4000.
www.airasia.com

Air Canada
Kuala Lumpur. *Tel* (03) 2148-8596. Singapore.
Tel 6256-1198.
www.aircanada.ca

British Airways
Kuala Lumpur. *Tel* (03) 2167-6006/2167-6188. Singapore. *Tel* 6622-1747. www.britishairways.com

Cathay Pacific
Kuala Lumpur. *Tel* (03) 2078-3377. Singapore. *Tel* 6533-1333
www.cathaypacific.com

China Airlines
Kuala Lumpur. *Tel* (03) 2142-7344. Singapore. *Tel* 6737-2211.
www.china-airlines.com

Emirates Airlines
Kuala Lumpur. *Tel* (03) 2072-5288. Singapore. *Tel* 6735-3535.
www.emirates.com

Garuda Indonesia
Kuala Lumpur. *Tel* (03) 2162-2811. Singapore. *Tel* 6250-5888. www.garuda-indonesia.com

Japan Airlines
Kuala Lumpur. *Tel* (03) 2161-1722. Singapore. *Tel* 6221-0522.

Jetstar
Singapore. *Tel* 6822-2288. www.jetstar.com

KLM
Kuala Lumpur. *Tel* (03) 2711-9811. Singapore. *Tel* 6737-7622.
www.klm.com

Malaysia Airlines (MAS)
Kuala Lumpur.
Tel (03) 7846-3000.
Singapore.

Tel 6336-6777.
www.malaysiaairlines.com

Qantas
Kuala Lumpur. *Tel* (03) 6279-5033. Singapore.
Tel 6415-7373.
www.qantas.com.au

Silk Air
Singapore. *Tel* 6223-8888. www.silkair.com

Singapore Airlines
Kuala Lumpur.
Tel (03) 2692-3122.
Singapore.
Tel 6223-8888.
www.singaporeair.com

Thai Airways
Kuala Lumpur. *Tel* (03) 2031-2900. Singapore.
Tel 1-800 2249-977.
www.thaiair.com

Tiger Airways
Singapore.
Tel 6538-4437.
www.tigerairways.com

United Airlines
Kuala Lumpur.
Tel (03) 2161-1433.
Singapore.
Tel 6873-3533.
www.ual.com

ARRIVING BY LAND

E & O Express
www.easternoriental express.com

Puduraya Bus Station
Kuala Lumpur.
Tel (03) 2070-0145.

Singapore Bus Station
Singapore.
Tel 1-800 2255-663.
www.sbstransit.com.sg

Singapore Train Station
Singapore. *Tel* 6221-3390.

Stesen Sentral
Kuala Lumpur.
Tel (03) 2279-8888.

ARRIVING BY SEA

Star Cruises
Malaysia.
Tel (03) 3103-1313.
www.starcruises.com

ORGANIZED TOURS

Thomson Worldwide
www.thomsonworldwide.co.uk

Traveling by Air

Malaysia has a very good network of internal flights, making air travel a comfortable and convenient way of getting around. The national carrier, Malaysia Airlines (MAS), is well-connected to almost all popular tourist destinations. Singapore itself is too small to require internal flights. With the advent of budget airlines, such as the hugely successful AirAsia, the much smaller Berjaya Air, and the new Fly Asian Xpress (FAX), the cost of flying has reduced considerably. Most big towns in Malaysia now have an airport, and it is easy to get tickets either through local travel agencies or by booking online. Flights are generally punctual, efficient, and inexpensive, which is particularly useful for visitors who want to see as much of the country as possible within a limited period of time.

Passengers waiting to check in at an airport counter

DOMESTIC AIRLINES

Until recently, Malaysia Airlines (see p342) had a virtual monopoly on all domestic flights throughout Malaysia. The situation has now changed with the arrival of AirAsia (see p342) and **Fly Asian Xpress (FAX)**, both of which offer low-cost, no-frills flights with limited seating space and payment for in-flight refreshments. AirAsia has now started to fly short-haul international routes, while FAX has taken over turbo-propeller plane services in Malaysian Borneo from Malaysia Airlines.

Berjaya Air offers a few flights from Kuala Lumpur and Singapore to some of the offshore islands, but prices are quite steep. Berjaya Air also claims that its Dash 7 aircraft is the biggest commercial aircraft to fly to the Tioman and Pangkor islands. Fares and availability can be checked and tickets booked online.

BERJAYA
Berjaya Air logo

DOMESTIC AIRPORTS

All Malaysian Airlines domestic flights depart from the state-of-the-art Kuala Lumpur International Airport (KLIA) (see p342), the largest and most well-connected airport in Malaysia. AirAsia operates out of its main base at the Low-Cost Carrier (LCC), located 12 miles (20 km) from KLIA, to which it is connected by shuttle buses. Berjaya Air operates out of Sultan Abdul Aziz Shah Airport, Kuala Lumpur's former international airport.

In Peninsular Malaysia, there are airports at Ipoh, Penang, Kuala Lumpur, Alor Setar, Langkawi, Kota Bharu, Kuantan, Kuala Terengganu, and Johor Bahru. Airports in Sarawak include Kuching, Sibu, Mukah, Miri, Bintulu, Belaga, Lawas, Mulu, Ba Kalalan, Long Akah, Long Banga, Long Lellang, Long Seridan, Bario, and Limbang. In Sabah, there are airports at Kota Kinabalu, Labuan, Kudat, Sandakan, Lahad Datu, Tawau, as well as Semporna.

The larger airports in all these states are serviced by both MAS and the fast expanding network of AirAsia. However, the smaller towns are connected in most cases only by the services of FAX.

FLIGHT NETWORK

While most major Malaysian towns are linked by direct flights, smaller towns also have connecting networks. In Peninsular Malaysia, most flights originate in Kuala Lumpur, flying to Pulau Tioman, Pulau Redang, and Pulau Pangkor. There are additional flights to Pulau Tioman from Selatar Airport in Singapore. Johor Bahru provides services to Penang, Ipoh, Kuala Lumpur, Kota Bahru, Kuching, Sibu, Miri, Kota Kinabalu, Sandakan, and Tawau.

In Malaysian Borneo, while the majority of flights originate in the provincial capitals of Kota Kinabalu and Kuching, it is also possible to make short hops without returning to the original point using the rural air services. Several 19-seater and 50-seater planes help maintain communications with the remote provinces. A visitor in Sarawak can therefore go from Kuching to Mulu via Sibu and Miri, or from Kota Kinabalu to Semporna via Sandakan in Sabah. There are also regular direct flights between both Miri and Mulu in Sarawak and Kota Kinabalu in Sabah.

A Fokker 50 turboprop, used for short-haul domestic flights, at Mulu

TICKETS AND RESERVATIONS

Tickets for flights on any of the airlines listed in the directory can be purchased from travel agents, although these days it is easier to book online with a credit card. All airlines permit online booking through their websites and e-tickets are becoming more common. While there is usually some flexibility about changing dates for reservations with major carriers such as MAS and Singapore Airlines, budget airlines do not allow rescheduling. Changing the date of the flight after making a booking with a budget airline requires payment of a penalty.

FARES AND SPECIAL DISCOUNTS

With the introduction of budget airlines in Southeast Asia, travelers have a wide range of travel options. However, there are no low-cost long-haul carriers to the region from Europe or USA. Also, by the time tax and fuel surcharges are added, flights are no longer as cheap as they first appear. Potential travelers need to weigh carefully the pros and cons of traveling with different carriers. It is also worth checking promotions and offers from MAS and Singapore Airlines before making any reservations. Passengers arriving by international flights can also get a Discover Malaysia pass issued by MAS, which entitles them to five domestic flights for just US$199. Groups of three or four passengers can get a 50 percent discount from MAS, applicable on trips between the peninsula and Malaysian Borneo and also between Sabah and Sarawak. For other routes in Malaysia a 25 percent discount is applicable. The Singapore Stopover Holiday offered by Singapore Airlines includes free bus rides and admission to several tourist attractions as well as special hotel rates and discounts at shopping outlets.

TRAVEL AGENCIES

Both countries have travel agents who assist visitors with travel arrangements, hotel bookings, and guided tours. **Asian Overland Services**, **Crest Travel and Tours**, **Discovery Tours and Travel**, **East West Executive Travellers**, **Excellence Holidays**, **Ezz Travel**, **J3 Travel**, **Honeyworld Holidays**, **Planet Travel**, **Jetliner Travel**, **Kennex Travel**, **Malaysia Tourism**, **STA Travel**, **Skyzone Tours and Travel**, **Transtar Travel**, **Pedati Saujana Holidays**, **Star Holiday Mart**, **TDK Travel and Tours**, and **TVI Holidays** offer planned holidays.

Travel agency signboards lining a street in Little India, Georgetown

DIRECTORY

DOMESTIC AIRLINES

Berjaya Air
Kuala Lumpur.
Tel (03) 7846-8228.
www.berjaya-air.com

Fly Asian Xpress (FAX)
Kuala Lumpur.
Tel (03) 8775-4000.
www.flyasianxpress.com

TRAVEL AGENCIES

Asian Overland Services
39–40 Jalan Mamanda 9, Ampang, Kuala Lumpur.
Tel (03) 4252-9100.

Crest Travel and Tours
111 North Bridge Rd, 05–08 Peninsula Plaza, Singapore.
Tel 6337-9189.

Discovery Tours and Travel
Tel 6733-4333. www. discoverytours.com.sg

East West Executive Travellers
Suntec Tower 5, Singapore. *Tel* 6238-8488. www.ewet.com

Excellence Holidays
Wisma Excellence, Kuala Lumpur. *Tel* (03) 2117-2929. www.excellence holidays.com

Ezz Travel
62E Ground Floor, Jalan Genuang, Segamat, Johor. *Tel* (07) 931-6601.

Honeyworld Holidays
24 Raffles Place, Singapore.
Tel 6532-2232.

J3 Travel
3 Pickering Street, Central Singapore. *Tel* 6327-4238. www.j3travel.com

Jetliner Travel
Lot 14 Level 2, Kota Kinabalu International Airport, Sabah.
Tel (089) 222-737.

Kennex Travel
Menara Pan Global, Lorong P. Ramlee, Kuala Lumpur.
Tel (03) 2031-8810. www.kennextravel.com

Malaysia Tourism
17th Floor, Putra World Trade Center, Jalan Tun Ismail, Kuala Lumpur.
Tel (03) 2163-0162.

Pedati Saujana Holidays
2A Bangunan MPSP, Kedah Darul Aman.
Tel (04) 425-2052.

Planet Travel
Block 925 Yishun Central 1, Singapore.
Tel 6286-9009. www.planettravel. com.sg

Skyzone Tours and Travel
Lot 3.05–08 Shaw Parade, Kuala Lumpur.
Tel (03) 2141-8588. www.skyzonetours.com

Star Holiday Mart
29/30 Duxton Road, Singapore.
Tel 6735-9009. www.starmart.com.sg

STA Travel
400 Orchard Road, Singapore. *Tel* 6737-7188 www.statravel.com.sg

TDK Travel and Tours
B6 Sri Dagangan 2, Kuantan, Pahang Darul.
Tel (09) 513-4466.

Transtar Travel
01–15 Golden Mile Complex, Singapore.
Tel 6299-9009. www.transtar.com.sg

TVI Holidays
1 Raffles Place OUB Center, Singapore.
Tel 6533-2533.

Traveling by Train and Boat

While domestic flights are cheap and convenient for visitors with limited time, boat and train travel offers travelers a sense of the geographical variety and richness of Malaysia and Singapore. The railway connects many major towns in Peninsular Malaysia, while visitors to Sabah can experience rail travel on a short stretch from Kota Kinabalu to Tenom. A range of boats is available to tourists, from dugout canoes to luxury cruise liners. Many, such as the *ekspres* boats of Sarawak, have a distinctive character found nowhere else in Malaysia. Boat and train journeys take longer than flights and are suitable for travelers on an extended holiday.

KTM Komuter train at a Malaysian station

RAILROAD NETWORK

The Malaysian railroad system, **Keretapi Tanah Melayu Berhad (KTM)**, is a modern, economical, and comfortable mode of transport. The railroad was the only way to get around the country before the construction of the peninsula's road network, and many of the stations in the interior still retain their original colonial architecture.

The network consists of two main lines, with a few minor branches running down to the west coast. From its starting point in Singapore, the West Coast line heads north to Kuala Lumpur, then on to Ipoh and Butterworth, before finally connecting at the border town of Padang Besar with Thai Railways.

The second route is the East Coast line, popularly known as The Jungle Railway *(see p149)*. Branching off the West Coast line at Gemas, about 37 miles (60 km) northeast of Malacca, it heads north through Kuala Lipis to Tumpat on the northeast coast near the Thai border. Most travelers heading to Thailand use the West Coast line, but it is possible to take the East Coast line up to Pasir Mas, and take a bus or taxi over the border to Sungei Golok, Thailand's southernmost railroad station.

In Borneo, the only railroad line is in Sabah, and visitors can ride the short stretch from Kota Kinabalu to Tenom, passing through the long gorge of the Sungai Padas *(see p181)*.

KTM also runs Komuter trains, an electrified short-distance train service connecting Kuala Lumpur to the surrounding suburban areas.

TRAINS

There are two types of trains: express trains that stop only at the main stations, and the slower and cheaper local trains that also stop at smaller stations. Express trains run only on the West Coast line, but local trains operate on both lines. Express trains usually consist of first and second class, while local trains are generally third class. All first- and second-class carriages have sleeper berths on overnight trains. All classes have air conditioning, which is generally very cold, making a jacket or blanket a necessity. Third-class carriages usually have fans. Free timetables are available online and at all KTM stations.

In a class of its own is the **Eastern & Oriental Express (E & O)**, which takes three days to get from Singapore to Bangkok. This train makes brief stops at Kanchanaburi in Thailand, Kuala Lumpur, and Butterworth, to allow passengers some time to sightsee in these towns.

TRAIN TICKETS, FARES, AND RESERVATIONS

Tickets can be purchased at all mainline stations, through the KTM website, or from travel agents. Fares depend on the type of train and class of carriage. Fares for first-class travel are about double the price of second class, which is approximately double that of third class. Sleeping berths are available for a small charge in addition to the basic fare.

Tourist rail passes offering unlimited train travel are also available. Visitors can pay US$35 for 5 days, US$55 for 10 days, and US$70 for 15 days. The passes are discounted by almost 50 percent for children. The fare from Singapore to Bangkok on the luxurious Eastern & Oriental Express is over US$1,500.

Advance booking is advisable for express trains if a sleeping berth is required.

Ticket barrier at a platform in Kuala Lumpur

Passengers boarding ferries on the Batang Rajang

BOAT FACILITIES, SERVICES, AND FARES

With regular services to popular destinations, boats and ferries are among the most popular ways to get to riverside towns and offshore islands. Most traditional bumboats have been replaced by faster and sleeker *ekpres* boats that offer basic seating with canopies for protection from the elements. Since they are intended to be used only for short journeys, there are usually no toilets or facilities for buying refreshments.

Although most boats are quite modern, safety precautions can be somewhat lax, with some operators overloading their vessels or not insisting on the use of life jackets. Services are also likely to be temporarily suspended due to inclement weather during the monsoon.

Boat fares vary according to the length of the journey and the condition of the vessel, but an average hour-long journey costs about RM15. Advance booking for tickets is not required, and payment can be made at the jetty or on board.

BOAT ROUTES AND CRUISES

In Malaysia, many major towns along the coasts and along rivers are connected by ferry, or *ekspres* boats. On the west coast of the peninsula, Butterworth is linked to Pulau Penang by a car ferry, which remains popular despite the existence of a road bridge between the mainland and the island. There is a twice daily ferry service to Pulau Langkawi from Penang, and hourly services both from Kuala Kedah and Kuala Perlis. Regular ferries run between Lumut and Pulau Pangkor.

On the east coast, there are several daily ferries from Merang to Pulau Redang and from Kuala Besut to the Perhentian Islands. Visitors to Pulao Tioman can get a ferry either from Peninsular Malaysia or take a catamaran from Singapore. There are no boat services connecting Peninsular Malaysia with Malaysian Borneo.

In Sarawak, longboats and *ekpres* boats are the principal methods of travel. They link Kuching with Sibu, Kapit, and Belaga along Batang Rajang, while in the north of the province, they are the main modes of transport along Sungai Baram. While there are no riverboat services in Sabah, a regular ferry runs between Menumbok and Pulau Labuan.

Visitors to Singapore can enjoy a cruise on a traditional bumboat along the Singapore River or around the southern islands. Several companies organize these cruises, including **River Boat**, **River Cruises**, **Watertours**, **Cruise Ferries**, **Penguin Ferry Services**, and **Eastwind Organization**.

Passengers purchasing tickets at a ferry port

DIRECTORY

RAILROAD STATIONS

Alor Star
Tel (04) 731-4045.

Butterworth
Tel (04) 323-7962.

Gemas
Tel (07) 948-2863.

Ipoh
Tel (05) 254-0481.

Johor Bahru
Tel (07) 223-4727.

Klang
Tel (03) 3371-9917.

Kuala Lipis
Tel (09) 312-1341.

Kuala Lumpur Sentral
Tel (03) 2730-2000.

Padang Besar
Tel (04) 949-0231.

Pasir Mas
Tel (09) 790-9025.

Singapore
Tel 6222-5165.

Tumpat
Tel (09) 725-7232.

RAILROAD NETWORK

Keretapi Tanah Melayu Berhad (KTM)
Tel (03) 2267-1200.
www.ktmb.com.my

TRAINS

Eastern & Oriental Express (E & O)
www.orient-express.com

SINGAPORE CRUISES

Cruise Ferries
Tel 6456-8518.

Eastwind Organization
Tel 6333-3432.

Penguin Ferry Services
Tel 6271-4866.

River Boat
Tel 6338-9205.

River Cruises
Tel 6336-6111.

Watertours
Tel 6533-9811.

Traveling by Road

The roads in Malaysia and Singapore are generally in very good condition and the network is comprehensive, making it easy to get around. There is an extensive and inexpensive bus system, and both state-run and private companies operate services that connect many major towns in Malaysian Borneo and most towns on the peninsula, with good connections to Singapore as well. Long-distance taxis are a good option for group travel, while car hire is reasonably priced and a good alternative for those who prefer flexible itineraries.

Long-distance luxury buses run by Transnasional

ROAD NETWORK

Peninsular Malaysia's road network is excellent, offering one of the best ways of exploring the country. The main road that runs along the peninsula is the North-South Highway, a six-lane toll road between Johor Bahru in the south and the Thai border. Route 8 goes up the east coast, linking Bentong, near Kuala Lumpur, with Kota Bharu in the north. Route 4 and Route 145 connect the east and west coasts of the peninsula. Various other roads connect towns in the interior.

Due to the rugged terrain, the network in Malaysian Borneo is limited. In Sarawak the only long-distance road runs up the coast between Kuching and Miri, although there are numerous good roads around Kuching itself. Sabah has a comparatively weak network, especially the roads in the interior; however, the road heading north and south along the coast from Kota Kinabalu is good.

Malaysia has two land bridge connections with Singapore – a causeway between Johor Bahru and Singapore and a second link between Tuas in Singapore and Geylang Patah in Malaysia.

LONG-DISTANCE BUSES

Traveling around Malaysia by bus is fast, comfortable, and cheap. Several private operators, including **Plusliner** and **Transnasional**, run air-conditioned luxury buses between major towns. Buses linking smaller towns make more stops and are not all air-conditioned. In rural areas, regular buses are replaced by minibuses or converted pick-up trucks. Other major bus operators include **Sri Maju**, **Transtar**, **Aeroline**, **Hasry Express**, **Biaramas**, **Tung Ma Express**, and **Tuaran United Transport**.

There are bus services to Singapore from several Malaysian towns, including Kuala Lumpur, Malacca, Ipoh, and Penang. Buses from Malaysia stop at the Ban San, Golden Mile Complex, or Lavender Street terminals.

Taxi stand sign

Travelers should note that long-distance bus terminals are often located on the outskirts of a town, requiring a local bus or taxi ride to get there, and that long-distance buses tend to set out in the early morning or evening.

BUS TICKETS AND FARES

Reservations for travel on buses are usually not necessary in Singapore and Malaysia, except during public holidays such as Christmas and Chinese New Year when many locals are traveling. Most people buy their tickets at the bus company office located at each bus station just before boarding a coach, but it is possible to book in advance to guarantee a place. Departure times are displayed on a placard in front of the office. Fares are reasonable and depend on the comfort provided by the bus.

LONG-DISTANCE TAXIS

Long-distance taxis or share taxis are worth considering, especially when traveling in groups of three or four. Solo travelers will need to wait until the driver has a full complement of four passengers, as these taxis operate on a shared-cost basis. The waiting time is usually not long, and is shorter early in the morning. It is also possible to charter the whole taxi for the price of four single fares. There is usually a long-distance taxi stand right next to the long-distance bus station in each town, with fares for various destinations posted on a board. Taxi fares are about double the bus fare, but the service is much quicker. Night journeys may have an additional fare.

A long-distance taxi

CAR AND MOTORBIKE RENTALS

Renting a car is an appealing way of exploring Malaysia, as it offers travelers the freedom to change their travel plans at will. Rental agencies usually require that drivers be over 23 years of age and have held a clean driving license for at least a year. Overseas visitors will need an International Driving License.

Car hire rates are higher in Malaysian Borneo than on the peninsula. While insurance is generally included in the price, it is wise to spend extra for Collision Damage Waiver (CDW) insurance, which covers costs resulting from accidents. Renting a car in Singapore costs more than in Malaysia, with rental and fuel costing almost double. There are also surcharges for driving hired cars from Malaysia to Singapore and vice versa.

Hiring a motorbike is less formal, and the guesthouse

Motorbikes lined up for hire outside a rental agency

owners or shops who rent them out rarely ask to see a license. Rental rates are reasonable, and this can be a good way of exploring islands, such as Pulau Penang and Pulau Langkawi, or attractions on the outskirts of cities.

All major rental agencies, including **Budget**, **Hertz**, **Avis**, and **Thrifty** are represented, along with local agencies, such as **Mayflower**, **Orix**, **Hornbill**, **Pronto**, **Extra**, **Kinabalu**, and **Popular**, which sometimes offer cheaper rates.

While renting from a local firm may be tempting, it could be a problem if the vehicle breaks down far from the rental office and the company has no local backup, so enquire about their network before signing a deal. Visitors should note that 4WD vehicles for rent are scarce, so those heading for the hills should employ a reliable tour operator who can provide an appropriate vehicle with a driver.

RULES OF THE ROAD

Vehicles drive on the left in both Singapore and Malaysia. The use of seat belts is obligatory, and within cities, the speed limit is 31 mph (50 km/h). Most road signs are self-explanatory, except for the ubiquitous *awas* in Malaysia, meaning "be careful." The permissable level of alcohol in the blood is 0.8 percent in Malaysia and there are heavy penalties for those convicted of drinking and driving.

DIRECTORY

Getting around KL & Singapore

Both Kuala Lumpur and Singapore are relatively easy to get around, as there is a variety of transport methods at a visitor's disposal. The Light Rail Transit (LRT) and Mass Rapid Transit (MRT) metro systems are swift and efficient. Bus lines cover both cities quite thoroughly, and metered taxis are convenient and easy to find. Some trishaws, or three-wheeled bicycle taxis, still ply the streets offering fun but expensive rides for tourists. The most enjoyable way of getting around is walking, but while Singapore is pedestrian-friendly, Kuala Lumpur is not easy to walk around. For travelers with limited time, it is worth considering an organized tour.

Fully air-conditioned MRT train traveling on an elevated track

Pedestrians window-shopping in Kuala Lumpur's Chinatown

WALKING

All the main areas of interest in Kuala Lumpur, such as the colonial district, Chinatown, and Little India, are close together and can easily be covered on foot. However, as six-lane roads and flyovers divide Kuala Lumpur into sections unconnected by sidewalks, strolling beyond these areas is unviable. Traffic is fast-moving and heavy, so visitors should always be alert.

The situation is better in Singapore. The city center is pedestrian-friendly and conducive to strolling around or window-shopping, especially along Orchard Road. The hot and humid climate of both cities requires precautions such as using sunblock, carrying enough drinking water, and limiting walks to a few hours to avoid exhaustion.

METROS

In Kuala Lumpur the LRT is a fast and economical way of getting around the city, with trains arriving every 5 to 15 minutes between 6am and midnight. It is possible to pay for a single trip, but it is better to get a Touch 'n Go card which is a stored-value ticket that can also be used on City Shuttle buses. LRT maps are available at all stations.

Singapore's MRT is often acclaimed as the best metro in the world because of its clean carriages, speedy service, and low prices. The most convenient way to pay is the stored-value ticket, called an EZ-link card worth S$15, which includes a S$3 deposit and is valid on all MRT and bus journeys. Any

LRT ticket, Kuala Lumpur

credit on the card can be reclaimed at a card outlet on departure. A Tourist Day ticket available for S$10 at MRT stations allows up to 12 bus or MRT rides a day regardless of the distance traveled. Smoking, eating, and drinking are prohibited on the MRT.

BUSES

Kuala Lumpur is well-served by buses, which run at close intervals between 6am and 11pm, although poor signage and problems with route information can occasionally cause visitors some confusion. One of the most useful lines for tourists is the City Shuttle, which links many downtown locations. The shuttle is operated by **Rapid KL**, who also run the LRT. A day ticket costs RM2, while the integrated bus and LRT daily pass costs RM7. City Shuttle route numbers are 101 to 115 and these buses can be identified by a red disk on the windscreen.

In Singapore there are two major bus companies, **SBS** and **SMRT**, who also run train and taxi services. As on the MRT, the easiest way to pay the fare is the EZ-link card, which must be tapped against a machine when boarding and leaving the bus. If paying by cash, drop the exact fare in the box as no change is given. A more tourist-oriented form of transport is the **Singapore Trolley**, which runs between the Singapore Botanic Garden and Suntec City, with a daily pass costing S$14.90.

Passengers waiting to board a city bus in Kuala Lumpur

TAXIS

Taxis can be particularly useful when arriving in an unknown city as they spare the need for prior knowledge of the city's layout, though such service comes at a price. In Kuala Lumpur, red and white taxis charge an initial fare of RM2 for the first mile, and 10 cents for every 220 yards (200 m) thereafter. Drivers often decline to use the meter with tourists, and try to agree on a fixed fare that is inevitably higher than the meter rate. Note that meters are also occasionally doctored. It is wise to confirm the usual fare for a planned journey with your hotel before setting out. Most fares in the city should be RM10, but 50 percent extra is charged after midnight.

Taxis are easily available on the streets of Singapore. They have a flag fare of S$2.50 for the first kilometer, and S$0.50 for each subsequent kilometer. There are, however, provisions for additional surcharges. **SBS Transit**, **Comfort Cabs**, **Sunlight Taxi**, **Radio Teksi**, **City Cab**, and **Smart** are among the taxi service providers here.

ORGANIZED TOURS

Taking an organized tour is the ideal way of seeing a city's major sights in relative comfort, and there are plenty of companies that offer such tours in both Kuala Lumpur and Singapore. In Kuala Lumpur, apart from grand

The enormous Petronas Towers, one of the highlights of a city tour

full-day tours or 3-hour city highlight tours, which take in the Petronas Towers, the Royal Palace, Chinatown, the Lake Gardens, and the National Museum, there are walking tours, architectural tours, and museum tours. **Tour East**, **Reliance Travel**, **Angel Tours**, and **Borneo Travel** in Kuala Lumpur offer a variety of engaging tour options.

In Singapore tours usually take in Orchard Road, Little India, and Chinatown, though specialist tours are also available, covering themes such as World War II sights, Asian cuisine, and Singapore's throbbing nightlife. For a more personalized tour, with a tailor-made itinerary, it is best to contact the **Registered Tourist Guides Association of Singapore**. **Holiday Tours**, **RMG Tours**, and **SH Tours** also organize packaged excursions of Singapore.

White taxi, Kuala Lumpur

Yellow taxi, Singapore

DIRECTORY

BUS COMPANIES

Rapid KL
No.1 Jalan PJU 1A/46, Petaling Jaya, Selangor, Malaysia.
Tel 1-800 388-228.
www.rapidkl.com.my

Singapore Trolley
Tel 6339 6833.

SBS
205 Braddell Road, Singapore.
Tel 1-800 2255-663.
www.sbstransit.com.sg

SMRT
Singapore. *Tel* 1-800 2255-663.
www.smrt.com.sg

TAXI COMPANIES

City Cab
Singapore. *Tel* 6552-2222.

Comfort Cabs
Kuala Lumpur.
Tel (03) 6253-1313.

Radio Teksi
Kuala Lumpur.
Tel (03) 9131-8080.

SBS Transit
Singapore. *Tel* 6555-8888.

Smart
Singapore. *Tel* 6485-7700.

Sunlight Taxi
Kuala Lumpur.
Tel (03) 9057-5757.

ORGANIZED TOURS

Angel Tours
Kuala Lumpur.
Tel (03) 2141-7018.

Borneo Travel
Kuala Lumpur.
Tel (03) 2161-2130.

Holiday Tours
Singapore. *Tel* 6738-2622.

Registered Tourist Guides Association of Singapore
Singapore. *Tel* 6339-2114.

Reliance Travel
Kuala Lumpur. *Tel* (03) 2148-6022. www.reliancetravel.com

RMG Tours
Singapore. *Tel* 6220-1661.

SH Tours
Singapore. *Tel* 6734-9923.

Tour East
Kuala Lumpur. *Tel* (04) 227-4522.
www.toureast.net

General Index

Acknowledgments

Dorling Kindersley would like to thank the many people whose help and assistance contributed to the preparation of this book.

Contributors
David Bowden is an Australian expatriate who has worked in Asia for over a decade. He now calls Malaysia home and writes and photographs for some of the leading national and regional newspapers and magazines.

Ron Emmons is a British writer and photographer who has lived in Thailand since the 1990s. He is author of the DK *Top 10 Travel Guide to Bangkok*.

Andrew Forbes has lived in Chiang Mai, Thailand for the past 20 years, where he is editor of CPA Media. He has visited Malaysia regularly over three decades and has contributed to the DK *Eyewitness Travel Guide to Vietnam and Angkor Wat*.

Naiya Sivaraj has been a traveler and writer for as long as she can remember, and has recently started to make a living by combining the two. She is currently pursuing a journalism program at UCLA.

Richard Watkins was born in Wales and is a freelance travel writer. He has written for a number of publications including various newspapers and magazines in UK, USA, and Australia.

History Consultant
Nicholas White is Reader in Imperial and Commonwealth History at Liverpool John Moores University, UK. He has written a number of books and articles on Malaysian history including (with J.M. Barwise) *A Traveller's History of South East Asia*, published by Windrush/Cassell, 2002.

Phrasebook Writer
E. Ulrich Kratz

Fact Checkers
Erik Fearn, Angelia Teo

Proofreaders
Shonali Yadav, Stewart J. Wild

Indexer
Jyoti Dhar

Design and Editorial
Publisher Douglas Amrine
List Manager Lucinda Smith
Managing Art Editor Jane Ewart,
Managing Editor Kathryn Lane
Project Editor Ros Walford
Senior Art Editor Paul Jackson
Project Art Editor Sonal Bhatt
Jacket Designer Tessa Bindloss
Senior Cartographic Editor Casper Morris
DTP Designers Jenn Hadley,
Natasha Lu
Production Controller Inderjit Bhullar

Design and Editorial Assistance
Alexandra Farrell, Jacky Jackson,
Helen Townsend

Additional Picture Research
Rachel Barber, Ellen Root

Additional Cartography
Base mapping for Kuala Lumpur derived from Netmaps.

Additional Photography
Irv Beckman, Simon Bracken, Gerard Brown, Andy Crawford, Peter Chen, Frank Greenaway, Benu Joshi, Barnabas Kindersley, Dave King, Colin Koh, Lawrence Lim, Ian O'Leary, Lloyd Park, Brian Pitkin.

Special Assistance
Many thanks for the invaluable help of the following individuals:

Jo Chua, Baba-Nonya Heritage Museum; Asma Adnan and Mohamad Redza, Islamic Arts Museum; Rohaya Juli, Money Museum; Noredah Othman, Sabah Tourism Board; Letitia Samuel, Sarawak Tourism Board; Serene Lim Si Si, Singapore Tourism Board; S. T. Ramish, Tourism Malaysia.

Photography Permissions
Dorling Kindersley would like to thank the following for their assistance and permission to photograph at their establishments:

Islamic Art Museum; Kompleks Budaya Kraf; National Art Gallery; National History Museum; Penang Museum and Art Gallery; Royal Museum.

Picture Credits

Placement Key: t=top; tc=top center; tr=top right; cla=center left above; ca=center above; cra=center right above; cl=center left; c=center; cr=center right; clb=center left below; cb=center below; crb=center right below; bl=bottom left; bc=bottom center; br=bottom right; ftl=far top left; ftr=far top right; fcla=far center left above; fcra=far center right above; fcl=far center left; fcr=far center right; fclb=far center left below; fcrb=far center right below; fbl=far bottom left; fbr=far bottom right.

Every effort has been made to trace the copyright holders, and we apologize in advance for any unintentional omissions. We would be pleased to insert the appropriate acknowledgments in any subsequent edition of this publication.

Works of art have been reproduced with the kind permission of the following copyright holders: *Homage to Newton*, 1985 © Kingdom of Spain, Gala – Salvador Dali Foundation, DACS, London 2008 221c.

The Merlion symbol has been used with the kind permission of the Singapore Tourism Board (Reference Number STB/J6/07) 204clb.

The publishers would like to thank the following individuals, companies, and picture libraries for their kind permission to reproduce their photographs:

ALAMY: 1Apix 326br; 2d Alan King 47c; AndyLim. com 186cl; Banana Pancake 187tl; Robert E. Barber 18bl; Bare Essence Photography 77tr; Beaconstox 322tl; Brandon Cole Marine Photography 326bl; Bruce Coleman Inc. 17bl; Comstock Images 18-19c, 195bl; David Noton Photography 72tr, 294cla; Dbimages 10bl; Reinhard Dirscherl 19tr, 326cr; Elvele Images 12cl; Espixx 292bl; David Fleetham 18clb; Simon Grosset 214cl; Kim Haughton 86; Hemis 21clb; Henry Westheim Photography 5tr, 112clb; Jack Hobhouse 54tr; David Hosking 16bc; Iconotec 141t; Images&Stories 153br; Jon Arnold Images 147cr; Jo Kearney 26cl; Jenny Matthews 218br; Neil McAllister 60tr, 345cr; Chris McLennan 297cla; Michele Molinari 186tr; David Moore 113cra; Roger Munns 18tl; nagelestock.com 11tr; Nic Cleave Photography 113crb; North Wind Picture Archives 34bc; Picture Contact 9tr, 11bc; Sergio Pitamitz 17cr; Wolfgang Pölzer 326cla; Robert Harding Picture Library Ltd 21tr, 61tl, 105bc, 178t; Scenics & Science 61cra; Neil Setchfield 62t, 125bl; Slick Shoots 234tr; Nick Simon 28tr; Stephen Frink Collection 18tr, 19tl, 19crb; Steve Allen Travel Photography 226clb; Laurie Strachan 295c, 296cla; Terry Fincher.Photo Int 173cb; Ozil Thierry 10tr, 51b; Tribaleye Images/ J Marshall 317tr; Carlos Villoch 326bc;

Rob Walls 20crb, 36bc; Maximilian Weinzierl 245bl; Terry Whittaker 17tr; David Wootton 21cra; Tengku Mohd Yusof 316cr; ANDYLIM CREATIVE: 131br; THE ASEAN SECRETARIAT: 44clb; ASIAEXPLORERS.COM: Timothy Tye 33c, 33bl, 339ftr, 339cr; TIMOTHY AUGER: 217c.

BABA-NONYA HERITAGE MUSEUM: Jo Chua 126clb, 126br, 127ca, 127bl; BERJAYA CORPORATION BERHAD: 344c; BES STOCK: Alain Evrard 330-1; THE BRIDGEMAN ART LIBRARY: Drum, Dong Son style, 2nd-1st century BC (bronze) (see also 232894), Vietnamese School/Musee Guimet, Paris, France, Lauros/Giraudon 33br, Sloane 197, ff.381v-382r: Plan of the city of Malacca, c.1511 (pen & ink with w/c), Barretti de Resende, Pedro (16th Century)/British Library, London, UK, © British Library Board. All Rights Reserved 35tr, The port and town of Malacca, Malaysia, illustration from 'Le Costume Ancien et Moderne' by Giulio Ferrario, published c.1820s-30s (coloured engraving), Zancon, Gaetano (1771-1816)/Private Collection, The Stapleton Collection 37crb, Sir Thomas Stamford Raffles (1781-1826), Lonsdale, James (1777-1839)/London Zoological Society, UK 38bl, Borneo: Signing of the Treaty for cession of Labuan, 1846/British Library, London, UK, © British Library Board. All Rights Reserved 40bc; BRUNEI TOURISM: 55tr, 152tr, 172cla, 172cl, 172bc, 173tl, 173br.

ADRIAN CHEAH: 317cb; CORBIS: 18cla, 331c; Atlantide Phototravel 105cr; Bettmann 44t; Tom Brakefield 151b; EPA/Ahmad Yusni 28bl,/Pool/Saeed Khan 45bl; Macduff Everton 9b, 202; Eye Ubiquitous 112cla; Free Agents Limited 199tr; Michael Freeman 31c, 35bl; Farrell Grehan 4br, 135cr; Peter Guttman 21br; Hamish Park 50cr; Chris Hellier 22br, 162bl, 163br; Dave G. Houser 318tr; Rob Howard 21cla, 327tl; Hulton-Deutsch Collection 20cra, 42bl, 43bc; Image Source 138bc; So Hing-Keung 28-29c; Earl & Nazima Kowall 20br, 113bc, 316bl; Bob Krist 59br; Frans Lanting 180bl; Charles & Josette Lenars 30cl, 295tl; Yang Liu 317c; Viviane Moos 20cl; Christine Osborne 316clb; Neil Rabinowitz 54cla, 87b; Robert Harding World Imagery/Louise Murray 170bl; Joel W. Rogers 162cl; Schlegelmilch 50bl; Shamshahrin Shamsudin 73b; Paul Souders 45tr; Stapleton Collection 32; Luca I. Tettoni 34bl; Nik Wheeler 17cl, 21c, 318bl; Lawson Wood 177tr, 194clb; Michael S. Yamashita 55tl; Zefa/Herbert Kehrer 169c,/Hugh Sitton 144-5,/Photex/Berverly Factor 18br; CPA MEDIA: 34tr, 34c, 36crb, 38tr, 38cla, 38-9c, 38br, 39tl, 39crb, 39bl, 39br, 40t, 40c, 41tr, 41bl, 41bc, 42tl, 42c, 42br, 43t, 65bl; David Henley 22tr, 111br; COURTESY OF THE THAI SILK COMPANY 92bl.

DEWAN FILHARMONIK PETRONAS, KUALA LUMPUR CITY CENTRE, MALAYSIA: 321br; DK IMAGES: FSTOP Pte. Ltd., Singapore 203cl, 242br, 243cla, 243cb, 338ca, 342tc, 346br, 350tr, 351bc.

FLPA: Minden Pictures/Frans Lanting 46-7,185br; FOREST RESEARCH INSTITUTE MALAYSIA: 76cb.

GENTING THEME PARK: 320br, GETTY IMAGES: Photographer's Choice/Guy Vanderelst 196-7; Robert Harding World Imagery/John Miller 8bl; Stone/Paul Chesley 20bl; The Image Bank 2-3; THE GRANGER COLLECTION, NEW YORK: 7c, 36tc, 37tl, 37bl, 37bc, 39cra, 40br, 157cb, 197c, 221tr, 269c.

HILTON KUCHING HOTEL: 293tr; ERIC HUNT: 185bl.

INTERCONTINENTAL HOTELS GROUP: 270br; ISLAMIC ARTS MUSEUM MALAYSIA: 4tr, 68tl, 68cla, 68clb, 69tl, 69cra, 69cb, 69bc.

JUDITH MILLER: Sloan 317cl.

LONELY PLANET IMAGES: Mark Daffey 170cl, 185tl; Richard L'Anson 227bc; Phil Weymouth 227tl.

MARY EVANS PICTURE LIBRARY: 41crb; MASTERFILE: Mark Downey 154cl, 324cl; John Foster 163tc; R. Ian Lloyd 8cr, 29tr, 44br, 49br, 54bl, 134bl, 172tr, 200bc; Brad Wrobleski 174; MONEY MUSEUM & ART CENTRE OF BANK NEGARA MALAYSIA: 35bc, 39tc, 39ca.

NATIONAL AERONAUTICS AND SPACE ADMINISTRATION: 14cl; NATIONAL ARCHIVES OF MALAYSIA: 187tr; NATIONAL GEOGRAPHIC IMAGE COLLECTION: Tim Laman 49t, 194cla; NATURAL VISIONS: Brian Rogers 186clb; NATUREPL.COM: Doug Perrine 17crb; NEGERI SEMBILAN TOURISM ACTION COUNCIL: Zainal Abidin Abu Samah 121crb, 121bl, 121br.

ORIENT-EXPRESS HOTELS TRAINS & CRUISES: 342br.

PHOTOBANK: 206; PHOTOGRAPHERS DIRECT: 42 Degrees South 35clb; Bare Essence Photography/Chan Tze Leong 54br; Graham Simmons 226tr; Tengku Mohd Yusof Photography 23br; PHOTOLIBRARY: Corbis Corporation 195cra, Digital Vision 132, 268-269; Earth Scenes/Animals Animals/James J Stachecki 20tr; David B Fleetham 188-189; Staub Frank 133b; Index Stock Imagery/Clineff Kindra 28cla,/Walter Bibikow 30tr; Jon Arnold Images/Walter Bibikow 27cra; Jtb Photo Communications Inc 27bl, 112tr, 227cr, 244cl, 315bl, 316tr; David Kirkland 175b; Pacific Stock/Perrine Doug 195tl; Photodisc/Emma Lee/Life File 98-99;

Photononstop/Maurice Smith 171br, Robert Harding Picture Library Ltd/ Richard Ashworth 30clb; Photo Researchers, Inc 245cra; PHOTOSHOT: NHPA/Gerald Cubitt 16cb,/John Shaw 17tc;/World Pictures/Eur 76tl.

RABANI: 182b; REUTERS: Zainal Abd Halim 1c, 21cb; Jason Lee 28br; Bazuki Muhammad 23crb, 53cr; Stringer Malaysia 23bc; ROBERT HARDING PICTURE LIBRARY: Reinhard D 194tr, 195crb; Robert Francis 184cl; Gavin Hellier 5cl, 25c; John Miller 88bl, 89cr; Louise Murray 194bc.

SABAH TOURISM BOARD: 181br, 184bl, 270cl; RADIN MOHD NOH SALEH: 26crb, 30bl, 30br, 143tc, 143cla, 143clb, 143cr, 143crb, 176bl; SARAWAK FORESTRY: 163cr; SARAWAK TOURISM BOARD: 51c, 55br, 157tr, 160c, 167c, 167bl, 190tr, 271tl, 292c, 322c, 324br, 326cl, 327br, 328br, 334tl, 335tl; SENTOSA ISLAND: 244tr, 245tl; SEPILOK RESORT: 271bc; SINGAPORE ART MUSEUM: 213bc; SINGAPORE TOURISM BOARD: 26tr, 199bc, 200cl, 201tr, 201bl; SUPERSTOCK: age fotostock 48bl; Murat Ayranci 56.

TOURISM MALAYSIA: 17bc, 19bl, 19br, 29c, 29bl, 29br, 30-1c, 31tl, 31tc, 31cr, 31bl, 31br, 45br, 48c, 50tc, 51tr, 52c, 53bl, 60br, 73tc, 77br, 91tl, 96c, 143bl, 150, 159cra, 171tl, 314tc, 316cl, 316cra, 317tl, 317cra, 319cr, 320tc, 321tr, 322br, 325br, 332tc, 332cl.

VIRTUAL MALAYSIA: 341tc.

WIKIPEDIA, THE FREE ENCYCLOPEDIA: 225tc; JOEY CE WONG: 138cla.

Front Endpaper: ALAMY: Kim Haughton fcla; CORBIS: Macduff Everton cr; MASTERFILE: Brad Wrobleski ftr; PHOTOLIBRARY: Digital Vision tc; SUPERSTOCK: Murat Ayranci cl; TOURISM MALAYSIA: cra.

Back Endpaper: KL MONORAIL SYSTEM SDN BHD.

Jacket images: Front: ALAMY IMAGES: Eye Ubiquitous / Paul Seheult c; James Davis Photography / James Davis clb. Back: ALAMY IMAGES: Reinhard Dirscherl cla; Neil McAllister bl; CORBIS: Jose Fuste Raga clb; DK IMAGES: tl. Spine: ALAMY IMAGES: Eye Ubiquitous / Paul Seheult t; CORBIS: Zefa / Hugh Sitton b.

SPECIAL EDITIONS OF DK TRAVEL GUIDES

DK Travel Guides can be purchased in bulk quantities at discounted prices for use in promotions or as premiums. We are also able to offer special editions and personalized jackets, corporate imprints, and excerpts from all of our books, tailored specifically to meet your own needs.

To find out more, please contact: (in the United States) SpecialSales@dk.com (in the UK) Sarah.Burgess@dk.com (in Canada) DK Special Sales at general@tourmaline.ca (in Australia) business.development@pearson.com.au

Phrase Book

Malay belongs to the Austronesian family of languages whose several hundred distinct variations cover the Indian and Pacific oceans. It is the national language of Malaysia, Brunei, and Singapore, and for many centuries has been the language of learning, diplomacy, and commerce in this region. One of its earliest scripts, a modified Perso-Arabic script called *Jawi*, was the means by which Islam was disseminated. *Jawi* is still widely used in Brunei today. Elsewhere, it has been replaced by the Latin script *Rumi*, which was not spelled uniformly until Malaysia, Indonesia, and Brunei agreed on a standard form of spelling. Prior to the 19th century, international trade and relations would have been unthinkable without the use of Malay, but after 1800, large-scale immigration from China and India resulted in the widespread use of Chinese and Tamil in Malaysia. Today, English is widely spoken, mostly in urban centers, but any effort made by visitors to speak Malay is usually appreciated, particularly in more remote parts of the country. Malay, whose official name is Bahasa Melayu, is often incorrectly called Bahasa, which means language.

Malay Pronounciation Guide

There are no strong stresses in the Malay language and most letters are pronounced in the same way as English. As a general rule, beginners are advised to stress the penultimate syllable. However, if this syllable contains a mute e, the stress moves to the final syllable.

a	as in f*a*ther
	or as in th*e*
	or as in b*u*t
e	like the "a" in m*a*chine when unstressed;
	or as in b*e*ll when stressed
i	as in tax*i*
	or as in Apr*i*l

o	as in m*o*rning
	or as in st*o*p
u	as in b*oo*t
	or as in g*oo*d
ai	as in *i*ce
	or as two separate sounds, as in Hawa*ii*
au	as in *ou*t
	or as two separate sounds, as in b*a-ut*
c	in between *tu*be and *ch*oose
j	in between *due* and *Ju*ne
k	as English "k" except in a final letter, when it becomes a glottal stop (brief pause)
ng	as in si*ng*er
ngg	as in lo*ng*er
ny	as in i*nnu*endo

In an emergency

Help!	Tolong!
Stop!	Berhentilah!
Call a doctor!	Panggil doktor!
Call an ambulance!	Panggil ambulans!
Police!	Polis!
Fire!	Api!
Where is the nearest telephone?	Di mana telefon yang terdekat?
Where is the nearest hospital?	Di mana hospital yang terdekat?
I am lost!	Saya sesat!
Do you need help?	Awak perlukan pertolongan?
I've been robbed!	Saya dirompak!
Go away!	Pergi!
I've had an accident.	Saya terlibat dalam kemalangan.

Communication essentials

Yes	Saya
No	Bukan/Tidak
Hello	Helo
Goodbye	Selamat jalan
Excuse me/ apologies	Minta maaf
Please	Tolong/silahkan
Thank you	Terima kasih
You are welcome.	Kembali.
Good morning	Selamat pagi
Good afternoon	Selamat petang
Good evening	Selamat malam
Good night	Selamat hari
How are you?	Apa khabar?
Madam	Puan
Sir	Encik (Ci')
Today	hari Ini
Tomorrow	Esok
Yesterday	Kelmarin
Later	Esok/Nanti

Now	Sekarang/Segera
What?	Apa?
When?	Bila?
Which one?	Yang mana?
Who?	Siapa?
Why?	Mengapa?

Useful phrases

Do you speak English?	Apakah berbahasa Inggeris?
I don't speak Malay.	Saya belum berbahasa Melayu.
I don't understand.	Saya kurang faham.
I/we want to...	Saya/kami mahu...
What is your name?	Siapakah nama?
My name is...	Nama saya...
Where is...?	Di mana...?
Is it close by?	Sudah dekat?

Is it far away?	**Masih jauh?**	doctor	**dokter**
Could you	**Minta perlahan**	faint	**pingsan**
please speak	**sedikit?**	fever	**panas (badan)**
drive/walk		high	**tinggi**
slower?		low	**rendah**
How do I	**Untuk ke...**	medicine	**ubat**
get to...?	**sebaiknya saya**	nurse	**perawat**
	naik apa?	pain/ill	**sakit**
Are children	**Adakah kanak-**	painkillers	**ubat penghilang**
allowed?	**kanak dibenerkan**		**kesakitan**
	masuk?	pregnant	**hamil**
I like...	**Saya suka...**	sanitary	
I don't like...	**Saya tidak suka...**	napkins	**tuala wanita**

Useful words

How many/	**Berapa**
much is it?	**harganya?**
Do you accept	**Credit card**
credit cards?	**boleh?**
This is too	**Ini terlalu**
expensive.	**mahal.**
buy	**beli**
cheap	**murah**
clothes	**pakaian**
expensive	**mahal**
market	**pasar/tamu**
price	**harga**
sale	**jualan (murah)**
sell	**jual**
shoes	**kasut**
shop	**kedai**
supermarket	**pasar raya**

address	**alamat**
Attention!	**Awas!**
bad	**buruk**
big	**besar**
clean	**bersih**
closed	**tutup**
cold	**sejuk**
dirty	**kotor**
door	**pintu**
empty	**kosong**
enough	**cukup**
entrance	**masuk**
exit	**keluar**
full	**penuh**
good	**baik**
hot	**panas**
less	**kurang**
more	**lebih**
pull	**dorong**
push	**tolak**
open	**buka**
quick	**cepat**
slow	**perlahan**
small	**kecil**
stairs	**tangga**

Nature and sightseeing

bay	**teluk**
beach	**pantai**
cape/	**tanjung**
promontory	
estuary/town	**kuala**
hill	**bukit**
information	**penerangan**
island	**pulau**
lake	**tasik**
mosque	**masjid**
mountain	**gunung**
paddy field	**sawah**
palace	**istana/astana**
park	**taman**
river	**sungai/batang**
square	**padang**
strait	**selat**
temple/shrine	**kuil**
tourist	**pejabat**
travel agency	**agensi**
	pelancongan
village	**kampung**

Transport

I would like to	**Saya mahu**
reserve a	**tempahkan**
seat.	**tempat duduk.**
Would you tell	**Tolong**
me when to	**beritahukan,**
get off?	**bila sudah**
	sampai?
How long	**Berapa lama**
does it take	**untuk ke...?**
to get to...?	
Which bus	**Bas mana**
goes to...?	**yang ke...?**
Where do I	**Di mana**
pay?	**tempat**
	membayar?
I need a	**Kami memerlukan**
mechanic.	**mekanik.**
I have a	**Tayarnya**
flat tire.	**kempis.**
aeroplane	**kapal terbang**
boat	**perahu**
bus	**bas**
bus stop	**stesen bas**
car	**kereta**
car baby seat	**tempat duduk**
customs	**cukai**
cycle	**naik baisikal**
petrol	**minyak/petrol**
return (trip)	**(perjalanan) pergi**
	balik
seat	**bayi**
single/one	**tiket sehala**
way (ticket)	**pergi balik**
taxi	**teksi**
timetable	**jadual waktu**
train	**kereta api**

Banks

Is there an	**Ada ATM?**
ATM?	
I want to	**Saya mau**
change	**tukar dollars/**
dollars/	**pounds...**
pounds...into	**menjadi ringgit**
Malay ringgit.	**Malaysia.**
money	**wang/duit**
change	**wang kecil**
change money	**tukar wang**
exchange rate	**kadar pertukaran**
traveler's	**cek**
checks	**kembara**

Colors

black	**hitam**
blue	**biru**
green	**hijau**
red	**merah**
white	**putih**
yellow	**kuning**

Health

antiseptic	**antiseptik**
blood pressure	**tekanan darah**
condom	**kondom**
contaceptive	**kontraseptif/**
	pencegah hamil
dentist	**dokter gigi**
diarrhea	**diarea/cirit-birit**

Directions

here	**di sini**
there	**di sana**
in	**(di) dalam**
from (where)	**dari (mana)**
left	**kiri**
right	**kanan**
straight on	**jalan terus**
in front of	**di hadapan**

Shopping

Do you have...?	**Apakah ada...?**
Can I have...?	**Minta...?**

behind	di belakang
at the corner	di simpang
near	dekat
far	juah
to	ke
north	utara
south	selatan
east	timur
west	barat
northeast	timur laut
northwest	barat laut
southeast	tenggara
southwest	barat daya

Staying in a hotel

I have a reservation.	Ada tempahan.
Do you have a room?	Ada bilik?
What is the charge per night?	Berapa semalam?
I want a double/ single room.	Saya minta bilik kelamin/ bujang.
I am/we are leaving today.	Saya/kami nak mendaftar kelaur hari ini.
double	kelamin
single	bujang
bed	katil/tempat tidur
key	kunci
lights	lampu
bathroom	bilik mandi
toilet	tandas
soap	sabun
towel	tuala
Open	Buka
Closed	Tutup
Emergency exit	Pintu kesemasan

Eating out

A table please.	Minta meja untuk.
May I see the menu?	Minta daftar makan?
I would like to order now.	Saya mau pesan sekarang.
I am vegetarian.	Saya vegetarian.
I don't eat...	Saya tidak makan...
The bill, please.	Minta bil.
breakfast	makan pagi
children's menu	menu kanak-kanak
dinner	makan malam
fork	garpu
glass	kaca mata
highchair	kerusi tinggi
knife	pisau
lunch	makan tengah hari
meat	daging

restaurant	restoran
seafood	makanan laut
snack	makanan kecil
spoon	senduk
vegetable	sayur

Menu decoder

asam	sour
ayam	chicken
ayer panas	hot water
ayer sejuk	cold water
ayer teh	tea
buah-buahan	fruit
domba	lamb
garam	salt
gula	sugar
ikan	fish
jus	juice
kelapa	coconut
kopi	coffee
manis	sweet
mee	noodle
merica	pepper
minuman	drink
nasi	steamed rice
pedas	spicy
pedih	bitter
sapi	beef
susu	milk
telur	eggs
udang	prawn/shrimp

Time and day

clock	jam
minute	menit
quarter hour	suku
second	detik
watch	jam tangan
hour	pukul
day	hari
week	minggu
month	bulan
year	tahun
morning	pagi hari
noon	tengah hari
midday	siang hari
afternoon	sore hari
evening/night	malam hari
What is the time please?	Sudah pukul berapa?
11.19 in the morning	pukul sebelas lewat sembilan belas menit pagi
1 o'clock	pukul satu
1.15 in the early afternoon (midday)	pukul satu lewat suku siang
3.45 in the afternoon	pukul empat kurang suku sore
6.30 in the early evening	pukul enam setengah sore

9.31 in the evening/ at night	pukul sepuluh kurang dua puluh menit malam
Monday	hari Isnin
Tuesday	hari Selasa
Wednesday	hari Arba
Thursday	hari Khamis
Friday	hari Jumaat
Saturday	hari Sabtu
Sunday	hari Ahad/ Minggu

Cardinal numbers

1	satu
2	dua
3	tiga
4	empat
5	lima
6	enam
7	tujuh
8	delapan
9	sembilan
10	sepuluh
11	sebelas
12	dua belas
13	tiga belas
20	dua puluh
21	dua puluh satu
22	dua puluh dua
30	tiga puluh
40	empat puluh
50	lima puluh
60	enam puluh
70	tujuh puluh
80	delapan puluh
90	sembilan puluh
100	seratus
1,000	seribu
2,000	dua ribu
10,000	sepuluh ribu
20,000	dua puluh ribu
100,000	seratus ribu
200,000	dua ratus ribu

Ordinal numbers

1st	pertama
2nd	kedua
3rd	ketiga
4th	keempat
5th	kelima
6th	keenam
7th	ketujuh
8th	kedelapan
9th	kesembilan
10th	kesepuluh
11th	kesebelas
12th	kedua belas
20th	kedua puluh
100th	keseratus
1000th	keseribu

DK EYEWITNESS TRAVEL INSURANCE

FOR PEACE OF MIND ABROAD
we've got it covered **wherever** you are

For an **instant quote** on quality worldwide travel insurance visit
www.dk.com/travel-insurance or call:

USA 1 800 749 4922 (Toll Free)
UK 0800 258 5363
Australia 1300 669 999
New Zealand 0800 55 99 11
Canada www.dk.com/travel-insurance
Worldwide +44 870 894 0001

Cover provided to residents of over 46 countries for virtually every kind of trip

Please quote our ref: Eyewitness Travel Guides

Insurance is arranged through and provided by Columbus Travel Insurance Services Ltd
(trading as Columbus Direct), Advertiser House, 19 Bartlett St, Croydon, CR2 6TB .
Columbus Direct is authorised and regulated by the Financial Services Authority.

COLUMBUS direct

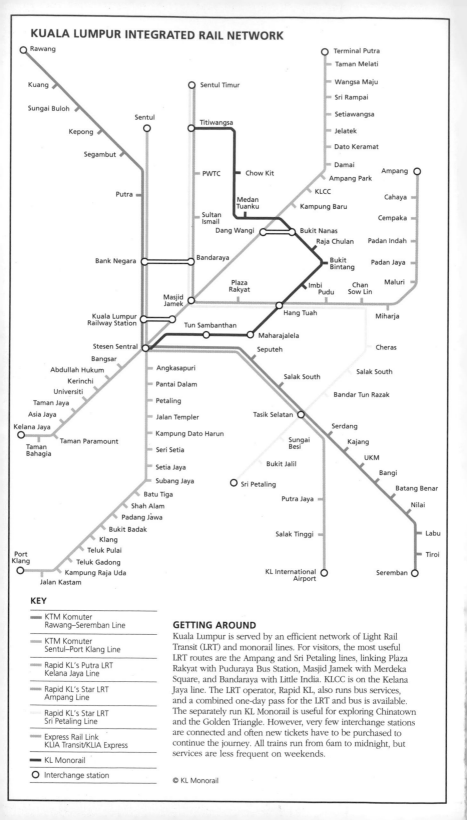

KUALA LUMPUR INTEGRATED RAIL NETWORK

Rawang
Kuang
Sungai Buloh
Kepong
Segambut
Sentul
Sentul Timur
Titiwangsa
Terminal Putra
Taman Melati
Wangsa Maju
Sri Rampai
Setiawangsa
Jelatek
Dato Keramat
Damai
Ampang Park
KLCC
Kampung Baru
Ampang
Cahaya
Cempaka
Padan Indah
Padan Jaya
Maluri
Putra
PWTC
Chow Kit
Medan Tuanku
Sultan Ismail
Dang Wangi
Bukit Nanas
Raja Chulan
Bukit Bintang
Bank Negara
Bandaraya
Plaza Rakyat
Masjid Jamek
Hang Tuah
Imbi
Pudu
Chan Sow Lin
Miharja
Kuala Lumpur Railway Station
Tun Sambanthan
Maharajalela
Seputeh
Cheras
Stesen Sentral
Bangsar
Abdullah Hukum
Kerinchi
Universiti
Taman Jaya
Asia Jaya
Kelana Jaya
Taman Bahagia
Taman Paramount
Angkasapuri
Pantai Dalam
Petaling
Jalan Templer
Kampung Dato Harun
Seri Setia
Setia Jaya
Subang Jaya
Batu Tiga
Shah Alam
Padang Jawa
Bukit Badak
Klang
Teluk Pulai
Teluk Gadong
Kampung Raja Uda
Jalan Kastam
Port Klang
Salak South
Bandar Tun Razak
Tasik Selatan
Sungai Besi
Bukit Jalil
Sri Petaling
Putra Jaya
Salak Tinggi
KL International Airport
Salak South
Serdang
Kajang
UKM
Bangi
Batang Benar
Nilai
Labu
Tiroi
Seremban

KEY

— KTM Komuter
Rawang–Seremban Line

— KTM Komuter
Sentul–Port Klang Line

— Rapid KL's Putra LRT
Kelana Jaya Line

— Rapid KL's Star LRT
Ampang Line

— Rapid KL's Star LRT
Sri Petaling Line

— Express Rail Link
KLIA Transit/KLIA Express

— KL Monorail

◯ Interchange station

GETTING AROUND

Kuala Lumpur is served by an efficient network of Light Rail Transit (LRT) and monorail lines. For visitors, the most useful LRT routes are the Ampang and Sri Petaling lines, linking Plaza Rakyat with Puduraya Bus Station, Masjid Jamek with Merdeka Square, and Bandaraya with Little India. KLCC is on the Kelana Jaya line. The LRT operator, Rapid KL, also runs bus services, and a combined one-day pass for the LRT and bus is available. The separately run KL Monorail is useful for exploring Chinatown and the Golden Triangle. However, very few interchange stations are connected and often new tickets have to be purchased to continue the journey. All trains run from 6am to midnight, but services are less frequent on weekends.

© KL Monorail